People
and Polity

People and Polity

The Organizational Dynamics of World Jewry

Daniel J. Elazar

WAYNE STATE UNIVERSITY PRESS   DETROIT   1989

Library of Congress Cataloging-in-Publication Data
Elazar, Daniel Judah.
  People and polity : the organizational dynamics of world Jewry /
    Daniel J. Elazar.   p.   cm.
  Bibliography: p.
  Includes index.
  ISBN 0-8143-1843-6 (alk. paper). ISBN 0-8143-1844-4 (pbk. :
    alk. paper)
  1. Jews—Politics and government—1948–   2. Israel and the
Diaspora.   3. Jews—History—1945–   I. Title.
DS140.E42 1989
909'.04924—dc19   88-17404
                                                                CIP

Daniel J. Elazar is president of the Jerusalem Center for Public Affairs, Senator N. M. Paterson Professor of Intergovernmental Relations at Bar-Ilan University, and professor of political science and director of the Center for the study of Federalism at Temple University. Dr. Elazar is the author of *American Partnership: Intergovernmental Co-Operation in the Nineteenth Century* and *American Federalism: A View From the States* among his other books on American politics. His most recent books include *The Jewish Polity: Jewish Political Organization from Biblical Times to the Present* (with Stuart A. Cohen), *Israel: Building a New Society,* and *Exploring Federalism.*

The manuscript was edited by Tom Seller. The book was designed by Joanne Elkin Kinney. The typeface for the text and the display is Galliard.

Manufactured in the United States of America.

People (pē·p'l). In sing. as a collective of unity c.pl. Nations, races (=L.populi, gentes). late ME. example: Should not a people seek their God? *Isaiah* viii, 19.

Polity (po·liti). 1538 [from the Latin politia and the Greek πολιτεια] a. A particular form of political organization 1597. b. An organized society . . . 1650.
example: Nor is it possible that any form of politie, much less politie ecclesiasticall should be good, unless God himselfe bee the authour of it—Hooker

—the *Oxford English Dictionary*

Contents

Preface

This volume is devoted to understanding the Jewish community as a polity, as a commonwealth that transcends, as it were, space, in the same way that, as a people, Jews have transcended time. As an organized people, Jews partake of an exceptional kind of political life, which, if still unusual today, may well be a form to which the world in general is moving. If Marshall MacLuhan is correct, the world is undergoing some retribalization. In many respects, the Jews are the modern tribe par excellence, the tribe that has kept pace with the movement of civilization without sacrificing its kinship structure while still managing to create a commonwealth that transcends territorial limits.

The Greeks, as usual, had a word for it. The Hellenistic world coined the term *politeuma* to describe phenomena such as the worldwide Jewish polity of that age, in which Jews simultaneously maintained strong political links, including citizenship, with their territorial polities, the Hellenistic cities, and with one another across lands and seas. A *politeuma* was an autonomous polity located within another polity but not federated with it. Baron defines a *politeuma* as "an organization of men of the same political status outside their native habitat . . ." and indicates that the term was also applied to the Greek, Idumean, Cretan, and Phrygian diaspora communities.[1]

The characteristic form of political organization in the modern epoch was the territorial nation-state, politically sovereign within clear boundaries, encompassing a territory over which complete authority was exercised by a particular government ostensibly in the name of the single nation that inhabited that territory. This is not the place to go into this theory of national territorial sovereignty and its consequences. At its best it was a founding and sustaining myth for states that were far from homogeneous despite their striving for homogeneity, often at the price of earlier identities, loyalties, and cultures. At its worst, it became a vehicle for unprecedented barbarism in the name of national unity and ethnic or racial purity.[2]

The Jews were caught in the middle of the struggle for modern statehood, particularly in Europe. First they lost their communal autonomy to the new nation-states and only after a struggle were they able to gain civil rights and citizenship in the new states in recompense. In the process, the Jewish people almost lost its polity. But the realities of Jewish existence were such that, even as emancipation of Jews as individuals was spreading throughout the world, new devices for Jewish corporate organization in the diaspora emerged, based on the exercise of necessary functions in the limited sphere that remained open for collective Jewish activity. In the postmodern epoch, these functions coalesced into activity spheres in which voluntary collective Jewish action was considered acceptable.

This development is simply a more blatant example of a general reality that has resurfaced in the postmodern epoch. If the modern epoch was characterized by a relent-

9

less pursuit of the territorial nation-state, the postmodern epoch is one in which humanity is trying to come to grips with an ineluctable pluralism that has prevented all but 10 percent of the world's states from having even a chance to become homogeneous. As Ivo Duchacek has pointed out, the other 90 percent of the world's politically sovereign states have substantial minorities, which must be accommodated. Even many of the remaining 10 percent have links to members of their nation who constitute minorities in surrounding states. As a consequence, simple territorial arrangements are increasingly being supplemented by nonterritorial ones to accommodate these minorities.[3] The Jews are both pioneers and beneficiaries of the new situation.

The study of the Jewish people as a polity is a proper, if neglected, element in the corpus of Jewish studies and a worthy subject of political research generally.[4]

The Jewish people has the distinction of being the longest lasting and most widespread "organization" in the history of the world. Its closest rival is the Roman Catholic Church, half its age. Curiously—and perhaps significantly—the two are organized on radically opposed principles. The Catholic Church is built on hierarchical principles from first to last and gains its survival power by their careful and intelligent manipulation.[5] The Jewish people is organized on federal principles from first to last and enhances its survival power by applying them almost instinctively in changing situations. The contrasting characteristics of these two modes of organization are intrinsically worthy of political and social investigation. So, too, is the role of the Jewish polity in the development and extension of federal principles, institutions, and processes.[6]

The Jewish polity emerges out of two sources: *kinship*—Jews are born Jews and, as such, are members of the tribe—and *consent*—they agree to be bound by their transcendant covenant. Most Jews cannot chose the ties of kinship. However, what Jews do with those ties is a matter of choice. Individually, every Jew in every age has consented to be Jewish—has voluntarily assumed the ties of *citizenship,* not simply the ties of kinship. This combination of kinship and consent lies at the very basis of the Jewish polity.

In modern times, the option not to consent expanded considerably in every respect. Today, it stands at what is probably an all-time high, even though modest counterpressures have begun to reemerge. Although modern civilization has influenced Jews to the extent that "being Jewish" is no longer an all-embracing way of life for most members of the Jewish community, the concept of and behavior involved in "being Jewish" remains far more broad-gauged in its scope and reach than the concepts of and behavior involved in being a member of a religious group only, hence its political dimension.

Consequently, the maintenance of Jewish life can be understood as a matter of familial solidarity, but it must also be understood in the light of the active will of individual Jews to function as a community. The "Jewish community" in the largest sense is defined as all those people born Jews or who have consciously and formally embraced Judaism though born outside the Jewish fold. At the same time, *Jews* can be fully understood only when they are linked by a shared destiny and a common communications network whose essential community of interest and purpose is reflected through an at times bewildering panoply of organizations.

In the end, though associational activity provides the motive thrust for the maintenance and continuation of Jewish life, the organic ties persist and are strengthened when the survival of the community seems to be at stake. Jews, even marginal ones, have a "sixth sense" about threats to their security and survival as Jews. Since the Holocaust of World War II, when the Jewish people lost one-third of its total number, that "sense" has been sharpened considerably.

What follows is a discussion of how the contemporary Jewish community has responded to the problems of transforming the passive bonds of kinship into active associational ties based on the bonds of consent; how its responses have been stimulated by the "sixth sense" mentioned above; and how the responses themselves relate to traditional patterns of Jewish organization. The sum of the discussion is generally optimistic, perhaps overly so. It is optimistic because organizationally contemporary Jewry has made great strides in the past forty years and progress on that front seems to be continuing. It may be overly optimistic because the organizational progress of the Jewish polity must be viewed in the context of the crisis of Jewish survival now besetting world Jewry. At times the gap between the organizational life of the community and most of the Jews in it seems to be growing to unmanageable proportions. The community's organizational successes may obscure its failure to mobilize most Jews to take their Jewishness with utmost seriousness. It should be borne in mind that the following discussion is presented with the knowledge that organization alone cannot solve that problem.

Part I of this work offers an overview of the foundations of the world Jewish polity and its reemergence as an active force on the world scene in our time, the reconstitution of the countrywide communities, which constitute that polity, the spheres of activity through which that polity carries out its functions, the domains into which those activities are organized, and the institutions, dimensions, and tasks of the renewed Jewish polity. It concludes by looking at the new Jewish public that has emerged in the postmodern epoch as citizens of that polity.

Part II focuses on the individual countrywide communities, which together constitute the Jewish polity. It begins with an examination of Israel as a Jewish state and focuses in turn on the Jewish communities of the Western Hemisphere and the British Commonwealth, Europe, the Muslim world, and the far-flung diasporas of Africa and Asia. It examines the institutions of each Jewish community and its organizational dynamics in the context of its overall Jewish condition. The book concludes with an examination of the problem of building citizenship in the Jewish polity now that it has been renewed under postmodern conditions.

This work is the product of the Study of Jewish Community Organization begun by the author in 1968 and conducted during the fifteen years from 1968 to 1983 in Israel and throughout the world. The list of people who made this study possible is an extensive one. First of all, I owe a debt of gratitude to the institutions involved in the sponsorship of this study. I was first asked to do this study by Dr. Stephen J. Roth of the Institute for Jewish Affairs in London, which provided the seed money for it and partial financing for the first two years. In that early period the Center for the Study of Federalism at Temple University became a cosponsor of the study and more than matched the financing from the institute. After 1970 the Jewish Community Studies Group, formed as a result of the project, became an active element in it. In 1972 the JCSG was incorporated as the Center for Jewish Community Studies (CJCS), which in 1976 became part of the Jerusalem Center for Public Affairs (JCPA). By 1972 the CJCS had full responsibility for the study, a responsibility it brought with it into the JCPA, which has housed the entire project ever since, providing the support needed for its completion.

The first step undertaken upon the initiation of the project in 1968 was to convene a working group to develop a theoretical framework and methodology for undertaking the project. Participating in that group were my colleagues A. A. Kessler, Charles S. Liebman, and Ernest Stock, and three research assistants, Steven A. Aschheim, Miriam Mundstuck, and Adina Weiss (now Lieberles). We seven hammered out the basic framework for the study, developed a set of initial theoretical statements, and undertook the first case studies on Belgium, Brazil, and South Africa. I owe them all a great debt. The products of that first year's workshop-seminar were presented at the World Congress for Jewish Studies in the summer of 1969 and later published in the *Jewish Journal of Sociology*. Each remains a seminal article in the field. Others who contributed to the workshop-seminar that year included Asher Arian and Ernest Krausz, both of whom presented papers at the World Conference of Jewish Studies, which contributed to the overall effort.

I also owe a particular debt of gratitude to those who joined with me to conduct the field studies of the communities. In the course of the study every one of the eleven largest Jewish communities, along with many of the smaller ones, was subject to a comprehensive "mapping." Besides those mentioned above, they include: Joseph Aron, Jennifer K. Bowerman, Dan Caspi, Alan M. Cohen, Benjamin Fain, Harriet Pass Friedenreich, Henryk Zvi Geller, Yaakov Glickman, Stephen R. Goldstein, Anna Gordon, Louis Greenspan, Ilan Greilsammer, Baruch Hazzan, Ephraim Inbar, Zachariah Kay, Seymour B. Liebman, Stephen Mandel, Peter Y. Medding, Edna Oberman, Esther Oren, Thomas L. Price, Marc Salzburg, Sheldon Schreter, Mervin Verbit, R. H. Wagenberg, Harold M. Waller, Simcha Werner, and Jonathan S. Woocher. Most of their studies and reports have been published by the Jerusalem Center for Public Affairs in Hebrew and English and some have also been translated into French, Spanish, and Portuguese. A list of the studies is provided in Appendix 1. I have drawn on their work for this volume and take full responsibility for my adaptation of their materials and the conclusions I have drawn from their studies.

Professor Moshe Davis of the Hebrew University's Institute for Contemporary Jewry and his colleagues, particularly Haim Avni, Paul Glickson, and Geoffrey Wigoder, also helped me during the first two years of the project. The institute provided me with my first academic base in contemporary Jewish studies as a visiting professor in the academic years 1968–69 and 1969–70. More than that, it helped provide the intellectual environment for identifying the questions to be studied and for learning what had been studied up till that time. The institute's oral history program, under the direction of Dr. Wigoder, cofinanced some of the initial interviews of Jewish community leaders who had found their way to Israel, transcriptions of which are on file in the oral history archive.

In the final writing of the book, I was assisted by several research assistants, including Jesse Fried, Edward Miller, Jami Rubin, and Joshua I. Shuman. I owe a special debt to JCPA staff researchers Alysa M. Dortort and Naomi Linder, who were responsible for bringing the final manuscript to publishable form, and to Carol S. Halberstadt and Mark Ami-El, who typed the various drafts. Special thanks are due the Lucius N. Littauer Foundation and its president William R. Frost for providing assistance in the final preparation of the manuscript.

While this volume stands fully alone, the reader might also wish to consult the other book-length studies that have emerged from the project, particularly *Community and Polity: The Organizational Dynamics of the American Jewish Community, Jewish Communities on the Great Frontier,* and *Israel: Building a New Society,* all by this author. For those wishing to place the contemporary Jewish polity in historical context, there is *The Jewish Polity* by this author and Stuart A. Cohen.

Every organized Jewish community is treated in this volume, although not all equally or even proportionately to their size. Those communities that we were able to examine more fully are discussed in greater detail and, more important, greater texture, going beyond organizational forms to look at organizational dynamics and occasionally content. It should be understood that this volume does not pretend to be a collection of exhaustive community studies. The basic works listed in Appendix 1 go further in that direction, in some cases, thoroughly, in others with much remaining to be done. Here, an effort has been made to present something of the texture of the community rather than encumber the reader with the details of community organization and history, always with the comparative dimension in mind.

The study of Jewish communities, especially contemporary communities, as polities is still in its infancy. It is my hope that this volume will advance that study and encourage others to pursue the many questions it should provoke.

Jersualem
Iyar 5747—May 1987

Notes

1. Salo W. Baron, *The Jewish Community: Its History and Structure to the American Revolution*, 3 vols. (Philadelphia: Jewish Publication Society of America, 1942), chap. 4.

2. See Daniel J. Elazar, "From the Editor of *Publius*—Federalism, Centralization, and State Building in the Modern Epoch," *Publius*, vol. 12, no. 3 (summer 1982), pp. 1–9; James W. Skillen and Stanley W. Carlson-Thies, "Religion and Political Development in Nineteenth Century Holland," *Publius*, vol. 12, no. 3 (summer 1982), pp. 43–64.

3. See Ivo Duchacek, "Antagonistic Cooperation: Territorial and Ethnic Communities," *Publius*, vol. 7, no. 4 (fall 1977), pp. 3–30; Daniel J. Elazar et al., *Handbook of Federal and Autonomy Arrangements* (forthcoming); Stephen Thernstrom and Ann Orlov, eds., *Harvard Encyclopedia of American Ethnic Groups* (Cambridge, Mass.: Harvard University Press, 1980).

4. The modern nation-state, despite its present currency, is but one form of polity. In recent years political research has come to recognize that there are other kinds of polities (or political systems, to use the term preferred among contemporary political scientists) existing alongside the nation-state even today. David Easton, Gabriel Almond, and Robert A. Dahl, among others, have pioneered in broadening the definition of political systems. See, for example, David Easton, *The Political System* (New York: A. A. Knopf, 1953); Gabriel A. Almond and James S. Coleman, eds., *The Politics of the Developing Areas,* (Princeton: Princeton University Press, 1960); and Robert A. Dahl, *Modern Political Analysis* (Englewood Cliffs, N.J.: Prentice-Hall, 1963). Dahl, for example, defines a political system as "any persistent pattern of human relationships that involves to a significant extent, power, rule, or authority . . . any collection of real objects that interact in some way with one another can be considered a system . . . ." This somewhat inadequate definition demonstrates the new breadth of the definitional framework being used to understand different forms of political order, or different polities. For a good collection of recent thought on this problem, see Roy C. Macridis and Bernard E. Brown, *Comparative Politics,* 3d ed. (Homewood, Ill.: The Dorsey Press, 1968). Robert J. Pranger offers an important and extremely relevant discussion of the larger questions of political order in *The Eclipse of Citizenship: Power and Participation in Contemporary Politics* (New York: Holt, Rinehart and Winston, 1968). Benjamin Akzin discusses this entire question in *State and Nation* (London: Hutchison University Library, 1964), a book that rests to a great extent on insights drawn from the Jewish experience.

5. See, for example, Edwin Samuel, "The Administration of the Catholic Church," in *Public Administration in Israel and Abroad 1966,* vol. 7, one of the few such studies available.

6. A few historians and social scientists have taken note of the covenant community as a distinct sociopolitical phenomenon from this perspective. Margaret Mead, for example, suggests that the Jewish polity and other covenant communities deserve special exploration; see her Introduction to Mark Zborowski and Elizabeth Herzog, *Life Is with People* (New York: Schocken Books, 1952). For an eloquent evocation of the spirit and character of the covenant community, see Page Smith, *As a City upon a Hill* (New York: Alfred A. Knopf, 1966).

Note on the Figures

The following conventions are used in the figures throughout this volume. *Keter Torah* officers and institutions are placed on the right axis of the triangle. *Keter Malkhut* officers and institutions are placed on the left axis of the triangle. *Keter Kehunah* officers and institutions are placed on the bottom axis of the triangle. Solid-line axes indicate that the relevant keter possesses identifiable officers and institutions. Broken lines axes indicate that the officers and institutions cannot presently be identified or are assumed not to have existed. Patterns of influence, authority, and communication are indicated as follows: solid-line arrows indicate continuous and/or direct patterns; broken-line arrows indicate intermittent and/or indirect patterns.

I

The Organizational Dynamics of Postmodern Jewry

1

The Foundations of the Jewish Polity[1]

Jews can be fully understood only when they are recognized as members of a polity—a covenantal community linked by a shared destiny, a promised land, and a common pattern of communications whose essential community of interest and purpose and whose ability to consent together in matters of common interest have been repeatedly demonstrated. In traditional terms, *Judaism* is essentially a theopolitical phenomenon, a means of seeking salvation by constructing God's polity, the proverbial "city upon a hill" through which the convenantal community takes on meaning and fulfills its purpose in the divine scheme of things.[2] From a more secular point of view (if such a distinction can be made), *Jewish peoplehood* has been the motivating force for communal life and creativity throughout the long history of the Jewish people. The power of this force has certainly been demonstrated in our own time with the restoration of the State of Israel.

The Jewish polity has some special characteristics. It is worldwide in scope but only territorial in a limited sense. It is not a state, although a state is an essential part of it.[3] It is authoritative but only for those who accept citizenship within it. It does not demand the exclusive loyalty of those attached to it, because many of its members share multiple loyalties.[4] And, finally, it exists by virtue of a mystique, an orientation toward a future that looks to the redemption of mankind.

Preeminently, the Jewish polity survives because of the Jews' will to carve out an area of autonomous existence amid polities that would absorb or eliminate them.[5] As it turns out, this is as true of Israel in its own way as it has been of the diaspora Jewish communities, just as it was true of all the earlier Jewish commonwealths.

It is always a mistake to underestimate the continuity of culture. Individuals are formed early in their lives by the cultures into which they are born. So, too, is a people. The seeds of whatever Jews are today were planted at the very birth of the Jewish people. Certain key characteristics visible then and deriving from those original conditions have persisted over time despite all the subsequent changes in the Jewish situation.

The Jewish polity is a product of a unique blend of kinship and consent. The blend is already reflected in the biblical account of its origins: a family of tribes that becomes a nation by consenting to God's covenant.[6] (It should be noted that the term *federal* is derived from the Latin *foedus* meaning covenant.) It continues to be reflected in later biblical narratives.[7]

Postbiblical Jewish history gave the blend a new meaning. That Jews were born Jewish puts them in a special position to begin with, one which more often than not forced them together for self-protection. Yet sufficient opportunities for conversion, assimilation, or the adoption of a posture of simple apathy toward any active effort to maintain Jewish life were almost always available as options. The survival of organized

17

and creative Jewish life, then, can only be understood in the light of the active will of many Jews to function as a community, in itself a form of consent ratified by repeated consensual acts over the millennia.

Beyond the sheer fact of communal survival, consent has remained the normal basis for organizing of the Jewish polity. Jews in different localities consented (and consent) together to form congregations and communities—in Hebrew the terms are synonymous.[8] They did (and do) this formally through articles of agreement, charters, covenants, and constitutions. The traditional Sephardi term for such articles of congregational-communal agreement, *askamot,* conveys this meaning exactly. The local communities were (and are) then tied together by additional consensual arrangements, ranging from formal federations to the tacit recognition of a particular *halakhic* authority, *shtadlan,* or supralocal body as authoritative.[9] When conditions were propitious, the de facto confederation of Jewish communities extended to wherever Jews lived. When this level of political existence was impossible, the binding force of Jewish law served to keep the federal bonds from being severed.

Covenantal Foundations

Jews have traditionally organized their communities into coherent bodies politic on a constitutional basis. In Jewish law, every Jewish community is a partnership of its members. Legally, communities do not exist apart from their members. There is no such thing as "the state" existing independently of the people in *halakhah,* or Jewish tradition. The ultimate constitutional basis of that partnership is the original covenant establishing the Jewish people, the covenant that tradition records as having been made between God and the twelve tribes of Israel at Sinai. From that covenant came the Torah, the traditional constitution of the Jewish people.

When Jews speak of Torah, they do not refer to the five books of Moses alone but to the Torah as it has grown, with the Talmud added to it, with the interpretations and commentaries added to both, in the light of the historical experience of the Jewish people. Until modern times, nobody disputed the traditional constitution. Jews accepted the Torah. They may have argued over its interpretation, but they accepted it. And out of that acceptance the Jewish polity was given constitutional form.

A covenant is a morally informed agreement or pact between parties having an independent and sufficiently equal status based on voluntary consent and established by mutual oaths or promises involving or witnessed by a transcendent authority. A covenant provides for joint action to achieve defined ends, limited or comprehensive, under conditions of mutual respect in a way that protects the respective integrities of all the parties to it. Every covenant involves consenting, promising, and agreeing. Most are meant to be of unlimited duration, if not perpetual. Covenants can bind any number of partners for a variety of purposes, but in essence they are political in that their bonds are used principally to create relationships best understood in political terms.

As much as covenant is a theological and a political concept, it is also informed by a moral or ethical perspective that treats political relationships in the classical manner. That is, it links *power* and *justice*—the two faces of politics—and preserves the classic and ancient links between ethics and politics. Again, the emphasis is on relationships rather than structures as the key to political justice. Structures are always important, but ultimately, no matter how finely tuned the structures, they come alive (or fail to) only through the human relationships that inform and shape them.

Covenant is tied in an ambiguous relationship to two related terms, *compact* and *contract*. On one hand, both compacts and contracts are closely related to covenant, and sometimes the terms are even used interchangeably. Moreover, covenantal societies tend to emphasize contractual arrangements at every level of human affairs. However, there are real differences between the three terms. Covenants and compacts differ from contracts in that the first two are constitutional or public and the last private. As such, covenantal or compactual obligation is broadly reciprocal. Those bound by one or the other are obligated to respond to one another beyond the letter of the law rather than to limit their obligations to the narrowest contractual requirements. Hence, covenants and compacts are inherently designed to be flexible in some respects and firm in others. As expressions of private law, contracts tend to be interpreted as narrowly as possible as to what the contract explicitly mandates.

A covenant differs from a compact in that its morally binding dimension takes precedence over its legal dimension. In its heart of hearts, a covenant is an agreement in which a higher moral force, traditionally God, is either a direct party to or guarantor of a particular relationship. A compact, based as it is on mutual pledges rather than guarantees by or before a higher authority, rests more heavily on legal as well as moral grounding for its politics. In other words, compact is a secular phenomenon.

This is historically verifiable by examining the shift in terminology that took place in the seventeenth and eighteenth centuries. Although those who saw the hand of God in political affairs as a rule continued to use the term *covenant,* those who sought a secular grounding for politics turned to the term *compact.* Though the distinction was not always used with strict clarity, it does appear consistently. The issue was further complicated by Rousseau and his followers, who talk about the social contract, a highly secularized concept, which, even when applied for public purposes, never develops the same moral obligation as either covenant or compact.

In its original biblical form, covenant embodies the idea that relationships between God and humans are based on morally sustained compacts of mutual promise and obligation. God's covenant with Noah (Genesis 9), which comes after Noah had hearkened fully to God's commands in what was, to say the least, an extremely difficult situation, is the first of many examples. In its political form, covenant expresses the idea that people can freely create communities and polities, peoples and publics, and civil society itself through such morally grounded and sustained compacts (whether religious or otherwise in impetus), establishing thereby enduring partnerships.[10]

The covenantal approach is clearly connected with constitutionalism. A covenant is the constitutionalization of a set of relationships of a particular kind. As such, it provides the basis for the institutionalization of those relationships; but it would be wrong to confuse the order of precedence. Again, the biblical model whereby a covenant provides the basis for constitutional government by first establishing a people or civil society which then proceeds to adopt a constitution of government for itself, is paradigmatic. Here the constitution involves the translation of a prior covenant into an actual frame or structure of government. Sometimes the constitution includes the covenant within it, serving both purposes simultaneously.

The American Declaration of Independence is an excellent example of a political covenant. The diverse inhabitants of the thirteen colonies reaffirmed that they consented to become a people. It was not without reason, therefore, that Abraham Lincoln fondly described the union created by that act as "a regular marriage."[11] The partners do not unquestionably live happily ever after, but they are bound by covenant to struggle toward such an end, a commitment well understood and made explicit by Lincoln during the Civil War.

The covenantal approach not only informs and animates the Jewish polity but represents the greatest Jewish contribution to political life and thought. It is possible that covenant ideas emerged spontaneously in different parts of the world. If covenant thinking is rooted in human nature as well as nurture, it is to be expected that some people everywhere would be oriented toward the idea somehow. However, it is not sufficient for random individuals to be disposed to it for an idea to take root and spread. Somehow a culture or civilization must emerge that embodies and reflects that idea.

The first such civilization or culture was that of ancient Israel whose people transformed and perfected a device originally developed among the west Asian peoples who inhabited the area. The first known uses of covenant were the vassal treaties through which the empire builders of west Asia secured the fealty of lesser peoples and their domains through pacts secured by oath before their respective deities.[12] These international or intra-imperial pacts laid out the form that covenants have taken ever since, which included five elements: a prologue indicating the parties involved, a preamble stating the general purposes of the covenant and the principles behind it, a body of conditions and operative clauses, an oath to make the covenant morally binding, and stipulated sanctions to be applied if the covenant were violated.

Either parallel to or derived from these ancient vassal covenants there emerged domestic political and religious usages of covenant. The two were connected in the Bible to form the classic foundation of the covenant tradition.[13] God's covenant with Israel established the Jewish people and founded it as a body politic, while at the same time creating the religious framework that gave the polity its raison d'être, its norms, and its constitution, as well as the guidelines for developing a political order based on proper, that is, covenantal, relationships.

Biblical adaptation of the forms of the vassal covenants involved a transformation of the purpose and content so great as to mean a difference in kind, not merely degree. A covenant was used to found a people, making their moral commitment to one another far stronger and enduring than that of a vassal to an imperial overlord. The Bible draws a distinction between "sons of the covenant," *bnei brit* in Hebrew, and "masters of the covenant," *ba'alei brit*. *Bnei brit* is used where the covenant has created a new entity whose partners are bound together as siblings in a family. The covenant that unites and forms the Jewish people in the biblical account and in all later Jewish history makes all Jews *bnei brit*. However, where the term used is *ba'alei brit,* the covenant is essentially an international treaty. It does not create a new entity but establishes a relationship of peace and mutual ties between separate entities that remain separate for all purposes outside the limited-purpose pact.

This new form of covenant was understood to be not simply witnessed by Heaven, but as bringing God in as a partner, thus informing it with religious value and implication for the Israelites, who saw no distinction between its religious and political dimensions. The covenant remained a theopolitical document with as heavy an emphasis on the political as could be. The strong political dimension reflected God's purpose in choosing one people to be the builders of a holy commonwealth that would be a model for all others.

It was only later with the rise of Christianity and the beginning of the long exile of the Jews from their land that covenant took on a more strictly religious character for some, in which the political dimension was downplayed, if not downright ignored by Christian theologians on the one hand and diminished by Jewish legists on the other. Christianity embraced the covenant idea as one of its foundations but reinterpreted the old biblical covenant establishing a people and a polity to be a covenant of grace between God and individual humans granted unilaterally and mediated by Jesus.[14] Jewish legists simply took the basic covenantal framework of Judaism for granted and concentrated on the fine points of the law as applied to daily living or the expected messianic redemption.[15]

In the Jewish world, the political dimension of covenanting received new impetus in the eleventh through fourteenth centuries to provide a basis for constituting local Jewish communities throughout Europe. That effort ran parallel to the establishment of municipal corporations throughout the continent, which were legitimized by royal charter, usually negotiated between the municipality and the throne.[16]

All this is well documented in Jewish sources. Because Jews were always moving, either by choice or by necessity, when they came to new places they had to organize communities, for Jews cannot function Jewishly without organized communities. It was to ease the process that model charters for setting up communities and communal institutions came into existence. Thus *Sefer HaShtarot* (The Book of Contracts), a late eleventh- or early twelfth-century compendium of model laws (significantly, in the form of contracts) by Rabbi Judah HaBarceloni, a Spanish Jew, includes model laws for every contingency, all of which are in accord with the Torah, that is, constitutional.[17] It is the first such compendium that we know of in Jewish history. Perhaps it is the first in history. It includes model charters for establishing welfare societies, for organizing synagogues, for providing assistance to widows and orphans, for establishing schools, and many others. Most especially, it includes a model charter for establishing a *kehillah,* a local community whose preamble reads as follows:

> We, the elders and leaders of the community of———due to our many sins we have declined and become fewer and weaker, and until only few have been left of many, like a single tree at the mountaintop, and the people of our community have been left with no head or *nasi,* or head justice or leader, so that they are like sheep without a shepherd and some of our community go about improperly clothed and some speak obscenely and some mix with the gentiles and eat their bread and become like them, so that only in the Jewish name, are they at all different. We have seen and discussed the matter and we agreed in assembly of the entire community, and we all, great and small alike, have gone on to establish this charter in this community.

The model charter continues to describe how the community, by this action, establishes its right to enact ordinances, establish institutions, levy and collect taxes—in short, carry on all the functions of a municipal government.

The principles of community enunciated in the foregoing document are clear. For the actions of a community to be legally binding in Jewish law, it had to be duly constituted by its prospective members, preferably through a constituent assembly and a constitutional document. They must be able to say that "we have met together as the elders, that we have discussed the matter, that we have agreed in assembly of the entire community." If these patterns were not followed the action would not be valid.

Covenant and the Origins of the Polity

Since its beginnings, political science has identified three basic ways in which polities come into existence: conquest, organic development, and covenant.[18] These questions of origins are not abstract; the mode of founding of a polity does much to determine the framework for its later political life.

Conquest can be understood to include not only its more direct manifestation, a conqueror gaining control of a land or a people, but also such subsidiary ways as a revolutionary conquest of an existing state, a coup d'état, or even an entrepreneur conquering a market and institutionalizing his control through corporate means. Conquest tends to produce hierarchically organized regimes ruled in an authoritarian manner: power pyramids with the conqueror on top, his agents in the middle, and the people underneath the entire structure. The original expression of this kind of polity was the pharaonic state of ancient Egypt. It was hardly an accident that those rulers who brought the pharaonic state to its fullest development had the pyramids built as their tombs. Although the pharaonic model has been judged illegitimate in Western society, modern totalitarian theories, particularly fascism and nazism, represent an attempt to give it theoretical legitimacy.

Organic evolution involves the development of political life from its beginnings in families, tribes, and villages to large polities in such a way that institutions, constitutional relationships, and power alignments emerge in response to the interaction between past precedent and changing circumstances with the minimum of deliberate constitutional choice. The result is a polity with a single center of power, dominated by an accepted political elite, controlling the periphery, which may or may not have influence at the center. Classic Greek political thought emphasized the organic evolution of the polity and rejected any other means of polity-building as deficient or improper. The organic model is closely related to the concept of natural law in the political order. Natural law informs the world and, when undisturbed, leads to a kind of organic development, which, in turn, results in this model of the polity.

The organic model has proved most attractive to political philosophers precisely because, at its best, it seems to reflect the natural order of things. Thus it has received the most intellectual and academic attention. However, just as conquest produces hierarchically organized regimes ruled in an authoritarian manner, organic evolution produces oligarchic regimes, which, at their best, have an aristocratic flavor and, at their worst, are simply the rule of the many by the few. In the first, the goal is to control the top of the pyramid; in the second, the goal is to control the center of power.

Covenantal foundings emphasize the deliberate coming together of humans as equals to establish bodies politic so that all reaffirm their fundamental equality and retain their basic liberties. Polities whose origins are covenantal reflect the exercise of constitutional choice and broad-based participation in constitutional design. Polities founded by covenant are essentially federal in the original meaning of the term—whether they are federal in structure or not. That is, each polity is a matrix compounded of equal confederates who come together freely and retain their respective integrities even as they are bound in a common whole. Such polities are republican by definition, and power in them must be diffused among many centers or the cells within the matrix.

Recurring expressions of the covenant model are found among the Jews, whose people started out as rebels against pharaonic Egypt; the Swiss, whose people started out as rebels against the Holy Roman Empire; and the Dutch, Scots, and Puritans who rebelled against the Roman Catholic hierarchy in the Reformation era. In the modern epoch, republicans who were rebels against either hierarchical or organic theories of the state adopted the covenant model in one version or another. Frontiersmen—people who have chosen to settle new areas where there are no established patterns of governance in

which to fit and who, therefore, have had to compact with one another to create governing institutions—are to be found among the most active covenanters.

What is common to all political societies rooted in the covenant idea is that they
have drawn their inspiration proximately or ultimately from its biblical source. There is
evidence of other contractual or oath-bound societies and, of course, constitutionalism of
various kinds exists outside the biblical tradition. But there is no evidence of any developed covenantal tradition that is not derived from the Bible.

The biblical grand design for humankind is federal in three ways. (1) It is based on
a network of covenants beginning with those between God and man, which weave the
web of human, especially political, relationships in a federal way—through pact, association, and consent. (2) The classic biblical commonwealth was a fully articulated federation of tribes instituted and reaffirmed by covenant to function under a common constitution and laws. Any and all constitutional changes in the Israelite polity were introduced
through covenanting, and even after the introduction of the monarchy, the federal
element was maintained until most of the tribal structures were destroyed by external
forces. The biblical vision of the restored commonwealth in the messianic era envisages
the reconstitution of the tribal federation. (3) The biblical vision for the "end of days"—
the messianic era—not only sees a restoration of Israel's tribal federation, but what is, for
all intents and purposes, a world confederation of nations, each preserving its own
integrity while accepting a common divine covenant and constitutional order. This order
will establish appropriate covenantal relationships for the entire world. Although it
shares many of the same positive ends, it is the antithesis of the ecumenical world state
envisaged by the Roman and Christian traditions, which see the merging of everyone
into a single entity. The biblical-covenantal-Jewish view sees peoples preserving their
own integrities within a shared whole.

Covenant theory emphasizes human freedom because only free people can enter
into agreements with one another. It also presupposes the need for government and the
need to organize civil society on principles that assure the maintenance of those rights
and the exercise of power in a cooperative or partnershiplike way.

Covenantal (or federal) liberty, however, is not simply the right to do as one pleases
within broad boundaries. Federal liberty emphasizes liberty to pursue the moral purposes
for which the covenant was made. This latter kind of liberty requires that moral distinctions be drawn and that human actions be judged according to the terms of the covenant.
This does not preclude changes in social norms, but the principles of judgment remain
constant. Consequently, covenantal societies, founded as they are on covenantal choice,
emphasize constitutional design and choice as a continuing process.

The Edah as a Classic Republic

The Jewish polity has followed the covenant model since its inception, adapting it
to variegated circumstances in which Jews have found themselves over the millennia—as
a tribal federation, a federal monarchy, a state with a diaspora, a congress of covenantal
communities, a network of regional federations or confederations, or a set of voluntary
associations.

The classic Hebrew name for this kind of polity is *edah*. The *edah* is the assembly of all
the people constituted as a body politic. *Edah* is often translated as congregation; that term
has a religious connotation today that it did not have when introduced in sixteenth- and

seventeenth-century biblical translations. Then it had a civil meaning as well. It was a "congregation"—an institutionalized gathering of people who congregate (come together) that meets at regular times or frequently for common action and decision making.[19]

In Mosaic times *edah* became the Hebrew equivalent of "commonwealth" or "republic," with strong democratic overtones. The idea of the Jewish people as an *edah* has persisted ever since and the term has been used to describe the Jewish body politic in every period to the present. In this respect, the term parallels (and historically precedes) similar phenomena such as the *landesgemeinde* in Switzerland, the Icelandic *althing,* and the town meeting in the United States.

The characteristics of the original *edah* can be summarized as follows:

1. The Torah is the constitution of the *edah*.

2. All members of the *edah,* men, women, and children, participate in some appropriate way in constitutional decisions.

3. Political equality exists for those capable of taking full responsibility for Jewish survival.

4. Decisions are made by an assembly that determines its own leaders within the parameters of divine mandate.

5. The *edah* is portable and transcends geography.

6. Nevertheless, for it to function completely, the *edah* needs Eretz Israel.

These basic characteristics have been preserved with such modifications as were necessary over the centuries. Thus, in biblical times, taking full responsibility for Jewish survival meant being able to bear arms. Subsequently, the arms-bearing measure of political equality gave way to one of Torah study. Today the diaspora measure is contributing to the support of Israel, while arms-bearing is again the measure in Israel. The principles of assembly, leadership, and decision making have remained the same although modes of assembling, leadership recruitment, and leaders' roles and responsibilities have changed from time to time. The portability of the desert-born *edah* is as notable a characteristic as is its attachment to Zion. The Torah has persisted as the *edah*'s constitution albeit with changing interpretations.

The regime most common in Jewish experience has been the aristocratic republic, in the classic sense of the term—rule by a limited number who take upon themselves an obligation or conceive of themselves as having a special obligation to their people and to God. For Jews, this has been manifested in some combination of a perceived obligation by those of greater status or wealth to use their privileged position to help other Jews and by those learned in Torah to serve the will of God by serving the community.

Jewish republicanism is rooted in a democratic foundation based on the equality of all Jews as citizens of the Jewish people. All Jews must participate in the establishment and maintenance of their polity, as demonstrated in the Bible—at Sinai, on the plains of Moab, before Shechem, and elsewhere—in *Sefer HaShtarot,* and in many other sources. Nor is that foundation merely theoretical; even where power may not be exercised on a strictly democratic basis, it is generally exercised in light of democratic norms.

There are problems associated with the use of these terms, but they do help us understand that the Jewish polity often has been governed by a kind of trusteeship. It is a trusteeship because the community is republican, because it is a res publica, a public thing or a commonwealth—a body politic that belongs to its members. The Jewish people is a res publica with a commitment to a teaching and law, which its members are not free simply to alter as they wish but must be maintained to be faithful to principles.

The Western world today takes the republican revolution for granted. Yet the republican revolution was one of the great revolutions of modernity. It is the foundation of modern democratic government. The West pioneered in the idea and practice of republican government. The Jews were among the first many centuries ago. Then came the Greeks and the early Romans. Except for a few outposts, including the Jewish *kehillah,* republicanism died under the realities of imperial Rome and medieval feudalism, replaced by absolutism. In modern times, a revolution was needed to restore the republican principle. Before the republican revolution, the prevailing view was that the state was the private preserve of its governors. When Louis XIV said "I am the state" he was articulating a classic antirepublican position.

The rise and fall of dictators in the Third World today shows the situation in a region that is in transition from prerepublican to republican government. It is no accident that most of the Arab states, after their revolutions in the 1950s and early 1960s, added the word *republic* to their new names, to signify that they sought to be part of the republican revolution. The Islamic world, far more than Europe, held to the notion for centuries that the organs of governance belonged to whomever held power. The people sought to stay clear of involvement with their governors. At best, the ruler was benevolent; he was Harun al-Rashid, who put on a disguise and wandered in the marketplace and, as he saw injustices, rectified them on the spot. He was a benevolent despot, but it was still despotism; it was not a republican government. More often than not, the despotism was just that, hence the postcolonial revolutions in the Arab world and the at least symbolic embracing of republicanism, which, in most Arab states, has yet to become real.

Still, an aristocratic republic always has a darker side in that it has a tendency to degenerate into oligarchy. The history of governance in the Jewish community has been one of swinging between the two poles of aristocratic republicanism and oligarchy. Though this is a perennial problem, the basic aristocratic republicanism of the Jewish polity has worked equally well to prevent absolutism or autocracy.

The Jewish people rarely has had anything like dictatorship and then only locally and de facto under unique circumstances. Jews are a notably intractable people, even under conditions of statehood where coercion theoretically has been possible; hence, dictatorship has not been an acceptable regime for Jews.

Nor have Jews in the past had anything like the open society of the kind envisaged by many contemporary Americans, in which every individual is free to choose his or her own "life-style." One of the reasons for this is that being Jewish and maintaining the Jewish polity has not been simply a matter of survival. It has also been a matter of living up to specific norms based on divine teaching and law, which establish the expectation that private and public life is to be shaped according to that teaching and law.

The Three Arenas of Jewish Political Organization

From earliest times, the Jewish polity has been organized in three arenas. Besides the *edah,* or national, arena, there are countrywide or regional, and local arenas of organization. The immediately local arena comprises local Jewish communities around the world of varying sizes, under varying forms of communal organization. Whether we are speaking of Yavneh or Saragossa, Mottel or Chicago, the local community remains the basic cell of Jewish communal life. Here the institutions that serve the Jewish community are organized and function.

Beyond the local arena, there is a larger, countrywide arena in which the Jews in particular regions, countries, or states organize for common purposes. The organizational expressions of that arena have included such phenomena as the Resh Galuta (Exilarch) and Yeshivot of Babylonia, the Vaad Arba Aratzot (Council of the Four Lands) of late medieval Poland, the State of Israel, the Board of Deputies of British Jewry, and the congeries of "national" (meaning countrywide) organizations of American Jewry framed by the Council of Jewish Federations. Fund-raising for Israel, for example, depends on work in local communities but is generally organized in this second arena on a country-by-country basis.

Beyond the second arena, there is the third, that of the Jewish people as a whole: the *edah*. This arena was extremely weak for nearly a millennium but has been given new institutional form within the last century, most particularly in our time. The *edah* is the main focus of the reconstitution of the Jewish people in our time.

This threefold division into separate arenas of governance, once formulated in early Israelite history, has remained a permanent feature of Jewish political life. This is so despite frequent changes in the forms of organization of the several arenas and in the terminology used to describe them.

The Bible delineates the first form in which these three arenas were constituted. The *edah* was constituted by the *shevatim* (*shevet,* tribe), each with its own governmental institutions. Each *shevet* was, in turn, a union of *batei av* (*bet av,* extended household). After the Israelite settlement in Canaan, the most prominent form of local organization was the *ir* (city or township) with its own assembly (*ha'ir*) and council (*sha'ar ha'ir* or *ziknai ha'ir*).

Subsequently, in the local arena, just as the *bet av* gave way to the *ir,* the *ir* gave way to the *kehillah* (local community) wherever the Jewish population was a minority. The *kehillah* became the molecular unit of organization for all postbiblical Jewry, especially because new *kehillot* could be established anywhere by any ten adult Jewish males who so constituted themselves. Although the *kehillah* survives in the diaspora, in contemporary Israel, the local arena is once again governed by comprehensive municipal units—cities or villages.

Similarly, the breakdown of the traditional tribal system (a phenomenon that long preceded the first exile) resulted in the replacement of the *shevet* by the *medinah* (properly rendered as autonomous jurisdiction or province in its original meaning), a regional framework, which embraces a congeries of *kehillot* that it unites in an organizational structure, as in Medinat Yehud (Judea in the Persian Empire). In the diaspora, the term *medinah* became almost interchangeable with *eretz* (country) to describe the intermediate arena, as in Medinat Polin (the organized Jewish community in Poland) in Eretz Lita (the organized Jewish community in late medieval Lithuania). In modern times, the term came to mean a politically sovereign state and is now used only in connection with Medinat Yisrael (the State of Israel).

The term *edah,* as an expression of the widest form of Jewish political association, retained its original usage unimpaired until transformed in colloquial modern Hebrew usage, where it came to denote a country-of-origin group in Israel. Occasionally, it was replaced by such synonyms as Knesset Yisrael. The *edah* managed to survive the division of Israel into two kingdoms, the Babylonian exile, and the Roman conquest of Judea by developing new forms of comprehensive organization. During the period of the second commonwealth (ca. 440 B.C.E.–140 C.E.) and again from the second to the eleventh centuries, it was particularly successful in constructing a fully articulated institutional framework that embraced both Israel and the diaspora. The breakdown of the universal Moslem empire and consequent demise of the *edah*-wide institutions of Resh Galuta and Gaonate in the middle of the eleventh century left world Jewry bereft of comprehensive institutions other than the *halakhah* itself. From then until the mid-nineteenth century, the *edah* was held together principally by its common Torah and laws as manifested in a worldwide network of rabbinical authorities linked by their communications (responsa) on *halakhic* matters. The revival of other *edah*-wide institutions in our own times is a principal subject of this book.[20]

The Three Ketarim

Classically, leadership in the Jewish polity has been divided and shared among three domains known in Hebrew as the three *ketarim* (crowns): the *keter torah,* the domain of the Torah; the *keter kehunah,* the domain of the priesthood; and the *keter malkhut,* literally, the crown of kingship but more correctly understood as the domain of governance. Each of these *ketarim* has functions it must perform if Jewish life is to be complete; hence, all are necessary for the survival and development of the *edah.*[21] There has never been a time when the *edah* has not in some way functioned through some kind of division of authority and powers among the three *ketarim.* This is not separation of powers in the modern sense. The *ketaric* division is for comprehensive polities that embrace more than the organs of government in the modern sense. Hence it comes before the executive-legislative-judicial division. Each *keter* combines a range of functions, institutions, and roles within its domain.

The *keter torah* embraces those responsible for the maintenance and application of the Torah, its laws, principles, and spirit in the life of the Jewish people and governance of the *edah.* Its roots go back to Moses, the first *navi* (prophet) and, as such, the first to bear that *keter.* After the age of prophecy, it passed to the *soferim* (scribes) and then to the Sanhedrin with its *hakhamim* (sages) and rabbis. In the traditional Jewish polity, its bearers functioned primarily as teachers and judges.

The *keter kehunah* embraces those who are responsible for the ritual and sacerdotal expressions of Jewish being, designed to bring Jews closer to Heaven individually and collectively (and hence to each other as Jews). From a public perspective, the functions of this crown play a major role in determining the fact and character of citizenship in the *edah.* Originally granted in the Torah to Aaron and his heirs, it is principally identified with the *cohanim,* but after the destruction of the Second Temple, its functions passed to other religious functionaries, principally *hazzanim* and, more recently, congregational rabbis, and generally were confined to the most local arena of Jewish organization.

The *keter malkhut* embraces those who are responsible for conducting the civil business of the *edah:* to establish and manage its organized framework, its political and social institutions, to raise and expend the money needed for the functioning of the *edah,* and to handle its political and civic affairs. Although, like the others, it is bound by the Torah-as-constitution, this *keter* has existed as a separate source of authority since the beginning of the *edah,* with its own institutions, responsibilities, and tasks. It is the oldest of the *ketarim,* emerging out of the patriarchal leadership of the original Israelite families. Later, it passed to the *nesi'im* (magistrates), *shofetim* (judges), and *zekenim* (elders), and then to the *melekh* (king). After the end of Jewish political independence in Eretz Israel, it was carried on by the Nasi (patriarch) in Eretz Israel and the Resh Galuta (exilarch) in

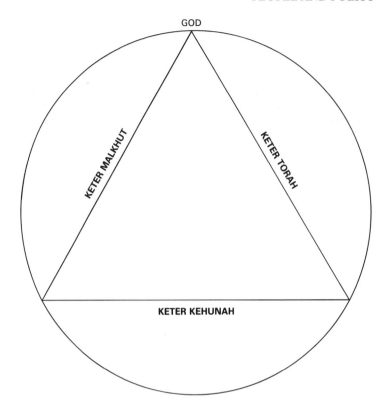

GOD

KETER MALKHUT

KETER TORAH

KETER KEHUNAH

Figure 1.1.   Constitutional structure of the *edah*.

Babylonia, the *negidim* of Spain, and the *parnassim* of the *kehillot*. Figure 1.1 is a generalized model of the structure of the *edah* following this division of authority.

Thus, one of the ways in which Jews tried to prevent the corruption of their governing bodies was through the division of powers in the polity. The legitimacy of the division is made explicit in many texts. For example, Bereshit Rabbah, the Midrashic commentary on the Book of Genesis, comments on the verse: "The scepter shall not depart from Judah, nor the ruler's staff from between his legs" (Gen. 49:10). According to the Midrash, the "scepter" is interpreted as the exilarchs in Babylon, who rule the people, Israel, with the stick; the "ruler's staff" are the patriarchs of the family of Rav, who teach Torah to the populace in the land of Israel.

Another explanation of the verse is offered: "The scepter is the Messiah, son of David (*Mashiah ben David*) who will rule over the kingdom, that is to say, Rome, with a stick. And the ruler's staff are those who teach *halakhah* to Israel." Even after the Messiah comes there will have to be a separation of powers, for even he is not to be trusted with all the powers alone. Even if he can rule over Rome, there still must be the great Sanhedrin to teach *halakhah* to Israel.

This traditional pattern underwent many changes in the modern epoch but continued to be the basic model for the *edah* and its *kehillot*, if only out of necessity because the classic division persisted in new forms. In the nineteenth century, the institutions of the *keter kehunah* became stronger at the expense of the others as Jewish life was redefined under modernity to be primarily "religious," even as Jews ceased to rely on the Torah as binding law. The synagogues became elaborate institutions and their rabbis the principal instrumentalities of the *keter kehunah*. Today, however, as we shall see, the Jewish polity is amid a resurgence of the *keter malkhut*. This is principally because of the reestablishment of a Jewish state in Eretz Israel, but it also reflects changes in the orientation of Jews in the diaspora.

The increasing narrowness of approach of the traditional bearers of the *keter torah*, coupled with the growing secularization of Jews, which made that sphere and the sphere of *keter kehunah* less attractive to them, all contributed to this power shift. In the political world, the domain with the key to political power obviously had an advantage. In addition, as the other two domains were fragmented among different movements, each claiming to be authoritative, the *keter malkut* became the only domain in which all groups would meet together, at least for limited political purposes, further strengthening the latter's position in the *edah*.

These shifts in power are only several of many in the history of the *edah*, part of the continuing and dynamic tension among the *ketarim*.

Representative Government in the Edah

Representative government in the *edah* subsequent to the biblical period represents, in many respects, a continuing effort to maintain ancient forms of participation in new guises, forms that have disappeared in other modern polities and are only now beginning to change for the *edah*. The basis of governance in the original *edah* (ca. 1280–1000 B.C.E.) was the assembly of all its citizens for covenanting and other fundamental constitutional questions, all adult males for deciding basic policy questions (such as declarations of constitutionally permitted wars), and the tribally selected *nesi'im* on an ad hoc basis for special tasks and a permanent basis for continuing ones. Governance between *edah*-like assemblies was in the hands of notables designated apparently by some form of consensus, based on the recognition of some families as leading ones. By the time of the institution of kingship (1000–722 B.C.E.), it was already apparent that the *edah* no longer attempted to assemble as a whole, although there were still assemblies of notables drawn from all the functioning tribes to play the role of the assembly of the whole. This system may have persisted in Judah after the fall of the northern kingdom (ca. 721–440 B.C.E.)—evidence is scanty—with assemblies of the Am Ha-aretz, consisting of local notables replacing assemblies of tribal leaders.

When Ezra and Nehemiah reconstituted the Jewish polity (ca. 440 B.C.E.), most of world Jewry continued to live outside Eretz Israel; hence assembly of the entire *edah* was impossible even in theory. It was then that a system of virtual representation was formally introduced through the establishment of the Anshei Knesset HaGedolah, which assembled in Jerusalem. This new body comprised 120 members symbolically representing a *minyan* (quorum of ten) from each of the twelve tribes and, hence, the *edah* as a whole, a sign that virtual representation was the intent behind its formation. It was really composed of people who lived in Judah plus one or two members from the communities of the exile who came to settle in Judah and could be added to the body, who spoke for the rest of the *edah*. The transportation technology at the time made any other system impossible.

This system of virtual representation continued through the next nine hundred years of Jewish history, even after the diaspora Jewish communities developed fully articulated governing institutions of their own. The only changes were that in some periods there was regularized representation from the diaspora in the *edah*'s sitting decision-making body, located in Jerusalem until 70 C.E. and subsequently in other parts of Eretz Israel. It ended only with the abolition of the Nesiut (patriarchate) by the Romans, ca. 429 C.E.

The *yeshivot* in Babylonia continued this pattern when power passed to them. They became the virtual representatives of the *edah* in its rule-making and adjudication functions, paralleling the Rosh HaGolah (exilarch), who was the *edah*'s chief magistrate. The *yeshivot* continued the tradition of bringing in people from around the Jewish world to the extent possible on a voluntary, personal choice basis, consisting of those who decided to come, study, and stay. This arrangement persisted for six hundred years, until the system was disrupted by the abolition of the office of Rosh HaGolah in 1042 C.E.

After that, the *edah* was unable to sustain equivalent common institutions, surviving as a communications network for *halakhic* decision making through correspondence rather than an assembly. Political organization was confined to local, countrywide, or, in rare cases, multicountry regions. Hence the system of virtual representation existed in principle rather than practice. The structure of the *edah* changed during the next nine hundred years, being expressed through a handful of notable *halakhic* figures whose decisions gained *edah*-wide acceptance or a handful of *shtadlanim* whose influential services were recognized *edah*-wide.

The problems of transportation and communication encountered by Ezra and Nehemiah in the fifth century B.C.E. remained unchanged until well into the nineteenth century C.E. At times, deterioration of conditions made the problems even greater. Not until the development of the steamboat, railroad, and telegraph did new technology make continental and intercontinental links feasible.

It was not until the World Zionist Congress in 1897 that an effort was made to establish a body representative of the *edah* in modern terms: through constituency elections of delegates to a worldwide congress in which all communities were potentially if not actually to be represented. Since that time, there has been a striving to establish such institutions. The WZO was and is a membership organization. It became worldwide in scope but never embraced a majority of the *edah* as members. The World Jewish Congress, established in 1936, tried to overcome that problem by being based on country affiliates, the major representative bodies from each countrywide Jewish community. However, its strength was and is concentrated in Europe and Latin America with no real presence in the world's largest Jewish communities—the United States, Israel, the Soviet Union, and France.

Framing organizations were established in the local and countrywide arenas by the end of the modern epoch or during the first generation of the postmodern epoch as a culmination of the modernization process. They were accompanied by a general revolution in transportation and communications based on air travel and the airwaves. Jews are now engaged in the reestablishment of effective, continuing *edah*-wide framing institutions, principally through the reconstitution of the Jewish Agency and the WZO. Because transportation and communication technologies now permit this, it is likely that something serious will come out of the effort. Nevertheless, this will not be the whole story, for there are structural limitations to the degree to which formal representatives of all segments of the *edah* can assemble on a regular basis. Thus we are returning to the situation of ancient Israel but on a worldwide scale. Leading figures representing the elements of the *edah* come together at regular intervals and are involved in consultations

Table 1.1
Jewish Population and Distribution by Continent (in thousands)

Continent	Year							
	1840		1900		1939		1982	
	Total	%	Total	%	Total	%	Total	%
Europe[a]	3,950	87.8	8,900	80.9	9,500	56.8	2,843	21.9
Asia	300	6.7	510	4.6	1,030	6.2	3,417	26.3
Africa	198	4.4	375	3.4	625	3.7	172	1.3
North America								
South America	50	1.1	1,200	10.9	5,540	33.1	6,478	49.9
Oceania	2	*	15	0.2	33	0.2	79	0.6
Total	4,500	100.0	11,000	100.0	16,728	100.0	12,989	100.0

*less than 0.1%

Sources:
1. Jacob Lestschinsky, *Tfutzot Yisrael ahar haMilhamah,* Tel Aviv, 1958.
2. *American Jewish Year Book, 1968* and *1984.*
[a]Including Russia.

Except for those in the Moslem countries that were soon virtually to disappear, the major functioning Jewish communities all had acquired sufficient size to become significant factors on the Jewish scene only within the previous two generations. In many cases, the original shapers of those communities were still alive, and many were still the actual community leaders. The Jewish world had been willy-nilly thrown back to a pioneering stage.

This new epoch is still in its early years, hardly more than a single generation old; hence, its character is still in its formative stages. Nevertheless, with the establishment of the State of Israel in 1948 the Jewish polity began a constitutional change of revolutionary proportions, inaugurating a new epoch in Jewish constitutional history. For the first time in almost two millenia, the Jewish people were presented with the opportunity to attain citizenship in their own state. Israel's very first law (Hok Ha-Shevut, the Law of Return) specified that every Jew had a right to settle in Israel and automatically acquire Israeli citizenship.

To date, only a fraction of the *edah* have taken advantage of Israel's availability. Most continue to live in the lands of the diaspora of their own free will. Hence the dominant structural characteristic of the *edah* continues to be the absence of a binding, all-embracing political framework, although it now has a focus. The State of Israel and its various organs have a strong claim to preeminence in fields that touch on every aspect of Jewish communal life. The Israeli leadership have argued consistently that Israel is qualitatively different from the diaspora and hence its centrality must be acknowledged. The American Jewish leadership, in particular, have taken the position that Israel is no more than first among equals. Nevertheless, the reestablishment of a Jewish state has crystallized the *edah* as a polity, restoring a sense of political involvement among Jews and shaping a new institutional framework in which the business of the *edah* is conducted.

The diffusion of authority and influence that continues to characterize the structure of the *edah* and its components has taken various forms in the new epoch. The *keter malkhut* has been transformed into a network of single and multipurpose functional authorities, most of which do not aspire to do more than serve their particular functions, but all of which acknowledge the place of the State of Israel at the fulcrum of the network. The *keter kehunah* has become a conglomeration of synagogue movements and their rabbinates, who are mainly responsible for ritual and pastoral functions. Each manages—independently—various ritual functions in a manner it deems appropriate to its own traditions, perspectives, and environment. That each of these movements has established a framework with worldwide aspirations, such as the World Union for Progressive Judaism and the World Council of Synagogues, merely underlines the new organizational character of the *edah*.

Sectoral segmentation is most prononounced in the *keter torah*. Contemporary Jews take their cues in this domain from a kaleidoscopic spectrum of authorities. Their range stretches from the Jewish professors and scholars who influence contemporary Jews' understanding of what is expected of them as Jews to the rabbinical leadership of the Conservative and Reform camps, who may use the traditional devices for ruling on matters of Torah but often in untraditional ways, to the heads of very traditional *yeshivot* and the *rebbes* of various émigré Hassidic communities who have reestablished themselves in the principal cities of Israel and the United States from which they have developed multicountry networks.

The fragmentation of the *keter torah* is both a reflection and an expression of the absence yet of a clear-cut, commonly accepted constitutional basis for the entire *edah*. The tendency toward a wide variety of interpretations of the Torah, which emerged during the modern epoch, has now become exacerbated. It is a sign of the times that if the Torah is to be included in the definition of the constitution, it has to be reinterpreted for Jews. The reality is that the norms by which Jews live their lives are interpreted through various prisms, of which the traditional prism is now only one. Still, it seems that most Jews perceive the Torah to be a constitutional referent in some way.

This fragmentation is further reflected in the multiplicity of camps and parties that exert influence on the life of the *edah* and its constituents. Broadly speaking, the principal camps can be termed: the Orthodox, the Masorati (traditional), who see themselves as continuing the ways of the Pharisees, the Liberal religious, and the Neo-Sadducees. The last includes Israelis seeking to express their Judaism through Israeli Jewry's emerging civil religion—Zionists—and those diaspora Jews who find their best means of Jewish expression in the communal institutions. These camps are separate but not mutually exclusive. Presented diagrammatically, they ought to be viewed as a triangle, a device that stresses their points of overlap as well as their distinctiveness (fig. 1.2). The Mizrahi Party, for instance, straddles the Zionist and the Orthodox camps, viewing its Zionism as one expression of its Orthodoxy. Increasingly, too, do the Conservative (Masorati) and Reform (Liberal) movements find themselves linked with Zionism. At the same time, the Neturei Karta, the secular Zionists, and the surviving classical Reform elements remain separated in their respective camps.

Whatever its form of organization, the primary fact of Jewish communal life today is its voluntary character. Although there are differences from country to country in degree of actual freedom to be Jewish or not, the virtual disappearance of the remaining legal and even social or cultural barriers to individual free choice in all but a handful of countries has made free association the dominant characteristic of Jewish life in the postmodern era. Consequently, the first task of each Jewish community is to learn to deal with this freedom. This task is a major factor in determining the direction of the reconstitution of Jewish life in this generation.

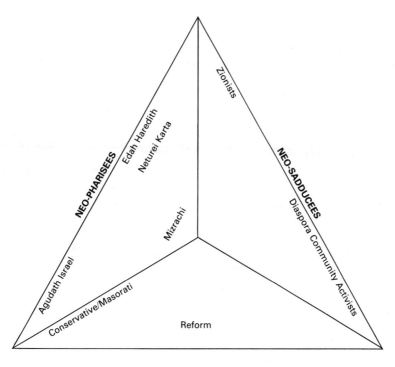

Figure 1.2.   Camps and parties of the *edah*.

The new voluntarism also extends into the internal life of the Jewish community, generating pluralism even in previously free but relatively homogeneous or monolithic community structures. This pluralism is increased by the breakdown of the traditional reasons for being Jewish and the rise of new incentives for Jewish association. This pluralistic Jewish polity can best be described as a communications network of interacting institutions, each of which, while preserving its own structural integrity and filling its own functional role, is connected to the others in a variety of ways. The boundaries of the polity, insofar as it is bounded, are revealed only when the pattern of the network is uncovered. The pattern stands revealed only when both its components are: its institutions and organizations with their respective roles and the way in which communications are passed between them.

The pattern is inevitably dynamic. There is rarely a fixed division of authority and influence but, instead, one that varies from time to time and often from issue to issue, with different entities in the network taking on different "loadings" at different times and relative to different issues. Because the polity is voluntary, persuasion rather than compulsion, influence rather than power, are the only tools available for making and executing policies. This, too, works to strengthen its character as a communications network because the character, quality, and relevance of what is communicated and the way in which it is communicated frequently determine the extent of the authority and influence of the parties to the communication.

The reconstitution of the *edah* is only in its beginning stages; its final form for this epoch cannot yet be foreseen. At this writing, the Jewish people is in the buildup period of the second generation of the postmodern epoch and is actively engaged in trying to work through a new constitutional synthesis, both political and religious. It is likely that the constitution for the new epoch will find its source in the traditional Torah as understood and interpreted in traditional and nontraditional ways. The continued reliance on the Torah as a constitutional anchor could not have been forecast during the first generation of the new epoch, when the late modern trend of secularization was still alive. But it is now fair to conclude that for most Jews, the Torah continues to serve as a constitutional foundation even though they no longer feel bound by its commandments as traditionally understood.

A second element in the new constitutional framework is the commitment to Jewish unity and peoplehood as embodied in the network of institutions serving the *edah*. This commitment is basically founded on a people-wide consensus. However, it is also acquiring a documentary base through congeries of quasi-covenantal constitutional documents generated in the new institutions of the *edah*. These may develop into a comprehensive postmodern constitutional supplement to the *edah*'s historic constitution, following the pattern of earlier epochs.

Notes

1. This chapter is based on material originally presented in four publications by the author, "The Reconstitution of Jewish Communities in the Post-War Period," *Jewish Journal of Sociology,* vol. 11, no. 2 (December 1969), pp. 187–226; "Kinship and Consent in the Jewish Community," *Tradition*, vol. 14, no. 4 (fall 1974), pp. 63–79; *Covenant and Freedom in the Jewish Political Tradition,* Annual Sol Feinstone Lecture (Philadelphia: Gratz College, March 1981); and *Participation and Accountability in the American Jewish Community* (New York: Council of Jewish Federations and Association of Jewish Community Organization Personnel, 1980).

2. The close connections between the theological and the political are made manifest in Jewish literature beginning with the Bible. In our time, Martin Buber has been the foremost expositor of those connections. See, in particular, his *Kingship of God,* trans. Richard Scheimann (London: G. Allen and Unwin, 1967). See also Hans Kohn, *The Idea of Nationalism* (New York: Collier Books, 1944), chap. 2; and Harold Fisch, *Jerusalem and Albion* (New York: Schocken Books, 1964).

3. Jews have always desired an independent territorial state, but they have desired it only as a means to a larger end and not as an end in itself.

4. Pranger, *The Eclipse of Citizenship,* following the Bible and Aristotle, among others, provides a useful discussion of citizenship as the creation of official identity, itself a culturally created necessity for every man that enables men to become fully human. The necessity for citizenship has become universal (p. 10): "In the language of psychology, citizenship supplies an integral segment of one's 'identity pattern,' something taken as second nature." It is in this sense that the concept is used here. See also Akzin, *State and Nation.* Relevant to the Jewish situation is D. F. Aberle et al., "The Functional Prerequisities of a society," *Ethics,* vol. 60, no. 2 (January 1950), pp. 100–110. On the compatibility of multiple loyalties, see Morton Grodzins, *The Loyal and the Disloyal* (Chicago: University of Chicago Press, 1957).

5. Pranger, *The Eclipse of Citizenship,* following Sheldon S. Wolin in *Politics and Vision* (Boston: Little and Brown, 1960), defines this phenomenon as the carving out of political space, space "shaped by a dualist structure of tangible objects and subjective perceptions which arranges a system of shared political meanings among citizens and also establishes these meanings in hierarchies of valued priorities." Pranger continues, "Around a nation are drawn a number of physical and non-physical boundaries within which citizens feel at home, outside of which they are foreigners. Such a space is molded by objective factors such as geographical frontiers, an economic system, a legal system, a common political language . . ., and by the special governmental institutions called offices. But one also discovers certain subjective perceptions and expectations that members share about correct political action, expectations drawn from the members' own individual needs and values and from the social symbolism attributed to boundaries, economics, language, and governments. These

symbolic perceptions may not find common agreement throughout a nation. Nevertheless, there are often common relationships between more specialized perceptions which entitle an observer to speak of a 'pattern' for even the heterogeneous political life of a Switzerland or an India . . . . In every political situation, no matter how transient, one can locate such patterns of civic expectations." Pranger defines this as the political culture of a "national state" but with a few modifications it is useful in defining the political space and culture of the Jewish polity. Thus, for example, this concept being related to the study of Jewish political life, the tangible objects are the patterns of community organization and activity; the subjective perceptions relate to the questions of individual identity and involvement. See also Daniel J. Elazar and Joseph Zikmund, eds., *The Ecology of American Political Culture: Readings* (New York: Thomas Y. Crowell, 1975), Introduction.

6. The biblical understanding of the covenant as a consensual, theopolitical act is discussed in George E. Mendenhall, *The Tenth Generation,* and in R. A. F. MacKenzie, S.J., *Faith and History in the Old Testament* (New York, 1963); see chap. 3, "Israel's Covenant with God."

7. The record of the reaffirmation of the covenant in the Bible is easily discernible in the text itself. Buber, *Kingship of God,* deals with this in his textual exegesis. See also the studies of Avraham Malamut, "Organs of Statecraft in the Israelite Monarchy," *The Biblical Archaeologist,* vol. 28, no. 2 (1965), pp. 34–51; G. E. Mendenhall, "Covenant Forms in Israelite Tradition," *The Biblical Archaeologist* vol. 17, no. 3 (1954), pp. 50–76; Hayim Tadmor, " 'The People' and the Kingship in Ancient Israel: The Role of Political Institutions in the Biblical Period," *Journal of World History* vol. 11, no. 1–2 (1968), pp. 46–68; Moshe Weinfeld, "The Transition from Tribal Republic to Monarchy in Ancient Israel and Its Impression on Jewish Political History," in Daniel J. Elazar, ed., *Kinship and Consent: The Jewish Political Tradition and Its Contemporary Uses* (Ramat Gan: Turtledove Publishing Co., 1981), pp. 151–66.

8. Leo Baeck discusses this phenomenon in *This People Israel: The Meaning of Jewish Existence* (Philadelphia: Jewish Publication Society of America, 1965). The historic evidence is mustered in Daniel J. Elazar and Stuart Cohen, *The Jewish Polity: Jewish Political Organization from Biblical Times to the Present* (Bloomington, Ind.: Indiana University Press, 1985).

9. See, for example, Louis Finkelstein, *Jewish Self-Government in the Middle Ages,* 2d ed. (New York: Jewish Theological Seminary, 1964); and H. H. Ben-Sasson, *Perakim beToldot haYehudim beYamei haBaynayim* (Chapters in the History of the Jews in the Middle Ages) (Tel Aviv: Am Oved, 1969).

10. See Daniel J. Elazar and John Kincaid, eds., *Covenant, Polity, and Constitutionalism* (Lanham, Md.: University Press of America and Center for the Study of Federalism, 1982) and Daniel J. Elazar, "Covenant as the Basis of the Jewish Political Tradition," *Jewish Journal of Sociology,* vol. 20, no. 1 (June 1978), pp. 5–37.

11. Daniel J. Elazar, "The Constitution, the Union, and the Liberties of the People," *Publius,* vol. 8, no. 3 (summer 1978), pp. 141–75.

12. See, for example, Delbert R. Hillers, *Covenant: The History of a Biblical Idea* (Baltimore: Johns Hopkins Press, 1969).

13. Ibid.

14. Ibid.

15. See Gordon Freeman, "Rabbinic Conceptions of Covenant," in Elazar, ed., *Kinship and Consent.*

16. See I. A. Agus, *The Heroic Age of Franco-German Jewry* (New York: Yeshiva University Press, 1969); Menachem Elon, "On Power and Authority: Halachic Status of the Traditional Community and Its Contemporary Implications," in Elazar, ed., *Kinship and Consent;* Gerald Blidstein, "Individual and Community in the Middle Ages," in Elazar, ed., *Kinship and Consent;* Elazar and Cohen, *The Jewish Polity,* esp. Epoch XI.

17. R. Judah HaBarceloni, *Sefer HaShtarot.*

18. In the words of *The Federalist,* force, accident, or choice. See Hamilton, Jay, and Madison, *The Federalist* (1788), no. 1.

19. Elazar and Cohen, *The Jewish Polity,* Introduction; Robert Gordis, "Democratic Origins in Ancient Israel: The Biblical Edah," in *Alexander Marx Jubilee Volume* (New York: Jewish Theological Seminary, 1950); Moshe Weinfeld, "The Transition from Tribal Republic to Monarch in Ancient Israel and Its Impression on Jewish Political History," in Elazar, ed., *Kinship and Consent.*

20. Elazar and Cohen, *The Jewish Polity.*

21. See Stuart A. Cohen, *The Concept of the Three Ketarim,* Working Paper No. 18 of Workshop in the Covenant Idea and the Jewish Political Tradition (Ramat Gan and Jerusalem: Bar Ilan University Department of Political Studies and Jerusalem Center for Public Affairs, 1982).

22. Howard M. Sachar's *The Course of Modern Jewish History* (New York: Dell Publishing, 1958) is a comprehensive source of the history of Jewish life in this period. The changes themselves are discussed by Jacob Katz in *Tradition and Crisis* (New York: Free Press of Glencoe, 1965) and Michael A. Meyer, *The Origins of the*

Modern Jew: Jewish Identity and European Culture in Germany 1794–1824 (Detroit: Wayne State University Press, 1967). See also Louis Finkelstein, ed., *The Jews: Their History, Culture, and Religion* (Philadelphia: Jewish Publication Society of America, 1960), 3d ed., 2 vols.; Salo W. Baron, "The Modern Age" in Leo W. Schwarz, ed., *Great Ages and Ideas of the Jewish People* (New York: The Modern Library, 1956), pp. 315–484.

23. For a brief exposition of this definition of the modern era, particularly as it applies to the United States, see Daniel J. Elazar, *Cities of the Prairie* (New York: Basic Books, 1970), Introduction and Appendix; and, by the same author, *Toward a Generational Theory of American Politics* (Philadelphia: Center for the Study of Federalism, 1968). The writer has discussed this periodization of Jewish history in "A Constitutional View of Jewish History," *Judaism,* vol. 10, no. 3 (summer 1961), pp. 256–64.

24. See Jacob Lestchinsky, *Tfutzot Yisrael Ahar haMilhamah* (The Dispersions of Israel after the War) (Tel Aviv, 1958) (Hebrew); Aryeh Tartakower, *HaHevrah haYehudit* (Jewish Society) (Tel Aviv: Massada, 1957–59) (Hebrew).

25. Yitzhak Ben-Zvi, *Toldot Eretz Yisrael beTekufah haOtomanit* (History of the Land of Israel in the Ottoman Period), (Jerusalem: Yad Itzhak Ben Zvi, 1955) (Hebrew); Robert Sherevsky, Avraham Katz, Yisrael Kolatt, and Hayim Barkai, *Meah Shanah ve'od 20* (One Hundred Years and Another 20), (Tel Aviv: Ma'ariv, 1968) (Hebrew).

26. It should be noted that most, if not all, of the first colonies were founded by covenants or articles of agreement, thus continuing the classic Jewish pattern. See Daniel J. Elazar, *Israel: Building a New Society* (Bloomington, Ind.: Indiana University Press, 1986).

2

A Generation of Reconstitution

Jews are known to live in 121 countries, 82 of which have permanent organized communities. At least 3 and perhaps as many as 12 others are remnant communities where a relative handful of Jews has custody of the few institutions that have survived in the wake of the emigration of most of the Jewish population. Fourteen more are transient communities where American or Israeli Jews temporarily stationed in some Asian or African country have created such basic Jewish institutions (for example, religious services and schools) as they need. Only 21 countries with known Jewish residents have no organized Jewish life.

The eleven largest countrywide communities contain more than 90 percent of world Jewry (table 2.1).[1]

For nearly two decades after World War II, the reconstruction and reconstitution of existing communities and the founding of new ones were the order of the day throughout the Jewish world. The Jewish communities of continental Europe underwent a period of reconstruction in the wake of their wartime losses, changes in the formal status of religious communities in their host countries, immigration to Israel, internal European migrations, and the introduction of new, especially Communist, regimes (table 2.2).[2]

The Jewish communities of the Moslem countries were transformed in response to the convergence of two factors: the establishment of Israel and the anticolonial revolutions in Asia and Africa. The greater portion of the Jewish population in those countries immigrated to Israel, and organized Jewish life beyond the maintenance of local congregations virtually ended in all of them except Iran, Morocco, and Tunisia (table 2.3).

The English-speaking Jewries and, to a lesser extent, those of Latin America, were faced with the more complex task of adapting their organizational structures to three new purposes: to assume responsibilities passed to them as a result of the destruction of European Jewry, to play a major role in supporting Israel, and to accommodate internal changes in communities still in the process of acculturation (tables 2.4 and 2.5).

Many of the transient Jewish communities in Asia and Africa were founded or given organized form in this period while others, founded earlier by Jews who followed the European colonial powers into Africa, transient merchants, and refugees were abandoned (tables 2.6 and 2.7).

At first, the patterns of countrywide Jewish communal organization followed those of the previous epoch with some modifications. But as the postmodern epoch begins to plant its own imprint on the *edah,* the differences in status and structure are diminishing. A common organizational pattern is emerging, consisting of several basic elements, including:

Table 2.1
Largest Countrywide Jewish Medinot / Aratzot

Country	Jewish Population
1. United States	5.9 million
2. Israel	3.6 million
3. USSR	2.0 million
4. France	535,000
5. United Kingdom	390,000
6. Argentina	300,000
7. Canada	308,000
8. South Africa	120,000
9. Brazil	110,000
10. Australia	90,000
11. Hungary	70,000

Governmentlike institutions, whether "roof" organizations, framing institutions, or separate organizations serving discrete functions, that play roles and provide services on all planes (countrywide, local, and intermediate), which, under other conditions, would be played, provided, or controlled—predominantly or exclusively—by governmental authorities. They are responsible for tasks such as external relations, defense, education, social welfare, and public (communal) finance. They include:

1. A more or less comprehensive fund-raising and social planning body.
2. A representative body for external relations.
3. A Jewish education service agency.
4. A vehicle or vehicles for assisting Israel and other Jewish communities.
5. Various comprehensive religious, health, and welfare institutions.

Localistic institutions and organizations that provide a means for attaching individual Jews to Jewish life on the basis of their most immediate and personal interests and needs. They include:

1. Congregations organized into one or more synagogue unions, federations, or confederations.
2. Local cultural and recreational centers, often federated or confederated with one another.

General purpose mass-based organizations, operating countrywide on all planes, that function to (a) articulate community values, attitudes, and policies, (b) provide the energy and motive force for crystallizing the communal consensus that grows out of those values, attitudes, and policies, and (c) maintain institutionalized channels of communication between the community's leaders and "actives" ("cosmopolitans") and the broad base of the affiliated Jewish population ("locals") for dealing with the problems and tasks facing the community in the light of the consensus. They include a Zionist federation and its constituent organizations and fraternal organizations.

Special interest organizations, which, by serving specialized interests in the community on all planes, function to mobilize concern and support for the programs conducted by the community and to apply pressure for their expansion, modification, and improvement.[3]

The first two of these types are embodied in the institutions that form the structural foundations of the community and the last two in organizations that function to activate the institutional structure and give it life. Institutions of the first type are easily identifiable in most communities. They include the boards of deputies founded by Anglo-Jewish

Table 2.2
Postwar Changes in Continental European Jewish Communities

COUNTRY	POSTWAR SITUATION
Albania	Diasappeared as organized community after Communist take-over
Austria	Reconstructed and reconstituted around a substantially different population
Belgium	Reconstructed and reconstituted, significant new settlement by eastern European refugees
Bulgaria	Limited reconstitution under limitations imposed by Communist regime after mass immigration to Israel
Cyprus	Jewish community emigrates leaving remnant with no organized Jewish life
Czechoslovakia	Partial reconstruction and limited reconstitution under Communist regime
Denmark	Reconstructed along prewar lines
Finland	Reconstituted with additions of refugee population
France	Reconstructed and reconstituted with substantially new population from eastern Europe; subsequently further reconstituted after North African influx
German Democratic Republic	Miniscule remnant community nominally reconstructed and reconstituted under Communist regime
German Federal Republic	Reconstructed and reconstituted with substantially different population including eastern European refugees and Israelis
Gibraltar	No significant constitutional change
Greece	Partially reconstructed and reconstituted around remnant population
Hungary	Partial reconstruction and limited reconstitution under Communist regime; flight of refugees in 1956
Italy	Partially reconstructed after formal restoration of prewar constitution
Liechtenstein	Jewish community slowly being liquidated through emigration
Luxembourg	Reconstructed and reconstituted
Malta	No significant organizational change but considerable emigration
Monaco	Small but stable Jewish community
Netherlands	Partially reconstructed and reconstituted with remnant population and addition of some refugees
Norway	Reconstructed with addition of some refugees
Poland	Extremely limited reconstitution under Communists with successive emigrations of surviving Jews
Portugal	Reconstituted to include remnants of wartime influx of refugees
Romania	Limited reconstitution under Communist regime, substantial immigration to Israel
Spain	Gained formal status as community; wartime refugee settlers founded communal institutions, subsequently taken over and reinforced by Sephardim from North Africa
Sweden	Reconstituted with addition of refugees and abolition of state-required community membership
Switzerland	Limited reconstitution to include wartime refugees
Turkey	Reconstituted after extensive immigration to Israel

COUNTRY	POSTWAR SITUATION
USSR	Only remnant of organized communal life survives war; underground community constituted in postwar generation
Yugoslavia	Reconstructed and reconstituted under Communist regime after substantial immigration to Israel

Table 2.3
Postwar Changes in Jewish Communities in Moslem Countries

COUNTRY	POSTWAR SITUATION
Aden	Entire community emigrated during decolonization
Afghanistan	Majority of Jews migrated to Israel leaving remnant behind
Algeria	Almost all Jews fled in the wake of the French evacuation, moving to France and essentially ending Jewish communal life
Egypt	Successive oppressions and migrations to Israel after 1948 virtually ended community's existence. Remnant that survived until the Israel-Egyptian peace treaty has resumed its links with the Jewish world
Iran	Community drastically reduced in size by immigration to Israel; later under severe strain in the wake of the Khomeini revolution but continues to function as in past with minor adjustments
Iraq	Mass migration to Israel reduced community to a tiny oppressed minority
Lebanon	Community weathered Arab-Israel conflicts until 1967. After outbreak of civil war in 1975, almost all the remaining Jews migrated but not to Israel
Libya	Migration to Israel accelerated after each Arab-Israel crisis; community finally ceased to exist after 1967 war
Pakistan	Most of small community emigrated, leaving a very small group to maintain a single congregation
Sudan	No organized community life
Syria	Oppression after 1948 led to migration of most Jews to Israel. Government pressure on remnant increased after Six-Day War. At present, Jewish population are prisoners of the state
Tunisia	Despite official attempts to encourage Jews to stay, most emigrated to Israel in successive waves after independence. Small communities remain
Yemen	All but a tiny handful left for Israel immediately after establishment of the state. There has been little contact with the remnant since then

communities, the American Jewish community federations and Council of Federations, the Canadian Jewish Congress, the Fonds Social Juif Unifié in France, and the like. The most important localistic institutions are the synagogues, which, by their very nature, are geared to be relatively intimate associations of compatible people. Even the very large American synagogues that lose their sense of intimacy are localistic institutions in this sense, in the overall community context.

The most important localistic organizations are family clubs, *landsmanschaften,* and other similar groups. Organizations in the third category differ widely from community to community. In the United States, B'nai B'rith and Hadassah come closest to perform-

Table 2.4
Postwar Changes in English-speaking Jewish Communities

COUNTRY	POSTWAR ADJUSTMENTS
Australia	Continued influx of refugees enhanced Jewish life and necessitated changes in its organizational structure to encompass the widened scope of Jewish activity and more intensely "Jewish" Jews
Canada	Pressures of "Americanization," suburbanization, and general homogenization of Canada led to weakening of Canadian Jewish Congress framework and strengthening of American-style community federations as bases of community organization
Ireland	Native-born generation comes to fore and emigration reduces community substantially. Provincial communities disappear leaving Dublin as sole locus of Jewish life
New Zealand	Continued emigration of younger generation has decreased Jewish population and weakened community structure
South Africa	Changes in the regime and the rise of a native-born generation in the community shifted emphases of communal institutions and dominant mode of Jewish identification, weakened Zionist Federation and strengthened the Board of Deputies while encouraging maintenance of high level of communal cohesion
South-West Africa/ Namibia	Small community of Jews engaged in business; functions as if its days were numbered
United Kingdom	Rise of last wave of immigrants and native-born generation challenges communal status quo from both left and right, weakening traditional institutions and strengthening new ones that reflect community's greater diversity
United States	Destruction of European Jewry decisively transferred world Jewish leadership role to the American Jewish community. This plus rise of a new generation and disappearance of immigrant ideologies led to significant organizational changes to meet their demands. The community also became more rooted in the general society

ing these functions, with a number of smaller countrywide organizations sharing in the task; in South Africa and much of Latin America the Zionist federations have assumed that role. The special-interest organizations are also readily identifiable in the various communities.[4]

In the smaller countrywide communities, th four kinds of roles may be compressed with fewer institutions and be filled incompletely as a consequence. However it is done, the functions must be institutionalized for an organized community to exist. The mapping of the community's organizational structure along the lines of this typology reveals many of the more permanent channels into which the community's communications network is set and also exposes the ways in which the channels are used.

Israel and the diaspora communities have retained or restored the tripartite structure of the three *ketarim*. For most, functions in each domain are now fulfilled by a variety of institutions, headed by formally elected officers and staffed by a professional civil service. Those institutions can be grouped into five activity spheres, whose *ketaric* alignment is shown in figure 2.1.

The government-like institutions are almost invariably associated with the *keter*

Table 2.5
Postwar Changes in Latin-American and Caribbean Jewish Communities

COUNTRY	POSTWAR ADJUSTMENTS
Argentina	Collapse of European-style *kehillah* institutions in late 1960s accelerated emergence of the sports clubs (community centers) as new building blocks for the community as whole. Simultaneously, a network of Conservative Jewish religious institutions developed as basis for religious identification for a growing number of Argentinian Jews
Aruba	Small community which maintains itself through occasional increments of Jewish retirees
Barbados	Jewish community partially Americanized as result of settlement of retired American Jews
Belize	No organized community life
Bolivia	Most of the prewar influx of refugees from Nazism left in the postwar period, leaving the community in a state of decline
Brazil	The community, previously fragmented among country-of-origin groups, succeeded in creating an umbrella confederation early in the 1950s
Chile	A tightly knit and well-organized community until the Allende revolution and counterrevolution. The latter provoked the flight of many Chilean Jews, some of whom later returned, substantially weakening the possibilities for extensive communal life
Canal Zone	Transient community of American service personnel and businessmen
Colombia	As the children of the original Jewish settlers leave to seek their fortunes elsewhere, the community declines
Costa Rica	Small community slowly declining because of emigration
Cuba	Community reached its demographic and organizational apogee in the 1950s and then declined precipitously after the Castro takeover in 1959. By the end of the postwar generation only a remnant remained, protected by the authorities but without any future as a community in a Communist state
Curaçao	Small community survives despite assimilation and emigration, with some reinforcements from American Jewish retirees
Dominican Republic	Remnant remains after the prewar Jewish refugees left
Ecuador	Refugees from Nazism slowly left after the war. Small community remains
El Salvador	Small community, barely able to maintain institutions
Guatemala	Small community maintains minimal institutions
Guyana	Community slowly declined in postwar years as young people seek opportunity elsewhere. Decline hastened on advent of independence
Haiti	Only unorganized remnants of Jewish community remain after the war
Honduras	Small and declining Jewish community
Jamaica	Small Jewish community reinforced by American retirees

COUNTRY	POSTWAR ADJUSTMENTS
Martinique	No organized community life
Mexico	Jewish community almost unchanged in its organizational structure from prewar period but transformed demographically as a native-born generation becomes predominant
Nicaragua	Jews abandon the country after Sandinista takeover fearing government-sponsored anti-Semitism
Panama	Small Jewish community continues to maintain basic Jewish institutions
Paraguay	Refugee community disperses after war leaving a nucleus that continues to maintain organized community life
Peru	Community slowly diminishing as native-born children seek opportunity elsewhere
Suriname	Small community continues to maintain organized framework despite assimilation
Venezuela	Community completes transition from immigrant to native-born generation. Rise in importance of Sephardic Jews
Trinidad and Tobago	Community continues to decline despite reinforcement by American retirees

Table 2.6
Postwar Developments in African Jewish Communities

COUNTRY	POSTWAR ADJUSTMENTS
Angola	Small Jewish community leaves after Portuguese grant colony independence
Burundi	No organized Jewish community life
Congo Republic	Handful of Jews remains after independence
Ethiopia	Situation continues to deteriorate first under imperial regime and then more drastically under Communist-oriented military government. Jewish population severely reduced through persecution and begins to flee in 1970s for transfer to Israel. Transfer of majority of Jews made in 1984–85
Kenya	Jewish community stabilizes after independence to become the center of Jewish life in East Africa
Nigeria	Transient Jewish community of Israelis develops in 1960s; is reduced in 1970s but begins to flourish again in the latter part of that decade
Mozambique	No organized community life
Senegal	No organized community life
Swaziland	No organized community life
Tanzania	No organized community life
Uganda	Organized Jewish life never strong; ceases after independence as most Jews leave
Zaire	Most Jews leave after independence; small congregation remains. Transient Israeli community provides continuing Jewish presence from 1960s on, with some interruptions
Zambia	Most Jews immigrate to Rhodesia after independence; nucleus remains to preserve congregational community
Zimbabwe	After Rhodesia's unilateral declaration of independence, Jews began to emigrate but substantial numbers remained to maintain a full range of communal institutions. Once Rhodesia became Zimbabwe, Jews began to leave at more rapid pace, leaving a remnant community, which still maintains an elaborate communal structure

Table 2.7
Postwar Developments in Asian Jewish Communities

COUNTRY	POSTWAR ADJUSTMENTS
Burma	Jews abandoned country in 1942 in the face of Japanese invasion. Although a few returned after the war, organized community life was not reestablished. In 1950s and 1960s a transient Israeli community develops and then leaves
China	Jewish population reaches apogee in World War II because of influx of refugees, almost all of whom leave after the Communist takeover in 1949. Organized Jewish life ceases in the 1950s, although a scattered handful of Jews remain
Fiji	No organized community life
Hong Kong	Small community is expanded by English-speaking businessmen, particularly Americans, in the postwar period
India	Two-thirds of Jewish community immigrates to Israel, others to the United States and Great Britain, ending Iraqi domination of the community and transferring communal control to the Bene Israel who continue to maintain a full range of communal institutions in a smaller, but stable, community
Indonesia	Jews are interned by Japanese during the war and leave after independence. Organized communal life ceases
Japan	Jewish refugee community disperses after war, but new community develops around American Jewish businessmen
Malaysia	Jews leave upon establishment of independence
Nepal	Transient community of Israelis develops in 1950s and continues on a much-reduced basis
Philippines	Most of prewar Jewish community emigrates in 1950s leaving small community reinforced by American Jewish businessmen
Ryukyu Islands (Okinawa)	Community develops under American occupation consisting of American Jewish servicemen and businessmen. It virtually disappears when islands are reunited with Japan
Singapore	Jewish community survives the war but suffers from slow emigration throughout the postwar period. Nevertheless, it continues to maintain its institutions
South Korea	Transient community of American Jewish service personnel with a few Jewish businessmen
Taiwan	Jewish community established by American Jewish businessmen and service personnel in the postwar period
Thailand	Jewish community established by American Jewish service personnel and Jewish businessmen from various parts of the world in the postwar period. Substantially reduced after the Americans leave Vietnam but continues to function minimally
Vietnam	Jewish community established by American Jewish service personnel and businessmen in the postwar period and abandoned when Americans withdraw from Vietnam

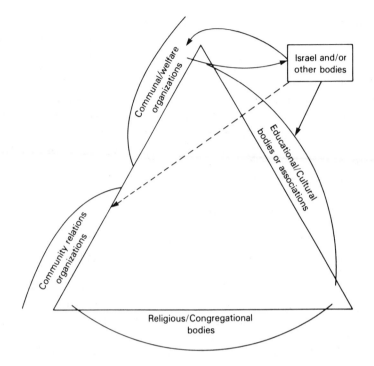

Figure 2.1.   Generalized model of the three *ketarim*
in diaspora communities.

malkhut. Until World War II those of the consistorial communities may have had to be
classified under the *keter kehunah* but since then, with one or two exceptions (Romania,
for example, where the Communist regime has insisted on preserving the principle that
being Jewish is exclusively a matter of religion), other institutions associated with the
keter malkhut have superseded them in this capacity. Only in the case of Agudath Israel
can one find an example of such institutions growing out of the *keter torah.*

The localistic organizations and institutions are primarily connected with the *keter
kehunah,* secondarily with *keter torah,* and only occasionally with *keter malkhut.* That is
because most of them are synagogues, schools, and *yeshivot.* Localistic bodies like *landsmanschaften,* which were strong in the days of the great Jewish migrations, have lost
much of their role as Jews have settled into their new places of residence. Today even
Jewish emigrants are more likely to seek ties with peers through synagogues and schools
than through secular country-of-origin societies, in part because of the decline of secularism as a motivating force in Jewish life and in part because mutual aid societies are less
needed in the era of the welfare state. The few secular localistic bodies that remain may
fall in the domain of the *keter malkhut* to the extent that they serve public purposes.

The general purpose mass-based organizations also fall principally within the *keter
malkhut,* although some, like the Hassidic groups, are more appropriately classified
under the *keter kehunah* and others like Agudath Israel fall into the *keter torah.* Special-
interest organizations are to be found in all three domains by their very nature.

Local communities, or *kehillot,* are organized in a manner suitable to each country
following regional patterns. Usually they are organized as federations of local organiza-

tions or institutions. Increasingly, they share a basic tripartite structure based on (1) synagogues, (2) communal-welfare institutions, and (3) representative or Zionist institutions, but the emphasis is different in different lands. Some of the more prominent variations include: (1) formal municipal governments functioning according to laws of the state (Israel); (2) Jewish community federations that link functional agencies for fund-raising and community planning (United States, Canada); (3) single congregations (for example, New Zealand); (4) congregations linked through community boards (for example, Stockholm); (5) federations of congregations (for example, Istanbul); and (6) federations or associations of social, political, and welfare institutions (for example, Buenos Aires).

The Jewish Polity: Key Questions

It is in this framework, then, that the problem of the organization of the Jewish polity in today's voluntaristic environment must be explored. A number of key questions can be raised about every Jewish community, regardless of its place in the typology presented above. Among those needing investigation, questions of structure and function, affiliation and strength, legitimacy and authority, power and influence, leadership and representativeness, decision making and conflict stand out.

The functions of the Jewish polity. What functions does the Jewish polity perform? How are they handled? What sets of priorities do they reflect? How well are they carried out? Obviously, the functions of every Jewish community revolve around the fundamental goal of Jewish collective and individual survival, both physical and cultural. In this respect, the Jewish polity is no different from any other. Accordingly, it may be hypothesized that, apart from the actual maintenance of the polity's institutions, its most important functions are defense and education.

In Israel, these two functions are handled in the manner of all states—an army, a school system, appropriate ministries, and so forth. In the diaspora, defense, in particular, has taken different forms in this generation. In most Jewish communities, local action against anti-Semitism has been supplemented by efforts to assist Jews in subjugated communities and, overwhelmingly, by assistance to Israel. Diaspora Jewry's aid for Israel really must be considered a defense expenditure in the sense that diaspora Jews look upon Israel's survival as vital to their personal security and self-respect and hence are willing to pour out support for it on a scale unprecedented in the annals of Jewish communal life. An analysis of the tone of the campaigns to raise funds for Israel confirms this thesis, and the longtime unwillingness to invest in Israel, that is, to deal with Israel on a business basis, by the same people who give great sums to the cause is revealing.

Education is a more problematic function because it involves and exposes all the ambivalences of contemporary Jewish life. The desire for survival is in conflict with the desire for full integration with the general society, or perhaps more accurately, into the worldwide cosmopolitan culture so attractive to people in all walks of life, especially students and intellectuals. A study of the educational function in each community not only leads to an understanding of its content and its place in the community's scheme of things but also serves as an important means of gaining insight into the community's values and self-image.

Similar insights may be gained, though to a lesser degree, from an examination of the other domestic functions of each community. Simply cataloguing the range of these functions is useful in this regard, while tracing the expansion or contraction of the range is a good way of assessing changes in the community as a whole, whether in regard to its internal strength, the external pressures on it, or its members' interest in maintaining their communal integrity.

Problems of affiliation. The question of affiliation with the Jewish community is easily disposed of in those few countries that still maintain formal registration under government auspices for all those who identify themselves as Jews. It is more difficult in the vast majority of countries that lack that convenience, for in those countries, not only affiliation but the form it takes is self-determined by every individual Jew. In some cases, membership in a roof organization is the accepted form for most Jews. In others, it is membership in certain core institutions (for example, synagogues) or organizations (for example, Zionist federations) which is demanded by the local value system for one to be considered part of the community. In yet other cases, the key to affiliation is contribution to the appropriate community fund.

Community strength. The measurement of the strength of any voluntary community is a difficult task. A study of the Jewish people as a polity is particularly useful in this regard because it suggests what is especially true in contemporary Jewish affairs: in an organized community, the whole is greater than the sum of the parts. Organization itself affects communal strength, intensifying communal life beyond what it might be if the aggregate Jewish behavior of individual Jews were to be the measure of Jewish strength. Thus, although individual Jews may or may not live intensely Jewish lives, the institutions and organizations in the community in which they may be involved make them more Jewish and thereby increase the overall strength of the whole and its parts.

Strength is a function of the actual exercise of influence that shapes action and, consequently, an organization that appears to have strength in the abstract may turn out to be relatively weak in specific situations or relative to particular issues. Organizations in the following categories are considered potentially strong:

1. Organizations membership in which the community deems mandatory for all Jews in good standing in the community. Numerical strength is one indication of which organizations have that status.

2. Organizations that furnish a high proportion of leaders for the community as a whole, whether as a result of democratic choice, for anachronistic reasons, or because they are themselves organizations of elites.

3. Organizations that are called on to be spokesmen for the community, at least in the fields of their recognized competence.

None of these three categories is individually determinative. Most Jews in a given community may belong to synagogues yet desire to minimize the communitywide influence of the synagogue movements. Organizations of elites may find their members occupying key positions in the community but adopting different roles and stances more appropriate to the specific positions they occupy. And nothing is quite so obvious as the weakness of a "recognized spokesman" when the establishment for which he (or it) speaks no longer has the confidence of the community's larger public. Perhaps some "triangulation" of all three will produce at least a rough guide to the problem of strength.

In Israel, of course, this is an issue of a different order entirely. There, the formal institutions of the state are obviously the centers of both authority and power. Any other ranking is secondary, although it is important not to underestimate the power of public nongovernmental bodies such as the Histadrut or Agudath Israel. Furthermore, because

Israel is a comprehensive, all-embracing Jewish society, it is necessary to include general economic and political as well as strictly Jewish measures to make any determination.

Patterns of Participation

The first task of every Jewish community is to learn to deal with the particular local manifestation of Jews' freedom to choose whether they wish to affiliate with it or not. This task is a major factor in determining the direction of the reconstitution of Jewish life in our time. It is increasingly true that diaspora Jews, if they feel Jewishly committed at all, feel that they are so by choice rather than simply by birth. Not that an organic tie does not underlie the fact of their choice, but birth alone is no longer sufficient to keep Jews within the fold in an environment as highly individualistic and pluralistic as the contemporary world. No one is more conscious of this than are the Jews themselves.

One result of that is that participation in Jewish life in the diaspora is exceptionally uneven. It was always true that some Jews participated in the life of their community more than others. What we know about humanity leads us to recognize that some people are more attuned to participation than others. Nevertheless, the intensely voluntaristic aspects of participation of all kinds in the contemporary would make the differences in willingness to participate even more important among diaspora Jewry.

Perhaps most important of all, participation actually defines the limits of the community. The Jewish communities in the diaspora are not communities of fixed boundaries within which all those born Jews find themselves and in which they are then moved to organize to meet their public needs, as in Israel. Instead, these communities consist of a series of concentric circles radiating outward from the hard core of committed Jews toward areas of semi-Jewishness on the other fringes where the community phases off into the general society. This new shape of diaspora Jewry is portrayed in idealized form in figure 2.2.[5]

The hard core of the Jewish community consists of Jews whose Jewishness is a full-time concern that informs every aspect of their lives, whether from a traditionally religious point of view, as ethnic nationalists, or because of their involvement in Jewish life "every day in every way." They and their families are closely linked in their Jewishness internally and to others with similar ties, so that their Jewish existence is an intergenerational affair. Our best estimate is that between 5 and 10 percent of the Jewish population in the diaspora fall into this category.

Surrounding this hard core is a second group consisting of those Jews continuously involved in Jewish life and consistently active in Jewish affairs, but to whom living Jewishly is not a full-time matter. They are likely to be the mainstays of Jewish organizations of various kinds and make Judaism a major avocational interest. Ten percent is a fair estimate of such Jews in the diaspora today.

A third group, surrounding the participants, consists of those Jews affiliated with Jewish institutions or organizations in some concrete way but are not particularly active in them. These would include synagogue members whose membership does not involve them much beyond the periodic use of synagogue facilities, at least for the rites of passage or for the High Holy Days. Also included here would be members of some of the mass-based Jewish organizations such as Hadassah and B'nai B'rith or any of the other charitable groups that are identifiably Jewish, whose membership reflects primarily private social interests rather than a concern for the public purposes of Jewish life. This is a large

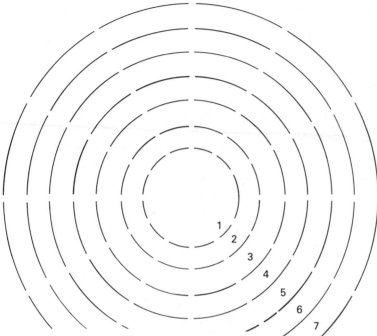

1. Integral Jews (living according to a Jewish rhythm)
2. Participants (involved in Jewish life on a regular basis)
3. Associated Jews (affiliated with Jewish institutions in some concrete way)
4. Contributors and Consumers (giving money and/or utilizing the services of Jewish institutions from time to time)
5. Peripherals (recognizably Jewish in some way but completely uninvolved in Jewish life)
6. Repudiators (seeking to deny or repudiate their Jewishness)
7. Quasi Jews (Jewish status unclear as a result of intermarriage or assimilation in some other form)

Figure 2.2.   The shape of contemporary diaspora communities.

category because it includes all those who recognize the necessity for some kind of associational commitment to Jewish life even if it is only for the sake of maintaining a proper front before the non-Jewish community. It is estimated to include 30 percent of the diaspora Jewish population.

Beyond that circle there is a fourth consisting of Jews who contribute money to Jewish causes and use the services of Jewish institutions periodically during their lifetimes, usually synagogues for the rites of passage. Perhaps another 30 percent of diaspora Jews fall into this category, some of whom have too-limited incomes to develop more formal or lasting attachments to Jewish life in an associational context that makes the payment of money a binding factor in the associational process.

Beyond the circle of contributors and consumers there is a circle of Jews who are recognizably Jewish in some way but completely uninvolved in Jewish life. Though they may be married to Jewish spouses and their children are unquestionably of Jewish descent, they have no desire even to use Jewish institutions for the rites of passage and insufficient interest even in such Jewish causes as Israel to contribute money. Perhaps 15 percent of diaspora Jewry fall into this category.

There is a small group of born Jews who actively reject their Jewishness. Once a significant group, it is a decreasing one, for the openness of society to Jews today has eliminated the necessity for active hostility on the part of those seeking to escape their Jewishness. Active rejection survives as a pathological syndrome among a handful of born Jews.

Finally, there is an unknown number of "quasi Jews" who are neither inside the Jewish community nor entirely out of it. These are people who have intermarried but have not lost their own personal Jewish "label" or who have otherwise assimilated to a point where Jewish birth is incidental to them in every respect. We can assume that between 5 and 10 percent of the known Jewish population fall into this category, plus an unknown number who are simply not reckoned in the conventional statistics.

The boundaries between these categories as well as their membership is quite fluid as is indicated in figure 2.2 by separating them with broken rather than solid lines. There is considerable movement in and out of all of them; more along the edges of each than across separated circles. Thus Jews in group two ("participants") are more likely to move into the hard core or out into more casual membership than to drop out altogether, while "peripherals" may move into the quasi-Jewish category with some ease or, under certain circumstances, will be easily brought into the category of "contributors and consumers."

Moreover, in times of crisis there will be general tightening of the circles. Thus the Six-Day War, the high point of Jewish identification in recent times, probably increased the extent and intensity of Jewish identification in all the circles, including the sixth, but only in relation to the prior stance of the individuals involved. Thus, "participants" may have become even more preoccupied with Jewish affairs during the period of the crisis and "peripherals" may have become contributors for the moment, but it was unlikely for peripherals to become participants. Such studies as we have indicate that even Jews who, at the time, were seen by their more committed fellows as "coming out of the wood-work" to identify and contribute were, in most cases, already passive synagogue members or at least on organizational lists as sometime supporters. Of course, we are speaking here about aggregates, not isolated cases.[6]

What this means is that the community is built on a fluid, if not on an eroding, base, with a high degree of self-selection involved in determining who is even a *potential* participant in the public life of the community. In all likelihood, only 20 percent of the Jewish population fall into that category and by no means all of them define their Jewish concerns as public ones. For many—even the hard core (Hassidic Jews, for example)—the concerns of the Jewish *community* are not their concerns. They are interested in leading private lives that are intensely Jewish but do not seek to channel their Jewishness into the realm of public affairs.

There is some evidence that the "bundle" of circles is getting looser and spreading out farther from the hard core. It is likely that a great gap is developing between circles four and five, so that the Jews who remain actively committed to Jewish life are growing closer to its center and those who are passively committed or less are drifting away. There were signs of this in 1967 and the phenomenon was clearly visible at the time of the Yom Kippur War. If this is so, the bases of Jewish communal life in the diagram are not only shifting but eroding, making the maintenance of a workable representative community an even more difficult problem for diaspora Jewry.

The implications of this for Jewish life are both important and frightening. It is clear that even the problem of defining who is in and who is out of the Jewish community at any given time becomes an increasingly difficult one. With the "intermarriage explosion" of recent years, the gray area of Jewishness has begun to reach into the more positively identified circle of Jews through family relationships. This is particularly problematic as we get a generation of semi-Jews who, in a world such as that of the United States, may associate with Jews and wish to marry Jews as often as they wish to marry non-Jews without having any real commitment to Jewish tradition or Jewish communal life.

As the most peripheral circles grow in size, we may find a startling decline in the number of Jews who can be identified as such. It is possible that several million present members of the Jewish community will simply disappear during the next generation or two because, although they may recall their Jewish ancestry, they will have moved so far into the gray area that they will be beyond reclamation by the community. Furthermore, if the circles grow apart as they seem to be, even among those who will remain there will be sharp divisions. The hard core who wish to preserve a Jewish way of life and those immediately surrounding it will, in natural response to their situation, tighten their own circles, and the more peripheral elements, in natural response to their situation, will be drawn ever farther into the gray area in which one generation will be Jewish and the next generation not.

The new voluntarism also extends into the internal life of the Jewish community, generating pluralism even in previously free but relatively homogeneous or monolithic community structures. This pluralism is increased by the breakdown of the traditional reasons for being Jewish and the rise of new incentives for Jewish association. The possibilities for organizing a pluralistic Jewish community have also been enhanced by these new incentives and the postmodern breakdown of the rigid ideologies that divided Jews in the last third of the modern era (mid-nineteenth to mid-twentieth centuries). Certainly, the creation of the State of Israel has given the Jewish people a new and compelling focus that enhances almost all Jews, and whose crucial role as a generator of Jewish ties, regardless of other differences, was decisively demonstrated at the time of the Six-Day War and in subsequent situations.[7]

Authority and Power

Legitimacy and authority. A major dimension of the modernization of the Jewish polity is the changing understanding of authority and legitimacy, which took on an entirely new look in the modern epoch and has undergone further changes in the postmodern epoch.[8] Authority in premodern Jewish history was not based on any human or social institution or agency, but on the universally accepted Torah, which was the source of legitimacy for the organizational structure of every Jewish community. Even when hierarchical devices were sometimes used to implement the authority of the Torah, the legitimacy of that authority was based on distinctly nonhierarchical principles. Today, of course, the traditional authority of the Torah is no longer universally accepted, and the Jewish community has apparently created substitute forms of authority, which, though far weaker and much less visible, nevertheless function to hold the community together for some purposes and enable it to achieve common goals.

For the last century or more, the Jewish community was without any widely accepted authoritative force. The one thing that united almost all Jews in those years was their desire to become part of the open society. The touchstone of Jewish authority, to the extent that there was one, was a common commitment to modernism or liberalism. Leadership passed to Jews who had "made it," in the larger society precisely because they had.

The establishment of the State of Israel created a new source of authority for Jews. Certainly after 1967 Israel has become the primary authoritative factor, uniting virtually all Jews. All this is not to say that Jews are no longer interested in or accept the Torah, however they interpret it, or that the shift is without problems. But the people who now speak with the most authoritative voice in the community are the people who speak in some way with the voice of Israel.

The authoritative role of Israel functions in two ways. First, Israel is itself authoritative; what Israel wants is interpreted to be what the Jewish community should want, and even those who wish to dissent from any particular Israeli policy or demand must be circumspect when they do so. Those Jews who reject Israel's claims on them are more or less written off by the Jewish community. They are certainly excluded from any significant decision-making role in the community.

Furthermore, people who claim to speak in the name of Israel or for Israel gain a degree of authority that places them in advantageous positions when it comes to other areas of communal decision making. This authoritative role has contributed as much to enhancing the Jewish community federations and their leadership as the sheer act of raising money. The two are closely interconnected. Even the synagogues, which are expected to be bastions of support for the Torah as the primary source of authority in the community, have come increasingly to rely on Israel and Israel-centered activities to legitimize their own positions. The shift in most American synagogues on Yom Kippur from fund-raising for synagogue needs to fund-raising for the sale of Israel bonds is an example.

Israel, however, is a human and secular source of authority, subject to all the weaknesses of all human and secular sources. Israel is the fulfillment of a messianic dream but it is not the coming of the Messiah because nothing human that we so far have seen is. So, though for the moment Jews have solved the problem of how to provide some measure of authoritative integration for the Jewish people, Israel does not solve the problem of restoring the kind of authority that will enable the Jewish polity to become the commonwealth that it properly should be.[9]

Power and structures. The question of authority, with its connotations of formality and legitimacy, leads naturally to the related question of influence in the community, with its connotations of informal power. Three basic forms of political control can be identified in the history of political systems: *autocratic, oligarchic,* and *polyarchic.* (The terms are used here in the most neutral sense implied by their Greek roots.) The Jewish polity or its components have experienced all three at one time or another.[10]

Under the *autocratic* form, a *single individual* (for instance, a *shtadlan*) or an organization functioning as a *corporate person* (for instance, a chief rabbinate) by being decisively involved in every significant community decision exercises well-nigh complete control over the community. From the evidence available, this has been a rare phenomenon in Jewish history and never a legitimate one. The most visible example is Herod's usurpation of power in ancient Judea, with Roman support. It is virtually nonexistent in the contemporary Jewish world, surviving principally in the Hassidic world and perhaps in the smallest communities or in some of the traditional *kehillot.*[11]

Oligarchy is a form of political control in which a substantially closed group of individuals, or interests represented by individuals, enjoys a virtual monopoly of power by keeping decisive control over significant community decisions within its confines. Undoubtedly more prevalent in the Jewish world than autocracy, several forms of oligarchic control are discernible. The simplest involves rule by a *single element* in the community—a small group with the same fundamental interests whose members are closely linked with one another through a network of interlocking relationships that holds power in its hands. To those who stand outside this kind of oligarchy, its rule seems no different from that of an autocracy. However, inside the controlling element itself, decision-making is collegial, if only because no individual is in a position to exercise control on his own.

The other two forms are more complex. A *multiple-element oligarchy* combines the leaders of a number of different elements in the community in the decision-making group, but the group remains self-selected and still stands in dominating relationship to the remainder of the community. Since each element in the coalition has its own sources of power, none can decisively influence community decision-making without the others. At the same time, the more elements represented in the oligarchy, the more open it becomes to various points of view in the community. A multiple-element oligarchy can be broadly based, quite responsive at least to the articulate publics in the community, and representative of the great majority (if not all) of its significant elements. In that case it can be considered a *representative oligarchy* or one which, in exercising its decisive influence over community decision making, gives every legitimate interest a share, albeit a highly structured one, in the process. Oligarchy has long been a common pattern of organizing power in Jewish communities, at least since the crystallization of the idea of the Jewish polity as an aristocratic republic during the Second Commonwealth.

Polyarchic systems of political control are those in which no single individual, group, or element nor any exclusive combination of elements can monopolize power or be decisively involved in every significant community decision. They are characterized by their openness and fluidity, to the extent that power is not only widely diffused, but different issues or situations are likely to change the influence of different groups, giving them greater or lesser roles in the decision-making process depending on their salience. Moreover, the leadership of these groups is more likely to change with some frequency.

In an *organized polyarchy* the elements, groups, and individuals active in the community are mobilized in routinized ways and exercise their influence through recognized channels. Because their participation is expected, coordination among them is possible on a regular basis. Where power is even more widely diffused and the participants less easily coordinated, a *fragmented polyarchy* exists. In a fragmented polyarchy it is difficult for both participants and observers to determine who has the power potential to achieve their goals. If sufficiently fragmented, a polyarchy may become chaotic, but because *chaotic polyarchy* would signify a community in dissolution, it is a rare phenomenon and, when it exists, it is ephemeral.

Given the thrust of Jewish political tradition and the circumstances of Jewish existence as a polity by choice, some limits and opportunities in contemporary Jewish political organization should be apparent. Only in Israel is it possible to maintain formal mechanisms of governance associated with a clearly bounded political system. Diaspora Jews cannot expect to establish their communities on the same basis as modern democratic states, by the votes of the people, pure and simple. There may be voting and elections but they are limited for two reasons. One is technical—the relatively low level of participation and turnout in a voluntary situation. The other is ideological—to survive as a people, much less a holy commonwealth, Jews must maintain standards regarding what a Jewish commonwealth should be. The result is a tendency toward multiple element or representative oligarchy, based, in part, on the tripartite division among the *ketarim* and, in part, on the informal distribution of power among organizations, institutions, and people.

Ideally, these oligarchic forms find expression in a kind of aristocratic republicanism, which leads to governance by what may be called a trusteeship, with a strong popular base and a higher legitimacy. The history of Jewish self-government can be understood as a continuing effort to maintain that trusteeship by combining its aristocratic and democratic bases. However, like every other form of government, aristocratic republicanism has its degenerative side. When aristocratic republics degenerate, they become oligarchies, in the narrower sense, or rule by a self-selected few for their private benefit. In any age and time, there is a continuing tension between the aristocratic republican ideal and the lower manifestations of reality. It is the problem of every generation to confront that tension and to seek to move the community in the direction of the higher, rather than the lower.

Jewish political tradition also speaks to this. For example, Rabbi Shlomo ben Aderet, known by the acronym of his name, Rashba, one of the great constitutional interpreters of the Spanish Jewish community in the fourteenth century, responding to questions put to him by the Jewish communities of Lerida and Saragossa, defined the problems of consent and obligation in ways that are applicable to the Jewish situation today. He was asked by the Jews of Lerida whether a community can unilaterally enforce its decisions against its members. His answer:

> In all matters of the community, no one part of the community is permitted to do as they please, unless the entire community consents. For the community are as partners in all communal responsibilities and in all communal appointments, such as tax collectors, unless there exist men who have been appointed to deal with communal affairs; those who are called by our sages the seven *tuvei ha'ir*. In most places, nowadays, the important men of the community direct the affairs of the community in consultation and agreement. In general, it is assumed that the individual avoids his own opinion, but if some of the community, even from among those who are not so great in wisdom, object, their objection is an objection. So long as they do not expressly accept, their objection stands. This is certainly so, where the objection is made by some of the men who are normally those to be consulted.[12]

Rashba is talking about an aristocratic republican system, but even the objection of the average Jew in the community stands. Jews, for good or for ill, persist in that course until this day. In no community is there a way to say to people who object that the objection is not an objection, even if the majority think it is not, because the objection will stand. That makes it difficult to govern Jews. Anybody who is involved in Jewish public life knows how difficult it is. Here we have testimony as to how difficult it was even in the Middle Ages, when the Jews were bound together as a group under their own laws, which their own governing bodies could enforce, and were not simply a voluntaristic society in the way of the contemporary world.

At the same time, the specific forms and procedures of communal governance can vary from place to place and time to time, as long as the principles are maintained. The Rashba's answer to the Jews of Saragossa:

The customs of different locales differ in these matters, for there are places where all matters are handled by their elders and advisors, and there are places where even the council can do nothing without the consent of the entire congregation in which there is found the agreement of all, and there are places which appoint for themselves a group of men whose direction they will follow for a given period of time in all matters related to the group.[13]

One of the factors that contributed most to the breakdown of the premodern Jewish community was that, on the eve of the modern epoch, the aristocratic republican ideal was all too often corrupted. Jewish communities fell under the rule of oligarchies that tried, one way or another, to protect their own privileges. Jews were not often in a position to feather their own nests, so it was not so much a question of getting rich, as avoiding the burdens that were imposed on the community as a whole. The evidence suggests that now there is less oligarchic rule in the Jewish communities of the world than was the case in many traditional communities for the previous several centuries. If the Jewish people has not achieved its aristocratic ideal, it is also far from its degenerative side.

The existing evidence suggests that most of the larger countrywide Jewish communities fall somewhere between multiple-element oligarchies and fragmented polyarchies. The greater number are concentrated in the middle; most of the smaller ones are either multiple-element or single-element oligarchies, perhaps by default. At its best, oligarchic control is a decent approximation of the ideal Jewish republic within the limits imposed by human nature. In more down-to-earth terms, oligarchies frequently come into existence because there are power vacuums to be filled, and there are only a few people interested in filling them. This is particularly true in contemporary Jewish life.

Finally, the special nature of the Jewish polity—its core of religious principles and behavior patterns that must be preserved if the community is to survive meaningfully, its lack of an all-embracing territorial base and the special problem that imposes, its dependence on a particular kind of dedicated leadership willing to assume grave burdens voluntarily—makes oligarchy a reasonable solution to its problems of governance. At the same time, the community's reliance on the consent of its members to survive, the voluntarism that informs that consent, and the same religious tenets that make survival meaningful demand a degree of democratic participation that under most circumstances has kept oligarchies representative.

Apart from the influences indigenuous to Jewish civilization, particular Jewish communities have always been influenced by the means of organizing power current in their host societies at any given time. In medieval Europe, this meant a strengthening of the hierarchical and autocratic elements in the community. Today this means democratization to a greater or lesser degree. The trend since World War II is in that direction, within and relative to the communities' different structural patterns and external environments.

Decision making and community conflicts. The substantive aspects of the decision-making process in Jewish communities lie outside the scope of this chapter. Nevertheless, it seems appropriate to set out what appear to be some general principles about decision making and conflict in the contemporary Jewish world. First, the ideological struggles of the modern epoch, whether involving emancipation, secularism, socialism, or Zionism, either have vanished or are vanishing from among the concerns of the decision makers, surviving only as anachronisms where the leadership has not changed. They have been replaced by essentially pragmatic concerns revolving around the great central principle of

Jewish survival. In the aftermath of the Holocaust and in the turbulence of the contemporary world, the survival question has taken on the most crucial importance in the minds of almost all Jews, whether of concern for the survival of Israel, concern about outbreaks of anti-Semitism, or concern about preserving communal unity at all costs.

In effect, then, no issue is allowed to emerge as a matter of public controversy if it is felt that such a controversy would threaten the unity of the polity. Because of that, if at all possible, open community conflict is confined to marginal matters that are not threatening. "Extremists" such as the militant Orthodox, idealistic youth, or intellectuals, who challenge the survival consensus by raising "controversial" issues are disliked and even feared by the great "respectable" center that dominates most, if not all, organized Jewish communities. And it is very easy to acquire the label of "extremist" simply by questioning decisions arrived at through the established patterns of decision making. By and large, these involve a quiet allocation of resources according to the hierarchy of interests of the community leaders with an emphasis on establishing and preserving an acceptable status quo.

Changes or innovations are introduced on an incremental basis only to raise as little controversy as possible. People working together over a long period of time learn how to satisfy each other's interests in this regard almost intuitively. Those who challenge this pattern and create "controversy" by doing so are likely to experience rejection even at the hands of those who agree with them in principle. In the end, serious conflicts that may occur in the community are likely to be personal rather than substantive in origin. The major exception to this picture is the conflict between the firmly Orthodox and most of the community over matters of religious law and practice.

The Federal Basis of the Polity

Federalism is the traditional way in which the Jewish people has maintained its unity in the face of the pressures of diversity.[14] At any given time, a wide variety of federal arrangements are to be found in the organized Jewish communities of the world. The Jewish community adapts its traditional forms to the environment of the host country so that its structure reflects local conditions while making possible (as far as possible) the achievement of the main purposes of corporate Jewish life. The structure that almost always emerges from the adaptation is based on federal principles and uses federal forms.

The pluralistic federalism of the voluntary community substantially eliminates the neat pattern of communal organization usually held up as the model by those concerned with "rationalizing" Jewish community life. Though smaller communities in different cultural settings are not likely to go all the way in the same direction, more and more the seemingly anarchistic American pattern is revealed as the paradigm of their development if not the vision of their future.

Certainly the model of a hierarchical organizational structure does not offer an accurate picture of the distribution of powers and responsibilities in any Jewish community today. Even in the more formally structured communities of Central Europe and Latin America, the institution that appears to be at the top of the pyramid is really dependent on, and often manipulated by, the institutions and organizations that would be placed farther down on the structure in any hierarchical scheme. The local community that "should" be on the bottom is the real center of power. For communities like the

United States, even the model as modified is useless. Nor is there a central governing agent in most communities that serves as the point at which authority, responsibility, and power converge. Even in the communities ostensibly dominated by a *consistoire,* the erstwhile central body has been shunted aside to become another specialized institution in an oligopoly, as in France where the Fonds Social Juif Unifié (FSJU) and the Comité Représentatif des Israélites en France (CRIF) now play an equal or superior role.

What is needed, then, is a more appropriate model of Jewish communal organization that takes realities and trends into account. The structure of the contemporary countrywide Jewish community is best understood as a multidimensional matrix that takes the form of an even more intensive communications network than the *edah.* In it the interacting institutions are informed by shared patterns of culture as well as activated by a shared system of organizations and governed by shared leadership cadres.

The character of the matrix and its communications network varies from community to community. The network may be connected through a common center that serves as the major (but rarely, if ever, the exclusive) channel for communication or it may form a matrix without any real center, with the lines of communication crisscrossing in all directions. Always, however, the boundaries of the community are revealed only when the pattern of the network is uncovered. As with the *edah,* the pattern stands revealed only when both its components are, namely, its institutions and organizations with their respective roles and the way in which communications are passed betweeen them. The pattern is a dynamic one, with the distribution of authority and influence varying according to the times, the issues, and the character, quality, relevance, and manner of what is communicated.[15] This organizational matrix overlays the concentric circles into which the Jewish people is divided in our times. The matrix is firm enough, but the concentric circles are fluid. The result is the erection of a strong building on a foundation of shifting sands. That indeed describes the contemporary Jewish situation.

Political Culture and Political Behavior

One of the major checks on the trusteeship is cultural. Jews approach the larger questions of governance with a moralistic outlook, expecting high standards of behavior, based on the principle that the polity must pursue justice and that those who lead it must do so as a public trust. The term, in talmudic times, for the elders of the city was *tuvei ha'ir,* the good men of the city. In reality, of course, they were not always good men, but what they were supposed to be was embodied in the concept. Any behavior that falls short of these standards has provoked sharp criticism from the days of the prophets to our own. One of the tasks of any Jew is to hold his leaders up to the measure of that criticism. In modern parlance, that is referred to as a "prophetic stance."

At the same time, Jews are individualistic in their personal behavior and demands, accepting the discipline of the community as binding only when they consent to it. Classical Hebrew has no word for *obey.* (It is true that a word has been created in modern Hebrew for military usage, but it has not caught on, even in the Israel Defense Forces, which is built, as much or more than any Israeli institution, on Jewish principles.) There is a word for *command: tsavot—mitzvot* are commandments but the response to commandments is to hearken—*lishmoa* in Hebrew. Implicit in the idea of hearkening is that every human being, as a free soul, must make a decision to respond, even to a commandment. He consents, or hearkens, to do what he hears. Ultimately, there is no way anybody can force somebody to do what he does not want to do. Ultimately, the individual makes the choice. Sometimes there is not much of a margin of choice. According to one Midrash, when God offered the Torah at Sinai, he held the mountain over the Jews and offered them the choice of accepting it or being buried. Even in that case there was a hearkening and there was the doing—in short, a choice. Most of the time there are better options than that.

Jewish individualism tends to be assertive, as well. No more need be said about that; only consider what it means in connection with communal governance.

Balancing Jewish moralistic and individualistic tendencies is a strong sense of traditionalism, which serves as an anchor for both. Traditionalism is the source of conservatism in Jewish life. There is nobody as "orthodox" in his way as an old Jewish radical; whatever ideology Jews adopt is ultimately made into a tradition, forcing its adherents to live intensively according to customs rooted in its principles. Things must be done according to precedent and without rocking the boat, even though, with their moralistic tendencies, Jews tend to look constantly for improvements and reform and, with their individualistic ones, Jews tend to be liberal.

There is a tension in all Jewish communities between traditionalism, moralism, and individualism. It is a tension that is not and cannot be definitively overcome. Instead, it is the kind of creative tension that helps define Jews as Jews. In every generation, Jews try to adjust to it as best they can.[16]

Finally, Jews always have messianic expectations, and approach political life with those expectations before them. Jews fight for messianic goals, hence their intense commitment to ideologies and causes. A messianic commitment can lead to fanaticism. There are no better fanatics than Jews. Why? Because to be messianic, one has to have passion and has to believe passionately. If one believes passionately that something is right, one will go to almost any lengths to achieve it. Fortunately, Jews have been taught so strongly by the Torah to minimize violence that even their worst fanatics tend to stop with the throwing of stones. But that comes right up to the edge.

Jews have messianic expectations of their leaders and institutions, magnifying their normal human failings because Jewish institutions are supposed to live up to the highest forms of aristocratic republicanism and to the highest manifestations of the teaching of the Torah. They are inevitably disappointed, because, being human, their leaders never do. In modern times, when the pull of a common law and a common way of life has been weakened, this has exacerbated divisions within Jewish life, at times to the point of self-destructive disunity.

Leadership and Representation

If the typology discussed above holds the key to the study of power and influence—and hence decision making—in Jewish communities, it can also be of use in dealing with questions of leadership and representation. For the Jewish community, as a voluntary polity dependent for its functioning on the free choice of individuals willing to do their share to make it function, is ruled by a governing circle composed of the people who choose to make its tasks theirs, either as professionals or as volunteers. The character of that governing circle both reflects the character of the population it serves and contributes significantly to the shaping of the character of the community itself.

The sheer range of communal functions today requires such a variety of talents to fill its many leadership roles that the kind of simplistic exercises in the description of leadership patterns in the Jewish community frequent in the past have been made obsolete. In a system in which a basically complex leadership network is further complicated in the diaspora by the division between professionals and volunteers, special questions arise as to the relationship between leadership and decision making. Still others involve problems of position and role, recruitment and training, and selection, mobility, and replacement of leaders of both types. The depth of our ignorance about such matters remains extraordinary.

The Community Constitution

Taken together, the structure and functions, means of affiliation and variations in strength, patterns of authority and distribution of influence, forms of leadership, representativeness and decision making give shape to the constitution which every community creates for itself over time. Not simply—or necessarily—a written frame of government, a constitution in this sense combines the formal ordering of institutions, organizations, and offices with sociologically determined distribution of power and a conception of the good Jewish community that rationalizes the entire social and legal structure and provides the community with its principle of distributive justice.[17] The identification of this broad constitution and its components takes us beyond the community's organizational "bundle" into the larger questions that make the structure meaningful. It is the first goal in understanding the Jewish people as a polity.

Notes

1. Jewish population figures are always problematic because most are based on estimates. Even census figures outside Israel rely on voluntary responses to questions about religion and ethnicity. Here I have used the figures provided in the *American Jewish Year Book 1983* and those provided by U. O. Schmelz in *World Jewish Population: Regional Estimates and Projections,* Jewish Population Studies Series (Jerusalem: Hebrew University of Jerusalem, 1981), reconciling discrepancies according to my best judgment in the light of our own field research.

2. The sources for the information in this and the following tables are cited in detail with each case study. Much is from the field notes of the Study of Jewish Community Organization.

3. An earlier version of this model was first presented in Daniel J. Elazar, "The Reconstitution of Jewish Communities in the Postwar Period," *Jewish Journal of Sociology,* vol. 11, no. 2 (December 1969), pp. 187–226.

4. "Structure," "function," and "role" in the sense used here should be understood as the patterning of interactions between institutions, organizations, and groups as well as the patterning of the institutions, organizations, and groups themselves. In this sense, we are concerned with these both as entities and as role players in the system. See Talcott Parsons and Edward A. Shils, eds., *Toward a General Theory of Action* (Cambridge, Mass.: Harvard University Press, 1951) for an elaboration of the concepts of role and the patterned interaction of roles.

5. I have elaborated on this model in *Community and Polity* (Philadelphia: Jewish Publication Society of America, 1976), p. 72.

6. A comprehensive view of the effect of the Six-Day War can be found in the section on "The Arab-Israel War of 1967," *American Jewish Year Book 1968,* vol. 69, pp. 115–32. Also see Ernest Stock, "How 'Durban' Reacted to Israel's Crises: A Study of an American Jewish Community," *Forum,* 1975; Peter Medding, "Toward a General Theory of Jewish Political Interests and Behavior," *Jewish Journal of Sociology,* December 1977.

7. See Milton Himmelfarb, *The Jews of Modernity* (New York: Basic Books, 1973); Charles S. Liebman, *The Ambivalent American Jew* (Philadelphia: Jewish Publication Society of America, 1976); Peter Y.

Medding, "Toward a General Theory of Jewish Liberalism" in Daniel J. Elazar, ed., *Kinship and Consent* (Washington, D.C.: University Press of America, 1983); Paul R. Mendes-Flohr and Jehuda Reinhartz, eds., *The Jew in the Modern World: A Documentary History* (New York: Oxford University Press, 1980); Calvin Goldscheider, *Jewish Continuity and Change: Emerging Patterns in America* (Bloomington, Ind.: Indiana University Press, 1986).

8. Charles S. Liebman, "Dimensions of Authority in the Contemporary Jewish Community," *Jewish Journal of Sociology,* vol. 12, no. 1 (June 1970), pp. 29–37.

9. For a discussion of "Israelolitry and Its Limits," see Elazar, *Community and Polity.*

10. For a more extensive treatment of the typology in a different but analogous setting, see Daniel J. Elazar, *Cities of the Prairie* (New York: Basic Books, 1970), chap. 5.

11. The patterns of Jewish political organization are treated in detail in Daniel J. Elazar and Stuart A. Cohen, *The Jewish Polity: Jewish Political Organization from Biblical Times to the Present* (Bloomington, Ind.: Indiana University Press, 1985). See also Salo W. Baron, *A Social and Religious History of the Jews,* 18 vols. (New York and Philadelphia: Columbia University Press and Jewish Publication Society of America, 1952–83); and Haim Hillel Ben Sasson, ed., *A History of the Jewish People,* contributions by A. Malamut (London: Weidenfeld and Nicholson, 1976).

12. I. Epstein, *The Responsa of R. Solomon ben Adreth of Barcelona* (New York: Ktav, 1968).

13. Ibid.

14. For an elaboration of the relationship between pluralism and federalism, see Daniel J. Elazar, "Federalism," in *International Encyclopedia of the Social Sciences* (New York: Macmillan, 1968).

15. Johannes Althusius was the first to present a comprehensive discussion of the political system as a communications network that deals in detail with the ideas advanced here and has the virtue of being the first systematic presentation of this theory. His *Politica methodoce digesta,* first published in 1603, is available in a modern edition edited with an extensive introduction by Carl J. Friedrich (Cambridge, Mass.: Harvard University Press, 1932). More recently, Martin Landau and Vincent Ostrom have taken up the same theme. See "Federalism, Redundancy, and System Reliability" by Martin Landau and "Can Federalism Make a Difference?" by Vincent Ostrom, both in Daniel J. Elazar, *The Federal Polity* (New Brunswick, N.J.: Transaction Books, 1974).

16. On these dimensions of political culture, see Daniel J. Elazar, *American Federalism: A View from the States,* 3d ed. (New York: Harper and Row, 1984), chaps. 5 and 6; *Israel: Building a New Society* (Bloomington, Ind.: Indiana University Press, 1985), chap. 11.

17. Norton Long discusses this "constitutions" approach to the study of politics in "Aristotle and the Study of Local Government," *Social Research,* vol. 24, no. 3 (autumn 1957), pp. 287–310, a modern adaptation of Aristotelian principles for the study of comparative government.

3

The Activity Spheres of the Jewish Polity

Every Jewish community is organized through a mixture of territorially and nonterritorially based institutions.[1] Local political units are, with some modifications, used as the basis for the organization of local Jewish communities throughout the world. At the same time, the ideological and functional divisions in the Jewish community, real or putative as they may be, also provide significant points for organization as do particular functions and some common interests, which are then linked to the territorial community through some common mechanisms.

The territorially based organizations such as the Jewish federations in the United States and Canada, local authorities in Israel, or the state boards of deputies in Australia are invariably the most comprehensive ones, charged with providing direction for the community or some fragmented segment of it. The ideological-, functional-, and interest-based organizations such as the synagogues or the social services agencies generally touch the more personal aspects of Jewish life. The two bases of communal organization are recognizably distinct as such, but the specific units of organization are usually demarcated much less distinctly.

Because of the nature of the Jewish community, the territorially based organizations do not necessarily have clear-cut boundaries. This situation is not a particular problem with Jews because Jewish political culture views boundaries from a West Asian rather than an Anglo-American perspective. For Jews, the world is divided into oases and deserts rather than into clear-cut territorial plots. Every oasis has a clear core and a shifting periphery as it fades into the desert at the shifting edge of the watered area, which changes with changes in the internal water supply of the oasis. The desert, in turn, belongs to nobody or everybody. Thus the periphery can expand or contract without significantly changing the character of the core. Both Jewish law and Jewish political organization are structured in this way. For traditional Jews, law consists of a hard, immutable core (the Torah), surrounded by layers of interpretive applications, each of which becomes bonded to the original over time, expanding the whole corpus. Thus, Jewish culture has come to look upon law as requiring a fixed core of observance with room for interpretation at the peripheries. Jews are bound to but not bounded by their law. Its observance is a personal responsibility reinforced by community expectations and pressures. Both clearly reflect the situation in the land of Israel and the Middle East as a whole.

Anglo-American institutions, on the other hand, took form in well-watered countries, where lands are divided by fixed boundaries that serve as receptacles. Status is determined by who is inside a particular set of boundaries and who is not. Normally, there are no lands outside boundaries in the Anglo-American world. For Anglo-Americans then, the core is far less important than the fixed boundaries.[2]

The components of the Jewish polity follow the Jewish pattern. The State of Israel is the best example. Even when diaspora Jewish communities are erected in fixed boundary systems, they tend to be fuzzy at the periphery and more clear-cut at the core, particularly in an age of voluntary affiliation. In many respects, the local territorial communities are simply aggregates of Jews in particular cities or, since the suburban emigrations, in the metropolitan areas that embrace the cities that once contained the community.

Much the same pattern prevails with regard to ideologically based organizations. By and large the ideologies of the late modern epoch have lost their power to attract. Once powerful Zionist movements survive as political parties, vehicles for individuals to obtain leadership positions in the Jewish community, or by performing specific tasks within the community. Organizations representing the non-Zionist secular ideologies hardly survive at all. The "oasis" pattern describes their reality.

The religious movements have faired better, particularly a resurgent Orthodoxy, only to emphasize further the distinction between core and periphery. Though the core of Orthodox Judaism has grown extensively, it is still true that, outside Israel and the United States, few members of Orthodox congregations throughout the world are seriously Orthodox. This is even more true of the Conservative and Reform movements, which are built around even smaller cores of serious Conservative and Reform Jews with large masses of more casual members attracted to their respective congregations by location, habit, family, and friendship patterns, if not by historical or geographic accident. Except for those core groups, congregational members are less interested in their synagogue's ideological affiliation than in how well it serves their personal religious needs.

Since 1967 new ideological movements have surfaced in Israel and the diaspora. Some, such as Gush Emunim and Shalom Achshav (Peace Now), represent emerging political alignments in Israel. Originally founded to express different positions regarding the future Jewish presence in the territories occupied by Israel as a result of the Six-Day War, both have become nuclei for a renewal of the struggle between left and right in the Jewish state.

In the United States, the Left, which had more or less abandoned Jewish communal involvement for several decades, returned to the arena with new organizations such as New Jewish Agenda and the Jewish Fund for Justice. In France, the Renouveau Juif combines ideological opposition to the rampant assimilationism among the Jews of that country, with an effort to strengthen commitment to Israel and to find a new place in the sun for French Jewry's new Sephardic majority.

Throughout the world a new ideologically militant Orthodoxy has emerged, using a new network of *yeshivot* as their nuclei. As yet these represent small if vital minorities within the Jewish people. Their vitality already has given them a weight beyond their numbers, but one would be hard put to say that they have reideologized the community, especially since, in the Orthodox camp, where ideology takes traditionally religious forms, ideological groupings have succeeded in maintaining themselves and their ideologies in organized form.

For the polity as a whole, ideologically based organizations have had more success on a worldwide or countrywide basis, where the absence of comprehensive territorial institutions has been marked, than on the local plane. All told, however, modernity emphasized the territorial over the nonterritorial elements wherever given half a chance and to reduce ideologically based organizations to functional specialists responsible for specific tasks.

A major result of this has been to limit the powers of the countrywide organizations in the diaspora and to make the primary locus of decision making for those communities local. This takes two forms. In one, the dominant local community either constitutes or captures well-nigh total control of the countrywide Jewish organizations, so that they, in essence, express the perspective and interests of that community. This is the pattern in countries like Sweden and France.

In the other form, the countrywide organizations are weak compared with the local ones and are either ignored or manipulated by the local ones as they deem necessary. That is the pattern in the United States and Brazil. In a few cases, Australia, South Africa, and Switzerland, for example, the countrywide organizations do have a significant independent standing. Only in Israel, where the countrywide organizations are either state institutions or closely intertwined with the state, do they play a dominant role as such, not as extensions of some local community or congeries of local communities.

What emerges is not a single pyramidal structure, not even one in which the "bottom" rules the "top" as is sometimes suggested on the organization charts. There is no "bottom" or "top" except on a functional basis for specific purposes (if then). This absence of hierarchy is the first element to recognize in examining how Jews make their institutions work.[3]

The Role of Functional Groupings

In the context described above, the institutions and organizations of the Jewish polity group themselves de facto in five major spheres of public activity: (1) religious-congregational, (2) educational-cultural, (3) external relations–defense, (4) communal-welfare, and (5) Israel–world Jewry (table 3.1).[4]

Religious-Congregational Sphere

The religious-congregational sphere falls principally within the domain of the *keter kehunah,* with a certain overlap into that of the *keter torah,* where its rabbinical leaders prefer to be located. From time to time, institutions from the domain of the *keter malkhut* impinge upon this sphere, but since the decline of the consistorially-based regimes in the Jewish communities that had them in the modern epoch, the institutions in this sphere have not had a serious role in that latter domain. Intervention in the other direction comes primarily in the *edah* arena.

Contemporary synagogues provide the immediately personal and interpersonal ritual-cum-social functions demanded by the community and, in most countries, do so primarily through highly independent individual congregations. The congregations have a monopoly of those functions locally; the synagogue confederations, rabbinical associations, seminaries, and *yeshivot* maintain a parallel monopoly of the community's organized religious and *halakhic* concerns countrywide (table 3.1). The only new-style institutions to have emerged in this sphere in the postwar period are the religious study and research centers. These include bodies such as CLAL in the United States and the Shalom Hartman Institute in Israel, which offer religious motivation and instruction to Jews seeking to reconnect with the Jewish religious tradition.

Table 3.1
Spheres, Institutions, and Organizations

SPHERE	LOCAL	COUNTRY-WIDE	WORLDWIDE
Religious-congregational	Synagogues Orthodox outposts Rabbinical courts Kashrut councils Local religious councils	Synagogue confederations Seminaries and yeshivot Rabbinical associations Rabbinical courts Ministry of religions study centers	Israeli chief rabbinate Knesset World synagogue leagues Agudath Israel Hassidic communities
Educational-cultural	Synagogue schools Communal and secularist schools Day schools Colleges of Jewish studies Central Agencies of Jewish education Jewish community centers Jewish studies programs in universities Local cultural institutions and groups	Countrywide Jewish educational bodies Countrywide associations of Jewish community centers Jewish colleges and universities Scholarly Associations Jewish foundations (e..g., National Foundation for Jewish Culture) Educational services of government bodies Educators' Associations Jewish cultural institutions and organizations study centers	Jewish Agency and World Zionist Organization Memorial Foundation for Jewish Culture Joint Distribution Committee Alliance Israélite Universelle Israel government Public affairs centers
External relations—defense	Local community relations councils Local chapters or offices of countrywide community relations bodies	Countrywide community relations organizations (e.g., CRIF, American Jewish Committee, boards of deputies) Jewish war veterans associations Professional associations Special-purpose groups (e.g., Soviet Jewry)	Consultative Council of Jewish Agencies Coordinating board of Jewish organizations World Jewish Congress Israel government World Council for Soviet Jewry WOJAC American Jewish Committee Anti-Defamation League Public affairs centers B'nai B'rith
Communal-welfare	Jewish federations Social service agencies Jewish community centers Local Jewish press Jewish hospitals/health care institutions	Council of Jewish Federations Councils of Jewish community centers Immigrant aid societies Boards of Deputies	Israel government Jewish Agency/WZO International professional/functional associations B'nai B'rith Joint Distribution Committee Public affairs centers
Israel-world Jewry	Jewish Federations Local Zionist chapters Local Israel bond office Local "friends" of Israel or overseas institutions	Council of Federations UJA/UIA Zionist organizations Israel bonds United HIAS Service "Friends" of Israel or overseas Institutions	Israel government Jewish Agency/WZO Jewish National Fund World Zionist Organization Joint Distribution ORT Claims conference Keren Hayesod Public affairs centers

Locally, the congregations may be supplemented by such manifestations of Orthodoxy (occasionally paralleled in the Conservative movement) as a rabbinical court and a *kashrut* council. In the larger communities, there are also *yeshivot* or branches of Hassidic movements that serve (and try to develop) special constituencies. In addition, intercongregational regional organizations and boards of rabbis are in the larger local communities.

Countrywide, the synagogues are organized according to one of four models, as unions, federations, confederations, or leagues or some combination thereof. France and Britain offer two models of synagogue unions. The French *consistoire*, established in Napoleonic times, follows a classically centralized model. It was a veritable instrument of the state for most of the nineteenth century, until the French separated church and state in 1905. It remained dominant in the community until World War II. Although the structure of the *consistoire* was changed from time to time, its basic form has remained constant. It is centered in Paris with regional consistorial bodies either subsidiary to Paris or dependent on it, with only Alsace-Lorraine outside the model because of its special political status as a disputed territory between Germany and France. The chief rabbi of the *Consistoire Central* is the chief rabbi of France. He is supported by a small *conseil laique*. All synagogues are technically the property of the *consistoire* in which they are located, and rabbis are formally appointed by the appropriate consistorial body.[5]

The United Synagogue, the dominant synagogue body in Britain, is somewhat less centralized in the British style. There, too, member synagogues are owned by the common body, which must approve the appointment of congregational rabbis, all of whom are under the authority of the Ashkenazic chief rabbi. In Britain, the board of the United Synagogue has greater authority vis-à-vis the chief rabbi than in France, because France is more hierarchical in its organizational culture. Boards in Britain consist of persons with independent bases in the community. Moreover, except in areas of doctrinal controversy, the United Synagogue rules its member congregations with a lighter hand, allowing a measure of decentralization roughly parallel to that which Parliament allows British local authorities.[6]

The South African Federation of Synagogues is a good example of the federation model. Individual congregations are independent to the extent that they are owned by their members who appoint their own rabbis but are bound closely with one another under the authority of the chief rabbi of South Africa.[7]

The American model offers the best example of the use of confederations and leagues. Three great synagogue confederations, for the Orthodox, Conservative, and Reform movements, plus a smaller one for the Reconstructionist movement and various subsidiary leagues within the Orthodox community embrace most of the permanent synagogues in the United States. However, because every congregation is independent and self-contained under the law—the private preserve of its members—there is no need for it to be a member of any larger body if its members choose not to be. Hence many congregations are independent and many others are nominal members of the countrywide bodies. Consequently, the latter have little power aside from that of professional placement. Even so, every congregation, no matter how committed it may be to its movement, hires its own rabbinical staff, under its own terms, in what amounts to a free market situation.[8] The controlling power of the individual synagogues in the religious-congregational sphere in the United States means that a large share of Jewish activity—involving nearly half the total local expenditure of American Jewry—is managed outside any communal decision-making system.

In 1926, in their common quest for an expanded role in American Jewish life, the three great synagogue confederations formed a league, the Synagogue Council of America. For a few years during the height of the "religious revival" of the 1950s, it tried to capture the leading role as spokesman for American Jewry. Nominally, it is the Jewish religious counterpart to the National Council of Churches and the Catholic Council of Bishops but does not actually play such a role. Its principal function today is to provide the only religious forum where representatives of Orthodoxy, Conservatism, and Reform still meet on common issues.

Each synagogue confederation has a seminary, which, because it is academic, projects itself on the American Jewish scene in a quasi-independent way. Even with the growth of Judaic studies programs in academic institutions, these seminaries remain the backbone of organized Jewish scholarship in the United States. Their alumni lead the congregations of American Jewry and, through their rabbinical associations, link their seminaries and the confederations.

There are also a growing number of *yeshivot* in New York and many other major Jewish communities that reflect the great growth and proliferation of the new ultra-Orthodox elements in the community. They preserve and extend traditional Jewish scholarship on a scale never before experienced in American Jewish history.

In Israel, the religious-congregational sphere is dichotomized between the formal institutions of the state and thousands of small independent congregations. Some have buildings and activities apart from worship services but most are limited to places of worship with traditional study circles attached and occasional events such as evenings of liturgical music or lectures by prominent rabbinical personalities. Through the Ministry of Religions and the local religious councils, the state provides a variety of religious services, mainly those falling within the framework of the *keter kehunah,* having to do with ritual expression. The state-appointed and supported rabbinical courts deal with the most practical manifestations of *keter torah,* particularly in matters of personal status, which are exclusively under their jurisdiction. Thus the Israeli dichotomy is such that the congregations themselves play no role in the governance of the Jewish polity and confine themselves to activities growing out of *keter kehunah;* the major governmental institution of the Jewish polity, the State of Israel, provides all other services directly.[9]

Since World War II, there have been some tentative but real steps toward the development of *edah*-wide institutions in the religious-congregational sphere. Formally, these include the world leagues of synagogues which are tied to each of the major branches of Judaism. Although they have developed a presence of sorts, they remain tertiary institutions in the overall scheme of things, established, maintained, and directed from the United States, or by Americans who have relocated in Israel. That they have emerged at all is testimony to the revival of the *edah* as a working entity in which the representatives of each *keter* feel that they must develop appropriate instrumentalities to be represented in that arena.

It is significant that the three *edah*-wide leagues have all joined the World Zionist Organization (WZO), which invited them to do so in an effort to strengthen its position on the Jewish scene vis-à-vis the reconstituted Jewish Agency, which is increasingly dominated by the local community federations. The WZO, in turn, has bolstered the three worldwide synagogue movements by providing them with a way to participate in world Jewish politics, and supplying them with funds enabling them to do so far beyond what their countrywide congregational bodies are prepared to provide.

Much stronger are the worldwide bodies of the ultra-Orthodox, including Agudath

Israel, Chabad, and other Hassidic communities that emanate from the religious-congregational sphere but extend their work beyond that sphere into most of the others. All of these bodies are considerably older than the world synagogue leagues, but all, even those whose movement antecedents go back to the eighteenth century, are essentially twentieth-century phenomena. Agudath Israel was founded in 1912 and, in many respects, serves as an umbrella organization for most of them. A federation of movements of the ultra-Orthodox camp, it is built around three recognizable elements from eastern Europe: the communities of the Lithuanian *yeshivot*, Polish ultra-Orthodoxy, and the Hungarian-Romanian Hassidic courts. Each of the three has its representatives on the movement's supreme body, the Moetzet Gedolei HaTorah (Council of Torah Sages) and the principal ones have their designated representatives in the Israeli Knesset through the party.[10]

Unlike the world synagogue leagues, Agudath Israel has structured a comprehensive subpolity which gives expression to all three *ketarim*. The Council of Torah Sages, representing the *keter torah*, obviously maintains the upper hand by explicit design, but this does not lessen the reality of a *keter malkhut*, which takes the form of a somewhat subordinate set of professional politicians occupying appropriate positions in the Jewish world, and a *keter kehunah* consisting of various Hassidic *rebbes* who dominate the member Hassidic communities. The various Hassidic groups have more or less elaborated structures with Chabad having the most extensive. Though they, too, emerge from this sphere to overlap into others, they are somewhat more confined to the mainstream concerns of the sphere, though in their own way.[11]

The Israeli rabbinate is a growing force in the religious-congregational sphere throughout the *edah* by virtue of its role in determining the personal status of individual Jews. In an age of jet travel and growing population interchange between Israel and the diaspora, such decisions have ramifications that reverberate throughout the Jewish world. In this connection, the Knesset is also acquiring influence in the religious-congregational sphere, the first "secular" body anywhere to do so, simply because of its central role in defining "who is a Jew" in a situation where religion and state are intertwined.

The religious-congregational sphere is in the curious situation of, on one hand, being a powerful influence on all Jews, yet unable to mobilize even half of them in any formal relationship to religious institutions in the diaspora. With the exception of the few communities that still maintain community-wide registration of Jews, membership in synagogues or congregations is voluntary and if one chooses not to affiliate with some religious body, one is simply not affiliated. Thus in the United States perhaps 50 percent of the Jewish community maintains a synagogue affiliation at any given time, though approximately three-quarters of all Jews will have been affiliated with a synagogue at some time or another in the course of their lives. In France, membership figures are even lower.

In Israel, where a different pattern of affiliation prevails, the "membership" figure is undoubtedly much lower, but then every Jew is linked to the religious-congregational sphere through his or her being bound as a Jew to *halakhic* laws of personal status through the state's rabbinate and religious institutions.

In a sense this situation reflects the different stages or directions of modernization in the Jewish world. In premodern times, all Jews were doubly bound by *halakhah* and by the social pressure of the community to be substantially observant. Today the binding force of *halakhah* on an other than voluntary basis has mostly disappeared except in

Israel, where it has been reduced to the area of personal status. So, too, social pressure no longer prevails except where people choose to be part of subcommunities of observant Jews. Otherwise, the character and extent of linkage with the religious-congregational sphere is a matter of individual choice, ranging from congregational affiliation to being part of a Jewish community in which the religious dimension is built in. The only issue in which all Jews may be subject to some kind of binding decision making is in determining Jewishness itself, that is to say, "who is a Jew," where, because of the influence of Israel, the decisions of its authoritative institutions on this question are authoritative for the Jewish world as a whole.

Educational-Cultural Sphere

The educational-cultural sphere can be defined clearly and the institutions that function in it are among the most separated in the Jewish world. As a result, the sphere is extremely fragmented. This is partly for substantive reasons. Because education is what it is, the principal vehicle for socialization of new generations, it obviously must reflect the ideological presuppositions of the current generation. Once the Jewish people ceased to be homogeneous and ideologies of Jewishness began to multiply, so too did the educational vehicles for their expression and transmission.[12]

The institutional divisions of modernity also contributed heavily to further fragmentation even where ideological differences did not come into play. Thus, for example, one can expect differences in educational approach between Orthodox and non-Orthodox, not to speak of the divisions between religious and nonreligious, Zionist and non-Zionist education, which emerged during the latter part of the modern epoch. But there are also divisions within each camp based on institutional interests. In the United States and Canada, for example, even synagogues of the same movement try to maintain their own schools for reasons of institutional self-preservation, which may or may not be valid but are perceived as vital. In the Western world, the synagogization of Jewish life was the principal institutional cause of the fragmentation. In eastern Europe and Israel, the growth of ideological divisions led to the same result. Both forms of fragmentation are now visible throughout the Jewish world.

There is also an environmental factor of importance. Part of the Jewish drive for emancipation included the drive for the right of entry into the educational systems of the host societies. Thus, for many, Jewish education was relegated to supplementary education and no more. With the decline of emancipationist expectations, there has been a return to the notion of providing comprehensive elementary and secondary education and, to some extent, tertiary education as well, through day schools or *yeshivot*.

This has led to the development of two parallel and usually separate systems of Jewish education in the diaspora—a network of day schools and another of supplementary schools. In most diaspora countries, every day school is independent of every other one rather than being part of a system. At most, the day schools are affiliated with some overarching Board of Jewish Education, or Va'ad Hinukh, which provides technical services and support and some subsidization but rarely functions as the guiding hand of an integrated system. The few exceptions are notable, in both their educational achievements and their professional quality.

In Israel the situation is much the same, even though education is, for the most part, state sponsored and almost entirely state financed. Recognition of ideological differences among the Jews of Israel has led to the emergence of several different school systems within the state framework or closely associated with it. These include: (1) the state schools, which are basically nonreligious; (2) the state religious schools, which follow the ideology of religious Zionism; (3) the kibbutz schools which, though part of the state system, reflect the respective ideologies of the kibbutzim in which they are located; (4) a new developing state traditional school network for those who want their children to learn Jewish tradition but in a non-Orthodox context; and (5) the independent schools, for the most part the schools of Agudath Israel, that are formally outside state control but are financed by the government. Finally, the ultra-Orthodox maintain a network of *heders*, Talmud Torahs, and *yeshivot*, entirely outside the system, which teach only traditional subjects and do not receive state funds.[13]

The tertiary educational structure of the Jewish world includes several categories of institutions: traditional *yeshivot*, modern rabbinical seminaries that also serve as institutions for developing scholars of Jewish studies, Jewish teacher-training schools, general universities under Jewish auspices, and Jewish studies programs in non-Jewish universities. Again, every one of these is independent of every other one, although some may be located in a movement or state framework. The closest thing to an integrated system of higher Jewish education is the network of universities in Israel, each of which is, for all intents and purposes, a national institution belonging to the Jewish people, subject to fiscal supervision by the Israel Council for Higher Education, a government agency that sets basic guidelines for who does what and who gets what in Israel.[14]

Adult and continuing education is the province of all the aforementioned tertiary bodies plus individual synagogues and various organizations serving their members or using adult education to increase membership. In the United States, for example, Hadassah, B'nai B'rith, and the American Jewish Committee have made notable efforts in adult Jewish education. The Council of Jewish Federations and the local federations have emphasized leadership development as a form of continuing education.

Adult Jewish education is particularly well developed in North America and particularly weak elsewhere. The concept of leadership development is in its infancy in the other diaspora communities. Continuing education is widespread in Israel where it has been developed on an institutionalized basis and through private study circles (comparable with the kind of *minyanim* that flourish by private initiative in Israel). These study circles are not necessarily religious in orientation; many are organized by nonreligious Jews to pursue the study of Jewish culture generally. Israel's Open University is emerging as a major factor in continuing education, especially in Jewish studies, and is also seeking to expand its role to the diaspora. It is a state-sponsored institution financed by a grant from the Rothschild family.[15]

Most *kehillot* and *aratzot* have some kind of central agency for Jewish education, a coordinating body which is rarely comprehensive, plus, perhaps, one or more countrywide bodies that sponsor, coordinate, or provide technical assistance to schools. They may also have one or more countrywide instrumentalities promoting some special aspect of Jewish education. The United States is an example of the last. The Jewish Education Service of North America (JESNA), which has replaced the American Association for Jewish Education, is a continental (including Canada) body, but it does not include Torah U'Mesorah, a countrywide coordinating body that sponsors Orthodox day schools. Parallel to both is the Coalition for Alternatives in Jewish Education (CAJE), a body developed out of the Jewish countercultural efforts of the late 1960s to try to infuse a new spirit into Jewish education through working directly with Jewish teachers. Although there is some cooperation between these bodies, either directly or through the medium of the federation movement, they remain quite separate.[16]

The South African Jewish community has a comprehensive South African Board of Jewish Education with real responsibilities. It works directly in the provinces of Transvaal and Natal and through a provincial board in Cape Province.[17] In Argentina, the Va'ad HaHinuj was founded to provide technical assistance to Jewish schools in the provinces but has gradually extended its role to include Buenos Aires.[18]

In the *edah* arena the strongest forces for Jewish education are those linked with the World Zionist Organization and the Jewish Agency. Together the two have seven departments that deal with Jewish education, the WZO Education Department, the Torah Education Department, and the Youth and Hehalutz Departments; the Agency has the Education Committee and the Youth Aliya Department. The last confines its attention to Israeli youth (although there are plans to expand it to serve diaspora youth temporarily in Israel); the others work principally in the diaspora. In addition, the WZO departments of Development and Services and Services to the Sephardi Communities play major stimulatory roles, the first principally in continuing education and leadership development and the second with the range of educational functions as they relate to Sephardim.

The Jewish Agency's Pincus Fund and the Joint Education Fund of the Agency, the WZO, and the government of Israel provide support for innovative educational programs throughout the Jewish world. This division of responsibilities is often decried but it has never been properly studied. Although clearly a result of political pressure, the pressure reflects real ideological and institutional divisions in Jewish life, which cannot be overlooked by any actors in the educational-cultural sphere.[19]

Besides the foregoing, the Memorial Foundation for Jewish Culture contributes to the support of educational institutions throughout the Jewish world from German reparations money. The American Jewish Joint Distribution Committee finances education programs mainly in Israel and in countries where disadvantaged Jews live unable to maintain their own systems unaided.

There are also the multicountry networks of Jewish schools established to help Jews raise themselves out of poverty to respectability. The oldest of these are the schools of the Alliance Israélite Universelle. Established by French Jewry in 1860, the Alliance served a combined purpose of helping Jews, principally in the Islamic world, enter modernity while preserving some measure of Jewishness. The Alliance schools have been in decline at least since World War II, in part because of the decline of French Jewry as a result of the Holocaust, in part because of the Jewish evacuation of the countries in which the Alliance worked, and in part because French language and culture no longer represent the gateway to modernity. Jewish schools emphasizing English became more popular among their prospective clients. The Alliance has tried to adapt by expanding its program in Israel and France in directions that give more emphasis to the Jewish component than previously.

A second worldwide network is that of the schools of the Organization for Rehabilitation through Training (ORT). Originally founded in Russia to provide vocational education for Jews in the modern world, they also were content with a modicum of Jewish content. The ORT schools continue to flourish in Israel and most of the same countries where the Joint Distribution Committee and the Alliance are active. They also maintain a few schools in Europe, which service Jewish refugees. Many of them offer the only Jewish education that their students are likely to get, but the main purpose remains vocational. As such, they serve non-Jews also. In Bombay, India, for example, the ORT school is considered to be a Jewish school, but only a tiny fraction of the student body is Jewish. ORT's success has led it to be commissioned to undertake projects for the United Nations in the Third World.

One other worldwide network is the Otzar HaTorah, established by Syrian Jews from the United States after World War II to provide a more traditional Jewish education in a modern framework for Jews in the Islamic countries. Otzar HaTorah, though Orthodox and thus different in its orientation from the Alliance schools, rapidly became popular because its language of general education was English. It offered young Jews entry into the postwar international scene dominated by the English language. Many families were willing to have their students receive an Orthodox education in return for that benefit. In Iran, for example, the Alliance schools, which had been brought to the country in the 1890s, were dominant until the British occupation of the southern half of Iran during World War II. At that point the Iranian Jews discovered that French was losing its predominance; when the opportunity presented itself, they shifted their children to the Otzar HaTorah schools. The Alliance schools were left for the poorest people, who had no choice.[20]

The larger dilemma of Jewish education is perhaps more clearly understood when we note that the principal leadership of the *edah* is associated with the *keter malkhut* while Jewish educators see themselves as related to *keter torah*. That alone would create some distance between the two, although one that could be bridged once it was recognized for what it is. The matter is further complicated by the fact that in the diaspora Jewish educators are too often subordinated to rabbinical leaders in the *keter torah* and, if they are not themselves rabbis, to congregational rabbis (*keter kehunah*) as well. Thus they have to struggle for position within their own *keter*.

The difficulties of Jewish educators are increased by the fact that there is no longer a clear-cut understanding of what should be the content and goals of Jewish education. In many cases, particularly in North America, the primary purpose of Jewish education is religious education in the narrowest sense, the transmission of "synagogue skills" to enable the next generation to function within the context of the North American synagogue. In Latin America and Europe, on the other hand, much of Jewish education is secular in orientation based on an equally limited Hebraism, with language skills monopolizing the Jewish curriculum. Although these are the two dominant minimalist approaches to Jewish education, there are contradictory maximalist approaches as well. There are the schools that emphasize the study of classic rabbinic texts as the be-all and end-all of Jewish study and those whose emphasis is on Jewish history and literature, with a number of variants within each group.

Moreover, outside Israel where Jewish education, however defined, is central to the curriculum, there are serious conflicts over the amount of time to be allocated to Jewish study. Whether in relation to day schools or supplementary schools, Jewish studies at the tertiary level or whatever, students and their parents are principally interested in acquiring the general education needed to pursue successful careers, and Jewish education is distinctly supplementary. Not only have the hours per week spent in supplementary schools declined, but even in those countries where most Jewish children go to Jewish day schools, the amount of time allocated to Jewish subjects in those schools is often quite limited.

Thus Jewish education and Jewish educators are caught in the middle in more ways than one, torn between their aspirations and the tasks thrust upon them, their self-esteem and their status in the larger realm of Jewish life, and the relationships across the *ketarim*. This also explains why so much of the leadership of the *keter malkhut* is estranged from Jewish education aside from formally acknowledging its importance in the abstract. Associated as they are with a different domain—one that contemporary Jewish education has not properly addressed—they do not have sufficient links with the domain with which Jewish education is identified to develop a truly serious commitment to it.

Jewish cultural activities are even more fragmented than educational ones, if that is possible.[21] Outside Israel, they are also more likely to be privately sponsored and financed. Diaspora Jewish public support for cultural activities is minimal, to say the least. In part this is because of the low level of Jewish culture among diaspora Jews with the possible exception of a few limited circles and partly because in the major concentration of diaspora Jewry, North America, support for cultural activities in general is considered more a matter for private than public concern by the society as a whole. There is probably more per capita support for Jewish culture by the French Jewish community because in France it is expected that culture will be publicly supported. In the other English-speaking countries, except Canada, the level of cultural expectation in the Jewish community is so low that even private support is rare. In Latin America, the situation is even worse.

Most local support for Jewish culture in the diaspora comes from private foundations or through the Jewish community centers, which may sponsor book fairs, art exhibitions, literary evenings, and the like. Countrywide, if there is a body that services the community centers, such as the National Jewish Welfare Board in the United States, it may also provide support services for those cultural activities and provide some stimulus for them. North American Jewry has the National Foundation for Jewish Culture, which provides direct support for some forms of Jewish culture and scholarship and also manages the Joint Cultural Appeal through which is channeled financing from local federations to a group of beneficiary agencies ranging from the Jewish Publication Society to the American Academy for Jewish Research and the Institute for Jewish Research (YIVO), most of which deal with scholarship rather than public culture. No such body exists in any other diaspora community.

Israel is the real heartland of Jewish cultural activities. There the instrumentalities and fiscal resources of the state are mobilized for cultural activities to a degree much greater than in any diaspora Jewish community, partly because the state sees its role as the guardian and promotor of Jewish culture as vital and partly because the government tradition out of which its founders came viewed this as an appropriate state role in the first place. State involvement ranges from the Academy of the Hebrew Language, the official body for determining Hebrew usage, to municipal subsidies of public nongovernment bodies in the promotion of lecture series, and everything in between. The Ministry of Education and Culture is just that. It does much more than oversee the state school system but touches every other aspect of education and culture, including radio and television, theater, the graphic and plastic arts, and Jewish scholarship.[22]

The preeminent cultural role Israel plays in the *edah* is tempered only by the degree to which knowledge of Hebrew is necessary to have access to the products of Israel's efforts. Because that is a serious barrier, many in the diaspora have maintained that Israel is doing too little, but that is principally because they do not have access to what is being done.

External Relations—Defense Sphere

The focus of this sphere has shifted under the changing conditions of Jewish history. For modern Jewry, external relations and defense were confined to representation of Jewish interests before non-Jewish governments and, later, community-relations efforts to improve relations with non-Jews.[23] As a result of the establishment of Israel, postmodern Jewry combines those diaspora forms with the classic devices of military defense and foreign relations among states. The role of the Israel Defense Forces and the Israeli Foreign Ministry in the defense of Jewish interests worldwide should not be minimized. Still, both are limited in their ability to defend Jews outside Israel. Hence community relations remains the first line of defense of the latter.

Outside North America, community relations is usually referred to as representation and is conducted by representative boards. In English-speaking countries these are usually called boards of deputies; in France, the Conseil Représentatif Israélite Français (CRIF); in Argentina, the Delegación de la Asociaciones Israelitas Argentina (DAIA); and so on. (See table 3.2.) For the most part these organizations are countrywide, perhaps with local branches, and are confederations or federations of all the organizations and institutions of standing in the communities they serve.

The first of these bodies, the Board of Deputies of British Jews, was established by Act of Parliament in 1760 as the official address for communication between the British government and the Jewish community. Most others were established by the Jewish community alone and do not have such official status, though they are usually recognized informally as the link.

Because the principal common concern of the newly emancipated Jews and later modern Jews in general was to promote good relations with the governments of their host societies, to secure full civil and political equality, these representative bodies soon became the dominant organizations in their communities. They attracted the highest status leadership (who in any case would have been the ones called on to represent the Jewish community to the non-Jewish world) and set much of the communal tone.

Among the European countries, only in France were these tasks retained by bodies emanating from the religious-congregational sphere, the *consistoire,* until almost the end of the modern epoch. Only in 1944, under the German occupation, when the need for a representative Jewish body whose sole function would be to protect Jewish interests vis-à-vis what was by then a very hostile outside world became fully apparent, did French Jewry organize CRIF. Outside Europe, similar bodies came into existence primarily in the wake of some major anti-Semitic incident. In Latin America, such incidents either involved actual pogroms, particularly about the time of World War I or Nazi-engendered anti-Semitic campaigns in the 1930s. In the British Commonwealth countries, the anti-Semitism that provoked organized Jewish response was less dramatic but was perceived as no less real a barrier to full Jewish equality. The South African Jewish Board of Deputies (SAJBD) is an exception in this regard; it was organized primarily to provide relief to Jewish refugees at the time of the Anglo-Boer War.

Despite their emergence as the most important communal bodies, they have been limited, by and large, to a representational role. The exceptions are in Canada and South Africa. The Canadian Jewish Congress (its different name in part reflected the influence of North American thinking) took on a broader governance role, especially in the education and cultural sphere.[24] As noted above, the SAJBD was founded to coordinate relief

Table 3.2
Principal Countrywide External-Relations Organizations

United States	France	Commonwealth Countries	Argentina
Conference of Presidents of Major American Jewish Organizations	Conseil Représentatif Israélite Français (CRIF)	Board of Deputies of British Jews	Delegación de la Asociaciones Israelitas Argentina (DAIA)
National Jewish Community Relations Advisory Council		Executive Council of Australian Jewry (ECAJ)	
American Jewish Committee		Canadian Jewish Congress (CJC)	
American Jewish Congress		South African Jewish Board of Deputies	
Anti-Defamation League of B'nai B'rith			
National Conference on Soviet Jewry			

work. Even after its focus changed to representational activities because of the rise of anti-Semitism in South Africa in the 1930s, it retained functions from other spheres.[25] All were seen as the principal government-like institutions of their communities and rapidly became the most important manifestations of the *keter malkhut*.

Another common characteristic was that all began as countrywide organizations. In the larger countries many later established regional or local branches, while maintaining the centrality of the countrywide body. This was even true in Australia where the principal bodies are the state bodies; they were established before Australia was unified, when each state was an independent British colony. Thus the locus of the external relations–defense function was and remained countrywide.

In Canada, the Canadian Jewish Congress established regional offices following the conventional regional groupings of Canada (that is, the Atlantic provinces, Quebec, Ontario, and the Western provinces), with the Quebec and Ontario offices being identical with the local Montreal and Toronto Jewish Congresses, respectively. In South Africa the original Board of Deputies embraced Transvaal, the Orange Free State, and Natal; Cape Province had its own Board of Deputies, reflecting the semi-independent status of Cape Town. Even after the two boards were integrated, Cape Town remained a subsidiary entity, which preserved much of its own integrity. These regional structures were the exception rather than the rule and, on the whole, the representative boards remained centralized institutions.

The Jews of the United States initiated their defense efforts in similar form but with a different result.[26] The first countrywide Jewish organization based on other than fraternal principles was the Board of Delegates of American Israelites, which was clearly modeled after the Board of Deputies of British Jews. Founded in 1859, its fate was suggestive of what would happen on the American scene, which was so different from that of other countries. In the United States, official channels between the government and the Jews were not welcomed and could not be sustained. Nor in those years were the problems of community relations sufficiently serious beyond the local arena to sustain a countrywide organization. The Board of Delegates played some role in combatting anti-Semitism during the Civil War, but that was the greatest domestic challenge that it faced. It made a more visible effort to mobilize the American government against denial of Jews the right to settle freely in Switzerland, but that remained more of a symbolic issue than a real one. When, after fourteen years, the board was absorbed by the newly founded Union of American Hebrew Congregations, the primary responsibility for defense against anti-Semitism passed into the hands of the leaders of B'nai B'rith who had local or national influence.

The intensification of anti-Semitism in the late nineteenth century led to new efforts to provide American Jewry with defense. The first of these was the American Jewish Committee founded in 1906, as a league of notables of German Jewish ancestry, the "who's who" of American Jewry, who were committed to quiet action to defend Jewish rights. For a while it was recognized as the preeminent voice of American Jewry because of the stature of its leadership. It was challenged in 1913 by the founding of the Anti-Defamation League of B'nai B'rith whose members sought a more militant way to fight vicious anti-Semitism after the Leo Frank case in Atlanta, Georgia, a blood libel in modern guise. Meanwhile, the American Jewish Committee tried to consolidate its position by stimulating the organization of local *kehillot* in major American cities, particularly New York, Philadelphia, and Chicago, which would have used the committee as their countrywide representative.

The *kehillah* experiment collapsed in all three cities for reasons that need not be explored here. A major reason was the rise of Eastern European Jewry to positions of greater power and their challenge to the German Jewish–dominated American Jewish Committee. That challenge led, after World War I, to the establishment of the American Jewish Congress, which was dominated by Eastern European Jews and Zionist in orientation.

Competition among the three "defense agencies" assured that none would become the spokesman for American Jewry. In 1944 a major effort was made by the Council of Jewish Federations to bring about their consolidation. The effort failed because of the strength of the vested interests supporting each body. The CJF had to back off, but it did give birth to the National Jewish Community Relations Advisory Council (NJCRAC), a CJF-founded and financed umbrella organization that fostered consultation between the big three, the more specialized countrywide bodies such as the Jewish War Veterans and the Jewish Labor Committee, and the local Jewish community relations councils. The latter had risen to prominence as Jewish community councils in the 1930s to combat anti-Semitism and the threat of nazism locally. Over time, the NJCRAC became another player in the game but never became more than a modest coordinating body.

The local Jewish community councils, however, attempted to be like the Canadian Jewish Congress in that they saw themselves as possible unifiers of the whole Jewish community for internal and external purposes. To assert this claim, they had to challenge the Jewish welfare federations, which had already acquired custody of fund-raising locally and beyond. They lost the struggle and were transformed from community councils into community relations councils with clearly defined representational responsibilities under the aegis of the federations that provided them with their funds. Thus in the United States the community relations bodies gradually ceased to be the dominant institutions of *keter malkhut,* ceding that role to the federations and their countrywide arm, the Council of Jewish Federations.[27]

In addition to the community relations council major American Jewish communities often have local offices or chapters of the American Jewish Committee, the Anti-Defamation League, the American Jewish Congress, the Jewish War Veterans, and the Jewish Labor Committee that also engage in community relations work, whether in cooperation with the Jewish Community Relations Council or independently. The classic pictures of fragmentation in American Jewish life are usually drawn from the community relations field, and it is in that field that the most publicized countrywide efforts have been made to bring order out of chaos.[28]

If we compare community relations with the educational-cultural or religious-congregational spheres where there are also many separate organizations involved, we find that, in the last two, the situation is so structured that the many separate organizations engage in little direct competition. In the first, the smaller number of separate organizations overlap one another because they deal with the same problems—often with the same explicit issues. Only in organizations with special referents such as the Jewish Labor Committee is this problem not an ever-present one. The effects of that competition are potentially great because they are directed toward matters that reach outside the Jewish community and directly affect its relations with the larger world. Consequently, a considerable amount of self-policing and specialization has developed in the sphere since 1944.

In the 1950s, in an effort to provide a single American Jewish public voice (as distinct from a formal lobby) to speak for Israel, American Jewry was stimulated by Nahum Goldmann to organize the Conference of Presidents of Major Jewish Organizations. After the 1967 war, most particularly after Yitzhak Rabin became Israel's ambassador to the United States, the Presidents' Conference, as it came to be known, emerged as the most important quasi-official spokesman for American Jewry on Israeli matters. It remains confined to matters relating to Israel and has never attempted to be more than that; as a loose league of organizations, its member bodies would prevent it from going beyond that specific concern.

The Presidents' Conference had about a decade of real prominence. Then, in the late 1970s, a combination of circumstances led the same people who were active in the federations (which by that time had become the true government-like institutions of American Jewry and the principal representatives of the *keter malkhut*) to become personally active in the America Israel Public Affairs Committee (AIPAC), the principal American Jewish lobby for Israel, whose strength increased proportionally and began to eclipse the Presidents' Conference. Today a new balance is in the making.

Thus the American experience is diametrically opposed to that of the rest of the world where representation has provided the focal point of Jewish unification under conditions of modernity. In the postmodern epoch, however, the American experience is being transplanted to the rest of the world. In country after country, the dominant bodies of the communal-welfare sphere that are parallel to the federations in the United States, such as the Fonds Social Juif Unifié in France and the AMIA in Argentina, are increasing in importance as the focal points of the *keter malkhut* and are subordinating the representative boards to them. Where this is not taking place, as in South Africa, the boards themselves have acquired or expanded their communal-welfare functions.

For the *edah* as a whole, there has been a clash between the two approaches. Because the Europeans were initiators of *edah*-wide efforts in this sphere in modern times, at first those efforts followed their mode. Historically there was a progression from individual *shtadlanim* (intercessors) from the major countries of western Europe who traveled singly or collectively around the world to defend Jewish interests, particularly in the matter of securing the emancipation and civil rights of Jews, to *shtadlanic* organizations sponsored by the Jews of each country, beginning with the Alliance Israélite Universelle in 1860 and including such bodies as the Anglo-Jewish Association and the Hilfsverein der Deutschen Juden, to the World Jewish Congress, founded in 1936.

The progression reflected the changing status of European Jewry. When the Alliance was established, its founders wanted it to be a multicountry association, worldwide in scope with members in every Western country. The governments of the several European powers, however, made it clear to "their" Jews that this would be objectionable because of European interstate rivalries. Hence it was only after the Jews felt secure enough to take matters into their own hands and the Jewish situation in Europe had so deteriorated because of the rise of totalitarian regimes after World War I that the Jews could take that next step.

The dominance of representative bodies in the *edah* persisted until World War II. In the end, it was the alliance between Israel and American Jewry that transformed the situation. Even before 1948, the Jewish Yishuv in Eretz Israel came to see itself as a state within a state, where defense was to be handled by military means, not simply by petitioning the nations. The role of the diaspora was to provide them with the money to build the Yishuv and the military means for its defense. They were able to mobilize the American Jewish fund-raisers who were then becoming more concerned with the rescue of victims of the Holocaust than with the traditional fight against anti-Semitism.

The diplomatic struggle of the Yishuv still required diaspora support and even leadership until the state was declared and leadership passed to the newly constituted government. After that, the diaspora role was redefined as limited lobbying for policies determined in Israel. Thus the external relations function was separated from defense and, in the process, somewhat downgraded.

All this culminated after the establishment of the State of Israel. The new state saw itself defending Jewish interests through the classic means of military force and interstate diplomacy and saw the diaspora Jewish community relations bodies as secondary instruments of Jewish national policy where the state could not directly intervene.

Meanwhile, in the diaspora, World War II brought an end to the era in which anti-Semitism was an accepted phenomenon. This meant that the battle for Jewish rights and dignity was progressively reduced to assaults on last bastions or concerned with peripheral matters rather than being a matter of life and death, thereby decreasing the importance of the community relations bodies. At the same time, issues of Jewish religious and cultural survival in an open society became more important; hence the internal life of the community began to take precedence.

All this was reinforced by a decline of the role of European Jewry in Jewish life because of the Holocaust and the destruction of the established European Jewish communities. The World Jewish Congress became increasingly dependent on the World Zionist Organization, which was increasingly dependent on the State of Israel. Meanwhile, other diaspora bodies, particularly from the United States, began to enter the international arena to increase the degree of fragmentation in it, in a manner reminiscent of the United States. So many Jewish bodies have consultative status before the United Nations and its agencies that there are two councils designed to coordinate their activities, the Consultative Council of Jewish Organizations and the Coordinating Board of Jewish Organizations.

Because support and assistance for Israel have become key items on the community relations agenda, the Israeli government has become a prime mover in this sphere.

Despite occasional protests to the contrary, Jewish action for Israel is conducted in close consultation with and in response to the initiative of the Israeli authorities. Because so much of the function now revolves around Israel, in some respects the Israeli role in the external relations–defense sphere may well be greater than its role in any other sphere of decision making in the diaspora.

The one great issue in which the diaspora has taken the lead is in connection with the efforts to secure the right of emigration for Soviet Jews. Although both Israel and diaspora authorities have been concerned about the issue, in the 1960s there was a difference of opinion on how best to proceed to secure Soviet government consent. The Israelis preferred quiet diplomacy, while diaspora Jews insisted on public activity. The latter won, in part because Soviet Jewish activists endorsed the public approach and diaspora Jewish organization for Soviet Jewry became a galvanizing element in the external relations–defense sphere, at least since 1967. Some of that energy has spilled over to diaspora efforts to work with Israel to rescue other beleaguered Jewries, particularly in Syria and Ethiopia.

The revival of anti-Semitism in the 1970s has restored a greater measure of importance to the diaspora organizations in this sphere but only within the new Jewish political framework, by which they remain ultimately subordinate to the institutions of the communal-welfare sphere in conjunction with the State of Israel. Today they are more like departments of foreign affairs than linking institutions of governance.[29]

Communal-Welfare Sphere

As late as the 1950s the communal-welfare sphere was simply another functional grouping among several, though considerably better organized internally in some countries, particularly the United States and Canada. There the various Jewish social service and welfare agencies plus the Jewish community centers had confederated a generation or more earlier. Today, the sphere is the locus of the principal government-like institutions of the *edah* and its countrywide and local arenas. Its principal institutions are usually the framing institutions for community organization in each arena, if not the focal points.

The emergence of the communal-welfare institutions in this new capacity was the result of a nearly generation-long struggle in the Jewish community. It reflected the change in Jewish priorities generated in part by the increased integration of Jews in their respective diaspora countries but, most importantly, by the rise of Israel. In the 1930s the countrywide community relations organizations plus their *edah* arena extensions were dominant in the Jewish world for all the reasons described above. By the end of that decade, it was apparent that community relations alone could not meet the challenge of anti-Semitism, that it was necessary to provide massive funds for resettling Jewish refugees and rebuilding Eretz Israel as a haven for them. This gave fund-raising an even higher priority than before and strengthened the instrumentalities of the communal-welfare sphere responsible for raising the needed money.

The linchpin of that transformation was an alliance between the Yishuv in Eretz Israel, later carried on and formalized by the state, and the federation movement in the United States to give the United Jewish Appeal the dominant role in fund-raising for Israel. David Ben-Gurion, first prime minister of Israel and architect of the strategy, made this alliance for both practical and political reasons. Practically, he saw that the Zionists in the United States did not have the capability of raising money in the way that the "non-Zionists" who led the federation movement did, and Israel needed the massive support that only the "non-Zionists" could provide. Moreover, because American Zionism was dominated by members of a rival political party, he did not object to cutting them out of a potential power base. As a result, the Zionist movement in the United States was left to wither, and the federation movement, through the United Jewish Appeal, which became its principal instrumentality for this purpose, flourished. The convergence of local and Israeli needs only strengthened this trend after the establishment of the state. The community-relations organizations could not withstand this new force. The North American situation is paradigmatic; hence it is worth describing in some detail. Although the local Jewish federations in the United States had already expanded to include fund-raising for overseas needs by the late 1930s, their pretensions to centrality in the community were limited on the domestic scene because they were primarily concerned with the traditional social service functions.[30]

Two decades later, the federations had been transformed into the major fund-raising bodies in the community. By the end of the 1950s, the federations realized that proper execution of their role as allocating agencies meant greater involvement in community planning of a scope that at least touched all the activities defined as being communitywide in any locality. At the same time, the old "German Jewish" leadership that had dominated the communal-welfare field was broadened to include eastern European Jews, selected from the same income, occupational, and observance levels. The former had, by and large, favored a restricted role for the federations while the latter took a much broader view.

The 1960s saw the federations undertake community planning on a large scale, beyond that required for the simple allocation of funds. They also acquired greater responsibility for and interest in Jewish education as well as continuing and even deepening their relationships with their constituent social service and welfare agencies. In the process, most made strong efforts to broaden their leadership base to include new segments of the community. In the 1970s many of the remaining constituencies—the Orthodox and the synagogues, for example—were brought in to a greater or lesser degree.

Parallel to the federations' increased fund-raising role was the development of a Jewish civil service, which found its principal place in the federations and their agencies. The Jewish social welfare institutions were among the first to move from voluntary to professional staffing, at the turn of the twentieth century when social work emerged as a profession. Thus, when service apart from social work began to emerge as a communal need, it is not surprising that it was given into the hands of professionals not only volunteers. The first of these professionals were drawn, for the most part, from the cadres of social workers who had become agency heads in the social service sphere. Others drifted into the field from other professions. All told, a small group of pioneers emerged to build the federation movement and in the process forge a new profession.

As the federations expanded, their need for a civil service grew. During the first half of the postwar generation, members of that civil service were recruited from the aforementioned sources, but in the latter half, schools of Jewish communal service were developed, some independently of the federations, others under federation stimulus, to provide a senior civil service trained specifically for the federation world. The result further strengthened the communal-welfare sphere as the locus of the framing institutions of postwar American Jewry.

All this has enhanced the central role of the federations locally and given them a real claim to being the umbrella organizations of their communities. There is no question that the key to the growth of the power of the local federations is that they have become the major fund-raising bodies on the American scene. Even though money and influence are not necessarily correlated on a one-to-one basis, there is unquestionably a relationship between the two. Locally, as agencies become more dependent upon the federation for money, they are more likely to be included in the ambit of federation planning and policy-making.

The same pattern has been repeated on the countrywide plane though in a less clear-cut way. The difference is that the Council of Jewish Federations (CJF) does not have fund-raising powers but, in the fashion of confederations, is dependent on assessments levied on the local federations. Consequently, it has no such fiscal power to exercise over the countrywide organizations parallel to the local community relations, social service, and educational agencies. The Jewish Welfare Board (JWB), for example (whose founding antedates the CJF), is financed in the same way—by dues from its local constituents and the local federations directly, thus limiting the possibility of direct CJF influence. Except for the National Jewish Community Relations Advisory Council, the national community relations and religious organizations are even more independent. Some of them also have special projects in the welfare field. Almost all of these originated before there was anything like the federation movement on the American Jewish scene; each organization made efforts to serve the broad needs of the Jewish community.

Still, influence of the CJF, however indirect, has been growing on those bodies that represent leagues of local agencies financed by their community federations, including the JWB, the NJCRAC, and the Jewish Educational Service of North America. The CJF actually precipitated the transformation of the American Association for Jewish Education into JESNA and is a critical force in keeping that agency alive. The role of the CJF has been growing primarily because it speaks in the name of the federations and can offer a forum that none of the other groups can. The CJF General Assembly, for example, has become the major gathering place for those people involved at the highest levels of communal decision making in American Jewry, including representatives of organizations only tenuously connected with it, if at all. Its development has followed a "snowballing" pattern; as it becomes more so, it continues to become even more so.

The CJF itself is part of a triangle of countrywide bodies responsible for fund-raising and disbursement. The second is the United Jewish Appeal, the major countrywide fund-raising arm of American Jewry. The UJA works primarily through the local federations, providing them with technical assistance while they run the campaigns, but also has created a countrywide network of fund-raising missions to Israel and big gifts solicitation. The third organization in the triangle, the United Israel Appeal, is the principal recipient of UJA funds for transmission to Israel and is responsible for oversight of the use of those funds in the name of the donors. As a result it is also the linking organization between the federations, the CJF and the UJA with regard to the governance structure of the Jewish Agency.

Unlike the situation in the United States, fund-raising for Israel in the rest of the diaspora remained in the hands of the World Zionist Organization through Keren Hayesod, the WZO fund-raising instrumentality established in 1920, and the local instrumentalities established under local law but within the Keren Hayesod framework. In those countries, the Zionist movement retained a greater measure of control until the 1960s when the American approach began to spread to them.[31]

The Canadian Jewish community was one of the first to begin to change. Canada had already been brought into the orbit of the American federation movement, and Jewish welfare federations had been established in almost every major Canadian community during the 1930s. Nevertheless, the Canadian Jewish Congress (CJC) with its local branches remained the principal framing institution of Canadian Jewry. Then, in the late 1960s and early 1970s, mergers were negotiated between the CJC and the federations. Locally the federations became the principal framing institutions, and the CJC retained community relations and cultural functions countrywide. This led to the strengthening of the United Israel Appeal of Canada as an independent Canadian body. Though remaining formally a part of Keren Hayesod, it began to function more like the United Jewish Appeal because it had the backing of the federations. This was followed by the establishment of the National Budgeting Committee, functioning out of the Canadian office of the Council of Jewish Federations, which is the vehicle for the local federations in Canada to allocate funds for countrywide projects. Canada also followed the American pattern of professionalizing its Jewish civil service with the same results.[32]

A similar transformation took place in France in a way appropriate to that country. There no local institutions have ever been able to compete with the central institutions of French Jewry, and whatever power struggles have taken place have been between the latter. After the role of the *consistoire* was drastically reduced, it seemed as if the CRIF would take its place, but the Fonds Socials Juif Unifié (FSJU), organized after the war through the efforts of the American Jewish Joint Distribution Committee to improve fund-raising in France, soon demonstrated that control of fund-raising almost inevitably led to concern for community planning and that together the two were the ticket for acquiring dominance in community affairs. Hence the FSJU has emerged in France as the parallel to the federation movement in North America with the CRIF becoming dependent on it.[33]

British Jewry remains the exception among the major communities. Its communal-welfare sphere continues to be divided among many separate organizations and institutions. The Board of Deputies remains the framing institution to the extent that British Jewry has one. Only in the early 1980s has the Jewish Welfare Board made even tentative steps toward integrating the sphere.[34]

In South Africa and Australia the boards of deputies have had to develop fund-raising mechanisms attached to them so that they could remain the framing institutions, then begin to undertake community planning and reduce the proportion of their time devoted to community relations. This transformation in South Africa was stimulated by local circumstances. After the Afrikaaner National party won power in 1948, the Board of Deputies began to retreat from a highly visible community relations posture so as not to provoke controversy within or outside the Jewish community. Thus it was searching for a new role, and with good timing, its needs coincided with the worldwide trend.[35]

In all these cases, specialization came later and slower than in the United States and Canada. For example, a Jewish civil service began to emerge only in the 1970s, visibly in South Africa and France, less so in Britain and Australia. These communities also have had more difficulty in linking fund-raising for Israel with fund-raising for local needs. The Israeli establishment has opposed that link, preferring to keep tighter control over the fund-raising for Israeli needs through an undiluted Keren Hayesod. Only in France have the local forces, led by the influential Rothschilds, been able to overcome that opposition. In the other communities a compromise was reached. In South Africa, for example, the two campaigns remain separate but are conducted in alternate years.

Similar developments took place in Latin America. The original organizations of

Argentinian Jewry, for example, were extensions of *landsmanschaften,* the leading one of which was the Ashkenazi burial society in Buenos Aires (the Hevra Kadisha Ashkenazi) founded in 1894, out of which developed the Asociación Mutua Israelite Argentina (AMIA). These bodies constituted the internal communal-welfare sphere, but they did so on a basis that gave the community no overarching organization. Not until 1939, in the face of rampant anti-Semitism stimulated by Nazi inroads into the large German population of Argentina, did the country-of-origin communities come together to form the Delegación de la Asociaciones Israelitas Argentina (DAIA), a defense organization on the classic model. The DAIA rapidly became the dominant spokesman for the community but confined its activities to defense, representation, and community relations.

After the establishment of the State of Israel, the AMIA became dominated by the Zionist parties, but it remained an Ashkenazi organization, even to the extent of conducting its meetings in Yiddish. The Sephardim organized parallel bodies, and, in 1965, a central organization. In the meantime, in 1952 the AMIA had established a Va'ad Ha-Kehillot (Council of Communities) to link Buenos Aires Jewry with 140 smaller Jewish communities in the country. In the 1970s, the Va'ad Ha-Kehillot expanded to include the Sephardim. It has become at least a modest umbrella organization for the entire community, whose principal responsibilities are in the communal-welfare sphere.[36]

In Brazil, Jewish life had a harder time developing; not until the beginnings of the postmodern epoch in 1946–47 were federations of Jewish organizations and institutions formed in the larger communities. These came together in 1951 to establish the Confederacao das Entidades Representatives de Collectividaide Israelitas de Brasil (Confederation of Jewish Representative Bodies in Brazil). In time, this body was renamed the Confederacao Israelita de Brasil (CIB), which merged representation and communal-welfare functions into a single confederal body. It links some two hundred institutions and organizations in eight Brazilian states. The basic activities of the community are conducted in the local *kehillot,* where communal-welfare institutions, combined with the Israel-overseas fund-raising bodies, are the strongest forces.[37] Mexico is the third largest Jewish community in Latin America. To the extent that it has an umbrella organization, the Comité Central, it is a community relations body closely connected with the World Jewish Congress and clearly in the external relations–defense sphere.[38] All told, the other Latin American Jewries follow much the same model. The World Jewish Congress is stronger in Latin America than in any other region of the world, itself a reflection of the continued strength of the community relations organizations in those communities.

In all of Latin America, there is little in the way of a Jewish civil service, and organized fund-raising for Israel is underdeveloped. Keren Hayesod basically solicits wealthy individuals rather than conducting a full-fledged campaign, in great part because organized fund-raising in general is underdeveloped and export of money problematic in Latin America. There Jews have been influenced by the underdeveloped civic life of their host countries and even where they have retained a willingness to contribute have done so on a sporadic and individual basis. Thus neither of the two pillars designed to strengthen the communal-welfare sphere has been as well developed as in North America or Europe. This is particularly visible in smaller Latin American communities. As the larger communities seek to build stronger internal institutions and as fund-raising for Israel becomes a more prominent communal activity and not simply the solicitation of wealthy individuals, this is slowly changing.

Although the Latin American section of the World Jewish Congress has no parallel in the communal-welfare sphere, Europe has developed a continent-wide institutional expression of this sphere parallel to the European section of the World Jewish Congress, the European Council for Jewish Community Services. The ECJCS was founded in the aftermath of World War II at the initiative of the Joint Distribution Committee (JDC) in close cooperation with the Council of Jewish Federations. For its first decades, it remained a weak reed. The need to rebuild the local communities after the war and the lack of any tradition of intercommunity cooperation in Europe were important constraints on its leadership. They were reinforced by the strong opposition of the leadership of the FSJU. Because France is by far the dominant community in Europe, its lack of cooperation invariably reduced the willingness to cooperate by others, even those smaller communities that needed the services of the European Council.

After a generation of local reconstruction, things took a new turn in the late 1970s. In 1979 the JDC, in an effort to change the situation, secured the appointment of a new executive director, an Israeli of European origin who had spent many years in the United States and came out of the American communal-welfare sphere, who laid the foundations for further change. When he returned to Israel after three years, his successor, herself French, was able to benefit from those foundations and from the fact that a new executive director had been appointed for the FSJU, who was more open to cooperative relations. This may be a sign that the new generation of European Jews is prepared to include European Jewish unity on its agenda.[39]

A new element that has appeared on the communal-welfare scene is the Israeli contingent in the form of the government of Israel and the Jewish Agency. The government of Israel has its special interest in diaspora Jewry as a support system for the state, which it pursues in many ways but is finding increasingly advantageous to pursue in the context of the communal-welfare sphere. The Jewish Agency, particularly since its reconstitution, has virtually co-opted the communal-welfare leadership as its "non-Zionist" representatives, in the process becoming the major *edah*-wide instrumentality of that sphere. This has created an even tighter bond between the institutionalized representatives of the world Zionist movement and the diaspora Jewish communities than ever before. The institutionalization of relationships is still in its incipient stage; its course will be charted over the next several decades.[40]

Israel–World Jewry Sphere

The origins of the last functional arena can be traced to the informal links among *shtadlanim* which became crystallized as a result of the Damascus blood libel of 1840. These *shtadlanic* efforts continued through the nineteenth century. Leading figures such as Moses Montefiore of Great Britain and Adolph Cremieux of France and, later, men like Lucien Wolfe of Great Britain and Benjamin Franklin Peixotto of the United States used their standing in their countries of residence and on the world scene, and the official positions sometimes gained because of their standing, to assist Jewish communities suffering persecution or seeking civil rights. Beginning with the establishment of the Alliance Israélite Universelle, the individual *shtadlanim* began to give way to *shtadlanic* organizations. After the opposition of the great powers prevented the Alliance from becoming a worldwide Jewish organization, every country developed its own, with informal links between them.[41]

The first worldwide organization for this sphere was the World Zionist Organization established in 1897. In the following years, the WZO established several subsidiary institutions such as the Jewish Colonial Trust (now Bank Leumi) and the Jewish National Fund. By World War I there was a substantial array of instrumentalities organized to function in this sphere as manifestations of the Zionist effort, including the various Zionist parties, organized as worldwide unions or federations.[42] The anti-Zionist Jewish socialists organized the Jewish Workers Bund later in 1897 and gave it wide scope in the years following. The non-Palestine-centered Zionists organized the Jewish Territorial Organization in 1905 and the ultra-Orthodox camp organized Agudath Israel in 1912.[43]

All these instrumentalities were to survive the war. In the interwar years, they were joined by the Keren Hayesod (1920) and the Jewish Agency for Palestine (1929). The latter became the first great link between Zionists and non-Zionists, although, until 1970, the link existed on paper more than in fact. Nevertheless, through the Keren Hayesod and the United Palestine Appeal, Zionists and non-Zionists developed other links to raise money for the Yishuv. In 1936 the World Jewish Congress was founded under the stimulus of the WZO to coordinate the Jewish struggle against nazism.

It was still hard to say in that period that Zionist or Israel-oriented enterprises constituted the focal point of the sphere because the countrywide bodies organized to serve other communities in the *edah* for non-Zionist purposes were equally important. For example, in 1914 American Jewry founded the American Jewish Joint Distribution Committee (the JDC or "Joint") as a federation of socialist, Orthodox, and general overseas relief agencies, which, by uniting, could better provide relief to Jews caught in war zones during World War I. After the war, the JDC continued to function as a relief agency in eastern Europe and the Islamic countries. Its avowed purpose was to help Jews integrate into their countries of birth or residence as equal citizens. In the interwar generation the "Joint" poured far more money into providing relief for Jews in the Soviet Union and for resettling them there than American Jewry was able to raise to support the resettlement of Eretz Israel, a tragic blunder whose consequences did not become apparent until the Holocaust.[44]

The rise of Hitler led to the transformation of this sphere, placing rescue and evacuation ahead of the struggle for local civil rights and assimilation, and increasingly turning to Eretz Israel and Zionism as every other possibility for massive Jewish immigration proved a false hope. The emergence of unified Zionist and non-Zionist fund-raising bodies, such as the United Jewish Appeal in the United States in the late 1930s, was the first step. After the magnitude of the Holocaust became apparent, there was a massive shift on the part of almost all concerned Jews to support the Zionist effort to establish a Jewish state.

Once this was achieved in 1948, Israel became the undisputed focal point of this sphere and the dominant element in it. This did not preclude, however, bilateral ties of other kinds crisscrossing the Jewish world. Thus the JDC not only began to focus its attention on work in the new Jewish state but also worked to improve the lot of Jews remaining in the Islamic countries and to rebuild the Jewish communities of postwar Europe. The American Conservative and Reform movements initiated efforts in Latin America and Australia to establish alternative forms of Jewish religious participation in communities that had been dominated by a stagnant and declining Orthodoxy. Later, the Jewish community center movement in the United States reached out to assist other communities in the development of equivalent institutions. Nevertheless, the basic ties were to or through Israel.

The Israel–World Jewry sphere has three interlocking elements, one concerned with fund-raising, a second with political activity, and a third with educational and social welfare services. Responsibilities for fund-raising are divided among the *magbit* organizations (Keren Hayesod and the United Jewish Appeal), the Israel Bonds organization, the Jewish National Fund, and the various "friends" of Israel or world Jewish institutions. Political activities are conducted primarily through the World Zionist Organization, which is composed of parties and movements at least nominally united into countrywide Zionist federations, and the World Jewish Congress with its regional apparatus. On a third plane are those country-specific bodies involved in external relations outside their borders, such as the American Jewish Committee.

Educational and social welfare services are conducted by bodies such as the JDC, ORT, the Alliance Israélite Universelle, and Otzar HaTorah. They are supplemented by the extension of countrywide bodies across international boundaries in the way that most countrywide organizations in the United States also function in Canada or the National Jewish Welfare Board of the United States has helped Jewish community centers in Argentina. In all these, the Jewish Agency is becoming more prominent as it emerges as the principal instrument of the *edah* in state-building in Israel and the preservation of Jewish life in the diaspora. The JDC has become the bearer of American Jewish "knowhow" and money wherever there are Jewish communities in need of redevelopment. The best cooperation, however, is likely to be found among the educational and social welfare institutions; this is true partly because of the important role played by the JDC as a financing instrumentality for most of them and the growing role of the Jewish Agency in that respect, with regard to educational activities.

The principal *edah*-wide fund-raising instrumentalities are those connected with Israel: the Keren Hayesod and the Jewish National Fund. Keren Hayesod functions in every country where it is permitted by local law, except in the United States; the Jewish National Fund (Keren Kayemet) functions in the United States as well. In recent years Keren Hayesod and the American United Jewish Appeal have begun to cooperate in the governance of the Jewish Agency and in specific fund-raising endeavors, particularly with the world's largest givers in the form of the International Leadership Reunion, an annual meeting of contributors of $250,000 or more, cosponsored by the two fund-raising bodies.

The potentiality for competition among the fund-raising organizations is great. Because the need to cooperate for the common good of Israel and the Jewish people is felt universally among them, a system of negotiated sharing has been developed through a network of agreements dividing the money or the campaign arenas. The basic agreements are those reached countrywide between the representatives of the local fund-raisers working through their local and countrywide bodies and the representatives of Israel, often on an annual basis. In some agreements, for example in the United States and France, the money raised annually in the local campaigns is divided. In others, for example in South Africa and Argentina, annual campaigns are alternated—one year for Israel and the next for local needs. In a few agreements, for example in Great Britain, separate and parallel campaigns are retained each year.

There are also agreements among the fund-raisers for Israel's general needs and the various "friends" groups, spelling out their jurisdictions and claims to methods of fund-raising. Thus in the United States the Israel Bonds organization has a "right" to make synagogue appeals, while direct solicitation on a mass basis is the province of the United Jewish Appeal through the federations. The "friends" chapters normally work with big givers through personal contacts, but after 1967 they were asked to suspend fund-raising except for capital expenditures and to support the Israel Emergency Fund. This arrangement was terminated in 1971. All these organizations are required to obtain local campaign clearances from the federations in each community, which limit their campaign time and solicitation sources. This system does not work as well in practice as in theory because it is difficult to stop people from soliciting or contributing money in an open, voluntary framework.[45]

The Zionist organizations cooperate closely in the world Jewry arena and less well in the others. Because they are tied to the great "national" (read "worldwide") Zionist parties that participate in the political life of Israel, they have a long and well-developed tradition of sharing power through such devices as proportional representation and the party key when it comes to Israel and *edah*-wide activities. However, they often have been less willing to cooperate on the local scene. In the United States, for example, only in 1970, after agreements reached in Jerusalem, did they respond to their growing weakness by creating a countrywide Zionist federation. It was paralleled by local Zionist federations in which each of the parties preserved its identity but functions under a common umbrella based on federal principles, for common purposes. This federative effort did not succeed in strengthening the Zionist movement as expected, for the countrywide and local federations remained more formal than real.[46]

"Games" and "Complexes"

Each of the five functional spheres may be considered a "game" in the framework of Jewish life, and the organizations and institutions relating to each a "complex" surrounding each game (see table 3.1). There is an indefinite and fluid number of games in the *edah* and its communities, depending on how the "cake" is cut in any particular circumstance; all, however, are based on the five functional spheres. The games may be subdivisions of those spheres or they may link more than one sphere. Thus, for example, the communal-welfare and Israel–world Jewry games are linked at some points into one communal-Israel–world Jewry "supergame." Furthermore, there are hospital games in the communal-welfare framework in which a particular hospital can be a separate game. The contents or boundaries of a particular game-and-complex can and do shift. It is possible for operational purposes to decide that an activity is a game in itself or to treat it as a part of a larger game. All activities in the community can be viewed and analyzed in relation to these games, however delimited.

There is relatively little shifting of participants from sphere to sphere, except where two or more spheres are linked in a supergame. Those serving the Jewish community in professional capacities (rabbis, communal workers, Jewish educators) shift least. Lower echelon volunteers may shift but are rarely involved in more than one sphere or game at a time. Important voluntary leaders can and do shift from game to game with greater ease or are involved in several games at once. In a particular sphere or game there may be considerable overlapping or revolving of leadership.

Because the games and complexes involve local, countrywide, and *edah*-wide "players" simultaneously, they are major vehicles for integrating leadership across all the arenas. There are few countrywide or *edah*-wide games not based on local leadership wearing other hats, except among the professionals charged with daily operating responsibilities. Thus the system of games and complexes reinforces the local basis of Jewish life even as it integrates Jewish activity from hometown to Jerusalem.

The five spheres originally began as relatively separate in their functioning but have since grown together inexorably. This reflects the contemporary human condition in which everything is becoming increasingly dependent on everything else. In an age of growing complexity, the possibility of separating institutions, activity spheres, or jurisdictions, has become increasingly limited in every part of the world, and the Jewish people is no exception.

If in particular local and countrywide arenas there remain exceptions to this rule, they are idiosyncratic. This chapter has reviewed how the communal-welfare and Israel–world Jewry spheres have come to embrace progressively the external relations—defense and educational-cultural spheres. The least integrated is the religious-congregational sphere. It may be more connected with the others in the *edah* arena than in some local communities, but is increasingly so in every arena. The future, then, requires an approach to Jewish life that is comprehensive and looks for consequences, anticipated and unanticipated, rippling through the system whenever action is undertaken in one or another of the spheres.

Notes

1. The combination of territorial and nonterritorial patterns of communal organization is clearly portrayed for the diaspora in the *American Jewish Year Book* (published annually since 1899 by the American Jewish Committee and the Jewish Publication Society of America). See also S. P. Goldberg, *The American Jewish Community: Its Structure, Role, and Organizations* (New York: Women's ORT Community Service Publication, 1968); Howard R. Penniman, ed., *Israel at the Polls: The Knesset Elections of 1977* (Washington, D.C.: American Enterprise Institute for Public Policy Research, 1979); Daniel J. Elazar with Peter Medding, *Jewish Communities in Frontier Societies: Argentina, Australia, and South Africa* (New York: Holmes and Meier, 1983).

2. Max Kadushin, *Organic Thinking: A Study in Rabbinic Thought* (New York: Jewish Theological Seminary, 1938); Elazar and Medding, *Jewish Communities in Frontier Societies,* pp. 80–82; Daniel J. Elazar, "Land Space and Civil Society in America," in *Land Settlement Policy* (Raleigh, N.C.: North Carolina State University, 1969).

3. Ernest Stock describes this phenomenon in "The Absence of Hierarchy: Notes on the Organization of the American Jewish Community," *Jewish Journal of Sociology,* vol. 21, no. 2 (December 1970), pp. 195–200.

4. See Daniel J. Elazar, *Community and Polity: The Organizational Dynamics of American Jewry* (Philadelphia: Jewish Publication Society of America, 1976), chap. 5.

5. Phyllis Cohen Albert, *The Modernization of French Jewry: Consistory and Community in the Nineteenth Century* (Waltham, Mass.: Brandeis University Press, 1977); Paula Hyman, *From Dreyfus to Vichy: The Remaking of French Jewry, 1906–1939* (New York: Columbia University Press, 1979).

6. *Chiai HaYehudim be-Britania* (Jewish Life in Britain), issue of *Tefutsot Yisrael,* vol. 21, no. 4 (winter 1983) (Hebrew); Sonia L. Lipman and Vivian D. Lipman, *Jewish Life in Britain: 1962–1977* (New York: K. G. Sauer, 1981); V. D. Lipman, ed., *Three Centuries of Anglo-Jewish History* (London: The Jewish Historical Society of England, 1961).

7. Elazar and Medding, *Jewish Communities in Frontier Societies,* chap. 12; Steven B. Aschheim, "The Communal Organization of South African Jewry," *Jewish Journal of Sociology,* vol. 12, no. 1 (June 1970), pp. 201–31. (Reprinted by the Center for Jewish Community Studies.)

8. *Yihudo veAtido shel Beit-HaKnesset beAmerica* (The American Synagogue: Its Uniqueness and Future), issue of *Tefutsot Yisrael,* vol. 20, no. 3 (summer 1982) (Hebrew); *Orthodoxim, Reformim, Conservativim: HaZeramim HaDatiyim beLevatehem* (Current Trends in Jewish Religious Life), issue of *Tefutsot Yisrael,* vol. 18, no. 1 (spring 1980) (Hebrew); Moshe Davis, *The Emergence of Conservative Judaism* (Philadelphia: Jewish Publication Society of America, 1963); Leonard J. Fein et al., *Reform Is a Verb* (New York: Union of American Hebrew Congregations, 1972); Leon Jick, "An Intimate Portrait of the Union of American Hebrew Congregations: A Centennial Documentary," *American Jewish Archives,* vol. 25 (April 1973), pp. 3–115; Charles S. Liebman, "Orthodoxy in American Jewish Life," *American Jewish Year Book 1965,* vol. 66, pp. 21–97; Gunther W. Plaut, *The Rise of Reform Judaism* (New York: World Union for Progressive Judaism, 1963–65); Marshall Sklare, *Conservative Judaism: An American Religious Movement* (New York; Schocken Books, 1972); Joseph L.

Blau, *Reform Judaism: A Historical Perspective* (New York: Ktav, 1973); Jacob Neusner, ed., *Sectors of American Judaism: Reform, Orthodoxy, Conservative, and Reconstructionism* (New York: Ktav, 1975).

    9. S. Z. Abramov, *Perpetual Dilemma* (Rutherford, N.J.: Farleigh Dickinson University Press, 1976); Zvi Yaron, "Religion in Israel," *American Jewish Year Book 1976*, vol. 76, pp. 41–90; Charles Liebman and Eliezer Don-Yehiya, *Religion and Politics in Israel* (Bloomington, Ind.: Indiana University Press, 1984).

    10. Menachem Friedman, *Havrah ve HaDat: HaOrthodoxiya Halo Tzionit be Eretz Yisrael 1918–1936* (The Non-Zionist Orthodox Movement in the Land of Israel) (Jerusalem: Yad Yitzhak Ben-Zvi, 1978) (Hebrew); Joseph Friedenson, *A History of Agudat Israel* (New York: Agudath Israel of America, 1970); Eliezer Don-Yehiya, "Origins and Development of the Agudah and Mafdal Parties," *Jerusalem Quarterly*, no. 20 (summer 1981), pp. 49–64; *Yaakov Rosenheim Memorial Anthology: A Concise History of Agudath Israel* (New York: Orthodox Library, 1968).

    11. Jerome R. Mintz, "Ethnic Activism: The Hassidic Example," *Judaism*, vol. 28, no. 4 (fall 1979), pp. 449–64; Harry M. Rabinowicz, *A Guide to Hassidism* (New York: T. Yoseloff, 1960); Israel Rubin, *Satmar: An Island in the City* (Chicago: Quadrangle, 1972).

    12. *Al Matzavoh shel HaHinukh HaYehudi be'-America* (On the State of Jewish Education in America), issue of *Tefutsot Yisrael*, vol. 18, nos. 2–3 (summer–fall 1980) (Hebrew). Especially in this issue, see Daniel J. Elazar, "The Civil Goals of Contemporary Jewish Education," pp. 61–70; Louis Katzoff, *Issues in Jewish Education* (New York: Bloch Publishing Company, 1949); Burt Jacobson, *Report of Work Conference on Current Concerns in Jewish Education* (New York: American Jewish Committee and American Association for Jewish Education, 1970); Hillel Hochberg, "Trends and Developments in Jewish Education," *American Jewish Year Book 1972*, vol. 73, pp. 194–235; Eduards Rauch, "Jewish Education in the United States, 1840–1920," unpublished Ph.D. dissertation (Harvard University Graduate School of Education, 1978); Walter Ackerman, "Jewish Education Today," *American Jewish Year Book 1980*, vol. 80, pp. 130–48; Lloyd P. Gartner, ed., *Jewish Education in the United States* (New York: Teachers College Press, 1969); Zvi Adar, *Jewish Education in Israel and in the United States,* trans. Barry Chazan (Hebrew University of Jerusalem, 1977); Alexander M. Shapiro and Burton I. Cohen, eds., *Studies in Jewish Education and Judaica in Honor of Louis Newman* (New York: Ktav, 1984).

    13. Eliezer Don-Yehiya, "Shituf ve-Conflict ben Machanot Politiim: HaMachanei HaDati ve Tnuat HaAvodat ve-Mashber Chinuch be-Yisrael" (Cooperation and Conflict between Political Camps: The Religious Camp and the Labor Movement and the Education Crisis in Israel), Ph.D. dissertation (Hebrew University of Jerusalem, 1977); Elad Peled, "The Hidden Agenda of Educational Policy in Israel: The Interrelationship between the Political System and the Educational System," Ph.D. dissertation (Columbia University, 1979). Also note that there is a state Arabic-language school system for the Arabic-speaking minorities.

    14. Arye Globerson, *Higher Education and Employment: A Case Study of Israel* (Hampshire, England: Saxon House, 1978); Augusta R. Auerbach, "Critical Issues in Israeli Universities," Ph.D. dissertation (Southern Illinois University at Carbondale, 1976); Max Rauch, "Higher Education in Israel," Ph.D. dissertation (University of Southern California, 1971); Shmuel Bendor, "University Education" (in Israel) in Asa B. Knowles, ed., *International Encyclopedia of Higher Education* (San Francisco: Jossey-Bass, 1977), pp. 2331–40; Council for Higher Education, Planning and Grants Committee, *Annual Reports*, nos. 1–10, Academic Years 1973–74 to 1982–83 (Jerusalem, 1975–84); *Higher Education in Israel: Statistical Abstract 1980–81* (Jerusalem, 1982); *The Higher Learning System in Israel* (Jerusalem, 1983) (Hebrew); Samuel Halperin, "The Decline (and Coming Fall?) of Israeli Higher Education," *Jerusalem Letter*, no. 75 (August 28, 1984).

    15. Samuel Halperin, *Any Home a Campus: Everyman's University of Israel* (Washington, D.C. and Jerusalem: Institute for Educational Leadership, Inc. and Jerusalem Center for Public Affairs, 1984); and *Al Matzavoh shel HaHinukh HaYehudi be-America.*

    16. Geoffrey E. Bock, *The Jewish Schooling of American Jews: A Study of Non-Cognitive Educational Effects,* Ph.D. dissertation (Harvard University, 1976): Alexander Dushkin and Uriah Engelman, *Jewish Education in the U.S.* (Jerusalem: Institute of Contemporary Jewry of Hebrew University, 1959); Adar, *Jewish Education in Israel and in the United States;* Gartner, *Jewish Education in the United States;* Daniel J. Elazar, "Jewish Education and American Jewry: What the Community Studies Tell Us," *Pedagogic Reporter* (March 1970); Alysa M. Dortort, "Federation Allocations for Jewish Education and Community Centers: A Comparison," *Jerusalem Letter,* no. 67 (November 24, 1983).

    17. Gustav Saron and Louis Hotz, *The Jews in South Africa: A History* (London and Cape Town: Oxford University Press, 1955); Elazar and Medding, *Jewish Communities in Frontier Societies;* Ascheim, "The Communal Organization of South African Jewry." Also, the annual article on South Africa in the *American Jewish Year Book* contains basic information on developments in the Jewish educational sphere.

    18. Elazar and Medding, *Jewish Communities in Frontier Societies;* Robert Weisbrot, *The Jews of Argen-*

tina: From the Inquisition to Perón (Philadelphia: The Jewish Publication Society of America, 1979); Seymour B. Liebman, *Argentine Jewry,* unpublished manuscript prepared for the Center for Jewish Community Studies (1975); Mordejai Herbst, *Kol Tora BeArgentina* (Buenos Aires: Departamento Religioso del Superior Rabinato de la Republica Argentina, 1970); Zevi Scharfstein, "Jewish Education in Latin America," in Central Yiddish Culture Organization, *The Jewish People: Past and Present,* vol. 2 (New York: Marstin Press, 1946–48), pp. 172–78; Olga M. de Winter, "La educación judía en la Argentina," *Comunidades judíos de latinoamerica 1966,* pp. 133–42; Simja Sneh, "La red escolar judía en la republica Argentina," *Comunidades judíos de latinoamerica 1968,* pp. 129–42.

19. The Jewish Agency for Israel, *Building Our Future: A Jewish Agency Program for Jewish Education in the Coming Decades—A Proposal* (Jerusalem: Jewish Agency for Israel, 1983); The L. A. Pincus Jewish Education Fund for the Diaspora, *Report* (Jerusalem, 1981) and *Report no. 3* (Jerusalem, 1983); The World Zionist Organization—The Press and Public Relations Bureau, *Jewish Education in the Diaspora* (Jerusalem: World Zionist Organization, 1971); Israel Ministry of Education and Culture, Jewish Agency for Israel and World Zionist Organization, *Joint Program for Jewish Education* (Jerusalem, 1982); Yehoshua Fagen, ed., *Chinuch ve Tarbut be-Golah Me Pe'elot HaMachlakah le Chinuch ve Tarbut be Golah* (Education and Culture in the Diaspora, from the Activities of the Department for Education and Culture in the Diaspora) (Jerusalem: World Zionist Organization, Department for Education and Culture in the Diaspora, 1971) (Hebrew).

20. Ernest Stock, "Jewish Multicountry Associations," American Jewish Year Book 1974–75, vol. 75, pp. 571–97; Arziel Eisenberg, ed., "The Early History of the World Council on Jewish Education 1960–66: A Story of Groping and Exploration" (New York, April 1967) (mimeographed); Ernest Stock, "Multicountry Agencies in Jewish Education," in H. S. Himmelfarb and Sergio Della Pergola, eds., *Jewish Education World-wide: Cross-Cultural Perspectives* (Jerusalem: Hebrew University, forthcoming).

21. Memorial Foundation for Jewish Culture, *Study Documents: Meeting of Board of Trustees,* presented at biennial meeting of Board of Trustees, July 23–26, 1984 (New York: Memorial Foundation for Jewish Culture, 1984); Immanuel Jakobovits, *The Cultural Condition of the Jewish People* (New York: Memorial Foundation for Jewish Culture, 1984).

22. "Israel: State of Cultural Life," in *Society* (Jerusalem: Keter Publishing House, Israel Pocket Library, 1974); S. N. Eisenstadt, *Israeli Society* (London: Weidenfeld and Nicolson, 1967), chap. 10; Haya Gratch, ed., *Twenty-Five Years of Social Research in Israel* (Jerusalem: Jerusalem Academic Press, 1973); Michael Curtis and Mordecai S. Chertoff, eds., *Israel: Social Structure and Change* (New Brunswick, N.J.: Transaction Books, 1973); Elihu Katz and Michael Gurevitch, *The Secularization of Leisure: Culture and Communication in Israel* (London: Faber and Faber, 1976).

23. Naomi W. Cohen, *Not Free to Desist: The American Jewish Committee, 1906–1966* (Philadelphia: Publication Society of America, 1972); Ann G. Wolfe, *A Reader in Jewish Community Relations* (New York: Ktav for Association of Jewish Community Relations Workers, 1975), chap. 2; Harry Schneiderman, ed., *Two Generations in Perspective: Notable Events and Trends 1896–1956* (New York: Monde Publishers, 1957); Max J. Kohler and Simon Wolf, "Benjamin F. Peixotto's Mission to Roumania," in Abraham J. Karp, ed., *The Jewish Experience in America* (Waltham, Mass.: American Jewish Historical Society, 1969), vol. 3, pp. 371–82. (For community relations in specific countries, see below.)

24. Canadian Jewish Congress, *Fifty Years of Service, 1919–1969* (Montreal: Canadian Jewish Congress, 1970); Harold M. Waller, *The Canadian Jewish Community: A National Perspective* (Jerusalem: Center for Jewish Community Studies, 1977); Stuart E. Rosenberg, *The Jewish Community in Canada,* 2 vols. (Toronto: McClelland and Stewart, 1970); M. Weinfeld, W. Shaffir, and I. Cotler, eds., *The Canadian Jewish Mosaic* (Toronto: J. Wiley, 1981).

25. *The South African Jewish Board of Deputies: The Story of Fifty Years, 1903–1953* (Johannesburg: South African Jewish Board of Deputies, 1953); S. A. Rochlin, "How the South African Jewish Board of Deputies Started," *Jewish Affairs,* vol. 18, no. 5 (May 1963), pp. 4–12; Gustave Saron, *The South African Jewish Board of Deputies: Its Role and Development* (Johannesburg: South African Jewish Board of Deputies, 1973).

26. Naomi W. Cohen, *Not Free to Desist;* John P. Roche, *The Quest for the Dream* (New York: Macmillan, 1963); Nathan C. Belth, ed., *Not the Work of a Day* (New York: Anti-Defamation League of B'nai B'rith, 1965); Yehuda Bauer, *My Brother's Keeper: A History of the American Jewish Joint Distribution Committee, 1929–1939* (Philadelphia: Jewish Publication Society of America, 1974); Elazar, *Community and Polity* and *Pluralism ve Shivion* (Pluralism and Equality), issue of *Tefutsot Yisrael,* vol. 19, nos. 2–3 (summer-autumn 1981) (Hebrew); Will Maslow, *The Structure and Functioning of the American Jewish Community* (New York: American Jewish Congress and American Section of the World Jewish Congress, 1974); Wolfe, *A Reader in Jewish Community Relations.*

27. Elazar, *Community and Polity;* Harry L. Lurie, *A Heritage Affirmed* (Philadelphia: Jewish Publica-

tion Society of America, 1961); Julian Freeman, *Organizing the American Jewish Community* (New York: Council of Jewish Federations, 1977).

28. Graenum Berger, ed., *The Turbulent Decades: Jewish Communal Service in America, 1956–1978,* 2 vols. (New York: Conference of Jewish Communal Service, 1981), chap. 8; Abraham G. Duker, "The Problems of Coordination and Unity," in Oscar I. Janowsky, ed., *The American Jew: A Reappraisal* (Philadelphia: Jewish Publication Society of America, 1964); Walter A. Lurie, *Strategies for Survival: Principles of Jewish Community Relations* (New York: Ktav, 1982); Chaim I. Waxman, *America's Jews in Transition* (Philadelphia: Temple University Press, 1983), chap. 9

29. Lurie, *Strategies for Survival* and "Thirty Years of Professional Development in Jewish Community Relations," *Journal of Jewish Communal Service,* vol. 58, no. 4 (summer 1982), pp. 284–92; Wolfe, *A Reader in Jewish Community Relations.*

30. For a history of the federation movement before 1960, see Lurie, *A Heritage Affirmed.* An overall portrait of the sphere can be found in Robert Morris and Michael Freund, eds., *Trends and Issues in Jewish Social Welfare in the United States, 1899–1958* (Philadelphia: Jewish Publication Society of America, 1966). For more recent developments, see Elazar, *Community and Polity;* Philip Bernstein, *To Dwell in Unity: The Jewish Federation Movement since 1960* (Philadelphia: Jewish Publication Society of America, 1983); and Ernest Stock, *Partners and Pursestrings* (Lanham, Md. and Jerusalem: University Press of America and Jerusalem Center for Public Affairs, 1986).

31. Ernest Stock, "Jewish Multicountry Associations" and "The Reconstitution of the Jewish Agency: A Political Analysis," *American Jewish Year Book 1972,* vol. 73, pp. 178–93; Nahum Goldmann, *The Autobiography of Nahum Goldmann,* trans. Helen Sebba (New York: Holt, Rinehart and Winston, 1969); Israel Goldstein, *My World as a Jew: The Memoirs of Israel Goldstein,* vol. 1 (New York: Herzl Press, 1984).

32. Daniel J. Elazar and Harold M. Waller, eds., *The Governance of the Canadian Jewish Community* (forthcoming); Harvey Rich, *The Governance of the Jewish Community of Calgary* (Jerusalem: Center for Jewish Community Studies, 1974); Jennifer K. Bowerman, *The Governance of the Jewish Community of Edmonton* (Jerusalem: Center for Jewish Community Studies, 1975); Louis Greenspan, *The Governance of the Jewish Community of Hamilton* (Jerusalem: Center for Jewish Community Studies, 1974); Alan M. Cohen, *The Governance of the Jewish Community of London* (Jerusalem: Center for Jewish Community Studies, 1974); Harold M. Waller and Sheldon Schreter, *The Governance of the Jewish Community of Montreal* (Jerusalem: Center for Jewish Community Studies, 1974); Zachariah Kay, *The Governance of the Jewish Community of Ottawa* (Jerusalem: Center for Jewish Community Studies, 1974); Yaakov Glickman, *The Governance of the Jewish Community of Toronto* (Jerusalem: Center for Jewish Community Studies, 1974); Edna Oberman, *The Governance of the Jewish Community of Vancouver* (Jerusalem: Center for Jewish Community Studies, 1974); Stephen Mandel and R. H. Wagenberg, *The Governance of the Jewish Community of Windsor* (Jerusalem: Center for Jewish Community Studies, 1974); Anna Gordon, *The Governance of the Jewish Community of Winnipeg* (Jerusalem: Center for Jewish Community Studies, 1974); Harold M. Waller, *The Canadian Jewish Community: A National Perspective* (Jerusalem: Center for Jewish Community Studies, 1977); Daniel J. Elazar, "The Jews of Quebec and the Canadian Crisis," *Jerusalem Letter,* no. 11 (May 19, 1978).

33. Marc Salzberg, "The Organized Jewish Community in France," unpublished Ph.D. dissertation (1974) and *French Jewry and American Jewry* (Jerusalem: Center for Jewish Community Studies, 1971); Ilan Greilsammer, *The Democratization of a Community: The Case of French Jewry* (Jerusalem: Center for Jewish Community Studies, 1979); "Jews of France: From Neutrality to Involvement," *Forum,* nos. 28–29 (winter 1978), pp. 130–46 (reprinted by Center for Jewish Community Studies); and "Le Juif et la Cité: Quatre Approches Théoriques," *Archive de sciences sociales des religions,* no. 46/1 (July–September 1978), pp. 135–51 (reprinted by Center for Jewish Community Studies).

34. *Chiai HaYehudim be-Britania;* Sonia L. Lipman and Vivian D. Lipman, *Jewish Life in Britain, 1962–1977.*

35. Elazar and Medding, *Jewish Communities in Frontier Societies;* Aschheim, "The Communal Organization of South African Jewry"; Gideon Shimoni, *Jews and Zionism: The South African Experience (1910–1967)* (London and Cape Town: Oxford University Press, 1980); Saron and Hotz, *The Jews in South Africa;* Gustav Saron, "The Making of South African Jewry: An Essay in Historical Interpretation," *South African Jewry* (Johannesburg: South African Jewish Board of Deputies, 1966).

36. Haim Avni, "Argentine Jewry: Its Socio-Political Status and Organizational Patterns," *Dispersion and Unity,* no. 12 (1971), pp. 128–62.

37. Miriam Mundstock, *The Jewish Community of Brazil,* unpublished manuscript prepared for the Center for Jewish Community Studies (1970); Robert M. Levine, "Brazil's Jews During the Vargas Era and After," *Luso-Brazilian Review* 5 (summer 1968), pp. 45–58.

38. *Ha-Yehudim be-Mexico ve be-Artzot America HaTichona* (The Jewish Communities in Mexico and Central America), issue of *Tefutsot Yisrael,* vol. 16, no. 1 (January–March 1978) (Hebrew); Seymour B. Liebman, *The Jewish Community of Mexico* (Jerusalem: Center for Jewish Community Studies, 1978).

39. Daniel J. Elazar, "The New Agenda of European Jewry," *Jerusalem Letter/Viewpoints,* no. 35 (October 17, 1984); Charles S. Liebman, *On the Study of International Jewish Political Organizations* (Jerusalem: Center for Jewish Community Studies, 1978); Ernest Stock, "Jewish Multicountry Associations" and "The Emerging European Jewish Community Structure," *Jerusalem Letter,* no. 46 (March 14, 1982).

40. Daniel J. Elazar and Alysa M. Dortort, eds., *Understanding the Jewish Agency: A Handbook* (Jerusalem: Jerusalem Center for Public Affairs, 1984); Zelig Chinitz, *A Common Agenda: The Reconstitution of the Jewish Agency for Israel* (Jerusalem: Jerusalem Center for Public Affairs, 1985).

41. Ismar Elbogen, *Century of Jewish Life* (Philadelphia: Jewish Publication Society of America, 1966); Howard Morley Sachar, *The Course of Modern Jewish History* (New York: Dell Publishing Co., 1958); Salo W. Baron, *The Jewish Community: Its History and Structure to the American Revolution,* 3 vols. (Philadelphia: Jewish Publication Society of America, 1942).

42. Elazar and Dortort, *Understanding the Jewish Agency;* World Zionist Organization, *Reports for the Period September 20, 1971–December 31, 1977* (Jerusalem: World Zionist Organization Executive, 1978), submitted to the 29th Zionist Congress in Jerusalem; Stock, "Jewish Multicountry Associations"; The World Zionist Organization, the Organization and Information Department, *The World Zionist Organization* (Jerusalem, 1972).

43. See Daniel J. Elazar and Stuart A. Cohen, *The Jewish Polity: Jewish Political Organization from Biblical Times to the Present* (Bloomington, Ind.: Indiana University Press, 1985), Epoch XIII: Voluntary Organizations. For general histories of the bund, the territorialists, and Agudath Israel, see *Encyclopedia Judaica.*

44. Herbert Agar, *The Saving Remnant: An Account of Jewish Survival* (New York: Viking Press, 1960); Bauer, *My Brother's Keeper;* Daniel J. Elazar, "Israel, American Jewry, and the Re-Emergence of a World Jewish Polity," in *Annual of Bar Ilan University Studies in Judaica and the Humanities XVI–XVII* (Ramat Gan: Bar Ilan University, 1979), pp. 89–126.

45. Elazar, *Community and Polity* and "Israel, American Jewry, and the Re-Emergence of a World Jewish Polity,"; Marc Lee Raphael, *A History of the United Jewish Appeal 1939–1982* (Providence, R.I.: Brown University–Scholars Press, 1982) and *Understanding American Jewish Philanthropy* (New York: Ktav, 1979).

46. *Yisrael veHatfutsot, HaTnuah HaTzionit, HaSochnut HaYehudit* (Israel and the Diaspora, the Zionist Movement, the Jewish Agency) (Jerusalem: World Zionist Organization, Press and Public Relations Bureau, 1970) (Hebrew); and Eliezer D. Jaffe, *Givers and Spenders: The Politics of Charity in Israel* (Jerusalem: Ariel Publishing House, 1985).

4

False Divisions and Real Domains

Understanding the Jewish polity requires the shedding of certain assumptions about contemporary Jewish life derived from the orientations of the Western Christian world in the modern epoch. One such assumption is that there is a real division in Jewish life between so-called religious and so-called secular activities. From that assumption follows another: secular activities for the Jewish people are public and religious ones are private.

It is also necessary to understand the relationship between "cosmopolitans" and "locals," a perennial division in human affairs, and how it influences organized Jewish life; between professionals and volunteers, a new division in diaspora Jewish life; and between civic and political conceptions of leadership that divide the contemporary Jewish world, most particularly Western Jewry and Israel.[1] Finally, it is necessary to understand the role of the three domains of authority integral to Jewish public affairs and their interrelationships.

"Religious" and "Secular"

Before the modernization of the Jewish community, it was impossible to draw a distinction between religious and secular activities, in whatever form of communal organization existed. In the very small communities, where most Jews lived until the urbanization of the nineteenth and twentieth centuries, one institution, known as the *bet knesset* (house of assembly), served as the locus of Jewish communal life. It included not only such acknowledged religious functions as prayer and study of sacred texts, but also social welfare, judicial, and general governance functions of the community. The *bet knesset* pattern often carried over into the few large urban Jewish communities where the Jews would be divided among a number of *kehillot*, each with its own *bet knesset*, often based on their region of origin and at times on the occupations of the members; these would be loosely linked in a citywide league or confederation, primarily for external-relations and defense purposes.

With the emancipation and consequent modernization of the Jews came a transformation of their institutions. Modern Jews tried to jettison the political dimensions of Jewish corporate existence and to emphasize the ritual cum ethical dimensions, which in the modern Western world were considered to be the province of "religion." The *bet knesset* was transformed into the modern synagogue, formally designed to be a place of prayer and ethical preaching (and teaching) and secondarily a place where Jews could gather socially. This new-style synagogue was deliberately defined as a religious institution and was stripped of those functions that were determined by modern society to be secular—initially, communal governance and increasingly, as the nineteenth century wore on, social services and education, which became the province of the state.[2] This distinction became most pronounced in western Europe and North America and was least visible in eastern Europe, the Balkans, North Africa, and western Asia, where modernization came more slowly, although by the end of the nineteenth century it was increasingly widespread even in those regions.[3]

This new distinction between "religious" and "secular" activities served not only modern diaspora Jews but also the Zionist movement. Although the harbingers of Zionism in the nineteenth century came out of traditional Judaism and saw their Zionist political activity as an extension of traditional Jewish political life, the organized Zionist movement was initiated by modern Jews. Most of them were secular in their own lives and accepted the modern distinction implicitly. Even when they were willing to give due regard to the religious dimension of Judaism, they did so on the basis of the distinction between religious and secular life. They saw Zionism as a secular political movement, like other nationalist movements that, while often seeking support of whatever religion was dominant in a particular national community, saw themselves as forces for the development of secular states. Thus Theodor Herzl made it a point to give the Jews of his restored Jewish state rabbis and synagogues, but he viewed both as being outside the political life of the restored Jewish commonwealth. Among more militant secularists, particularly those in the socialist camp, the religious dimension was to be stamped out in favor of a new secular belief system rooted in socialism.

In the West, where the host societies emphasized church-state separation, this division was carried furthest. In the East, including the State of Israel, religion and state invariably remained linked to the extent of state recognition of and support for some religions. This did not eliminate, however, the distinction between religious and secular even in those societies. Those matters having to do with religious ritual observance and ethical teaching and preaching were assigned to the recognized religious institutions; the rest of the activities of civil society were deemed to be the province of the state or voluntary secular organizations.

Outside Israel, the activities that belonged to the synagogues and their confederations were labeled "religious" and, until recently, were rarely touched by the polity. Community relations, welfare, social service, and Israel-oriented concerns of the polity were treated as "secular" and, with few exceptions, located in the institutions of the community outside the province of the synagogues. In between were the educational functions, which were sometimes treated as "religious" and sometimes as "secular" and often suffered because they fell between the two schools.

This new understanding of the character of the Jewish community was deepened in the diaspora in the early years of the twentieth century by the self-imposed division between those Jews concerned with their "shuls" and those who, though perhaps members of synagogues, were more interested in welfare and community relations activities which they saw as divorced from "religion." This led to the rise of two separate groups of Jewish activists, a situation reinforced by the other divisions referred to above.

Because religion was now defined as a private matter, the synagogues were conceived to be private institutions, the province of their members and their members alone, and the activities now defined as secular were increasingly regarded as public, that is, as belonging to the whole Jewish community. In their emphasis on the personal needs of their members, synagogues became localistic institutions while the public services became the province of the cosmopolitans. Under the new system, congregational rabbis became "professionals"—paid functionaries of their congregations rather than judges in matters of Jewish life responsible to the community as a whole.

Shortly after the rabbis became functionaries, professionalization was also introduced into the other communal institutions. The two types of professionals were recruited and trained from different groups. The rabbis were recruited from among those with spiritual aspirations and trained in seminaries; the Jewish civil servants were primarily drawn from secularist environments and trained as social workers.

Despite all the forces making for separation, the division could not and did not remain a hard and fast one. It has been breaking down since the end of World War II. In the United States, as synagogues grew in power in the 1950s, they began to see themselves as the true custodians of Jewish life. They claimed authoritative roles in areas previously reserved to the "secular" side, particularly in the provision of services for middle income families who were synagogue members or prospective members. Although they were unsuccessful in this effort, it contributed to breaking down the sense of division.

The thrust of Jewish tradition militated against such a separation as being artificially enforced. Those concerned with the "secular" side became more involved in Jewish life and saw their activities not as simple social services to immigrants that supplemented government services or provided services where government services did not exist but as functions with a specifically Jewish content. They began to think of them as no less "Jewish" in the traditional sense than the functions of the synagogues. Nevertheless, although ideologically and functionally the lines between the two are weakening, structurally the separation between "religious" and "secular" institutions is real.

The division in Israel was sharper than that in the diaspora in ideological terms, but because religious and secular were organized into political camps, they were also more intertwined. The main thrust of the Zionist movement was secular, either in the sense of nineteenth-century liberalism with its emphasis on relegating religion to the private sphere and separating religion and state, or in the way of militant socialism, which saw religion as, at best, an anachronism if not a brake on progress. Thus in Israel the Zionist enterprise was not only defined by most of those engaged in it as secular, but, unlike most diaspora Jews, they saw themselves as secularists by ideology.

Religious Zionists developed their own version of Zionism early on, which synthesized Torah with *derekh eretz*—the ways of the world—but to maintain their synthesis in a secularist environment, they had to develop separate institutions within the framework of the Zionist movement from cradle to grave.[4] Thus the division between religious and secular took on a new meaning, first in the Zionist world and then in Israel. There, too, however, the division proved to be unrealistic because of the Jewish way of life. Religious Zionism, from the first, engaged in activities that in other societies would have been labeled secular, though from within a religious framework, including the establishment of religious kibbutzim, banks, and social welfare institutions.

The socialists tried hard to re-valuate traditional Jewish festivals, taking old bottles and filling them with new wine, recognizing that Jews wanted to maintain at least the externalities of the traditional Jewish calendar and other traditional Jewish symbols.[5] The liberals soon discovered that the *raison d'être* of the Jewish people lay in the maintenance of respect toward the Jewish religious tradition and the cultivation of a civil religion that emphasized public manifestations of that respect. Thus slowly but surely the rapprochement and intermixture emerged in Israel, linking the two divisions institutionally if not ideologically. As part of the coalition agreement, which maintained the Zionist movement intact despite internal ideological differences, first the Yishuv and then the new Jewish state pledged to maintain public support for basic religious institutions such as the Sabbath, observance of *kashrut* in all public facilities, and state support for religious institutions.[6]

During the first generation of statehood, strong efforts were made to preserve the ideological purity of the secularists. Thus in Israel's Proclamation of Independence there is no direct reference to the name of God, but instead a euphemism, the Rock of Israel, which is accepted by religious traditionalists but can be otherwise interpreted by secularists if they so choose. Contrast this situation with what took place twenty-eight years later, after the Entebbe raid in 1976. When the special session of the Knesset, called to offer public thanks to the heroes of that raid, was opened by the late Israel Yeshayahu, then speaker of the Knesset and a Labor party leader, he mounted the podium, placed a *kippa* on his head, and read from the Book of Psalms. The act symbolized the change that had taken place in the intervening generation.

The emergence of an Israeli civil religion rooted in Judaism was paralleled in the diaspora. Even those who chose the so-called secular route for communal activities increasingly developed a belief system rooted in Jewish religious tradition.

"Public" and "Private"

The putative division between the "religious" and "secular" sectors of the Jewish community was reinforced by implicit assumptions as to what is "public" and what is "private" in contemporary Jewish life. In the diaspora there was a notion that because being Jewish is considered a private matter by the larger society, all Jewish communal activities are private. This view has broken down only recently, partly under the impact of Israel and partly as a result of the efforts of students of the Jewish community who have emphasized the degree to which the collective efforts of the community must be considered public from a Jewish point of view, however they are defined by the external world.

Thus in the United States and Canada the activities sponsored or financed by the federations and their constituent agencies have come to be viewed as the public activities of the Jewish community. The argument for "communal responsibility" essentially has been an argument designed to define them in that manner. Synagogues, on the other hand, are still regarded as private activities, the exclusive province of their members. Decisions about the establishment of synagogues, their location and relocation, their membership, their religious ideology and practice, their programs and the amount of money charged to participate in those programs, the physical plant constructed to house them, what is done with the plant when it is no longer needed—all are the private preserves of congregational members or leaders regardless of overall community interests or needs.

In communities where synagogues are owned by congregational unions as in Britain and France, this view of their private character is less pervasive. This is true even for congregations in the communities that are outside the mainstream synagogue unions, because many of them, are part of larger movements in the Orthodox world, whether Agudath Israel or Chabad or whatever, where traditional modes of thought prevail and the public/private distinction is nonexistent.

Synagogues are considered private associations in Israel no less than in most of the diaspora. This might seem surprising to outsiders, because most synagogues receive government subsidies for construction and maintenance. However, this merely follows the Israeli pattern: the government subsidizes many private bodies if they are considered to serve public purposes. Because most Israeli synagogues are small by contemporary diaspora standards, rarely consisting of more than two hundred people, their private character is made real by their limited activity as houses of prayer and perhaps study.

A parallel development has taken place in Latin America with regard to the *deportivos,* or sports centers, the Latin American equivalent of the Jewish community centers of North America. In those much more secularized communities, the *deportivos* were established as private clubs in the same way that synagogues were established in North America (and in contrast to the way the Jewish community centers there were established, as public institutions). For many years they were considered strictly private associations outside the purview of the organized Jewish community.

As they grew larger and more important as places for Jews to gather and express their Jewish identity, the *deportivos* began to acquire a public dimension as instrumentalities of the Jewish community. Their leaders began to see themselves as public figures. In Argentina, for example, the leaders of the *deportivos* came to challenge the establishment for control of the AMIA and the DAIA, the two major instrumentalities of Argentinian Jewry. They offered the first competition to the party system borrowed from Europe and Israel, which dominated those institutions until the 1970s. Once the *deportivos* began to be perceived in this light, it was a short step toward raising the issue of how they could become true community centers and provide public expressions of Jewishness. At that point they even sought assistance from the Jewish community centers of North America to help them undergo this transformation.

All this is not to suggest that there is no private sphere in Jewish life, or that there should not be. It suggests only that the lines between public and private institutions are not that distinct in any Jewish polity, even in the diaspora where some Jewish institutions are defined by the external society as private. This is equally true in Israel where the Zionist enterprise emphasizes the public dimension of even the most private activities (the kibbutz, for example, which sought to transform the family connection into a public one). The public dimension was not only emphasized over the private but also was politicized to the extreme, with ideological considerations transformed into contests for political power in every possible sector of life.[7] In this respect, the Zionist experience was the obverse of that of the diaspora in the modern epoch, where Zionism emphasized privatization even of the public dimension. In the end, however, both dimensions have been moving toward a common position somewhere in the middle.

"Cosmopolitans" and "Locals"

It is more realistic to view the conventional distinction between public and private institutions in Jewish life today as a reflection of the dichotomy between "cosmopolitans" and "locals."[8] Cosmopolitans are those who see the whole community as a single piece and maintain connections and involvements across all of it. Although their cosmopolitanism is first defined in relation to a particular community, as Robert Merton has shown, once they develop a cosmopolitan outlook toward their community, they almost invariably take a cosmopolitan view of the larger world of which that community is also a part. Locals are those whose involvement and connections are confined to a small segment of the total community—a neighborhood, a particular social group, or, in Jewish life, a particular synagogue, organization, or club. Their involvement rests overwhelmingly on their commitment to the point of attachment that does not extend to the community as a whole except indirectly. Moreover, their perceptions of the larger world are also limited, based as they are on their local involvements.

All people are either cosmopolitans or locals in the same sense that all are either liberals or conservatives. Apparently, this is a natural division in society. Concurrently, all cosmopolitans have clearly localistic needs—the need to be tied to something more intimate than the community in the abstract, or even to a set of institutions that must inevitably be depersonalized to some degree. And locals can be mobilized for cosmopolitan purposes when those purposes are made to strike home at the source of their involvement. Thus every polity needs institutions devoted to serving cosmopolitan and local needs as well as the local needs of cosmopolitans and the cosmopolitan needs of locals.

In the Jewish polity, as in all others, most governing bodies combine cosmopolitan and local representation, leading to conflict within them along cosmopolitan-local lines. Still, the government or government-like organizations and agencies generally emphasize cosmopolitan concerns and consequently are more likely to attract cosmopolitans to leadership positions in them. The synagogues, *landsmanschaften,* country clubs, and lodges, on the other hand, represent local needs and interests. That is their primary role. Consequently, they are more likely to attract locals as leaders. The exceptions are the cosmopolitans who lead synagogues and the like with predominantly cosmopolitan memberships, who are interested in serving their own local needs, and the cosmopolitan rabbis and others who are leaders of locals because they need a congregational or equivalent institutional base.

Professionals and Volunteers

The other major division among decision makers in the diaspora is that between professional and voluntary leaders, with the professionals further subdivided into those whose training is obtained through rabbinical institutions and those whose training is through secular professional schools. Professionalization is unquestionably a modern phenomenon. Traditional society is characterized by other distinctions, either determined by birth (for example, priests) or the voluntary shouldering of special religious obligations. Those who held formal responsibility in the traditional Jewish community were called from the ranks of the community, on a voluntary basis. Even the emergence of a professional rabbinate came late in Jewish life, on the eve of the modern epoch, and did not really become widespread until almost the end of that epoch. The rabbis of earlier ages were proud that they supported themselves as craftsmen, businessmen, or physicians.

The oldest equivalent of a paid professional class in Jewish life is the priestly caste associated with the *keter kehunah,* which was based on descent rather than professional skills. Some priests devoted their time fully to the service of the sanctuary and were compensated by a share in the sacrificial offerings. With the destruction of the Temple in Jerusalem, a priesthood supported by the people came to an end; today the very limited functions of the priestly caste are voluntarily maintained. A new class of professionals has developed in the *keter kehunah* including congregational rabbis, *hazzanim* (cantors), *shohetim* (ritual slaughterers), and peripheral positions such as choir directors and clerks of local religious councils in Israel.

The gradual professionalization of the rabbinate added that dimension to the *keter torah,* which more recently has also acquired other professions, principally in the realm of Jewish education. Professionalization has become equally widespread in the *keter malkhut.* One of the great achievements of the contemporary Jewish polity has been the development of a civil service that is second to none in the world, including the civil service of the best governments. Today that civil service is fully articulated and extends into every imaginable field. It has training schools, professional associations, journals, and jargon—all the elements of a profession. If we attach to it the Israeli civil service, which serves the Jewish state in the way of any state service, we can estimate that a significant share of the work force of the Jewish people is on the Jewish public payroll.

The American Jewish community has the most professionalized leadership of any in the world, probably the most of any in Jewish history. The roots of this undoubtedly lie in the commitment to professionalization that envelops the larger American society. The United States began this commitment in the 1840s, and, since then, true professionalism has become as much a hallmark of the American approach to doing the world's work as splendid amateurism was of the British approach more than a century ago. The American Jewish community has imbibed that commitment to professsionalism and has consistently moved to professionalize its organizations and institutions.

Today, the day-to-day business of the American Jewish community is almost exclusively in the hands of professionals. Because these professionals are involved with the daily problems of the community, they usually are committed to their careers throughout their adult lives and are trained to occupy the positions they hold. Consequently, they exercise great influence in the decision making of the community.

Professionalization has not taken root nearly as well in the rest of the Jewish world. The idea of a Jewish civil service has now emerged in countries like France, South Africa, and, to a lesser extent, Australia, but is still much more limited than in the United States. The International Conference of Jewish Communal Service has been organized as the *edah*-wide professional association for the Jewish civil service, and it is trying hard to promote the idea, along with standards and training.

Originally, the Jewish civil service was recruited from two sources: immigrants and the lower middle class. The more "Jewish" the occupation, the less attractive it was to Jews seeking careers. Many of the most able senior Jewish professionals among the founders of the senior Jewish civil service in effect "backed into" their careers out of force of circumstances. This is a problem that the Jewish civil service has overcome in the United States but still must overcome in the diaspora.

In Israel, public service is considered a desirable career for middle-class Israelis and serves many of the same functions of upward mobility. It is almost a natural choice for university graduates who have not specialized in a technical field and are not interested in going into business. Until recently, the latter was frowned on as a proper pursuit in a society informed with socialist ideas. This is now changing as business becomes a respectable and even attractive career.

On the other hand, there has been no diminution in the number of voluntary leaders in the diaspora. Parallel roles for professionals and volunteers have crystallized in almost every Jewish organization and institution, allowing for extensive participation by both. What is less fixed is how they relate to each other. Generally speaking, there is at least an underlying tension between the two groups, though not necessarily an unproductive one.

This tension is most noticeable in the synagogues where it is likely to lead to confrontations from time to time. In part, the intimacy of the leadership circle in the synagogue creates an arena for conflict that might not exist in other institutions. More-over, the gap in interests and values between the professionals led by the rabbi and the voluntary leadership is likely to be greater in the synagogue than elsewhere. The rabbi is not only committed to providing overall leadership for his particular synagogue but also must be committed to some transcendent norms and religiously prescribed patterns of behavior. These may or may not be shared by the voluntary leadership. At the same time, neither can do without one another as is conceivably possible in other Jewish institutions.

The tension is further exaggerated because each element has a special claim to the central authoritative role. The rabbi's claim is based on his role as spokesman for the transcendent dimensions of Judaism; the claim of the voluntary leadership is based on the nature of congregational government in both the Jewish and American traditions (not to mention that they provide the money for the operation of the institution). Consequently, conflicts between the professional and voluntary leadership of synagogues have at times attained legendary proportions in Jewish life. Because both sources of authority are institutionalized in the congregational framework, the tension is inevitable.

In other diaspora bodies, as a rule, wherever the requirements of the profession are most exclusive and demanding, and the need for professional expertise established, separation of professional and volunteer roles is the norm. Wherever the line between professional and volunteer competence is least distinct, their roles tend to be mixed. Thus in Jewish education and some Jewish social services, operational control and much policy-making power are placed in the hands of professionals; they are viewed as specially trained experts who bring to their tasks an expertise that endows them with a special role. The voluntary leadership often confines itself to developing or approving general policy and finding the necessary monetary and community support for the enterprise. They intervene more actively only when the professionals fail to provide the requisite leadership.

In community relations and fund-raising, the lines that divide professionals and volunteers are blurred. Professionals are often treated as if they cannot claim much in the way of special expertise (other than the expertise of experience) for handling what are essentially political or public tasks. In fact, they may have substantial influence because of their special training and, most important, because they spend all their working time at what they do, enabling them to know the situation better than the voluntary leadership. Like all professionals, their special power is based on the extent to which they control the amount and kind of information that reaches their volunteer counterparts. Their control of in-house planning, their ability to influence strongly the appointment of voluntary leaders to particular office, and their providing of continuity in the life of the organization also add to their power.

Some of the volunteers too, may also have special talents, capabilities, or connections, particularly political ones, which place them in strategic positions in organizations. From these positions they play major roles in the decision-making process hardly different from those of the professionals. In such cases, volunteers and professionals are often found working in tandem on common problems with minimum conflict.

To be a voluntary participant in the diaspora one must be able to take time—sometimes large quantities of time—away from one's career or business and be prepared to spend one's own money on travel, because it is expected that voluntary leaders will not take money from the organizations they serve. Aside from successful businessmen and lawyers associated with law firms where there is a tradition of allowing members to participate in Jewish communal life, the only people who can contribute the requisite time are academics, and they are limited by their lack of money required to maintain an active role. Thus, willy-nilly, wealth becomes an important factor determining who the voluntary leadership will be. On the local plane, this demarcation is not as stark as it seems. It is far less true for small synagogues and clubs (the most local institutions of all) and most true for the United Jewish Appeal or Keren Hayesod.

Even where wealth is of great importance, it does not function as the only measure of leadership. The wealthiest men are not necessarily the most important leaders. There is apparently some threshold of prosperity past which most persons are equal in the pursuit of leadership roles. A man of modest means (from the perspective of the very wealthy) may choose to allocate a high proportion of his resources to the Jewish community and get recognition accordingly; a man of great means may not be willing to make such a major allocation and be rejected accordingly.

Moreover, beyond the willingness to give there must be a willingness to serve. Once again, large contributors may or may not choose to be participants, and smaller ones may be willing to provide more of their time, energy, and talents. Evaluation of one's contribution is usually based on the norm in the group from which one is drawn. Thus an academician can become a "large contributor" on the basis of what is, in absolute terms, a small amount of money. Finally, certain "old families" feel responsibility for communal affairs and are recognized in their communities as leaders on the basis of longstanding precedents, even if they cannot compete in wealth with newer elements. The only exceptions to this are the Zionist parties and organizations like the Jewish War Veterans, which, because they draw their membership from a population with modest incomes, have traditionally provided subsidies to enable their leadership to function in that capacity.

In Israel, the Jewish communities of eastern and central Europe before the Holocaust, and the Latin American Jewish communities until the 1970s, there is or was a class of professional Jewish politicians who hold elective offices in the community and are paid salaries for doing so. This class has severely limited the role of volunteers in those communities and, in some respects, has even hindered the development of a civil service, because the politicians are not prepared to relinquish power to it. Where this is the case, relations between professional politicians and professional civil servants take on a character of their own. The politicians have special responsibility for political mobilization and policy-making.

Elsewhere, lack of a recognizable group of politicians does not eliminate the need for people to fill political roles. Thus it falls to people drawn from ostensibly nonpolitical channels to play the roles of political mobilization and decision making that are the province of politicians in other systems without being perceived—or perceiving themselves—in that light. As a result, volunteers, social workers, rabbis, businessmen, and, occasionally, academics may assume the tasks of professional politicians without either being chosen for that role through normal political means or recognized for what they are.

As the role of professional civil servant grows, new problems develop. The privatization that is taking place in contemporary society has a natural tendency to strengthen the roles of professionals in every area, to transfer more responsibilities to the civil service. This trend is reinforced by the universal truth that all contemporary societies have discovered: once professionalization is introduced and a civil service built, it is a natural tendency for the civil service to take on even more, simply because it is involved every day in every way and what it does represents the major career interest of the people who are involved in doing it.

Government or government-like bureaucracies not only respond to issues with which they identify but also create new issues and initiate demands to deal with them. This tendency can be balanced in situations in which there is a strong republican regime functioning but where the public declines and the res publica becomes weakened; there are insufficient checks and balances, and the civil servants begin to take over responsibility because they feel that if nobody else will do the job, they must. Besides, they feel that because they have been appointed to undertake those tasks, they have a right to do them. There is some justice in this kind of attitude, but it does result in new problems of who leads and by what authority.

In Israel at the upper levels of decision making, the line between politicians and civil servants is often blurred. Patronage still figures extensively in appointments to responsible positions in what is formally defined as the civil service, and people often move from the civil service to political offices. This not only leads to a rather politicized top echelon in the government of the state and in its local authorities, but also in the Jewish Agency/WZO complex, where it has led to serious misunderstanding and conflict between the Israeli and diaspora leadership.

Because the principal offices of the Jewish Agency and the WZO are located in Israel, the top positions in those offices are filled in the Israeli pattern on the basis of political involvement and connections rather than on the basis of the distinction between professionals and volunteers common in the diaspora and particularly in the United States. The diaspora leadership keeps insisting that the professional/volunteer distinction be introduced into the Jewish Agency, but the Israelis cannot even understand it, much less accept it. Jewish Agency department heads are professional politicians and receive salaries for occupying their positions full-time. They do not see themselves as voluntary leaders nor do they appreciate that as an appropriate posture. Their directors-general, who are presumably the equivalent of agency executive directors in the diaspora and hence "should" be professional civil servants, are often subordinate professional politicians, following the pattern of many of the government ministries. Those that are not, often are technocrats who have moved into their positions from other realms and do not see themselves as part of the continuing civil service of their departments. The diaspora has slowly succeeded in expanding the number of technocratic directors-general (as distinct from politicians) without bringing the Israelis to abandon their overall understanding of the role of the department heads and the relationship between department heads and their directors-general. This has become one of the major structural issues of the emergent world Jewish polity.

The situation in Israel arose, in part, because of the political nature of Jewish affairs in the Zionist movement and in part because of the lack of men of social standing or wealth who could assume leadership roles on a noblesse oblige or *pro bono* basis. Moreover, the ideological orientation of Zionism led to the concept that officeholders represent constituencies and hence cannot be independent volunteers. Both the socialist and then the statist thrust of the movement and the state led to the conviction that such positions should be career positions; that is, public people should make their careers in public life and be compensated for doing so rather than entering public life after making money outside. Zionism in that sense was in no small measure a revolt against the domination of Jewish life by the wealthy in the diaspora. Hence, Zionists are strongly

committed to compensation for leadership as an egalitarian and democratizing measure
that enables anyone to aspire to the highest positions in Jewish life.[9]

The Ketarim as Real Domains

There is a more accurate and intrinsically more Jewish way to understand the
divisions in Jewish public life, identified in chapter one: the division into the three
domains or *ketarim*. These classic models tell us more about Jewish public affairs than any
other models we might choose.[10] Once we understand that authority and power in the
community are shared among the representatives of the three *ketarim,* the discussion
shifts from what has become the conventional one of who is entitled to do what in the
Jewish community—rabbis or laymen, synagogues or federations—to one of how each of
these institutions is to be understood and what its role and functions are to be in the
overall scheme of things.[11]

The leaders in the communal-welfare, Israel–world Jewry, and external relations–
defense spheres have assumed the mantle of *keter malkhut.* Most of the issues that have
developed with regard to this domain have to do with the intra-*ketaric* competition, such
as the conflict between the Israeli and diaspora leadership within the Jewish Agency or
jurisdictional disputes among organizations in the same sphere. Some echoes of such
earlier contests remain but only in relation to specific functions, not overall role. No
doubt there will continue to be controversies of this kind between the spheres, and there
will never be a time without controversy, but there is no longer a struggle for control of
the *keter malkhut* as such.

Today the *keter kehunah* is mostly in the hands of rabbis and *hazzanim.* Although
there are some authoritative personalities in other spheres of Jewish life who play a
sacerdotal role on the symbolic level for the *edah* as a whole, this function is basically a
local one. The question of who is a rabbi has reemerged lately as a major issue around the
question of ordination of women. The issue first confronted Western Jewry 150 years
ago when non-Orthodox movements emerged that required rabbis who functioned in
other than the traditional pattern and were trained accordingly. The result then was that
the *edah* (although not all its parts) recognized non-Orthodox rabbis but, in the process,
shifted the rabbinate as a whole from the *keter torah* to the *keter kehunah,* de facto if not
de jure.

An even more important question is, Are rabbis' functions a matter of private right
or are they public responsibilities? This is an issue that is perhaps most strongly manifested in the Reform movement, where every rabbi is entitled to decide personally how to
conduct conversion and whether or not to perform mixed marriages. Whatever the stance
of the movement's majority it sees such decisions as private ones in which every rabbi is
sovereign. Yet the question is not so easily disposed of. Is every rabbi authorized to
decide who is a Jew without being responsible to any system? Are these public responsibilities? Is this part of the privatization of Jewish life, and is it going to have a great effect
on the definition of citizenship in the Jewish polity? This is a question of citizenship, of
who is eligible to be part of the Jewish people. The notion that any person may privately
decide who is eligible to be part of the Jewish people is a problematic one from the
perspective of the polity no less than from a traditional religious perspective.

With regard to the *keter torah,* a major contemporary issue is who represents the
keter. There are several claimants for prime roles as its representatives. First of all, there is

a struggle among the Orthodox and non-Orthodox religous movements for authority in this domain. The Orthodox Jews, or at least their leadership, insist that their Torah sages and rabbis are the only legitimate bearers of the *keter torah;* the non-Orthodox insist that all rabbis are equally legitimate. There is a secondary struggle within Orthodoxy but, with a few exceptions, even where they disagree, Orthodox groups accord legitimacy to one another.

The core governance institutions of the *keter torah* are the *yeshivot* and rabbinical seminaries linked with the various movements whose leaders function as such in that *keter.* For the ultra-Orthodox, these *yeshivot* constitute or are represented either in the Bet Din of the Edah Haredit, the Moetzet Gedolei haTorah of Agudath Israel, or the new Moetzet Hakhmei haTorah of Shas, its breakaway Sephardic offshoot. In religious-Zionist circles, the *yeshivot* share their power with the chief rabbinates. The Jewish Theological Seminary is the power center of the Conservative movement; in the Reform movement, the Hebrew Union College–Jewish Institute of Religion must share power with the Central Conference of American Rabbis.

On an individual basis, today authoritative scholars, most of whom hold rabbinical ordination (*semikha,* a grant of authority), are the principal bearers of *keter torah.* Few, if any, hold puppits. Most are Torah scholars at *yeshivot,* seminaries, or universities who possess the personal ability to reach out. The title rabbi may add to their status but it does not define it. A few are professors whose scholarly attainments are less traditional but who play a similar role. Finally, there are the *rebbes* and "gurus" who, for their own personal followers, are seen as bearing the *keter torah.* By and large, the elements of the professoriate who find themselves in the *keter torah* have no direct governance role but are influential because of their connections with the *keter malkhut,* whose leaders have, in effect, anointed them as bearers of Torah.

A second issue is more critical than ever before, and that is, What constitutes "Torah"? Between the time of the Karaite schism in the eighth century of the common era and the nineteenth century, a common traditional understanding of Torah prevailed. Even those who rejected Judaism shared in that common understanding. Since the rise of Reform, that understanding has faced one challenge after another. Today we are seeing even greater competition for the definition of Torah, including some very strange definitions. In one sense, this is a tribute to the strong hold that the principle of Torah retains on Jews of all kinds, so much so that every ideological claim on Jews as Jews must find its link with Torah. But some of the claims attack the very foundations of reasonable understanding of what is expressed in the Torah and its tradition.[12]

A third issue, growing out of the second, is, How do Jews see themselves bound by Torah? For both the *am* and the *edah,* Torah is constitutional. However much room there may be for interpretation and choice in the tradition, it is not merely a nice set of ideas and traditions to be taken or left as one pleases. Contemporary Jewry has recognized the truth of this in at least one modest way, by introducing some standards of Jewish observance such as *kashrut* (dietary laws), *motzi* and *birkat hamazon* (blessings before and after the meal), or *kiddush* and *havdalah* (sanctification of the beginning and end of the Sabbath) where appropriate in Jewish public institutions (including those of the State of Israel) and at public functions. On a private level, the issue is nowhere nearly as resolved. Moreover, Jewish public institutions have not really grappled with the constitutional character of Torah outside the ritual sphere, all too often reducing its role to questions of ritual observance and generalized moral exhortation.

All these are issues that will continue to confront the institutions of the Jewish polity because there are practical decisions to be made in the community about each. Sooner or later every institution confronts the necessity to make such decisions, must decide who will participate in making them, and will be called to account for them by one constituency or another.

In a sense, the institutions have addressed themselves to these issues in two ways. One is by providing money to help educate the next generation, including the future bearers of the *keter torah*. Beyond that, the institutions of the *keter malkhut,* to a great extent, have been the legitimizers of the new authoritative scholars who have challenged the congregational rabbis for major roles in the *keter torah.* This is a reflection of how, in the postmodern epoch, the *keter malkhut* has become a major source of authoritative recognition for most Jews. This is true not only of the professors who are featured at their functions from time to time, only a few of whom are brought to teach Torah. To an extent even major figures in the traditional rabbinate have acquired authority beyond their immediate circles because of recognition by the *keter malkhut* and its leadership, whether through election as chief rabbis in Israel and those diaspora communities that maintain that institution and place it in the jurisdiction of the *keter malkhut,* or by common consent.

Note, for example, the role that leadership has played in the rise to universal prominence of the Lubavitcher Rebbe (who certainly does not see their recognition as in any way authoritative) and his Chabad movement and the expansion of its influence in contemporary Jewish life—through contributions as private individuals, through opening doors to community institutions, and simply by lending Chabad their prestige. The same thing occurred with Rav (Rabbi Joseph) Soleveichik. In a more subtle way, Jewish institutions began to seek his counsel. No board or executive meeting decided that he was the new authoritative personality. Rather, it happened within the informal dimensions of the *keter malkhut.*

What this suggests is that in the perennial competition among the three *ketarim,* today the *keter malkhut* has the upper hand, marking the end of a period of one thousand years or more in which the *keter torah* had the upper hand. The breakdown of the traditional community, the secularization of Jewish life, and the reestablishment of the Jewish state have all led in that direction, but it is only in this generation that Jews are beginning to feel its consequences.

In a large measure, the increasingly dominant role of the *keter malkhut* comes from its function as the only domain where Jewish unity can be maintained under current conditions. Thus the Orthodox camp refuses to sit together with representatives of non-Orthodox movements in the framework of the *keter torah* because that would mean recognition of the legitimacy of those movements in that *keter.* (In truth, the ultra-Orthodox will not sit with the mainstream Orthodox either.) Much the same is true for the *keter kehunah,* although there the record is mixed in some diaspora communities, especially in the United States. Yet all camps and their subdivisions will sit together in the institutions of the *keter malkhut,* whether the World Zionist Organization, the World Jewish Congress, the Knesset and government of Israel, countrywide boards of deputies, or local federations, because only in the other domains does the Orthodox camp insist on maintaining its monopoly. That strengthens the role of the *keter malkhut* immeasurably.

Another factor strengthening the *keter malkhut* is the role of Israeli leadership. During the first postmodern generation, the Israeli leadership was given a major role in that *keter* by virtue of Israel's status as the Jewish state. Israeli leaders will continue to play a major role, even if they will not necessarily continue to be accepted in as uncritical a manner as was true in the first generation, because of recent changes in Israel and in Israel-diaspora relations. The new intimacy established between Israel and the diaspora since 1967 has had a temporary deflating effect, but in the long run it should create a new and stronger basis on which Israelis can play a leadership role, rooted in mutual acquaintance and understanding.

The 1970s witnessed the emergence of a new world Jewish leadership. The catalyst for this development was the reconstitution of the Jewish Agency in 1970. The reconstituted Agency offered a forum for leaders of the diaspora communities to become involved in Israel and world Jewish affairs in other than philanthropic ways. Once tasted, this became a very attractive opportunity. Moreover, as a forum, it brought together Jewish leaders from different parts of the world and from different modes of Jewish involvement, creating bonds among them whose implications are just beginning to be manifested.

In sum, when we look at the classic Jewish model of the three *ketarim,* we see that the issues of Jewish leadership have been conceptualized incorrectly for many years. That question was phrased too often as "Who will lead the Jewish community?"—as if there were to be one leader, one institution, or one narrow group that was to do so. But the Jewish community classically is governed through a kind of mixed system of checks and balances represented by the division of authority and power among the three *ketarim.* That pattern persists.

Another question is how new issues are raised and placed on the Jewish agenda. In a polity based on trusteeship, it is not possible to rely on the trustees to look for all the new issues. All that can be expected from the trustees is that they be willing to respond to issues raised elsewhere. The trustees are busy dealing with existing issues and maintaining consensus.

When the new issues that well up are major ones, of critical import, they are most likely to gain recognition through at least a modicum of confrontation. That is part of the natural history of such things and it is not a bad thing. Not every confrontation need lead to change. What can be expected is that the trustees will be brought to respond in some appropriate way because of the values they and their colleagues share. What is bad is when there is polarization that cannot be bridged.

Generally speaking, contemporary Jewry has not done badly in that regard. As a result there is general consent, at worst, grudgingly given, to the present system, even by its declared critics. However, it is necessary to make a constant effort to keep the *edah* from simply becoming a new kind of oligarchy, either of the interested volunteers or the professionals. The Jewish civil service must be encouraged to regulate itself. That is necessary but not sufficient, because no person or group can be the judge of his or its own cause. Hence all segments of the polity must work together to create the appropriate relationship among the bearers of the three *keterim* and between the leadership circles and the Jewish public, as appropriate manifestations of the continuing yet reconstituted *edah.*

The distribution of powers within the ketarim. Because the tasks of the *keter kehunah* are primarily technical, governance in that domain is structured along the lines of separate functional authorities for each task, no one of which has real authority or power beyond its immediate sphere of responsibility. This is true whether we are speaking of *hazzanim* in synagogues or local religious councils in Israeli towns. The only exceptions are where the instrumentalities of this *keter* overlap into those of the *keter torah* and derive a broader authority from the latter.

The *keter torah* has claims beyond the immediate functional interests of that domain, or, perhaps more accurately, because the immediate functional responsibilities of that *keter* according to its ideology extend to every corner of Jewish life, the governance claims of its instrumentalities can extend as widely as they desire. By and large, however, even those who assert the maximum sphere of influence do not seek to govern directly every aspect of Jewish life. Instead, they claim to have a veto or, at most, certain policy-making powers with regard to areas outside those immediately associated with *keter torah*.

Even the Council of Torah Sages only seeks direct governance of the *yeshiva* world and is content with making policy or vetoing acts of those subordinate to it in the other domains. In Mizrahi/National Religious party circles, the domain of *keter torah* is even more circumscribed. The leaders who have chosen to function in the domain of the *keter malkhut* possess final decision-making authority within the bounds of the Torah as constitution and are not expected to turn to representatives of the *keter torah* for policy guidance in matters about that sphere. That is why the Mizrahi and its offshoots were known as "anticlericalists" in the religious camp, one of the elements that set them apart from Agudath Israel. For those who are not religious, the role of the *keter torah* is at most a limited symbolic one, and the authority of the rabbis is confined to ritual matters that fall in the sphere of the *keter kehunah*.

Perhaps the strongest claimants for an overarching role for the representatives of the *keter torah* outside Agudath Israel are the leaders of the Conservative and, to a lesser extent, the Reform movements. The Conservative movement, in particular, is rabbi dominated in a clerical sense, perhaps more so than any other movement in Jewish history. Moreover, its rabbis see a role for themselves extending beyond their pulpits or seminaries. Although they advance that claim, it is not one necessarily honored by the *ba'alei batim* in the movement.

The issue in the Reform movement is more clouded, because its lay leadership has always claimed equality with the rabbinate. Even so, because it is a movement that emphasizes the religious dimension of Judaism above all others, its rabbis assert serious claims of dominance in Jewish life, although in a more circumscribed sphere, for they are not necessarily interested in extending Torah to all aspects of life.

The *keter malkhut* itself has developed more elaborate and intricate governance structures as it has increased in power in the Jewish polity. What is important to note, however, is the degree to which those structures resemble one another, whether in Israel or the diaspora. This common governance structure can be described as congressional (as distinct from parliamentary, presidential, or separation-of-powers, or any nonrepublican system) in the sense that it is based on assemblies, on congresses of delegates who come together to constitute a common body without surrendering their responsibilities as delegates.[13] The structure includes two or three planes, serving the *edah,* its *medinah* and *aratzot,* and their *kehillot.* Governance in each plane begins with a large forum designated as the principal decision-making body, in which all the elements federated together to form the entity are represented. This large body will meet infrequently, either annually or only every several years if it serves the *edah* as a whole or some major segment of it, quarterly or annually for countrywide communities (except for Israel's Knesset that meets for extended periods throughout the year), and monthly or quarterly if it serves a local *kehillah.* It elects a smaller board to handle continuing policy-making responsibilities on a regular basis, which meets more frequently, usually once a month or more. Either the assembly or the board chooses an executive committee, which handles the daily business of governance. The executive committee usually shares responsibility collectively, although the chairman or president may have some special status as its convener and spokesman.

The congressional principle of representation of the federated bodies usually continues to have importance in both the board and executive committee as well as the assembly, although the smaller the body, the more the element of collective responsibility is present. Although, in theory, the larger bodies are superior to the smaller, in fact, as in parliamentary systems, the smaller direct the larger. At best the larger exercise veto powers over policy proposals generated by the smaller ones, or, where there are three planes, perhaps the larger two have something of a check-and-balance relationship with each other.

This pattern is carried over to the other arenas as well. The growth of Jewish population and its concentration in larger metropolitan centers means that, except in the smallest communities, even the local arena cannot function on the basis of the assembly of all citizens. The congressional model, then, serves as a substitute like that of the limited town meeting in New England. The advantage is that in the local arenas, there can be real representation of different constituencies, not only virtual representation. The governance structure that has emerged reflects this pattern.

Leaders with Multiple Roles

The other dimension of representative government in the Jewish polity is that Jewish leaders wear many different hats; hence both representatives and represented appear simultaneously in many forums and either represent or need to be represented in many different forms. Jews, if active at all, are members and even active in many overlapping organizations and institutions. Many Jews belong to more than one synagogue, not to speak of membership in a number of different Zionist or other organizations, besides contributing to the *magbit* or paying taxes to the Israeli government or whatever.

This is not simply a contemporary phenomenon; it was always true to a greater or lesser extent. Even in the small medieval community, Jews who were members of a common *kahal* were also members of different *hevrot*. They sought to express themselves through the *kahal* as a whole and through the special interests of the *hevrot*.

Given the amorphous nature of the community's boundaries and the absence of one comprehensive set of institutions or instruments of governance, this weaving of many nets serves to strengthen Jewish unity and make more intensive use of Jewish talent. Hence it is accepted as inevitable and necessary, in Israel and in the diaspora. There is every reason to believe that, like the congressional system, it is part and parcel of Jewish political culture.

Both these dimensions reflect how the Jewish polity is one of those that is built from the ground up, that is, from the smallest arena to the largest rather than vice versa. In this respect it is like the Swiss and American polities, whose origins were to be found in the *Landesgemeinde* and the town meeting, respectively, as well as in larger arenas. The result of this ground-up construction is that political life begins with all citizens expecting to participate as equals, an expectation that they retain even after larger arenas have been established, and which they seek to transfer to these larger arenas in some appropriate, if lessened, way. Like the Americans and the Swiss, the Jewish polity has had to maintain some kind of primary citizen involvement through appropriate mechanisms applied to its very different and unusual situation. The vulnerability of these systems to large scale public initiatives, whether in the form of demonstrations, as in the State of Israel, or in some other way, is a constant reminder of where the locus of power lies.

All this stands in sharp contrast to polities organized from the top down in which citizens do not expect to participate continuously but merely to be consulted, or to ratify, or to choose which elites will govern them—all of which leads to a different approach to representation. This is the difference between the parliamentary and the congressional systems, despite their external structural similarities. Parliaments developed in hierarchical polities to modify the control exercised by those on the top (usually monarchs) by requiring them to secure the approval of representatives of the people or the various estates of the realm before pursuing their policy ends; congressional systems developed from the bottom up or, more accurately, from smaller to larger arenas.[14]

Notes

1. This typology was first presented in Daniel J. Elazar, *Community and Polity: The Organizational Dynamics of American Jewry* (Philadelphia: Jewish Publication Society of America, 1976), chap. 8.

2. "Development of the American Synagogue," *Modern Judaism*, vol. 4, no. 3 (October 1984), pp. 255–73; W. Gunther Plaut, *The Growth of Reform Judaism* (New York: World Union for Progressive Judaism, Ltd., 1965); and Salo W. Baron, *The Jewish Community: Its History and Structure to the American Revolution*, 3 vols. (Philadelphia: Jewish Publication Society of America, 1942).

3. Charles S. Liebman and Eliezer Don-Yehiya, *Civil Religion in Israel: Traditional Religion and Political Culture in the Jewish State* (Berkeley: University of California Press, 1983); Jacob Katz, *Out of the Ghetto: The Social Background of Jewish Emancipation, 1770–1870* (Cambridge, Mass.: Harvard University Press, 1973); Raphael Mahler, *A History of Modern Jewry, 1780–1815* (New York: Schocken Books, 1972).

4. Liebman and Don-Yehiya, *Civil Religion in Israel* and *Religion and Politics in Israel* (Bloomington, Ind.: Indiana University Press, 1984); Gary Schiff, *Tradition and Politics: The Religious Parties of Israel* (Detroit: Wayne State University Press, 1977); David Vital, *The Origins of Zionism* (Oxford: Oxford University Press, 1975).

5. Berl Katznelson, "Revolution and Tradition," (1934) in Arthur Hertzberg, ed., *The Zionist Idea* (New York: Atheneum, 1981); David Ben-Gurion, *Rebirth and Destiny of Israel* (New York: Philosophical Library, 1954); Eliezer Don-Yehiya, "Hilon, Shlilah ve-Shiluv; Tfisot shel ha-Yahdut haMesorati ve-Musagahah be-Tzionut ha-Sococialisti," (Secularization, Negation, and Integration: Concept of Traditional Judaism in Zionist Socialism), *Kivunim*, no. 8 (August 1980), pp. 29–46 (Hebrew).

6. See S. Z. Abramov, *Perpetual Dilemma* (Rutherford, N.J.: Fairleigh Dickinson University Press, 1976); Liebman and Don-Yehiya, *Religion and Politics in Israel*.

7. S. N. Eisenstadt, *Israeli Society* (London: Weidenfeld and Nicolson, 1967); Yuval Elizur and Eliahu Salpeter, *Who Rules Israel?* (New York: Harper and Row, 1973).

8. Daniel J. Elazar with Douglas St. Angelo, "Cosmopolitans and Locals in Contemporary Community Politics," in *Proceedings of the Minnesota Academy of Science* (May 1964); Alvin W. Gouldner, "Cosmopolitans and Locals: Toward an Analysis of Latent Social Roles," *Administrative Science Quarterly* (1958), nos. 2, 3, 4; Robert K. Merton, *Social Theory and Social Structure*, 2d ed. (Glencoe, Ill.: The Free Press, 1957); Carle Zimmerman, *The Changing Community* (New York: Harper and Bros., 1938).

9. Dan Horowitz and Moshe Lissak, *The Origins of the Israeli Polity: Palestine under the Mandate* (Chicago: University of Chicago Press, 1978).

10. Stuart A. Cohen, *The Concept of the Three Ketarim*, Working Paper No. 18 of Workshop in the Covenant Ida and the Jewish Political Tradition (Ramat Gan and Jerusalem: Bar Ilan University, Department of Political Studies and Center for Jewish Community Studies, 1982).

11. See Daniel J. Elazar and Stuart A. Cohen, *The Jewish Polity: Jewish Political Organization from Biblical Times to the Present* (Bloomington, Ind.: Indiana University Press, 1985), pp. 258–303.

12. For example, the activities of Zalman Schachter and his associates, and advocates of restoration of the practice of circumcision of females.

13. For the definition of *congress*, see the Oxford English Dictionary. On forms of representative

government, see Edmund Burke, *A Letter to the Sheriffs of Bristol* (Cambridge: Cambridge University Press, 1936); Alfred de Grazia, *Public and Republic: Political Representation in America* (New York: Knopf, 1951) and *Apportionment and Representative Government* (New York: Praeger, 1963); John Stuart Mill, *Considerations on Representative Government* (New York: Liberal Arts Press, 1958); Carl J. Friedrich, *Man and His Government: An Empirical Theory of Politics* (New York: McGraw-Hill, 1963); Lewis Anthony Dexter, "The Representative and His District," *Human Organization,* no. 16, pp. 2–13; "Representation" in David Sillo, ed., *International Encyclopedia of the Social Sciences,* 18 vols. (New York: Macmillan, 1968–79), pp. 461–79.

14. A full examination of the representative institutions of the Jewish polity as examples of congressional government has not yet been undertaken. It is one of the many tasks ahead in the study of Jewish political institutions and behavior.

5

The Institutions of the Renewed Polity

First Steps toward Jewish Polity in Modern Times

A primary characteristic of the Emancipation era was the effort of Jews in the Western world to redefine themselves politically as citizens of their states, though of a different religious persuasion. With that came the effort by many to detach themselves from the common fate of fellow Jews. This effort received its strongest formal expression in the formulations of the Napoleonic Sanhedrin where Jews, under some duress, abjured any transnational ties. Nevertheless, the Jews were at least ambivalent about this aspect of their search for emancipation and citizenship as individuals. No longer comfortable speaking about their brethren as members of a common nation, English-speaking Jews in the nineteenth century coined the term *coreligionists,* a philological barbarism designed to reflect the persistance of ties but on a limited and careful basis.[1]

A change in name did not change reality, however; the common interests of Jews the world over did not disappear. Those interests intensified during the nineteenth century. Significantly, the attitude of the European nation-states, new or old, where most Jews lived, did not shift either. Despite their demands that "their" Jews become citizens or subjects on an individual basis, they still viewed the Jews as a separate group. Thus, the Congress of Vienna in 1815 addressed the "Jewish question" as part of its agenda; since then hardly any important international meeting has been without some Jewish issue before it.[2]

At first, the Jewish question was addressed without the direct involvement of the Jews themselves. This was not a situation that the Jews could tolerate. Even under conditions of emancipation and denationalization, they were not prepared to allow others the exclusive right to determine their interests and destiny. Moreover, not even all emancipated Jews had abandoned the sense of nationhood. It was precisely in the United Kingdom and the United States, where Jews were most free to become citizens on an individual basis, that many felt least constrained to abandon the sense that a Jewish nation existed. Early in the twentieth century, the term *peoplehood* came into use to provide a more acceptable expression of that sentiment.

The first Jewish political responses (as distinct from philanthropic ones) to trans-state Jewish problems were made through individual notables working quietly behind the scenes on behalf of Jewish interests—a revival in new form of *shtadlanut,* which had prevailed in medieval Europe. At the beginning of the nineteenth century the Board of Deputies of British Jews made representations to the British and foreign governments about the situation of Jews in other lands, but they were more symbolic than real until

112

the *shtadlanim* began acting with the board's blessing. The greatest Jewish *shtadlan* of the nineteenth century was Sir Moses Montefiore, but he was by no means the only one.

By and large, these *shtadlanim* were activated on behalf of Jewish brethren in lands not yet touched by emancipation or where promises of emancipation were not fulfilled, chiefly Eastern Europe and the eastern Mediterranean, plus North Africa. The first intervention to attract worldwide attention came in 1840 in the case of the Damascus blood libel. It was undertaken strictly by individual *shtadlanim,* but, significantly, the *shtadlanim* from the major western European countries found it in their interest to coordinate their work in what was perhaps the first modern *edah*-wide expression of Jewish political activity. The construction of the first housing outside the walls of the Old City of Jerusalem was a classic example of this trend. Montefiore of Great Britain was entrusted with money bequeathed by Judah Touro of the United States to be used for the Jewish poor of Eretz Israel. The result: Mishkenot Sha'ananim.

As the western European great powers became increasingly involved in the internal affairs of the Ottoman Empire, the Jewish notables capitalized on their positions in their respective powers (particularly Austria, France, Great Britain, and, later, Germany) to intervene on behalf of their brethren. Similarly, the Board of Deputies of American Israelites, founded in 1859, included among its purposes the defense of Jewish interests overseas. Nevertheless, even though it was the first countrywide Jewish body organized on democratic principles, its efforts were made meaningful (as much as they were) by quasi-*shtadlanic* methods. The offices of the United States government were used to obtain consular or ministerial appointments for American Jewish notables in countries where they had an interest in working for the improvement of the condition of the Jews. Thus armed with American government credentials, the notables could enhance their *shtadlanic* roles.[3]

Between the 1840s and the 1870s the number of problems requiring such joint action grew, or, at the least, the concern of the western Jewish communities with those problems expanded. As involvement increased and a pattern of response emerged, more institutionalized methods of handling the increased work load were introduced in the form of *shtadlanic* organizations. They also found it advantageous to cooperate with one another. In this way, interventions were regularly carried out in Russia, in Romania, the Ottoman Empire, and North Africa and in other countries as needed.

Shtadlanut was able to hold its own as long as the large body of Jews was not awakened politically. The emergence of the Zionist movement changed all that. Theodor Herzl's convening of the first Zionist Congress in 1897 marked a turning point in worldwide Jewish organization. Herzl transformed the basis of Jewish contacts with foreign powers and the character of the demands Jews made by the establishment of the World Zionist Organization. One of the principles of the Basel program was "the organization and uniting of the whole of Jewry, by means of appropriate institutions, both local and international," thus serving notice that the Jews were prepared to act as a body, organized democratically on a worldwide basis to achieve their political goals.

The Zionists were opposed by the notables and their organizations as much for ideological reasons as for any others. The notables were committed emancipationists and bitterly opposed to the revival of Jewish nationalism. For the remainder of that generation, the struggle between the two approaches continued, culminating in the victory of the Zionists during World War I in the course of the struggle over the Balfour Declaration.[4] After the end of that war, *shtadlanut,* even in its institutionalized form, receded into the background, and the field of worldwide Jewish activity was taken over by multicountry organizations with avowedly, if not exclusively, political goals. The basis for a worldwide Jewish polity was now in place.

In the interim, the first worldwide Jewish fraternal organization had also emerged, significantly, an American Jewish creation. The B'nai B'rith was founded in New York in 1843 as a modern expression of the Jewish desire to maintain communal bonds in a secular age. It rapidly spread to every part of the United States where Jews lived. In 1882, the first overseas lodge was founded in Germany and, by the turn of the century, even Eretz Israel had a lodge. In the United States, B'nai B'rith was a broad-based organization; in Europe and the Middle East it became an elite group. Until the end of the nineteenth century, its leaders also played local roles as *shtadlanim*. In some countries they still do. Subsequently, the international leadership became active in the world Jewish arena.[5]

The victory of the Zionists meant far more than the ultimate establishment of a Jewish State. It marked the reestablishment of a Jewish political consciousness, either willingly or reluctantly, and the reestablishment of a sense of Jewish peoplehood with all that this implied. The form of the Jewish polity today is the direct product of the Zionist victory; Jewish responsibilities to contemporary events are based on the "facts" that the Zionists established among the Jews and within the non-Jewish world.

The Forging of a New Jewish Polity in the Twentieth Century

While the beginnings of an institutionalized structure for world Jewry were developing, massive demographic changes were taking place in the Jewish world. The world Jewish population grew geometrically as the conditions under which the Jews lived improved. From an estimated 2.5 million in 1800, the number of Jews in the world increased to 10.5 million a century later and to 16.5 million in 1939.[6]

The Jews also began to evacuate what had been the major centers of Jewish life in the Old World and to establish new centers in the New World of the great European frontier, North and South America, South Africa and Australia, or in France and Great Britain—areas utterly peripheral to Jewish life for centuries. This process, which had become a flood by the end of the nineteenth century, was given additional impetus by World War I and the Russian Revolution. It received its final aspects as a result of World War II, the Holocaust, and the establishment of the State of Israel.

By the middle of the twentieth century, not a single Jewish area of settlement that had been prominent at the time of the American and French revolutions remained in the forefront of Jewish life, and hardly a single Jewish community remained undisturbed anywhere in the world. The eastern European Jewish centers were destroyed, either physically or socially. Even in the Soviet Union, most Jews were no longer located in the areas of traditional Jewish settlement. The establishment of the State of Israel effectively ended organized Jewish life in the Arab lands. Even the centers that had emerged in continental Europe in the nineteenth century were either physically destroyed or so reduced in numbers and morale as a result of the Holocaust that they were unable to play their earlier role. The United States had emerged as the largest Jewish community functioning as a unit under one government in all Jewish history. Most Jews of the world lived in English-speaking countries and had adopted English as their native language. Hebrew, the language of Israel and Israelis, had been restored to its premier place in

Jewish civilization. Yiddish, Ladino, and other diaspora Jewish languages survived as remnants, primarily in Latin America, Canada, and (paradoxically enough) Israel, rather than in the lands of their origin.

While this process was going on, new organizations had emerged to serve world Jewry.[7] The Americans contributed the Joint Distribution Committee (JDC). In 1929 the Jewish Agency was organized to unite world Jewry in the effort to rebuild Eretz Israel. In 1936 the World Jewish Congress (WJC) was organized, mostly by the Jewries of Europe, to try to protect Jewish rights in an age of growing Fascist anti-Semitism. From the beginning, these organizations developed areas of functional specialization, the first two by design and the last by virtue of its situation.

Crowning the creation of new centers and new organizations was the renewal of independent Jewish national existence in Eretz Israel within a politically sovereign state. As a state, Israel transformed all previous relationships among Jewish communities. A state, possessing political sovereignty with the powers and responsibilities that go with it, could not be treated simply as another Jewish community on the world scene. At the same time, because it had a relatively small percentage of the total number of Jews in the world (only in the 1970s did it become the second largest Jewish community, today approximately three-fifths the size of the largest), it could not become the sole voice of the Jewish people, either internally or externally, much as its leaders would have liked it to. Thus the blessings of statehood brought a new set of political problems for the Jewish people—good problems but problems nevertheless.

The first formal effort to define the role of the state as the spokesman for the Jewish people took the form of an exchange of letters between David Ben-Gurion, then Israel's prime minister, and Jacob Blaustein, then president of the American Jewish Committee, in 1950. The committee was at that time the leading *shtadlanic* organization in the United States and was known as non-Zionist. Following a modified version of the emancipationist ideology, Blaustein wanted to make it clear to the world and to the Israelis that Jews of the diaspora were citizens of their respective countries, owed no political allegiance to Israel, and did not see Israel as their political spokesman in Jewish affairs. Ben-Gurion, interested in strengthening Israel's alliance with the Jewish notables in the United States and not eager to start a war with them, more or less accepted Blaustein's terms and limited Israeli claims along those lines.

A generation later their correspondence reads like an anachronism, but it must be remembered that the first generation of leaders to face these problems was a product of the last generation of the nineteenth century when the struggle between the Zionists and the *shtadlanim* was at its height. Thus the understanding and assumptions they brought with them were those of a much earlier age. The Ben-Gurion-Blaustein agreement reflects the effort of two men of good will trying to come to grips with a new situation, but bound by their own experience and even the phraseology of an earlier age.[8]

What characterized the first two generations of the twentieth century, when this new Jewish polity was being forged, was growing collective political action on a wide variety of fronts, coupled with strenuous denials of its being political. Only now, in the second generation of Jewish statehood and postwar reconstruction, has a generation of Jewish leaders emerged whose formative experiences have taken place in this new context and who are able and willing to face up to it and its implications. This new generation is not afraid to talk about Jewish political interests and to make Israel the major subject on their political agenda.

The Six-Day War and the Yom Kippur War six and a half years later did much to end this dichotomy. If anything, the Jewish people in their numbers demonstrated how open they were to recognizing the political realities of the State of Israel and their attachment to it. Jews who in no overt way differed from their neighbors in their private lives were prepared to go into the streets in frankly political demonstrations for Israel. This marked a reversal of the emancipationist dictum of *Haskalah* poet Y. L. Gordon, "Be a Jew in your home and a man in the street"; Jews who no longer knew how to be Jews in their homes went into the streets to demonstrate their Jewish attachments.[9]

New Structures and Relationships

During and after World War II, other Israeli and American Jewish organizations and institutions also became involved in the world Jewish scene. The American Jewish Committee undertook to develop an international program of some scope after World War II. The B'nai B'rith and ADL expanded their operations outside the United States. The three American synagogue movements established worldwide associations. Israel, in the meantime, was busy establishing offices or tributary organizations to raise money to assist in the rebuilding of the land or to provide support in other ways. Thus, in the years between 1945 and 1955, a subsidiary network of worldwide organizations was developed, focusing either on the United States or Israel, but also involving Jewries in many other countries.[10] Table 5.1 catalogues the existing Jewish multicountry organizations.

The multiplication of organizations led to a concern for restructuring the institutional framework of the emerging Jewish polity to limit duplication and promote coordination. Some bodies, new and old, were working at cross purposes with one another, some in the pursuit of different goals, but many in the pursuit of the same ones. In a manner familiar to American Jews, the community relations organizations presented the biggest problem. The number of defenders of Jewish interests that came forward was such that, at times, the efforts at defense were jeopardized. For example, once the Jewish-Catholic rapprochement began, it became difficult for the Vatican to decide which among the many Jewish claimants to talk to. In time, a coordinating body was established to speak with a harmonious set of voices, if not a single voice.

In the aid-to-Israel sphere, the multiplicity of organizations seeking to assist the Jewish state also led to demands for coordination. As Israel began trying to assist the diaspora in strengthening Jewish life, it initially did so in a manner that paid little attention to the established framework within the various diaspora communities. The Israelis were called to task and demands for coordination were raised.

One possible focal point for coordination might have been the World Jewish Congress, but the Holocaust had destroyed whatever base it had by reducing the European Jewish communities to secondary or tertiary status on the Jewish map. Nahum Goldmann, the founder and leader of the WJC, remained the preeminent political figure in the diaspora. He was successful in coordinating efforts to secure German reparations through the World Conference on Material Claims against Germany (1951). Among its other activities, it entered into partnership with the JDC to assist in the rebuilding of Jewish life in Europe and with the Jewish Agency to assist in the rebuilding of Israel. Goldmann, recognizing the new limits on the WJC, took the lead in trying to stimulate a coordinating agency for those Jewish organizations involved in multicountry activities, out of which emerged the now defunct World Congress of Jewish Organizations (COJO) in 1958. At the time, this move was welcomed by the Jewish Agency, which underwent reconstitution itself to include non-Zionist and Zionist elements in 1970.[11]

At first, those advocating structural changes to reflect the new realities sought an overarching framework that would unite all bodies serving the Jewish people. This dream has never been abandoned in theory, but in practice the Jewish people has come to make do with a far looser structure, a number of separate "authorities" with specialized areas of activity loosely tied together through coordinating councils. The Claims Conference, the JDC, and the Jewish Agency are examples of such authorities.

This situation has developed pragmatically on a de facto basis. It has never been formally recognized or given any formal legitimacy by participants in or commentators on the world Jewish scene. Now, however, it is fair to suggest that for the indefinite future, world Jewry will be united only through the formal mechanisms of coordinating councils and the more important informal mechanism of overlapping leadership. Apparently the Jewish people does not seek a more comprehensive framework on a worldwide basis, particularly given the nature of contemporary Jewish life (most Jews are not even aware of the network that exists, even if they are interested in Jewish survival), while Jewish leadership is extremely wary of anything that gives rise to thoughts of the "elders of Zion." Moreover, the religious and ideological differences that divide Jewry prevent unity on anything other than a loose confederative basis.

The authorities that do exist and their coordinating organizations are dominated by Israel and American Jewry, sometimes by the one, sometimes by the other, and sometimes on a shared basis, depending on which authority is involved. The structure of the authorities is such that other Jewish communities are represented and even well represented, and the representatives of the stronger among them can play important roles.

Perhaps the major problem facing multicountry Jewish bodies other than the functional authorities is not how to coordinate activities among themselves in a better way but how to link themselves with the realities of Jewish life in a world in which most Jewish activity is carried on locally in a large number of communities. Even the countrywide organizations and institutions of most Jewries are weak except insofar as they confine their activities to purposes that require the concentration of a critical mass (e.g., fund-raising for Israel, representation before the government, support of a seminary, or a placement service providing assistance to localities seeking professional personnel) or serve, for all intents and purposes, one very large local community. If the countrywide bodies tend to be weak, the worldwide ones are no more than forums where leaders in their respective communities can regularly meet to exchange views, almost totally outside the awareness of the communities they purport to lead and with minimal effect on the activities or the quality of life within them.

The Constitutional Structure of the Edah[12]

Today's world Jewish polity comprises a network of single and multipurpose functional authorities, no single one of which encompasses the entire gamut of Jewish political interests, although several have attempted to do so. They include the following categories:

1. National institutions—for example, the Jewish Agency for Israel, World Zionist Organization, Jewish National Fund

2. Multicountry associations—for example, ORT, World Jewish Congress

3. Educational institutions under the auspices of the entire Jewish people—for example, the universities in Israel

Table 5.1

A Typology of Jewish Multicountry Associations

Name of Association	Service Religious	Service Education Culture	Service Welfare Community Organization	Political Rights	Political Ideology
Agudath Israel World Organization	X*				Y*
Alliance Israélite Universelle[1]		Y	Y	Y	
B'nai B'rith International Council		X	X		
Conference on Jewish Material Claims against Germany			X		
Consultative Council of Jewish Organizations				X	
European Council of Jewish Community Services		Y	Y		
International Conference of Jewish Communal Service			Y		
Jewish Agency for Israel	Y	X	X		Y
Jewish Colonization Association		X	X		
Maccabi World Union					
Memorial Foundation for Jewish Culture	Y	X			
Mizrachi World Union	X				Y
ORT (World ORT Union)		X			
OSE (Oeuvre de Secours aux Enfants)[2]			X		
Women's International Zionist Organization		X	X		Y
World Conference on Soviet Jewry[3]				X	
World Council of Synagogues	X				
World Federation of YMHAs and Jewish Community Centers			X		
World Jewish Congress				X	
World Sephardi Federation	Y	Y	X		X
World Union of Jewish Students		X			Y
World Union for Progressive Judaism	X				
World Zionist Organization		X			X
Zionist Youth Movements (Bnei Akiva, Habonim, etc.)		Y			X

*X = primary; Y = secondary.

[1] Although no longer multicountry by our criteria, the Alliance began its career in 1860 as the first "universal" Jewish association in modern times; it therefore deserves a place in this table.

[2] OSE is included because of its historic multicountry character; today, to all intents and purposes, it is a French organization.

[3] This is an ad hoc association with a single purpose. Unlike the more permanent multipurpose political associations, it has been able to enlist across-the-board participation.

Table 5.1—
Continued

Name of Association	Goals			Structure and Membership			Mode of Operation		
	Fraternal		Youth	Federative	Unitary	Individual Membership	Operational	Consultative	Distributive
	General	Special Interest	Sports						
Agudath Israel World Organization	X			X			X		
Alliance Israélite Universelle[1]					X		X		
B'nai B'rith International Council				X			Y	X	
Conference on Jewish Material Claims against Germany				X					X
Consultative Council of Jewish Organizations				X				X	
European Council of Jewish Community Services				X				X	
International Conference of Jewish Communal Service	X					X		X	
Jewish Agency for Israel				X			X		
Jewish Colonization Association					X				X
Maccabi World Union			X	X			X		
Memorial Foundation for Jewish Culture				X					X
Mizrachi World Union				X			X		
ORT (World ORT Union)				X			X		
OSE (Oeuvre de Secours aux Enfants)[2]					X		X		
Women's International Zionist Organization				X			X		
World Conference on Soviet Jewry[3]				X			Y	X	
World Council of Synagogues				X				X	
World Federation of YMHAs and Jewish Community Centers			X	X				X	
World Jewish Congress				X			X		
World Sephardi Federation		X		X			X		
World Union of Jewish Students		Y	X		X		X		
World Union for Progressive Judaism				X			Y	X	
World Zionist Organization				X			X	Y	
Zionist Youth Movements (Bnei Akiva, Habonim, etc.)		Y		X			X		

4. Organizations under local sponsorship whose sphere of activity is multi-country—for example, the Joint Distribution Committee

Ernest Stock has grouped the multicountry associations by their principal goals (a more inclusive list appears in table 5.1, pages 118–119):

Principal Goal Characteristics	*Organization*
Political–general purpose	World Zionist Organization
Political–special purpose	World Conference of Soviet Jewry
Distributive	Conference on Material Claims against Germany
Services–operational	World ORT Union
Services–coordinating	European Council of Jewish Communities
Religious	World Union for Progressive Judaism
	Agudath Israel World Organization
Association–fraternal	B'nai B'rith International Council
Association–special interest	World Sephardi Federation
	World Union of Jewish Students

Instruments of the Keter Malkhut

The most concrete manifestation of the shift to preeminence of the *keter malkhut* was the emergence of a coherent set of institutions for that domain on an *edah*-wide basis (fig. 5.1). Those institutions are increasingly tied together by a sense of common purpose, shared leadership, and programmatic collaboration. Most of them are outgrowths or continuations of the organizations that emerged toward the end of the previous generation, including such key or exemplary bodies as:

Jewish Agency for Israel. Originally established by the World Zionist Organization and selected non-Zionist community leaders in 1929 to represent world Jewry in mandated Palestine, the Jewish Agency (JAFI) became the principal governing body of the Jewish "state within a state" before 1948. With the establishment of the state, many of its original functions and most of its key people were transferred to the new government. For a while, it seemed as if the very existence of the agency as a separate organization was in doubt. It survived because of the convergence of two needs. Those who remained with the WZO wanted to keep it as their vehicle for political participation, and the United States tax laws required a nongovernment vehicle for channeling American money into Israeli development.

Its status as the arm of world Jewry was reaffirmed in 1952 through a covenant between the WZO and the State of Israel affirmed in a constitutional act of the Israeli Knesset. Its principal responsibility under the covenant was to handle the immigration and settlement of Jews into Israel.

Because it also remained entirely in the hands of the WZO, the agency's position was ambiguous to say the least. According to Zionist theory, the WZO spoke for the Jewish people, but in reality Zionist organizations in most diaspora communities were then already losing power and influence, thus making it impossible for them to speak for their communities. This was particularly true in the United States where the Zionist movement never achieved a power position that came close to the Zionist model and after 1948 rapidly lost whatever influence it had.

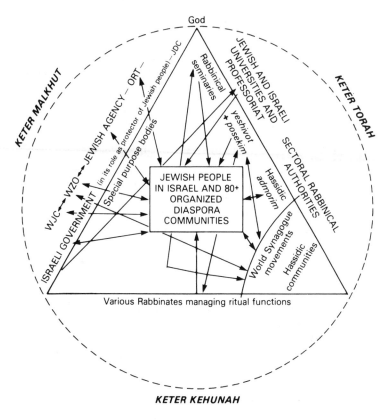

Figure 5.1.   Contemporary organization of the *edah*.

During the next fifteen years, the agency became rooted-in as part of the system of governance of the Jewish state while at the same time becoming more and more an arm of the state as its independence diminished. This led to dissatisfaction on the part of the diaspora contributors to the UJA and Keren Hayesod, which, in turn, stimulated the constitution of 1969–70 under the leadership of the late Louis Pincus and of Max Fisher. They saw the need to overcome the agency's problematic position and to give it a proper one in the constellation of the world Jewish polity as well as the State of Israel.

The reconstitution separated the WZO and agency and restructured the agency's governing organs so that the "non-Zionist" representatives of the diaspora communities through their fund-raising arms were included in them as equal partners. The change was formally marked by a second covenant between the agency and the state. The agency that emerged this time was not simply an instrumentality of the Israeli government, designed to achieve limited political and institutional ends; it was, at least potentially, an instrumentality of the Jewish people and a key element in the reemerging world Jewish polity.[13]

A new structure emerged from the reorganization. The Jewish Agency Assembly of more than four hundred members was established to be the basic sounding board and policy-making body, the Board of Governors of more than sixty members became the principal governing body, and the Executive the body handling day-to-day matters. As is always the case in parliamentary systems, the Executive became the body with the real power. The Board of Governors struggled valiantly to find a governance role for itself, inasmuch as its members were scattered over the world and could meet only a few times a year for brief periods. The assembly at best briefly reviewed policy matters but did not really find an effective role, something that generated much frustration for many diaspora members who wanted their participation in the assembly to be meaningful, especially because it came at substantial personal expense.

The Jewish Agency functions in education, housing, immigration, settlement, and urban rehabilitation, and provides social services. It remains closely tied to the WZO, which is, in many respects, its alter ego for work in the diaspora. More recently, the assembly has found its voice, the Board of Governors has found ways to effectively assert its authority, and the Executive has become more responsive to both.[14]

Because the Jewish Agency has become the principal forum for diaspora Jewry to participate in *edah*-wide activities and especially the common tasks of the Jewish people in Eretz Israel, its status and importance have risen rapidly since its reconstitution. It has become the major arena for the internal politics of the *edah* and has attracted many talented and effective diaspora leaders who come to it through a network of organizations— Zionist, fund-raising, and communal-welfare—of which it is rapidly becoming the nexus for *edah*-wide business. The expansion of its mandate in the early 1980s to include work in the diaspora to promote Jewish education and Aliya has been paralleled by the increase in diaspora community interest in its workings, which strengthens it further.

World Zionist Organization.[15] The WZO was founded at the first Zionist Congress (1897) to attain a "legally secured, publicly recognized national home for the Jewish people." That goal was reached when the Balfour Declaration became part of the League of Nations Mandate for Palestine (1922). Britain acknowledged the WZO as the "Jewish agency" charged with representing the world Jewish interest in the implementation of the Mandate. It transferred that status to the separately constituted Jewish Agency in 1929. The two merged again in the 1940s after the withdrawal of the non-Zionists from the Agency over the question of Jewish statehood. In 1971, when the Jewish Agency was reconstituted, the WZO resumed its independent status. The WZO retains a 50 percent partnership in the Jewish Agency, thereby preserving for itself a key—some would say dominant—role in the agency's work.

Today the WZO is charged with implementing the "Jerusalem Program" of 1968, which defines the aims of Zionism as "the unity of the Jewish people and the centrality of Israel in Jewish life; . . . the preservation of the identity of the Jewish people through the fostering of Jewish and Hebrew education and of Jewish spiritual and cultural values; (and) the protection of Jewish rights everywhere." This makes explicit the new role of the WZO as a diaspora-oriented body, though its original purpose had been to harness efforts of world Jewry for the Yishuv. In part, its functions are those that cannot be subsumed under the headings for which tax-exempt philanthropic money in the United States and elsewhere is contributed. For example, although agricultural settlement money for new immigrants is the domain of the Jewish Agency, the WZO finances and administers agricultural projects in the administered territories, because it is understood that the United States Internal Revenue Service does not want tax-exempt money to be used across the 1949 armistice lines.

Structurally, the WZO is a federation of ideological movements. Most of these constituent bodies have been linked with an Israeli counterpart since the development of the prestate Zionist party system. Increasingly, however, they imperfectly reflect the changes that have occurred in the Israeli party system. The World Confederation of General Zionists, for example, retains nomenclature that ceased to exist in Israel in the

1960s and is often referred to as the "nonparty party." In addition, there is a second tier of nonparty member organizations including the Women's International Zionist Organization (WIZO), the three worldwide synagogue movements, the World Maccabi Union, and the World Sephardi Federation, which have limited voting rights.

The WZO is governed by the World Zionist Congress, which, in theory, is an elected parliament. The more than six hundred seats in the congress, which meets every four years, are allocated geographically in the following proportions: 38 percent for Israel, 29 percent for the United States, and 33 percent for the other diaspora countries. In Israel, delegates are allocated to the Zionist political parties (that is, all except the Communist and exclusively Arab parties) in proportion to their representation in the Knesset. Each party then designates its delegates accordingly. The voting outside Israel is largely by party lists. In recent years, the parties in the various countries have negotiated the division of their country delegations roughly in proportion to their respective memberships, to avoid holding elections. This led to serious problems of credibility so, in 1986 the Zionist General Council voted to require actual elections as provided by the WZO constitution. Accordingly, elections were held for the 1987 Congress.

The Congress elects the Executive, in which the major parties are represented, and the General Council. The General Council meets once or twice a year between congresses. Governance of the WZO is in the hands of a wall-to-wall coalition on the principle that Zionist work is above party wars, with the chairmanship of the Executive and the Congress normally in the hands of the party at the head of the Israeli government at the time or a party in coalition with it.

The party composition of the Zionist movement long antedates the establishment of the state. Almost from its inception, the congresses were assemblies of parties as well as of delegates. Despite a widespread desire for structural changes after 1948, the WZO found it impossible to transcend the party structure, which undoubtedly reduced its effectiveness as a mass movement in the diaspora.

The WZO, as an *edah* instrumentality, never functioned as a representative body in Eretz Israel. After 1917, democratically elected parliamentary bodies were introduced to speak for the Jewish Yishuv. The Zionist parties contested with one another for seats in those bodies.

Periodically, attempts have been made to dilute the political character of the WZO by permitting individuals to affiliate directly with countrywide Zionist federations without first joining political groups and through the affiliations of the nonpolitical groups mentioned above as associate members. Full membership, however, remains reserved for the political groups while offices and rewards are distributed according to a modified party key.

In the federated structure that is the WZO, the influence of the Israeli center is greater than the sum of its parts. This is because the center represents Israel to the diaspora bodies: it originates programs, has a highly articulated bureaucracy, and allocates the financial resources. The status of the WZO in the diaspora is weakened by the lack of clarity about its tasks in the era of statehood. The effect of the late David Ben-Gurion's openly critical attitude toward the WZO has not yet worn off. The aims of the WZO are broad enough, and its apparatus wide-ranging enough, for it to assume the character of a conglomerate among multicountry Jewish organizations; but its party political structure sets limits to its acceptance on a broad popular basis.

World Jewish Congress.[16] The World Jewish Congress (WJC) has as its main purpose the defense of Jewish rights, and to that end it aims to be representative of the widest possible spectrum of world Jewry. It is an avowedly diaspora-oriented organization. Its specific activities in recent years have included intervention on behalf of Jews in Arab countries; pressure for the prosecution of Nazi war criminals and for indemnification payments to their victims; contacts with Christian church bodies on questions of Israel and anti-Semitism; cultural assistance to small Jewish communities; relations with international organizations, including the International Committee of the Red Cross, the Organization of American States, and the Council of Europe; espousal of the cause of Soviet Jewry; maintaining Jewish contacts with the Third World; and support of Israel in its diplomatic struggles.

Like the WZO, the World Jewish Congress has a federative structure. In theory it is a confederation of countrywide representative community bodies, with the general body deliberately limiting itself in scope. The members—independent community organizations—are free to determine their own policies locally. The WJC's constitution prohibits it from operating or speaking in a country unless its local constituents agree, except where no organized community exists or where a community cannot freely express its will.

On the other hand, the WJC may set up branches in countries without representative organizations or where the leading groups are unwilling to participate. Thus, when the Board of Deputies of British Jews refused to affiliate, the WJC established a British Section. In the United States, the American Jewish Congress initially functioned as the American arm of the WJC. When differences arose between the two groups, the WJC established a North American Section, which has recently begun to enroll rabbinical and congregational associations as affiliates. Conversely, the Canadian Jewish Congress and DAIA (the representative organization of Argentine Jewry) are, as representative organizations, directly affiliated with the WJC.

The WJC Executive works through four regional branches, each with its constitution—in North America, South America, Europe, and Israel—that mediate between the parent body and affiliates. The European branch, which operates primarily in western Europe, also maintains ties with community organizations in the Communist bloc. The Israeli branch does not have constituent organizations. Composed in keeping with the ubiquitous party key, its eighteen members are drawn from the spectrum of parliamentary parties.

Because its members are organizations, the number of individuals actually associated with the WJC is small. Some 400 to 500 delegates attend the quadrennial assemblies. Between assemblies, an executive committee of 120 meets annually, to which every member organization sends at least one delegate. There are also a governing council of 35, a secretary-general in Geneva, and a director-general in New York, since 1981 the center of its governance. Its cultural department is headquartered in Israel, its political department in Paris, and its policy research institute is in London. Among the members of the governing council is a strong contingent of prominent rabbis and diaspora Zionist leaders.

The WJC has complemented the WZO in areas where the latter could not operate, but it has also been the WZO's potential rival. For this reason, the Zionist leadership's attitude toward the WJC has always been one of ambivalence. In the 1930s, Dr. Chaim Weizmann, as the WZO president, stayed away from the founding assembly of the WJC, persisting in his resolve to avoid diaspora Jewish politics. Although most of the Zionist Congress voted to designate the WJC as the most suitable instrument for the protection of Jewish rights, thereby ensuring WZO representation in (and in recent years subsidization of) the WJC, the concern that diaspora interests might compete with those of the Yishuv was never far submerged and has surfaced again in the era of the state. The notion of an organization representing world Jewry which might hold a position independent of Israel has little appeal to the state's policymakers.

A second, equally substantial element in the inability of the WJC to become the representative organization of world Jewry was the unwillingness of the major Jewish organizations in the United States and Britain to become part of the WJC structure. The real bases of the WJC are in Latin America and Europe. It may well be the dominant regional Jewish organization in Latin America, but that region is not strong enough on the world Jewish scene to be a real power base. The diminution of Europe's strength after the Holocaust, coupled with the emergence of the European Council of Jewish Community Services as an increasingly important regional force, has weakened the role of the WJC on that continent. Finally, the dominance of the WJC by Nahum Goldmann and his coterie of supporters for the entire postwar generation weakened the organization internally by discouraging new leadership and externally by making Goldmann's agenda—and quarrels—its own.

Conference on Jewish Material Claims against Germany.[17] The Conference on Jewish Material Claims against Germany (Claims Conference) is a model of an effective, special purpose, multicountry association. It was formed to undertake two tasks: to press (in conjunction with the government of Israel) Jewish claims against Germany and to distribute the funds received among eligible beneficiaries. The conference was established in 1951 on the initiative of the Israeli government and the WZO-Jewish Agency and with the assistance of the WJC. Twenty-two organizations from the United States, England, Canada, Australia, South Africa, France, and Argentina participated. Protracted negotiations led to separate agreements by the German Federal Republic with Israel and with the Claims Conference.

In its distributive phase there was remarkable consensus among the many divergent organizational interests represented—this despite strong ideological opposition to the idea of accepting payments from Germany, which only gradually receded. The success of the Claims Conference in both its diplomatic and distributive tasks can be attributed to the following factors:

1. Its representative character
2. Its clearly delimited goal
3. The challenge of bona fide diplomatic activity with two sovereign states in place of the lobbying and shadowboxing that is normally the lot of nonsovereign entities
4. The opportunity to be a full-fledged partner of Israel in the negotiations
5. The high caliber of the negotiators
6. The early agreement on criteria and priorities for the distribution of money
7. The utilization of established facilities rather than becoming an operating agency or creating new instrumentalities

The Claims Conference ended its active role in 1965 with the fulfillment of its goal. Its formal existence is maintained for the performance of certain limited, ongoing tasks. Among these are monitoring the implementation of German legislation on restitution; pressing for further legislation, especially in East Germany; administering a fund for former community leaders; and supporting non-Jews who had helped rescue Jews and who are in financial difficulty.

By 1965 the Claims Conference had allocated $110 million, of which three-fourths was applied to the relief, rehabilitation, and resettlement of Nazi victims outside Israel and the rest used mainly for cultural and educational reconstruction. Grants were made to some 250 Jewish communities and institutions in thirty countries, primarily in Europe, and for research and publications by authors who were Nazi victims. Institutions for the commemoration of the Holocaust were also beneficiaries.

Memorial Foundation for Jewish Culture.[18] In 1964 the Claims Conference established the Memorial Foundation for Jewish Culture to serve as a living memorial to the six million who perished in the Holocaust and transferred to it the funds that had remained after German payments ceased. This base endowment of about $10 million was augmented by additional amounts in subsequent years, so that the foundation has been able to distribute about $1.25 million annually. The Memorial Foundation maintains quite an elaborate apparatus for the implementation of a financially modest program. It has forty-seven member organizations, each of which sends three representatives to the board of directors. Eighteen organizations are of the multicountry type (thirteen have "World" in their names) and twenty-nine are territorial, the latter including five academic and cultural groups in Israel. Thus the Memorial Foundation is even more inclusive than the Claims Conference. Like the latter, it has a small professional staff, whose job consists mainly of sifting applications for support (these amount to several times the available financing) and making recommendations for allocations to the board and the 25-member executive committee.

World ORT Union.[19] The World ORT Union is a service agency that is multicountry in all aspects: functional, administrative, and financial. ORT now trains Jews and others in sophisticated technological specialties. Operations are conducted in twenty-four countries, and more than 100,000 students are enrolled in vocational training courses of a wide variety, making ORT the largest nongovernmental system of vocational education in the world. ORT also conducts training programs in Third World countries, sponsored and financed by the United States foreign aid program, the Swiss foreign ministry, and by various international institutions, primarily the World Bank.

Its major center of activity is Israel, with an enrollment of some sixty thousand. Other programs are in Iran, Ethiopia, Morocco, and India; in Argentina, Venezuela, and Uruguay; in France, Italy, and the United States.

The World ORT Union, seated in Geneva, is a federation of autonomous national organizations, constituted as an association according to the Swiss civil code. It provides its local affiliates with financial subsidies, training of personnel, and overall planning. The union is governed by a congress meeting every six years, to which member organizations send elected delegates. A central committee of 150 meets between congresses; it elects an executive committee of twenty to forty members, which convenes biennially. The president of the World ORT Union is an American, as is its executive director; the executive chairman is French. In the lower administrative echelons, the staff is multinational.

The World ORT is an effective multicountry body because:

1. It is a single-purpose organization that has been able to adapt its program to changing circumstances and requirements.

2. Its nonpolitical nature has assured its entry and acceptance in nonwestern countries, especially in the Moslem world. (Operations in eastern Europe, which continued in the postwar period, have since been phased out.)

3. Its major emphasis has shifted to Israel, making a substantial contribution to filling that country's need for technically trained people.

4. In its training program, ORT has maintained professional standards that have given it international recognition.

5. In its financing, it has combined local support for local programs, inter-*edah* allocations (in the United States through the JDC), and non-Jewish financing.

6. It accomplished a shift in leadership from eastern Europe to the United States and by that succeeded in selling the ORT idea to the American Jewish public and becoming a beneficiary of federated fund-raising in the United States.

7. Its federal structure makes possible participation by representatives from all its multicountry membership and provides a forum for bridging differences in approach.

Joint Distribution Committee.[20] A major share of multicountry activity in education, welfare, and community organization is performed by organizations sponsored by individual countrywide communities. Outstanding among them is the American Jewish Joint Distribution Committee (JDC), the chief overseas welfare agency of American Jewry and one of the two partners in the United Jewish Appeal. Although sponsored and governed by American Jews, its staff is multicountry and its range of operations is probably greater than that of any other Jewish body.

The JDC organizes and finances rescue, relief, and rehabilitation programs for imperiled and needy Jews throughout the world; conducts a wide range of health, welfare, education, and rehabilitation programs; and provides aid to cultural and religious institutions. It serves some 430,000 Jews in twenty-five countries, including Israel. It contributes financially to the support of many other Jewish organizations, and it works with most of the other *edah* bodies in the fulfillment of its mission. Its headquarters are in New York, with regional headquarters in Paris and Jerusalem.

The evolution of the JDC since its founding in 1914 reflects the transformations that have taken place in Jewish life in the twentieth century. Its beginnings were in ad hoc relief, an American Jewish response to World War I, the first of the great crises to bring disaster to Jews in the twentieth century. As such, it became the embodiment of Jewish unity when under siege, as American Jews from all the ideological camps—Socialist, Orthodox, and Progressive—found a way to join with one another despite their great ideological differences to provide relief and rescue for fellow Jews.

After the war's end, the Russian Revolution and the various eastern European regional wars created new needs, and the JDC was institutionalized as a permanent instrument for American Jewish relief efforts. It became a classic emancipationist institution, committed to enabling and even encouraging Jews to find their way within the countries in which they were located. In part, this was an American Jewish response to the severe limitations placed on immigration to the United States, but it is of great significance that effectively the response was anti-Zionist.

This orientation did not change until the impact of Nazism became apparent and the JDC had to reevaluate its stance. Even so, not until the takeover of the eastern European countries by Soviet-sponsored Communist regimes that sooner or later expelled the JDC, charging it with being a foreign agent, did the "Joint" truly shift its orientation. At approximately the same time, early in the 1950s, Ben-Gurion persuaded the JDC to undertake major responsibilities for the relief of the elderly and chronically ill refugees who had come to Israel as part of the mass immigration in the years immediately following the establishment of the state. This brought the "Joint" to Israel in a major way. Since then, there has been a consistent expansion of the JDC role in the Jewish state, most recently moving from relief, rehabilitation, and institutional support to concerns such as the improvement of civic life and local government in Israel.

In the meantime, the major thrust of the JDC relief activities outside Israel was shifted to the remnant Jewish communities in the Islamic world. In addition, the JDC played a major role in rebuilding European Jewry in the aftermath of World War II and continues to play a significant, if reduced, role in encouraging European Jews to strengthen their Jewish institutions. The JDC also returned to eastern Europe during a thaw in the cold war and continues its work there in a low-key way.

The JDC is held in high respect within the Jewish world and has succeeded in penetrating into places where Jewish institutions are usually forbidden or severely limited. Its success stems from its constant striving to be a professional rescue and relief organization, nonpolitical, and dedicated to maintain as low a profile as needed to achieve its tasks.

Alliance Israélite Universelle.[21] The France-based Alliance Israélite Universelle has an illustrious record of establishing educational institutions in the Moslem world. With the demise of Jewish communities in those countries and shift in the locus of Jewish life from the Francophone and Anglophone communities, it declined on the world scene although it continues to do important work in Israel.

By keeping a low profile, the Alliance has managed to maintain schools in those Arab and Islamic countries where Jews are severely restricted or even persecuted. In this it has no doubt enjoyed support from the French government, which tends to maintain close ties with those regimes. Most recently it has tried to stimulate an institutional revival through serving Jews from North Africa and western Asia who have settled in France, providing them with educational institutions and assistance for existing institutions, particularly through its teachers seminary.

Like the JDC, the Alliance is a living witness to the change that has taken place in Jewish thinking about emancipation and nationhood. Alliance schools were originally known for their emancipationist and assimilationist orientation. In many cases, their effect was to weaken Jewishness in the name of modernization.[22] Now its major activities are in Israel where its most successful new project has been the sponsorship of a teachers seminary linked with the Hebrew University, designed to train teachers for Jewish subjects in Israeli nonreligious schools in such a way that the curriculum of those schools will be more Jewishly informed.

European Council of Jewish Community Services.[23] The most recently established multicountry aasociation of consequence is the European Council of Jewish Community Services, a regional body serving as a forum for European Jewry. Its membership includes some seventy communities in eighteen European countries. The council is the successor to the Standing Conference of European Jewish Communities, which was organized by the JDC in the 1950s. Its purpose was to stem the slow disintegration of Jewish life in postwar Europe and to help the communities transcend their local preoccupations in the search for common solutions. When the conference was transformed into the council, its offices were moved to Paris and a French communal worker was appointed as secretary general in place of a JDC staff member, completing the organization's "Europeanization." (As a sign of the times, English is the predominant language, and the council's publication, *Exchange,* is in English.)

The turning point in the council's role from a liaison body into a larger multicountry Jewish organization came in May 1972. At a meeting in Berlin, its governing assembly adopted a five-year program, which provided for commissions on fund-raising, young leadership training, and social services, and activated a Europe-wide community center association. In scope and functions, the European Council is similar to the Council of Jewish Federations (CJF) in the United States and maintains consultative contact with its American counterpart.

Government of Israel. The government of the State of Israel now acts as a principal defender of the physical welfare of the Jewish people under certain circumstances (for example, dealing with Nazi war criminals and terrorists) and maintains that it does so in the name of the *edah.* Thus, the security forces of Israel sometimes defend all Jews, the Knesset of Israel plays a major role in defining their status as Jews, and the prime minister or president sometimes speaks in their name.

Instruments of the Keter Torah and Keter Kehunah

Because the new pluralism in Jewish life has generated differing interpretations of the Torah-as-constitution, the *keter torah* is organized on clearly sectoral lines. Within it, older institutions and officers continue to serve various segments of the *edah* in more or less traditional ways. At the same time, others have changed and new institutions have emerged to serve other groups in new ways and to maintain traditional patterns.

Outstanding among the survivors from the previous epoch are a limited number of *posekim* (*halakhic* decisions) with *edah*-wide influence in their own camp and some similarly placed *yeshivot.* The chief *posekim* of the ultra-Orthodox are organized in the Moetzet Gedolei haTorah (Council of Torah Greats). Hassidic groups, whose centers are now transplanted either to Israel or to the United States, also survive (although their principal officer is now usually a *rebbe,* not a *tzaddik*). Conspicuous among those groups are the Chabad (Lubavitcher) Hassidim, one of the few Hassidic sects that attempts to reach out to the *edah.* More recently, a Sephardic Moetzet Hakhmei haTorah (Council of Torah Sages) has emerged, comprising leading *posekim* in the Sephardic world.

Non-Orthodox representatives of this *keter* are found primarily in or around seminaries of their movements, reflecting the combination of rabbinical and professorial status that marks the effort of the non-Orthodox to combine modern and traditional form. Because the Reform movement is much less oriented to the concept of the *keter torah* than the Conservative, this phenomenon is more pronounced among the latter. In recent years, both movements have been given increasing emphasis to the rule of their rabbinical associations in deciding issues of Jewish law and custom.

Prominent among the new institutions in this *keter* are the professors of Jewish studies at Israeli and other universities who have acquired status as constitutional commentators and guides. These, and others drawn from the intellectual community, address themselves to Jewish concerns in an academic fashion; in so doing they lay the groundwork for new interpretations of the Torah-as-constitution.

The domain of the *keter kehunah* embraces various rabbinates and synagogue bodies that are occupied with ritual functions and their management. Some instruments of this *keter* have become more highly organized than at any time since the destruction of the Second Temple. The world synagogue movements and the organized rabbinates in the United Kingdom and Israel are outstanding examples. The rabbinates are important because they provide examples of how *medinah*-based instruments of this *keter* now attempt to perform an *edah*-wide function. For example, the Israeli chief rabbinate provides direct services for some small communities (e.g., Iran, India) as does the United Kingdom rabbinate of the United Synagogue for some communities in countries that once were part of the British Empire. The World Council of Synagogues (Conservative, established 1957) and the World Union for Progressive Judaism (Reform, established 1926) are associations of countrywide congregational bodies.

Countrywide Communities within the Edah[24]

As an independent state with a Jewish majority, where Jewish culture is dominant, Israel stands in a class by itself. In the diaspora, American Jewry is the only community which, along with Israel, can function fully as Jewish community, self-sufficient in its Jewish resources; more than that, it adds significantly to the sum of Jewish civilization in its own community and beyond. Without entering into the normative argument of Israel's centrality in Jewish life, empirically it must be understood that Israel and the American Jewish community are the strong centers of Jewish activity today. There are those who would argue that the six million Jews in the United States are not as culturally creative or as Jewishly aware as the three and a half million in Israel; however, nobody who knows the American Jewish community can deny that it plays a role in contemporary Jewish life and in Jewish history that goes far beyond simply sustaining Jewish existence.[25]

Ranking below Israel and American Jewry is a second category of diaspora communities. It comprises the communities that are potentially self-sufficient Jewishly but whose power to add to the sum total of Jewish civilization is limited to what they can do within their own borders except for periodic contributions by a few exceptional institutions or individuals. They can create and maintain institutions, even produce their own leaders, but their influence rarely extends beyond their own jurisdictions. These self-sufficient communities include the Jewries of France, Great Britain, Canada, and perhaps South Africa and Argentina. As self-sufficient communities, they can contribute to the overall work of world Jewry and demand a voice in matters affecting world Jewry. (Argentina is included in this category although a combination of local circumstances had made it less than self-sufficient in the recent past.)

A third category comprises Jewish communities that, with some assistance from the outside (for example, they usually must import rabbis and Hebrew teachers), can maintain a viable Jewish life for their members. These communities may not be in danger of disappearing but are not likely to play significant roles on the world Jewish scene. There are many such communities. Typical of them are Australia, Brazil, and Switzerland.

A fourth category comprises communities with small Jewish populations that, despite their organizational integrity, are in constant danger of disappearing because of assimilation or emigration. These communities possibly have the means of those in the third category so far as they are sufficiently well organized to maintain their viability, but the combination of their small populations and the openness of the host environment works to reduce their chances of survival. The Scandinavian communities exemplify this group.

Most recently there has grown a fifth category comprising communities that may be termed protectorates of Israel and American Jewry. These communities maintain their internal institutions but are dependent on either one or both of the two great centers, not only for sustenance of their Jewish life but also for direct guidance and even programmatic activity to sustain them. The first four categories of communities can be found throughout Jewish history. It is unclear whether the fifth category is a new one or whether it simply represents the reemergence of a phenomenon that has existed in the Jewish past. For our purposes, however, it can be treated as a new phenomenon, a product of twentieth-century upheavals with hardly an echo before World War I.

Postwar Iran is a classic example of such a protectorate,[26] especially before the Khomeini revolution. Then a Jewish community of 80,000, it had the means, in principle, to be viable with a minimum of public assistance. The character of Iranian Jewry, however, led them to rely heavily on the Israeli ambassador to guide their internal decision making, on Israeli teachers to provide Jewish education in their schools, and on the American Joint Distribution Committee and Otzar Hatorah and the Alliance to maintain the schools and the community's social welfare institutions and to provide organizational guidance for the community. Although the community was not always willing to acknowledge its protectorate status, it was reaffirmed well-nigh daily. In a different way, Soviet Jewry is also a protectorate, unable to operate legitimately as a community under Soviet rule. As much as there is any kind of organized Jewish life, it is dependent on the work of Israeli and American Jews in tandem with local activists, whether Zionists or Hassidim.[27]

Protectorates are indigenous Jewish communities whose direction and principal activities have passed to outsiders from the major centers. Another category of community comprises colonies, planted by Jews from the major centers. Both Israeli and American Jewries have developed colonies in the postwar period, principally in Asia and Africa but also to a limited extent in the Caribbean. Israelis have done so primarily in connection with their missions for the Israeli government or private companies. Where they are present in sufficient numbers, they have created replicas of Israeli schools to serve their children's needs and other institutions on a modest scale to serve their own. American Jews have done so primarily as a result of American military activities in the aftermath of World War II. Where American forces have been stationed long enough to attract Jews with military and civilian occupations, they have created communities. The Jewish communities in Japan, Okinawa, and Thailand are examples. These communities are small, do not count for much on the world Jewish scene, and may well be temporary, as some have already proved to be.[28]

Finally, there is a category of communities in dissolution, generally outside the orbit of world Jewry for reasons peculiar to their internal situations. At best, they are protected from time to time by other Jewries, almost in the manner of the nineteenth century, through sporadic intervention often by way of third parties. These are primarily communities in eastern Europe and the Arab countries.

Notes

1. *The Oxford English Dictionary* indicates that this neologism was first used in 1842.

2. See Charles S. Liebman, *On the Study of International Jewish Political Organizations* (Jerusalem: Center for Jewish Community Studies, 1978) and Mala Tabory and Charles S. Liebman, *The Study of International Jewish Activity: An Annotated Bibliography* (Ramat Gan: Bar Ilan University Department of Political Studies, 1986).

3. For a superb case study of one such example, see Lloyd Gartner, "Roumania, America, and World Jewry: Consul Peixotto in Bucharest, 1870–1876," *American Jewish Historical Quarterly*, vol. 28, no. 1 (September 1968), pp. 25–117.

4. See, for example, Stuart Cohen, "The Conquest of a Community? The Zionists and the Board of Deputies in 1917," *Jewish Journal of Sociology*, vol. 19, no. 2 (December 1977), pp. 157–84. (Reprinted by the Center for Jewish Community Studies, 1978.) For the Zionist war on *shtadlanut*, see Charles S. Liebman, "Diaspora Influence on Israel: The Ben-Gurion–Blaustein Exchange and Its Aftermath," *Jewish Social Studies*, vol. 36, nos. 3–4 (July–October 1974), pp. 271–80. (Reprinted by the Center for Jewish Community Studies, 1978.)

5. Paul Goodman, *B'nai B'rith: The First Lodge of England 1910–1935* (London: published by the Lodge, 1936); Walter M. Schwab, *B'nai B'rith: The First Lodge of England—A Record of Fifty Years* (London: O. Wolff, 1960); E. E. Grusd, *B'nai B'rith: The Story of a Covenant* (New York: Appleton-Century, 1966); M.

Bisgyer, *Challenge and Encounter: Behind the Scenes in the Struggle for Jewish Survival* (New York: Crown Publishers, 1967); Itzhak Alfassi, ed., *Misdar B'nai B'rith be-Yisrael* (B'nai B'rith Order in Israel) (Tel Aviv: B'nai B'rith in Israel, 1966) (Hebrew); Deborah Dash Moore, *B'nai B'rith and the Challenge of Ethnic Leadership* (Albany: State University of New York Press, 1981).

    6. Estimates of Arthur Ruppin in the *American Jewish Year Book* as presented in Raphal Patai, *Tents of Jacob* (Englewood Cliffs, N.J.: Prentice-Hall, 1971), p. 79.

    7. The two best sources of multicountry Jewish organizations are Ernest Stock, "Jewish Multicountry Associations," *American Jewish Year Book 1974–75*, vol. 75, pp. 571–97 and Josef J. Lador-Lederer, "World Jewish Associations," *Encyclopedia Judaica Yearbook 1973* (Jerusalem: Keter, 1973), pp. 351–56.

    8. See Liebman, "Diaspora Influence on Israel."

    9. Daniel J. Elazar, "The United States of America: Overview," in Moshe Davis, ed., *The Yom Kippur War, Israel, and the Jewish People* (New York: Arno Press, 1974), pp. 1–35.

    10. For a running account of developments on this front, see the *American Jewish Year Book,* published annually by the American Jewish Committee and the Jewish Publication Society of America.

    11. See Ernest Stock, "The Reconstitution of the Jewish Agency," *American Jewish Year Book 1972,* vol. 73, pp. 178–93; and Charles S. Liebman, "Does the Diaspora Influence Israel? The Case of the Reconstituted Jewish Agency," *Forum,* no. 23 (spring 1975), pp. 18–30. Both articles have been reprinted by the Center for Jewish Community Studies, 1978.

    12. For a more detailed review, see Stock, "Jewish Multicountry Associations" and Daniel J. Elazar and Stuart A. Cohen, *The Jewish Polity: Jewish Political Organization from Biblical Times to the Present* (Bloomington, Ind.: Indiana University Press, 1985), pp. 258–303.

    13. Zelig Chinitz, *A Common Agenda: The Reconstitution of the Jewish Agency for Israel* (Jerusalem: Jerusalem Center for Public Affairs, 1985); Stock, "The Reconstitution of the Jewish Agency," pp. 187–88; and Liebman, "Does the Diaspora Influence Israel?"

    14. Daniel J. Elazar and Alysa M. Dortort, eds., *Understanding the Jewish Agency: A Handbook* (Jerusalem: Jerusalem Center for Public Affairs, 1984).

    15. Zionist General Council, *Addresses, Debates, Resolutions, June–July 1978* (Jerusalem: The Zionist Executive, Organization and Information Department, 1978); "Caesarea Crossroads," *Forum,* no. 41 (spring/summer 1981), pp. 1–52; Joseph Heller, *The Zionist Idea* (New York: Schocken Books, 1949); David Vital, *Zionism: The Formative Years* (Oxford: Clarendon Press, 1982); Chaim Weizmann, *Trial and Error: The Autobiography of Chaim Weizmann* (New York: Harper and Row, 1949); The World Zionist Organization, the Organization and Information Department, *The World Zionist Organization* (Jerusalem, 1972); and Stock, "Jewish Multicountry Associations."

    16. On the World Jewish Congress, see Nahum Goldmann, *The Autobiography of Nahum Goldmann,* trans. Helen Sebba (New York: Holt, Rinehart and Winston, 1969); Lador-Lederer, "World Jewish Associations"; Stock, "Jewish Multicultural Associations"; Melvin I. Urofsky, *A Voice That Spoke for Justice: The Life and Times of Stephen S. Wise* (Albany: State University of New York Press, 1982); George Garai, ed., *Four Years in Action: A Record of the World Jewish Congress, 1936–1976* (Geneva: World Jewish Congress, n.d.).

    17. On the Claims Conference, see Stock, "Jewish Multicountry Associations"; "Conference on Jewish Material Claims against Germany," *Encyclopedia Judaica,* vol. 5, pp. 872–73; Conference on Jewish Material Claims against Germany, *Five Years Later: Activities . . . 1954–1958* (New York: Conference on Jewish Material Claims against Germany, 1959); and Lucy S. Davidowicz, "Conference on Jewish Material Claims against Germany," *American Jewish Year Book 1953,* vol. 54, pp. 471–85 and *American Jewish Year Book 1960,* vol. 61, pp. 110–27. Also see Annual Reports of Conference on Jewish Material Claims against Germany (1954–).

    18. On the Memorial Foundation, see Stock, "Jewish Multicountry Associations" and Memorial Foundation for Jewish Culture, *Study Documents—Meeting of Board of Trustees,* presented at biennial meeting of Board of Trustees, July 23–26, 1984 (New York: Memorial Foundation for Jewish Culture, 1984). Also see annual volume of the *American Jewish Year Book.*

    19. On ORT, see *Eighty Years of ORT,* Historical Materials, Documents, and Reports (Geneva: World ORT Union, 1960); Jack Rader, *By the Skill of Their Hands: The Story of ORT,* rev. ed. (Geneva: World ORT Union, 1965); Leon Shapiro, *The History of ORT* (New York: Schocken Books, 1980).

    20. There are several histories of the JDC, including Herbert Agar, *The Saving Remnant: An Account of Jewish Survival* (New York: Viking Press, 1960) and Yehuda Bauer, *My Brother's Keeper: A History of the American Jewish Joint Distribution Committee, 1929–1939* (Philadelphia: Jewish Publication Society of America, 1974). See also Daniel J. Elazar, "Israel, American Jewry, and the Re-Emergence of a World Jewish Polity," in *Annual of Bar Ilan University Studies in Judaica and the Humanities 16–17* (Ramat Gan: Bar Ilan University, 1979), pp. 89–126.

21. On the Alliance Israélite Universelle, see Phyllis Cohen Albert, *The Modernization of French Jewry: Consistory and Community in the Nineteenth Century* (Waltham, Mass.: Brandeis University Press, 1977); Paula Hyman, *From Dreyfus to Vichy: The Remaking of French Jewry,* 1906–1939 (New York: Columbia University Press, 1979); Michael M. Laskier, "The Alliance Israélite Universelle and the Struggle for the Recognition within Moroccan Jewish Society: 1862–1912," in Issachar Ben-Ami, ed., *The Sephardi and Oriental Jewish Heritage Studies* (Jerusalem: The Magnes Press, 1982); André Chouraqui, *Cent ans d'histoire l'alliance israélite universelle et la renaissance juive contemporaire, 1860–1960* (Paris: Presses Universitaires de France, 1965); and Alliance Israélite Universelle, *Les droits de l'homme et l'éducation* (Paris: Presses Universitaires de France, 1961).

22. See, for example, Mair José Bernadette, *Hispanic Culture and Character of Sephardic Jews,* 2d ed. (New York: Hermon, 1981).

23. On the ECJCS, see Daniel J. Elazar, "The New Agenda of European Jewry," *Jerusalem Letter/ Viewpoints,* no. 35 (October 17, 1984); Liebman, *On the Study of International Jewish Political Organizations;* Ernest Stock, "The Emerging European Jewish Community Structure," *Jerusalem Letter,* no. 46 (March 14, 1982) and "Jewish Multicountry Associations."

24. All these communities are discussed in depth in Part 2 of this work; hence documentation of this section is confined to specific cases.

25. The case for American Jewry is fully stated in Steven M. Cohen, *American Modernity and Jewish Identity* (New York: Tavistock Press, 1983); Chaim I. Waxman, *America's Jews in Transition* (Philadelphia: Temple University Press, 1983); Arnold M. Eisen, *The Chosen People in America* (Bloomington, Ind.: Indiana University Press, 1983); Henry L. Feingold, *A Midrash on American Jewish History* (Albany, N.Y.: State University of New York Press, 1982); Charles Silberman, *A Certain People.*

26. See Daniel J. Elazar, *The Jewish Community of Iran* (Jerusalem: Center for Jewish Community Studies, 1975).

27. Gunther Lawrence, *Three Million More?* (Garden City, N.Y.: Doubleday, 1970); Gitta Amipaz, *Jews in the Soviet Union* (Jerusalem: Israel Information Center, 1977); Richard Cohen, *Let My People Go* (New York: Popular Library, 1971); Meir Rosenne, "Some Legal Aspects of the Struggle for the Rights of Jews in the Soviet Union," *Israel Law Review,* vol. 9 (1984), pp. 588–93; Stephen J. Roth, *The Helsinki "Final Act" and Soviet Jewry* (London: Institute of Jewish Affairs, 1976); William W. Orbach, *The American Movement to Aid Soviet Jews* (Amherst: The University of Massachusetts Press, 1981).

28. Elazar, "Israel, American Jewry, and the Re-Emergence of a World Jewish Polity," p. 103.

6

The Jewish Agency and Israel-Diaspora Relations

Enhancing Interorganizational Collaboration

As the postwar generation passed into history, the massive and continuous emergency effort by Israeli and American Jewry to rescue Jews or to reestablish Jewish life also ended. Although this reduced the need for some activities by those centers, it has also created the need for new kinds of activity that require greater endurance and will need to be continued indefinitely. Thus, one of the first areas to be explored in Israel-diaspora relations is how the instrumentalities of the *edah* work out long-term means for cooperating to provide services to the Jewish world. Characteristic of the contemporary situation is that, where outside assistance or intervention is involved, it does not come simply from one center or the other but almost invariably from both.

We have already referred to Iran. There, even before the turn of the century, the Alliance Israélite Universelle was established to provide basic education for Iranian Jewry. Its entry into the country was facilitated through negotiations by the *shtadlanic* institutions with the then rulers of Iran and only after the application of considerable pressure by the Western powers, triggered by the *shtadlanim*. The Alliance was dominant until World War II, when the Iranian Jews perceived that French influence was on the decline in the world and the American influence on the rise. At that point two American-sponsored institutions, the Joint Distribution Committee and the Otzar Ha-Torah (an organization established to build and maintain religiously oriented schools for Jews in the Middle East), came into Iran to undertake social and educational activities. The two have been there ever since.

The Jewish Agency also arrived in Iran during the war, and, with the establishment of the State of Israel, an Israeli presence was also established. The Israelis' first efforts were directed toward encouraging the mass immigration of Iranian Jewry to Israel. By the mid-1950s, when it became apparent that tens of thousands of Jews would stay in Iran, the Israelis changed their orientation to include efforts to influence the Jewish community remaining in the direction of Zionism, aliya, and financial support of the Jewish state.

In pre-Khomeini Iran the Israel embassy was a major influence in the Jewish community. The Jewish Agency conducted fund-raising and aliya campaigns and, whenever the Iranian government permitted it, sent *shlihim* to work with Jewish youth. The Israeli chief rabbinate served as the court of last resort for the *halakhic* problems of Iranian Jewry, and the young rabbis in the community, insofar as there are any, have been trained in Israel. Support for internal social and educational needs was (and continues to be) provided by the JDC and, for education, by the Otzar HaTorah and the Alliance, the JDC working closely with the two. The professional leadership of the JDC originally consisted of American and British Jews. Subsequently, Israelis joined the staff. The Alliance relied more heavily on local people, with an occasional French Jew. Otzar HaTorah relied on local people, with Israelis filling the top professional positions. The Jewish schools, run directly by the Iranian Jewish community with the support of the JDC, used Israeli personnel whenever the government permitted them to do so, and they were then employed by the local schools.

The intermixture reflected the emerging worldwide Jewish civil service whose main people are drawn from several countries. Many have made career commitments to that civil service and not to any particular community in which they may be serving. (The first Israeli to serve with the JDC in Iran received his training and first fieldwork experience in Jewish community centers in the United States, went on to join the JDC staff in Geneva, developing cultural programming for European Jewry, returned to Israel to work with local community centers and Project Renewal, and then went to the United States as a community *shaliah*.)

The interlocking framework was developing even as tensions between the JDC and the Agency continued on the old basis. The JDC was committed to strengthening Jewish life in Iran; the Agency wanted to encourage the Iranian Jews to leave. Whatever the antagonisms between them, they did develop patterns of cooperation to advance the common goal of strengthening the Jewish life of Iranian Jewry to the point where neither can operate without the other.[1]

Argentina is another example of the intervention of the two centers. A community of more than 300,000 Jews, at one time it was at least self-sufficient, if not more. However, the combination of the breakdown of civil society in Argentina in the 1960s and the failures of the indigenous Jewish leadership to adjust to new world conditions forced the community into a struggle for its viability. In that struggle, it turned to the two great centers for support. It was encouraged to do so by the leaders of both centers, who understood that the sixth or seventh largest concentration of Jews was an asset that could not be abandoned to its own fate.

From the first days of Israel's independence, the Israeli role was actively welcomed and encouraged in Argentina. The original response of the Argentinian non-Jews was to recognize Israel as the *madre patria* (the mother fatherland) of Argentinian Jewry parallel to the mother fatherlands of Argentinians of Spanish, German, Italian, and other extractions.[2] For Jews, this was a strong basis for an identity that was primarily secular, in a community whose institutions were so dominated by Zionists that the only parties that contested for control of them were the political parties supported by their Israeli counterparts. As time went on, the Israeli ambassador became an increasingly important figure in the decision making of Argentinian Jewry, and Israeli assistance in the form of *shlihim*, teachers, and rabbis became greater. In the late 1960s, as some communal institutions began to disintegrate, the Argentinian dependence on Israel grew even more, almost as if Israel was called upon to replace a local lack of will and also finance certain communal functions.

Argentinian Jewry was less open in its welcome of American Jewish support, principally because of the endemic Latin American hostility to the big brother from the North. Nevertheless, shortly after World War II, the American Jewish Committee opened an office in Buenos Aires to help the Argentinian Jews deal with problems of anti-Semitism and to link them more closely with the rest of the Jewish world. Subsequently, the Conservative movement sent a rabbi to Argentina who, after considerable struggle, managed to build a substantial network of congregations affiliated with the United Synagogue, with ancillary activities including a theological seminary, a Ramah camp, and a variety of educational programs. Through them he actually transformed the religious life of Argentine Jewry. More recently the National Jewish Welfare Board has developed a technical assistance program for the Jewish sports clubs.

The principal point of sharing between Israeli and American Jewry is to be found in the special assistance programs of the Jewish Agency, which were launched with the endorsement of the American representative. Although Israeli and American activities have been less closely related in Argentina than they were in Iran because of the differences between the communities, the fact that both major centers have seen fit to devote considerable effort to Argentina is testimony in and of itself.

In France, a much larger and stronger Jewish community (where local forces play a much more important role and the respective interests of the two outside centers can be better articulated on the ground), the cooperation between the JDC and the agency is less visible. The JDC's work in stimulating the creation of the Fonds Social has a direct payoff in the improvement of fund-raising for Israel. There the work of the JDC was carried out by a group of American Jewish social workers who spent their careers in Europe rebuilding European Jewish life, many of whom have since retired to Israel.[3]

Europe remains the most important arena for Israeli and American Jewish efforts. The efforts of each often have been in different directions, although the gap has narrowed considerably in recent years. The cross-purposes at which the principal representatives of the two major communities worked in the interwar generation were to leave their scars well into the next generation, nor did the Holocaust entirely put an end to them. In the aftermath of World War II, the agency and the JDC again found themselves working in the same field and at cross-purposes. By then, the ideological commitment of the JDC to discourage Jews from leaving their European lands of origin had disappeared. The JDC leadership, however, was strongly committed to the notion that the Jews who did want to resettle in Europe should be assisted and those who did not wish to settle in Israel were entitled to seek other homes with the support of world Jewry. The Jewish Agency, on the other hand, was committed to convincing the survivors to wait demonstratively in the displaced-persons camps until they could leave Europe for Israel and to discourage those who chose not to.

Matters were further complicated by the American-sponsored immigrant aid societies (the HIAS of today), whose avowed task was to assist Jewish displaced persons wanting to immigrate to the United States. Particularly between 1945 and 1947, when no Jewish state was immediately in the offing and the doors to Palestine were officially closed, the American organizations felt a moral responsibility to assist Jews to enter the United States. At the same time, the representatives of the Jewish Agency wanted all the displaced persons to stand fast in the camps so as to intensify the problem and stimulate world support for Jewish statehood. Even so, the common interest of the parties in rescuing Jews and in helping them rebuild their lives brought them together in cooperative activity in the camps, albeit antagonistic cooperation.

The issue was resolved by the establishment of the state and the immigration of most of the displaced persons to Israel. In the end, the JDC assisted in that immigration and established its own institutions in Israel to assist those unable to become self-supporting there. It also continued to assist the survivors who remained in Europe to rebuild Jewish life there. After a while, the Israelis were reconciled to the realities of the renewal of a European diaspora, though on a limited basis, and they, too, began to work among European Jewry to tie them closely to Israel in commitment, if not through aliya. The story of the role of the American Jewish community in the reconstitution of European Jewry in the postwar generation and in the development of new institutions to meet their needs has yet to be told.

The recent conflict over the question of the *noshrim* (Jewish émigrés from the Soviet Union who choose not to go to Israel) is reminiscent of that earlier struggle. The Israeli position, fully supported by the Zionist movement, is that Jews who leave Russia because they have requested to immigrate to Israel as part of the reunification of families scheme (the formal reason why the Russians let them go) should be required to complete the journey. At the least, if they drop out they should not be eligible for assistance from other Jewish sources. The diaspora position, most prominent among the American Jewish leadership, is that the issue is one of rescuing Jews, which is a Jewish responsibility under any circumstances, and the destination of any Jews so rescued should be their personal choice.[4]

The latest front where American and Israeli efforts to serve the rest of the diaspora are now coming to the fore is in the provision of rabbis and teachers for those communities unable to train their own. The American Jewish community began by taking a few students from Latin America, Europe, and even India into its seminaries in the immediate postwar period. Today American rabbis are themselves going out to serve communities overseas. Mention has been made of Argentina. The chief rabbi of Sweden is a Philadelphian who is a graduate of the Jewish Theological Seminary. Japan invariably has an American rabbi.

Israel's importance here (which is of ancient vintage) is also growing, in both ways. Students come from various parts of the world to study in Israeli *yeshivot* and then go back to serve in their communities; Israelis who train for the rabbinate in Israel go out to serve communities in the diaspora from East Asia to Chile. Here Israel has even developed mechanisms for cooperative activity with diaspora communities other than the United States. So, for example, the Indian Jewish community, which has no rabbi, periodically sends young men to study in Israel to learn to be at least *shohetim* and *mohelim*. For years, the Jewish Agency *shaliah* in Bombay was from the Torah Education Department. He served as a conduit for rabbinical matters, passing on requests for such things as divorces or conversion of *olim* to the rabbinate in Israel, providing them with the pertinent information as needed, and then executing their decisions. For conversion of *olim* to Israel, a complex procedure was developed. After the local *shaliah* undertook to train prospective converts, he provided them with certificates which they could bring with them to Israel. They were then sent via Turkey where the chief rabbi would convert them before their arrival in Israel, thus avoiding any problem with the local rabbinate of the kind that made integration of Indian Jews particularly difficult in the 1950s.[5]

Thus, willy-nilly, a partnership between Israeli and American Jewry has been forged to serve Jews living outside the two centers. Each center has created its own instruments for the tasks at hand. This partnership, initially antagonistic, has become increasingly so, as the issues that once divided them have diminished. To date, this kind of coordination has developed on an ad hoc basis. This means that what has developed is real and in response to real needs and is not simply "window dressing" to serve some external demands.

Shaping a New World Leadership

The first thing achieved by the reorganization of the Jewish Agency was the emergence of a more broadly-based world Jewish leadership tied into the countrywide and local communities of the diaspora. The world Zionist movement had developed a worldwide leadership much earlier, a leadership that continued to exist after the establishment of the state, even if much diminished in power and influence. But the Zionist leadership never attained the comprehensive scope it sought. Now, in the reconstituted Jewish Agency, the merging of Zionist and community leaders, the men and women who speak for the diaspora communities, particularly those of the United States, offered an opportunity for the emergence of a truly comprehensive Jewish leadership. The Jewish Agency provided an arena within which such a leadership could work, and the people who entered that arena, on the whole with strong and impressive credentials, were ready to take advantage of the opportunity. If anything, the first decade was a period of frustration for many as the opportunities to function developed more slowly than they would have liked. Nevertheless, during a decade of exposure to one another, that leadership began to take shape.[6]

To understand the wider meaning of this, we must go back to the formal reconstitution, to examine:

1. The expectations of those involved in it
2. The structures that emerged from it
3. The functions entrusted to the reconstituted Jewish Agency, the relationships that developed between the agency and its various parts, the new leadership of the State of Israel, and the diaspora communities

As is inevitable in human affairs, there were mixed expectations about what the reconstitution was designed to accomplish. Probably the most minimal expectations were those of many in the Israeli government and the WZO leadership who hoped that the change would be cosmetic and not alter established patterns. The community leaders, however, saw the change as an opportunity to raise the level of efficiency in the agency, to gain greater accountability of the money they were raising for Israel, and to sharpen the agency's policy focus and functions.

Those who initiated the reconstitution—mainly insiders in the Jewish Agency—expected to build a more effective instrumentality for the achievement of the agency's mission in Israel and for the involvement of the diaspora in that mission.

As the process developed, those who wanted minimal changes found that their expectations would not be borne out. Those who expected an easy transition to a new era were also disappointed. Pressures from the reconstituted governing bodies led to improved agency budgetary practices, opened up agency activities for discussion and consideration, and in a limited way began to influence the choice of officeholders in senior agency positions. Each step meant a struggle, but with each advance, the agency acquired greater independence and began to work truly as an arm of the Jewish people. Although progress in that direction has been slow, there is every sign that it is steady.

The division between Zionist and community leaders is greatest in matters of governance. The community leaders feel far more frustrated about the lack of an appropriate role because their experiences abroad have been in exercising real power and not simply in participating in general debate. The top Zionist leadership, however, tends to be concentrated in Israel and to sit on the Executive. Not only are they more accustomed to the general debate, but they can transcend it by exercising power through day-to-day roles as heads of departments within the agency. In sum, on paper the new structure under the reconstitution offered a fair framework for joint activity; but it quickly became a source of endless frustration and puzzlement for many of the most active and committed participants in the agency's work.

Although the reconstitution did not change the functions of the Jewish Agency, it did set in motion a process that has led to changes in implementation and continues to move toward further changes. Parallel to the reconstitution was the decision by the Israeli government to assume responsibility for the absorption of immigrants, leaving the Jewish Agency which had previously dealt with Aliya and absorption only with Aliya. Matters have not worked out precisely as intended, but the agency's role in absorption has been substantially diminished.

Similarly, while the reconstitution was being implemented, the role of the agency in rural settlement was declining, mostly because the bulk of the job had already been done. Moreover, the agency could not directly undertake construction of settlements across the Green Line because of presumed American political constraints. Hence this task was formally assigned to the WZO. At the same time, the role of the agency in urban areas began to grow. During the 1970s it continued to grow, culminating in 1977 in the launching of Project Renewal. The previous policy of the Israeli government, which had prevented the agency from working directly with municipal governments in common programs, was reversed so that the agency was given a direct role in urban redevelopment. Thus the agency acquired a new frontier in the 1970s, one whose possibilities and problems seem unlimited.[7]

Other shifts in agency functions began to be manifested. The agency's role in Israeli higher education, once fiscally overwhelming, began to diminish after a struggle between the agency and the Israeli government as to whether the former would have a say in the expenditure of the funds it provided. The government quashed the agency's bid for more than token influence, and since then the agency has introduced and implemented a plan to substantially cut back its share of the higher education budget.[8]

There have been shifts in social welfare spending within Israel, with the role of the Jewish Agency slowly being reduced in that sphere. On the other hand the agency has begun to take on greater responsibility for Jewish education in the diaspora, a matter of shared concern for all Jewish leaders.[9] All these changes are in progress and their results remain to be seen. All are symptomatic of what some diaspora leaders have suggested as a basic shift in the agency's mission, from rebuilding the Jewish national home in Eretz Israel to forging stronger links between Israel and the diaspora.

Reconstitution has brought in its wake a new set of relationships in the agency and between the agency and other forces in the Jewish polity. In the agency, the first new relationship was between the Zionists and the community representatives. Formally, matters were worked out quickly. Beyond the formal level, the relationship is still uncertain and often uneasy. There is also the relationship between the agency and the WZO, which remains quite ambiguous and a subject of much concern.[10]

The relationship between the agency and the government of Israel, as noted above, is moving toward greater independence for the former. This, too, is an issue in flux, with the government reluctant to encourage such independence but increasingly forced to do so by the diaspora community representatives. Project Renewal has been a major factor in making the change real and may prove a decisive one. Through Project Renewal, for example, Israeli local government authorities have developed ties not only with the agency but also with their twinned diaspora communities. It has not taken long for local leaders to perceive that such ties, especially with the diaspora communities directly, can be invaluable in helping them in their efforts to gain more for their communities from the powers-that-be in the state.[11] This has served to weaken the otherwise hierarchical relationship between state and local government by introducing the *edah* as a third party.

There is also a changing relationship between the agency and the diaspora communities. Once viewed strictly as a conduit for philanthropic contributions to help Israel's people and as a vehicle for helping diaspora fund-raising efforts by the care and feeding of missions to Israel, the Jewish Agency has begun to be perceived as the diaspora's instrumentality in Israel and, for purposes outside Israel, to be what it always purported to be, a "national institution" belonging to the entire *edah,* which needs to be treated and developed as such, and, if necessary, reorganized further.

Beyond Formalism: The Achievement of Caesarea

The next major step forward was the Agency Board of Governors' retreat at Caesarea in February 1981. There, after a decade of sitting around the same tables to discuss business, but always maintaining their formal roles, the Zionist and community leaders had an opportunity to discover the people behind the roles. This apparently had a decisive effect upon most of the participants and marked a significant advance in the integration of this new Jewish leadership.[12]

In the decade between the reconstitution of the Jewish Agency and the meeting at Caesarea, the possibilities that lay within a reconstituted Jewish Agency as potentially the preeminent worldwide functional authority of the Jewish people were exposed. It was demonstrated that there could be a world Jewish leadership drawn from the *keter malkhut*. Much remains to be done, however, to translate that potentiality into reality. Most important is the need to break out of the limitations of formalism, which, not surprisingly, accompanied the first decade of the reorganized agency. That was the principal task of Caesarea.

The principal expectation of the organizers of the Caesarea meeting was integrative: to bring together the leadership of the Jewish Agency and help them understand one another so that they could explore together the goals, purposes, and functions of the Jewish Agency with a view toward moving the agency a major step along the road toward fulfilling its potential. By most accounts, this integrative expectation was met. This led to the establishment of six special commissions of the Board of Governors. Their task was to continue the review process begun in Caesarea—to examine the governance, finances, and management of the agency, its goals and objectives, and its special role in Jewish education and aliya. Substantively, a decision was made at Caesarea to shift the Jewish Agency from some present functions to emphasize aliya and Jewish education in the diaspora. This was a momentous decision because it drastically changes the agency from an essentially Israel-oriented authority to one that is seeking to play a major role in every part of the Jewish world. Because of its implications, it is not a decision that could be taken lightly. That only these two substantive functions were deemed to be worthy of separate commissions is telling.

The Problem of Interorganizational Cooperation

What Caesarea left out was the question of relationships between the agency and the rest of the world Jewish polity. Most immediately, its relationships with the government of Israel are frequently overpowering in their effect on the agency's work, the lion's share of which is within the boundaries of the state. In particular, the agency's relationship with the Israeli political party system is at issue, since the parties continue to dominate the choice of department heads and other personnel and, through them, the agency Executive and daily operations.

Conversely, the relationship between the agency as an adjusting body and the American Jewish community has been based on the latter's insistence on stringent limits to agency activities in the United States. The policy that the agency is not to work within the American Jewish community except in limited and supplementary ways has been in effect at least since 1960.[13]

In the late 1950s the Jewish Agency, eager to promote day schools, decided to provide direct subsidies to a Jewish day school in at least one American Jewish community, after the school's request had been turned down by the local Jewish federation, then firmly opposed to the day schools as a communal solution to the problem of Jewish education. The leadership of the local federation, which included some of the top leadership in the United Jewish Appeal countrywide, acted quickly and firmly to prevent the agency from doing so, on the grounds that money collected through the federation for use in Israel was not to be used to bypass federation policies in their own community. The agency reluctantly was forced to retreat and a countrywide policy was established in the wake of that experience. Since then, the agency has provided funds for educational programs in Israel serving American Jewry with the active cooperation of the local communities but has refrained from trying to bypass them and certainly not to counteract local policies.

French Jewry has tried to take a similar stance in recent years, though with less success since the agency already has a well-established role in France.[14] It is a sign of the times that some of the same people who were directly responsible for limiting the agency's scope in their diaspora communities were, as members of the Board of Governors, participants at Caesarea.

The relationship between the agency and other Jewish multicountry functional authorities will have to be clarified. For example, it has been noted that since World War II, the agency or WZO and the Joint Distribution Committee have been involved in a kind of antagonistic cooperation. In the past, before the establishment of the State of Israel, there was a genuine conflict. Now nothing is inherent in the goals of the agency or the JDC as presently defined that demands the perpetuation of such tensions. On the contrary, the new concern of the agency with urban redevelopment in Israel and Jewish education in the diaspora will demand closer cooperation between the two authorities.

To take another example, direct relations between the Jewish Agency and the World Jewish Congress have been confined to a few select issues, such as the rescue of Soviet Jewry; at the same time the WZO has close ties with the WJC. For many years it was probably the WZO that kept the WJC alive. More recently, since the accession of Edgar Bronfman to the presidency of the WJC, there has been a new infusion of energy and money into the organization, and some effort has been made to distance it from its previous backer. Unlike the JDC, which maintains a low profile in its activities, the WJC lives primarily off its public visibility. Hence, its announcements often lead to confrontation with the WZO–Jewish Agency complex. Here, too, a new relationship may need to be developed.

Three crucial issues that must be addressed here are issues of access, representation, and feedback. With other *edah*-wide organizations, the active participants have tended to become isolated—a closed circle in which people increasingly talk to people in their arena alone and have less and less to communicate to the other arenas where the real action is found. This situation exacerbates the perennial question raised in almost all the arenas, How representative are those who speak in the name of the Jews?

The Jewish Agency in its new form as a more broadly based representative body, may become the vehicle concerned Jews are seeking to frame the *edah*. The agency, however, must first resolve its own questions of access and representation. By creating an arena for a new and more broadly based world Jewish leadership and recruiting important people to participate in that arena, the reconstituted Jewish Agency has done much to create such a leadership. It is, however, the nature of the arena that, as the leadership forms, it, too, becomes increasingly isolated from the other arenas of Jewish activity. The extent of that isolation need not be overdrawn; each leader in the Board of Governors wears many hats and has many connections with other areas of the Jewish world. Still, as time goes by, their experiences remove them from their peers who have not shared those experiences. This has been the fate of other congeries of "world Jewish leaders," who have ultimately come to dance only with one another. It may be an inevitable concomitant, because people have only so much time and energy and cannot work in all arenas at once. It is a problem, though, precisely because of the issues of access, representation, and feedback, which accompany Jewish organizations today.

Questions also have been raised about how the leaders of the world Jewish polity achieve their leadership positions, because elections to them are mostly pro forma ratifications of slates presented by closed nominating committees, and only people with sufficient time and money can offer themselves for leadership roles, especially beyond the local arena. This is particularly blatant because real or nominal responsibility for choosing representatives is in the hands of either the World Zionist Organization, which favors a narrow circle of politicians, or the Keren Hayesod and the United Israel Appeal, the two major bodies responsible for fund-raising in Israel, who naturally favor big contributors.

In one sense, neither grouping can make a serious claim to being representative. In the diaspora, the lack of bounded polities makes it almost impossible to choose representatives on a popular democratic basis. Those countries that have communal elections have registered such low turnouts that their elections are frequently manipulated by small blocs that can gain disproportionate influence over the electoral process. Thus the "democratic elections" approach cannot offer much improvement. In Israel, the one bounded polity in the system, where a representative leadership could be chosen, the party system is such that those elected are hardly more representative of the community than those elected in the diaspora communities.

On another level, however, it can be argued that the leadership is not entirely unrepresentative. Moreover, if it is understood as a reflection of the *keter malkhut,* which represents only the civil dimension of the Jewish body politic and not the spiritual, religious, or intellectual aspects, a case can be made that it is not unduly unrepresentative in comparison with other systems of representation.

What is lacking, however, is proper access and feedback. Appropriate channels are only now being developed to provide Jews with access to their representatives on the agency governing bodies, whether from the Zionist parties or from the communities. People can always talk to one another and the Jewish world is not so big that any leaders are unreachable, but that is too haphazard a situation for effective access. How does a local community in Israel or the diaspora communicate its interests to the Jewish Agency? In North America, the establishment of committees on the Jewish Agency by the CJF and the larger community federations has introduced new channels of communication that are becoming institutionalized. The restructuring of the board of the UIA in the United States to include representatives from the community federations is another step in that direction. Until recently few local leaders, not to speak of other Jews, followed or were sufficiently aware of the work of the agency to communicate their concerns. Development of institutionalized channels of access has already begun to change that.

Parallel to the question of access is that of feedback. How does the work of the agency and its various instrumentalities and governing bodies get brought to the attention of the other arenas or, for that matter, to parallel bodies in the *edah* arena? There are few institutionalized channels of feedback, something clearly reflected in the problem of isolation noted above.

There is also the issue of accountability. The Jewish Agency is another example of a trusteeship institution in the history of the *edah*. Trusteeship is a useful device, but it is effective only if there is some way to keep the trustees accountable. Accountable to whom? It can be suggested that Jewish institutions must be accountable to those Jews involved in Jewish life, who have gone beyond their kinship ties to demonstrate their citizenship in the Jewish body politic. The effort to develop better means of accountability must be high on the contemporary Jewish political agenda.

It is the resolution of these problems of expectation, structure, and relationship that must precede decisions about changing the functions of the instrumentalities of the *edah*. There is too little public concern over *what* or *how well* these bodies do. Most discussions are confined to *who* does what. A major shift in emphasis, however—especially in the directions suggested—could lead to serious disputes unless these other problems are addressed and progress is made toward their resolution.

Assuming that the Jewish people is not seeking to establish a world Jewish parliament, it still requires effective national institutions to do its work as an *edah*. No other institution has a better claim to playing a preeminent role than the Jewish Agency; to do so, however, it must be ready to confront the difficult questions, draw the appropriate conclusions, and make the needed changes.

The Expansion of the Diaspora Role in Agency Affairs

The issue is considerably more complex when it comes to the participation of each center in the affairs of the other. Israel has been notably reluctant to encourage diaspora involvement in policies affecting it directly, even where diaspora money is involved. Until the mid-1970s diaspora Jews were reluctant to press matters. For example, where Israel has demanded Jewish mobilization in the United States on its behalf, American Jewry has been content to follow the Israeli lead on the grounds that Israel's vital interests are those most immediately affected. Similarly, American Jewry has strongly resisted Israeli attempts to intervene in its communal affairs for many of the same reasons. Though from time to time Israel has shown more interest in doing so, it generally has respected American Jewish wishes and pulled back when asked to do so. In matters affecting world Jewry, because they are the major centers of Jewish life, both feel free to act for the resolution of world Jewish problems or in the defense of world Jewish interests.

During the past generation a standoff prevailed. More recently, the diaspora attitude has changed, and American Jewish leaders in particular are demanding a greater share in decision making in matters they see as affecting Jews as Jews, in Israel or

elsewhere. In recent years, they have openly challenged Israeli policy about the resettlement of Russian Jewish émigrés and have begun to assert themselves in the Jewish
Agency.

At that, American Jewish communities remain reluctant to see agency money spent
in the United States, fully understanding the implications of such a policy shift, even
when the money would be spent for mutually acceptable programs. Given that the local
federations have been reluctant to strengthen the Council of Jewish Federations by
giving the Council more money to operate or finance programs, it is not surprising that
they are even less interested in giving their money to the Jewish Agency to use as the
agency determines in the federation's own jurisdictions.

The Israeli effort to limit American Jewish involvement in its internal affairs can be
both difficult and easy to implement. It can be difficult because diaspora Jews can
maintain that the money whose expenditure they want to influence, or at least participate
in supervising, is raised by them for purposes in Israel, and that they are entitled to be
assured that the funds are being spent for those purposes and efficiently at that. For
American Jewry, this interest is even stronger because their contributions are exempt
from American taxes when they are used for humanitarian purposes and are expended by
instruments fully or substantially controlled by the American donors.[15]

On the other hand, because Israel is an independent state with great status in the
eyes of diaspora Jews and because it is in continued crisis, which makes diaspora Jews less
willing to press Israelis hard and aggravate their problems, it can be easy for the Israeli
government to limit American Jewish influence in the internal affairs of Israel. To some
extent the Israelis have had to accommodate the demands of American law to insure the
continued tax exemption so important in assuring that funds keep flowing from American Jewry. That accommodation has been made through the Jewish Agency.

The vehicle for doing so has been the United Israel Appeal, the successor to the
prestate United Palestine Appeal, which was a Zionist instrumentality for raising money
for the Zionist enterprise in Eretz Israel. The old UPA joined with the JDC to form the
UJA in 1938. As the UJA became stronger, the UPA, transformed into the UIA after
1948, increasingly lost its identity. Then, in the late 1950s, it was reorganized as the
vehicle to give the UJA some means to make the Jewish Agency accountable for the tax-
exempt money it was pouring into Israel. During the 1960s and 1970s, as the Jewish
Agency underwent its reconstitution, the UIA first lost and then regained its role on an
expanded basis, as the Jewish community federations through the CJF sought simultaneously to strengthen their hand vis-à-vis the UJA and also follow the use of the money
they raised. Through all of these reorganizations, the UIA remained the only institutional framework in the United States which brought together leaders of the Zionist
movement with leaders of the federations and the UJA. Hence its role became pivotal
even as it had to maintain a low profile because of the wishes of its constituent elements.
Its principal function today is to keep the Jewish Agency accountable under the terms of
the United States tax code and in light of the concerns of American Jewry for efficiency
and fiscal responsibility.

Since the reconstitution, there has been a series of contests over the proper role of
the diaspora communities. One of the first examples was the struggle over increasing the
role of the Jewish Agency in supervising the expenditure of its funds by Israel's institutions of higher education. By the early 1970s, between three-fifths and two-thirds of the
total budget of Israel's universities came from the Jewish people by way of the Jewish
Agency, compared with less than 10 percent from the government of Israel (the rest came

from direct contributions and tuition). The agency's funds were channeled to the universities through a government body, the Council for Higher Education, in which the agency had only one representative, or essentially no voice. The diaspora leaders in the agency, led by the Americans, decided that, because they were providing much of the total, they should have a greater share in supervising the expenditure. Through the UIA, they established a task force and appointed a distinguished American Jewish leader, Dean William Haber of the University of Michigan, to undertake the study and negotiations to achieve their ends. The government representatives and those of the universities resisted and, after some negotiation, the status quo ante was reaffirmed with minor changes. In response, the agency reduced its share to 10 percent of the total higher education budget as the price for having only token representation and no control. The issue was buried and no diaspora voice was raised in protest, no doubt because the diaspora Jewish leaders were themselves ambivalent about the matter and did not consider it of first priority. Subsequently, a "trade-off" arrangement was made; the Israeli government granted an amount equivalent to the Jewish Agency's transfer to the Council on Higher Education, to service the Jewish Agency's debt.

More visible and vital were the two contests for the chairmanship of the Executives of the World Zionist Organization and the Jewish Agency, the first of which took place after the sudden and unexpected death of Pinhas Sapir and the second after the May 1977 Israeli elections. After Sapir's death, Arye Leon Dulzin, treasurer and senior Likud representative for both bodies, became acting chairman of the two, as he had been once before after the equally sudden and unexpected death of Louis Pincus. Though on the previous occasion Dulzin had agreed to accept the decision of the Labor party to install Sapir and had not contested Sapir's election, when the Labor party this time indicated that it was going to back Yosef Almogi for the two positions (a strong figure in Israeli internal politics but a man who had never had any significant association with the agency or with diaspora Jewry), Dulzin decided to fight. He based his hopes on the response of diaspora Jewry, particularly the Americans, with whom he had developed connections over the years, and much of his appeal was based on what he hoped would be a diaspora Jewish reluctance to accept the apparent *diktat* of the ruling Israel Labor party. However, Dulzin was disappointed to find a sharp division in the ranks of the diaspora leadership. The foremost American leaders were not particularly predisposed toward his candidacy, in part because of a reluctance to oppose the Israeli establishment, in part because they disagreed with Dulzin's stated opposition to the recent Israel–Egypt Sinai disengagement agreement. Thus Dulzin failed to make the issue one of Israel versus diaspora and lost honorably in a political contest that saw Almogi win supporters from both groups.

Things took a different turn in 1977–78. It did not take long for those involved in the work of the Jewish Agency to realize that Almogi, whatever his other talents, was not suited for the chairmanship. His term was generally a disappointment and a strong interest developed in replacing him. The Israeli Knesset elections of May 1977 provided the catalyst for change. The Likud victory meant that, according to the Zionist political tradition, Likud should name a new chairman of the WZO and Jewish Agency Executives at the next opportunity. Almogi took advantage of this tradition to announce his resignation, despite pressure from segments of the Labor party leadership who urged him to remain so as to retain Labor control of at least that instrumentality.

Dulzin again announced his intention to stand for the chairmanship, this time with the backing of a party that would have the majority at the next World Zionist Congress. Once again, certain elements of the Labor party, with their allies in the WZO, tried to build a coalition against him. This time, the non-Zionist diaspora Jewish leadership in the agency made it clear that they would not condone any such arrangement and that they expected Dulzin to be elected by the WZO and then by the Jewish Agency as a matter of course. The Labor effort collapsed, and Dulzin was duly elected at the congress in February 1978.

The aftermath of the 1978 congress led to another conflict which demonstrated the growing strength of the diaspora community representatives. Part of the shift in party control after the May 1977 Knesset elections was manifested in the shifting of portfolios in the WZO and Jewish Agency Executives. Several portfolios are held jointly by the same person for both bodies under the terms of the reconstitution agreements. The diaspora representatives' position has been that those joint portfolios should be given to the best person, without regard to party considerations. This is a position that is unheard of in Israel where every public office is handed out according to some party key.

In the past, the diaspora representatives have had to concede to the realities of Israeli politics. This time, in part because of the change in party control and in part because of their growing strength, they were able to take a stand. Thus, they insisted on screening the party nominees who emerged from the Zionist Congress, and behind the scenes once or twice even tried to influence the nominations, all as part of an "advise and consent" policy included in the reconstitution agreements. Thus, they pressured the Labor party to retain Raanan Weitz as head of the Settlement Department in the face of a different Labor party choice, strictly on the basis of an assessment of the candidates' capabilities. They also insisted on screening the proposed candidates for treasurer of the Jewish Agency nominated by the Zionist parties, which led to the Board of Governors choosing Labor's Akiva Lewinsky over Likud's Yoram Aridor after Lewinsky made a better impression when interviewed. Finally, the non-American diaspora leadership had a major hand in designating the new chairman of Keren Hayesod.

Prime Minister Begin took strong umbrage at this intervention, seeing it as a frustration of his party's success at the polls. A long, public fight ensued, which ended in a comprehensive compromise. What he and his colleagues in Herut failed to understand was that they had come to power at the end of an era, in a period of transition when the old rules were changing and new ones were being formulated. Their rise to power was possible only because of the general changes taking place in Israeli politics; however, those changes meant that the new power holders would not enjoy exclusive rights over the fruits of victory in the same way as their predecessors. The result demonstrated that a change had indeed occurred in the allocations of power between Israel and the diaspora in the national institutions.

The new power of the diaspora communities was made even more manifest in 1983, when Raphael Kotlowitz was replaced as head of the Aliya Department of the Jewish Agency. Kotlowitz, a longtime Herut activist, had suffered from bad relations with the community leaders for years. Their acquiescence to his election in 1978 came only after the forceful invervention of Menachem Begin himself. In the intervening years, Kotlowitz further alienated his diaspora associates, and they insisted that he be replaced at the end of his term.

After a protracted struggle, which began before the thirtieth Zionist Congress in December 1982 and concluded at a special meeting of the Board of Governors in Atlanta in November 1983, Kotlowitz was formally rejected and Herut invited to submit a new nominee. The party responded by nominating Ariel Sharon and the community representatives prepared to cast another veto. They were spared the need to do so by the action of the Zionist General Council, which has to approve party nominees before they are submitted to the Jewish Agency Board of Governors. In an unprecedented action, the General Council rejected Sharon by a substantial vote, holding that his controversiality in the diaspora rendered him inappropriate for the position. There is little doubt that its courageous step was a result of the new sense of the Jewish Agency fostered by the reconstitution. With it, "advised consent" became established procedure.

It would be inaccurate to assume that the foregoing contests were simply between Israel and the diaspora. On most issues there is no natural division between the two; the divisions cut across both. All of this reflects the growing intimacy between Israel and the diaspora in matters relating to the national institutions. Take the matter of access. Today any significant diaspora Jewish leader can speak to anybody in any ministry, not to mention the Jewish Agency, about any matter in which his constituency has a direct interest. In this respect, diaspora Jewish leaders have as much or more access as most Israelis, including most Israeli local government officials—the leaders most close with Israel citizenry—for example. All Israeli first-line officeholders, not to speak of second and third echelon people, regularly appear before diaspora groups in Israel and abroad and are available for meetings with the diaspora leadership far more than they appear before Israeli groups or are regularly available to Israeli lower level leadership. Israelis perceive that it is easier for diaspora Jewish leaders, even of the second and third echelon, to see the prime minister than it is for any Israeli outside the Knesset.

Whether the diaspora leaders have real influence as a result is another matter. Most appearances are one-way streets, which has to do as much with the situation as with the desires of the Israelis. The Israeli leadership may or may not be open to diaspora ideas. It is equally true that many diaspora leaders are not sufficiently involved or well informed to use the access they have. Significantly, when they are involved or informed and do wish to use that access (as in the "Who is a Jew?" issue), they do so. It may even be said that they get results, depending on the constellation of factors influencing Israeli policy-making on an issue.

The initiation in 1978 of Project Renewal as an Israeli government–Jewish Agency–diaspora–local community partnership to rehabilitate Israel's disadvantaged neighborhoods marked a new step in the development of a relationship based on active diaspora involvement in Israel at the grass roots. This new project offered great potential for the development of a new matrix of relationships—local community to local community and among the representatives of larger arenas. The relationship was beset with difficulties at the beginning, as might have been expected; in short order, however, it became one of real partnership, so much so that the situation is not likely to return to the status quo ante even after Project Renewal is completed.[16]

Project Renewal was the catalyst for changing the structure of the relationships between Israel and the diaspora. During the first generation of statehood, contact between Israel and the diaspora was like contact between two pyramids that touched at their tips. No more than a handful of leaders on each side had regular and meaningful contact with one another. In Israel, the prime minister, a few of his ministerial colleagues, the chairman of the Executive of the Jewish Agency, and a few of his departmental colleagues handled almost all the regular contacts with a handful of diaspora leaders. The latter were drawn from the very top echelons of the fund-raising organizations or, in a few instances, from the community relations bodies. After the Six-Day War, the ties began to stretch further down the pyramid. Project Renewal transformed the two pyramids into a single matrix. Not only were the ties between the top leadership intensified, but ties were developed between the second and third echelon leaders and then betwen ordinary Jewish activists and their Israeli counterparts through Project Renewal committees and volunteer programs. This transformation has not only helped further the integration of the Jewish people into a single entity, but also has made it impossible for the business of the *edah* to be conducted in the old pyramidal manner. The implications of this are yet to be fully felt.

Precisely because diaspora leaders are not present day to day and are not inside Israeli society—the very things that make them diaspora leaders, namely, being in the diaspora and being inside other Jewish societies—means that their ability to use their access is limited. By the very nature of the situation, there is no remedy for this nor should there be. Perhaps there are a few people who can be sufficiently inside both Israel and some diaspora Jewish society to have influence in both but it is likely to be a modest influence, because of the time and locational factors involved, and this ability is not given to more than a handful.

As Charles Liebman has pointed out, the degree of influence by the leaders or groups from one center on the internal life and activities of the other depends on three conditions: (1) how serious the desire for influence is, (2) how focused the effort is to bring influence to bear and perhaps how persistent as well, and (3) whether the particular group has strong allies in the other center. Thus Orthodox Jews have had more influence on religious issues in Israel than any other diaspora group because they best meet the three conditions. The issue is of extreme importance to them, they are willing to make focused and persistent efforts to exert their influence, and they have strong allies in Israel.[17]

Similarly, the concern of Conservative and Reform Jews to gain official recognition in Israel has been limited in the sense that only recently have the "heavyweights" in their movements have not thrown their weight behind the effort. The effort has been sporadic and diffused, and those leading it had no strong allies within Israel. Nevertheless, when changes were proposed in the laws defining "Who is a Jew?" that would have substantially affected Conservative and Reform conversions, the two groups did get together and make a serious and focused attempt, for which they found allies in Israel and succeeded in tabling the matter whenever it has been raised.

Similar examples can be found in the other direction. Israeli efforts to influence Jewish education in the United States have been ambivalent, unfocused, and sporadic. Moreover, for a long time the Israelis had no firm allies in the United States except on the level of glittering generalities because they have made only recently an effort to develop close links with American Jewish educators. Hence their influence has been minimal. In the one or two areas where this is not so, it is precisely because in those program areas serious, focused, continuous efforts have been made in alliance with American Jewish counterparts. Cooperation in Israel programming and summer camping are examples of this, as are the community *shaliah* and scholar-in-residence programs.

On the other hand, in fund-raising, the Israelis have been extremely serious. Their efforts have been focused and undeniably persistent, and they have strong local allies. The results speak for themselves. Despite periodic demands in the diaspora communities for reconsideration of the amounts allocated for Israel's needs, existing funding levels are at least maintained. From this, at least one point should be clear. Even under the best of circumstances, influence requires strong commitment, diligent work, and proper support. There is no avoiding that, no matter what frameworks are developed.

Proper Frameworks for the Relationship

Although the major issues facing Israel-diaspora relations are not necessarily structural ones, nevertheless, the issue of proper frameworks for the evolving relationships in the context of the emergent world Jewish polity is important. Such frameworks are not simply structural but also psychological.

During the past generation, the relationship between Israel and diaspora Jewry has progressed from vague linkage to interdependence and is now approaching integration. In the years immediately after World War II, at the time of the creation of the state, American Jewry in particular saw its relationship to the Jewish community in what was then called Palestine as some kind of vague link between "coreligionists" who needed their help like any other Jewish community in trouble. (The term was still very much in vogue, even though thoroughly lacking in relevance when applied to the predominantly secular and, in those days, still antireligious population of the modern Yishuv.) Whatever American Jewry did was done for "them" to solve their problems and to relieve the sufferings of the survivors of the Holocaust.

Even after the state was declared, the links between Israel and much of world Jewry remained vague. Despite discussions in some quarters suggesting elaborate formal frameworks for structuring those links—Mordecai Kaplan's plan for a new Jewish covenant and constitution immediately comes to mind—during the 1950s and most of the 1960s the perception of the links became, if anything, even more tenuous. The new world Jewries were busy completing their transition from immigrant communities into established ones and the surviving old world Jewries were in the throes of reconstruction, while Israeli Jewry was busy trying to establish itself in the years following the mass emigration.

It took the Six-Day War to demonstrate that the ties that bound Israel and the diaspora were ties of mutual interdependence, that all elements in the world Jewish polity were dependent on one another for their status and security to a greater or lesser degree. In reaction to this discovery, efforts were made at the end of the decade to create frameworks that would express this interdependence. The reconstituted Jewish Agency was the first among them.

The Yom Kippur War moved the Jewish world from interdependence toward integration, as it became apparent that the fate of almost every Jew was dependent on what happened in Israel. In the first place Jewish institutions, even those such as synagogues not directly associated with Israel, became increasingly dependent for their fiscal survival on conditions in Israel, as crises there changed the direction of local fund-raising efforts in every diaspora community. Beyond that, individual Jews began to perceive how closely integrated their fate was with the Jewish state, not only because the Israeli Knesset played a major role in defining "Who is a Jew?" (the only body in the world, religious or secular, able to do so and make its decision mean something for all Jews), but also because even the ebb and flow of anti-Semitism has come to depend on conditions in Israel.

The United Nations General Assembly session of 1975, highlighted by the passage of the resolution equating Zionism with racism, made this even more apparent. It is understandable that the resolution could cause great fears among Jews in Latin America and behind the Iron Curtain where anti-Semitism, whether official or unofficial, is widespread and any excuse for anti-Semites to act is usually exploited. What is significant is that American Jewry, which does not stand to suffer from increased anti-Semitism in the American context, felt equally jittery and insecure. In short, the psychological framework in which diaspora Jewry operates now relies heavily on the security and well-being of the State of Israel to assure the mental health, if not the physical security, of Jews outside the state, wherever they may be.

The psychological framework of Israeli Jews has also undergone changes since 1967. The often emphasized contempt of Israelis for diaspora Jewry that was so prevalent until the Six-Day War has essentially disappeared. In its place, the Israelis have come to view diaspora Jewry as brethren in every respect. The major popular argument about the diaspora in Israel today is whether to refer to diaspora communities as Israel's only permanent allies or to suggest that, because Jews are one people, describing any part of them as allies of any other diminishes the ties between them. At the same time, the Israelis' self-confidence about the greater security of Jews in Israel as compared with the diaspora has diminished.

Still, the Israelis' psychological framework defining Israel as the only center of the Jewish people remains intact. Without going into the question of the centrality of Israel, it is clear that for most Israeli leaders the notion that there may be another center of equal or nearly equal importance is not an acceptable one.[18] This is not as difficult a problem for the Israeli man-in-the-street, who is constantly being impressed with the possibilities for Jewish life in the United States from what he sees and hears, either personally or through the mass media.[19]

Throughout most of Jewish history, there was more than one center of Jewish life at the same time. Empirically, the model for Jewish life is not that of a center with peripheries but of two or more centers or even congeries of centers bound together in a common network or matrix. For Jews, Jerusalem is the center of the world—certainly the center of the Jewish world; yet acknowledging its status as center does not require acknowledging its absolute supremacy over every part of the Jewish body politic. For Americans, Washington is the capital of the United States and even the free world; it receives respect and consideration as such. Yet Americans do not attribute to Washington centrality in American life because it is the capital. Americans know that New York and Los Angeles and Chicago and Houston and San Francisco (to mention but a few places) are also centers that are equal to or exceed Washington for certain purposes, even if they are not equal to one another.

Jews are bothered by many questions about who they are and where they are going. The Israel-diaspora issue is but one of these questions. In this respect, as in others, Israeli Jews have turned out to be no different from their diaspora brethren. For Israelis are not like Frenchmen, Englishmen, or Russians who are attached to their country simply because it is their country. In this respect they are more like Americans who love their country precisely because of the special vocation or purpose which they see entrusted to it.[20]

During the recent wars, Israeli and diaspora Jewries have discovered that their vocation is a common one, rooted in their common Jewishness, that there is no separate Israeli vocation, although there is a separate Israeli citizenship open to Jews and non-Jews and different diaspora citizenships of which Jews partake without giving up their Jewishness. Learning that lesson was not easy either for Israeli or diaspora, especially American, Jews. Both groups saw themselves as having a destiny set apart from the common Jewish destiny and, by implication, a separate vocation. Diaspora Jews have had to discover the limits of the emancipationist ideology and the truth that to pursue a

Jewish vocation there must be a Jewish polity. Israeli Jews have had to discover that the reestablishment of a territorial state possessing political sovereignty as currently understood does not, and cannot, end the Jewish condition; at best it can transfer that condition to its original home where Jews have created opportunities to turn it to advantage. For both, then, the events since 1967 have brought the beginning of new wisdom. For that wisdom to flower, Jews need to understand better the Jewish vocation and the necessary role of the political aspect of Jewish life, both in Israel and in the world Jewish community, in giving it means for proper expression.

Notes

1. Daniel J. Elazar, *The Jewish Community of Iran* (Jerusalem: Center for Jewish Community Studies, 1975).

2. See Moshe Davis, "Centers of Jewry in the Western Hemisphere: A Comparative Approach," *Jewish Journal of Sociology,* vol. 5, no. 1 (June 1963), pp. 4–26.

3. Marc Salzburg, "The Organized Jewish Community in France," unpublished Ph.D. dissertation (1974) and *French Jewry and American Jewry* (Jerusalem: Center for Jewish Community Studies, 1971); Iland Greilsammer, *The Democratization of a Community: The Case of French Jewry* (Jerusalem: Center for Jewish Community Studies, 1979); "Jews of France: From Neutrality to Involvement," *Forum,* nos. 28–29 (winter 1978), pp. 130–46, and "Le Juif et la cité: quatre approches théoriques," *Archive de sciences sociales des religions,* no. 46/1 (July–September 1978), pp. 135–51. (Reprinted by Center for Jewish Community Studies.)

4. See Tefutsot Israel, vol. 16, no. 2 (April–June 1978): "The 'Noshrim'—Jewish Emigrés from the USSR. Avoiding Israel," Daniel J. Elazar, co-editor.

5. Daniel J. Elazar, Field Notes—Indian Jewish Community, August 1970.

6. Ernest Stock, *Partners and Purse Strings: The History of the United Israel Appeal in America* (Lanham, Md.: University Press and Jerusalem Center for Public Affairs, 1986); Zelig Chinitz, *A Common Agenda: The Reconstitution of the Jewish Agency for Israel* (Jerusalem: Jerusalem Center for Public Affairs, 1985); Daniel J. Elazar and Alysa M. Dortort, eds., *Understanding the Jewish Agency: A Handbook* (Jerusalem: Jerusalem Center for Public Affairs, 1984).

7. See Daniel J. Elazar, Gerald B. Bubis, Moshe Hazani, and Hillel Frisch, *Project Renewal: An Introduction to the Issues and Actors* (Jerusalem: Center for Jewish Community Studies, 1980); Daniel J. Elazar, Paul E. King, and Orli HaCohen, *The Extent, Focus, and Impact of Diaspora Involvement in Project Renewal,* Report 1—*Interim Report* (Jerusalem: Jerusalem Center for Public Affairs, August 1982), Report 2—*Six Case Studies of Diaspora-Neighborhood Linkage* (JCPA, May 1983), Report 3 (JCPA, August 1984), and Report 4—*Review of the Jewish Agency Renewal Department Role* (JCPA, February 1985).

8. Liebman, "Does the Diaspora Influence Israel?"; Elazar and Dortort, *Understanding the Jewish Agency,* pp. 37–89.

9. The Jewish Agency for Israel, *Building Our Future: A Jewish Agency Program for Jewish Education in the Coming Decades, A Proposal* (Jerusalem: Jewish Agency for Israel, 1983); The L. A. Pincus Jewish Education Fund for the Diaspora, *Report* (Jerusalem, 1981) and *Report No. 3* (Jerusalem, 1983); The World Zionist Organization—The Press and Public Relations Bureau, *Jewish Education in the Diaspora* (Jerusalem, 1971); Israel Ministry of Education and Culture, Jewish Agency for Israel, and World Zionist Organization, *Joint Program for Jewish Education* (Jerusalem, 1982); Yehoshua Fagen, ed., *Hinukh ve-Tarbut be-Golah MePe'elut HaMahlakah le Hinukh ve Tarbut be-Golah* (Education and Culture in the Diaspora from the Activities of the Department for Education and Culture in the Diaspora) (Jerusalem: World Zionist Organization, Department for Education and Culture in the Diaspora, 1971) (Hebrew).

10. Chinitz, *A Common Agenda,* chap. 4 and Amnon Hadary, "From Herzl to Herzliya," *Forum,* no. 50, pp. 1–8.

11. Elazar, King, and HaCohen, *The Extent, Focus, and Impact,* Reports 1–4.

12. For a discussion of the Caesarea meeting and its implications, see Chinitz, *A Common Agenda,* chap. 5; Hadary, "From Herzl to Herzliya"; Daniel J. Elazar, "The Jewish Agency and the Jewish People after Caesarea," *Forum,* nos. 42–43 (fall/winter 1981), pp. 1–14.

13. See Daniel J. Elazar, *Community and Polity: The Organizational Dynamics of American Jewry* (Philadelphia: Jewish Publication Society of America, 1976), pp. 248–51.

14. Salzburg, "The Organized Jewish Community in France" and *French Jewry and American Jewry.*

15. For an extreme statement of this position, see Eliezer Jaffe, "Non-Conventional Philanthropy," *Moment,* vol. 4, no. 5 (May 1979), pp. 63–64; "Wanted: A New Agency," *Moment,* vol. 8, no. 4 (April 1983), pp. 62–63; and "Beyond the Jewish Agency," *Jerusalem Post* (June 25, 1984), p. 7.

16. Elazar, King, and HaCohen, *The Extent, Focus, and Impact,* Reports 1–4; The International Committee for the Evaluation of Project Renewal, *Annual Report for 1982* (Jerusalem: The Government of Israel—The Ministry of Housing and the Jewish Agency–Project Renewal Department, March 1983); *Annual Report for 1983* (Jerusalem: The Government of Israel—The Ministry of Housing and the Jewish Agency–Project Renewal Department, February 1984).

17. Charles S. Liebman, *Pressure without Sanctions: The Influence of World Jewry on Israeli Policy* (Cranbury, N.J.: Fairleigh Dickinson University Press, 1976).

18. On the centrality of Israel, see Nathan Rotenstreich, *Essays on Zionism and the Contemporary Jewish Condition* (New York: Herzl Press, 1980) and "Israel's Exile in American Jewish Thought," *Forum,* nos. 28–29 (winter 1978), pp. 27–37; and Eliezer Schweid, *Israel at the Crossroads* (Philadelphia: Jewish Publication Society of America, 1973).

19. Hanoch Smith and the Smith Research Center, *Attitudes of Israelis towards America and American Jews* (New York: Institute on American Jewish–Israeli Relations, October 1983).

20. For an analysis of the meaning of this difference, see Charles S. Liebman, "The Rise of Neo-Traditionalism among Modern Orthodox Jews in Israel," *Megemot* 27 (May 1982), pp. 231–50; and Charles S. Liebman and Eliezer Don-Yehiya, *Civil Religion in Israel: Traditional Religion and Political Culture in the Jewish State* (Berkeley: University of California Press, 1983).

7

The New Jewish Public

The reemergence of the institutions of the *keter malkhut* as the dominant ones in the *edah* and in most of its countrywide and local communities is part of a profound shift in the locus of power in the Jewish polity. This is not merely a superficial institutional revision but a change in the socioreligious orientation of the Jews who constitute the Jewish body politic. This change completes the abandonment of what had become traditional Jewish society nearly eighteen hundred years ago by all Jews, including those who cling to the old ways most tenaciously. Perhaps 80 percent of world Jewry today no longer see themselves bound by *halakhah,* however much they may or may not see themselves as "religious" or "good Jews" and however much they may preserve in their lives Jewish traditions and mores. But even the other 15 percent live in ways that are radically different from those of the traditional society from which they or their fathers emerged.[1]

Accompanying this change is another one of nearly equal historic aspect—the approaching end of the fundamental geocultural division that dominated the Jewish people for the past millenium, namely, the division between Sephardim and Ashkenazim. With all the subdivisions in each group, each represented a geocultural "whole" in its own right. These divisions became basic to Jewish life in the eleventh century, with the emergence of a self-sustaining Jewish community in Europe north of the Alps and the breakup of the Arab caliphate, which ended the rule of the Resh Galuta (exilarch) and the *gaonim* of Babylonia over world Jewry. In due course, each of these major groups and many smaller ones in them developed their own customs and traditions within the framework of *halakhah* or compatible with it, including languages, and appropriate orientations to the Muslim and Christian worlds around it.

These divisions have broken down through a combination of emigration and modernization. As Jews were detached from the environments in which the separate traditions flourished, they had to adapt to radically new conditions of modernity in different places, be it in the secularized West or in the renewed Jewish state. There they added such extensive new elements to their lives as to foreshadow the beginning of a new set of divisions in the Jewish people. The Jewish people is in the throes of that transformation now.

Although these transformations began during the modern epoch, until the last generations of that epoch most of world Jewry, though not its cutting edge, still lived within the old frameworks, *halakhic* and geocultural. The Holocaust ended that situation and the postmodern epoch began with most Jews living outside the four ells of the *halakhah* and away from the old bastions of Sephardic and Ashkenazic Jewry. Now, in the second generation of the postmodern epoch, a new Jewish public is emerging whose relations with its Jewishness are more likely to be expressed idologically and institutionally through the *keter malkhut* than through the *keter torah*. The fundamental sociocultural patterns of this new public are more likely to be shaped by whether its members live in Israel or the diaspora than whether they are Ashkenazim or Sephardim. All this is leading to a new division that is likely to be particularly important in shaping Jewish life in this epoch. At the same time, and somewhat paradoxically, the Jewish world today is faced with a revival of Sephardic and Orthodox self-assertiveness.

Sephardim and Ashkenazim

At a time when more than 80 percent of the Jewish people are of Ashkenazi descent and heritage, suddenly Jews are confronted with a resurgent Sephardic drive for recognition in the Jewish fold. Today Sephardim constitute about 18 percent of world Jewry and will exceed 20 percent by the end of the century. This is a dramatic reversal of the demographic trend that has prevailed since Sephardim and Ashkenazim emerged as separate groupings within the Jewish people in the eleventh century. At the end of that century, nearly 96 percent of world Jewry was Sephardic. It was only in the middle of the fourteenth century that the percentage of Ashkenazim reached that of the Sephardim today. Although the Ashkenazic percentage continued to grow, it was the modern epoch that transformed the situation radically. In 1650, 65 percent of world Jewry was still Sephardic. The Ashkenazim became a majority in the eighteenth century, but it was not until the nineteenth century brought a population explosion in Europe that the ratio shifted dramatically. At their high point in 1930, 92 percent of world Jewry was Ashkenazic.

That same population explosion did not catch up with the Sephardic world until the twentieth century, when the Ashkenazic birthrate began to decline, leading to the shift now in progress, which began in the 1930s. The Holocaust accelerated the new trend. Although the Sephardim suffered great losses as well—the great Judesmo (Ladino)–speaking reservoir of Sephardic culture in the Balkans was destroyed as fully as was the great Yiddish-speaking reservoir in Eastern Europe and even North African Jews were deported to the camps—Ashkenazic losses were not only substantially greater in absolute terms, but also their major demographic reservoir was materially affected.

Even more decisive is that today the Sephardim are heavily concentrated in the State of Israel, which is the only major Jewish community with a positive birthrate, and the Ashkenazim are concentrated in the diaspora where most Jewish communities have negative birthrates. Moreover, the Sephardic birthrate is at the high end of the scale in Israel (although it is adjusting downward) and probably also in the diaspora.

There are 2.5 million Sephardim in the world today, more Sephardic Jews than there ever were, just as there are vastly more Ashkenazim. In the fourteenth century, when the ratios were precisely reversed, there were some 2 million Jews in the world. That number was not exceeded until the eighteenth century when the Ashkenazi population began its rapid growth.[2]

Raw demographics are misleading unless the location of the two groupings is taken into consideration. About 60 percent of Israel's population is now Sephardic, and that percentage is growing. In contrast, almost 97 percent of the Jewish population of the United States is Ashkenazic. (The ratio of Sephardim to Ashkenazim in the United States is about that of the ratio of Jews to the general American population.) Soviet Jewry is also largely Ashkenazic, and French Jewry, the third largest diaspora community, now has a Sephardic majority. In sum, the major centers of world Jewry are equally divided between Sephardim and Ashkenazim.

The Sephardim in Israel now are beginning to come into their own and are likely to become the dominant political force by the end of this generation or the beginning of the next. Similarly, the Sephardim are on their way to becoming the dominant force in the French Jewish community.

The term *Sephardi* is often restricted to the descendants of Jews from Spain, but it can be used properly to describe the Jewish world of western Asia and the Mediterranean basin, with their eastern and western extensions in the modern epoch—from Hong Kong to Seattle. Historically, the Jews in that part of the world shared the same patterns of *halakhic* expression, a common cultural base, and certain patterns of communal organization, tied together by a close-knit communications network that took shape initially in Eretz Israel and Babylonia. It gained its full form in the Iberian Peninsula, and then was developed and preserved in the Ottoman Empire, from Morocco to Mesopotamia, where the exiles from Iberia found refuge.[3]

Conversely, the term *Ashkenazi* was originally applied to the Jews of northern France and the Rhineland. Later it became the universal term for the Jewries of Europe north of the Alps (with their eastern and western extensions in the modern epoch—from China to Hawaii), whose shared *halakhic* patterns, common cultural base, and forms of communal organization and governance differed from those of their Sephardic brethren in the context of their common Jewishness, linked by their own parallel communications network developed during the same thousand years.[4] In essence, Sephardic Jewry is the Jewry of the south, distinct from Ashkenazic Jewry, which is the Jewry of the north.

This is not to suggest that two Jewries developed out of that thousand-year separation. Quite to the contrary, what is amazing is the degree to which the two groupings remained interconnected. To some extent those connections were maintained through interregional migration, although mass migrations between the two spheres occurred only at certain crucial turning points in Jewish history, and most migrations were from east-to-west-to-east within each sphere. What kept them bound together was a common constitutional and legal framework that preserved their shared *halakhic* and religious grounding despite regional variations. This common framework was maintained by a continuous flow of constitutional, legal, cultural, and intellectual communications between almost all parts of the Jewish world.[5]

Nevertheless, differences did develop, perhaps because Ashkenazic Jewry lived in a predominantly Christian environment for most of that thousand years, and Sephardic Jewry (except for the Jews of Italy and, for a brief period, most of the Jews of Spain) lived in a predominantly Muslim environment. Nor should we overlook the cultural differences between the Mediterranean world and northern Europe, which have been noted by historians since the days of the Roman Empire.[6]

Beyond these immediate differences, Sephardic culture came to represent the classical strain in Jewish civilization, and Ashkenazic culture came to represent the romantic strain. Every healthy civilization requires both classic and romantic forms of expression and an intertwining of the two; hence, it is no surprise that Jewish civilization found a way for both its classic and romantic modes to be expressed.[7]

Sephardim in Ferment

The Sephardic world is in ferment for two reasons: (1) underrepresentation of Sephardim in positions of power and influence in the political life of Israel and communal life in many Jewish communities in the world, and (2) the exclusion of the Sephardic cultural heritage from contemporary Jewish culture, even from the culture taught to their own children in the schools, media, and other public institutions.

The first situation is changing for the better. In Israel, the rise of the Likud to power brought vastly increased opportunities for Sephardim, which they are properly exploiting in the best sense of the term. Sephardim are rapidly moving forward in public life and will do so even more rapidly as the generation progresses. In the latter half of the first generation of Israeli statehood, Sephardim acquired equal representation in municipal offices as talented young Sephardim entered politics on the local plane. In this generation, Sephardim have moved toward proper representation on the state plane, led by leaders from development of towns and *moshavim* to achieve new positions and growing stature in the state arena. There will still be a need for Sephardic pressure, of course, to achieve full opportunity, because nobody vacates power positions voluntarily; essentially, however, normal pressure should bring this struggle to a successful conclusion in short order.[8]

The image of the Sephardim in Israel is that of Jews from the Afro-Asian countries who were brought to the state after 1948, and in the minds of many Ashkenazim are still "new immigrants" although they have been in the country for more than a generation. In fact, they represent only one segment of the Israeli Sephardic population. The modern resettlement of Eretz Israel actually was begun by Sephardim from Spain who came in regular waves at least once every hundred years beginning in the thirteenth century. Until the mid-nineteenth century there were almost no Ashkenazim in the country. From 1840 to 1948, there was an intensification of this immigration, particularly from the countries of the Mediterranean littoral, from the Balkans and Syria through Morocco. The Sephardim maintained their majority in the land until the 1860s and their political dominance until the British conquest of the country from the Ottoman Turks in 1917.

Although the absolute number of Sephardic *olim* was smaller than the number from eastern Europe in the interwar generation, a far higher percentage of the total Sephardi population came to settle in Eretz Israel throughout the entire period. For example, one quarter of Salonikan Jewry came in the 1920s and 1930s. Moreover, Sephardim kept coming after the end of the mass immigration and, except for the Russian-Jewish Aliya in the 1970s, constituted the largest source of *olim* throughout the first generation of statehood. The situation in the diaspora is more complex. The Sephardim remain a majority in the original areas of Sephardic settlement, around the Mediterranean Basin and in western Asia, but all of these are remnant or declining communities.[9] The two exceptions are Spain, which is a small but growing community as a result of the settlement of Moroccan Sephardim in its major cities in recent decades, and Italy, a unique community within the Sephardic world, which is holding its own.[10]

Morocco remains the one country in North Africa where Jews are free to build a future, but even there the emigration of Jews continues. The fourteen thousand Jews remaining there represent no more than 7 percent of the Jewish population that lived in Morocco at the time of the reestablishment of the State of Israel and perhaps a third of those who remained when Morocco regained its independence. Moreover, the community, although having enough human and fiscal resources to take care of itself, has become reliant on outside, principally Ashkenazic, aid, whether through the Joint Distribution Committee or the Chabad movement, which in its great energy has been able to turn many Moroccan Sephardim into Lubavitcher Hassidim with olive complexions, in total disregard of their own cultural heritage.

Future generations will chronicle the contributions of North African Jewry to the

Sephardic world in the decades since the breakup of their communities in the wake of the establishment of the State of Israel. Beginning in the early 1950s, Moroccan Jewry became the primary reservoir for Sephardic leadership in much of the Sephardic world. Their presence is notable from Israel to Sydney. But that reservoir has now almost dried up. In the Jewish communities of east Asia, the Sephardim represent about half the population and play important roles in sustaining the communities that themselves remain of little importance on the world Jewish scene.

In France, Sephardim are slowly gaining control over the community, but in the process are merging with the Ashkenazim to form a new French Jewry.[11] In Switzerland, they represent a strong and wealthy minority with influence accordingly. The percentage of Sephardim in the rest of Europe is too small to be significant. The most that can be said about the European situation is that small groups of Sephardic émigrés from the Islamic countries have established residence in the major cities of that continent, have become wealthy, and are now beginning to surface as actors on the world Jewish scene.

In Britain, the Sephardic minority is prestigious but so small that, however distinguished, it carries little weight as a group in the overall community. Nor can it produce intellectual and spiritual leadership but instead imports that leadership, principally from the Sephardic reservoir in Morocco.[12]

Latin America has the greatest concentration of Sephardim outside Israel and France, comprising approximately 20 percent of the Jewish population in each Latin American country. They have generally gone their own way because the dominant Ashkenazic community refused to accept the Sephardim as equals, even denying the legitimacy of their *kashrut* on the grounds that their kosher slaughtering does not meet Ashkenazic *halakhic* standards. Hence the Sephardim built their own communal institutions, generally synagogue-based, and usually failed to get together among themselves, because of their different countries of origin.[13] Much the same has been true among the Ashkenazim in Latin America, but they at least formed umbrella organizations. In recent years, there has been a marked improvement in this situation, both in a revival of Jewish interest in the Sephardic community and a greater willingness on the part of both Ashkenazim and Sephardim to begin to build links between the two subcommunities. Nevertheless, these efforts are still in their early stages.

While the number of Sephardim in North America has grown and become more visible, their percentage of the Jewish population of either Canada or the United States is too small to make their collective presence meaningful. Only in Montreal and Seattle, where they constitute 15 to 20 percent of the Jewish population, is a Sephardic presence felt. Nevertheless concern with the place of the Sephardim in Israel has led Ashkenazi Jews of both countries to pay more attention to the Sephardim in their midst.[14]

Much the same is true of the other English-speaking countries. There are a handful of Sephardim in South Africa, mostly refugees from once flourishing if small Jewish communities in the Belgian Congo and the Rhodesias, and percentagewise, a slightly larger concentration in Australia, where Adelaide, one of the smaller Jewish communities in that country, has a Sephardic majority.[15]

Where the Sephardim constitute less than 10 percent of the population, sooner or later they assimilate into the larger Ashkenazic community. Where they constitute 20 percent or more, they are struggling to retain their separate identity, and are even undergoing something of a cultural revival now that they have the economic wherewithal and leisure time to search for their roots as the Ashkenazim are also doing. Today, however, they are doing so while seeking a place in the larger Jewish community and ending their isolation from it, an isolation as much imposed by the Ashkenazim as by their own separate heritage. In those few living Jewish communities where the Sephardim constitute a majority, they are now trying to make their majority status felt by seeking a proportionate role in the governance of the overall community.

The Cultural Issue

The cultural issue is likely to become the big issue and the more difficult one as the political issue passes. There are already important signs that this is so. As Sephardim become better established in Israel and their diaspora communities, economically and politically, they have the leisure to reflect on the process of their adjustment, which, particularly in Israel, stripped them of so much of their heritage, and to demand remedial steps accordingly.

The problem is particularly acute in Israel. The strength of Jewish culture in the diaspora is much weaker, and there is little preserved of the original Jewish cultures, Ashkenazic or Sephardic; hence, there is less sense of deprivation. True, such phenomena as neo-pseudo–Hassidism and *shtetl* appreciation leave the Sephardim out; usually, however, Sephardim constitute small minorities of the Jewish population, and there is little they can do in response except try to encourage the revival of a measure of their own culture in the same manner.

In Israel, however, the Sephardic majority feels culturally put upon. This is not only a response to the prevalent Ashkenazi myth that the Sephardim are culturally inferior; the roots are far deeper than that.

When the first Ashkenazim came to Eretz Israel in the nineteenth century, first as members of the old Yishuv (namely, as Jews who came to Jerusalem and other holy cities to live as Jews of Mea Shearim do today) and then as *halutzim* in the first and second aliyot, they found a dominant Sephardic community whose leaders were actively promoting the revival of Jewish life in Eretz Israel in their own way. The first Ashkenazim merely sought independence from that community, but beginning with the Zionist Aliyot they sought dominance on Zionist grounds. As long as the Ottoman Turks ruled in the country the old Sephardic elite remained in power. With the coming of the British, the situation shifted and the *halutzim* took over, excluding all others, Sephardim and Ashkenazim alike.

The Third Aliyah brought with it a Russian Zionist culture and imposed it as the norm in Eretz Israel. When the mass migration of Sephardim came after the establishment of the state, they were taught that this was the normative Israeli culture and often were forcibly assimilated to it. The secular and socialist parties gained control over the lives of most of the new immigrants so most of their children were sent to be educated in secular Zionist institutions, and made to abandon their religious and other traditions and practices. The religious parties were equally if not more Ashkenazic, so the Sephardim who came under their influence, particularly the children, were also pressed with Ashkenazi molds. Thus, with the best intentions, the Sephardim had their culture eroded from under them, in addition to having the problems of adjustment that all immigrants have and the extra problems of being misunderstood by the Ashkenazi majority.

As long as the Sephardim were persuaded that the Ashkenazim were right—that Zionist socialism *à la Russe* was superior (the code word is "Western")—they accepted this situation and even worked hard to adjust to it. But, after the decline and fall of the

Labor establishment in the 1970s, with its weaknesses and corruption exposed, the Sephardim began to question whether the Ashkenazim were right and began to assert their cultural interests and values.[16]

This is not the place to go into detail on the subject. Suffice it to say that many Sephardim now are searching for their roots on the assumption that their culture is at least equal if not superior to Ashkenazi culture. So, for example, in religion, the Ashkenazi world is polarized between the Orthodox and the secularists who reject each other's way of life while the Sephardim remain open to one another, with the religious refusing to reject those who have drifted from religious observance and those who have drifted still maintaining a positive attitude and frequently some participation in traditional religious practices. More and more Sephardim are convinced that they have something special to offer the religious life of the country and a vital role to play in shaping the Jewishness of the Jewish state. In style and manners, music and cuisine, the Sephardim feel that they have as much or more to offer to the emerging Israeli culture than do they Ashkenazim. There is now a revival of Sephardic literary and theatrical efforts, which, although usually unrecognized outside Sephardic circles (in part because of subliminal biases and in part because of differences in style), are of serious quality and sooner or later be taken into account within Israel's high culture.

This cultural thrust shows that most Sephardim in Israel have "made it" and that the stereotype of the Sephardi as a poor person living in a semi-slum is grossly inaccurate. Even if most of those in that category are Sephardim, they constitute a maximum of 30 percent of the Sephardic population in Israel; the other 70 percent are integrated economically within Israeli society, and they now have the time to consider questions of the spirit. Because matters of culture are always more difficult to resolve than questions of political power, this issue is likely to be a more difficult one for Israel and the Jewish would to deal with, but it must be addressed in the best possible way. Doing so is not a question of one side making concessions to the other; instead, it is a question of appropriately reintegrating the romantic and classic strains of Jewish civilization so that each may make its contribution to the Jewish culture now emerging.

What all this suggests is the last gasp of the division into Ashkenazic and Sephardic spheres and the reintegration of the Jewish people around new dimensions of unity and other lines of division. The task of the current generation is to bring about the reintegration in a way that all parties can make an equal contribution so that Jewish life and culture will be enriched and the best of earlier strains in Jewish civilization will be carried over into whatever will emerge in the future.

The New Sadducees

The processes that accompanied the emergence of Zionism, the resettlement of Jews in their land, and the reestablishment of the Jewish commonwealth have also brought about the reemergence of the classic threefold division that has shaped the internal life of the Jewish people whenever Jewish life has been centered in Eretz Israel. Those divisions are best known by the names attached to them in the Second Commonwealth: Pharisees, Sadducees, and Essenes.[17] These three parties, as they are referred to by historians, or camps, to use a more appropriate term that reflects the internal complexity of each and is compatible with modern Hebrew usage, acquired their identities under these names in the last centuriees of the Second Commonwealth. Each camp, however, can be traced at least to the Davidic monarchy when the Jewish people was divided into monarchists supporting the Davidic line, supporters of the prophetic school later identified with Elijah, and groups of ascetics such as the Rehabites who abjured town life.[18]

Much has been said about the normalization of the Jewish people through the rebuilding of Zion, all of which assumes a change that will make the Jews "like all the nations." There is every reason to believe that normalization, for Jews, means the active restoration of these three camps in Judaism and Jewish life. That the current revival of Jewish national existence in the land has led to a revival of those two of the three camps which had disappeared during the long exile is the most clear-cut step toward truly Jewish normalization yet taken.

The Sadducees (including their predecessors) were the first camp in preeminence for over a millenium, from the time of King David to the end of the major Jewish revolts against Rome (roughly 1000 B.C.E.–135 C.E.). They were preeminently the party of Jewish statehood, in the sense that their Jewishness was principally expressed through the political institutions of a state and those religious institutions, such as the priesthood and the Temple, intimately bound up with statehood. In sum, they were most closely identified with the institutions of the *keter malkhut,* although they also sought to co-opt the institutions of the *keter kehunah* to serve the purposes of *keter malkhut* and to extend the influence of the *keter malkhut* over the *keter torah*.[19]

With the destruction of the state and the transformation of the Jewish settlement in Eretz Israel into a community existing on Roman sufferance, the Pharisaic system of Jewish life, with its special emphasis on the individual internalization of Jewish norms, became dominant. It ultimately came to embrace almost all Jews who remained in the fold. The Pharisees anchored their system in the *keter torah*. After the destruction of the Temple, they gained control of the principal instrumentalities of the *keter malkhut* in Eretz Israel and put down a challenge by the surviving priestly representatives of the *keter kehunah* to co-opt them. Because of the prominence of the Temple and its ritual in the *halakhah* of the Pharisees, it is worthwhile recalling that the Temple came into existence to emphasize the new statehood of David and Solomon and became the keystone of the renewed statehood of the Hasmoneans. The Pharisees, as part of their preemption of centrality in Jewish life, co-opted the Temple as a symbol *after* it was destroyed.[20]

The Pharisaic system emphasized schools as the principal institutional expression of organized Jewish life and the locus of such political power as remained in Jewish hands, scholars as the principal spokesmen for the Jewish people, and the individual observance of a portable Law as the touchstone of Jewish identification and self-expression. It was uniquely adapted to the needs of the times. Thus the diaspora experience strengthened the Pharisaic camp in every respect. Lacking a proper political base, the Saducean camp ultimately disappeared. Significantly, the last bastion of Sadducee ideology was in Babylonia, where the conditions of Jewish autonomy made the exilarch a focal point for its expression. But even the exilarch eventually had to come to terms with the heads of the academies and became tied to them.[21]

The Essenes emphasized small collectivist communities as the means to fulfill the precepts of the Torah. They required the protection of a strong Jewish presence and power to maintain a shielded existence as a separatist messianic minority in the Jewish fold. Once that was gone, they could not sustain their colonies.[22] Hence they simply disappeared when Jewish political autonomy was irrevocably lost, as their Rehabite predecessors had with the destruction of the First Commonwealth.

The Rise of the Neo-Sadducees

Pharisaic Judaism held fast for nearly eighteen hundred years and, with one important exception—the Karaite challenge—was almost unchallenged for fifteen hundred
years.[23] This is not to suggest that every Jew in the premodern world lived according to
the *halakhah* as then interpreted, nor was there a uniform interpretation of *halakhah* in all
times and climes. We have enough evidence of Jewish deviation from Pharisaic norms,
even on the part of devout Jews, to know that this was not so; Pharisaic Judaism,
however, was the norm and all recognized it as such even if all individuals did not meet it
in the normative way. At the same time, Pharisaic Judaism was not Orthodoxy, which is a
modern invention. It was the form and fabric of a tradition society, which meant that
there was considerable latitude within and among Jewish communities in *halakhic* interpretation as long as the differences could be contained in the traditional society.

Once the Pharisaic camp had won, it was no longer a camp within a larger framework
but provided the framework itself. Only with the coming of the modern epoch in the
seventeenth century did the order it imposed on the Jewish people begin to break down
under the pressures of emancipation and modernization. By the early nineteenth century,
assimilation was rampant among those Jews who had left the traditional society. Because
the only Judaism they knew was Pharisaic, once they no longer accepted that, they were in a
position to break completely to the point of conversion to a nominal Christianity in order
to advance in the world around them. This provoked several responses.

One was the emergence of the Reform movement, which rejected Pharisaic Judaism entirely by rejecting the binding character of the *halakhah,* emphasizing instead the
importance of religion in the western Protestant sense as a means of connecting people to
the transcendent deity rather than binding them to transcendent norms. The Reform
movement rejected the *keter torah* for a new, sanitized version of the *keter kehunah,* which
emphasized prayer in local "temples" under rabbis who served as ministers. Reform also
rejected the *keter malkhut* by denying that Jews were a people and rejecting all Jewish
national goals.[24]

For those Jews who wanted less radical religious reform, historical, later Conservative, Judaism became the vehicle. The advocates of historical Judaism still saw themselves
in the Pharisaic camp in that they recognized the binding character of *halakhah,* but they
wished to stimulate *halakhic* change in keeping with modern times. In their efforts to be
good citizens of the countries in which they lived, they minimized the claims of the *keter
malkhut.* Their reliance on the new-style synagogue as their major vehicle also brought
them to renew and emphasize the *keter kehunah,* though in the guise of reforming the
keter torah.[25]

In response to assimilation and these reform tendencies, those who saw themselves
as remaining faithful to Pharisaic Judaism developed Orthodoxy, which is as much a
modern movement as the other two. It was based on a new ideology emphasizing the
immutability of Pharisaic forms and a set of doctrines that rejected the idea of change in
the *halakhah.* The new Orthodoxy eventually sought to foster greater adherence to the
minutiae of the *halakhah* as a demonstration of one's full commitment to Judaism.[26]

For some time, the only nonreligious alternative to Pharisaic Judaism was assimilation, through either the adopting of local nationalisms or socialism.[27] Even the
Sabbatean movement (an effort to break with Pharisaism) at the beginning of the modern epoch, which was certainly not ideologically assimilationist, led in that direction.[28]

Only with the rise of modern Jewish nationalism and, most particularly, Zionism did another alternative emerge. That alternative eventually became what may properly be called the Sadducean option, an authentically Jewish option based on the conditions of modernism and resting on much the same kind of political and high cultural base identified with the Sadducees of two millenia earlier.

The re-creation of Jewish national life in Eretz Israel that followed brought about the reestablishment of the tripartite framework that had informed earlier Jewish commonwealths. Even a variation of Essenism reemerged in the form of the kibbutz, whose collectivism, we now know since the discovery of the Dead Sea Scrolls and related materials, represents a recurring phenomenon in Jewish life—an effort to express Jewish messianic aspirations in the framework of a community of the chosen expected to lead but, in the end, protected by the larger Jewish society.

Once Pharisaic Judaism lost its dominant position, the Pharisees again became a camp. Today the Pharisaic camp can be defined as comprising Jews who see in *halakhah* the unifying principle of Judaism. After a century or more of retreat, that camp is again advancing. Its adherents have taken the offensive after years of being on the defensive and have now developed institutions designed to "convert the Jews." Their camp represents perhaps a quarter of the population of Israel, and perhaps 15 percent of world Jewry can be considered part of it. If we include *halakhically*-committed Conservative Jews, perhaps one-fifth of world Jewry would fall into the Pharisaic camp.

Of those among the remainder of world Jewry who identify Jewishly in some conscious way, most may be considered Sadducees or, more accurately, neo-Sadducees. Today's Sadducees include Israeli Zionists, diaspora Jews who seek to be Jewish through identification with the Jewish people as a corporate entity, its history, culture, and tradition, but without necessarily accepting the authority or centrality of *halakhah* in defining their Jewishness. In essence, these people tend to have a political commitment to Judaism in the broadest sense. Thus they are firmly committed to the Jewish people, either as a whole or as it exists in Israel, seeing in the expression of peoplehood or nationhood what can be termed a religious obligation, though often in the sense of a civil religion.

The fate of the Conservative and Reform movements in this regard is instructive. Each defines itself in modern religious terms. The Conservative Jews are ambivalent when it comes to *halakhah*. Some, probably no more than one-fifth of their claimed membership, see themselves as continuing *halakhic* Judaism, and the rest have no ideology, only ties to Conservative synagogues. Their ideology as Jews undoubtedly stems from their strong commitment to the State of Israel, reinforced by a deep feeling that Jews everywhere share a common fate whether they will it or not. In short, they remain Jewish for Sadducean reasons. This is even more so in the Reform movement, which continues to reject the binding character of the *halakhah* in the name of religious liberalism even though it has abandoned its initial anti-Zionism and, on the contrary, has tried to link the movement with Israel in concrete institutional ways.

Increasingly, these Neo-Sadducees have come to understand that the maintenance of Jewish peoplehood is a political act. Formerly, there were those who explicitly sought to deny the political aspects of their position, arguing that what was involved was cultural expression, but in recent years they have come to understand how profoundly political their commitment is.

A few may be defined as Essenes—those who, in the Essene tradition, have sought to create total messianic societies in the framework of this world. Most are in the kibbutzim. In the late 1960s, an effort was made to develop what must be defined as an American Jewish Essene movement through the organization of communes and *havurot* on or near college campuses in the United States.[29] Lacking the protection of appropriate political frameworks, that effort has produced limited results except insofar as the *havurot* became surrogate synagogues and hence within the *keter kehunah*.

Coming to Grips with a Pluralistic Judaism

It has been suggested here that Zionism is preeminently a Sadducean movement, even though there has been a Pharisee wing of Zionism from the first and contemporary Essenes are principally connected with the Zionist enterprise. The Zionist movement was the first to recognize that the survival of the Jewish people in a post-Pharisaic age required a political revival. Consequently, it was the first movement to redefine Jewish life in explicitly political terms, relating to Jewish history and tradition through that perspective.

Almost all Israel's present political leadership and most of the diaspora leadership are effectively in the Sadducean camp. They have created an alliance with those Pharisees who have joined them in the common enterprise. The Pharisees have had to join that enterprise principally on Sadducean terms, although they have been able to wring concessions from the Sadducees with regard to the public maintenance of Pharisaic norms, because for the Sadducean camp Jewish unity is important enough to warrant them. Moreover, the Sadducees' nostalgia for Jewish tradition makes those norms more acceptable, particularly because they have nothing workable to put in their place.

That implicit understanding of what the Mizrahi's alliance with the World Zionist Movement meant led to the deep conflict within the Orthodox camp during the early days of the Zionist revolution. The Agudath Israel sought to remain authentic *perushim* (they used—and use—the term) in the sense of being utterly willing to be separated from most Jews to maintain what they believed was the only correct approach to Judaism. Mizrahi was prepared to "taint itself" by association with the new non-Pharisaic majority to advance what it believed were common Jewish goals, which it understood as valid in the Pharisaic tradition.[30]

Although the Pharisaic camp has a special commitment to *halakhic* Judaism as we know it, many Sadducees also share a strong commitment to Jewish religious tradition and practice. Many are traditional or observant Jews by any standard. A few are even "orthoprax": they practice *halakhic* Judaism without being Orthodox in their fundamental ideological commitments, which are Sadducean. Still, Pharisees and Sadducees alike tend to look upon them as less authentic in their Judaism, because we are still living in the shadow of Pharisaic dominance. After all, a significant number of Jews now in Israel came from communities where the Pharisaic tradition continued its dominance unbroken during their own lives there, although, naturally, their number is decreasing. Moreover, a two thousand-year tradition is not forgotten overnight.

Nevertheless, by now several generations of Jews have grown up outside any Jewish *religious* tradition and cannot cope with the religious aspect of their Jewishness. Because of them and the renewed Jewish state that inevitably pursues political goals, the Jewish people now must reconcile itself to the renewed classic party division in Jewish life and, whatever their individual commitments, to expect the continuation of a strong Sadducee camp. As Jews, they must insist that the Sadducean camp begin to understand itself for what it is and develop an appropriately articulated Jewish framework in which to work. They cannot simply transform those elements off Pharisaic Judaism that are appealing into a kind of civil religion that is either no more than residually Jewish or that uses Jewish forms to promote non-Jewish content. The ancient Sadducees may not have accepted the Pharisaic understanding of Judaism, but they, too, shared a religious conception of Jewish existence. Although that task falls upon the entire Jewish people, it is of particular concern and relevance to Israel, which, as the center of the Jewish world and the only place where an autonomous Jewish culture flourishes, must make a greater effort to make that culture truly Jewish in one way or another.

A civil religion indeed has emerged in Israel.[31] It represents the first articulation of a revived Sadducean approach to maintaining the rhythm of Jewish life. No civilization can exist without having a rhythm. A great part of the genius of Judaism is found in the way it establishes a rhythm for all Jews. Normally, the life rhythm of a civilization is associated with a particular locale. Pharisaism was (and is) particularly adept in the way it transformed that rhythm into a portable one, which could be carried into exile in every diaspora. Zionism-as-Sadduceanism has emphasized the revaluation of traditional Jewish rhythms in ways that are tied to the Israeli locale but influenced by a universal culture.

Those in the Pharisaic camp will undoubtedly argue that the neo-Sadducean civil religion is not enough, and properly so—in its present form they are right and they may even be right for the long term. But with some four-fifths of world Jewry outside the Pharisaic camp, a Sadducean Judaism will develop whether the Pharisees will it or not. The only open question—a big one—is, What will be its content?

The trend is toward separate Judaisms on one level, despite the Sadducean borrowing of Pharisaic practices for their civil religion. Israel may well come to be divided into the two if not three separate communities. On the other hand, their continued willingness to work together in the institutions of the *keter malkhut,* however strong their divisions in the other *ketarim,* offers an opportunity for maintaining Jewish unity under these new conditions. Let us hope that, in the Third Commonwealth, the intense conflicts that marked the Pharisee-Sadducee relationship in the Second Commonwealth will be avoided for the sake of the Jewish people.

Neo-Sadducees and the Jewish Political Tradition

Interaction between the two camps should not only be fostered for the sake of Jewish unity, but also for the fullest expression of the Jewish spirit. Precisely because the Sadducean camp has roots in the political expression of Judaism and Jewishness, the neo-Sadducees need a living Jewish political tradition. It, too, should be rooted in Jewish sources and experience, in light of their first principles and because they cannot depend on the *halakhah* to provide them the continuity that a tradition and a way of life offer. In short, the neo-Sadducees require a comprehensive political tradition in the way that Pharisees require a comprehensive *halakhic* tradition.

To suggest that the Sadducees are in special need of a Jewish political tradition is not to suggest that the Pharisees do not need one. To the contrary, just as Pharisaic Judaism managed to absorb the ideology and symbols of the Davidic line and the Temple ritual, the two most important Sadducean traditions, in order to provide a comprehensive approach to Judaism and Jewishness, so, too, have the Pharisees had to relate to the Jewish political tradition.

Why, then, has that tradition become obscure in Pharisaic Judaism? Under the conditions in which Pharisaic Judaism originally developed, it had become dangerous for Jews to have political consciousness as such. The consequences of three anti-Roman rebellions demonstrated that. So the Pharisees absorbed and hid that tradition in the mainstream of the *halakhah,* carefully avoiding any reference to it as a political tradition. In subsequent ages, this tradition survived and even thrived within the four ells of *halakhic* Judaism, in the life of Jewish communities wherever Jews settled. We are just now discovering how well it did.[32]

As a consequence, we have a paradoxical situation today. The Jewish political tradition in its most authentic form lives in the Pharisee camp, but the Pharisees themselves are least willing to recognize it as a *political* tradition. Consequently they have done relatively little to come to grips with the problems of statehood in a *halakhic* framework. The Sadducees, on the other hand, although far more open to building their Jewishness on a political tradition, have ignored that tradition and have built their political ideologies on foreign traditions, mostly imported from Europe.

For the Sadducees to recover the tradition, they must learn not only from their experience as Jews confronting political situations, but by drinking deeply from sources preserved by the Pharisees. Similarly, although the Pharisees can continue to live off their own sources, to cope with statehood they must acquire Sadducean concerns and even norms to some degree. At a time when the Jewish people is threatened with breaking apart into separate camps or communities, most especially in Israel, this interdependence is a positive element, a basis on which to rebuild a more united Jewish people and a more Jewish state.

Notes

1. The estimates are my own, based on the estimated percentage of Orthodox Jews in Israel, the United States, and elsewhere in the diaspora and an estimate of the number of non-Orthodox Jews who consider *halakhah* to be binding. See "Who Is a Jew and How? The Demographics of Jewish Religious Identification," *Jerusalem Letter/Viewpoints* no. 53 (September 24, 1986).

2. See Raphael Patai, *Tents of Jacob* (Englewood Cliffs, N.J.: Prentice-Hall, 1971), chap. 5.

3. Patai, *Tents of Jacob;* Richard D. Barnett, ed., *The Sephardi Heritage: Essays on the History and Cultural Contribution of the Jews of Spain and Portugal* (London: Vallentine, 1971); Jehuda Wallach and Moshe Lissak, eds., *Atlas Carta leToldot Medinat Yisrael, Shanim Rishonot* (Carta's Atlas of Israel, The First Years, 1948–1961) (Jerusalem: Carta, 1978), pp. 72–78 (Hebrew); Haim Beinart, *Atlas Carta LeToldot Am Yisrael be-Yamai HaBeinaim* (Carta's Atlas of the Jewish People in the Middle Ages) (Jerusalem: Carta, 1981) (Hebrew); Evyatar Freisel, *Atlas Carta LeToldot Am Yisrael be'Zman HaHadash* (Jerusalem: Carta, 1983) (Hebrew).

4. Zvi Ankori, "Origins and History of Ashkenazi Jewry," *Forum,* nos. 46/47 (fall/winter 1982), pp. 149–75; Abraham Joshua Heschel, *The Earth Is the Lord's* (New York and Philadelphia: Harper and Row and Jewish Publication Society of America, 1950).

5. Daniel J. Elazar and Stuart A. Cohen, *The Jewish Polity: Jewish Political Organization from Biblical Times to the Present* (Bloomington, Ind.: Indiana University Press, 1985); Raphael Halperin, *Atlas Etz-Hayim* (Tree of Life Atlas), 10 vols. (Tel Aviv: "Ruah Ya'akov," 1948–1982) (Hebrew).

6. See Robert Lopez, *Birth of Europe* (New York: M. Evans and L. B. Lippincott, 1966); Henri Pirenne, *A History of Europe,* 2 vols. (Garden City, N.Y.: Doubleday Anchor Books, 1958).

7. Heschel, in his loving description of the Ashkenazic culture of Hassidic eastern Europe, *The Earth Is the Lord's,* dwells on this difference between Ashkenazim and Sephardim and in the process describes the two strains from an Ashkenazic perspective. Although many aspects of Herschel's highly romanticized effort to distinguish between the two expressions of Jewish culture are highly subjective, he did capture the essence of the difference between the Sephardic and Ashkenazic worlds and, in doing so, put his finger on the distinction between the classical and romantic approaches to Jewish life. See also Daniel J. Elazar, "Sephardim and

Ashkenazim: The Classical and Romantic Traditions in Jewish Civilization," *Judaism,* vol. 33, no. 2 (spring 1984), pp. 146–59.

8. See Szewach Weiss, "Local Government in Israel: A Study of Its Leadership," Ph.D. dissertation (Hebrew University of Jerusalem, 1968) and Daniel J. Elazar, "Israel's New Majority," *Commentary,* vol. 75, no. 3 (March 1983), pp. 33–39.

9. Daniel J. Elazar, Harriet Pass Friedenreich, Baruch Hazzan, and Adina Weiss Liberles, *The Balkan Jewish Communities: Yugoslavia, Bulgaria, Greece, and Turkey* (Lanham, Md. and Jerusalem: University Press of America and the Center for Jewish Community Studies of the Jerusalem Center for Public Affairs, 1984). Maurice Roumani et al., *The Case of the Jews from Arab Countries: A Neglected Issue* (Tel Aviv: World Organization of Jews from Arab Countries, 1983); Ernest Stock, "Jews in Egypt—1983," *Jerusalem Letter,* no. 60 (June 15, 1983); Hayyim J. Cohen, *The Jews of the Middle East 1860–1972* (Jerusalem: Israel Universities Press, 1973); "Lebanese Jews Shrink to 200," *Jerusalem Post* (October 29, 1980); Pearl Miller, "The Jews of Damascus," *Jerusalem Post Magazine* (December 23, 1977) and "Stranger in Damascus," (December 25, 1977); Richard Ben Cramer, "Trapped in Syria: A Prayer for 'Next Year . . .'," *The Philadelphia Inquirer* (April 30, 1978); George E. Gruen, *Syrian Jews Face Perilous Future,* Foreign Affairs Department Background Memorandum (New York: American Jewish Committee, Foreign Affairs Department, March 16, 1981); Daniel J. Elazar, *The Jewish Community of Iran* (Jerusalem: Jerusalem Center for Jewish Community Studies, 1975). See the field notes of Daniel J. Elazar on the Jewish community of Afghanistan. Also see Reuben Kashani, "Yehudei Afghanistan" (The Jews of Afghanistan) in *Tefutsot HaGolah,* vol. 16, nos. 69–70 (1975); *The Jewish Communities of the USSR,* an unpublished report prepared as part of the Study of Jewish Community Organization under the auspices of the Center for Jewish Community Studies (1973); Joshua Rothenberg, *The Jewish Religion in the Soviet Union* (New York: Ktav Publishing House, Inc., 1971); Yitzhak Ben Zvi, *The Exiled and the Redeemed,* trans. I. A. Abbady (Jerusalem: Yad Yitzhak Ben Zvi, 1976); Flower Elias and Judith Elias Cooper, *The Jews of Calcutta* (Calcutta: The Jewish Association of Calcutta, 1974); Daniel J. Elazar, *The Jewish Community of India,* unpublished report prepared for the Study of Jewish Community Organization under the auspices of the Center for Jewish Community Studies (1976); *India Jewish Year Book 1969* (Bombay: Abi-Emu Publishers, 1969). M. D. Japheth, *The Jews of India: A Brief Survey* (Bombay: M. D. Japheth, 1969); Schifra Strizower, *The Bene Israel of Bombay* (New York: Schocken Books, 1971); Ezekiel N. Musleah, *On the Banks of the Ganga: The Sojourn of Jews in Calcutta* (North Quincy, Mass.: Christopher Publishing House, 1975); Eliya Ben Eliahu, *Indian Jewry '84* (Haifa: Ben Eliahu, 1984). See field notes of Daniel J. Elazar on the Jews of south Asia. Also see Abraham Kotsuji, *From Tokyo to Jerusalem* (New York: Bernard Geis Associates, 1964).

10. Henryk Zvi Geller, *The Jewish Community of Italy,* unpublished report prepared for the Study of Jewish Community Organization, under the auspices of the Jewish Community Studies Group, Jerusalem and Philadelphia (1973).

11. Ilan Greilsammer, *The Democratization of a Community: The Case of French Jewry* (Jerusalem: Center for Jewish Community Studies, 1979), "Jews of France: From Neutrality to Involvement," *Forum,* nos. 28–29 (winter 1978), and "Le Juif et la cité: quatre approches théoriques," *Archive de sciences sociales des religions,* no. 46/1 (July–September 1978); S. Trigano, "Zionism as a Strategy for the Diaspora: French Jewry at a Crossroads," *Jerusalem Letter/Viewpoints,* no. 32 (April 1984).

12. Vivian D. Lipman, *Social History of the Jews of England* (London: Watts and Co., 1954); A. M. Hyamson, *The Sephardim of England: A History of the Spanish-Portuguese Community, 1492–1959* (London: Methuen, 1951).

13. Haim Avni, "Argentine Jewry: Its Socio-Political Status and Organizational Patterns," *Dispersion and Unity,* vol. 12 (1971), pp. 128–62; Elazar with Medding, *Jewish Communities in Frontier Societies;* Mordechai Mevorach, *Report on a Visit to the Sephardi Communities of Latin America* (Jerusalem: World Zionist Organization, the Department for Zionist and Social Activity among the Sephardi and Oriental Communities, 1977); Jacob Beller, *Jews in Latin America* (New York: Ktav, 1971); Nissim Elnecavé, "Sephardic Jews in Argentina," *Dispersion and Unity,* vol. 2 (June 1960), pp. 56–57; Mauricio Pitchon, "The Sephardic Jewish Community of Chile," unpublished manuscript, Jerusalem Center for Public Affairs Archives; Frances P. Karner, *The Sephardics of Curaçao: A Study of Sociocultural Patterns in Flux* (Assen: Van Gorcum and Co., 1969); Enrique Ucko, *La fusion do los sefardies con los dominicanos* (Ciudad Trujillo, Dominican Republic: Imprenta "La Opinion," 1944); Seymour B. Liebman, *The Jewish Community of Mexico* (Jerusalem: Center for Jewish Community Studies, 1978).

14. Harold M. Waller and Sheldon Schreter, *The Governance of the Jewish Community of Montreal* (Jerusalem: Center for Jewish Community Studies, 1974). Marc D. Angel, "The Sephardim of the United States: An Exploratory Study," *American Jewish Year Book 1973,* vol. 74, pp. 77–138, and *La America: The Sephardic Experience in the United States* (Philadelphia: Jewish Publication Society of America, 1982); Daniel J.

Elazar et al., *Sephardic Jewry in the United States: A Preliminary Profile* (Jerusalem: Center for Jewish Community Studies, 1978); Hayyim Cohen, "Sephardi Jews in the U.S.: Marriage with Ashkenazim and Non-Jews," *Dispersion and Unity,* vols. 13–14 (1971–72), pp. 25–33; David Pool and Tamar de Sola, *An Old Faith in the New World* (New York: Columbia University Press, 1955); Abraham D. Lavander, ed., *A Coat of Many Colors: Jewish Subcommunities in the United States* (Westport, Conn.: Greenwood Press, 1977).

15. Daniel J. Elazar with Peter Medding, *Jewish Communities in Frontier Societies: Argentina, Australia, and South Africa* (New York: Holmes and Meier, 1983), pp. 242–43, 309.

16. Daniel J. Elazar, "Israel's New Majority," *Commentary,* vol. 75, no. 3 (March 1983), pp. 33–39, *The Sephardim Today* (Chappaqua, N.Y.: Rossel Books, forthcoming) and "A New Look at the Two Israels," *Midstream,* vol. 24, no. 4 (March 1978), pp. 3–10; Michael Inbar and Chaim Adler, *Ethnic Integration in Israel* (New Brunswick, N.J.: Transaction Books, 1977); Shlomo A. Deshen, "Political Ethnicity and Cultural Ethnicity in Israel during the 1960s," in Abner Cohen, ed., *Urban Ethnicity* (London: Tavistock, 1974); Lee Dutter, "Eastern and Western Jews: Ethnic Divisions in Israeli Society," *Middle East Journal,* vol. 31, no. 4 (autumn 1977), pp. 451–68; Sammy Smoocha, *Israel: Pluralism and Conflict* (London: Routledge and Kegan Paul, 1978); *HaBayia HaEdatit: Hemshechiot veShinui* (The Ethnic Problem in Israel: Continuity and Change), special issue of *Megamot Behavioral Sciences Quarterly,* vol. 28, nos. 2–3 (March 1984) (Hebrew).

17. Haim Hillel Ben Sasson, ed., *A History of the Jewish People,* contributions by A. Malamut (London: Weidenfeld and Nicholson, 1976); Louis Finkelstein, *The Pharisees: The Sociological Background of Their Faith,* 2 vols., 3d rev. ed. (Philadelphia: Jewish Publication Society of America, 1962) and *Pharisaism in the Making: Selected Essays* (New York: Ktav, 1972); George Foot Moore, *Judaism in the First Centuries of the Christian Era,* 3 vols. (Cambridge: Harvard University Press, 1927–1930); Leo Baeck, *Pharisees and Other Essays* (New York: Schocken Books, 1966); Travers R. Herford, *The Pharisees* (London: G. Allen and Unwin, 1924).

18. Ben Sasson, ed., *A History of the Jewish People;* John Bright, *A History of Israel,* 2d ed. (Philadelphia: Westminster Press, 1972); Martin Noth, *The History of Israel* (London: A and C Black, 1960).

19. Stuart A. Cohen, *The Concept of the Three Ketarim,* Working Paper No. 18 of Workshop in the Covenant Idea and the Jewish Political Tradition (Ramat Gan and Jerusalem: Bar Ilan University Department of Political Studies and Center for Jewish Community Studies, 1982); Abraham Malamat, ed., *The Age of the Monarchies: Political History, The World History of the Jewish People, First Series,* vol. 4–i (Jerusalem: Massada Publishing Co., 1979); Haim Tadmor, "The People and the Kingship in Ancient Israel: The Role of Political Institutions in the Biblical Period," in H. H. Ben Sasson and S. Ettinger, eds., *Jewish Society through the Ages* (New York: Schocken Books, 1973); Solomon Zeitlin, *The Rise and Fall of the Judean State: A Political, Social, and Religious History of the Second Commonwealth,* 3 vols. (Philadelphia: Jewish Publication Society of America, 1968–1978).

20. Elazar and Cohen, *The Jewish Polity,* pp. 121–34; Gedaliah Alon, *The Jews in Their Land in the Talmudic Age (70–640 C.E.),* trans. and ed. Gershon Levi, vol. 1 (Jerusalem: Magnes Press, 1980); Jacob Neusner, *From Politics to Piety: The Emergence of Pharisaic Judaism* (Englewood Cliffs, N.J.: Prentice-Hall, 1973).

21. Jacob Neusner, *There We Sat Down: Talmudic Judaism in the Making* (Nashville: Abingdon Press, 1972); S. M. Wagner and A. D. Breck, eds., *Great Confrontations in Jewish History* (Denver: University of Denver, 1977); Ralph Marcus, "The Hellenistic Age," in Leo Schwarz, ed., *Great Ages and Ideas of the Jewish People* (New York: Random House, 1956), chaps. 5 and 6.

22. Flavius Josephus, *The Second Jewish Commonwealth,* ed. Nathan Glazer (New York: Schocken Books, 1971); Moore, *Judaism in the First Centuries of the Christian Era;* R. Travers Herford, *Judaism in the New Testament Period* (London: Lindsey Press, 1928); Christian David Ginsburg, *The Essenes: Their History and Doctrines* (New York: S. Weiser, 1972).

23. Zvi Ankori, *Karaites in Byzantium: The Formative Years, 970–1100* (New York and Jerusalem: Columbia University Press and the Weizmann Science Press of Israel, 1959).

24. Gunther W. Plaut, *The Rise of Reform Judaism* (New YorK: World Union for Progressive Judaism, 1963–65); Sefton D. Temkin, "A Century of Reform Judaism in America," *American Jewish Year Book 1973,* vol. 74, pp. 3–75.

25. Moshe Davis, *The Emergence of Conservative Judaism* (Philadelphia: Jewish Publication Society of America, 1963; Marshall Sklare, *Conservative Judaism: An American Religious Movement* (New York: Schocken Books, 1972).

26. Charles S. Liebman, "Orthodoxy in American Jewish Life," *American Jewish Year Book 1965,* vol. 66, pp. 21–97; Reuven P. Bulka, ed., *Dimensions of Orthodox Judaism* (New York: Ktav, 1983).

27. Howard M. Sachar, *The Course of Modern Jewish History* (New York: World Publishing Company, 1958).

28. Gershom Scholem, *Sabbatai Sevi, The Mystical Messiah,* trans. R. J. Zwi Werblowsky (Princeton: Princeton University Press, 1973).

29. Gerald B. Bubis, Harry Wasserman with Alan Lert, *Synagogue Havurot* (Jerusalem and Washington, D.C.: Center for Jewish Community Studies and University Press of America, 1981); Daniel J. Elazar, "An Academic Havurah," *The Reconstructionist,* vol. 28, no. 7 (May 18, 1962), pp. 5–10; Elaine Shizgal Cohen, "A Gathering of Communities," *Congress Monthly,* vol. 46, no. 8 (December 1979), pp. 13–14; Jeffrey Oboler, "The First National Havurah Conference," *Congress Monthly,* vol. 46, no. 8 (December 1979), pp. 12–13; Barbara Pash and Marc Silver, "What's a Havurah?" *Present Tense,* vol. 5, no. 3 (spring 1978), pp. 6–8; Sandra King et al., "The Havurah Experience," *The Reconstructionist,* vol. 43, no. 4 (May 1977), pp. 15–19; Jacob Neusner, *Contemporary Jewish Fellowships in Theory and in Practice* (New York: Ktav, 1972); Bernard Reisman, *The Chavurah: A Contemporary Jewish Experience* (New York: Union of American Hebrew Congregations, 1977).

30. Charles S. Liebman and Eliezer Don-Yehiya, *Religion and Politics in Israel* (Bloomington, Ind.: Indiana University Press, 1984); Eliezer Don-Yehiya, "Hilon, Shlilah ve-Shiluv; Tfisot shel ha-Yahdut HaMesorati ve-Musagahah be-Tzionut ha-Sococialisti" (Secularization, Negation, and Integration: Concept of Traditional Judaism in Zionist Socialism), *Kivunim,* no. 8 (August 1980) (Hebrew) and "Origins and Development of the Agudah and Mafdal Parties," *Jerusalem Quarterly,* no. 20 (summer 1981); Ervin Birnbaum, *The Politics of Compromise: State and Religion in Israel* (Rutherford, N.J.: Fairleigh Dickinson University Press, 1970); Gary Schiff, *Tradition and Politics: The Religious Parties of Israel* (Detroit: Wayne State University Press, 1977).

31. Liebman and Don-Yehiya, *Civil Religion in Israel* and *Religion and Politics in Israel,* chap. 4; Shalom Lilker, "Kibbutz Judaism: A New Tradition in the Making," Ph.D. dissertation (Hebrew Union College–Jewish Institute of Religion, 1972).

32. Elazar, *Kinship and Consent* and *The Book of Joshua as a Political Classic: A Commentary,* rev. ed. (Jerusalem: Center for Jewish Community Studies, 1980), *The Constitutional Periodization of Jewish History: A Second Look,* rev. ed. (Jerusalem: Center for Jewish Community Studies, 1980), *Covenant as the Basis of the Jewish Political Tradition* (Jerusalem: Center for Jewish Community Studies, 1977); Elazar and Cohen, *The Jewish Polity;* Cohen, *The Concept of the Three Ketarim;* Gordon Freeman, *The Rabbinic Understanding of Covenant as a Political Idea* (Jerusalem: Center for Jewish Community Studies, 1977); Peter Medding, *Towards a General Theory of Jewish Political Interests and Behavior* (Jerusalem: Center for Jewish Community Studies, 1977).

II

Centers of the Reconstituted Commonwealth

8

Israel as a Jewish State

For all its striving for normality, Israel remains a curious kind of state, probably without any contemporary or modern parallel. Formally, Israel is built on the modern European model of statehood, behind which is a theory that views states as reified polities, existing apart from their citizens and sovereigns in all things, the cornerstones of all political life, and the primary focus of human loyalty (or at least that human loyalty that is not transcendent). Yet Israel as a Jewish state must inevitably reject that conception of statehood to be true to itself and the purposes for which it was founded.

Aside from the weight of the Jewish political tradition, which, though hardly recognized for what it is, still animates the attitudes of Jews towards political institutions including states, three principal factors force the rejection of European conceptions of statehood in practice and require a conception more appropriate to the Israeli situation: (1) Israel is the state of the Jewish people, (2) Israel is only one of the states in Eretz Israel, and (3) Israel as a state is a compound polity. The result is to lead toward a definition of statehood that may be sui generis to the Jewish people but in certain aspects resembles the democratic conception of the polity that prevails in the United States and other new societies.

Statehood and the Jewish Political Tradition

Before examination of the three factors, a word is in order about the idea of statehood in the Jewish political tradition.[1] There is no doubt that the idea of the Jewish people living independently in their own land stands at the heart of the Jewish political tradition. No matter how reckoned in the traditional sources, the fulfillment of the *mitzvot* in their completeness depends on the existence of a Jewish polity in Eretz Israel.[2]

Though important to enable the Jewish people to fulfill the tasks for which they were commissioned by God, the polity is not an end in itself. It is a means to that end but no more. Classic Hebrew reflects this. There is no generic term for *state* in the Bible or the Talmud. The Hebrew term *medinah,* now used for state, appears in both; in the Bible it refers to a political jurisdiction with local autonomy (the equivalent of a *Land* in German or one of the fifty states of the United States), that is, a territory under a common *din* (law) whose identity is marked by having its own political institutions but is not independent and certainly not politically sovereign in the modern sense.[3] In the Talmud, the term is used even more vaguely from a political perspective, as in *medinat hayam,* roughly translated as some distant jurisdiction.[4] Only in modern times has *medinah* come to be used to describe a "sovereign state."[5]

171

Hebrew, and therefore the Jewish political tradition, has different terms for different political systems. Each term focuses on a particular relationship between governors and governed. Thus the rich political terminology of biblical Hebrew described relationships rather than "states," using terms such as *edah, malkhut* (kingship), *mamlakhah* (dominion—the term closest to state in the modern sense), and *kahal* (congregation—in its civil sense).

In the biblical view, peoples, nations, and languages have the kind of permanence as entities that states have in modern European political thought. What is not fixed for peoples is the form of regime or political structure under which they operate. Peoples, nations, and languages are concrete, hence they are permanent; states are abstractions, hence they are identified only as they are manifested as regimes.

The chief reason for the classic Jewish rejection of state sovereignty in its European form rests with the strong belief that ultimate sovereignty reposes in God alone and that humans exercise delegated powers under the terms of God's covenants, which give the people an effective share in the exercise of sovereign powers. The *edah* is the primary delegatee of the power to govern the Jewish people, acting either as a whole or in conjunction with officers and institutions that it establishes under God's providence. Together, the *edah,* its officers, and God establish regimes through subsidiary covenants under the terms of the original covenant between God and Israel as embodied in the Torah. Under such a system there can be no reified state.[6] A state is a receptacle through which the true exercisers of sovereignty can establish a political order but has no life apart from them—something closer to a *medinah* in the biblical sense.

Until the rise of Zionism, the concept of statehood found little place among those Jews concerned with political matters. Even in Zionist theory, there was a great hesitancy to advocate statehood in that sense. Some Zionist theorists, such as Ahad Ha'am in the secular camp, and various religious Zionists sought to avoid statehood, seeing it as dangerous or improper for Jews.[7] Others, such as Martin Buber, who could see the need for political independence, developed a concept of statehood far more in keeping with the Jewish political tradition. Buber, indeed, drew heavily on that tradition to express his own radical conception of what a Jewish polity should properly be.[8]

Whatever Zionist theorists may have desired, events created a consensus that political independence was not only desirable, but was only achievable through statehood. Today, with insignificant exceptions, Israelis and other Jews do not regret that turn in the pursuit of the Zionist goal. The only question is, What kind of statehood? Under what view or conception of the state?

In the early years of Israel's independence, a special effort was made to strengthen the institutions of the state. Ben-Gurion's well-known *mamlakhtiut* (statism) policy was part of that effort. While Ben-Gurion understood the limits of *mamlakhtiut,* the policy as it gained currency led to a tendency to idolize the state and its most attractive instrument, the Israel Defense Forces. Subsequent events have turned Israelis away from that emphasis and have led them to reconsider the question of what statehood means in a Jewish state.

Israel as a Politically Independent Jewish State

The State of Israel is sui generis in the Jewish world because it is a Jewish society functioning in a self-consciously Jewish manner in an epoch that witnessed the disappearance of the last of such societies in the diaspora. Thus, although most of its government institutions are adapted from liberal European models, they are described in Israel in a political terminology which invokes the slogans and symbols of earlier epochs of Jewish rule in Eretz Israel.[9]

This is most evident in the institutions of the Israel government. Following the threefold division of Jewish political institutions, it is possible to view the institutions of the Jewish state as shown in figure 8.1.

The government of Israel comprises the *keter malkhut*. The other *ketarim* are independent to a degree but the government does play a role in organizing them. An examination of the institutions of the polity shows how this is so. As a matter of historical continuity, their names either continue or are derived from biblical political terminology.

Israel's supreme legislative body is the Knesset (assembly), a term first used to describe the Anshei Knesset Ha-Gedolah, the institution established in Jerusalem for the same purpose when the Jews returned from the Babylonian exile twenty-five hundred years ago. It is elected by universal adult suffrage on a party (*miflagah,* from the biblical *peleg*) list basis through proportional representation. Like the Anshei Knesset Ha-Gedolah, the Knesset has 120 members, equivalent to a *minyan* (quorum for constitutional and religious purposes) from each of the historic twelve tribes, to symbolize that it represents the entire people.

The *memshalah* (government)—a term signifying rule over equals, first used in the first chapter of Genesis for that purpose—is organized as a cabinet with collective responsibility. It must have the confidence of the Knesset. The *rosh memshalah* is head of the government; *rosh* is used in a similar political context in the Bible; as prime minister he must be a member of the Knesset. The members of the government are called *sarim* (ministers; singular: *sar*), the biblical term for such officers. Most are also the political

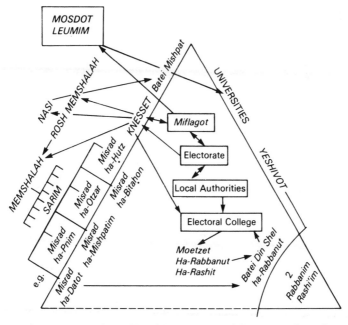

Figure 8.1.   The political institutions of the State of Israel.

heads of *misradim* (departments; singular: *misrad*), a biblical term, used then in reference to the Temple organization. They include: *otzar* (treasury, a biblical term for the same office), *hutz* (foreign affairs), *bitahon* (defense), *p'nim* (interior), and *datot* (religions).

The head of the Israeli state is the *Nasi* (president), the biblical term for magistrate or chief magistrate, used exclusively for the equivalent of president for more than two thousand years. The *bet mishpat* (courts; plural: *batei mishpat*), a new combination of biblical terms to distinguish civil courts from *batei din,* the traditional term for *halakhic* courts.

In the *keter torah,* the supreme state body governing Jewish religious activities is the *Moetzet HaRabbanut HaRashit* (Council of the Chief Rabbinate), a body elected by the Knesset. Its name is a combination of traditional terms; the term *rav* is talmudic and has been used consistently for the same purpose for two thousand years or more. The *rabbanim rashi'im* (chief rabbis), Sephardi (formally titled Rishon leZion, the first of Zion), and Ashkenazi preside over the Moetzet HaRabbanut HaRashit. Under their jurisdiction are local *batei din* (courts; singular: *bet din,* a traditional term in use for thousands of years): rabbinical courts established under state law with exclusive jurisdiction in personal status matters and concurrent jurisdiction in most civil matters.

Unofficial bodies bearing authority within this domain include two rabbinical councils commanding the allegiance of large numbers of Jews; the Moetzet Gedolei HaTorah of the ultra-Orthodox Ashkenazim and the Moetzet Hakhmei Hatorah of the Sephardim. Certain *yeshivot* are also informal centers of halakhic authority. The term was introduced in Babylonia eighteen hundred years ago as the Hebrew equivalent of Sanhedrin, the Hebraized Greek equivalent of *knesset.* To round out the picture, the universities, formally secular institutions, not only enjoy the special status reserved by Jews for institutions of learning but have, from the first, been entrusted with the task of serving the Zionist enterprise. Several employ professors in certain fields who have become the principal articulators of non-Orthodox Jewish visions and teachings associated with them, especially Zionism.

The tasks of the *keter kehunah* are chiefly handled by the Ministry of Religious Services plus different instrumentalities of the *keter torah.* Most are handled locally by the *moetzot datiot* (local religious councils).

Local authorities in Israel can be understood as *kehillot* following a similar model (see figure 8.2). The terminology of local government parallels that of the state government. A municipality is either an *ir* (city, a biblical term), a *moetzah mekomit* (local council), or a *moetzah azorit* (regional council). The mayor is *rosh ha'ir* (head of the city) or *rosh ha'moetzah* (head of the council). The legislative body is always the *moetzah.* The other terminology is the same.

The proportional representation system makes the Knesset broadly representative of the organized political groups in the polity on a consociational basis. Every *memshalah* is a coalition of parties, established under a formal constitutional agreement (*heskem*) negotiated by the parties. It must function in such a way as to allow its members much latitude and enable them to gain rewards for their constituents in return for participating in the coalition.

The Knesset frequently functions more as a sounding board for the broader interests of Israel and the Jewish people than as a legislative assembly in the conventional parliamentary sense. This fits well with the traditional role of the principal political assemblies of the Jewish people, which were designed to reflect the views of the *edah* and to reach an operative consensus on issues rather than legislate. The *memshalah* is responsi-

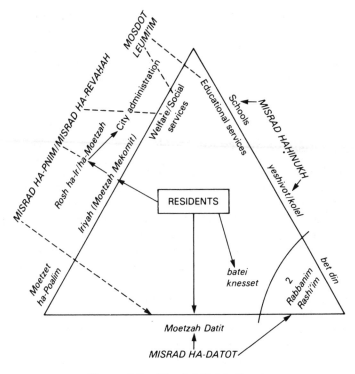

Figure 8.2.   The *kehillah* in Israel.

ble for formulating legislation and policy that can be modified by the Knesset, but are rarely rejected unless the responsible ministry has utterly failed to do its homework. The Knesset exercises most of its power through its committee system, something uncharacteristic of most parliaments but a classic aspect of congressional government. Committees are the source of such independence as the Knesset has vis-à-vis the *memshalah* and are so structured as to give the opposition members significant weight so that they will help guarantee that independence.

In the local arena, the law was amended in the late 1970s to institute direct election of mayors. This could have led to the introduction of a presidential system in the local arena, with the mayor substantially independent of his council and with nearly full authority to control the executive branch. In fact, the weight of tradition has led mayors to organize coalitions based on the distribution of seats in their local councils in a manner like the system in the state arena.[10] The relationship between the Knesset and *memshalah* and council and executive is best described as that of two unequal congressional bodies that nevertheless check and balance each other.

Israel is formally a secular, democratic state, the only one in the Middle East besides Turkey, but its calendar and rhythm are deliberately Jewish in the same way that the calendars and rhythms of the states of the Christian world are Christian, and of the Muslim world, Muslim. The Sabbath and Jewish holidays are official days of rest in Israel. Public and government bodies display Jewish symbols, whether *mezzuzot* on every doorpost in every public building or Hanukkah lights on top of the city hall at the appropriate season. The Israel Defense Forces, El Al the national airline, and all other public institutions maintain Jewish dietary laws and an agreed-on modicum of Sabbath observance. Hebrew is the official and principal language of the country (Arabic is also an official language and English a recognized one). Because language is the principal bearer of culture, it strengthens the Jewish cultural identity of the state. Even the most secular Israeli public figures use biblical and talmudic expressions in their speeches and discussions as a matter of second nature.

Israel as a State of the Jewish People

All the evidence indicates that a very large majority of the Jews of Israel view it as the state of the Jewish people.[11] Every coalition agreement forming a government reaffirms this view as the official policy of the government and the state. True, a small but vocal minority rejects this understanding. But no matter how vocal, it is small and appears to be growing smaller, having reached its high point in the late 1950s and early 1960s when *mamlakhtiut* was also at its apex. The trend toward the separation of Israel from the Jewish people was strong then and had at least the latent sympathy even of much of the establishment.[12]

The majority, who view Israel as the state of the Jewish people, are of two orientations: those who see the Jewish people of Israel as practically coterminous with the Jewish people and those who see the state as the center of a larger people. The first group is mindful of the existence of the diaspora but considers it to be merely an appendage of the state, probably transitory, either because diaspora Jews will be compelled to move to Israel sooner or later because of anti-Semitism or because they will assimilate into the societies in which they are located. From this perspective, practically speaking, the Jews who count are the Jews of Israel.[13]

Those in the second group not only recognize that the diaspora will continue to exist but that Israel has only one quarter of the Jews in the world while the largest Jewish community, that of the United States, has two million more Jews than the Jewish state. They argue that, because Israel is the only independent Jewish state and is the focal point of Jewish tradition, it is central to Jewish existence and far more important than mere numbers would indicate. However, they are also prepared to see it as one unit in a polity that has others.[14]

The second view is more accurate. Even if weakened by assimilation, at least some diaspora communities will continue to be organized and powerful in their own right. This is not to suggest that such communities will be independent of Israel; to the contrary, they are strengthened by Israel (just as the reverse is true). The Jewish world is too interdependent for any other course; as a body politic its parts interact to strengthen one another. Perhaps ironically, some diaspora communities will be strengthened by Israeli *emigrés,* some of whom have assumed important positions in those communities. Thus Israel is both a Jewish state sui generis and a Jewish community related to other Jewish communities on what could be considered a federal basis. Moreover, most Israeli Jews see the fostering of that relationship as one task of the state.

The principal institutional manifestations of this relationship are the national institutions functioning in the state's territory. In addition to the Jewish Agency and the World Zionist Organization, responsible for the settlement of the land and the Zionist education of Jews in Israel and outside, and the Jewish National Fund (JNF), responsible for land development wherever the Israel Lands Authority is not empowered to act, there are other national institutions. Technically, Bank Leumi, as the bank of the World Zionist Organization, is one, as is El Al, which is jointly owned by the state and the Jewish Agency and is known as the national airline. The Hebrew University and the other universities, a major share of whose funding and boards of governors are drawn from the Jewish community worldwide, and the National Library on the Hebrew University campus are also.

The relationship between the Jewish Agency and the State of Israel was institutionalized in the 1952 covenant between the World Zionist Organization and the state, ratified by the Knesset. Through the agency and its related organizations, the Jewish people undertake settlement, social, and educational projects throughout Israel, in rural and urban areas and often in cooperation with the local authorities. The different bodies have regional and local offices throughout the country that serve local populations as if they were government agencies.

The relationship between the state, the agency, and the universities has been institutionalized through the state's Council for Higher Education. Budgeting and policymaking are shared by the council, the universities' "national" governing boards, and each university's senate. These are roughly the equivalent of state, federal, and local bodies, if one were to translate them into political terminology. Tel Aviv, Haifa, and Ben-Gurion universities were founded by their municipalities, which continue to make their contribution as well. The others also get some support from the budgets of the local governments in whose jurisdictions they are located.

The Israeli government also seeks to institutionalize the relationship between Israel and the diaspora communities through common organizations and associations structured along functional, professional, ideological, and social lines. So, too, Israelis are represented in many world Jewish bodies through a network of nongovernmental organizations functioning in the state, such as the Israel section of the World Jewish Congress, the Israel Council of the World Zionist Organization, and the like. The Law of Return guarantees every Jew (except those fleeing criminal prosecution) the right of entry into Israel and immediate citizenship; in effect it obligates the state and local governments to provide all services to all Jewish immigrants from the moment of their settlement. (Because of the dominant political culture, such services and benefits are extended immediately to all those accepted as residents of the state.) There is much misunderstanding about the Law of Return. Israel has immmigration laws like those of other countries, with permits issued upon application and naturalization following in due course. However, because Israel is considered the state of the Jewish people, Jews enter as if they were engaging in interstate migration in the American manner. Similar laws hold true in other countries for those considered their nationals even if born outside their borders.

Israel as a State in the Land of Israel

The present State of Israel, with or without the territories occupied as a result of the Six-Day War, does not encompass the entire land of Israel, what Aryeh Eliav—noted for his willingness to cede the territories occupied by Israel in 1967 to a Palestinian state—has referred to as "the land of the twelve tribes."[15] Recognizing this does not mean espousing irredentism. The historical record shows that, even in the heyday of Jewish national existence in the land, it was more common than not for the land to be divided among several states. Only the Davidic and Hasmonean empires briefly succeeded in bringing the whole of Eretz Israel under a single Jewish government, at a price that few Israelis would wish to pay. Thus, although reestablishing Jewish national existence in the land should be seen as a proper exercise of the Jewish people's religious and historical rights, complete redemption of the land may well be "forcing the end."

That the State of Israel embraces less than the land of Israel has several important implications. First, there is a difference between the religious commitment to the land and loyalty to the state; the two are not identical. One should love Eretz Israel in its entirety beyond the boundaries the state. From a religious perspective, a good Jew must be committed to the state for what it is but should not make that commitment monistic; it is part of one's multiple commitment to the land, the people, the Torah, and God. This further reduces the tendency to view the state as an end in itself. Many secular Jews have emphasized, mistakenly, love of state as the equivalent of love of country. Religious Jews have not had that problem to the same extent, though some have also been susceptible to it.

Recognizing that Eretz Israel must presently be shared with another people does not require Jews to give up their love for it. Perhaps the day will come when peace permits the settlement of Jews in all parts of the land, even outside the territories embraced by the State of Israel. Even if those Jews are citizens of another state, the difference in their relationship to the land will be there. That is why Jordan excludes Jews as residents—out of fear for the consequences of that attachment.

Israel as a Compound Polity[16]

Many students of the Israeli political system have been misled by the apparent simplicity of the state's government. For those familiar with western European and American institutions, where polities are well-nigh territorially based, government is organized fairly simply on two or three levels or planes (state and local, or federal, state, and local); where the greatest complexity is in the overlapping of local governments, the Israeli political system is complex, in that it typifies the region in which it is located and the people it serves.

The State of Israel is a compound in several ways. First, although conceived as a Jewish state, it is also compounded of several different ethnoreligious minorities besides the Jewish majority: Muslim Arabs; Christians, mostly Arab, divided into several churches; Druse; Bahai; Circassians; and Samaritans, each with its own socioreligious structure and legal status, institutional frameworks, and government support.[17] In this respect, Israel is but a more enlightened example of a phenomenon among all Middle Eastern states: they have ethnic minorities that either must be accommodated in this way (as was once true in Lebanon), severely repressed (as in the case of the Kurds in Iraq), expelled (as were the Jews in several Arab states), or destroyed (as were the Armenians in Turkey). In a sense, this represents a partial adaptation of the millet system of Ottoman times and earlier, in which each group was constituted as a separate community with internal autonomy.[18]

Israel is also a republic compounded of different religions, each recognized and supported by the state yet claiming its own higher source of authority. Among the minorities, religious belief and practice is high and even among the Jewish majority it is significant, with perhaps one-fourth of the population quite religious in practice and another 40 to 50 percent selective observers of Jewish tradition. Even the so-called secular Jews expect to express their Jewishness through certain religious symbols and accept the institutionalization of the Jewish religion as befitting a Jewish state. While there are periodic calls for particular reforms, there are few people in any of the communities who are opposed to the present arrangement.[19]

The religious communities have their own institutional structures, recognized, and in many cases, chosen under state law because they provide state-supported services.[20] Thus each religious community has its own religious courts whose judges hold commissions from the state on the basis of qualifications determined by each religious community. They are selected by the appropriate bodies of each religious community under procedures provided by state law. These courts administer the religious laws of their community, each of which has its own legal system for matters of personal status. Religious law stands in relationship to the secular law of Israel roughly as state law stands in relationship to federal law in a federation with a dual legal system.

For the state these religious groups obtain their powers through state law, but for the religious communities their powers flow directly from God and their law represents Divine will. For them (and this is true for the Jewish religious authorities as much as for any of the others), the state should have only a minimal role in determining their powers other than that to which they are willing to acquiesce. It would be correct to estimate that one-third of Israelis hold the religious law of their communities in higher regard than the law of the state, including a small group of Jews, perhaps several hundred, who reject the state law altogether.

Each of the several communities represents a further compound in its ranks. Every Arab city or village is a compound of extended families—really clans—so much so that voting and office holding, decision making, and the distribution of political rewards are dependent on the competition or cooperation among the extended families in each locality. Every so often a group of young people emerges to challenge this arrangement and there is talk that the Arabs are modernizing and will no longer be bound by this kind of familial loyalty, but every time all but the most radical of the young end up following the lead of their families in these matters.[21]

The Jewish community in Israel is a compound of a different sort. Originally based on federal connections between groups from different countries or regions or between different Zionist movements, today it is compounded of communities of culture and communities of interest.[22]

There are two kinds of communities of interest: those with a religious or ideological base, usually referred to as movements, and those whose concerns are primarily with the management of power or the securing of economic or social goals. These communities of interest are reasonably well known, although perhaps too little attention has been paid to how they relate to each other and have since the beginning of the Zionist enterprise. Thus the different groups of socialist Zionists, each with its ideology, began to erect their settlements and institutions in the country. Paralleling them were Zionists with a liberal (in the European sense) ideology and others whose ideology was primarily derived from traditional religion, ranging from religious socialists who based a modern collectivist ideology on ancient religious sources, to the religious right that would not accept any kind of secular behavior in the state-to-be.

Each of these movements, except the extreme religious right and Communist left, sought to create a comprehensive range of institutions, a kind of nonterritorial state of its own but in the framework of the Zionist effort. They also wanted the effort to succeed, so they federated in roof organizations and institutions through which they could pursue the common objective, even while contesting with one another about the shape of the state to come and the vision that would inform it. This federation of movements became the basis of the present party system, which organizes and informs Israel's political system.[23]

The transition from the settlement stage when ideological democracy was dominant to a stage of rootedness when territoriality asserts itself may have weakened the system. Nevertheless, the state's institutional infrastructure continues to reflect those prestate federal arrangements through the party system and the Histadrut. The arrangements inform even ostensibly neutral government offices, state and municipally owned companies, cooperatives, and voluntary bodies in which offices are allocated by party no less than in the overtly political institutions.

Today, as in the past, the country is divided into three "camps": labor, national (Hebrew, *leumi*), and religious. With all the changes that have taken place in recent years, including the great weakening of concern with parties and ideologies in the Israeli body politic, these three camps persist. They persist partly for party political reasons and partly as a reflection of the real divisions that separate Israel's political activists, even if they are unideological.

Contrary to the conventional wisdom, the three camps do not relate to one another on a left-right continuum but stand in something like a triangular relationship to one another (see figure 8.3). For a long time, preoccupation with European models prevented students of Israeli politics from seeing that there never was a time when Israel, and the Zionist movement before it, did not operate on that basis. Thus for certain purposes, each camp is left or right depending on what aspect of a particular Zionist vision is involved.

The camps are divided into parties, in some cases along left-right lines, often antagonistic to one another. The size of each camp is not fixed, either in relation to the total population or to other camps, but whatever the fluctuations, the camps persist. Their persistence is reflected in the stability of camp (as distinct from party) allegiance in Knesset elections.

At one time, almost all services provided citizens were provided through the parties, or, for Labor, through the Histadrut, which united the labor camp. Again the analogy to a federal system is apt. Just as in a federal territorial polity one must be a resident of a state to avail oneself of the services of the polity, so, too, in prestate Israel it was necessary to be linked to a party or camp.

With the establishment of the state, the government took over more and more of the services, beginning with the military services (until 1948, the movements actually had separate paramilitary formations), continuing with the schools (which were divided into trends to accommodate the different social, political, and religious attitudes within the Yishuv), and most social services. The parties or camps, however, still control sports (teams in all league sports, for example, are organized by party, although the divisions have become meaningless now that the players are recruited strictly by ability), health insurance, ordinary medical facilities, and banking. Even those functions that have been absorbed by the formal institutions of government maintain an informal division by party key for employment purposes.

Today these manifestations of the old divisions are diminishing. More and more services are provided neutrally by the state or local governments or, more often, through cooperative arrangements involving the two. Party influence is strongest in the government structure and primarily touches those who pursue public careers rather than the

Figure 8.3.   The three camps and the parties (1984).

public at large, although in a government-permeated society this is a significant bastion of party strength.

The raison d'être for many of the original ideological divisions has so weakened that only in the religious camp do ideological justifications remain strong enough to create demands of prestate intensity, and they are accommodated by allowing parallel institutions in many fields. Schools are the best example. The expectation is that, aside from the division between the strictly religious and the non- or not-so religious, the ideological divisions will become weaker unless there is a strong upsurge of secular ideology but not necessarily disappear. In part, they are being replaced by new issue and cultural orientations that continue to give each camp its identity but without the earlier institutional apparatus.

Similarly, those communities that acquired a primarily territorial identity are becoming increasingly important as the polity makes the transition from its ideologically rooted founding to being more settled. Whatever the criticism sometimes raised against territorially based communities, it is generally recognized that the territorial expression of interest is natural to any society and is reenforced by strong Zionist desire to achieve greater rootedness in the country. The political parties may oppose the shift to territorially based representation on ideological grounds, but they do so primarily because of self-interest, to protect their power bases.

Circumstances have led to the emergence of a state that is more or less organized to accommodate some of the complexities of its population but in a formal structure borrowed from another context. That structure goes against the grain of most of the realities of Israeli society and politics and has had to be accommodated to those realities by a heavy reliance on extralegal methods. The mismatch has led to an increasing impairment in the governance of the state, of which one manifestation is a tendency to ignore the law to make things work.

Although something can be said for having allowed the system to develop pragmatically, as it has, focusing on the relationships desired in each instance rather than in the formalities of the structure, a point comes where structure is crucial, if only because of how it influences relationships. Israel has now reached that point, evidenced by the demands for structural reform that abound as many Israelis have begun to perceive, even dimly, that the structure of their governing institutions does not square with their expectations as citizens. The diehard resistance to those structural changes by those in power only adds weight to the evidence.

Much of the structure also goes against the grain of the Jewish political tradition. This is not readily perceived by a population that remains unaware of that tradition, even though it is the effect of the behavioral aspects of that tradition on a structure derived from nineteenth-century European models that has led to the mismatch. Nor are Israelis particularly aware that their polity is compounded. Even those who would be, for the most part look at the system through glasses colored by nonindigenous ideologies or methodologies that lead them away from a proper perception of the reality in which they live. Thus many in the religious camp have not come to grips with the pluralistic compound in the state, the labor camp has not come to grips with the changed character of the emerging territorial democracy, and the camps are only beginning to come to grips with the existence of a substantial and growing Arab minority.

After the Six-Day War, the camps seemed to be diminishing as political as well as social factors in Israeli society. The movement from ideological to territorial democracy was predominant in the first generation of Israeli statehood (1948–1977). David Ben-Gurion led the way after 1948 in his emphasis on *mamlakhtiut* (statism) in place of the earlier political ideologies, state provision of public services previously provided by the parties or camps, and a shift from socialism to a quasi-state capitalism in the economic sphere for pragmatic reasons. But he merely prefigured and strengthened what is a natural phenomenon in any new society: the decline of the founding ideologies as the society takes shape and the founders are succeeded by later generations who are where they are because they were born there and not because they have chosen to be builders of a new society because of prior ideological motivation. Every new society has passed through a similar transformation.

By the late 1960s, the new political leadership was, with a few exceptions, also nonideological, with leanings in one direction or another derived from the old ideologies, but basically pragmatic in orientation and concerned with new problems about which the old ideologies had little to say. Although the parties kept up some pretense of ideological commitment, almost everyone knew that this was merely a front designed to pay due obeisance to the *halutzic* spirit of the past. This was most true of the Labor Party, which had become a broad-based coalition of sectors and factions. It was least true of the religious parties which had living ideologies from which they drew, although there, too, the largest—the National Religious Party (NRP)—had become so pragmatic in practice that its ideology was only minimally relevant.

Hence, it was not surprising that after the Six-Day War, the emergence of new issues about the future of the administered territories and the negotiation of peace with the Arabs should lead to the breaking off of fringe elements from one camp and their movement to another, which had not previously happened in Israeli politics. That, plus the defection of many previously Labor voters to the Likud and the tendency of the young to vote Likud no matter how their parents voted, led many to believe that the camps were breaking down.

The 1984 elections suggested that matters were not so simple. It is true that the old ideologies have faded further, yet the camps are holding together well. Voter shifts and party divisions still are more likely within camps than across them. Thus the labor camp embraces the Labor party, Mapam (which broke its alliance with the Labor party rather than enter the national unity government), and Shulamit Aloni's Citizens' Rights movement, a Labor party breakaway now positioning itself on the "new left."

The Likud was founded as a union of the two major parties of the national camp—Herut and the Liberals—and acquired La'am in 1969, the one breakaway from the Labor camp that moved as a body across camps, In 1981, Tehiya broke away from Likud, yet remained in the same camp. So, too, did the smaller fragments under Yigal Hurvitz and Ezer Weizman (Yahad), which broke away in 1984. Both were identified by voters as being fully within the civil camp. Weizman's later decision to join the Labor Party led to a negative response among his voters, who never expected such a turn of events.

Since the establishment of the state, the religious camp has won between twelve and eighteen seats in every election, with the number usually thirteen to sixteen. On one occasion, almost the entire camp was united; on others it was divided between two parties: the National Religious Party and Agudath Israel. Occasionally, Poalei Agudath Israel would run independently and win a seat. In 1984, the religious camp was fragmented among five parties that together won thirteen seats. What is significant is that all five—the NRP, Agudath Israel, Matzad-Morasha, Sephardi Torah Guardians, and Tami—have stayed in their shared camp, however hostile the relationships among them.

If camps do not survive for ideological reasons, why do they? I would suggest that they have come to reflect different facets of Israel's emerging political culture, especially voter affinities in political expectations and style. Political scientists have referred to these as matters of "persuasion" rather than ideology—a somewhat vague set of orientations rather than a clear-cut doctrine specifying programs and goals. These differences in persuasion are still effective in shaping the configurations of Israeli politics and the limits of voter change. Such shifts as are taking place, among younger voters and Sephardim (the two groups overlap considerably), reflect a sorting out of persuasions because of generational change.

The Conflict of Cultural Inheritances

The political culture of Israel is compounded of several elements that have yet to become fully integrated.[24] Three major political strands can be isolated. The most visible was the conception of state and government imported from eastern and central Europe by most of the pioneering generation and built into the state's institutions at every turn. Its four salient elements, for our purposes, are: (1) a strong statist-bureaucratic orientation, (2) a perception of public officials as standing in a superior relationship to the general public by virtue of their role as servants of the (reified) state, (3) expectations of heavy state involvement in the economic and social spheres as normal and even desirable, and (4) strong support for centralization of power. Political organization is expected to be centralized, hierarchical, and bureaucratic.[25] Although much of this went against the ideology of the *halutzim,* which emphasized participatory democracy in face-to-face communities and cooperative institutions, in the end this political cultural orientation strongly influenced their expectations of the new state.

The second political cultural strand was also imported. Although primarily associated in the public mind with Jewish immigrants from West Asia and North Africa, it can be found among those European Jews who came to Israel directly from the *shtetl* (the Yiddish term for the east European townlet where the average Jew lived at the turn of the century) or a *shtetl*-like environment and were not previously acculturated to the larger European environment. This political culture also perceives the governing authority as a powerful force existing outside and independent of the people, but it sees government as more malevolent and more limited, the private preserve of an elite, serving the interests of that elite. Government is perceived personally as a ruler with whims rather than as the comprehensive and reified state of the first political culture. Individuals imbued with this political culture perceive themselves to be subjects of the ruler, not participating citizens. As subjects they seek to avoid contact with the government or anyone associated with it, insofar as possible, for safety's sake. When they must deal with officials, they usually take a petitionary approach, humbly requesting consideration of their needs and recognizing the superior power of the official without necessarily endorsing his authority. The state is not looked upon as a vehicle that provides services or social improvement. Instead, the hope is that its role will be as limited as possible so that the rulers will interfere in the lives of their subjects as little as possible.

The third political cultural strand grows out of the indigenous political experience of the Jewish people in their own communities. It is civic and republican in its orientation and views the polity as a partnership of its members, who are equal citizens and who are entitled to an equitable share of the benefits resulting from the pooling of common resources. There is no reified state nor do rulers rule by whim. The leaders of the community are perceived to be responsible to its members, who entrust the leaders with authority and have their own civic obligations to fulfill. The role of the community in dealing with human needs is perceived to be substantial but never all-embracing.

Whereas the first two political cultures see authority and power as hierarchical, Jewish political culture sees it as federal. In this view, it is the product of a series of covenants (or partnership agreements) derived from the great founding covenant of the Jewish people and reaching down to the immediate compacts that establish individual communities in the body civic or politic and affirm the equality of the partners and the authority of the institutions they serve.

Though this strand is as old as the Jewish people, the circumstances of Jewish political life since the loss of independence some two thousand years ago, and particularly since the rise of the modern nation-state in the last three hundred years, were such that Jewish communities could not preserve their political autonomy unadulterated. Consequently, the Jewish strand was frequently more latent than manifest. Every Jewish community, however, maintained some internal political organization, which, even when not conceived to be political by its members, acculturated them into patterns of political behavior vis-à-vis one another and the community. This civic strand is spread across almost the entire Jewish population of Israel, which means that, more than any of the others, it provides common points of reference and possibilities for communication among Jews from widely different diaspora environments.[26]

To some extent, Israeli civil society is already an amalgam of the three strands, with different institutions reflecting one strand more than the others. In other respects, the three stand in tension and even conflict. Thus the Israeli bureaucracy is European in style and structure, but the army—the most fully Israeli institution—comes far closer to the model of authoritative relationships rooted in Jewish political culture.[27] The subject strand, whose legitimacy is in doubt everywhere, and which is rapidly disappearing, remains visible, if at all, among certain strata in the development towns.

Yet, underneath these, the upward thrust of the previously latent Jewish political culture is becoming increasingly evident, though far from unilinear in its progress. Take the role of the Supreme Court in relation to the Knesset. Following European models, the Knesset is formally the highest repository of authority or political sovereignty in the state, with its supremacy specified in law and taken for granted in practice. Parliamentary systems normally do not give their supreme courts power to declare acts of parliament unconstitutional. Therefore, Israel makes no formal provision for judicial review of legislative acts of the Knesset.[28]

Courts, however, have always held authoritative positions in Jewish life, and Jewish political culture has emphasized judicial decision making as being of the highest importance. The Supreme Court of Israel has taken its obligations seriously and in 1969, asserted a limited power of judicial review, effectively declaring an act of the Knesset to be unconstitutional by holding that it was unenforceable.[29] The Knesset accepted the court's ruling and, in response, passed a revised act designed to accommodate its constitutional objections. In doing so, it effectively affirmed at least a limited power of judicial review as part of the state's constitutional framework and moved Israel a step away from the European models and closer to a model indigenous to the Israeli situation. Since then, the constitutional role of the Supreme Court has continued to grow, with almost no opposition.[30]

Though a common political culture is still in its formative stages, some of its elements can already be identified. First, there is the strong sense of national unity—one might say embattled national unity—which pervades the country, the effect of Israel's immediate security position and the history of Jewish isolation and persecution in the larger world. Because the security situation is a continuation of Jewish history in a new context, this element is rooted deeply in the psyches of Israeli Jews.

Similarly, a common sense of vocation, or at least a strong feeling of need for such a sense, is inherited from Jewish political culture. Until the 1950s, this sense of vocation was manifested through the Zionist vision of rebuilding Israel to redeem the Jewish people. Since then it has become somewhat blurred as it has become ideologically simplified and intellectually broadened. The revival of elements of the Zionist mystique after 1967 gave it new life for a few years, although by the late 1970s, there was a strong feeling abroad that this sense of vocation needed renewal. What was clear was that Israelis, as Jews, took the need for a sense of vocation for granted and felt uneasy when it was weak.

The federal element (in the social even more than the political sense) is an important part of Israel's emergent political culture. We have already noted the use of federal principles in the foundation of the state's institutions. These institutional arrangements are the most visible manifestations of the federal principles that permeate Israeli society and its political culture, from its congregational religious organization to its system of condominium housing. Even though it has no acknowledged federal structure in its polity, contractual government, the consociational diffusion of power among its political parties and movements, and negotiated collaboration are elements of the Jewish political culture that are finding expression, though imperfectly, in the restored Jewish state.[31]

Constitutionalism, republicanism, and desires for self-government are also deeply rooted in the emergent political culture of Israel. Whatever the problems faced by the country, threats to constitutional legitimacy or the republican form of government are not among them. Precisely because such threats are almost unthinkable, we know that cultural rather than simply strategic or expediential supports for constitutionalism and republicanism are involved.

In other matters, the shape of the emergent political culture is more equivocal. Impressionistic observation reveals that a change is taking place in the relationship between the bureaucracy and the public. The bureaucrats may not be becoming more efficient, but they are becoming less officious, accepting their role as public servants rather than officials of the state.

The same equivocal situation prevails regarding the role of the citizens. Israelis generally assume that citizens should be concerned with civic matters, and citizen participation in elections as voters is particularly high. Nevertheless, attempts to develop widespread political participation beyond the elections have run into difficulties because of the party system, where centralized control and adherence to the ideological symbols and forms of an earlier generation discourage participation by those not "political" in Israeli parlance (that is, those who do not make politics the overriding concern in their lives). This is slowly changing through public action and the acts of many individual citizens, which together are bridging the gap between cultural expectations and accepted political practice.

So, too, the public's expectations of politicians are reasonably high. The people demand a high standard of behavior by those they entrust with power, yet are still devising ways to impose sanctions if they do not meet that standard. Questions of political morality in this sense have become major issues, beginning with the 1977 elections.

Political Response

As Israel passes through its second generation of statehood and its fifth of pioneering, its political system is responding to the demands of Jewish state-building. This response can be viewed through the developing structure of Israel's constitution, the republican government in Israel, and the quality of Israeli democracy.

Constitutionalism. The covenant idea, with its underlying premise that civil society is really a partnership among the compacting individuals, is basic to Israel as a new society in the modern sense and as the heir to the Jewish political tradition. The idea of constitutional legitimacy flowing from covenantal consensus has moved in an unbroken line from the Israelite tribal federation through the *kehillot* of the diaspora to the kibbutzim of modern Israel. As a proper Jewish polity, the State of Israel was inaugurated through a covenant, which, as has been common since 1776, was called a Declaration of Independence. That document, the only one in the entire history of the state signed by every political party from Agudath Israel to the Communists, presents the state's founding consensus and the principles on which it is built, neatly balancing Jewish historical aspirations, traditional themes, and the universalism and pluralism of modernity. As such, it has acquired constitutional standing and moral force in the eyes of the Israelis. It is taught as the embodiment of the principles of the Israeli polity.[32]

Israel is committed to the adoption of a formal written constitution and first tried to write one in 1949. The first Knesset was actually elected as a constituent assembly. The series of compromises involved in the decision to postpone the writing of a constitution need not concern us here. Suffice to say that a reluctance growing out of just those problems of creating a new political cultural synthesis indigenous to the new society described above lay at the root of the decision. The problems of religion and state, the precise forms of political institutions, the degree of government centralization and intervention into the economy, and the extent to which individual rights needed constitutional safeguards were basic constitutional questions deemed worth deferring on that account.[33]

Instead, a standing Constitutional, Legislative, and Judicial Committee was established in the Knesset and charged with the responsibility of drafting Basic Laws, chapter by chapter, for submission to the Knesset. There approval by an absolute majority (at least sixty-one votes) gives them constitutional status. In accord with the political theory under which the state operates, the final document will be called a Basic Law and not a constitution (a term apparently reserved for use by the Jewish people as a whole). By 1988, nine Basic Laws had been enacted. They and the other documents deemed to have constitutional status are listed in table 8.1.[34] By now, a constitutional tradition that goes beyond those documents has taken root in the state.[35] Israel's constitution, like the British, is not written in a single document although, also like the British, it is based on a set of constitutional documents. These include the Declaration of Independence, the Law of Return, the Basic Laws, the covenant between the state and the World Zionist Organization/Jewish Agency, the Harari resolution enacted by the Knesset in 1950 establishing the process of constitution-making, and perhaps one or two other pieces of legislation. The essence of Israel's constitution, again like the British, is its ancient constitutional tradition, as adapted to contemporary conditions, as reflected in almost all of the aforementioned documents.

Republicanism and democracy. In Israel representative government was originally conceived to be government through representative institutions (that is, parties and

Table 8.1
The Constitution of the State of Israel

I. Basic Constitutional Texts

The Declaration of Independence	1948
The Law of Return	1950
World Zionist Organization—Jewish Agency (Status) Law	1952

II. Basic Laws

The Knesset	1958
Israel Lands	1960
The President of the State	1964
The Government	1968
The State Economy	1975
Israel Defense Forces	1976
Jerusalem, Capital of Israel	1980
The Judicature	1984
The State Comptroller	1988

movements) rather than representative individuals. This approach is now under some attack in a developing struggle over the means of representation and the constitution of the institutions themselves.

In the governing institutions themselves, in place of the integration of powers common in parliamentary institutions there is a continuing, if halting, trend toward separation of powers. The government (cabinet) has become increasingly independent of the Knesset and vice versa. The ability of the government to achieve independence is not difficult to fathom. The central problem in parliamentary systems all over the world is how to make legislatures more than simply routine ratifiers of executive proposals.

Israel has not solved this problem, but it has developed and institutionalized the unparliamentary device of standing committees with areas of responsibility somewhat akin to the American model that help the Knesset preserve some of its independence within the limits dictated by the parliamentary system and to shape government proposals into better legislation. These standing committees include representatives of government and opposition parties. Meeting behind closed doors, they allow members of the minority parties to influence legislation through their talents in a way that would be impossible if they had to act openly in an arena where their suggestions had to be judged on a partisan basis.[36]

The expansion of the bargaining arena must be considered another aspect of republicanism in Israel. As befits a society whose origins lie so heavily in covenantal arrangements, bargaining and negotiation are important features of Israel's political process, though, as befits a society torn between formal institutions representing the statist-bureaucratic political culture and tendencies reflecting the others, much of the bargaining is conducted despite the formal structure rather than in harmony with it. The Knesset committee system is simply one way in which it has been institutionalized without overt political change. The government is hardly more than a coalition of ministries, each delegated broad powers by the Knesset and the realities of coalition politics so that it can almost legislate in it its own field. These ministries negotiate with their clients, their local government counterparts, the prime minister, with one another, and the corresponding Knesset committees to implement their programs.

Most Jews who have settled in Israel came after the state was established. They usually had low expectations about government services and even lower expectations about their ability to participate in or even influence government policies. The expectations of the Arabs were even lower. Many of the Jews, however, were ambivalent; they saw the new state as a messianic achievement and hence expected its government to solve problems of housing and employment in a paternalistic way. In a sense, their outlook reflected a temporary synthesis between subject and statist political orientations.

As the population acquired an understanding of democratic government, their demands intensified; some groups, once passive, became almost unrestrained in their insistence on having their way. With this escalation of demands came an escalation of complaints about how services were delivered. Individuals would seek to influence those responsible for service delivery when it affected them, relying on personal contacts, but still did not see themselves as participants in the general political process. This has now changed, as most Israelis have been socialized into the political system, and the subject political culture has well-nigh disappeared. A new synthesis of civic and statist political orientations has emerged, whereby Israeli citizens expect the state to be dominant in meeting their needs in a framework of expected government responsiveness to a more involved public.

Whether these changes can overcome bureaucratic inertia and the formally hierarchical structure of the system is an open question. What is clear is that the political culture of Israel acts in contradictory ways. As much as the statist aspect is a force, it acts as a strong bulwark against the myriad of explicit and implicit contractual arrangements and the accompanying bargaining and negotiation that inform the system. As the civic aspect becomes stronger, it acts as a catalyst for change. Perhaps as the Israeli political culture becomes more consistent and harmonious, the combination will prove to be unworkable and one aspect or another will undergo serious modifications, but there is no reason to expect far-reaching institutional change in the near future.

Religion and Politics

Last in the discussion of Israel as a Jewish state is the operational relationship between religion and politics in it.[37] Increasingly, Jewish religion has become important in Israel's civic culture. The movement in this direction is unmistakable. Relations between religion and politics in Israel can be understood only by understanding the five forms of religious expression influential in the state today.

First, there is mainstream Orthodox Judaism as reflected by the established organs linked to the state. These include the chief rabbinate, the local religious councils, the rabbinical courts, and the state religious educational system. For the most part, this is the religion represented by the National Religious Party, which has been a coalition partner in every lasting government since the state was established, and even before. It has exercised a predominant, though by no means exclusive, influence over the public expression of religion in Israel.

Second, there is the popular religion of the broad public, a combination of residual folk traditions, of commonly accepted Jewish practices, and elements of an Israeli civil religion. Even though no more than a quarter of Israelis define themselves as *dati* (religious), which in the Israeli context means Orthodox, probably the largest single body of Israelis—the estimates are 40 to 50 percent—define themselves as *masorati* (traditional). For the Israelis, that is an umbrella term which includes people highly observant by any standards, those who simply maintain certain home customs, and those who observe almost nothing but consider themselves believers. Even among the 25 percent who define themselves as *hiloni* (secular), many retain substantial elements of folk religion in their lives—certain Sabbath observances in the home, avoidance of overt mixing of meat and milk, and the like—though they will define themselves as secular because, for them, these practices represent a comfortable kind of "Jewishness" rather than manifestations of religious belief. Popular religion is well rooted in Israel, in almost every quarter. It is undergoing radical change now, because of the transformation of many of the roughly 55 percent of Israelis of Afro-Asian backgrounds, who now are losing their traditional ways as did so many of the Jews who came from European backgrounds a generation or two earlier.

Third, there is the civil religion.[38] In a sense, civil religion represents the point of intersection between establishment and popular religion. The transformation from the use of "Rock of Israel" to the reading of the Psalms in a neotraditional manner in the Knesset reflects the emergence of a civil religion that is grounded in traditional Judaism but is not traditional religion. In chapter 7 it was suggested that it reflects the reemergence in new ways of Sadducean Judaism, the civil religion in Israel before the destruction of the Second Commonwealth and the great Jewish dispersion. In this respect it is different from the talmudic or Pharisaic Judaism embodied by Israel's establishment religion and which was the dominant Jewish religious expression for at least sixteen hundred years. This neo-Sadduceanism is based on the centrality of Jewish public life for the expression of Judaism. The developing civil religion in Israel tries to make sacred those expressions of Jewish moralistic nationalism associated with the state and to infuse them with traditional religious forms.[39]

There was always a degree of this, when even the most secularist *halutzim* took Jewish festivals and reinterpreted them in ways that gave expression to the values of the Zionist revival.[40] In recent years, celebrations that were entirely secular even when they relied on adaptations of traditional Jewish forms have been fused with Jewish religious symbolism and modes of behavior. For example, Israeli Independence Day has increasingly taken on the elements of a religious holiday. It is expected that the president of the state and the prime minister will go to evening and morning religious services on that day. Those services, parts of the regular daily prayer cycle, now include recitation of traditional prayers of praise and thanksgiving for Israel's independence. The religious establishment is also trying to develop some kind of recognition of Israeli Independence Day as a holiday that can be institutionalized in the Jewish calendar. Jerusalem Day, the anniversary of the liberation of the Old City and the Temple Mount according to the Jewish calendar, is also acquiring the status of a religious holiday.

Fourth, there is ultra-Orthodox religion, so called because it is even more extreme in its expression of classic talmudic Judaism than establishment religion. It is most visible through the people who make the headlines by throwing stones at autos that travel through or near their neighborhoods on the Sabbath, who protest the immodesty of women dressed in modern fashion, and the like. They number a few thousand at most by the broadest definition. Most of the ultra-Orthodox community, comprising several hundred thousand people, are counted among the Agudath Israel and the numerous Hassidic sects that express themselves with greater moderation.

The ultra-Orthodox constitute a state within a state. They maintain their own schools, institutions, rabbinical courts, and the like. There are points of intersection between them and the larger polity, but usually the polity tries to leave them alone, to give them the same support as any other group, but to get them to leave the state alone. This is an uneasy relationship that usually leads to sporadic conflict around critical issues, but this should not obscure the routine coexistence that exists at other times.

Fifth, there is an emergent nonestablishment Judaism, the Masorati (Conservative) and Yahadut Mitkademet (Reform) movements, which together are approaching fifty congregations in strength. With Masorati congregations now being formed throughout the country, two Reform and one Masorati kibbutzim on the land, and of both rabbis now being ordained in Israel, it is reasonable to conclude that these nonestablishment movements are in the country to stay. Although they are formally unrecognized, there are increasing contacts between them and the authorities in their daily activities and, in some respects they have tacit recognition. For example, under a minister of education from the National Religious party, the Ministry of Education supported the establishment of schools reflecting the Masorati approach in the framework of the state educational system. The number of these schools is growing and more are being established as the demand appears. Different congregations have obtained land for buildings from the municipal authorities, and occasionally Masorati rabbis have been authorized to perform marriages.

It is important to understand that the government of Israel does not control or try to control the religious establishment. Instead, the religious communities and groups use state instrumentalities to further their own ends. Headline-grabbing events notwithstanding, relations between the religious and nonreligious in Israel are quite routine.

The Religious Parties in Israeli Politics

Because of the pervasiveness of religious concerns in Israel, most of the five groupings or positions find political expression through the party system. Where the need for political expression is reinforced by the desire to benefit from the instrumentalities of the state—whether institutional control, financial support, recognition of legitimacy, state enforcement or religious norms, or any combination of these—the likelihood of acting through a political party is greatly increased.

An examination of Israeli politics since 1949 reveals that a governing coalition is formed when major shares of two of the three camps can be combined. Until the 1977 elections, coalitions usually comprised two-thirds of the labor camp plus two-thirds of the religious camp plus a small crossover from the national camp. In the Begin-led coalition, the same principle was observed but in reverse. Almost the entire national camp, except the Independent Liberals, linked with the entire religious camp. This, more than any mathematical formula, explains the basis of coalition formation in Israeli politics.

The shift toward greater concern for Jewish tradition by the pacesetters of Israeli society reflects two factors: the perennial search for meaning characteristic of Jews, including Israeli Jews, and the concern for the Jewish future of Israel. These factors are mutually reinforcing and are appropriate in a world where religious concern is rising.

Four of the five forms of religious expression are represented in the political process by parties (see table 8.2), and the fifth may have found a vehicle for gaining representation despite its reluctance to do so. Establishment religion has the National Religious Party (Mafdal) and its offshoots. Popular religion found its expression in Tami in 1981 and among the Shas voters in 1984. Ultra-Orthodox religion has its voice in Agudath Israel and the Shas leadership.

Civil religion found its partisan in the Likud, the work of Menachem Begin. Using the approach developed by his mentor, Ze'ev (Vladimir) Jabotinsky, Begin cultivated the synthesis between nationalist politics and Jewish religion, hence, his emphasis on Jewish ceremony and observance as part of the public life of the state. In this he was ahead of his Herut party colleagues (except the Sephardim). But he was very close to his constituency and found a common language with his closest potential coalition partners. No doubt part of the reason that voters who previously supported Mafdal voted for Likud in 1981 was that they felt Begin had a properly positive attitude toward religion and religious tradition.[41]

Begin's constituency was undoubtedly drawn heavily from among those deeply rooted in the popular religion, the Sephardic *shomrei masoret* (observers of the tradition) and their Ashekanzic counterparts. Outsiders have asked how Begin—so much the quintessential Polish Jew—managed to appeal to the Sephardim. Much of the answer lay in this sharing of a common popular religion to which he gave expression officially and privately. For the Sephardim, he is an authentic Jew even if his customs are different from theirs, unlike the Labor party leaders who impress them as being not very "Jewish" at all, because they seem to have no links with religious tradition.

Table 8.2
Religious Expression and Party Alignment

Religious Expression	Political Party
Establishment religion	Mafdal (National Religious Party)
Popular religion	Tami and Shas
Civil religion	Likud
Ultra-Orthodox religion	Agudath Israel
Nonestablishment religion	(Citizens Rights Movement)

Only nonestablishment Judaism is unrepresented in the political sphere, in great part because it is an expression of Western, particularly American, ideas about the relationship between religion and state and the need to maintain separation between them. Those views are reinforced by the interests of nonestablishment Jews in Israel that require a separation between establishment religion and politics if nonestablishment Judaism is to gain the full recognition that it seeks.

Recently, a growing minority among the nonestablishment leadership has begun to understand that the situation in Israel is different from that in the United States and for nonestablishment religion to get its share of the pie, it must have representation in the political arena. This minority has worked in two directions. Some, particularly in the Reform movement, have tried to form an alliance with the Labor Alignment to get Labor to endorse the full recognition of their movements. At one point in the 1981 campaign, this approach was gaining ground. Thinking it was really going to win an absolute majority of seats in the Knesset, Labor was willing to take that position even at the cost of alienating its former coalition partners from the religious camp. However, once it became apparent that Labor would not win that majority and, indeed, was struggling for its political life, its leaders tried to back away from that position—unsuccessfully as it turned out, because they had become identified by Orthodox and non-Orthodox alike as now committed to an anti-Orthodox stance.

Others have become involved in the parties of the *sabra* reform movement, including the short-lived Democratic Movement for Change and Shinui but particularly in the Citizens' Rights Movement (CRM). The CRM has offered these people hospitality but it would be premature to suggest that it has become the political expression of nonestablishment Judaism. Nevertheless, more than any other party, it has that potential.

The obverse of this is the spread of elements of religious expression into the national camp. Picking up on Begin's model, the Likud is increasingly committed to express some combination of civil and popular religion. Rather than following the "modernization" model posited by many social scientists that, as its population becomes "modernized," Israeli politics will move toward separation of church and state or at least greater secularization, there is every sign that we are witnessing the opposite. As Israel becomes further removed from its founding generation, its Jewish majority is even more concerned about the state's Jewish authenticity and is looking for ways to link the state to forms of Jewish religious expression that will reaffirm and strengthen that authenticity.

The civil religion emerging in Israel is essentially neo-Sadducean. That is, the religious forms are designed to bolster ties with the state and its institutions rather than treating the state and its institutions as handmaidens of the Jewish religious vision. That is what separates the national from the religious camp when push comes to shove. But, because a majority of the religious camp places a high value on the state and its institutions as instruments to achieve the religious vision, in practice the difference often becomes irrelevant. Menachem Begin was the fullest expression to date of using neo-Sadduceanism as a bridging rather than a divisive force. The Labor leaders are also neo-Sadducees but their expression of that tendency emphasizes its divisive side. Which version of the civil religion will win out remains to be seen, but the signs point to a public desire for it to be bridging rather than divisive. It is unlikely that this sentiment will or can be ignored by any major political party in Israel.

Notes

1. Daniel J. Elazar, ed., *Kinship and Consent: The Jewish Political Tradition and Its Contemporary Uses* (Lanham, Md.: University Press of America and Center for Jewish Community Studies, 1981); Eliezer Schweid, *Israel at the Crossroads,* trans. Alton Meyer Winters (Philadelphia: Jewish Publication Society of America, 1973); Menachem Elon, "The Sources and Nature of Jewish Law and Its Application in the State of Israel," *Israel Law Review,* vol. 3 (1968), pp. 88–126, 416–57.

2. Ervin Birnbaum, *The Politics of Compromise: State and Religion in Israel* (Rutherford, N.J.: Farleigh Dickinson University Press, 1970); Yehuda Gershuni, "The Torah of Israel and the State," *Tradition,* vol. 12, nos. 3–4 (winter-spring 1972), pp. 25–34; "Jewish Law in the State of Israel," in *Proceedings of the Rabbinical Assembly,* no. 36 (1974); Norman L. Zucker and Naomi Zucker, *The Coming Crisis in Israel: Private Faith and Public Policy* (Cambridge, Mass.: MIT Press, 1973).

3. The term first appears in 1 Kings 20:14–19 in Ahab's administrative devision of the northern kingdom; there the *medinot* are no more than administrative districts with a minimum of autonomy. In Megillat Esther the term is used to describe what today would be termed autonomous regions or provinces in the Persian Empire.

4. Gittin 3:3.

5. Eliezer Schweid, "The Attitude toward the State in Modern Jewish Thought before Zionism," in Elazar, ed., *Kinship and Consent.*

6. Daniel J. Elazar, chaps. 1–5 of *The Covenant Idea in Politics,* Workshop in the Covenant Idea and the Jewish Political Tradition, Working Paper no. 22 (Jerusalem and Tel Aviv: Center for Jewish Community Studies and Bar Ilan University Department of Political Studies, 1983).

7. Arthur Hertzberg, ed., *The Zionist Idea* (New York: Athenum, 1969); Harold Fisch, *The Zionist Revolution* (London: Weidenfeld and Nicolson, 1978); Ben Halperin, *The Idea of the Jewish State* (Cambridge, Mass.: Harvard University Press, 1961).

8. Martin Buber, *Kingship of God* (London: G. Allen and Unwin, 1967) and *Paths in Utopia* (New York: Macmillan, 1950).

9. Daniel J. Elazar and Stuart A. Cohen, *The Jewish Polity: Jewish Political Organization from Biblical Times to the Present* (Bloomington, Ind.: Indiana University Press, 1985).

10. Daniel J. Elazar and Haim Kalchaim, eds., *Local Government in Israel* (Lanham, Md.: University Press of America and Jerusalem Center for Public Affairs, 1988).

11. Charles S. Liebman and Eliezer Don-Yehiya, *Civil Religion in Israel: Traditional Religion and Political Culture in the Jewish State* (Berkeley: University of California Press, 1983) and *Religion and Politics in Israel* (Bloomington, Ind.: Indiana University Press, 1984); Simon Herman, *Israelis and Jews: The Continuity of an Identity* (New York: Random House, 1970); S. Z. Abramov, *Perpetual Dilemma* (Rutherford, N.J.: Fairleigh Dickinson University Press, 1976).

12. Yonathan Ratosh, "The New Hebrew Nation," in Ehud Ben Ezra, ed., *Unease in Zion* (New York: Quadrangle Books, 1974), pp. 201–34; Baruch Kurzweil, "The New 'Canaanites' in Israel," *Judaism,* vol. 2, no. 1 (January 1953), pp. 3–15; Georges Friedmann, *The End of the Jewish People?* (Garden City, N.Y.: Doubleday, 1967); Uri Avnery, *Israel without Zionists* (New York: Macmillan, 1968).

13. See, for example, the discussions in the publications of the Study Circle on World Jewry in the Home of the President of Israel, *Thirteenth Series—1983–84,* 9 vols. (Jerusalem: Shazar Library, the Institute of Contemporary Jewry of the Hebrew University of Jerusalem, 1983).

14. Hanoch Smith and the Smith Research Center, *Attitude of Israelis towards America and American Jews* (New York: Institute on American Jewish-Israel Relations, October 1983); Herman, *Israelis and Jews;*

Drora Kass, *Israeli and American Jews—Toward a Meaningful Dialogue* (New York: The American Jewish Committee, Institute on American-Israeli Relations, 1984).

15. Arie Lova Eliav, *Land of the Hart: Israelis, Arabs, the Territories, and a Vision of the Future* (Philadelphia: Jewish Publication Society of America, 1974).

16. S. N. Eisenstadt, *Israeli Society* (London: Weidenfeld and Nicolson, 1967); Daniel J. Elazar, *Israel: Building a New Society* (Bloomington, Ind.: Indiana University Press, 1986); Leonard J. Fein, *Politics in Israel* (Boston: Little, Brown and Company, 1967); Dan Horowitz and Moshe Lissak, *The Origins of the Israeli Polity: Palestine under the Mandate* (Chicago: University of Chicago Press, 1978); Howard Penniman, ed., *Israel at the Polls 1977* (Washington, D.C.: American Enterprise Institute for Public Policy Research, 1979).

Leharkiv, used to describe the organization of a polity or government, means "to compound" and the word is also used to describe complexity. It reflects the expectations inherent in the kind of environmental and cultural matrix in which the Jewish people has always been embedded and in which Israel must function today. Being basically covenantal, Jewish political life is reflected in the idea that bodies politic are compounded from different entities that retain their integrities even in the larger whole. This carries over into the shaping of the Israeli polity.

17. Jacob M. Landau, *The Arabs in Israel: A Political Study* (Oxford: Oxford University Press, 1969); Ian Lustick, *Arabs in the Jewish State: Israel's Control of a National Minority* (Austin: University of Texas Press, 1980); Sammy Smoocha, "Control of Minorities in Israel and Northern Ireland," *Comparative Studies in Society and History,* vol. 22 (April 1980), pp. 256–80; Ori Stendel, *The Minorities of Israel* (Jerusalem: The Israel Economist, 1973).

18. Yitzhak Ben-Zvi, *Toldot Yisrael be-Tekufah haOtomanit* (History of the Land of Israel in the Ottoman Period) (Jerusalem: Yad Itzhak Ben-Zvi, 1955) (Hebrew); Robert Sherevsky, Avraham Katz, Yisrael Kolatt, and Hayim Barkai, *Meah Shanah ve'od 20* (One Hundred Years and Another Twenty) (Jerusalem: Ma'ariv, 1968) (Hebrew). For an up-to-date review of the situation in the contemporary Middle East, see Michael Curtis, ed., *Religion and Politics in the Middle East* (Boulder, Colo.: Westview, 1981).

19. Liebman and Don-Yehiya, *Civil Religion in Israel, Religion and Politics in Israel,* and "Traditional Judaism and Civil Religion in Israel," *Jerusalem Quarterly,* no. 23 (April 1982), pp. 57–69.

20. Henry E. Baker, *The Legal System of Israel,* 2d ed. (Jerusalem: Israel Universities Press, 1968); Meir Silverstone, "Personal Status in the Israel Legal System," *Public Administration in Israel and Abroad 1971,* vol. 12, pp. 14–24; Stendel, *The Minorities of Israel;* Philip L. Culberston, "The Anglican Family Court in Israel and the West Bank," *Journal of Church and State* (spring 1981), pp. 285–308.

21. Ilene Beatty, *Arab and Jew in the Land of Canaan* (Chicago: Henry Regnery Company, 1957); Michael Curtis et al., eds., *The Palestinians: People, History, Politics* (New Brunswick, N.J.: Transaction Books, 1975); Landau, *The Arabs in Israel;* Hillel Frisch, "The Arab Vote in the 1984 Elections," in Daniel J. Elazar and Howard Penniman, eds., *Israel at the Polls, 1981* (Washington, D.C. and Bloomington, Ind.: American Enterprise Institute for Public Policy Research and Indiana University Press, 1986); Ian Lustick, "Israel's Arab Minority in the Begin Era," in Robert Freedman, ed., *Israel in the Begin Era* (New York: Praeger, 1982) and *Arabs in the Jewish State;* William B. Quadt, Fuad Jabber, and Anne Mosely Lesch, *The Politics of Palestinian Nationalism* (Berkeley: University of California Press, 1973); Sabri Jiryis, *The Arabs in Israel,* trans. from the Arabic by Inea Bushnaq (New York: Monthly Review Press, 1976); Walter Schwarz, *The Arabs in Israel* (London: Faber and Faber, 1959); Moshe Shokeid, "Strategy and Change in the Arab Vote: Observations in a Mixed Town," in Asher Arian, ed., *Elections in Israel 1973* (Jerusalem: Jerusalem Academic Press, 1975), pp. 145–66.

22. Eisenstadt, *Israeli Society.*

23. Horowitz and Lissak, *The Origins of the Israeli Polity.*

24. The concept of political culture is discussed in Gabriel A. Almond and Sidney Verba, *The Civic Culture* (Princeton, N.J.: Princeton University Press, 1963); Lucian Pye and Sidney Verba, eds., *Political Culture* (Princeton, N.J.: Princeton University Press, 1965); Daniel J. Elazar, *American Federalism: A View from the States,* 3d ed. (New York: Harper and Row, 1984), chaps. 5 and 6 and *Political Culture, Working Kits No. 1 and 2* (Philadelphia: Center for the Study of Federalism, Temple University, 1969).

25. Israel's emerging political culture is the subject of a major study of the Jerusalem Center for Public Affairs, and this section reflects the interim results of that study. See Elazar, *Israel: Building a New Society,* chap. 10. Leonard J. Fein presents a picture of this strand of Israel's political culture in *Politics in Israel,* chaps. 2 and 3 as do Gerald Caiden, *Israel's Administrative Culture* (Berkeley: Institute of Governmental Studies, 1970) and Eva Etzioni-Halevy, *Political Culture in Israel* (New York: Praeger, 1977). Also see Gabriel A. Almond, "Comparative Political Systems," *The Journal of Politics,* vol. 18 (1956), pp. 391–409, for suggestive comments

on the political culture of continental Europe. An expanded exposition of his thesis can be found in Almond and Verba, *The Civic Culture.*

26. Almond and Verba, in *The Civic Culture,* discuss this. See also Edward Banfield, *The Moral Basis of a Backward Society* (New York: Free Press, 1958).

27. The fullest discussions of Jewish political culture presently available are Daniel J. Elazar, ed., *Kinship and Consent: The Jewish Political Tradition and Its Contemporary Manifestations* (Washington: University Press of America and Center for Jewish Community Studies, 1982) and Elazar and Cohen, *The Jewish Polity.* I have suggested ways in which it can be pursued in my bibliographic essay "The Pursuit of Community: The Literature of Jewish Public Affairs, 1965–1966," *American Jewish Year Book, 1967* (Philadelphia: American Jewish Committee and Jewish Publication Society of America, 1967), vol. 68; and my article "The Reconstitution of Jewish Communities in the Post-War Period," *Jewish Journal of Sociology* (December 1969) offers a good starting point for its investigation. See also Salo W. Baron, *The Jewish Community* (Philadelphia: Jewish Publication Society, 1942), 3 vols.; Irving Agus, "The Rights and Immunities of the Minority," *Jewish Quarterly Review,* vol. 45, pp. 120–29; Gedalia Alon, *Mekharim B'toldot Yisrael* (Research in Israeli History) (Tel Aviv, 1957–58), vol. 2, pp. 58–74; and Jacob Katz, *Tradition and Crisis* (New York: Free Press, 1961), chaps. 1–5.

Fein, *Politics in Israel,* chap. 5, describes the bureaucracy. Caiden's *Israel's Administrative Culture* includes a useful chapter on Israel's administrative culture. An excellent description of the federal (in its social sense) character of the army is provided by S. L. A. Marshall, "Israel's Citizen Army," in *Swift Sword* (New York: American Heritage, 1967), pp. 132–33. See also Amos Perlmutter, *Military and Politics in Israel* (Totowa, N.J.: Frank Cass, 1969).

28. See Yehoshua Freudenheim, *Government in Israel* (New York: Oceana Publications, 1967). The situation in classic parliamentary democracies is portrayed in John C. Wahlke and Alex N. Dragnich, eds., *Government and Politics* (New York: Random House, 1966).

29. *Berman v. Minister of Finance and State Comptroller.*

30. Amnon Rubinstein discusses this question in "Supreme Court vs. the Knesset," *Hadassah Magazine,* vol. 51, no. 7 (March 1970). For a fuller account of this transformation, see his *Ha-Mishpat Hakonstitutioni shel Medinat Yisrael* (The Constitutional Law of the State of Israel), 2d ed. (Jerusalem: Schocken, 1984) (Hebrew).

31. There is good reason to believe that the federal element is present in all the new societies, derived, at least in part, from their origins as contractual partnerships. This is true even in those societies where no visible federal structure is involved. Contractual government, the constitutional diffusion of power, and negotiated collaboration seem to be characteristic of their polities. See Daniel J. Elazar, *Exploring Federalism* (University, Ala.: University of Alabama Press, 1987).

32. Horace M. Kallen, *Utopians at Bay* (New York: Theodor Herzl Foundation, 1958); Yigal Aricha, "Megillat HaAtzmault—Hazon ve-Mitziut," (Declaration of Independence—Vision and Reality), Seminar Paper, Bar Ilan University, Department of Political Studies, 1983) (Hebrew).

33. For a history of this effort, see Emanuel Rackman, *Israel's Emerging Constitution 1948–1951* (New York: Columbia University Press, 1955); David Ben-Gurion, "Laws or a Constitution," in *Rebirth and Destiny of Israel,* ed. and trans. from the Hebrew under the supervision of Mordecai Nurock (New York: Philosophical Library, 1954), pp. 363–79; J. Albert, "Constitutional Adjudication without a Constitution: The Case of Israel," *Harvard Law Review,* vol. 82 (1969), pp. 1245–65; Daniel J. Elazar, "A Time of Constitutional Milestones in the History of Israel," *Jerusalem Letter/Viewpoints,* no. 34 (June 12, 1984); Eli Likhovski, "Can the Knesset Adopt a Constitution Which Will Be the 'Supreme Law of the Land'?," *Israel Law Review,* vol. 4 (1969), pp. 61–69; Meir Shamgar, "On the Written Constitution," *Israel Law Review,* vol. 9, no. 4 (October 1974).

34. See Israel's Basic Laws in *The Constitution of the State of Israel* (Jerusalem: Jerusalem Center for Public Affairs, forthcoming), Part 2.

35. Rubinstein, *Ha-Mishpat Hakonstitutioni shel Medinat Yisrael,* chap. 1.

36. See Lester Seligman, *Leadership in a New Nation* (New York, 1964).

37. Two general overviews of the relationship between religion and state in Israel, from diametrically opposed perspectives, are Abramov, *Perpetual Dilemma* and Zvi Yaron, "Religion in Israel," *American Jewish Year Book 1976* (New York: American Jewish Committee and Philadelphia: Jewish Publication Society of America, 1975), vol. 76, pp. 41–90.

38. The definitive study of Israel's civil religion to date is that of Charles S. Liebman and Eliezer Don-Yehiya, *The Civil Religion of Israel* (Berkeley and Los Angeles: University of California Press, 1984).

39. See Daniel J. Elazar, "The New Sadducees," *Midstream,* vol. 24, no. 7 (August-September 1978), pp. 20–25.

40. Eliezer Don-Yehiya, "Hilon, Shlilah, ve-Shiluv: Tfisot shel ha-Yahadut HaMesorati ve-Musagahah be-Tzinout Ha-Socialisti," (Secularization, Negation, and Integration: Concepts of Traditional Judaism in Zionist Socialism), *Kivunim,* no. 8 (August 1980), pp. 29–46 (Hebrew).

41. Daniel J. Elazar, "Religion and Polities in the Begin Era," in Robert Friedman, ed., *Polities in the Begin Era* (Boulder, Colo.: Westview Press, 1984).

9

Jewish Frontier Experiences in the New World

If the State of Israel is one key to the new shape of world Jewry, the New World Jewries of the Western and Southern hemispheres constitute the other. European Jewry is depleted and tired, and can no longer bear the mantle of diaspora leadership. That mantle has passed to the New World, particularly to the Jewish community of the United States, but also to communities such as Argentina, Canada, South Africa, Brazil, and Australia, the sixth, seventh, eighth, ninth, and tenth largest Jewish communities in the world. The frontier experiences of these new Jewries, all effectively the products of the last century, have shaped them into something at least as unprecedented on the Jewish scene as the modern State of Israel. Their emergence as fully articulated communities with highly articulated organizational structures is the story of the completion of the adaptation of the Jewish people to modernity. Hence, it should be no surprise that they are the cutting edge of the Jewish diaspora in the postmodern epoch.

The great Jewish migrations of the modern epoch did not really touch the Western and Southern hemispheres, apart from the United States, until that epoch was in its last generations. True enough, small groups of Jews settled in Latin America as early as the sixteenth century when "New Christians" (Marranos) came with the Conquistadores in an effort to escape the Inquisition in Spain and Portugal. But the transplantation of the Inquisition to the New World, coupled with the normal course of assimilation, eliminated any serious crypto-Jewish presence by the end of the seventeenth century. The contemporary Jewish communities in those countries did not emerge until well into the nineteenth century.[1]

Individual Jews began to drift to the United States as early as the 1620s. The first community was established in 1654 with the arrival in New Amsterdam of twenty-three ex-Marranos who had been expelled from Brazil after the Portuguese reconquered it from the Dutch. Since then, there has been an organized Jewish community in the United States. It was augmented by a regular flow of immigrants, slowly for the first 150 years, then picking up the pace until it became a flood after the beginning of the great migration in the 1880s.[2]

Under French rule Jews were banned from New France (Canada) just as they were from France proper. Only with the British conquest in 1759 could Jews appear openly in that land. Jewish merchants accompanied the conquering British and organized communities in Montreal and Trois Rivières in the 1760s. Canada was almost entirely avoided by the nineteenth-century German and central European Jewish immigrants, because the United States was the land of opportunity and Canada was a backwater. Hence it was the eastern European Jews who were the real founders of the Canadian Jewish community, at the very end of the nineteenth century.[3]

Jewish convicts were among the very first settlers in Australia beginning in 1788 and enough even came as free men and women to organize a congregation at the beginning of the nineteenth century.[4] The Jewish presence in South Africa only became a reality at the beginning of the nineteenth century because before the British conquest it was illegal to profess Judaism openly in the Dutch South African colony. Assimilated Jews and converts to Christianity did reach South Africa as early as the latter half of the seventeenth century, but not until the late eighteenth century did the first identified Jews appear. There were enough of them to form a congregation in the early nineteenth century at the same time as their brethren in Australia.[5]

For Jews, those lands were the last frontier of the diaspora, one that proved attractive only after other lands of immigration had closed their doors. As a result, only now has the Jewish population in them become predominantly native born, with all that the change implies. In Australia and South Africa native-born people predominated two and three generations ago, only to be submerged by subsequent mass migrations. In Latin America, the children of the first migrants either left or became assimilated into the Christian majority and the communities had to be refounded in the latter years of the nineteenth century.

Jews and the Great Frontier

These communities exist by virtue of the great frontier of Europe, which began with the voyages of discovery in the late fifteenth century and persisted until our own time.[6] The land frontier, opened in the new territories discovered by European explorers, was based on rural pursuits, whether agricultural or extractive. It was the classic frontier of the modern epoch. In distinction to earlier colonization experiences, the modern frontier was not a temporary phenomenon that lasted only as long as there was free land. Instead, wherever it took root, it generated a chain reaction that in turn opened new frontiers.

Vast territories of the modern land frontier, far away from the original bastions of civilization, had to be explored, tamed, and settled. To do this effectively, men invented a technology that generated an urban-industrial frontier—a coming together of people in cities not to serve agricultural hinterlands but to concentrate and apply technology so as to create wealth—ultimately making the agricultural hinterland dependent on them. Early in the nineteenth century, the first signs of this urban-industrial frontier appeared in the United States.[7] During that century, it spread in varying degrees to other frontier countries, reflecting in each country the kind of land frontier that preceded it.

The American experience is the classic example of the classic frontier.[8] Except for a few minor colonization experiments, late in the history of the American land frontier, Jewish participation in that frontier followed the usual pattern of Jewish participation in American society. Jews often were prominent in the commerce associated with the opening and settlement of the land. Thus there were few Jewish trappers, farmers, or cowboys, but from the mid-seventeenth century Jews were involved in land speculation, the fur trade, and in peddling, which assured that commercial goods reached the frontier.

Jewish involvement in the land frontier reached its height in the Old Northwest, where Jewish peddlers became local merchants and then developed the great department store chains that grew to dominate so much of American merchandizing, and in the trans-Mississippi West where a few Jews were involved in mining and railroad building and many more in making life on those frontiers possible through the contributions of commerce. Still, the number of Jews involved in the rural–land frontier was small, in part because the Jewish population in the United States was small throughout most of the land frontier period.[9]

It was the urban-industrial frontier that offered extensive opportunities for the absorption of the mass Jewish emigration from eastern Europe.[10] Far more Jews benefited from the urban-industrial frontier than the land frontier, but the direct Jewish contribution to the opening of that frontier was no greater. The peddlers of the land frontier became the merchant princes of the urban frontier, and new industries, such as the garment industry, flourished under Jewish leadership. Nevertheless, the great industrial enterprises of that frontier in the United States remained in the hands of the older stock American (or immigrants from that same stock) and often deliberately excluded Jews.[11]

The process followed classic lines in South Africa, where the original outposts of the Dutch East India Company had in two centuries developed into a true land frontier that might have ended had gold not been discovered on the Rand, creating a link between the extractive aspect of the land frontier and the emerging urban-industrial frontier in other parts of the world.[12] This gave South Africa the resources to begin to develop an urban-industrial frontier. This transformation came precisely when Jews were arriving in the country in force, so that they could participate as pioneers in this last stage of the land frontier and in the transition to the later frontiers.[13]

As a group, Jews missed the Dutch colonial portion of the South Arican frontier, but they were very much a part of the British portion. The Litvaks came early enough in the history of the Boer republics to be pioneers of at least the urban frontier and not simply immigrants. This was not quite as true of the early arriving Anglo-Jews in the Cape Province, although they, too, were founders in Natal and in the outlying areas of the Cape. The Jews who came to the South African diamond and gold fields in the late nineteenth century were particularly well suited to the frontier, bringing with them energy and a willingness to explore new possibilities. They were embraced by a local population that stood at the threshold of adaptation to the urban-industrial frontier and that needed the skills the Jews could provide, particularly in the commercial realm, to link them to that new frontier.

The frontier had its least impact in Latin America, whose first settlement had come before the beginning of the modern epoch and without what later became the pioneering impulse. To a great extent, Latin America was a transplantation of the feudalism of late medieval Spain. During some three hundred years of colonial status, a premodern society became entrenched in the settled areas of the region and was hardly changed even by the settlement of uninhabited areas after independence. When urbanization came to Latin America, it was in the European style rather than a continuation of the great frontier.[14] As a result, when the Jews came, they did not so much participate in a pioneering enterprise as try to fit into a society that was experiencing all the tensions of modernization associated with Europe and the Third World—a common Latin American synthesis.

In essence Latin America represented an aborted frontier. The implantation of a *regimen de castas* (society of castes) in the manner of the corporate society of medieval Castille, whereby groups of people were distinguished from one another hierarchically by their racial origins, was the antithesis of the frontier ethos. Its impact on Latin America as a whole is clearly visible by the fact that nearly five hundred years after Columbus, the Americas south of the Rio Grande are still considered a developing area and part of the Third World.

For Jews this regimen meant exclusion from the body politic, which was fully open only to Roman Catholics of appropriate ancestry. Nor was the authoritarianism that developed early in Latin America conducive to Jewish involvement. Again, it ran against the frontier spirit and also stood in sharp opposition to Jewish political culture. Thus Jews could not side with the conservative establishment that made the Latin American independence movements and built the Latin American states. They perforce had to side with the most radical forces seeking a total reconstruction of Latin American society based on the attitudes of the age of reason if they were to hope to become part of it.

The other alternative was to build their own separate lives, maintaining contact in the external society only for unavoidable economic and social purposes. Most of the immigrant generation chose that course, but as time goes on those native to their respective countries who stay seem to be choosing the former. In the end, most of the Jews who did choose to emigrate to Latin America chose Argentina, Brazil, Chile, and Uruguay where the forces of modernization and whatever remnants there were of the frontier played some role in nation-building, and avoided Mexico, Central America, and the Andean republics until they were needed as places of refuge.

The Jewish colonization movement in Argentina in the last generation of the nineteenth century was the one Jewish activity closely linked with that country's rural-land frontier. Between 1889 and World War I, more than three thousand Jewish families founded or settled in agricultural colonies on vacant lands in Argentina and thereby established the most important indigenous tradition of Argentinian Jewry. Hardly more than twenty thousand Jews ever lived in the colonies (the peak was in 1925), and less than a third of those families now are connected with them in any way, but the fact that Jews had some share in the settlement of Argentina is important in shaping Argentinian Jewry's self-esteem as Argentinians.[15]

Canada followed the classic frontier pattern in part because of its vast continental expanse and in part because of its proximity to the United States where it benefited from a shared North American frontier.[16] Even more than Argentina and South Africa, Canada was a place where the Jews from eastern Europe had an opportunity to participate in the land frontier. Baron de Hirsch tried to establish Jewish agricultural colonies in the Canadian West, as in Argentina, but they failed. Jews homesteaded on an individual basis, and many more drifted westward to the small towns of the Canadian great plains in what were soon to become the prairie provinces, at the time that they were being settled. Thus the Jews of Manitoba, Saskatchewan, and Alberta share a land frontier tradition with their Canadian compatriots. Some were there with the first founders of the major cities on the Canadian prairies. Jews were among the primary recorders of that frontier experience in Canadian literature and the arts. While that was happening, Montreal, Toronto, and other cities were becoming the loci of an urban industrial frontier that attracted most of the Jews who came to Canada. Jews made major contributions to that frontier, although limited by the dominance of the old Canadian families and the degree to which Canada developed industrially as a branch of the United States.[17]

Australia had the primary ingredient of a true frontier in the sense of an empty land open to settlement, but because its first settlers were convicts, deported either against their will or to avoid hanging, the pioneering spirit was not encouraged. Nevertheless, the openness of the land had its effect, reinforced in the mid-nineteenth century by the arrival of voluntary immigrants who came in search of fortunes. Even then, the frontier was distorted, though not beyond recognition, by the land itself. Because most of Australia was desert, the frontier of settlement could not advance along a single line. Instead, the settlers concentrated in cities, merging the urban and land frontiers. Because of Australia's sparse population and distance from markets, no strong industrial frontier emerged. Instead, the cities maintained themselves by being bases for the extraction of natural resources.[18] As individuals, the early Jews were thrust into a pioneering framework, but most of them came too long after the first frontier stage of Australian society had passed to participate in the initial frontier experience.[19]

The urban-industrial frontier gave rise to a metropolitan-technological frontier. The completion of the first stage of industrialization—which gave birth to cities as wealth generators in their own right—led to new technologies involving the internal combustion engine, telecommunications, and synthetics. These made possible the automobile, the airplane, the telephone, radio and television, and plastics. These technological changes so greatly altered the world people lived in and the way they settled that world as to remake it. Metropolitanization became the dominant settlement pattern. People flocked to urban areas, leaving the rural environment to an ever decreasing minority; but they rebuilt those urban areas as congeries of suburbs—low density settlements surrounding a central city rather than as separate cities in the old urban style.

These metropolitan regions provided the opportunity for a life-style that embodied "rural" amenities such as single-family homes, lawns, and privacy, with the advantage of urban services. The regions were linked internally by roads and telephones and externally by airplanes and the mass media. They rested on a synthetics-plastics base and generated a new range of occupations and a new way of life based on consumption. This contrasts sharply with the great urban agglomerations of the Third World, which do not reflect an advancing frontier but instead modernization with its concomitant miseries, as in nineteenth-century Europe, but intensified by the lack of infrastructure.[20]

Jews were ideally suited for pioneering on the metropolitan frontier; it was heavily based on communications and Jews have been oriented toward the center of the communications network wherever they have been. Thus, in the frontier countries, Jews concentrated in metropolitan areas, and in the major ones at that, where they were prominent in precisely those branches of the economy that typified the metropolitan frontier.

Jewry in the United States flowered on the metropolitan frontier. Jews were leaders in developing and applying the technologies that opened and shaped the metropolitan frontier, and they were quick to take advantage of the opportunities that frontier provided. They were especially prominent in the communications and construction industries; suburban land development became a heavily Jewish activity and Jews were part of the vanguard in post-World War II suburbanization.[21]

Again, the impact of the frontier was least in Latin America. The Argentinian example is typical. Buenos Aires became the greatest metropolitan center in Argentina, but in a manner that combined Third World and nineteenth-century European patterns rather than because of any frontier change. The Jews concentrated in Buenos Aires because it was the capital, but however great their contribution to Argentinian society— and it has undoubtedly been great, because they are one of the few energetic elements in the country—it is an extractive rather than pioneering contribution; energetic elements in modernizing societies of that kind do less to build for the future than to make the present profitable and comfortable. Moreover, the growth of Buenos Aires has in many respects come at the expense of the rest of the country—again, an antifrontier phenomenon.[22] This situation is even more pronounced in the other Latin American countries, most of which have not even had anything like a metropolitan-technological frontier and where life is concentrated in the capital cities for other reasons. The exception is São Paulo in Brazil, where the Jews play a role like that in Canada.

Two-thirds of South Africa's Jewish population is located in the Johannesburg metropolitan area. Still, this is less than the perhaps 90 percent concentrated in the Argentinian capital. Moreover, following the pattern of earlier frontiers, the metropolitan frontier is real in South Africa, an extension and new manifestation of the great frontier, now in the process of transforming the South African polity and society.[23] Jews are also in the other metropolitan areas, particularly Cape Town and Durban, in significant numbers, so that their weight is felt throughout South African society.[24]

Most of the Jews who settled in Australia after World War II were drawn to the metropolitan frontier, and in one sense they can be seen as among its pioneers. However, because most were immigrants who had not gone through a period of acculturation, they played a less visible role on the current frontier than the far smaller number of their brethren had in the days of the land frontier.[25]

Whatever the relationship of different waves of Jewish settlers or generations of Jewish residents to particular frontier stages in the new worlds, where the frontier has existed, it has had a major impact on how Jews have related to the larger society and on how the environment has shaped their institutions and behavior. For the most part, this influence has moved toward integrating Jews as individuals with the life of the larger community and transforming Jewish institutions into expressions of the new synthesis of the Jewish heritage and the new environment. Conversely, in Latin America, where no proper frontier persisted, Jews have continued to be more isolated from the larger society, and their institutions have adapted less to the new environment.

Fragment Civilizations

Louis Hartz, in his important book, *The Founding of New Societies,* has referred to these frontier societies as fragments that broke off from European civilization and had to implant themselves in new soil, pursuing lines of development that reflected their European heritage but were, nevertheless, substantially different because of the transplantation.[26] These fragments began their separate development from the point at which they were separated from European civilization, often maintaining patterns common to the civilization they left behind in forms that remained frozen or took radically different directions from those of the original civilization, which continued to undergo adaptations of its own.

If there is any process in this sequence, it is how these fragments of civilization were self-consciously conservative in their earliest stages, as the pioneers of the new settlements tried to retain the only civilization they knew. Then, once rooted, the settlements took off in directions appropriate to the new environment, directions that were possible precisely because the population had become more self-confident and at home. The Jewish settlements in the Western and Southern hemispheres followed this pattern. They began as fragments of different Old World Jewries, making every effort to maintain familiar ways during the period of settling in, and only later began to move toward the more relaxed development of indigenous patterns.

The tendency of Jewish immigrants who tried to remain Jews but were not learned in Jewish matters was to identify their Jewish memories of the "old home" as the sum and substance of Jewishness and to be most fearful of any changes. This tendency was reinforced by their minority status in the new countries. It was reflected in the efforts of the Spanish and Portuguese Jewish immigrants to British North America in the seventeenth and eighteenth centuries to preserve their Portuguese ritual and organization; the eastern European Jewish immigrants to Latin America in the late nineteenth and early twentieth centuries trying to preserve Yiddish as the basis of Jewish life, and the commitment of large segments of early Australian and South African Jewry to maintain the Anglo-Jewish style in their synagogues and institutions. This need was intensified by the Jewish fear of assimilation into a non-Jewish environment if old moorings were let loose.

Eventually the Jews who immigrated to the countries of the New World had to adapt to their new environments. Despite the common thread of the frontier experience, each of the communities came to differ significantly from the others.

The Jews who came to the United States found themselves in a pluralistic society, from the first, initially pluralistic Protestant and later pluralistic Christian. An Americanized set of British norms constituted the accepted way of life but did not impose any strong orthodoxies other than a commitment to becoming American and speaking English. Thus the Jews were able to use their great talent for adaptation to become speedily Americanized. At the same time, the United States offered them the opportunity to preserve their Jewishness within that Americanized framework with no overt restrictions.

The Jews arrived in the United States in time to participate in almost all the events of American history. Even though their numbers were small during the colonial period and the Revolutionary and founding generations, there were enough for them to be partners in the American myth with their own heroes in the pantheon. That is one of the reasons why the Jews of the United States feel themselves to be Americans in every respect. Because American society was a fully new society, based on a new covenant designed to create a new people from the immigrants who reached its shores, the American environment made it easy for later generations of Jewish immigrants to adopt the American forefathers as their forefathers and to consider themselves the descendants of Washington, Jefferson, and Lincoln.

Because the Jews alone among immigrant groups to the United States had no nostalgia for the lands they left behind, they threw themselves into becoming Americans—probably more than any other group not originally from Britain. As a result, most rapidly dropped any customs and traditions that, to them, interfered with becoming fully American. They did so more rapidly than their brethren who immigrated to other New World countries, not only because they had to work on the Sabbath to survive, but also because the customs that they had taken for granted in the old world seemed "un-American," in the sense that they separated Jews from other people. Moreover, because American society did not encourage any religious orthodoxies, Jews did not even try to maintain a nominal Orthodox framework. By the same token, they were happy and even eager to develop adaptations that would enable them to continue to be Jews in the American context. Following the American style they experimented with new forms of Jewish religion, which gave birth to the Reform, Conservative, and Reconstructionist branches of Judaism and a new kind of Jewishness by the middle of the twentieth century.[27]

Public education was the norm in the United States, and the Jews rapidly made that norm theirs. Admission to the public schools was the badge of equality in American society. Hence, until well into the post-World War II generation, American Jews overwhelmingly opposed separate Jewish day schools, an attitude that did not begin to change until the 1960s, when the public school began to be seen as educationally inferior by many Americans of similar socioeconomic status. Jewish education became a matter of supplementary education—first in the Protestant manner of the Sunday school and only much later in the form of serious afternoon schools, which have always had difficulty taking root in the American environment.[28]

The Jews who settled in Latin America found themselves immersed in an Iberian civilization whose roots were premodern and which, even as it developed different national personalities, had difficulty shaking off its late medieval configuration. As Iberian countries, they were also Roman Catholic and had to pass through a modernization process as in other Roman Catholic countries. Moreover, the Jews arrived late, long after their host polities had been formed, missing three centuries of colonial history and the crucial first generations of national independence. That, when added to the problem of finding a place in strongly Roman Catholic societies, meant that they could only be a foreign element, a group of outsiders. Today, even the Jewish youths who seek to become fully part of their host countries do so primarily through leftist activities—which is merely another form of alienation.

The Jews who came to Latin America from the Middle East—either Sephardim of Spanish ancestry, who had the language and mannerisms of the Hispanic world, or Arabic-speaking Jews, who belonged to a shared Mediterranean culture—were less alienated than the Ashkenazim. Over the generations, they had developed mechanisms for institutional survival under conditions like those they found in the New World. So, although their external conformity was far greater than that of their Ashkenazi brethren, internally they also created and preserved the kind of institutional framework that works in an Hispanic environment. Thus they preserved their Jewishness while acclimating more to the Latin culture than the Ashkenazim.[29]

Most Jews who came to Argentina were Yiddish speakers from eastern Europe, particularly from Poland and Galicia. Their outlook was heavily influenced by the revolutionary currents that had swept their part of the world in the nineteenth century. They were foreign to the Latin world in speech, manner, and outlook, but their energetic volubility squared well with the Latin way of life. After a period of development, their communal organizations, like the institutions of Argentina, became forums for grand debates rather than effective vehicles of governance. Wanting to perpetuate the way of life they had brought with them, they became even more alienated from the Argentinian environment so strange to them, in turn alienating their children from themselves and from Argentina.[30]

Australia was from the first a fragment of British—perhaps even English—civilization in its eighteenth-century manifestations: fully Protestant with a strong Methodist emphasis, rapidly modernizing, reformist, and liberal. But it was a fragment drawn overwhelmingly from one class of English society—the lower class—sprinkled with a few sons of the aristocracy, usually black sheep who had to settle far from home for one reason or another. Only since World War II has Australian society become ethnically hetereogeneous, as a result of the immigration of Europeans from many backgrounds. This homogeneous British fragment tried to create a miniature English civilization on the other side of the globe. The Jews who came, most of whom also had English backgrounds, could do no less—nor did they wish to. Hence, the first synagogues in Sydney and Melbourne to this day maintain a "high church" atmosphere found in only a few congregations in England and an occasional South African snyagogue dating from the same period.

The first Jews to settle in Australia, like many of the first non-Jews, were exiled there because of criminal activities. However, most were not hardened criminals but persons who had been driven to crime by the dire circumstances of late eighteenth-century urban England. Hence their origins had scant long-range influence on the shape of either Australia or Australian Jewry.[31] The British Jews who came to Australia in the nineteenth century were augmented by a sprinkling from central Europe. Their common denominator was necessity or adventurousness that led them to so remote a frontier. It was only much later, after the turn of the century, that Jews coming from eastern Europe reinvigorated the already assimilating community. The form of their communities continued to follow the Anglo-Jewish pattern, even when they were no longer Anglo-Jewish in membership.

After the first wave of eastern European immigration tapered off in the 1930s, it was followed by a small wave of German Jewish refugees fleeing Nazism. Significant about that wave was that, whether assimilationist or not, its members found it hard to consider assimilation an alternative, because of their experiences in Europe. Some of them became pillars of the Jewish community in Australia, even though they privately maintained an assimilationist ideology.

The arrival of a large number of eastern European Jews after each of the world wars utterly transformed the community. First, their numbers overwhelmed those who were already there. Beyond that, because these were reluctant emigrants—those who had left only because of war and Holocaust—meant that far more were committed to maintaining Orthodox Jewish life. They were extremely strong willed about it. Thus Australia came to be the only new society in which most of the immigrants came with strong prior commitments to creating a traditionally oriented Jewish community. They immediately established educational and religious institutions for this purpose and directed their communal efforts to that end. They turned to the previously established institutions only when it became apparent that influence in them would be useful for advancing their basic goals.

Thus, day schools, once strongly opposed by the Australian Jewish mainstream as "ghettoization," sprang up overnight as soon as the new immigrants had resources to establish them. By the early 1960s, within half a generation of the new Australians' arrival, every significant trend in Jewish life was represented by a day school. By that time, these highly Jewish Jews were also beginning to be elected to important positions in the state boards of Jewish deputies.

The Canadian situation was more complex because the Jews came to a polity founded by two principal fragments: one French and one English, neither of which was hospitable to Jews. Almost all the Jewish immigrants to Canada came from eastern Europe where they were far removed from either French or English civilization. Like the situation in Argentina, almost none of the founders of the Canadian Jewish community passed through the original founding civilization of the country in the Old World before reaching Canadian shores. Hence, unlike the situation in Australia and South Africa, they did not come with an acquired cultural patina to help them meld with the local population.

On the other hand, Canadian Jewish institutions emerged directly out of the vitality of eastern European Jewry to be Canadianized from that starting point, rather than having to introduce that vitality into the bland Jewish institutions of the post-Emancipation West. The Jews who founded the Canadian Jewish community were more "Jewish" in cultural, national, and religious senses than those who founded the American Jewish community. This has had profound consequences on slowing the rate of assimilation within Canadian Jewry and creating an institutional fabric that is more traditional and separatist than its counterpart south of the border. The Jews of Canada have re-mained a separate and distinctive group. In some respects they are caught between Canada's two founding communities; in other respects they can take advantage of post-war Canada's shift from biculturism to multiculturism, as have other European groups such as Italians, Ukrainians, and Germans, who immigrated to Canada and found them-selves in the same situation.[32]

Canada became a multicultural society in the framework of a federal system that, since confederation in 1867, has seen the provinces grow in strength and increase their political power and sense of identity. One result of this is that Canada has no New York, no city that served as the major magnet for the Jewish immigrants. Jews settled almost equally in Montreal and Toronto, even though the first had some edge until the postwar period. Smaller numbers concentrated in the major cities of other provinces. Thus, the combined effect of Canadian federalism and the frontier led to the creation of a multicentered Jewish community resting on two more or less equal anchors with institu-tions structured accordingly.

This has generated certain anomalies. By and large, the Jewish settlers were more in sympathy with the Protestant English Canadians who were the dominant group, even though the Anglophones rejected them through "genteel" anti-Semitism, which was strong in the last generation of the nineteenth century and the first generation of the twentieth. They were far removed from the Roman Catholic French Canadians, who were equally anti-Semitic but might have sought out the Jews as allies against the English had the Jews been open to such an alliance. As a result, even the Jews who settled in the province of Quebec chose to assimilate into the Anglophone rather than into the Franco-phone community, much to the disgust of the French majority. This was to come back to haunt the Jewish community in the 1970s.[33]

Canadian Jews also remained more traditional than their counterparts in most of the other countries of immigration. Among the modified versions of eastern European institutions transplanted to Canada was Orthodoxy, to which most Canadian Jews contin-ued to adhere for a long time after their American counterparts had abandoned it. To this day most synagogues in Canada are Orthodox, with the Conservative movement second and the Reform movement considerably farther behind. Ultra-Orthodoxy, however, has probably made fewer inroads in Canada than in other communities like it. There is a growing ultra-Orthodox population, but it is much less influential in religious affairs because mainstream Orthodoxy remains strong, with a committed group and not merely Jews who are nominally Orthodox for public purposes. The latter situation allows ultra-Orthodoxy to take advantage of the vacuum created by it.

The Jewish immigrants established an all-embracing representative organization, the Canadian Jewish Congress, by the end of the community's first generation. They also retained Yiddish as a spoken and written language longer than the other English-speaking communities. All this was encouraged by their marginal position in Canadian society, which treated them ambivalently, opening its doors to them as individuals but keeping a distance from them as Jews.

Public schooling has been much less a political-cultural norm in Canada than in the United States or France. In Quebec, separate Francophone and Anglophone school systems were recognized as the basis of public education and were tied to the dominant Roman Catholic and Protestant churches. The Jews, eager to enter non-Jewish society, rejected the opportunity to establish a parallel Jewish school system and were content with being defined for school purposes as Protestants. Nevertheless, a Jewish day school system developed in Montreal when day schools were confined to the ultra-Orthodox in New York and one or two other cities in the United States. They were subsidized by the Quebec government and attracted many Jewish children. Today the day schools enroll two-thirds of the Jewish school population in that province.

In unilingual Ontario where public schools were the norm, they were also more Protestant without the restraints of separation of church and state as defined in the United States or France. While most Jews took advantage of the public schools, some wanted to give their children a more intensive Jewish education. They chose day schools that were not stigmatized as being separatist. Hence Toronto now has a network of Jewish day schools, and every Jewish community in the province has its day school. Public schools were much more likely to be the norm in the prairie provinces and British Columbia, and day schools were longer in taking root. The Jews who settled in those regions established communal Talmud Torahs that provided almost as rigorous a Jewish education through a supplementary educational framework for several generations of children.

During the first two generations of the nineteenth century—the formative ones for the Jews in South Africa—most of the Jews were Anglicized before their arrival. Hence, they fitted in well with the increasingly dominant British group, especially in the Cape region. Later the immigrants were overwhelmingly Litvaks (Jews of Lithuanian origin), whose resolution, intensity, and seriousness of purposed fitted in well with the Afrikaners among whom most of them settled. The Litvaks were given to institution building, particularly in the educational sphere, where South African Jewry has been notably successful.[34]

Even after the original Jewish settlers were submerged by the many arriving Litvaks, they gave the Jewish community its framework and at least its external tone, in the way that German Jews in the United States set the institutional and cultural patterns for the later Eastern European immigrants. This was particularly evident in the religious-congregational sphere, where Anglo-Jewish forms of synagogue organization, ritual observance, and nominal Orthodoxy became the norm. The South African Federation of Synagogues was a modified version of the United Synagogue of Great Britain, although under South African conditions, the member congregations retained greater independence than those of the United Synagogue, as the difference in the names of the two framing bodies indicates. Each congregation was a separate and self-governing corporation, but the Federation maintained strict control over standards for congregational rabbis and in ritual matters, which, in turn, has led most South African Jews to be nominally Orthodox, affiliated with Orthodox synagogues but far from Orthodox in their own observance.

The influence of Anglo-Jewry remains particularly strong in the Cape Province and Natal, the bastions of British civilization in the Republic. When the Litvaks began to arrive, they settled principally in the Transvaal—the greatest of the Afrikaner strongholds—and also in the Afrikaner areas of the other provinces. Litvaks had a cultural affinity to the Afrikaners, so links between Jews and Afrikaners were forged with relative ease, even though in the end the influence of Anglo-Jewry formally won out. Most Litvaks became English- rather than Afrikaans-speaking, and they also modeled their institutions on those of Anglo-Jewry. Still the links were real. Individual Jews became closely tied to Afrikaners, contributing to the development of the Boer republics and even to the growth of Afrikaans literature, a number of whose leading figures are Jewish.

The influence of the Litvaks was particularly strong in Jewish education. They emphasized separate Jewish schools from the first, although it took a generation or more of struggle before Jewish day schools became the predominant way of schooling for Jews in South Africa. The transformation took place after World War II and was undoubtedly encouraged by the realities of a bilingual, multiethnic society. The Afrikaners, the politically dominant group, developed the public school system as a vehicle for perpetuating Afrikaner culture, nationalism, and religion. Thus a substantial day school movement developed throughout South Africa. Unlike the situation in Australia, almost all the schools were nominally Orthodox and some extremely so. There was little room for non-Orthodox day schools in the South African context. Today, more than half the Jewish children in South Africa study in day schools, with proportions reaching more than 90 percent in the smaller communities.

Jews as a group became more important in the South African mosaic than in any of the other countries. The United States came close second after World War II and more recently may even have moved into first place. Individual Jews rose to higher positions in public life in Australia than in the other countries, including two governors-general and the highest-ranking Australian military commander in World War I. In South Africa, the British imperial representatives and those of the Afrikaner community shared or struggled for dominance in public life, to the exclusion of other groups. Argentinian public life is simply closed to non-Catholics except where Jews' economic skills have brought them into temporary positions of responsibility. As the Canadian Jewish community took root, many of its best talents were drained off to the United States in the way that other Canadians moved southward seeking opportunity. Only in the latter part of the postwar generation did Jews begin to surface as moderately significant figures in Canadian life.

The Succession of Generations

Just as humanity puts its changing imprint on space through the continuing frontier, it shapes time through the passage of generations. The generational rhythm that shapes human history reflects the nexus between human biology and civilization that leads to a patterning and repatterning of events at intervals of between twenty-five and forty years—usually between thirty and thirty-five. During this period the particular population cohort that sets the pace in any civil society reaches maturity, assumes positions of responsibility, and then passes from the scene as a result of death or retirement. Each generation confronts its own set of issues, which emerge from those dealt with in the previous generation. It more or less satisfactorily defines those issues and then deals with them so that new issues emerge from them to confront the next generation.[35]

Different rhythms. The order and timing of the Jews' arrival in each country contributed significantly to their adaptation and development.

From the first, the generational rhythm of American Jewry coincided with the generational rhythm of the United States. Even the arrival of the Jewish settlers fortuitously came near the beginning of the second generation of American history, enabling them to fit into the rhythm from the moment of their arrival. First came the Spanish and Portuguese, the Marranos or descendants of Marranos, who laid the congregational foundation for the community. They absorbed the first waves of Ashkenazim who followed them, maintaining the Spanish and Portuguese ritual and ways even after the Ashkenazim became a majority in the mid-eighteenth century.

In the generation immediately after American independence, there was an immigration of English Jews who were absorbed by the older Spanish and Portuguese institutions. Then, in the first generation of the nineteenth century, the German or, more accurately, the central European Jews came. They transformed American Jewry in two generations, placing the stamp of German Jewish culture on it. In the last generation of the century, after 1880, they were inundated by the masses of eastern European Jews, who kept many of the forms established by their German predecessors but gave them a new style and content.

A second immigration of the Sephardic Jews at the turn of the century paralleled that of the eastern Europeans but, because they were an infinitesimal percentage of the Jewish population, they have gone unnoticed. Thus contemporary American Jewry has an institutional structure introduced by Sephardic and German Jews but shaped by those from eastern Europe. The post-World War II migrations of Holocaust survivors, Sephardic Jews, Soviet Jews, and Israeli *yordim* have continued the stream of Jewish immigration to the United States but they came to an organizationally completed community.

In the larger Jewish communities of Latin America, eastern European and Mediterranean immigrants began to arrive at about the same time, late in the nineteenth century well after the establishment of the generational rhythm of their host societies. As it turned out, their communal processes came to fit into that rhythm much better than they came to integrate culturally. The tone for the Jewish community was set by the eastern Europeans; the Mediterraneans set their own tone and have maintained it. After the rise of Hitler, small numbers of German and central European Jews came. They had to fit into an eastern European world and, except as much as the first generation created and preserved its institutions, have generally done so. This is exactly the reverse of the process in North America, for example, where the Germanicized Jews preceded those who came directly out of eastern European culture by two generations, and thus set the patterns to which the others had to adapt.

In many of the smaller Jewish communities of Latin America, no organized Jewish life existed before the rise of Nazism, and their founding settlers were German and central European refugees. Even if they stayed on, many of their children subsequently left for more cosmopolitan countries and larger Jewish centers. The exceptions in those communities were Sephardi Jewish traders who found their way at the turn of the century and organized small congregations. All remained outside the generational rhythm of their host countries.

Canadian Jewry dates back some 230 years to the second generation of the eighteenth century and the British conquest of French Canada. Because Jews were not allowed to settle in French Canada, they had no share in the French colonial experience there. But because the first of them arrived at what was, in effect, the beginning of a new generation, the Jews easily adjusted to the rhythm of the British colonial experience. They were too few, however, to matter in other than the mythic aspects of Canadian Jewish history. The few Jewish settlers were mainly from England, a mixture of Ashkenazim and Sephardim. Many stayed for a short while and then returned to England or moved to the United States.

The next three generations found Canadian Jewry languishing in the backwaters of world Jewry. Canada attracted few immigrants as long as the United States was the unadulterated land of opportunity in the minds of Europeans. The Jewish community was kept alive by the handful of English Jews who crossed the Atlantic to its shores. As a result, there was a hiatus in the rhythm of the Canadian Jewish community, although the experiences of the Jews who came and remained continued to fit well into the progression of Canadian history.

It was only with the beginning of the mass emigration from eastern Europe in the 1880s, and particularly with the introduction of restrictions on immigration to the United States by the American government at the end of the nineteenth century, that Jews began to seek Canada as an alternative. The eastern European influx also came fortuitously at the beginning of a new generation in Canadian history, particularly in the opening of the West for settlement, so that the Jews fit in harmoniously. Eastern European Jewry simply took over the community; their predecessors had insufficient weight to dictate even the forms of communal life and organization. Thus the Canadian Jewish community is basically a twentieth-century phenomenon, founded by eastern European Jews who came to an essentially empty land, Jewishly and generally, and founded their institutions from scratch.

The development of the South African Jewish community came relatively late in South African history. As indicated above, from the beginning it was well integrated with the generational rhythm of the country and Western civilization.

The Jews of Australia were founders from the start. They were among the first arrivals in 1788 and were involved in every subsequent wave of immigration to now. The Australian Jews can also be said to have matched the shifting profile of immigrants to Australia—from the first ones who came as convicts to the latest Israeli *yordim* who are technically skilled settlers of the kind whose immigration is being encouraged in the aftermath of the great postwar immigration. Moreover, the generational timing was such that Australia was the one new society in which intensely Orthodox Jews took part in the mainstream of communal life. At the turn of the century, during the great immigrations to the other societies, Orthodoxy was under assault by liberal religion reflecting the dominant liberal ideology of the fin de siècle years and strengthened by the pervasive optimism of that period. By the late 1940s, after the rise of communism, fascism, and two world wars, optimistic liberalism was no longer so powerful a force, and Orthodoxy was beginning its resurgence along with fundamentalist religions outside the Jewish world. Thus, the pressure on the Orthodox to change was far less than before. Australian Jewish society is a reflection of this change.

Points of comparison. Several points of comparison run through the generational rhythms of the New World communities. On a continuum of Jews as founders in each country, Latin America would be at one end, South Africa and Canada in the middle, and the United States and Australia at the other end. Also, each entered the sequence of waves of migration at its own moment.

All began to suffer from anti-Semitism in the last generation of the nineteenth century. Modern racism took shape in the generation that began in the late 1870s and lasted until World War I, when Western imperialism was at its height. Northern Europeans rejected all others as lesser breeds and created elaborate theories to justify their attitudes. The Western world saw itself as a great civilizing force confronting inferior nonwhite elements. This view became strongest in the Anglo-Saxon and Teutonic countries, whose people saw themselves as the culmination of civilization and even doubted the "whiteness" of the "inferior" peoples of southern and eastern Europe, including Jews.[36] Even those not swayed by the new anti-Semitism saw the Jews as an Oriental people. It is no wonder that the Jews suffered as a result. But while racism toward others continued in the next generation without intensifying, toward Jews it was transformed into a murderous force.[37]

In their drive for acceptance by non-Jewish society, the Jews more or less accepted this characterization; many tried to remake themselves accordingly. Thus, acculturation was one of their primary goals, even if this meant a level of assimilation beyond that to which they consciously aspired. Their host societies, which welcomed them with greater or lesser willingness, expected them to become fully acculturated if not assimilated. In the United States—the most open and tolerant of the countries at that time—Americanization was considered the sine qua non for all immigrants. The other societies expected no less, though in different ways.[38]

After World War II most of the world repudiated racism, and anti-Semitism was also rejected, chiefly because of the Holocaust. In all the New World countries there was a decline in anti-Semitic expression—its near disappearance in the United States, a marked decline in Australia, Canada, and South Africa, and a much lesser decline in Latin America. Revelation of the horrors of the Holocaust led to a change in the hearts and minds of those who were moderately afflicted with the virus, forcing those with deeper prejudices to go underground.[39] Today, in a new generation, there are signs that anti-Semitism is growing again, feeding on the ignorance of a generation that does not know the evils of Nazism.[40]

The generation that matured after World War II was also less committed to homogenization. Anticolonialism replaced the white man's burden as the accepted standard, even in the West. The definition of "whiteness" had been expanded even earlier to include all Europeans, and racial barriers between whites and nonwhites were beginning to break down. Even in the centralized societies of the West, a new pluralism was stirring and there was a greater willingness to tolerate differences.[41]

Not that the new Jews of Australia—even the Orthodox among them—did not acquire the external manifestations of Australianness as quickly as possible. To the contrary, they made every effort to do so. But alongside these external manifestations they preserved much more of a public display of their Jewishness, to say nothing of what they maintained in their homes and institutions, more than any previous generation of immigrant Jews had felt comfortable in doing.

In Latin America in contrast, local xenophobic tendencies were exacerbated by the anticolonialist ideology, making Jewish differences even more suspect. In South Africa, because the dominant Afrikaners were white, their efforts to stay in power were interpreted by many as a continuation of colonialism. No matter how much the Afrikaners tried to explain that they had become an indigenous African people, their skin color placed them on the colonialist side. The Jews as whites were made even more welcome than they had been in South Africa because they were white, and were even encouraged to maintain their way of life in the context of the Afrikaners' plans for a multinational, multicultural society of unequals.

Jews were never as freely admitted to the upper echelons of Canadian society as they finally came to be admitted in the United States. In Quebec the French desire for emancipation from what they perceived to be colonial restraints led to a xenophobia that was reinforced by the tendencies toward anti-Semitism fostered by the traditional Roman Catholic church. Even after the 1960s, when the French Canadians turned secularist with a vengeance, they brought with them much of this anti-Semitic baggage, and many of their intellectuals became strong supporters of the Palestinian Liberation Organization and vigorously anti-Zionist. "Zionist" rapidly became a code word for "Jew."

In English Canada, the class system, much stronger than that in the United States, maintained the more subtle anti-Semitism of the British elite and hence excluded Jews.

This was particularly true in Ontario, the great bastion of Anglo Canada and the country's most powerful province. It was much diluted in the West, where, like in all frontier societies, there was greater opportunity for minorities.

The acceptance of multiculturalism and ethnic pluralism as official Canadian policy during the post-World War II generation offered the Jews an easy way to maintain their identity as Jews once they had acquired the elements of Canadian culture expected of all Canadian citizens. These were less pronounced than in Australia—for example, Canada accepted language differences as a reasonable form of pluralism—and considerably less than in South Africa where the official policy was to enshrine group differences, not simply recognize them. The Jews have been able to take advantage of those opportunities in Canada; yet because they are located in the most important centers of Canadian life, they have a harder time preserving the external manifestations of ethnic separatism to which more isolated groups cling.

It was in the United States that integration of the Jews into the larger society went furthest in the postwar period. When World War II ended, few Jews were in the elite professions, banking, heavy industry, or the universities, and even the most successful Jews were confined to the margins of what was then defined as respectable activity. In a generation all this had changed and almost every door was open to Jews. In universities where no Jewish professor could be found before 1950, Jews were chosen as presidents in the 1970s. Only a few small bastions of the old elites remained closed to Jews as they did to all outsiders, but every other aspect of public and private life was opened, including the family, as the soaring Jewish intermarriage rate indicated.

Another common element in the generational rhythm was the confrontation with communism that touched most of these Jewish communities from the middle of the interwar generation to the early stages of the postwar one. The messianic expectations nurtured by the Russian Revolution, coupled with the Great Depression, led a small but significant number of Jews to embrace communism in the 1920s and 1930s. In all the major New World communities except the United States, those Jews made significant efforts to capture the principal communal institutions. In Argentina, Canada, and South Africa, the effort was made early; in Australia, where in the 1930s Jewish institutions were still predominantly in the hands of the old establishment, it was not made until immediately after World War II. In each instance, the effort was defeated, mainly because of Jewish disillusionment with, even revulsion against, the Communist movement as its brutal and repressive record became known.[42]

Finally, the resurgence of Jewish corporate identity, a major feature of the postwar generation, is notable in the New World communities. Initiated by the Jews' new pride in and concern for Israel, it was nurtured by the transformation of organic Jewish ties into associational ones, the revival of ethnicity around the world, and a growing consciousness that Jews everywhere confronted common issues. The postwar generation has witnessed the revival of Jewish commitment to a Jewish polity, a commitment evident in the Jewries of the Western and Southern hemispheres.

Notes

1. See Seymour B. Liebman, *The Inquisitors and the Jews in the New World* (Coral Gables, Fla.: University of Miami Press, 1974) and Martin A. Cohen, ed., *The Jewish Experience in Latin America* (New York: Ktav Publishing House, 1971).

2. Henry L. Feingold, *A Midrash on American Jewish History* (Albany, N.Y.: State University of New

York Press, 1982) and *Zion in America* (New York: Hippocene Books, Inc., 1974); Lee. M. Friedman, *Early American Jews* (Cambridge, Mass.: Harvard University Press, 1934) and *Jewish Pioneers and Patriots* (Philadelphia: Jewish Publication Society of America, 1942); Oscar Handlin, *Adventure in Freedom: Three Hundred Years of Jewish Life in America* (New York: McGraw Hill, 1954); Anita L. Lebeson, *Jewish Pioneers in America: 1492–1848* (New York: Behrman House, 1931) and *Pilgrim People* (New York: Harper and Bros., 1950); Jacob Rader Marcus, *Early American Jewry,* 2 vols. (Philadelphia: Jewish Publication Society of America, 1955) and *The Colonial American Jew, 1492–1776,* 3 vols. (Detroit: Wayne State University Press, 1970); Abraham J. Karp, *Haven and Hope: A History of the Jews in America* (New York: Schocken Books, 1985).

    3. Louis Rosenberg, "Some Aspects of the Historical Development of the Canadian Jewish Community" and *Chronology of Canadian Jewish History* (Montreal: Canadian Jewish Congress, 1959); Stuart E. Rosenberg, *The Jewish Community in Canada* (Toronto: McClelland and Stewart, 1970–71); B. G. Sack, *History of the Jews in Canada,* trans. Ralph Novek (Montreal: Harvest House, 1960); A. J. Arnold, "Jewish Pioneer Settlements," *The Beaver,* (autumn 1975), pp. 20–26; M. M. Lazar and Sheva Medjuck, "In the Beginning: A Brief History of Jews in Atlantic Canada," *Jewish Historical Society of Canada* (fall 1981); and *Jews on the Fringe: The Development of the Jewish Community of Atlantic Canada,* Occasional Papers of the International Education Center (Halifax, Nova Scotia, 1983); Jonathan D. Sarna, "Jewish Immigration to North America: The Canadian Experience (1870–1900)," *Jewish Journal of Sociology,* vol. 28, no. 1 (June 1976), pp. 31–41; Erna Paris, *Jews: An Account of Their Experience in Canada* (Toronto: Macmillan in Canada, 1980); Harry Gutkin, *Journey into Our Heritage: The Story of the Jewish People in the Canadian West* (Toronto: Lester and Orpen Dennys, 1980).

    4. See C. A. Price, *Jewish Settlers in Australia* (Canberra: Australia National University, 1964).

    5. See Louis Herrman, *A History of the Jews in South Africa* (London: U. G. Hancz, 1930) and Gustav Saron and Louis Hotz, eds., *The Jews in South Africa: A History* (Cape Town: Oxford University Press, 1955), chap. 1, "Cape Jewry before 1870" by Louis Herrman.

    6. For an understanding of that phenomenon, see Frederick Jackson Turner, *The Frontier in American History* (New York: Holt, 1921); Walter Prescott Webb, *The Great Frontier* (Boston: Houghton Mifflin, 1952); Ray Allen Billington, *America's Frontier Heritage* (New York: Holt, Rinehart and Winston, 1966); Louis Hartz, *The Founding of New Societies* (New York: Harcourt, Brace and World, 1964); George Wolfskill and Stanley Palmer, eds., *Essays on Frontiers in World History* (College Station, Tex.: Texas A&M University Press, 1983).

    7. For a full exposition of this thesis, see Daniel J. Elazar, *The Metropolitan Frontier: A Perspective on Change in American Society* (New York: General Learning Press, 1973).

    8. Turner, *The Frontier in American History;* Billington, *America's Frontier Heritage;* Webb, *The Great Frontier.*

    9. Friedman, *Jewish Pioneers and Patriots;* Harold I. Sharfman, *Jews on the Frontier* (Chicago: Henry Regnery Company, 1977) and *"Nothing Left to Commemorate": The Story of the Pioneer Jews of Jackson, Amador County, California* (Glendale, Calif.: The Arthur H. Clark Company, 1969); Jacob Rader Marcus, *Memoirs of American Jews 1775–1865,* 3 vols. (Philadelphia: The Jewish Publication Society of America, 1955–56); Alfred Apsler, *Western Pioneers* (Philadelphia: Jewish Publication Society of America, 1960); Kenneth Libo and Irving Howe, *We Lived There Too* (New York: St. Martin's/Marek, 1984); Harriet and Fred Rochlin, *Pioneer Jews: A New Life in the Far West* (Boston: Houghton Mifflin Company, 1984).

    10. Elazar, *The Metropolitan Frontier* and *Cities of the Prairie: The Metropolitan Frontier and American Politics* (New York: Basic Books, 1970).

    11. Daniel J. Elazar with Peter Medding, *Jewish Communities in Frontier Societies* (New York: Holmes and Meier, 1983).

    12. See C. F. J. Muller, ed., *Five Hundred Years: A History of South Africa,* 2d rev. and ill. ed. (Pretoria and Cape Town: Academica, 1975); Shula Marks and Anthony Atmore, eds., *Economy and Society in Pre-Industrial South Africa* (London: Longman, 1980), esp. Martin Legassick, "The Frontier Tradition in South African Historiography," pp. 44–79 and Stanley Trapido, "Reflections on Land, Office, and Wealth in the South African Republic, 1850–1900," pp. 350–68.

    13. Herrman, *A History of the Jews in South Africa;* Saron and Hotz, *The Jews in South Africa: A History;* Elazar with Medding, *Jewish Communities in Frontier Societies;* and Gideon Shimoni, *Jews and Zionism: The South African Experience, 1910–1967* (Cape Town: Oxford University Press, 1980).

    14. See Tomas Roberto Fillol, *Social Factors in Economic Development: The Argentina Case* (Cambridge, Mass.: The M.I.T. Press, 1961); Russell H. Fitzgibbon, *Argentina* (Dobbs Ferry, N.Y.: Oceana Publications, 1974); Charles Gibson, *Spain in America* (New York: Harper and Row, 1966); Alan Gilbert, *Latin American Development: A Geographical Perspective* (London: Penguin Books, 1974).

15. Haim Avni, *Argentina: Ha-Aretz He-Ye'uda* (Argentina: The Promised Land) (Jerusalem: Magnes Press, 1973) (Hebrew); Robert Weisbrot, *The Jews of Argentina from the Inquisition to Perón* (Philadelphia: Jewish Publication Society of America, 1979).

16. William Metcalfe, ed., *Understanding Canada* (New York: New York University, 1982); J. M. S. Careless, ed., *Colonists and Canadians* (New York: St. Martin's, 1971); D. G. Creighton, *A History of Canada: Dominion of the North* (Boston: Houghton Mifflin, 1958); H. A. Innis, *The Fur Trade in Canada,* rev. ed. (Toronto: University of Toronto Press, 1956); A. R. M. Lower, *Colony to Nation* (New York: Longmans, 1958); E. W. McInnis, *Canada: A Political and Social History* (Toronto: Holt, Rinehart and Winston, 1969).

17. Arnold, "Jewish Pioneer Settlements"; Lazar and Medjuck, "In the Beginning" and "Jews on the Fringe"; Paris, *Jews;* Arthur Chiel, *The Jew in Manitoba* (Toronto: University of Toronto Press, 1961); Arthur D. Hart, ed., *The Jews in Canada: A Complete Record of Canadian Jewry* (Toronto: Toronto Jewish Publications, 1926); Stephen Speisman, *The Jews of Toronto* (Toronto: McClelland and Stewart, 1979); Louis Rosenberg, "Some Aspects of the Historical Development of the Canadian Jewish Community"; Joseph Kage, *Immigration and Integration in Canada* (Montreal: Jewish Immigrant Aid Services, 1966).

18. See Donald Horns, *The Lucky Country* (Melbourne: Penguin Books, 1966); George Nadel, *Australia's Colonial Culture* (Melbourne: F. W. Cheshire, 1957); Gordon Greenwod, *Australia: A Social and Political History* (Sydney: Angus and Robertson, 1955).

19. I. Getzler, *Neither Tradition nor Favour: The Australian Chapter of Jewish Emancipation* (Melbourne: Melbourne University Press, 1970); J. S. Levi and G. F. J. Bergman, *Australian Genesis: Jewish Convicts and Settlers, 1788–1850* (Adelaide: Robert Hale, 1974); C. A. Price, *Jewish Settlers in Australia.*

20. Elazar, *The Metropolitan Frontier.*

21. James Yaffe, *The American Jews* (New York: Random House, 1968); Sarah Blacher Cohen, ed., *From Hester Street to Hollywood* (Bloomington, Ind.: Indiana University Press, 1983); John Higham, *Send Them to Me: Jews and Other Immigrants in Urban America* (New York: Atheneum, 1975); Albert I. Gordon, *Jews in Suburbia* (Boston: Beacon Press, 1959); Irving Howe, *World of Our Fathers* (New York: Harcourt Brace Jovanovich, 1976); Marshall Sklare and Joseph Greenbaum, *Jewish Identity on the Suburban Frontier: A Study of Group Survival in the Open Society,* vol. 1 of the Lakeville Studies (New York: Basic Books, 1967); Benjamin B. Ringer, *The Edge of Friendliness: A Study of Jewish-Gentile Relations,* vol. 2 of the Lakeville Studies (New York: Basic Books, 1967).

22. Seymour B. Liebman, *Argentina Jewry: Its History, Ethnicity, and Problems,* unpublished report prepared for the Center of Jewish Community Studies, 1975; Weisbrot, *The Jews of Argentina;* Elazar with Medding, *Jewish Communities in Frontier Societies.*

23. Muller, ed., *Five Hundred Years;* C. W. DeKiewiet, *A History of South Africa, Social and Economic* (London: Oxford University Press, 1941); E. A. Walker, ed., *The Cambridge History of The British Empire,* vol. 8: South Africa, 2d ed. (Cambridge: University Press, 1963) and *A History of Southern Africa,* 3d rev. ed. (London: Longmans, 1957).

24. Elazar with Medding, *Jewish Communities in Frontier Societies;* E. Bernstein, "A Bird's Eye View of South African Jewry Today," in *South African Jewry,* 1967–68 (Johannesburg: South African Jewish Board of Deputies, 1968); Allie A. Dubb, *Jewish South Africans: A Sociological View of the Johannesburg Community* (Grahamstown: Institute of Social and Economic Research, Rhodes University, 1977).

25. Elazar with Medding, *Jewish Communities in Frontier Societies* and Peter Y. Medding, ed., *Jews in Australian Society* (Melbourne: Macmillan/Monash, 1973).

26. Hartz, *The Founding of New Societies.*

27. See Marshall Sklare, *America's Jews* (New York: Random House, 1971); Daniel J. Elazar, *Community and Polity: The Organizational Dynamics of American Jewry* (Philadelphia: Jewish Publication Society of America, 1976); Steven M. Cohen, *American Modernity and Jewish Identity* (New York: Tavistock, 1983); Charles S. Liebman, *The Ambivalent American Jew* (Philadelphia: Jewish Publication Society of America, 1973); Milton Himmelfarb, *The Jews of Modernity* (Philadelphia: Jewish Publication Society of America, 1973).

28. Walter I. Ackerman, "Jewish Education Today," *American Jewish Year Book 1980,* vol. 80 (New York and Philadelphia: American Jewish Committee and Jewish Publication Society of America, 1979), pp. 130–48; Judah Pilch, ed., *A History of Jewish Education in America* (New York: The National Curriculum Research Institute of the American Association for Jewish Education, 1969).

29. Martin A. Cohen, *The Jewish Experience in Latin America;* Nissim Elnecavé, "Sephardic Jews in Argentina," *Dispersion and Unity* (June 1960), pp. 56–57 and "Yehudim Sephardim be-Olam" (Sephardic Jewry in the World), *Bi-Tfutzot HaGolah,* nos. 44–45 (summer 1968), pp. 138–49 (Hebrew); Weisbrot, *The Jews of Argentina.*

30. Avni, *Argentina: HaAretz HeYe'uda;* Liebman, *Argentina Jewry;* Weisbrot, *The Jews of Argentina.*

31. Elazar with Medding, *Jewish Communities in Frontier Societies,* part 4.

32. M. Weinfeld, W. Shaffir, and I. Cotler, eds., *The Canadian Jewish Mosaic* (Toronto: J. Wiley, 1981).

33. Daniel J. Elazar, "The Jews of Quebec and the Canadian Crisis," *Tefutsot Yisrael,* vol. 15, no. 2 (April–June 1977), pp. 7–11.

34. Gustave Saron, "The Making of South African Jewry—An Essay in Historical Interpretation," in *South African Jewry* (Johannesburg: South African Jewish Board of Deputies, 1966).

35. For a fuller discussion of the generational rhythm, see Danield J. Elazar, "The Generational Rhythm of American Politics," *American Politics Quarterly,* vol. 6, no. 1 (January 1978), pp. 55–90 and "Generational Breaks" in Nissan Oren, ed., *When Patterns Change: Turning Points in International Politics* (New York and Jerusalem: St. Martin's Press and Magnes Press, 1984). For the application of the thesis to Jewish history, see Daniel J. Elazar, *The Constitutional Periodization of Jewish History: A Second Look* (Jerusalem: Center for Jewish Community Studies, 1979).

36. Max Horkheimer and Samuel H. Flowerman, *Studies in Prejudice* (New York: Harper and Brothers, 1950); Bruno Bettelheim and Morris Janowitz, *Dynamics of Prejudice* (New York: Harper and Brothers, 1950); John Higham, "Social Discrimination against Jews in America, 1830–1930," *Publication of the American Jewish Historical Society,* vol. 47, no. 1 (September 1957), pp. 1–33 and *Strangers in the Land* (New York: Atheneum, 1975); Lee J. Levinger, *Anti-Semitism in the United States: Its History and Causes* (New York: Bloch Publishing Co., 1925); Jacob Katz, *From Prejudice to Destruction: Anti-Semitism 1700–1933* (Cambridge, Mass.: Harvard University Press, 1980).

37. Bernard Lazare, *Antisemitism: Its History and Causes* (New York: International Library Publishing Co., 1903); Anatole Leroy-Beaulieu, *L'Antisémitisme* (Paris: Calmann Lévy, 1897); Joseph Reinach, *Historie de l'affaire Dreyfus,* 7 vols. (Paris: Editions de la Revue blanche, 1901–11); S. Ettinger, ed., *Anti-Semitism in the Soviet Union: Its Roots and Consequences* (Jerusalem: The Hebrew University of Jerusalem, the Center for Research and Documentation of East-European Jewry, 1983); Peter G. J. Pulzer, *The Rise of Political Anti-Semitism in Germany and Austria* (New York: Wiley, 1964); Judd Teller, *Scapegoat of Revolution* (New York: Scribner's, 1954); Leon Poliakov, *The History of Anti-Semitism,* 3 vols. (London: Routledge and Kegan Paul, 1974–75); Katz, *From Prejudice to Destruction.*

38. Werner Keller, *Diaspora: The Post-Biblical History of Jews* (New York: Harcourt, Brace and World, Inc., 1966); Paul R. Mendes-Flohr and Jehuda Reinharz, eds., *The Jew in the Modern World* (New York: Oxford University Press, 1980).

39. Will Herberg, *Protestant-Catholic-Jew: An Essay in American Religious Sociology* (New York: Doubleday/Anchor Books, 1960); "Anti-Semitism," in *Encyclopedia Judaica,* vol. 3, pp. 136–38; Arnold Foster and Benjamin F. Epstein, *The New Anti-Semitism* (New York: McGraw Hill Book Company, 1974), chap. 1.

40. Foster and Epstein, *The New Anti-Semitism;* Nathaniel Weyl, *The Jew in American Politics* (New Rochelle, N.Y.: Arlington House, 1968), chap. 16; "Anti-Semitism Today: A Symposium," special issue of *Patterns of Prejudice,* vol. 16, no. 4 (October 1982); Sander Diamond, *The Nazi Movement in the United States 1924–1941* (Ithaca: Cornell University Press, 1974); Michael Dobkowski, *The Tarnished Dream: The Basis of American Anti-Semitism* (Westport, Conn.: Greenwood Press, 1979); Paul E. Grosser and Edwin G. Halperin, *The Causes and Effects of Anti-Semitism: The Dimensions of Prejudice* (New York: Philosophical Library, 1978); Robert J. Marx, "The New Anti-Semitism and the Old," *Journal of Reform Judaism,* vol. 27 (spring 1980), pp. 1–11; Kalman Sultanik, "Antisemitism: An Overview," *Forum,* no. 36 (fall/winter 1979), pp. 83–97.

41. See Murray Friedman, "Religion and Politics in an Age of Pluralism, 1945–1976: An Ethnocultural View," *Publius,* vol. 10, no. 3 (summer 1980), pp. 45–80 and Morris Dickstein, *Gates of Eden: American Culture in the Sixties* (New York: Basic Books, 1977).

42. Little has been written about these Communist efforts. This writer and the staff of the Study of Jewish Community Organization have interview data on the subject, now in the archives of the Jerusalem Center for Public Affairs. See also Gideon Shimoni, *Jews and Zionism: The South African Experience 1910–1967* (Cape Town: Oxford University Press, 1980).

10

The State of American Jewry

The United States, with close to six million Jews (more than half of all the Jews in the diaspora and some 40 percent of all the Jews in the world today), like Israel, stands in a class by itself.[1] A large, fully modern society built on principles of individualism, pluralistic in the full sense of the word, settled by several significantly different waves of adventurous Jewish immigrants who shared one common commitment, that of seeking new lives as individuals, was not conducive to the development of sufficient homogeneity to permit the emergence of a neat communal structure. Consequently, every effort to create even so much as a single nationwide "address" for American Jewry has failed.

Nor is this situation without precedent. No Jewish community approaching the size of the American one has ever succeeded in creating a neat structure for itself, complete with "roof" organization and all the other accoutrements. The vaunted *kehillot* of other times and climes were developed for much smaller communities. From Roman times to the modern epoch, probably none exceeded a few tens of thousands in population and most were far smaller than that. In the seventeenth century, for example, there were only three cities in Europe with ten thousand Jews or more: Amsterdam, Istanbul, and Salonika. Even the largest countrywide communities did not exceed a few hundred thousand. Thus the cities with the largest Jewish populations in the United States—New York, Los Angeles, Philadelphia, Chicago, Boston, Miami—are larger than all but a handful of countrywide communities that have existed over the long history of the Jewish people.

The American Jewish community is built on an *associational base* to a far greater extent than any other in Jewish history. That is, not only is there no compulsion, external or internal, to affiliate with organized Jewry, but there is no automatic way to become a member of the Jewish community. Nor is there even an ambiguous way to do so. All connections with organized Jewish life in America are based on voluntary association with some particular organization or institution, whether in the form of synagogue membership, contribution to the local Jewish Welfare Fund (usually considered an act of joining the community as well), or affiliation with a B'nai B'rith lodge or Hadassah chapter.

This associational approach is typically American, a reflection of a social order that is based on chosen affiliation rather than descent. Americans do not like to think of themselves bound to anything by birth; hence they seek to transform all organic ties into associational ones. Even such organic entities as the family frequently take on an associational character in American Jewish life: the development and spread of the "family club," a formal association of relatives, in the 1930s is a case in point.

The usual pattern for affiliated Jews—like their fellow Americans—is one of multiple association. Memberships in different organizations reinforce one another, creating a network of ties that bind the individual who chooses to become enmeshed in them more firmly to the community. Without that associational base, there would be no organized Jewish community at all; with it, the community attains the kind of social and even legal status that enables it to fit well into the larger society of which it is a part.

Although some of its organizations sometimes succeed in developing from the top down, *the institutions of the American Jewish community are essentially local* and, at most, loosely confederated with one another for limited purposes. The three great synagogue movements, for example, are confederations of highly independent local congregations, linked by vague persuasional ties and a need for technical services. The confederations function to provide the requisite emotional reinforcement of those ties and the services desired by their member units. Like the other countrywide organizations, they combine countrywide identification with local attachments.[2]

Sooner or later, all large countrywide Jewish organizations have found that their survival is contingent on developing a local base to accommodate the powerful combination of American and Jewish penchants for organization along federal principles.[3] Excepting a few institutions of higher education (and formerly a few specialized hospitals, now nonsectarian), all Jewish social, welfare, and educational institutions are local in name and in fact, some loosely confederated on a supralocal basis and most not.

The key to American Jewish communal organization is its flexibility and that flexibility is reflected institutionally in the federal character of Jewish association. It has already been noted that the application of federal principles first applied in the federation of the twelve tribes has undergone many permutations in the long course of Jewish history. Today in an era of atraditionalism, it is one tradition not being abandoned by Jews.

Today, the *government-like institutions* of the American Jewish community include the Jewish community federations and those institutions and organizations dedicated to serving community-wide needs that are associated with them. In a typical community, they will include a Jewish community center, a central agency for Jewish education, a Jewish community relations council, social welfare institutions to deal with problems ranging from adoption to aging, a Jewish hospital, a welfare fund, and cultural societies with community-wide appeal.[4]

The most important *localistic institutions* are the synagogues, which are geared to be intimate associations of compatible people. Even the large American synagogues that lose their sense of intimacy remain localistic institutions in this sense. (The contradictions between size and function may be a major part of the problem of the contemporary American synagogue.) Other organizations include lodges, family clubs, *landsmanschaften* (associations of emigrants from the same town in the "old country"), and occasional "secular" societies that act as synagogue surrogates for those who proclaim their secularism. With some specific local exceptions, all are on the decline.

In the United States, B'nai B'rith and Hadassah, with lodges or chapters in almost every organized Jewish community, are mass-based mobilizing organizations but they attract their members primarily for localistic reasons. They are supplemented by smaller countrywide organizations such as the American Jewish Committee, American Jewish Congress, National Council for Jewish Women, and the different Zionist groups (of which Hadassah is formally one) most united in the American Zionist Federation.[5]

Although the *special interest organizations* are best identified locally, there are some common patterns countrywide. Local groups serving such diverse interests as support of

Jewish and Israeli institutions of higher learning, Jewish-sponsored hospitals and medical centers, vocational training programs for Jews in other countries, and a variety of Jewish eleemosynary and cultural institutions, abound.

In the smaller communities, the four roles may be compressed in fewer institutions or be filled incompletely but the functions must be institutionalized somehow for an organized community to exist.

To unite these independent associations are *overlapping local and supralocal federations* designed for different purposes. The most powerful are the local federations of Jewish agencies and their countrywide confederation, the Council of Jewish Federations (CJF), which have become the framing institutions of American Jewry and its *kehillot*. They are the only ones able to assert near-universal membership and all-embracing purposes, though not even the CJF has the formal status of a country wide "roof body."[6] Other federal arrangements are limited to single functions and their organizations rarely have more than a consultative role or power of placement or accreditation.[7] This confederative structure of American Jewry is manifested through a matrix comprising many institutions and organizations tied together by a crisscrossing of memberships, shared purposes, and common interests, whose roles and powers vary according to situation and issue.

Following the classic Jewish pattern, the American Jewish polity can be portrayed according to the *ketarim* among which the organizations are divided (figure 10.1):

KETER MALKHUT

Conference of Presidents of Major Jewish Organizations. Confederation of more than thirty organizations organized to speak for American Jewry before the United States government in matters relating to Israel.

Council of Jewish Federations (CJF). Confederation of 211 Jewish community federations in the United States and spokesman for them in matters of countrywide concern.

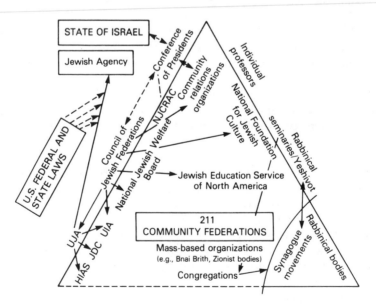

Figure 10.1. The contemporary organization of the United States Jewry.

Secretariat of Large Cities Budgeting Conference, American Jewry's major instrument for promoting fiscal accountability. Speaks for local federations in relations with UJA, Jewish Agency, and countrywide functional confederations. The annual General Assembly of CJF is the most important single gathering of American Jewry.

Hebrew Immigrant Aid Society (HIAS). Major instrumentality for transportation and absorption of Jewish refugees in the United States.

Jewish Education Service of North America (JESNA). Countrywide service agency for Jewish education.

Jewish Welfare Board (JWB). Countrywide service agency for Jewish community centers, directly handles several countrywide social service responsibilities, such as organizing and coordinating the military chaplaincy.

Joint Distribution Committee (JDC). Joint operating arm of the American Jewish community for providing relief and rehabilitation services to Jewish communities overseas.

National Foundation for Jewish Culture. Countrywide service agency for Jewish cultural activities. Administers Joint Cultural Appeal, which funds nine specialized cultural agencies.

National Jewish Community Relations Advisory Council (NJCRAC). Countrywide confederation and service agency for local Jewish community relations council and most "national" Jewish community relations organizations.

United Israel Appeal (UIA). Joint instrumentality of the Jewish community federations and the American Zionist bodies for transmitting and overseeing UJA funds spent by the Jewish Agency.

United Jewish Appeal (UJA). Major fund-raising instrumentality for general Israel and overseas purposes, including refugee resettlement. Jointly established and owned by Joint Distribution Committee (JDC) and United Israel Appeal (UIA) with Hebrew Immigrant Aid Society (HIAS) as beneficiary.

KETER TORAH

Principally in the hands of the rabbinical seminaries of the major religious movements and, to a lesser extent, their rabbinical bodies. For Orthodox camp, *yeshivot* and individual heads of *yeshivot* are authoritative. For non-Orthodox, some professors of Jewish studies are also authoritative.

KETER KEHUNAH

Principally in the hands of synagogue movements and their rabbinical bodies that are concerned with sacerdotal matters and ritual observance.

A parallel model has emerged in the local arena. It is portrayed in figure 10.2.

The Evolution of the American Jewish Polity

In the earliest period of Jewish settlement in the United States, the small and relatively homogeneous community achieved local unity through a system of local congregations resembling that presently found in countries like New Zealand: Jews in each city joined together to create a common congregation that provided all the communal services (religious, social, and educational) they desired, directly or through its *hevrot*. Jews from all parts of the world joined these community congregations, accepting the ritual and organizational patterns of their Sephardi founders as their own. Between 1654 and the end of the eighteenth century, "community" and "congregation" were synonymous.

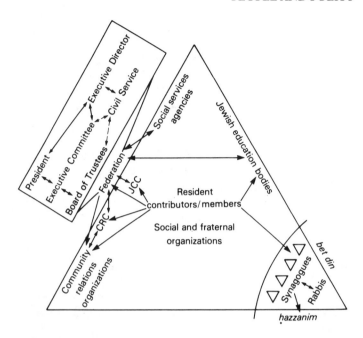

Figure 10.2.   United States Jewry: A generalized model of
the *kehillah*.

The emigrants from western and central Europe who arrived in the late eighteenth and early nineteenth centuries put an end to that kind of unity. The new immigrants wanted their own synagogues, first to preserve their particular Orthodox traditions and later to institute reform. So ended the single congregation community in the larger cities. Jewish organizational life was still basically local and congregational, but rudimentary social services and educational institutions at least nominally independent of any congregation began to emerge by midcentury. Even they were dominated by leaders of particular congregations wearing different hats.

From the late 1850s to the early 1880s, the growing American Jewish community experimented with its first countrywide organizations, including a representative Board of Deputies of American Israelites, modeled on the Board of Deputies of British Jews. The experiment was launched with great difficulty and failed almost immediately. Neither it nor its more narrowly based successor, the Union of American Hebrew Congregations (the name reveals how contemporaries still perceived Jewish life as concentrated in the synagogue and potentially unifiable on a congregational basis), could achieve universality. The divisions between traditionalists and liberals, not to speak of differences in country of origin, were already too great for reaching accommodation on the religious front while the geographic spread of the country hampered unity on any other basis.[8]

Whether any similar experiment would have succeeded became a moot point when the mass of emigrants from eastern Europe created the largest and most diverse Jewish community in history. Even local communities lost whatever unity they might have had previously under the impact of the new arrivals. The new immigrants' own efforts to introduce community structures based on European models failed as fully as the earlier efforts to introduce the Anglo-Jewish model. European rabbis sent to the New World to create orderly religious institutions retreated in disorder, and even such American-generated efforts to adapt European forms as the New York "kehillah" failed because of American conditions.[9]

Nevertheless, the new immigrants brought with them or stimulated by their arrival the beginnings of a system of Jewish communal life that turned out to be more suited to the American environment and, despite appearances to the contrary, has been able to mobilize Jewish energy for the great tasks that have confronted American Jewry. That system began in the closing years of the nineteenth century but its development is chiefly a twentieth-century phenomenon.

The roots of the present system are to be found in the response of the Jews already established in the United States by 1880 to the needs of the new immigrants as they perceived them, as modified by the organizational demands generated by the new immigrants for and by themselves. Their response led to the creation of organizations of all four types: welfare federations, "defense" agencies, congregational "roof" organizations and seminaries in the first category; Orthodox, Conservative, and Reform synagogues, *Landsmanschaften* and fraternal organizations in the second; organizations such as B'nai B'rith (expanded from its earlier form), the American Jewish Congress, and the Zionist groups in the third; and a welter of "national" and local groups in the fourth. At first, connections between these multifarious organizations and groups were minimal if not nonexistent. No real communications network existed on either the countrywide or local planes.

World War I brought the first real steps toward the creation of such networks. The unification of overseas welfare activities under the newly formed Joint Distribution Committee was the first successful effort to link old-line ("German"), Orthodox, and secularist elements into a common framework. Although the war also produced abortive attempts at creating mass Jewish unity countrywide, in the aftermath of their failure new efforts were generated on the local plane to link the diverse elements in the community for at least limited welfare and "defense" purposes. During the 1920s, the welfare federations and community councils, the institutions that best embodied these efforts, took root locally and began to coalesce countrywide.

The demands on the American Jewish community beginning in the late 1930s led to a growing recognition of the need to reconstitute the community's organizational structure at least to rationalize the major interinstitutional relationships and generally tighten the emerging matrix. These efforts at reconstitution received added impetus from the changes in American society and the Jews' place in it after 1945. They signaled the abandonment of earlier chimerical efforts to create a more conventional organizational pyramid in imitation of foreign patterns, which would have been out of place on the American scene.

Trends in Jewish Organization after World War II

The aftermath of World War II brought an intensification of the prewar trends in response to the conditions of postmodernity. American Jewry had become the foremost Jewish community in the world, nearly ten times larger than its nearest functioning counterpart. It had access to most of the wealth that world Jewry could mobilize to undertake the tremendous tasks of relief and reconstruction that confronted it because of the Holocaust, tasks to be increasingly concentrated in building the new State of Israel as the first demands of postwar relief were satisified.

At home the barriers against full participation in American society rapidly fell away. The opening of the metropolitan frontier found the Jews in the vanguard of the movement to the suburbs or, at the least, out of old neighborhoods to suburbanlike areas in the central cities, as settlers and developers. Both developments meant that institutional adaptations to new life-styles were required.[10]

Locally and then countrywide through the Council of Jewish Federations and Welfare Funds, the federations and their constituent agencies gained in strength. The major impetus behind their gain was their emergence as the dominant fund-raisers in the Jewish community. Pioneering in "single drive" fund-raising, the federations became the powerhouses behind an unprecedented voluntary effort. The exciting tasks of raising money for postwar relief and the rebuilding of Israel, which captured the imaginations of American Jews and most of the money raised from them, stimulated a phenomenal increase in the amounts contributed for all Jewish communal purposes. The impetus provided by "Israel" also redounded to the benefit of domestic Jewish needs, because the larger sums forthcoming from the coordinated drives were so allocated as to increase local resources too.

The federations did not (and, with rare exceptions, do not) subsidize synagogues or the functions that had come under the synagogues' wing. By tacit agreement they were left to raise their own money and also did so with remarkable success. Nevertheless, though large amounts were raised for the construction and maintenance of synagogues in the same period, synagogue fund-raising had neither the excitement nor the demands for continuity that abetted the annual federation "drives." Their great efforts were necessarily "one-shot" affairs and their annual needs remained relatively limited. Even so, by the 1960s the amount raised and spent for the maintenance of synagogues approximated the federations' allocations for other local purposes.

Not surprisingly, the federations attracted leadership, voluntary and professional, of the highest caliber available to the Jewish community. In time that leadership, at least partly because of the nature of the tasks that confronted it, began to see Jewish communal problems as connected with one another. Federation leaders began to be concerned with the broad range of Jewish needs, not simply with overseas relief or with the welfare functions that had been traditional to the federations in the pre-World War II period.

By 1960, most major Jewish federations were engaged in community planning of some sort, were supporting Jewish educational and cultural programs and welfare, defense, and overseas services, and were beginning to think of themselves as the central bodies for Jewish communal endeavor in their metropolitan areas. Increasingly after 1960, federations began to define the range of their interests as embracing almost the total Jewish community, excluding only the synagogues. On the countrywide plane, the Council of Jewish Federations and Welfare Funds began to strengthen its position, often providing the impetus for local federations to become involved in one area or another that previously had been defined as outside their purview.

During this period, there was also a sorting of roles among the countrywide organizations, many of which had aspired to the central role being assumed by the federation movement. Thus, the Zionist organizations, the American Jewish Congress, the American Jewish Committee, and B'nai B'rith began to edge away from the task of providing government-like services, to redefine themselves as the mass-based organizations whose principal task was to influence the community agenda.

The end result was the creation of interlocking and countrywide networks of institutions and organizations implicitly based on the principles delineated above. This system worked best in the local arena where the tasks were most concrete, the needs most apparent, and the resources most easily mobilized. Its capacities were more limited in the countrywide arena where symbolic issues and matters of personal and organizational prestige often dominated Jewish communal politics, causing interpersonal and interorganizational rivalries. These often obscured the real trends and limited the exercise of the real organizational strength of the American Jewish community.

The one set of organizations willing to challenge the federation movement were the three synagogue movements—in their congregations, as separate movements, and in combination through the Synagogue Council of America. The 1950s were particularly propitious for the synagogues to assert themselves. The apparent redefinition of Jewishness as an exclusively religious phenomenon to increase its appeal to a new generation of Americanized Jews strengthened the hands of those who claimed to be the spokesmen for Judaism as a religion.

While the federations were expanding their operations in the communitywide arena and involving the "cosmopolitans," first and foremost the synagogues were pioneering the suburban frontier in the most immediately local arenas and attracting wide support from the "locals." Because the synagogues were best geared to satisfy the immediate personal needs of their members or potential members, they had a great opportunity to reach out to a new generation looking for institutionalized ways to express their Jewishness yet largely estranged from the traditions of Jewish observance. Their growing monopoly of the celebration of the Jewish "rites of passage" insured them of a steady and even growing membership.

The synagogues' position was enhanced by the impact of the metropolitan frontier. The Jews who settled in the great cities during the heyday of the urban frontier settled in neighborhoods where their organic links were as strong if not stronger than their associational ones. This was as true of the more assimilated central European Jews "uptown" as of the eastern European immigrants in the great "ghettos." Whether or not one formally joined a synagogue, in those neighborhoods a Jew was surrounded by family and friends, businesses and institutions, all operating in a substantially Jewish milieu.[11]

The move to the suburbs broke up the old neighborhoods and, with each successive move outward from them lessening the proximity of Jews to one another, weakened the extent to which the immediate environment was "Jewish." Under such conditions, Jews who earlier had maintained their Jewishness through organic relationships had to seek more formal associational ties simply to keep those relationships alive. The local synagogue offered the easiest and most acceptable (in the American context) means of making the transition. Consequently, synagogue membership soared in the 1950s, paralleling developments in the churches that were affected by the metropolitan frontier in similar, though not identical, ways. Whether those membership gains represented a "return" to Judaism as was assumed at the time or simply a transition to more formal affiliation by those already committed, as demanded by changed circumstances, is a question that remains unanswered.

The resurgent synagogues capitalized on their position by reaching out to all new functions. They became the primary custodians of Jewish education, establishing synagogue schools on their premises as a means of attracting more members, adapting those schools to the conditions of suburbia, and creating an ideology of synagogue-centered Judaism to justify the trends they initiated, almost eliminating the private and communal

Hebrew schools of the previous era. They became the primary organizers of the youth, either on a congregational basis or through local chapters of their countrywide organizations, virtually replacing the Zionist organizations and offering strong competition to B'nai B'rith. They began to undertake recreational and social services that had been the province of the Jewish community centers and the local Jewish welfare agencies. To play their expanded role, synagogues had to become large institutions, often with memberships of more than one thousand families. Synagogues with fewer than four hundred families came to be considered less than viable.

As the leaders of the synagogue bodies tried to bring more functions into their synagogues, they increasingly came into conflict with the leaders of the federation bodies whose conception of the tasks of the community was also expanding. The struggle between the federations with their constituent agencies and the countrywide synagogue bodies with their constituent congregations was a classic manifestation of the "cosmopolitan-local" dichotomy. The "cosmopolitans" of the Jewish community focused on typically cosmopolitan interests ranging from local community to world Jewry. The focus of the locals was equally and typically localistic, whether in reference to immediate congregations or to the interests of the separate "branches" of Judaism in their competition with one another and with the extra-synagogue elements in the community.

While this was happening on the local plane, the countrywide synagogue bodies were also claiming a special importance in American Jewish life. This effort transcended their earliest efforts to foster congregations of their respective "persuasions" in a rough competition for the unaffiliated, challenging all other countrywide bodies in the process. In external relations the Synagogue Council of America began to develop relations with its Protestant and Roman Catholic counterparts and to act as the Jewish "religious" spokesman on the national plane. Though their challenge was only marginally successful, it represented a continuing area of contention in American Jewish life.

American Jewish Organization Today

The trends of the postwar period culminated in the early 1960s. The ostensible religious revial ended; membership in synagogues stabilized and then, by the mid-1960s, began to decline. New challenges emerged to threaten the other established organizations. By the end of the 1960s the trend toward sorting out the elements in the organizational structure of the community and harmonizing them in a common communications network had taken another step forward, partly because of the decline of one segment of the structure and partly because of the redefinition of the other.

The synagogues represented the declining element. It was not that their loss of membership was decisive, for despite the reversal of the earlier trend, actual losses were still moderate. Although the losses increased in the early 1970s, the synagogues stabilized by mid-decade and even began to grow again by 1980.

What did happen was that a convergence of events robbed the synagogues of much of the basis for asserting primacy. The changed American attitude toward establishment religion made the Jewish expression of that—the synagogue—far more vulnerable to criticism, especially from youth. Many of those young people found meaning in Jewish ethnicity when ethnic nationalism was on the upsurge around the world. The Six-Day War, in June 1967, made it clear to Jews that it was not simply a common religious affiliation that bound Jews together but a common fate as a people, symbolized and reaffirmed by the State of Israel and the Israeli-Arab conflict.[12]

The continued expansion of federation functions in the 1960s and 1970s made them even more attractive to young adults seeking leadership roles in the community. Even the oppositionists in the community moved from attacking the synagogues to attack the federations. Those from within the religious community who opposed the establishment either turned Orthodox or developed *havurot,* thereby creating a device that is now beginning to have serious positive impact on the religious-congregational sphere.

The situation stabilized in the mid-1970s. As the revolts of the 1960s played out, a reaction set in, with the synagogue benefiting from it like other established institutions in American society. The trauma of the Yom Kippur War and Israel's weakened position thereafter reduced its share of American Jewish attention and reawakened an interest on the part of American Jews to seek American Jewish solutions for their Jewish problems. Again the synagogue benefited. The synagogues themselves began to experiment with adaptations to their changed circumstances—some ridiculous and others sensible, some far beyond the pale of anything previously known in Jewish life, others creative adaptations of Jewish tradition.

The demise of other Jewish organizations as effective forces in the community left the synagogues along with the federations as the main pillars of Jewish life. If the synagogues no longer attracted memberships of the kind that they did at the beginning of the generation, they were still the only institutions in the American Jewish community able to bring together regularly large numbers of Jews. Although the number of Jewish "troops" was diminishing, the synagogues had those "troops" such as they were.

While the synagogues were on the decline, the federations were busy redefining their role in an expansive manner. In the 1960s, the federation accepted the day school as a needed instrument of Jewish survival and made support of day schools part of Jewish communal policy. In general, they increased their support for Jewish education and culture. They also embraced the public observance of Jewish religious practices and encouraged traditional and observant Jews to become involved in their ranks, thereby building bridges to segments of the Jewish community that had been outside their purview. The decade culminated in the federations taking the most effective action to reach out to disaffected Jewish youth. They developed extensive campus activities programs and brought key young leaders into the federation orbit. All this strengthened the federations as framing institutions of the community.

New organizational and functional patterns also began to emerge in response to the dissatisfactions that surfaced since the mid-1960s. The organization of religious rites and worship, the central concerns of the Jewish revival of the 1950s, was the issue that provoked the greatest dissatisfaction in the 1960s. The ferment among the younger generation led to an assault on the large suburban congregation, which they rejected as offering inauthentic modes of religious observance. They attacked the impersonality of the large synagogues and the lack of the sense of congregation, all of which they saw as having replaced the more intimate traditional synagogue. Those young Jews looking for an authentic religious experience responded with new ways to organize their religious life. The result was the development of *havurot* and the increase in small congregations devoted primarily to worship and fellowship.[13]

These innovations represent a return to traditional standards though in a new format. Thus it is not surprising that the pioneers of these responses to American

Judaism were traditionally minded Jewish academics and scientists who, in the late 1950s and early 1960s, began to establish their own Orthodox synagogues, committed to the meticulous observance of Jewish law and to the style of congregational organization common before the day of the large synagogue. This style emphasized small membership comprising families highly committed to one another and looking for interpersonal interaction aside from that built around the worship experience proper. This effort was paralleled on the other end of the spectrum by the founding of Reconstructionist Fellowships in the place of formal congregations.[14]

Since the mid-1960s this pattern has been followed with considerably more fanfare by academics and intellectuals from Conservative and to some extent Reform backgrounds, primarily through *havurot* and *havurah*-related activities.[15] Although most of these experiments ran out of steam by the mid-1970s, they infused a dynamism into Jewish religious life that has carried over beyond the limits of the original efforts to effect mainstream congregations also. Orthodoxy has embraced the small congregation as its norm. The large synagogue remains the norm in the Conservative and Reform movements because most Conservative and Reform Jews do not look for greater involvement; they want the synagogue to remain a service center and no more. Even so, in many cases the minority seeking more or the rabbis themselves have introduced *havurot* into their synagogues with some success.[16]

On another front, there has been a resurgence of Orthodox Judaism in the United States. By 1980 there were at least 50 percent more serious Orthodox Jews than in 1960. They comprise 10 percent of American Jews. Moreover, those who define themselves as Orthodox really are; indeed, with the move to the right in religious observance, they are even more Orthodox than the seriously Orthodox of the previous generation. Meanwhile, the nominally Orthodox Jews of past generations have all but disappeared.

The resurgence of Orthodoxy is an even more important phenomenon organizationally, because Orthodox Jews commit major parts of their time, effort, and money to building institutions that reflect their point of view, whether *yeshivot* or Hassidic empires. Thus, Orthodox Jews probably represent at least one-third of those American Jews seriously committed to maintaining Jewish life, and their institutions may account for an even greater share of the institutional effort in that direction. If this writer's calculations are correct, in the entire Conservative movement there are no more than fifty thousand Jews who live according to Conservative religious standards. About the same number of Satmar Hassidim (the most extreme of the Hassidic sects) gathered in a stadium in Long Island in December 1984 to celebrate the wedding of two descendants of the Satmar *rebbe*. There are probably ten Hassidic *rebbes* with more followers than the Reconstructionist movement, often hailed as the fourth branch of American Judaism. American Jewish institutions are just beginning to accommodate this new Orthodox reality.

Organization for defense took on new forms in the post-World War II era. The beginning of that period had witnessed some degree of rationalization of the organizational structure for external-relations matters; its end witnessed a serious if still limited assault on such organizations by those who felt that they were no longer needed.[17] Action against anti-Semitism was replaced by efforts to overcome the last barriers to full Jewish participation in American life, to help other groups, particularly blacks, achieve equality in American society, and to assist Jews in subjugated communities. The organized Jewish community was in the forefront of the civil rights movement, fighting social discrimination, seeking rapprochement with the churches, and resisting atavistic elements. American Jewry, understanding that the threat of local anti-Semitism had substantially diminished, now saw its primary defense task as the maintenance of Israel, not only as a place of Jewish refuge or a haven for Jewish refugees, but also as a sign of the new and improved Jewish status in the world.

As is usual in any civil society, defense took priority in Jewish organizational life; the support of Israel stood above everything else in the hierarchy of organizational goals. The priority position of Israel brought Jews more actively into the political arena in Washington and in the states and, ultimately, brought the federation leadership to the forefront of this effort.

The Six-Day War brought an abrupt end to the era of relative calm. Jewish human relations professionals found that they still had to battle for the Jews. In the aftermath of the war, anti-Semitism became somewhat respectable, particularly as the New Left began attacking organized Jewry under the rubric of "anti-Zionism." By that it encouraged the reemergence of right-wing anti-Semites, who had been quiet for fear of public rejection. Moreover, the more militant blacks rejected Jewish assistance in their own struggle and identified with anti-Jewish elements in the Israel-Arab conflict. Consequently, Jewish external relations began again to revolve around the defense of more straightforward Jewish interests and led to a strengthening of Jewish organizational capabilities in that direction.[18]

Just before the Yom Kippur War in 1973, dissenting groups emerged to suggest a different set of priorities for American Jewry. Dissent became an issue after the "Peace for Galilee Operation" in Lebanon in 1982. For a while it appeared that large segments of American Jewry were falling away from their staunch support of Israel. In fact, most of the dissent was confined to a few headline-makers, leaving the vast majority of Jews faithfully in the Israeli camp, even if many had doubts about the policies of the then current Israeli government.[19]

Defense of the State of Israel will continue to dominate the foreign relations concerns of American Jewry in the future. The feelings of isolation generated in the period immediately preceding the Six-Day War and after, because of Israel's apparent lack of allies other than world Jewry, has heightened American Jewry's sense of solidarity with the state and even its sense of "apartness" from non-Jews. Thus events reversed the trend of the 1950s and 1960s.

The trends in educational organization are more problematic, because education involves and exposes the ambivalences of contemporary Jewish life—the desire for group survival in conflict with the desire for full integration with the society or, perhaps more accurately, with the worldwide cosmopolitan culture attractive to the middle and upper classes, particularly the students and intellectuals among them. Jewish education after World War II combined an increase in enrollment in Jewish schools with a concomitant decline in the number of hours of instruction and the breadth of the curriculum. This trend was stimulated by the transfer of elementary and most secondary education to the synagogue, which made the teaching of "synagogue skills" and loyalties primary, to the exclusion of more substantive materials. The more intensive Talmud Torahs nearly disappeared.

Enrollment in Jewish schools peaked around 1962 and has been declining since, though it may now have stabilized again. The drop in Jewish births coupled with the continued diffusion of the Jewish population into suburbia and the increased demands of the public schools on their students have made supplementary Jewish schooling more difficult, thereby encouraging further reductions in hours and content.[20]

The drive for intensive Jewish education by a minority of Jews, however, has led to the simultaneous development of a substantial day school movement. Initially an Orthodox effort, in the 1960s the Conservative Movement began to develop its Solomon Schechter schools and in the 1970s the Reform Movement joined the trend. This represents a sharp change of direction for American Jews. During the modern epoch Jews tried desperately to break down all barriers that might keep them out of general schools and were even willing to sacrifice the Jewish education of their children for integration. No group in the United States has been more fervent in its support of the public schools than the Jews, who correctly perceived that American free, nonsectarian public education was the ultimate fulfillment of the Jews' emancipationist and integrationist dreams. Today, however, one-fourth of all students enrolled in Jewish schools, nearly one hundred thousand in number, attend all-day schools, and almost every Jewish community of over three thousand has at least one such school. Moreover, the Jewish federations, which for years avoided giving any assistance to such schools, have now made them significant beneficiaries, if not constituent agencies.

The day school movement was at first strengthened by many Jews being caught in changing neighborhoods where the public schools deteriorated before they were ready to move. Faced with the problems that this presented, they determined to send their children to private schools whereupon they chose Jewish private schools as a matter of preference. The continued decline of the public schools even in stable neighborhoods encouraged the trend. But parental recognition that the day school was the only possibility for their children to gain a Jewish education was the decisive factor.[21]

The 1960s also witnessed the development of programs of Jewish studies in secular colleges and universities. Originally masked under titles like "Near Eastern Studies" or "Semitic Languages and Literatures" in the few institutions where they existed, Jewish studies programs were pushed into the limelight at the end of the decade because of the blacks' struggle for similar programs. As blacks began to demand "black studies" programs in the universities, young Jews countered by demanding more extensive Jewish studies programs under that explicit label, with no masks. Today hundreds of colleges and universities have Jewish studies programs, and the Association for Jewish Studies, the professional association of college teachers in the field, has more than one thousand members. This has led to more college-age Jews exposed to Jewish education, often for the first time in a scholarly and systematic way, and has also created a market for Judaic scholars.[22]

Among the initial casualties of the Jewish studies programs were the Hebrew colleges, the independent institutions of higher Jewish education under Jewish communal auspices. It is true that few students took advantage of those colleges, but when it became possible to obtain academic credits toward a regular degree, many of those who did moved over to those programs. By the mid-1970s, however, it had become apparent that there were limits to Jewish studies programs in general universities. First, few offered more than elementary courses. Beyond that, they could not offer specialized professional programs to prepare students for positions in the Jewish community. Consequently, the Hebrew colleges started such programs, often in conjunction with general universities, and began to revive. The Jewish community began to realize that university Jewish studies programs, though important, would not be the salvation of higher Jewish education but that some judicious mixture was required.

Trends in the welfare field are mixed. As the welfare state became more deeply rooted and even resumed expansion, functions performed by private or public nongovernmental agencies became beneficiaries of government support at ever higher levels. Functions of the Jewish community were no exception, so that today Jewish welfare organizations are increasingly financed from non-Jewish, usually government sources and in return, are required to provide their services on a nonsectarian basis. Jewish hospitals, developed to provide Jewish doctors places to practice medicine when other hospitals would not have them, now represent a major Jewish contribution to the service network of the inner city in many communities. This pattern is likely to continue. There remain some specifically Jewish welfare services: those that treat middle-class ailments, primarily psychiatric ones, services to the aged, and services to populations left behind in changing neighborhoods.

By the end of the postwar generation, many Americans had begun to question the welfare state and, after 1977, began to back away from some of its more far-reaching elements. The election of Ronald Reagan to the presidency of the United States in 1980 marked a real turning point, bringing about federal cutbacks in many programs including some on which the Jewish community had come to depend. Still, the Reagan experience demonstrated that major elements of the welfare state are here to stay, and Jewish communal institutions will continue to be involved with government and other public nongovernment bodies in the provision of services. Thus the trend in the 1980s is toward somewhat greater commitment of Jewish resources to social welfare programs because of diminished government financing but without any major changes in Jewish communal priorities.

The enforcement of community norms has undergone great change. In the American context, the organized Jewish community cannot enforce traditional Jewish law. At the same time, new norms have developed that are subtly enforced by the community's organizational network. These norms revolve around support of Israel and "giving": assuming one's share of the financial obligations of the community. "Israel" has become the primary norm in an increasingly secularized Jewish community with almost all Jewish organizations sharing in the enforcing of the norms that relate to it and, in a sense, have taken the place of the old *halakhic* or God-centered norms even in many synagogues. Today, someone who refuses to support Israel is, in effect, read out of the Jewish community. The only issue that remains is the extent of dissent from particular Israeli government policies permissible among supporters of the state.

Because some common norms are necessary for the maintenance of a voluntaristic community, it is not surprising that supporting Israel is only one aspect of an emerging American Jewish civil religion.[23] Students of American Jewish life have identified the components of this civil religion, which include some Jewish observance, acceptance of pluralism in the Jewish community, a set of positive self-images and expectations about the special character of Jews and the Jewish people, and a strong commitment to Jewish self-expression through associated activity. This civil relgion first became visible toward the end of the 1960s; in the 1980s it has become widespread. Hence norm enforcement based on the canons of this civil religion will continue to be a task in Jewish organizational life. After three hundred years of secularization and assimilation, there is strong evidence that a revived concern with Jewish tradition is leading to its acceptance as a norm. Although different groups in Jewry will be entitled to define "Jewish tradition" in different ways, identification with that tradition and acceptance of the responsibility for maintaining, fostering, and extending it is reemerging as a core norm in Jewish life, embraced and enforced by all Jewish organizations.

In the realm of Jewish public finance, Jews continue to rely on voluntary giving to maintain their organizational structure and activities.[24] In recent years all major Jewish organizations have increased their demands on the members of the community to meet expanded needs at home and abroad. There is every reason to believe that these demands will continue at a high level. High levels of giving have been maintained since 1967 and 1973, even under the less tense circumstances of the subsequent years, but still the burden is assumed by only a fraction of Jews who could share it. The amount raised by the federations could be at least doubled if the Jews who could afford to contribute seriously but do not, were to do so. In the meantime, "real dollar" totals have dropped.

A few years ago there were some warnings that the new generation would be likely to reduce its giving to Jewish causes as the children of this generation of rich Jews pursue academic and professional careers rather than continue in the entrepreneurial ways of their fathers and hence would have less disposable income upon which to draw. It now seems that this is not the case; a new generation of entrepreneurs is emerging to replace the previous one. Moreover, the establishment of a prosperous upper middle class as the basis of the Jewish community has made available a great deal of money that must be garnered through smaller individual contributions but can be mobilized for Jewish causes.

One consequence of this has been the spread of causes seeking support. There is every reason to believe that the share of Jewish public funds raised through federated giving mechanisms is declining, even though the absolute dollar amount is increasing, as newly affluent Jews find more focused causes to which they contribute. This is true even with regard to Israel. In the early 1980s the annual amount donated to the UJA for transfer to Israel was about $300 million. The Israeli universities were raising another $100 million and Hadassah over $50 million for their projects in Israel. When contributions to other Israeli-based organizations are added to those two figures, it becomes apparent that the UJA provides no more than 60 percent of American Jewish money raised for Israeli purposes.

From Fragmentation to Reintegration

The thrust of the modern epoch, beginning in the mid-seventeenth century and accelerating thereafter, fragmented world Jewry. The tight communal organization of the Middle Ages was the first to give way. It was followed by the abandonment of life according to Jewish law by a growing number of Jews (a majority by the twentieth century). In the past two generations, even traditional ties to the community were abandoned by most Jews as they looked for full integration as individuals with the larger society, leading to what seemed to be the ultimate fragmentation of world Jewry. In all of this, American Jewry was in the vanguard. Traditional communal organization never existed in America because it never had any legal support. Life according to Jewish law was never the way of the majority, nor was life according to Jewish tradition. Pursuit of individual goals was always much more possible in the New World than anywhere else.

Then, in this generation, when fragmentation reached new heights, a movement to reintegration with new vehicles and norms began to gain momentum. The Holocaust brought a reconsideration of the need for Jewish unity. It, plus the sheer passage of time, contributed to the postmodern breakdown of the rigid ideologies that divided Jews in the last century of the modern epoch. Most important, the creation of the State of Israel has given Jews a new and compelling focus that continues to enhance the interest of many in being Jewish.

Accompanying this rediscovery of community has been a reintegration of the organizational components of the Jewish community, leading to the emergence of a more clear-cut structure and communications network linking them. More important, there has been an increase in the commitment of organizations of different kinds to the wholeness of the Jewish way of life. The rediscovery is rooted in the acceptance of a new pluralism in Jewish life. Organized pluralism leads to federalism, the traditional way Jews have maintained their organizational structures. All this may well represent a beginning in the effort to overcome the modern fragmentation of Jewish life. The American Jewish community in the second postwar generation continues to pursue this reintegration, which also affects the reintegration of American Jewry with world Jewry.

Notes

1. This chapter draws heavily on the author's book, *Community and Polity* (Philadelphia: Jewish Publication Society of America, 1976 and 1981).

2. *Yehudo beAtido shel Beit-HaKnesset be America,* issue of *Tefutsot Yisrael,* vol. 20, no. 3 (summer 1982) (Hebrew); *Orthodoxim, Reformim, Conservativim—HaZeramim HaDatiyim be Levtahim,* issue of *Tefutsot Yisrael,* vol. 18, no. 1 (spring 1980) (Hebrew); Moshe Davis, *The Emergence of Conservative Judaism* (Philadelphia: Jewish Publication Society of America, 1963); Leonard J. Fein et al., *Reform Is a Verb* (New York: Union of American Hebrew Congregations, 1972); Charles S. Liebman, "Orthodoxy in American Jewish Life," *American Jewish Year Book 1965,* vol. 66, pp. 21–97; Gunther W. Plaut, *The Rise of Reform Judaism* (New York: World Union for Progressive Judaism, 1963–65); Joseph L. Blau, *Reform Judaism: A Historical Perspective* (New York: Ktav Publishing House, 1973); Marshall Sklare, *Conservative Judaism: An American Religious Movement* (New York: Schocken Books, 1972); Sefton D. Temkin, "A Century of Reform Judaism in America," *American Jewish Year Book 1973,* vol. 74, pp. 3–75; Reuven P. Bulka, ed., *Dimensions of Orthodox Judaism* (New York: Ktav Publishing House, 1983).

3. Walter A. Lurie, *Strategies for Survival: Principles of Jewish Community Relations* (New York: Ktav Publishing House, 1982); Philip Bernstein, *To Dwell in Unity: The Jewish Federation Movement in America since 1960* (Philadelphia: Jewish Publication Society of America, 1983); R. M. MacIver, *Report on the Jewish Community Relations Agencies* (New York: National Community Relations Advisory Council, 1951); Ann G. Wolfe, ed., *A Reader in Jewish Community Relations* (Ktav for Association of Jewish Community Relations Workers, 1975).

4. Hafederatziot HaYehudit: Kehillah Nusah America (The Jewish Federation: "Kehillah" American Style), issue of *Tefutsot Yisrael,* vol. 20, nos. 1–2 (spring 1982) (Hebrew); Bernstein, *To Dwell in Unity;* Harry L. Lurie, *A Heritage Affirmed* (Philadelphia: Jewish Publication Society of America, 1961).

5. Deborah Dash Moore, *B'nai B'rith and the Challenge of Ethnic Leadership* (Albany: State University of New York Press, 1981); Edward E. Grusd, *B'nai B'rith: The Story of a Covenant* (New York: Appleton-Century, 1966); Naomi W. Cohen, *Not Free to Desist: The American Jewish Committee, 1906–1966* (Philadelphia: Jewish Publication Society of America, 1972); Nathan C. Belth, ed., *Not the Work of a Day* (New York: Anti-Defamation League of B'nai B'rith, 1965); Y. Shapiro, *Leadership of the American Zionist Organization 1877–1930* (Urbana, Ill.: University of Illinois, 1971); Melvin I. Urofsky, *We Are One! American Jewry and Israel* (Garden City, N.Y.: Anchor Press/Doubleday, 1978); Ira Hirschmann, *The Awakening: The Story of the Jewish National Fund* (New York: Shengold Publishers, 1981); Marvin Feinstein, *American Zionism 1884–1904* (New York: Herzl Press, 1965); Raphael Patai, ed., *Encyclopedia of Zionism and Israel,* 2 vols. (New York: Herzl Press/McGraw-Hill, 1971); Joan Dash, *Summoned to Jerusalem: The Life of Henrietta Szold* (New York and Philadelphia: Harper and Row and Jewish Publication Society of America, 1979); Rose Zeitlin, *Henrietta Szold: Record of a Life* (New York: Dial, 1952); Judah J. Shapiro, *The Friendly Society: A History of the Workmen's Circle* (New York: A Doron Book, Media Judaica, 1970).

6. On the CJF, see Lurie, *A Heritage Affirmed* and Bernstein, *To Dwell in Unity.*

7. On the special purpose roof organizations, see Graenum Berger, ed., *The Turbulent Decades: Jewish Communal Service in America 1958–1978,* 2 vols. (New York: Conference of Jewish Communal Service, 1981); Julian Freeman, *Organizing the American Jewish Community* (New York: Council of Jewish Federations, 1977); Will Maslow, *The Structure and Functioning of the American Jewish Community* (New York: American Jewish Congress and American Section of the World Jewish Congress, 1974); Wolfe, *A Reader in Jewish Community Relations.*

8. On nineteenth-century efforts to foster American Jewish unity, see Harry Simonhoff, *Saga of American Jewry, 1895–1914: Links of an Endless Chain* (New York: Acro Publishing Company, 1959); Henry L. Feingold, *Zion in America* (New York: Hippocene Books, Inc., 1974); Maurice J. Karpf, *Jewish Community Organization in the United States* (New York: Arno Press and The New York Times, 1938 and 1971); Isaiah M. Minkoff, "Development of Jewish Communal Organization in America," in Harry Schneiderman, ed., *Two Generations in Perspective* (New York: Monde Publishers, Inc., 1957), pp. 110–38; Chaim I. Waxman, *America's Jews in Transition* (Philadelphia: Temple University Press, 1983); Naomi W. Cohen, *Encounter with Emancipation: The German Jews in the United States, 1830–1914* (Philadelphia: Jewish Publication Society of America, 1984); Abraham J. Karp, *Haven and Hope: A History of the Jews in America* (New York: Schocken Books, 1985).

9. For examples of the former, see Moses Rischin, *The Promised City: New York's Jews 1914–1970* (New York: Harper Torchbooks, 1970) and Naomi W. Cohen, *Not Free to Desist;* Hyman B. Grinstein, "The Efforts of East European Jewry to Organize Its Own Community in the United States," *Publication of the American Jewish Historical Society,* vol. 49, no. 2 (December 1959), pp. 73–89; and Jeffrey Gurock, *When Harlem Was Jewish 1870–1930* (New York: Columbia University Press, 1979). On the *kehillah,* see Arthur A. Goren, *New York Jews and the Quest for Community: The Kehillah Experiment, 1908–1922* (New York: Columbia University Press, 1970).

10. See Marshall Sklare, ed., *The Jews: Social Patterns of an American Group* (New York: Free Press, 1958) and *Conservative Judaism;* Marshall Sklare and Joseph Greenbaum, *Jewish Identity on the Suburban Frontier: A Study of Group Survival in the Open Society,* vol. 1 of the Lakeville Studies (New York: Basic Books, 1967).

11. See Irving Howe, *World of Our Fathers* (New York: Harcourt Brace Jovanovich, 1976); Deborah Dash Moore, *At Home in America: Second Generation New York Jews* (New York: Columbia University Press, 1981).

12. On the effect of the 1960s and the Six-Day War see Moshe Davis, ed., *The Yom Kippur War: Israel and the Jewish People* (New York: Arno Press, 1974) and David Sidorsky, ed., *The Future of the Jewish Community in America* (New York: Basic Books, 1973); Steven M. Cohen, *American Modernity and Jewish Identity* (New York: Tavistock, 1983); Waxman, *America's Jews in Transition;* Arnold M. Eisen, *The Chosen People in America* (Bloomington, Ind.: Indiana University Press, 1983).

13. See Bernstein, *To Dwell in Unity* and *Hafederatziot HaYehudit,* issue of *Tefutsot Yisrael.*

14. See Charles S. Liebman, *Aspects of the Religious Behavior of American Jews* (New York: Ktav, 1974) and "Reconstructionism in American Jewish Life," *American Jewish Year Book 1970,* vol. 71, pp. 3–99; Max J. Routtenberg, *Decades of Decision* (New York: Bloch Publishing Company, 1973); Norman B. Mirsky, *Unorthodox Judaism* (Columbus: Ohio State University Press, 1978); Gilbert S. Rosenthal, *The Many Faces of Judaism* (New York: Behrman House, 1978).

15. See Jacob Neusner, *Contemporary Judaica Fellowship in Theory and Practice* (New York: Ktav, 1972); Bernard Reisman, *The Chavurah: A Contemporary Jewish Experience* (New York: Union of American Hebrew Congregations, 1977).

16. See Gerald B. Bubis, Harry Wasserman with Alan Lert, *Synagogue Havurot* (Jerusalem and Washington, D.C.: Center for Jewish Community Studies and University Press of America, 1981); Daniel J. Elazar and Rela Geffen Monson, "The Synagogue Havurah: An Experiment in Restoring Adult Fellowship to the Jewish Community," *Jewish Journal of Sociology,* vol. 21, no. 1 (June 1979), pp. 67–80.

17. Wolfe, *A Reader in Jewish Community Relations;* Karp, *Haven and Home;* Lurie, *A Heritage Affirmed;* MacIver, *Report on the Jewish Community Relations Agencies;* Berger, *The Turbulent Decades;* Arthur Hertzberg, *Being Jewish in America: The Modern Experience* (New York: Schocken Books, 1979).

18. Arnold Foster and Benjamin F. Epstein, *The New Anti-Semitism* (New York: McGraw Hill Book Company, 1974); Leonard Dinnerstein, ed., *Anti-Semitism in the United States* (New York: Holt, Rinehart and Winston, 1971); Milton Ellerin, *The AWACs Debate: Is There an Anti-Semitic Fallout?* Trends Analyses Report (New York: American Jewish Committee, 1982); Gregory Martire and Ruth Clark, *Antisemitism in the United States: A Study of Prejudice in the 1980s* (New York: Praeger, 1982); Nathan Perlmutter and Ruth Ann Perlmutter, *The Real Anti-Semitism in America* (New York: Arbor House, 1982); Harold E. Quinley and Charles Y. Glock, *Anti-Semitism in America* (New York: Free Press, 1979); Jacques Givet, *The Anti-Zionist Complex* (Englewood, N.J.: SBS, 1982); Jonathen S. Kessler and Jeff Schwaber, *The AIPAC College Guide: Exposing the Anti-Israel Campaign on Campus,* AIPAC Papers on U.S.-Israel Relations (Washington, D.C.: American Israel Public Affairs Committee, 1984); *Anti-Semitic Incidents in the Community . . . Coping with Eruptions . . . Preventing Future Outbreaks* (New York: American Jewish Committee, 1982); Earl Raab, "Anti-Semitism in the 1900s," *Midstream,* vol. 29, no. 2 (February 1983), pp. 11–18; Leon Hadar, "Anti-Semitism

in America," *Jewish Affairs,* vol. 37, no. 1 (January 1982), pp. 53–57; *Anti-Semitism in the United States,* vol. 1–The Summary Report (New York: Yankelovich, Skelly and White, Inc. for American Jewish Committee, 1981); *Anti-Semitism: Perceptions and Realities in 1980. Guidelines for Community Action* (New York: American Jewish Committee, 1980); *Extremist Groups in the United States: A Curriculum Guide* (New York: Anti-Defamation League of B'nai B'rith, n.d.); Hertzberg, *Being Jewish in America;* Gerald S. Strober, *American Jews: Community in Crisis* (Garden City, N.Y.: Doubleday, 1974).

19. Steven M. Cohen, *Attitudes of American Jews toward Israel and Israelis,* the 1983 National Survey of American Jews and Jewish Communal leaders (New York: Institute on American Jewish-Israeli Relations, the American Jewish Committee, 1983); "American Jews and Israel: Pragmatic, Critical, but Still in Love," *Jerusalem Letter,* no. 65 (November 13, 1983) and "Israeli Emigrés and the New York Federation: A Case Study in Ambivalent Policymaking for Jewish 'Communal Deviants,' " *Jerusalem Letter,* no. 71 (June 19, 1984).

20. Walter Ackerman, "Jewish Education Today," *American Jewish Year Book 1980,* vol. 80, pp. 130–48; Lloyd P. Gartner, ed., *Jewish Education in the United States* (New York: Teachers College Press, 1969); Zvi Adar, *Jewish Education in Israel and in the United States,* trans. Barry Chazzan (Jerusalem: Hebrew University of Jerusalem, 1977); Alexander M. Shapiro and Burton I. Cohen, eds., *Studies in Jewish Education and Judaica in Honor of Louis Newman* (New York: Ktav, 1984); Hillel Hochberg, "Trends and Developments in Jewish Education," *American Jewish Year Book 1972,* vol. 73, pp. 194–235; *Al Matzavoh shel HaHinukh HaYehudi be-America* (On the State of Jewish Education in America), issue of *Tefutsot Yisrael,* vol. 18, nos. 2–3 (summer-fall 1980) (Hebrew); Fred Massarik, "Trends in U.S. Jewish Education: National Jewish Population Study Findings," *American Jewish Year Book 1977,* vol. 77, pp. 240–50; Mark E. Schlussel, "Jewish Education in Transition: A Layman's View," *Jewish Education,* vol. 50, no. 1 (spring 1982), pp. 22–27.

21. Harold S. Himmelfarb, *The American Jewish Day School: A Case Study* (New York: American Jewish Committee, 1980); Joseph Kaminetsky, ed., *Hebrew Day School Education: An Overview* (New York: National Society for Hebrew Day Schools, 1970); "The Mystique of the Jewish Day School," *Jewish Education,* vol. 50, no. 3 (fall 1982), pp. 38–41; A. I. Schiff, *The Jewish Day School in America* (New York: Jewish Education Committee, 1966); Samuel Heilman, *Inside the Jewish School: A Study of the Cultural Setting for Jewish Education* (New York: American Jewish Committee, 1983); Fradle Pomerantz Friedenreich, "The Unwritten Curriculum in the Jewish School," *Jewish Education,* vol. 52, no. 1 (spring 1984), pp. 3–9.

22. See Moshe Davis, ed., *Contemporary Jewish Civilization on the American Campus: Research and Teaching* (Jerusalem: Institute of Contemporary Jewry, The Hebrew University of Jerusalem, 1974); Samuel Z. Fishman and Judyth L. Saypal, eds., *Jewish Studies at American and Canadian Universities: An Academic Catalog* (Washington, D.C.: B'nai B'rith Hillel Foundations and the Association for Jewish Studies, 1979); Arnold J. Band, "Jewish Studies in American Liberal-Arts Colleges and Universities," *American Jewish Year Book 1966,* vol. 67, pp. 3–30; Leon A. Jick, ed., The Teaching of Judaica in American Universities: The Proceedings of a Colloquium (New York: Association for Jewish Studies, 1970).

23. This civil religion has been extensively studied by Jonathan Woocher and others. See Woocher, "The 'Civil Judaism' of Communal Leaders," *American Jewish Year Book 1981,* vol. 81, pp. 149–69, *"Civil Judaism" in the United States* (Jerusalem: Center for Jewish Community Studies, 1978), and *"Civil Judaism": The Religion of Jewish Communities* (New York: National Jewish Conference Center, 1979); Charles S. Liebman and Eliezer Don-Yehiya, *Civil Religion in Israel: Traditional Religion and Political Culture in the Jewish State* (Berkeley: University of California Press, 1983).

24. On the trends in Jewish giving, see Steven Martin Cohen, "Trends in Jewish Philanthropy," *American Jewish Year Book 1980,* vol. 80, pp. 29–51 and "Will Jews Keep Giving? Prospects for the Jewish Charitable Community," *Journal of Jewish Communal Service* (autumn 1978), pp. 59–71; Samuel C. Heilman, "The Gift of Alms: Face-to-Face Almsgiving among Orthodox Jews," *Urban Life and Culture* (January 1975), pp. 371–95; Marc Lee Raphael, *A History of the United Jewish Appeal 1939–1982* (Providence, R.I.: Brown University–Scholars Press, 1982) and *Understanding American Jewish Philanthropy* (New York: Ktav, 1979); Milton Goldin, *Why They Give: American Jews and Their Philanthropies* (New York: Macmillan, 1976); Jacob Neusner, *Tzedakah: Can Jewish Philanthropy Buy Jewish Survival?* (Chappaqua, N.Y.: Rossel Books, 1982); Abraham J. Karp, *To Give Life* (New York: Schocken Books, 1981).

11

Jewries of the British Commonwealth

Besides the nearly six million English-speaking Jews in the United States, another half million Anglophone Jews live in other countries of the Western and Southern hemispheres, founded or developed by the British during their period of imperial expansion. Today all are independent states, most members of the British Commonwealth. Even without the Jews of Great Britain proper, these two groups of Anglophone Jews comprise about 60 percent of diaspora Jewry.

Regardless of the intensity of their Jewish attachments, almost all the Jews in these countries have been culturally assimilated into the wider society. Accordingly, they see Jewish attachment as "religious" identification and every individual as having free choice in the matter. Yet there is an equally strong feeling that somehow Jews stand apart from the majority population of British stock and can never bridge that gap. That contradiction is echoed by the larger society. Thus the associational aspects of Jewish affiliation are overtly more important than the organic aspects, but the latter remain real.

The community structure is built around associational premises from top to bottom. The communities have no special status in public law. At most, there is a "roof" organization formally or tacitly accepted as the "address" of the Jewish community for limited purposes and subsidiary institutions occasionally accorded government support (along with similar non-Jewish institutions) for specific functions. Nor do the communities have any strong tradition of communal self-government to call upon. All are entirely products of the modern epoch, hence their founders were either post-emancipation Jews or Jews wanting the benefit of emancipation and desirous of throwing off the burden of an all-encompassing corporate Jewish life.

Eleven of these countrywide communities have representative boards, usually called boards of deputies, as their principal spokesmen. Usually these representative boards formally embrace the other Jewish institutions and organizations in the community that otherwise are, for all practical purposes, independent of and often equal to them in stature and influence. Fund-raising, religious life, and the social services are under auspices other than the nominal roof organizations. Communities with representative boards are also constructed on federal lines. At the least, the boards become confederations of institutions and organizations; and in the federal or quasi-federal countries, they also become territorial confederations.

The boards emphasize their role as ambassador of the Jewish community rather than its governing body. This tendency has been accelerated since World War II by the "coming of age" of the last great wave of immigrants and the consequent diminishing of the earlier homogeneity which characterized most of these communities. The increase in competing interests, the decline in religious commitment, and the growth of assimilatory tendencies have also contributed to this change.

Canadian Jewry

According to the 1981 Canadian census, there are 308,000 Jews in Canada, an increase of approximately 8 percent since the 1971 census. Under the new method of questioning religious, ethnic, and linguistic attachments used in the census, it is possible that this figure slightly underestimates the actual number. More than two-thirds of the Canadian Jews are in Toronto and Montreal, Toronto exceeding Montreal for the first time in the history of Canadian Jewry.

Canadian Jewry wages a constant struggle to maintain its identity in the shadow of American Jewry. Nevertheless, as a community, it has a sense of purpose and is better organized countrywide than any other major Jewish community in the English-speaking world.[1] It, too, underwent a reconstitution in the first postwar generation, also shifting from the centrality of the external relations–defense sphere and the institutions that dominated it to a framework shared by those institutions and those of the communal-welfare and Israel-*edah* spheres. What was unique about the reconstitution was that it did not mean displacement of one by the other but the merger of the two on both the countrywide and local planes. Initiated by the local federations, the process was almost a textbook example of a federated community in action.

The reorganized structure is located in the domain of the *keter malkhut*. Its principal countrywide instrument is the Canadian Jewish Congress (CJC).[2] Long undisputed leader of Canadian Jewry, the CJC was founded in 1919 as a representative board to give Canadian Jewry a single voice in its relations with the non-Jewish authorities. All Jewish organizations in the country belong to the Congress and send delegates to its Triennial Assemblies (figure 11.1).

From the first, the CJC had two characteristics. It was a union of provincial or regional congresses, each of which related to its provincial authorities as appropriate, as the CJC related to the federal government. It had a far broader scope than representative boards in other countries, principally because, as an expression of Jewishness in a multicultural situation, it was concerned with religious and cultural life as well as community relations. As such it attracted the cream of the community leadership in every sphere, not only in the political. It was and is a prime expression of the *keter malkhut* in its most articulated modern version. Because one manifestation of late modern eastern European Jewry was a strong secularist movement, that, too, was brought to Canada. The CJC benefited from the secularist input, which wanted a separate set of institutions for the *keter malkhut* no less than did the more assimilated voluntary leadership, which wanted a properly respectable vehicle to liaise with the authorities.

Unlike the parallel bodies in other countries, the CJC was not founded to combat anti-Semitism. Instead, it grew out of the interest of Canadian Jews in having a voice in world Jewish affairs, particularly about the rebuilding of Eretz Israel and the reconstruction of European Jewry. Until the founding of the CJC, two groups vied for that role. The first was the old established Montreal Jewish community leadership who played the typical role of notables but who had no counterparts in the other communities. Neither they nor any of the other old family leaders could maintain their positions in the face of the highly active eastern European immigrants.

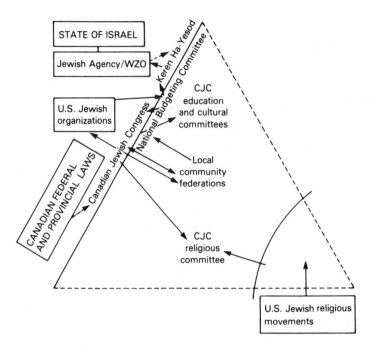

Figure 11.1. The institutional structure of the Canadian Jewish community.

The other competitor was the Zionist Organization of Canada (ZOC), founded in 1899. By that time there were Zionist groups in nine communities across the country. Hence the ZOC was the first countrywide Canadian Jewish organization. Nevertheless, it was not all-embracing enough to substitute for the emergent CJC. After first opposing the establishment of the CJC, the ZOC joined the other elements of the community to participate in the March 1919 founding. The only group not to join the CJC at first was the miniscule Reform movement, which finally came around in 1933.

The CJC is governed by a national assembly, which meets every three years to consider the state of Canadian Jewry and to elect the national council and officers. The national assembly is composed of delegates appointed or elected by hundreds of member organizations throughout the country. Membership is open to every kind of group. There are also some individuals elected at large. The national council meets annually and elects an executive committee, which numbers approximately seventy-five. The Canadian Jewish Congress is an open body. There are regular contests for the presidency and there are power struggles in the organization.

From the first, the CJC dominated the community relations sphere and the cultural segments of the educational-cultural sphere. The communal-welfare sphere remained divided among many local organizations until the Jewish community federation idea was imported from the United States in the 1930s, a generation after its emergence there. Not until the end of that decade did the federations become the principal vehicles for supporting local welfare and social service institutions. The synagogues dominated the religious-congregational sphere, and Jewish education was in the hands of numerous independent Hebrew and Yiddish schools, day and supplementary. Fund-raising for

Israel was the province of Keren Hayesod rather than an indigenous equivalent to the American United Jewish Appeal.

All this changed in the postwar generation. In the first half of that generation, fund-raising for Israel became the province of the federations and the United Israel Appeal (UIA) of Canada, a constituent organization of Keren Hayesod, which gained increasing independence from the parent body in Jerusalem. Thus by the middle of the 1960s the federations had come to play an important role in the Israel-overseas sphere.

At that point the discussions about a merger of the federations and the CJC local branches began to bear fruit. By the end of the generation, in the mid-1970s, such mergers had taken place in every major community so that Canada had reestablished on the local plane the kind of coherent structure it had consistently sought countrywide: an overarching instrumentality bringing together the three spheres dominated by the cosmopolitans in Jewish life. As a result, much of the educational-cultural sphere was also brought into the orbit of the federations. Even the synagogues were closely connected to the overall community structure because of their traditional links to the CJC. In 1983 eleven communities had federations: Calgary, Edmonton, Hamilton, London, Montreal, Ottawa, Saint Catherines, Toronto, Winnipeg, Windsor, and Vancouver.[3]

Countrywide, the CJC as the only comprehensive countrywide organization continues to be the formal voice of Canadian Jewry; however, it must share power with the Canadian Zionist Federation in matters relating to Israel and B'nai B'rith in community relations because of the realities of power distribution in Canadian Jewry. The principal mechanism for fund-raising for Israel is lodged with the United Israel Appeal. In 1974, the Canadians added the National Budgeting Conference (NBC), an instrumentality of the local federations to make allocations to Canada-wide organizations.

The NBC is a uniquely Canadian phenomenon. Although the local Jewish federations in Canada had joined the Council of Jewish Federations (CJF) to make it a North American movement, they tried also to develop a separate Canadian forum. To do so, a Canadian office of the CJF was established to provide CJF services in their own country. But that kind of technical assistance body—the maximum attainable in the United States—was not sufficient for the strong countrywide organization of Canadian Jewry. Hence after the mergers of the CJC and the local federations, the Canadians turned to the development of a joint instrumentality that would allocate funds for countrywide needs. The CJC was catalytic in this effort, because it offered a way to guarantee it adequate financing.

The other significant countrywide organizations are B'nai B'rith District 22, covering all of Canada, Hadassah-Wizo, the United Jewish Relief Agencies (UJRA), and the Jewish Immigrant Aid Services (JIAS). Another reflection of the cooperative orientation of the Canadian Jewish community is in the countrywide activities carried out jointly by the major organizations, at times on a less-than-friendly basis. One of these is the Canada-Israel Committee (CIC), which handles Canadian Jewry's lobbying for Israel and is sponsored jointly by the CJC, the Canadian Zionist Federation, and B'nai B'rith. For domestic matters, the National Joint Community Relations Committee is sponsored by the CJC and B'nai B'rith.

These joint activities also show the limitations of the CJC's role. Even though in theory it should be the dominant countrywide organization, it does not have the political power needed to maintain that dominance. It lacks political power in no small measure because it has no separate fund-raising capability and is dependent on money raised through the combined campaigns.

The only real effort at overarching countrywide organization in the religious-congregational sphere is through the Religious Affairs Committee of the Canadian Jewish Congress. In the past, that committee has defended *shehitah* and worked to find ways to make it compatible with changes in Canadian slaughtering laws, has defended the religious interests of Jews in the Canadian armed forces, and, in general, has given Canadian Jewry a voice in the religious concerns of the country.[4] The committee is also a facilitator of meetings of rabbis and synagogue lay leaders throughout the country. Beyond that, it does not seek to invade the religious-congregational sphere beyond playing a limited, coordinative role, seeing that sphere as belonging to the *keter torah* and *keter kehunah*.

Canadian synagogues are normally identified with Orthodoxy in its different strains. In the nineteenth century, some of the congregations looked to Great Britain whence came their rabbis and to the chief rabbi of the British Empire for *halakhic* guidance. But that disappeared with the coming of the eastern European immigrants who had no associations with that Jewish imperial tradition. There are more than 175 Orthodox congregations in the country. There are also some two dozen Conservative synagogues, including most of the oldest congregations, those that date before the great immigration. The Reform movement has lagged much further behind. Before 1953 there were only three Reform temples in the entire country: one each in Montreal, Toronto, and Hamilton.

All the major synagogue movements of the United States have a presence in Canada. The Conservative congregations are affiliated with the United Synagogue of America. The Conservative rabbis of Canada have an association of their own that also is part of the Rabbinical Assembly of America. The Reform movement maintains a Canadian Council of Reform Congregations affiliated with the Union of American Hebrew Congregations. The Orthodox Rabbinical Council of America maintains a branch association in Canada, although membership in the Union of Orthodox Jewish Congregations is only moderately widespread. Canadian Jews interested in the rabbinate study at the theological seminaries of the different movements in the United States.

The educational-cultural sphere is included in the realm of the *keter torah*. In addition to the extensive elementary and secondary educational systems, these are Jewish studies programs in the major universities, including programs at McGill and York Universities in Montreal and Toronto, respectively to train Jewish teachers. Canadian Jewry also has a rich cultural life in proportion to its size, serious adult Jewish education, an intellectual and academic community devoted to Jewish issues, and a literary community that deals with Canadian Jewish life from the inside.

Outside Montreal and, to a lesser extent, western Canada, Winnipeg in particular, day schools did not develop until the postwar generation. Now every significant Jewish community that can maintain one has its day school, and the day school networks in Toronto rival those in Montreal. The percentage of Jewish children attending day schools is high in most communities, about 50 percent in Toronto, two-thirds in Montreal, and exceeding 80 percent in Edmonton. On the other hand, most Jewish day schools cover the elementary grades only. Toronto is increasingly the exception to this. Jewish education, like Jewish life generally, is weakest in the Atlantic provinces where the Jews are scattered among communities too small for maintaining day schools.[5]

In many respects Canada is the very model of a modern Jewish community. The convergence of factors and forces that made that community has given it special character. Canadian Jews and others are fond of saying that Canadian Jewry is a generation behind

American Jewry. Organizationally this is not true; it has a separate character entirely, but sociologically it may well be. Hence it remains to be seen if there will be an erosion of Jewishness in the Canadian Jewish community like that in the United States since the mid-1960s. If so, then even the organizational structure of Canadian Jewry may suffer.

It may be that, because other factors come into play, the time lag may allow a sufficiently high percentage of Canadian Jews to escape the American experience and keep Canada different. The general Canadian environment, with its emphasis on bilingualism and multiculturalism, strengthens that possibility. So, too, does the more negative aspect of Canadian uniqueness: the greater prevalence of anti-Semitism than in in the United States, especially in more established circles. It may be genteel anti-Semitism but it exists nevertheless and the Jews feel it.

In all this Canadian Jewry offers another demonstration of the importance of good organization. In politics the whole, if properly organized, is greater than the sum of its parts. That is true in the United States where a community that stands on an eroding demographic base is strong because of its organizational capability. Canada does not yet have the eroding base, but it has even greater organizational capability, which is a major plus.

Anti-Semitism in Canada is aggravated by the special problem of the French Canadians, particularly the Quebecois, and their desire for national self-expression in the Canadian federation. The rise of French Canadian nationalism in Quebec since 1960 has brought with it a deterioration of relations between the French Canadians and the Jews. The Quebec nationalists who in the 1960s encouraged the immigration of French-speaking North African Jews as part of their effort to increase the French-speaking population have apparently concluded (not incorrectly) that, given the choice, even those Jews will identify with the Anglophones rather than with the Francophones. Moreover, those nationalists have identified with the Third World, including the Palestine Liberation Organization, making the Jewish position even more uncomfortable.

As a result, Montreal, the country's leading Jewish community for two hundred years, has lost its preeminence to its rival, Toronto. Young Jews, faced with living in a Francophone society governed by a group at least moderately hostile to Jewish aspirations for self-expression, have immigrated to the latter city. Although the panic of the early 1970s has abated somewhat as the Partie Quebecois lost strength and then office, and the Jewish emigration from Montreal has slowed, the future prospects of that community are still less than rosy.

Toronto is booming Jewishly as in every other way, offering attractive opportunities to Jews and to other Canadians. Meanwhile in the west, the Jews who do not leave the region are moving to Vancouver where the climate is better. Winnipeg, with the worst climate of any of the major Canadian cities, is losing Jewish population rapidly as its economy stagnates. Calgary and Edmonton are growing slightly in response to Alberta's economic boom.

The South African Jewish Community

Today there are approximately 118,000 Jews living in South Africa. Almost half live in Johannesburg (about 57,500). Cape Town is the second largest center, with about 25,650 Jews, and Durban has 5,990. The others are spread throughout the country, from substantial Jewish centers such as Port Elizabeth to the smaller rural communities.

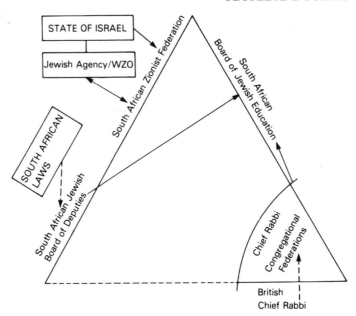

Figure 11.2. The institutional structure of the South African Jewish community.

South African, like Canadian, Jewry is noted for its comprehensive, coherent countrywide organization.[6] (See figure 11.2.) The South African Jewish Board of Deputies (SAJBD) is even more comprehensive than the Canadian Jewish Congress because it includes the United Communal Fund, the principal local fund-raising mechanism, in its domain. Also, there are no separate local or regional comprehensive Jewish bodies. The Board of Deputies directs Jewish affairs in the Transvaal (Johannesburg), which has more than two-thirds of the Jewish population of South Africa. Cape Province (Cape Town) has a subsidiary Board of Deputies and a committee of the board directs affairs in Natal (Durban). The board has its parallels in other spheres such as the South African Federation of Synagogues.

Provincial boards of deputies were established in 1903 and 1904 to handle the problem of Jews dislocated by the Anglo-Boer War. They united as the SAJBD in 1912, two years after the formation of the Union of South Africa. From the first, it was a representative body dominating the external relations–defense sphere. For the next generation and a half, the communal-welfare sphere was fragmented among many small welfare societies, but after World War II the board took steps to bring some order into that sphere and came to dominate it. It also developed close ties with the educational-cultural and religious-congregational spheres through the United Communal Fund, leaving only the Israel-*edah* sphere outside its purview.

The board acts as spokesman for the community in matters of Jewish interest. It maintains a vigilance against anti-Semitism and deals with anti-Semitic incidents as they occur. It attempts to foster better group relations between Jews and non-Jews. It is also formally concerned with coordinating Jewish communal work. The United Communal Fund (UCF), which helps finance other Jewish organizations, is administered by the board.

As its name implies, the board was established with the British model in mind. However, it subsequently expanded its functions beyond the scope of those of the British board. Thus the board operates a welfare department, which deals with personnel problems, unemployment, naturalization, and other matters, and administers the UCF. It promotes adult education programs, provides services to the campus community, maintains a chaplaincy program for Jews in the armed forces, and, working with other bodies, provides religious and educational services to the country communities. It maintains a communal library and archives and fosters research in South African Jewish history and demography. It publishes the monthly magazines *Jewish Affairs,* a principal source of Jewish information and ideas, and *Buurman* in Afrikaans to explain Jews and Judaism to that community. More recently, it has come to see itself as the instrument for community planning.

The board relates to the community through its constituent organizations. Affiliation is contingent on the single requirement than an organization be "any group of Jews organized for an authentic Jewish object." There is an affiliated membership of about 330 organizations constituting the range of institutional life. The board holds a biennial congress at which delegates from the affiliated organizations elect the executive council. Provincial councils are similarly elected by constituent bodies in their areas. Functional responsibilities are discharged by countrywide and provincial committees formed for that purpose. Most of the continuing work of the board is carried on through those committees.

In its early years, the board was preoccupied with immigration issues. In the 1930s, the immigration question was linked with the problem of growing anti-Semitism. Before World War II there was a serious but unsuccessful attempt by a group of Jewish leftists to take over the board and use it like a mouthpiece for their political activities. All three issues were characteristic of "new world" Jewish communities in those years, however unique their expression in the South African context.

A truly unique issue confronting the board and South African Jewry is the tragic dilemma of conscience arising out of South Africa's race problem. Whatever the opinions of individual Jews (which undoubtedly range across most of the spectrum of white opinion in the country but with a strong tendency toward its liberal end), after the National party came to power in 1948, the official Jewish stance expressed by the board was to maintain good relations with the Nationalists and avoid taking a stand on apartheid. This policy prevailed until the changes of the 1970s, which opened the door to bridge-building to the nonwhite peoples. Today the board openly supports political change in South Africa.

As much as South African Jewry is unified on the political level, it is basically divided in the fund-raising sphere. The situation is characteristic of Anglo-Jewry. It is notable that the pluralistic American Jewish structure has developed a centralized financial framework, while centralized South Africa has only a limited degree of coordinated finance. Until 1949 there was no centralization of local fund-raising whatsoever; each organization was left to its own resources. The UCF brought together for fund-raising purposes the Board of Deputies, the South African and Cape Province Boards of Education, the Federation of Synagogues, and other organizations, at first fifteen and today eighteen in all. It was a bold experiment, inasmuch as it included both "national-traditional" and "Reform" religious and educational institutions.

Reorganization of the UCF altered the past patterns whereby individual institutions—welfare, religious, social—garnered most of their support through private campaigns, special donations, and membership subscriptions. The UCF campaigns alternate every other year with Zionist fund-raising for Israel through the Israel United Appeal. The UCF began as an autonomous organization, although intimately involved with the Board of Deputies, which is dependent on it for almost its entire budgetary allocation. In 1972 the UCF became a department of the board.

Like the other British imperial offshoots, South African Jewry is nominally Orthodox. Most of its synagogues are united in the South African Federation of Synagogues with their own chief rabbi. Formally, he still turns to the British chief rabbi if he needs an outside opinion on matters of *halakhah,* although, like chief rabbinical authorities in other diaspora communities, he increasingly turns instead to the Israeli chief rabbinate.

The Federation of Synagogues is responsible for the functioning of the *bet din.* There is, however, little coordination of congregational life or synagogue planning. Much of this is, perhaps, explicable by the localistic nature of congregational life. Viewed in the context of the wider community, synagogues operate mainly in locally bound milieus. Synagogue affiliation as a way of membership differs from that of, say, the Zionist movement. Rabbis can seldom receive federation or congregational "mandates" because the synagogue members hold diverse communal attitudes, and commitments cut across many more strata of opinion than in other goal-oriented institutions. The loose structure of the Orthodox movement is further compounded by the Cape having a separate and autonomous Union of Orthodox Hebrew Congregations with its own chief rabbi.

Although the congregations are bound to the chief rabbi and the services remain fully Orthodox in form, most congregants are lax in their religious behavior, following patterns common in the Conservative movement in the United States. As a result, many committed Orthodox have broken away to found their own congregations. An ultra-Orthodox community has developed in recent years with its own congregations, schools, and *yeshivot.* This community has become more separatist as part of the general move to the right in the Orthodox world and is beginning to develop internal institutional competition. Originally affiliated with Agudath Israel, recently Chabad has entered the South African scene and begun to develop its own institutional network.

There is also a small Reform movement in South Africa, with congregations in the major cities. The Union for Progressive Judaism links them countrywide. The movement is subject to intense pressure by the Orthodox rabbinical establishment, which would like to ostracize it.

The major rival to the Board of Deputies over the years has been the South African Zionist Federation, which actually antedates the board as a countrywide organization. It was established in 1898, in the midst of the Anglo-Boer War, following the First Zionist Congress. South African Jewry was strongly Zionist from the first and was one of the first communities to become thoroughly Zionized. Hence the Zionists dominated the Israel-overseas sphere in an almost undisputed way for three generations. Contacts and fund-raising for Israel (through the Israel United Appeal) were the province of the Zionist Federation.

The federation is not merely a confederation of South African Zionist parties, like most other countrywide Zionist federations. It centralizes and coordinates, formulates policy, and initiates activity. Its organizational efficiency has been commented on by many overseas observers.

The federation undertakes many tasks besides managing the Israel United Appeal. It fosters Aliya programs (despite the disappointing facts associated with the recent wave of emigration, the number of South African *olim* relative to other western countries is high), publishes a weekly newspaper and other publications that circulate countrywide, and conducts educational and cultural activities for all age groups. Affiliated with the Zionist Federation is the South African Maccabi Association (seven thousand members in sports-crazy South Africa), which promoted South Africa's participation in the international Maccabi games in Israel every four years until Israel was forced to ban South African teams in 1985 to comply with international Olympic rules. Moreover, because South African racism is a barrier to the linking South African Jewry with many world Jewish organizations apart from the World Zionist Organization (the World Jewish Congress, for example, is non grata in South Africa because of its strong antiapartheid position), the links with the WZO became the principal institutional links between South African Jewry and the *edah*.[7]

All this has been changing in recent decades, partly because of the decline of the Zionist movement worldwide, which has also had its effect on the Zionist Federation in South Africa, and partly because of the strengthening of the instrumentalities of the communal-welfare sphere into which the Board of Deputies moved in the post-World War II generation. The reconstitution of the Jewish Agency has added to this shift, because the South African representatives to the Jewish Agency Assembly and Board of Governors, while formally chosen by Keren Hayesod, are major givers who have come to dominate the campaign in South Africa as elsewhere in the Jewish world. Thus donors are replacing Zionist politicians as South Africa's representatives on the world scene. The selfsame donors prefer to focus their local Jewish activities on the Board of Deputies rather than the Zionist Federation.

The structure of authority among the several countrywide organizations is parallel, not hierarchical. That is, each body has actual as well as formal autonomy in its own sphere of communal responsibility. The Zionist Federation usually defers to the Board of Deputies in community relations matters. Non-Zionist organizations usually defer to Zionist organizations in Israel-related matters. The same pattern applies to the nonreligious organizations with respect to religious affairs, and so on.

This pattern of mutual deference has not always prevailed. The present situation is the product of a long, often stormy process. The delineation of separate functional responsibilities was a gradual process. In the pioneering days of the community, the synagogue performed most of the communal tasks usually associated with other institutions. Thus it carried out educational, financial, and social functions besides strictly religious affairs. Later, for a brief period toward the end of the nineteenth century, the Zionist Federation—the only organization with institutional links throughout the country—became concerned with extra-Zionist activities. It saw itself as the guardian of Jewish interests in South Africa and the vital force in community affairs, and undertook immigration and naturalization work.

It is hardly surprising, then, that when the idea of a Board of Deputies—which would carry out those functions not strictly within the scope of the Zionist organization—was voiced, it met with opposition. This conflict was exacerbated by the fact that the Litvaks were particularly strong in the Zionist Federation while the Board of Deputies was an expression of the Anglo-Jewish leadership and their approach to communal organization. It was mitigated, however, by important communal leaders, such as Rabbi J. H. Hertz, who were both Zionists and leaders of the Anglo-Jewish elements in the community.

When, after much conflict, the board was finally established, it took several years before the functions of each body became clear. The federation continued to insist on its right to take parallel action with the board. Eventually the delineation of functions became clearer and more accepted, particularly during the 1930s. The growth of political anti-Semitism in South Africa and the urgent question of accepting German Jewish refugees from Nazism made "Jewish defense" a community priority and led to a substantial strengthening of the Board of Deputies. Today there is mutual recognition of each other's functions, although differences of outlook on some issues persist.

In the educational-cultural sphere, the percentage of Jewish children in Jewish primary and secondary schools in South Africa is one of the highest of any major Jewish community. Several of them are large, flourishing institutions by any standard. Jewish day schools cover much of the Jewish ideological spectrum. Nevertheless, a mainstream South African approach that can be described as "national-traditional" has become dominant. Thus the curriculum almost always includes Orthodox religious observance and emphasis on the centrality of Israel.[8]

The South African Board of Jewish Education (SABJE), founded in 1929, is the body responsible for the educational policy, financing, and coordination of most of South African Jewish education and is preeminent in that sphere. The board is an autonomous body funded in part through the UCF. It is an example of changing priorities and innovative leadership in the community. Formed at first by a small determined minority who perceived the need for community responsibility for Jewish education long before that view penetrated community consciousness, it was beset for years by community apathy and financial difficulties. Changing community conceptions of the place of education in communal life were to a large extent a product of the efforts of the board's leadership. Today, Jewish education is the major beneficiary of the UCF.

The board introduced a new atmosphere into Jewish education in South Africa. At first, it helped create a network of educational services ranging from nursery school through secondary education. Its staff also serves Hebrew schools not directly under its control, in an effort to maintain standards. The orientation of the board is Zionist and Orthodox, reflecting the dominant streams of organized South African Jewry.

Jewish education in South Africa is confined principally to school-age children. There is little in the way of an adult Jewish education. Few communal resources are devoted to stimulating adult Jewish culture. The Board of Deputies has made some efforts in that direction, and for a while a small group of Jewish Communists did the same for their own purposes. More recently, following the North American lead, South African Jews have sponsored the establishment of Jewish studies programs at the University of Cape Town and Witwatersrand University in Johannesburg. The problem remains, however: even if South Africa does produce indigenous talent to staff its Jewish studies programs or its rabbinate, most leave for other countries and, except for rabbis, the community does not offer sufficient monetary incentive for non-South Africans other than Israelis to come and fill the gap. Hence the Jewish studies programs have had to limp along with rotating, part-time people brought in from Israel or occasionally Britain and North America, and even the elementary and secondary schools rely heavily on Israeli teachers for Jewish subjects. The problem is compounded by the worsening South African political situation.

The intensity of provincial activity differs from province to province. Thus the Council for Natal Jewry has established a powerful coordinating structure and the historic position of Cape Jewry also gives the Cape Board a strong role. Often, however, what are deemed "provincial" matters are in reality confined to the one or two main centers of the province. Thus the differing strengths of provincial bodies may relate to the power of leading local communities and their varying desires for independent communal activity. The pattern usually is one in which authority is concentrated in the countrywide body, although neither the provincial nor the countrywide organizations would define their relationship in such terms. Thus relations between the Cape Board and the SAJBD really reflect the state of relations between the Cape Town and Johannesburg communities.

The dynamic center of both general and Jewish life in South Africa is undoubtedly Johannesburg. Given the demographic structure—half of South African Jewry lives in Johannesburg—it is hardly surprising that all the countrywide Jewish institutions are housed there. However, Cape Town's status as legislative capital and first South African city, its longer history of Jewish communal life, and its sheer physical distance from Johannesburg have contributed to enhancing its status and its role. The Cape community—Johannesburg leaders complain—is a world of its own. The Cape desire for autonomy is reflected at the institutional level: the Cape Board of Education acts as an autonomous body separate from the South African Board of Education. Similarly, the United Hebrew Congregations of the Cape is a separate body independent of the control of the Federation of Synagogues of South Africa. (The *South African Jewish Year Book* lists these two *Cape* institutions under the heading "National Institutions.") Although the Board of Deputies and the Zionist Federation include the Cape under the same organizational umbrellas, relations are also often strained. Nevertheless, common commitment to unity is so strong that these divisions would not endanger the basic unity of South African Jewry.

In South Africa, as elsewhere, most Jewish activity is local. In urban communities where there is an organized network of communal institutions there is usually a proliferation of organizations and activity. Some of the organizations such as sports clubs may be purely local; others may be chapters of provincial or countrywide institutions. On this plane volunteer affiliation and activity are most intense.

Although they are gradually disappearing in a rapidly industrializing society, a special pattern of communal organization can still be observed in the rural communities. What characterizes this life is its reliance on the single congregation rather than on a network of institutions. The Board of Deputies has a special department to serve these communities, which concentrates on the more isolated rural towns.

What emerges from this picture of communal structure? The profusion of organizations on all planes does not necessarily mean a "pluralistic" diffusion of power along American lines, where it is difficult to locate the source of decisions affecting the overall community, or the kind of separatist fragmentation characteristic of Argentinian Jewry. The evidence points to South Africa as a clear example of structured power. The countrywide institutions, each in its specific sphere of functional competence, formulate policy. These institutions are not merely the sum of their parts: to a large degree they initiate, coordinate, and even control. In a homogeneous community this kind of authoritative action is, within limits, effective. The importance of the provincial and local planes lies in their "community-involving" activities. This, in turn, serves as a balancing force. Though the countrywide institutions are more concerned with community-wide questions, in local organizations individual identification is given scope, and personal involvement is intense.

South African Jewry benefits from having its Jewish identity as secure as is possible in a voluntary situation because of the nature of South African society, which usually is referred to as multiracial but probably is better described as multitribal. The Jews benefit from being one of the white tribes. It is relatively difficult for Jews to assimilate because they must then attach themselves to some other tribe. At the same time, South African Jews feel that they are living on the edge of a volcano because of the growing black-white conflicts.

The positive Afrikaner attitude toward the Old Testament, not necessarily paralleled by a positive attitude toward real Jews, has permitted and even encouraged the Zionist tendencies of South African Jewry as being in keeping with Scripture. Hence the most national forms of Jewish self-expression are also the most acceptable in the South African context. Nevertheless, most South African Jews believe that they are sitting on their suitcases and do not see a long-term future for their children in South Africa even if they themselves have no intention of leaving.

After the troubles in the mid-1970s and again a decade later, there was substantial Jewish emigration. Considering South African Jewry is ostensibly Zionist and the emphasis on Zionism in South African Jewish education, one might have expected that most of these emigrants would have gone to Israel. It is true that South Africa has a higher percentage of *olim* than other English-speaking communities, but only a quarter of those emigrating chose the Jewish state. The other three-quarters immigrated to North America, Britain, or Australia, where many have made important contributions to strengthening Jewish life.

Most of the emigrants were professionals whose education enabled them to start again. Those in commerce and industry were less likely to emigrate because they could not transfer their assets in sufficient amounts to resume the life-style to which they had become accustomed in South Africa. The professionals preferred to resume their practices in countries where they knew the languages and could practice their professions in ways like those at home. The phenomenon of South African emigration highlights one paradox of the Jewish people in our time: the failure to take up the challenge of the Jewish state even by many who were educated to believe that challenge is central to contemporary Jewish existence.

The Australian Jewish Community

The Jewish population of Australia increased from twenty-four thousand in the mid-1930s to eight-five at the beginning of the 1980s. Ninety percent live in Melbourne and Sydney and 7 percent in the other state capitals.

The locus of Jewish organization in Australia is found in the state boards of deputies, which are, in effect, the local framing institutions of Australian Jewry. This is because Australia is a federal system spread over a continent whose six states each encompass imperial domains territorially (with the smallest, Tasmania, being an island), but whose populations are for the most part concentrated in one or at most two metropolitan areas per state. Thus Australia is a collection of metropolitan city-states and its Jews, even more metropolitan than the general Australian population, reflect this situation in their organizational structure.[9]

The major Jewish concentrations in Australia are in Sydney and Melbourne, which have a relationship like that of the Jewish communities of Montreal and Toronto; roughly coequal in size, importance, and activity, each with its own special character and with a built-in rivalry between the two. This has led to a pattern of rotation of the countrywide leadership between them. So, too, Perth, the third largest community, plays a role in the Australian constellation like Vancouver or Winnipeg. The other communities are considerably smaller. Adelaide is dominated by a recently arrived Sephardi population, which make it exceptional in the overwhelmingly Ashkenazi Australian Jewish milieu. Tiny communities exist in Brisbane and Canberra. Tasmania, which had a small but flourishing Jewish community 150 years ago, has had a declining Jewish population for at least two generations.[10]

The general pattern of Jewish communal organization in Australia is like that in Britain, South Africa, and Canada, except that the locus of power is in the state organizations. The spheres are more loosely connected and some are internally less unified than in Canada and South Africa, resembling Britain.

The state boards of deputies are linked through the Executive Council of Australian Jewry (ECAS) in a countrywide confederation whose principal responsibility is to maintain links with the Australian federal government in matters of Jewish concern and with the World Jewish Congress. It has maintained its position as official representative in all communications with federal ministers by ensuring that approaches in areas such as Israel and immigration are made in conjunction with the relevant national bodies (the Zionist Federation and the Australian Jewish Welfare and Relief Society).

Comprising delegates from each state, the Executive Council of Australian Jewry meets twice yearly; in the interim its affairs are administered by an executive body that moves every two years between Melbourne and Sydney. The integration provided by a countrywide executive body with officers from each state has not yet developed. Rather than establish truly countrywide executive bodies, the common practice in Australia is to rotate the executive between Sydney and Melbourne, with all members of the executive being from the one city, and with a provision for conferences every six months. The resulting countrywide body for that period is really the relevant local body in another guise.

This has been both cause and effect of the intense jealousy and rivalry in Australian Jewish community politics between Melbourne and Sydney, and of the ensuing problems of coordination. Petty parochial and personal differences and united reflexive opposition to the opposite state are not uncommon. Historical antipathies have been exacerbated by each community having a period of total control followed by a complete lack of control. The continuation of this practice reflects the financial costs of having members regularly travel interstate for meetings. Being a confederation of umbrella organizations, the Executive Council has less access to funds than the local groups themselves. The practice has also made it difficult to develop professional staff because of the mobility problem.

Until the end of World War II the leadership of Australian Jewry was in the hands of the prestigious congregations, particularly the two great synagogues of Melbourne and Sydney, where the old established elites ruled. The rabbis of those congregations remained at their posts for many years and acquired power and prestige accordingly. The opening of the postmodern epoch brought the rise of the representative boards as the principal loci of communal authority and power (see figure 11.3). This change reflected the postwar transformation of Australian Jewry. At that point, the rabbis generally withdrew from leadership of communal organizations and representative bodies. The constitutions of the boards specifically state that they are not to make any pronouncements on matters of religious law.

The boards of deputies in each state and the Executive Council of Australian Jewry not only had to struggle with the synagogues, but also had a long, bitter conflict with the Communist-dominated Jewish Council to Combat Fascism and Anti-Semitism. During

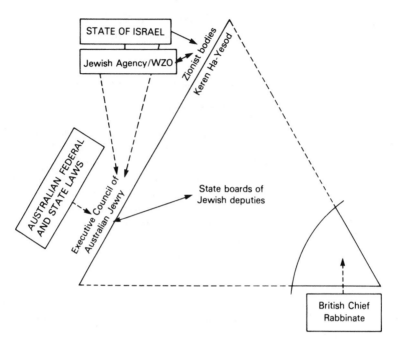

Figure 11.3.   The institutional structure of the Australian
Jewish community.

World War II the latter body had been entrusted with representational responsibilities
because of its expertise and great political awareness. When after the war it was revealed
as a Communist front organization, the Jewish community fought to eliminate it from
the scene. The representative boards' victory over the Communists marked a commitment by the Jewish community to an independent view of Jewish political interests, with
Jewish interests as defined by communal consensus as the touchstone of their policy-
making. This means that the boards do not involve themselves in political matters where
Jewish interests are not involved, and when they enter the arena it is only to advance
Jewish interests.

Both conflicts came to a successful conclusion by the middle of the 1950s when the
representative boards established a legitimate claim to sole authority in the external
representation of Jewish communities. As part of the constitutional settlement of the late
1940s, the representative boards agreed to exclude themselves from dealing with religious questions and ecclesiastical matters, but there is no clear understanding as to what
constitute such questions and matters. That issue is a source of modest communal
conflict to this day.

Since the broadening of the representative bodies in the 1940s, none of the top
representative leaders have been highly identified with synagogue leadership, which
generally seems content to remain within the congregational confines. Recruitment of
the board executive bodies has come more from the outside than from the ranks of
delegates to the boards. Individuals have been recruited for the executive bodies either
because they may have demonstrated leadership qualities and been successful in business
or the professions, or because they lead groups or institutions whose representation on

the executive body is thought necessary for harmonious communal functioning. In major fund-raising activities, ability to raise money will grant entry to the leadership; and the top positions go to those who also happen to be major donors.

There are three basic distinguishing characteristics of Jewish leadership in Australia. As a group, the leaders are representative in terms of values and countries of origin. There is a consistent pattern of functional representation and integration, of ensuring that the top organizations in the community include and actively involve leaders of the major communal agencies. As a group, it is narrow in composition, because leadership is voluntary and unpaid. Without seriously contested elections and salaried offices there is little way the politically motivated and ambitious can rise to positions of leadership without ample means. Moreover, because elections are rarely contested, the transmission of leadership is by cooptation and recruitment in narrow and known circles.

The religious-congregational sphere follows the nominally Orthodox pattern of Anglo-Jewry with a substantial gap between the public forms maintained in the synagogues and other public institutions and events, and the private observances of most Australian Jews. On the whole, Australian Jews are more religiously observant than in their sister communities. Nevertheless, religious organization remains confined to the congregational plane. Australia does not have a chief rabbi of its own; the community still accepts the authority of the British chief rabbi. Realistically, this means that there is a continuing absence of recognized religious authority. The official *batei din* have no authority over rabbis who are not members, and scarcely any over the rabbis who *are*. Matters such as *shehitah* are handled by the representative boards.[11] There is not even an organization of Orthodox rabbis in anything more than name. The absence of rabbinical organization is symptomatic of the continued general lack of organization in the religious sphere. There is no meaningful congregational body or association uniting the Orthodox synagogues on either a state or countrywide basis. There are embryonic bodies on paper but they lack power, authority, and prestige. It has also recently become common for the new, fully observant congregations to establish their own *batei din,* thus further reducing the possibilities of unified religious authority.

Since World World War II, a separate ultra-Orthodox community has grown up, comprising primarily refugees from the Holocaust who never passed through the Anglo-Jewish crucible. For example, the three old established congregations in Melbourne, where few apart from the rabbi and the cantor are fully observant, were supplemented by new traditional congregations in which the leading members and probably about 10 percent of the membership are fully observant. There are also smaller, more informal and intimate synagogues where most members are strictly observant. They have replicated the range of factions in the ultra-Orthodox world—Hungarian, Agudath Israel, and Lubavitch. In Melbourne, about 57 percent belong to the new traditional congregations, and about 9 percent to the strictly observant.

In all, approximately 8 to 10 percent of the Melbourne community are strictly observant. For Sydney the estimate is 4 percent. Their significance lies not in numbers but in the growth for the first time of a solid and self-sustaining core of observant Orthodoxy. This solid core has established an impressive network of religious and educational institutions. The core group has wider influence in the Jewish community than its numbers, being the center of a community in which Orthodoxy is dominant. The core thus becomes the reference group for the whole community; even the unobservant Orthodox regard it as the legitimate upholder of correct tradition and practice.

Each major community has at least one Liberal or Reform congregation but the

Reform movement is as weak in Australia as it is in South Africa. Sephardic communities have developed in Sydney, Melbourne, Perth, and Adelaide. In the first two cities they have established independent Sephardic congregations. In Adelaide the community's Sephardic majority control the Adelaide Hebrew Congregation.

Conflict between the rabbinate and the representative leaders of the community through the boards and the Executive Council of Australian Jewry is new in Australian Jewry. A major conflict developed in the early 1960s with the proposed Commonwealth Marriage Bill, which asked each religious group to nominate its marriage celebrants for government registration. The Executive Council of Australian Jewry used this as an opportunity to receive permanent legislative recognition as the representative body of Australian Jewry, and tried to have the Orthodox and Liberal rabbis forward their names through it. Neither group of rabbis agreed, for several reasons, but what united them was their view that marriage was a religious matter and therefore the ECAJ should have nothing at all to do with it. Each group feared that one day the council might fall into the hands of the other and would exclude them; the Orthodox also had religious qualms about the council certifying Liberal marriage practices.

Their joint refusal and effective demand to register directly and separately led the Commonwealth government to propose that Jewry be declared two denominations. This was the last thing the Jews wanted. Eventually, the Commonwealth government came to a decision that reflected the reality of Jewish congregational life. It declared Judaism to be one denomination and permitted each congregation to forward the name of its celebrant separately and directly. It also permitted any group of four congregations to register jointly.

Australia is also like Canada and South Africa in the educational-cultural sphere, with a very high percentage of Jewish children attending Jewish primary and secondary day schools (up to 48 percent in Melbourne and Perth), which cover the range of contemporary Jewish ideologies, although most are Orthodox in orientation. The larger schools are world renowned and all are independent or at least governed separately.[12]

Beyond the primary and secondary levels, Jewish studies programs are just beginning to appear at the universities. There are university departments in Melbourne and Sydney that teach Hebrew, Bible, and cognate studies, but do not attract many Jewish students. In recent years in Melbourne a Department of Jewish Studies was established in the College of Advanced Education; to date its offerings have been limited. The Lubavitcher Hassidim have established a Yeshiva Gedola (talmudic academy) and a Jewish studies institute for girls, and two *kollelim* have been organized.

There is relatively little in the way of Jewish cultural expression. As in South Africa, Australian Jewish journals of opinion have occasionally been published, usually as the passion of one or two people who have seen to it that they continue to appear, but which disappear when those people leave the scene. There are some signs that the funds and interest needed may become more available in the future. Australia does have a group of Jewish academics interested in Jewish social research and Jewish public affairs who have worked together on different projects and provide a certain intellectual leavening because they make themselves available to Jewish groups. The recent establishment of the Australian Institute for Jewish Affairs may help catalyze their efforts.

Because Australia is an acceptable place to live, it can draw on resources of American and British Jewry as well as Israel for teaching personnel and rabbinical leadership. In the past, rabbis and teachers were brought from Britain. In the postwar generation, the United States and Canada also became recruiting grounds. Now Israel is playing an increasing role in this respect.

The communal-welfare sphere in Australia is better integrated than the educational-cultural sphere. After the amalgamation of the different groups into the Australian Jewish Welfare and Relief Society (AJWRS), it became the central and coordinating body in each state and countrywide in all spheres of social and welfare services. It handled the early administrative arrangements for immigration with the Commonwealth government, arranging for suitable guarantees and sponsorship where required. At first, some of the *landsmanschaften* established accommodation centers for immigrants from their home regions, but with the slowing down of immigration the AJWRS assumed sole control of this activity. It looked after the immigrants on arrival, ensuring accommodation, arranging employment, and providing loans and other economic assistance to enable the newcomers to become self-supporting. The funds for these purposes came from local and overseas sources, and through the banking system by guarantee.

After its success in dealing with immigration, the society eventually expanded its activities to become the community's central social service agency. It deals with all kinds of problems affecting youth, the unmarried, orphans, the aged: alcoholism, delinquency, drugs, and so on, as well as continuing its traditional economic assistance. It became increasingly professionalized and has been a major force in the rationalization and coordination of social services to minimize overlap and duplication. It was instrumental not only in centralizing most of the main services in its own framework, but also in establishing state Jewish social service councils to coordinate the activities of the other groups working in the field. The major service outside its direct control is the provision and administration of the communal old-age homes, which are run by separate organizations. Some homes, such as the major one in Melbourne, operate on a larger scale, with total budgets exceeding those of the society. The AJWRS is only loosely linked with the major framing institutions of Australian Jewry.

The ECAJ dominates the external affairs–defense sphere. The Israel-overseas sphere is dominated by the Keren Hayesod and the Zionist Federation, with the first much more important than the second. The Zionist movement in Australia goes back to the days of Herzl and even before, as in other major Jewish communities, but never achieved the dominance it did in South Africa. The Australian situation is more like Britain, where the movement had to struggle hard with an older generation of rooted Australian Jews who opposed Zionism as threatening their position in Australian society. The struggle between the Zionist movement and the Australian Jewish establishment paralleled that of the struggle between British Zionists and the Anglo-Jewish Association and ended in the same way at approximately the same time.

The establishment of Israel resolved the great debate in Australian Jewry about a Jewish state and extinguished the problem of dual loyalties and dual nationality that had concerned some. But when the euphoria of the establishment of the state had subsided, undercurrents and antagonisms overshadowed by the great debate surfaced and aroused considerable communal tension. Although there was no open opposition to the State of Israel, there was considerable opposition to the Zionist movement that claimed to be its spokesman. The conflict was between an Israeli orientation and a local community orientation, and which should have supremacy. Admitting the primacy of Israel's interests, many local communal leaders were not prepared to grant a privileged position to Zionist leaders as spokesmen for the Jewish community in matters affecting Israel; they asserted their right to speak for the community in this regard. Similarly, they refused to accept the local Zionist leadership's definition of Israel's needs and how these should be related to local needs.

Already in 1948 the issue was joined over whether Australian Jewry should assist or encourage Jews in Europe to immigrate to Australia. Some Zionist leaders argued strongly that Jews should now be encouraged and assisted to immigrate only to Israel, and that therefore Australian Jewry should actively discourage further Jewish immigration. Moreover, in their view it was futile to plan for long-term Jewish cultural and communal survival outside Israel. The majority at a special conference of the Executive Council of Australian Jewry convened to consider the matter decided to accept the principle of the immigrants' free choice and to give them full assistance if they decided to come to Australia. They further decided under no condition should inducements be offered to help choose Australia, as apparently had been done until then.

There were also differences over the allocation of money raised and methods proposed by the United Israel Appeal for increasing donations. Proposals to tax all Jewish communal appeals for Israel to pay for state board and Executive Council administrative activities were regularly opposed by the Zionist movement. As the biggest appeal, its contribution would be the largest, and it refused on principle to divert money collected for Israel to local purposes. Such opposition usually generated counterclaims of "Zionist domination."

The Jewish communal leadership kept these tensions to a minimum through various strategies of cooperation. First, as already noted, representative leadership meant commitment to Israel even if not to formal Zionist activity. Second, Zionist leaders were incorporated into top community leadership positions. Third, in putting the case of Israel to the government, the Executive Council included Zionist leaders in all delegations.

The Six-Day War produced an outpouring of feeling that completely eradicated previous antipathies and tensions and significantly changed the status of Israel and Zionism in the communal structure. These feelings and changes were reinforced by the 1973 war. World Jewry's intense support for Israel during the wars led Zionists to become committed to diaspora Jewish life without their previous equivocations. Israel's problems became the major concern of the Jewish representative bodies, which effectively settled all claims for primacy or supremacy.

The wars also transformed Jewish giving in Australia, as elsewhere. Unprecedented amounts were donated in 1967, and the new levels have been maintained ever since, with a particularly dramatic jump in 1973. These increases, the more sophisticated methods of fund-raising, and the obvious need dissolved most older antipathies and criticisms.

After 1973, Australian Jews set up a professionally directed office to lead their political and representational activity for Israel. Although first established by the Victorian Board for Jewish Deputies and the Executive Council of Australian Jewry, who later became equal partners with the Zionist movement, it is now clear that because the resources are those of the Zionist movement, it supplies much of the day-to-day direction and decision-making authority. Official approaches to the Commonwealth government are still the province of the Executive Council, but much of the preparatory work and the intensive lobbying is carried out through the Zionist movement's professionally directed office. This upgrading of professional activity within the framework of the Zionist movement, with the partial displacement of other communal leaders, has not proved to be easy.

Even as the Australian Zionist Federation (AZF) has grown in power vis-à-vis the Executive Council, it has been losing power to the fund-raisers. The emergence of fund-raising for Israel as the principal Zionist activity ultimately led to a semi-autonomous body whose activities now overshadow those of the Zionist Federation. The fund-raisers are becoming dominant in the Israel-*edah* sphere in Australia as elsewhere. The main leaders of the United Israel Appeal (UIA) have in recent years risen in significance, compared with the leaders of the Zionist Federation. Although the UIA continues to function through the Keren Hayesod, it is essentially an independent Australian body that now also controls Australia's seats on the governing bodies of the Jewish Agency. This new leadership is beginning to make itself felt throughout the Australian Jewish community.

The state boards of deputies are organizations of organizations. Not having direct membership, their claims to representation stem from the spread of membership of their constituent organizations. Almost all major Jewish organizations are affiliated, and none of those that are not affiliated challenge the umbrella organizations' claims. At this juncture only a few of the more traditional Orthodox groups—such as the Lubavitcher Hassidim and a self-contained, semiseparatist, and highly organized Hungarian and Czech community—remain unaffiliated. They are, however, forced to recognize the boards' authority when they seek communal funds, and therefore must fit into the authorized fund-raising cycle.

Despite being umbrella organizations, the boards, because of pressure from European-influenced activists and because of a desire to be as representative as possible, have tried to relate to the members of the communities as individuals. That at least one-third of the Jewish community does not belong to any Jewish organization or congregations creates a problem of representation and weakens the boards' claims to speak for the whole community. Attempts were therefore made to develop systems of direct election of delegates. But community interest in the boards has been low; in surveys in Melbourne more than two-thirds knew little or nothing about what the Victorian Jewish Board of Deputies did.

Not surprisingly, attempts at direct election of delegates in Melbourne generated little interest; it was hardly to be expected that those Jews who did not find any Jewish congregation or organization of interest would be interested in a body even further removed from their immediate lives. Hence the elections were used by large, well-organized groups that could turn out votes to increase their representation without necessarily broadening the community base as intended. For many years the Jewish Ex-Servicemen's Leagues won those elections because they represented the only organized groups that made an effort to compete in them. Because their leadership was more local than cosmopolitan, the publicly elected representatives did not strengthen the boards in any particular way. As a result, even the limited system of direct election was abandoned.[13] In Sydney 50 percent of the delegates are elected, but here again most are already organizationally committed, and participation in elections is patchy. No attempts have ever been made to have direct elections for executive positions; these have always been confined to the assembled delegates.

The boards coordinate the activities of the functioning bodies in the community in the most general way. They clear a path in fund-raising by allocating authorized times of appeal, and they provide a forum for organizations to be informed about activities in the community. They are thus important in providing a sense of community merely by bringing together at regular intervals representatives of almost all major Jewish organizations and activities.

The functional activities—welfare, education, youth, synagogues, Zionism, culture, and fraternal association—are the province of the individual organizations, which jealously maintain their autonomy. Until the recent change in New South Wales, none of the boards raised money collectively. Consequently, they do not use budgeting to reflect collective views of communal priorities and needs, as is done in other countries. Nor can they use budgetary allocations to innovate, support worthwhile initiatives, or to introduce more rational planning and efficient resource allocation and prevent duplication of costs and facilities.

The boards are financially dependent on affiliation fees, and this has limited their activities and the degree of professionalization and policy execution, even in their function of representation and spokesmanship. Some leaders who devote time, money, and effort to these activities are probably not greatly disturbed by this phenomenon, which casts them into the public arena, gains them media exposure, and increases their communal status and prestige.

The roof bodies thus operate at a remove from the communities' ongoing functions, the expansion of which has been accompanied by a decline in the boards' authority. In the 1930s their authority (which was challenged) derived from the prestige and status of the individual leaders. In the 1940s and early 1950s their authority stemmed from the significance of the internal conflicts and from their activity on questions of Jewish immigration, Israel, and anti-Semitism. In time they have become less known and hence less authoritative to the average member of the community, but have remained significant to the affiliated organizations.

In recent years even the latter concern has declined somewhat; attendances are poor; elections for executive positions are rarely contested; there seem to be few controversial issues; much of the important representational activity about Israel, about which there is widespread consensus, has been taken over by the Zionist movement. Above all, delegates have lost their sense of political efficacy as activity is increasingly restricted to the executives. The executives are firmly in control; the boards serve merely as a legitimating device to enable the executive to operate independently.

Whether it is a matter of not having suitable channels for communication and consultation, or whether it simply reflects the desire of the executive to keep matters restricted to a small circle, the current situation is one of tight executive control, few opportunities for outside influence, and little public awareness of executive activity. Thus the common affairs of the Jewish communities are controlled by a small group of individuals formally elected annually by organizational representatives, in elections where competition for places is more the exception than the rule.

The Australian Jewish community may have fewer links and less integration among the five spheres than any other examined so far. In part, this reflects how Australian Jewry is a generation behind the other major Jewish communities in its development, just as Australia is behind its sister countries. Hence there has been less pressure to build links. The complexities of contemporary life are only now beginning to engulf Australia, forcing closer links among the spheres as has happened in other Jewish communities. This process will likely be accelerated in the next generation, but in the interim it is possible to look at Australia and see the kinds of separation that were common elsewhere until the 1960s.

The one imponderable on the Australian Jewish scene is the new wave of emigration from South Africa. In the 1980s, Australia apparently became the favorite place for South African Jews seeking to relocate. Similar in climate, culture, language, and rhythm, it offered the advantages of virtually an all-white continent with a great future in front of it, also in the southern hemisphere. By 1986 at least ten thousand South African Jews had settled in Australia, adding 15 percent to the Jewish population of that country. The

Jewish community of Perth, for example, went from fifteen hundred to five thousand souls as a result of the South African immigration. Even if no more South African Jews were to come, Australian Jewry would have been affected. If the immigration continues as it is likely to do, the face of the community may be changed once again.

The Zimbabwean Jewish Community

Before Rhodesia became Zimbabwe, about ten thousand Jews had settled there, coming from eastern Europe and to a smaller extent from the eastern Mediterranean, particularly the Isle of Rhodes, by way of South Africa, between 1890 and World War I. They were among the first white settlers of Southern Rhodesia, entering with the British. These Jewish pioneers rapidly established themselves in local commerce, mining, and such industry as there was and prospered mightily. They built Jewish communities in the principal cities founded by the British and established a board of deputies serving Southern Rhodesia, Northern Rhodesia (now Zambia), and Nyasaland (now Malawi), besides a full range of local institutions like those developed in South Africa: Orthodox synagogues, day schools, a Zionist Federation, and an active Keren Hayesod.[14]

With the coming of African decolonization in the 1960s, the Jewish community began to decrease. When Zambia and Malawi gained independence, many Jews left those countries although about three hundred remain in Zambia and a few score families still live in Malawi. At that time, Southern Rhodesia declared its independence of Britain to preserve white dominance. As Rhodesia, it held out for more than a decade before its white population was forced to capitulate to the black majority. In the interim, the Jewish population decreased by several thousand but six thousand Jews remained in Rhodesia when the transfer of power took place.

In the initial phases of the new regime, tens of thousands of whites, among them approximately forty-five hundred Jews, left the country, many for South Africa. Then it became apparent that, however insistent the blacks were in taking full political control, the new regime would respect white economic, civil, and social rights. Because Rhodesia had not been an apartheid society, racial integration did not prove to be an insurmountable obstacle. Consequently, after the initial flight, the exodus slowed and then stopped. In the mid-1980s, as the troubles in South Africa increased, there was even a reverse flow of whites who returned to an apparently stable Zimbabwe.

Today about fifteen hundred Jews remain in the country, a figure that seems to have stabilized. They continue to maintain the full range of Jewish institutions, although the community is necessarily no more than a shadow of its former self. Nor is its future as certain as that of the other white groups. Before winning power the Zimbabwean-backed leadership had taken support from the Palestine Liberation Organization, hence the Zimbabwean government today is friendly with the PLO and will have nothing to do with Israel. The Jewish community has adopted a low profile, but it seems to be surviving on an attenuated basis.

The New Zealand Jewish Community[15]

Jews began to settle in New Zealand as early as 1829, with the arrival of the first English settlers. The first congregation was founded in Auckland in 1840 under the leadership of David Nathan, whose family remains the dominant Jewish family in New

Zealand to this day. The Jewish community in Wellington was founded three years later, and communities were founded in Christchurch and Dunedin in the 1860s.

New Zealand's isolation led to a slow, modest increase in the Jewish population over the years, with almost all Jews settling in Auckland and Wellington. New Zealand's restrictive immigration policy assured that almost all Jewish settlers came from Britain. A very small number came from eastern Europe or Germany but, like many other countries, New Zealand's borders were closed to Jewish refugees in the Hitler period. Thus the Anglo-Jewish model has been easily maintained. It has also been easy for the Jews to assimilate into the general population and many have done so over the years.[16] In the 1870s a Jew was prime minister and there have been several Jewish mayors in the major cities.

Each local community is built around a single congregation-center, formally Orthodox, although Auckland and Wellington also have small Liberal congregations. Auckland also has a small, seriously Orthodox congregation. The Jewish community follows the pattern of formal Orthodoxy and individual laxity characteristic of Anglo-Jewry. The religious situation is reflected not only in the decline of *kashrut* observance, but in the inability of even the Orthodox congregations to maintain three services daily. Both the Orthodox and Liberal congregations hold services only on Sabbaths and holidays.

Aside from the congregations, there are B'nai B'rith lodges in Wellington and Auckland, established in 1960 and 1961 respectively. Neither is particularly strong. All told, there are between four thousand and five thousand Jews in New Zealand today.

Power in the community is vested in the voluntary leadership of three congregations, many of whom are the descendants of the old families, who more or less inherit their positions by virtue of their family standing. There is a dwindling base from which voluntary leadership can be drawn; rabbis and other Jewish professionals must be brought in from the outside and are hard to recruit. Liberal congregations have the advantage of temporary rabbinical services from students at the Hebrew Union College–Jewish Institute of Religion who come out on their vacations. Because it does not have enough rabbis, the community does not have a Beit Din of its own, but relies on Australia.

Auckland has a day school, which survives by admitting non-Jewish children to augment its small Jewish enrollment potential. Wellington has not been able to do even that. An hour of Sunday school is what most Jewish children receive in the way of Jewish education.

Young people who want a more substantial Jewish education must go to Australia or elsewhere. There are two youth movements, Bnei Akiva and Habonim, which cooperate with each other.

There are Zionist Information Offices in Auckland and Wellington, a chapter of the Friends of the Hebrew University, and a New Zealand Jewish Students Association. WIZO is probably the most active Zionist body. The community is served by the *New Zealand Jewish Chronicle*.

The more energetic of New Zealand's Jewish youth leave the country after graduation from university. Those who are active in Jewish affairs at least try to settle in Israel. Others go to Australia.

Although the three major congregations are leagued in a common New Zealand Jewish Council, it only acts on the rare occasions when there is a need to bring a Jewish matter to the attention of the New Zealand government. The other countrywide Jewish activities are the Magbit under the aegis of Keren Hayesod, which is also conducted locally for all intents and purposes, the Jewish National Fund, and the Zionist Federation, which is quite weak. New Zealand Jews began raising money for the Jewish Yishuv in Eretz Israel as early as the Crimean War; by 1862 the first Jew from Israel had reached the country on a fund-raising mission. Fund-raising for Israel has continued ever since.

New World Congregational Communities

The six small island communities in the Caribbean are organized primarily as *local congregations* or *congregation-centers* (see figure 11.4). They include Barbados (population 70), Dominican Republic (100), Jamaica (350), Netherlands Antilles (700), Suriname (500), and Trinidad and Tobago (500). Although founded by Sephardim—ex-Marranos or their descendants—most were shaped by Dutch, English, and, more recently, American Jews and share the characteristics of those Jewries: full voluntarism and identification primarily through religious institutions. Their lack of size and the low level of interest of most local Jewish residents keep organized Jewish life in a neat framework that may mask grave weaknesses of morale and commitment.

These communities have been less affected organizationally than the larger communities by postwar changes. Although assimilation has been hastened, the rise of Israel has given them a previously lacking focus of interest, which they cultivate assiduously, as an anchor. Also, they are now attracting a small but steady immigration of American Jews.[17]

As the first permanent Jewish communities in the New World, they had a flourishing Jewish life during most of the seventeenth and eighteenth centuries, but have been in serious decline since the nineteenth. Marranos, who tried to distance themselves from the Inquisition by coming to the New World, benefited from the Dutch and English conquests in the Caribbean to emerge openly as Jews. They brought prosperity to the region

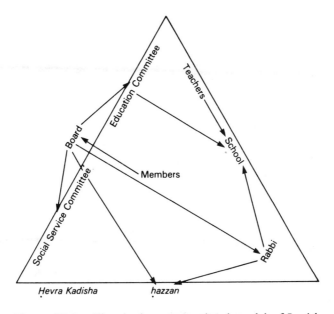

Figure 11.4.   The single congregational model of Jewish communal organization.

in return and built a network of organized communities, which at one time were a vital part of the Jewish world.[18]

The Jews of these communities went through the processes of settlement and acquisition of civil and political rights at the same time as the Jews of the Netherlands and England. In most cases, they became much more prominent in public affairs than their brethren back in the Old World because they represented a larger share of the white population and were, perhaps, the most energetic of the Europeans. In Suriname, a Jewish mini-state known as Joden-Savanne developed in the seventeenth century with an autonomous court and governing institutions in the framework of Dutch rule.

In the nineteenth century, the changing world economic situation and the abolition of slavery destroyed the economic base of the Caribbean region, and the Jews who had not assimilated began to emigrate in search of opportunity elsewhere, usually to the United States. Since then the Caribbean Jewish communities have been in general decline. This decline became more precipitous in the twentieth century because the small communities remaining were even more prone to losses through intermarriage and assimilation.

Today a maximum of five thousand Jews are left in the Caribbean region, most scattered among the island microstates and hence broken up into communities of a few hundred at most, unable to gain even the advantage of modest but growing numbers. Their synagogues are monuments to an unusual Jewish life that flourished during the first half of the modern epoch, and their survivors maintain syntheses of Portuguese rites, local culture, and American Reform and Conservative inclinations. With the recent rediscovery of the Caribbean as a vacation area and a tax haven, there has been a slight influx of Jews, mostly Ashkenazim from the United States. Besides adding population to existing communities, some five hundred of these Jews have settled in the Bahamas, others have scattered to other islands in the Caribbean, and there remain a hundred unorganized Jews in Haiti. If they combine with the twenty-five hundred American and Cuban Jews who have settled in Puerto Rico, these new settlers may at some point generate some new life in the Caribbean communities. Otherwise, their numbers in any one place will be too small to make a difference.

Jamaica. When the British conquered Jamaica from Spain in 1655 they were assisted by Sephardi Jews living on the island, who became protected subjects of the new rulers. The British conquest enabled the Jews to establish a community, and throughout the rest of the century there were additional inmigrations from South America and England. Jews, however, did not get full political rights until 1831, after which they became prominent in local public life. After a hiatus in the mid-nineteenth century, a new wave of immigration came at the century's end from the Levant, but many Jews also left the island because of the changed economic situation in the Caribbean.

Although Jews have established congregations in cities around the island in the past, at present about 90 percent of the 350 Jews remaining live in the Kingston area. The first congregations followed the Portuguese rite. An Ashkenazi congregation was established later. Efforts to merge them failed until 1921 when the original congregation Shaare Shalom became the United Congregation of Israelites. In its ritual it combines Sephardi, Conservative, and Reform practices. Jamaica is a congregational community and the United Congregation of Israelites maintains a home for the aged, a day school, and a supplementary religious school.

Netherlands Antilles. About seven hundred Jews live in this island polity, which is an associated state of the Netherlands. Jewish communities are found on Aruba and Curaçao. The first Jews settled in Aruba in 1753. The Jewish population dropped to no more than fifty throughout the nineteenth century, but after 1924 other Jews settled on the island from the Netherlands, Suriname, and eastern Europe. A Jewish center was established in 1942 and in 1946 a Jewish community was officially organized. A synagogue building was dedicated in 1962. The sole Jewish official is a *hazan*-teacher.

In Curaçao the Jewish community was founded as Mikveh Israel in 1651, but Jews were on the island from the time of the Dutch conquest in 1634. The Jewish community consisted almost entirely of Portuguese Jews linked to Amsterdam. It was legally recognized from the first, and the Jews have been fully active in the social, civic, and political life of the island.

The community grew during the seventeenth and eighteenth centuries, but throughout most of the eighteenth century it was involved in a series of disputes that required the intervention of the States-General in Holland and the local authorities. Matters improved in the nineteenth century, but internal rivalries continued to divide the community and led to the establishment of Temple Emanuel in 1864 as the first Sephardi Reform congregation in the world. Mikveh Israel and Emanuel merged in 1934, joined the World Union for Progressive Judaism, and adopted the Reconstructionist prayer book. A few Ashkenazim settled in Curacao after 1926, formed a club in 1932, and established a synagogue, Shaare Tzedek, in 1959.

Suriname. Suriname was a Dutch possession from the first generation of the seventeenth century until it gained independence at the end of the first postwar generation. Hence it was open to Jewish settlement at the very outset of the modern epoch. Jews had settled locally by 1639 and the community already had a rabbi by 1643. Hence Suriname is the oldest continuous Jewish community in the Western Hemisphere.

Groups of Jews continued to settle in Suriname throughout the seventeenth century, mostly fleeing the Inquisition in other parts of the Latin America or coming from the Sephardi congregations of western Europe. In the late seventeenth century there was a virtually independent Jewish state in Suriname, Joden Savanne, dominated by Jewish plantation owners who were probably the most powerful single economic force in the colony. The Portuguese Jewish settlers were joined by German Jews, who formed their own separate congregation in 1734. Although the number of Sephardim declined, the German Jewish community continued to grow and by 1836 exceeded the number of Sephardim.

The nineteenth century was one of economic decline because of the abolition of the slave trade in 1819 and the emancipation of the slaves in 1863. Suriname's plantation economy, which emphasized the growth of sugarcane, required cheap labor, and efforts in the late nineteenth century to maintain prosperity failed. Still, the Jewish population stood at fifteen hundred at the century's end. It declined rapidly after that, to about 750 in the mid-1920s and about five hundred today. The community is still organized into two Orthodox congregations: Neve Shalom and Sedek y Shalom. While the first was originally Ashkenazi and the second Sephardi, both now follow the Sephardic rite.[19] Regular services are held at Neve Shalom, which was restored in 1982–83. One hazzan serves both.

Notes

1. On Canadian Jewry, see, for example, Daniel J. Elazar and Harold M. Waller, eds., *The Governance of the Canadian Jewish Community* (Washington, D.C. and Jerusalem: University Press of America and Jerusa-

lem Center for Public Affairs, forthcoming); Stuart E. Rosenberg, *The Jewish Community in Canada* (Toronto: McClelland and Stewart, 1970–71); B. G. Sack, *History of the Jews in Canada,* trans. Ralph Novek (Montreal: Harvest House, 1960); M. Weinfeld, W. Shaffir, and I. Cotler, eds., *The Canadian Jewish Mosaic* (Toronto: J. Wiley, 1981).

2. Canadian Jewish Congress, *Fifty Years of Service, 1919–1969* (Montreal: Canadian Jewish Congress, 1970); *President's Report, National Reports, Regional Reports* (in one volume), Canadian Jewish Congress, 17th Plenary (Toronto, June 15–18, 1974); Harold M. Waller, *The Canadian Jewish Community: A National Perspective* (Jerusalem: Center for Jewish Community Studies, 1977); and Weinfeld et al., eds., *The Canadian Jewish Mosaic.*

3. Harvey Rich, *The Governance of the Jewish Community of Calgary* (Jerusalem: Center for Jewish Community Studies, 1974); Jennifer K. Bowerman, *The Governance of the Jewish Community of Edmonton* (Jerusalem: Center for Jewish Community Studies, 1975); Louis Greenspan, *The Governance of the Jewish Community of Hamilton* (Jerusalem: Center for Jewish Community Studies, 1974); Alan M. Cohen, *The Governance of the Jewish Community of London* (Jerusalem: Center for Jewish Community Studies, 1974); Harold M. Waller and Sheldon Schreter, *The Governance of the Jewish Community of Montreal* (Jerusalem: Center for Jewish Community Studies, 1974); Zachariah Kay, *The Governance of the Jewish Community of Ottawa* (Jerusalem: Center for Jewish Community Studies), 1974); Yaakov Glickman, *The Governance of the Jewish Community of Toronto* (Jerusalem: Center for Jewish Community Studies, 1974); Edna Oberman, *The Governance of the Jewish Community of Vancouver* (Jerusalem: Center for Jewish Community Studies, 1974); Anna Gordon, *The Governance of the Jewish Community of Winnipeg* (Jerusalem: Center for Jewish Community Studies, 1974).

4. Rosenberg, *The Jewish Community in Canada;* Evelyn Latowsky, "Three Toronto Synagogues: A Comparative Study of Religious Systems in Toronto," unpublished Ph.D. dissertation (University of Toronto, Department of Anthropology, 1969); Albert Rose, ed., *A People and Its Faith* (Toronto: University of Toronto Press, 1959); Michael Brown, "The Beginnings of Reform Judaism in Canada," *Jewish Social Studies,* vol. 34 (1972), pp. 322–42; Stuart Schoenfeld, "The Jewish Religion in North America: Canadian and American Comparisons," *Canadian Journal of Sociology,* 3 (1978), pp. 209–31; Morty Lazar and Sheva Medjeck, "Surveying Various Dimensions of Jewish Identification in Atlantic Canada," unpublished paper delivered at sixteenth annual meeting of Atlantic Association of Sociologists and Anthropologists, Sackville, N. B., Canada (March 1981).

5. Yaacov Glickman, "Ethnic Boundaries and the Jewish Parochial School in Toronto: The Inevitability of False Expectations," paper presented at the Conference of the Canadian Ethnic Studies Association held in Quebec City, November 4–6, 1977; United Jewish Welfare Fund of Toronto, *Study of Jewish Education* (Toronto: United Jewish Welfare Fund, 1975); Weinfeld et al.; Rosenberg, *The Jewish Community in Canada;* Elazar and Waller, *The Governance of the Canadian Jewish Community.*

6. Daniel J. Elazar with Peter Medding, *Jewish Communities in Frontier Societies* (New York: Holmes and Meier, 1983); Gustav Saron and Louis Hotz, eds., *The Jews in South Africa: A History* (Cape Town: Oxford University Press,1955); Steven Aschheim, "The Communal Organizations of South African Jewry," *Jewish Journal of Sociology,* vol. 12, no. 1 (June 1970), pp. 201–31.

7. Gideon Shimoni, *Jews and Zionism: The South African Experience, 1910–1967* (Cape Town: Oxford University Press, 1980).

8. Elazar with Medding, *Jewish Communities in Frontier Societies;* Edgar Bernstein, "A Bird's Eye View of South African Jewry Today," in *South African Jewry 1967–68* (Johannesburg: South African Jewish Board of Deputies, 1968). Also, the annual article on South Africa in the *American Jewish Year Book* contains basic information on developments in the Jewish educational sphere.

9. On Australian Jewry, see Elazar with Medding, *Jewish Communities in Frontier Societies;* Peter Y. Medding, ed., *Jews in Australian Society* (Melbourne: Macmillan/Monash, 1973); Walter Lippman, "Demography of Australian Jewry: Analysis of 1971 Census" (mimeographed) (Melbourne, 1975); and S. Encel, B. Buckley, and J. Sofer Schreiber, *The Sydney Jewish Community* (mimeographed) (Melbourne, 1972).

10. Encel, et al., *The Sydney Jewish Community;* L. M. Goldman, *The Jews in Victoria in the Nineteenth Century* (Melbourne: privately published, 1954); G. Solomon, "A Community History of Jewish Education in New South Wales and Victoria, 1788–1920," Ph.D. dissertation (Monash University, Melbourne, 1973); Ronald Taft and Geulah Solomon, "The Melbourne Jewish Community and the Middle East War of 1973," *Jewish Journal of Sociology,* vol. 26, no. 1 (June 1974), pp. 57–73; Peter Y. Medding, *From Assimilation to Group Survival: A Political and Sociological Study of an Australian Jewish Community* (Melbourne: F. W. Cheshire, 1968); S. Rutland, "The Jewish Community in New South Wales 1914–1939," M.A. thesis (University of Sydney, 1978).

11. Elazar with Medding, *Jewish Communities in Frontier Societies;* C. A. Price, *Jewish Settlers in Australia* (Canberra: Australia National University, 1964); Peter Y. Medding, "Orthodoxy, Liberalism, and Secularism in Melbourne Jewry," in *Jews in Australian Society*, pp. 41–60.

12. Elazar with Medding, *Jewish Communities in Frontier Societies;* I. Getzler, *Neither Toleration nor Favour: The Australian Chapter of Jewish Emancipation* (Melbourne: Melbourne University Press, 1970); Yosef Goell, "The Boomerang Effect," *Jerusalem Post* (June 3, 1983), pp. 4–5; G. Solomon, "A Community History of Jewish Education in New South Wales and Victoria" and "HaHinukh HaYehudi be-Australia," (Jewish Education in Australia) (Hebrew) *Tefutsot Yisrael*, vol. 17, no. 2 (June 1979), pp. 91–113.

13. Medding, *From Assimilation to Group Survival*, chap. 2.

14. See the field notes of Daniel J. Elazar on the Jewish community of Rhodesia (Zimbabwe). See also B. A. Kosmin, *Majuta: A History of the Jewish Community in Zimbabwe* (Gwelo: Mambo Press, 1981); Manyama Ngangura, "Future Bleak for Jews As Whites Flee Zimbabe," *The Canadian Jewish News* (October 17, 1984), p. 9; Geoffrey Wigoder, "The Jews of Rhodesia," *Jerusalem Post* (March 23, 1976).

15. For recent developments, see Stephen Levine, "New Zealand Jewry in Transition," *Jerusalem Letter* (1987) and the *American Jewish Year Book*. See also the field notes of Daniel J. Elazar on the Jewish community of New Zealand.

16. Geoffrey Wigoder, "The 5,000 Jews of New Zealand," *Jerusalem Post* (August 3, 1978); Lazarus Morris Goldman, *History of Jews in New Zealand* (Wellington: A. H. and A. W. Reed, 1958).

17. Ben Barber, "Endgame in Sosua," *The Jerusalem Post Magazine* (March 19, 1982), pp. 7–8; Lorna J. Sass, "Caribbean Jews: New Year in the Oldest Synagogue," *The Washington Post*, pp. D1, D4; Geoffrey Wigoder, "Rich and Vanishing Jews of Curaçao," *Jerusalem Post* (July 4, 1978) and "Settlers in the Sun," *The Jerusalem Post Magazine* (April 3, 1981), pp. 12–13; Frances P. Karner, *The Sephardics of Curaçao: A Study of Sociocultural Patterns in Flux* (Assen: Van Gorcum Ltd., 1969); Celia S. Rosenthal, "The Jews of Barranquilla," *Jewish Journal of Sociology*, (1956), pp. 262–74; Gaye Applebaum, "Jewish Family May Be the Last in Fading Montego Bay Community," *The Canadian Jewish News* (March 24, 1983), p. 53.

18. Zvi Loker, "Jewish Presence, Enterprise, and Migration Trends in the Caribbean," in Jeffrey K. Wilkerson, ed., *Cultural Traditions and Caribbean Identity: The Question of Patrimony* (Gainesville, Fla.: Center for Latin American Studies, University of Florida, 1980); Jacob Rader Marcus, "The West Indies and South American Expedition of the American Jewish Archives," *American Jewish Archives*, vol. 5, no. 1 (January 1953), pp. 5–21; Issac S. Emmanuel and Suzanne A. Emmanuel, *History of the Jews of the Netherlands Antilles*, 2 vols. (Assen and Cincinnati: Royal Van Gorcum, Ltd. and American Jewish Archives, 1970) and *Precious Stones of the Jews of Curaçao*, 2 vols. (Assen: Van Gorcum, Ltd., 1957); B. W. Korn, "Barbadian Jewish Wills," in *Bicentennial Festenschrift for Jacob Rader Marcus* (Waltham, Mass.: American Jewish Historical Society, 1976).

19. Hyman Kisch, "The Jewish Settlement from Central Europe in the Dominican Republic," Ph.D. dissertation (Jewish Theological Seminary, 1970); Mark Wischnitzer, "Historical Background of Settlement of Jewish Refugees in Santo Domingo," *Journal of Social Studies*, vol. 4, no. 1 (1942), pp. 50–58. On the Jewish community of Suriname, see P. A. Hilfman, "Notes on the History of the Jews in Suriname," *Publications of the American Jewish Historical Society*, no. 18 (1909), pp. 179–208; Beller, *Jews in Latin America;* Emmanuel, *History of the Jews of the Netherlands Antilles;* Manfred Lehmann, "Our Own Banana Republic," *The Jerusalem Post Magazine* (April 7, 1978), pp. 6–7.

12

Argentina and Brazil: Similarities and Contrasts

In the 1970s Latin American Jewry crossed the same threshold that United States Jewry did right after World War II, when the first generation passed from the scene and their native-born descendants assumed the central roles in communal life. But Latin America is not like the United States. In many respects, Latin America represents the most difficult context for Jewish life outside the Communist bloc. The countries of Latin America have old, established cultures with clear identities on one level. Yet they suffer from classic Third World problems of underdevelopment, a sense of inferiority vis-à-vis the developed countries, and a penchant for xenophobia that accompanies those two phenomena. Because of the peculiarities of the established Latin American cultures, even the Jews who have been attracted to assimilate within them do so with reservations. They are more likely to become revolutionaries than integrated into the mainstream societies of the countries of their residence.[1]

The Jewish Confrontation with Latin America

Increasing numbers of Latin American Jews are in limbo, neither identifying with the ways of their parents and grandparents nor finding a place in their host countries. As a result, most have developed a strong penchant to concentrate on money-making and leisure time activities, with their businesses and their sports, or, more properly, country clubs being central in their lives. The fact that the major binding Jewish institution in most Latin countries is the sports club speaks for itself.

Because of the difficulties they have in assimilating without ceasing to be Jewish, their closeness to an immigrant past, and their identification with Israel as their *madre patria,* there is a Jewish nucleus interested in promoting a strong separate Jewish existence. That nucleus focuses on Jewish integral (meaning comprehensive) schools, which have the advantage of attracting a very high proportion of Jewish youth because of the high quality of the general education they offer, particularly in contrast with the government schools. Such schools are the one visible achievement of the Jewish communities of Latin America. The separation of the Jewish population from the general population, coupled with the lack of adequate public educational facilities, has led every Jewish community in Latin America to establish Jewish day schools.

The first international census of Jewish schools in the diaspora, conducted in the early 1980s, covering kindergarten through secondary education, reported 159 Jewish schools in Latin America—103 in Argentina, 22 in Brazil, and 33 in the other countries. They enrolled more than 47,000 students; more than 21,000 in Argentina, more than

10,000 in Brazil, and more than 15,000 in the other countries, principally in the kinder-gartens and elementary schools. Overall, somewhere between 61 and 65 percent, nearly two-thirds of all school-age Jewish children, were enrolled in Jewish schools at the time of the census, with between 62 and 66 percent of the Jewish children in Argentina, 47 to 51 percent in Brazil, and 69 to 73 percent in other countries. Because the free diaspora world average was estimated in the same census at 41 to 45 percent, even Brazil's relatively low figure was above average.

The primary purpose of these schools is to provide a good general education for Jewish children to enable them to advance in life, and in some day schools the Jewish educational component is minimal. In others, however, Jewish schools have succeeded in teaching the students to speak Hebrew. Latin American Jews have a penchant for learn-ing foreign languages, which, in many ways, is the Latin American measure of being cultured. One of the strengths of the Jewish schools is that they are so good that in many of the smaller Latin American countries children of the non-Jewish elite, including the highest government officials, attend them to benefit from the quality education they provide.

Judith Laikin Elkin and others have suggested that Zionism is the religion of Latin American Jews. A recent survey by the London-based Institute of Jewish Affairs discov-ered that out of 510 Jewish faculty members at Mexican universities, only 143 belonged to synagogues, that is *kehillot,* while 406 contributed to the Magbit. Communal elections to the major *kehillot* are conducted along Israeli lines with the local political parties reflecting the Israeli and Zionist party system. The Israeli ambassador is automatically regarded as one of the community leaders, while the Magbit is perhaps the most unifying force in community after community.

The Israeli presence in Latin America is especially vital in the educational system. Between the two education departments of the World Zionist Organization, approxi-mately 150 Israeli teachers are regularly present in the region, fully or partially paid from Israeli or world Jewish sources. A very high percentage of indigenous Latin American Jewish teachers have received all or part of their training from the Hayim Greenberg and Gold Institutes in Jerusalem, the first for secular and the second for religious schools.

Traditional religion, on the other hand, plays a very minor role in what are basically secular communities. Its status is further diminished by the lack of religious functionar-ies, which dates to the earliest days of Latin American Jewry. One proof of how impor-tant the lack of such leadership is is found in the success of Conservative Rabbi Marshall Meyer, who in twenty-five years of service in Buenos Aires, built a Conservative move-ment that has mobilized thousands of otherwise irreligious Argentinian Jews, bringing them to some form of Jewish religion and actively into Jewish institutions. The Ortho-dox rabbis who are available, except for a few Israelis who have come to try to stimulate commitment to Judaism, are religious functionaries in the narrow sense.

Until the 1960s there were no locally born rabbis in Latin America. In that decade some Latin American Jews trained for the rabbinate in the United States came back home to take congregations. In 1962 Rabbi Meyer founded the Seminario Rabbinico. Only about 10 percent of its more than 300 students are in the eight-year rabbinical program. It was only a decade later that it began to produce indigenous rabbis for Latin American Jewry. Its graduates now are serving in congregations in Argentina, Brazil, Chile (both major congregations), Colombia, Peru, and Venezuela. Perhaps as a result of the Conser-vative movement's success, Israeli and other Orthodox groups, including Agudath Israel, Mizrachi, Chabad, and Satmar, have begun to send Israeli-trained rabbis and to train

Latin American students for the rabbinate in Israel to try to develop a parallel revival in the direction of Orthodoxy.

There is also a small Reform, or Progressive, movement, principally in Argentina and Brazil. By Reform or even Conservative standards, their religious practices are very traditional. What makes them unique is their outreach to youth through youth groups and summer camps and even more important, their willingness to convert non-Jews who wish to marry Jews and to bring them into the Jewish fold. Those conversions, of course, are not recognized by the Orthodox rabbinate.

Thus there is something of a captive audience for the other Jewish survivalist parties—Zionist, religious, Yiddishist—to try to influence. Whether they influence that audience beyond those who naturally lean in their direction is a matter of conjecture. Radical leftist views are at least as strong a force among the youth as is Jewish nationalist sentiment and probably much stronger. The two are not necessarily mutually exclusive; radical sentiments are often expressed even in the Jewish setting, often to the discomfiture of Israelis and Zionist elders, especially when in support for the Palestinian Arabs' demands for statehood.

Anti-Semitism. As a result of the Inquisition and the powerful role of the Catholic church, Latin America, especially the Hispanic countries, became anti-Semitic before Jews openly resided in them. This continuation of medieval anti-Semitism was further fueled by the post-independence struggle between the church and the liberal, meaning anti-clerical, forces. By and large the struggle was won by the conservatives, even if certain lip service came to be paid to liberal doctrines.

The only countries where church disestablishment can be said to be at least formally complete are Chile and Mexico, and full disestablishment there came only in the 1920s. Most countries at least require that the president must be a Roman Catholic. Even in Argentina and Uruguay, where the tendency is to separate church and state in practice, there is no formal separation, and Jews have had to struggle for rights that in the English-speaking world were taken for granted, such as the right to perform Jewish marriages or to have their children registered without being baptized (a right achieved in Argentina only in 1877). The Argentinian military establishment remains closed to Jews, who cannot rise above the rank of captain. In most countries, anti-Semitism is chronic and endemic, mitigated only by the Latin American character, which keeps it from being systematic.

Today anti-Semitism in Latin America is linked with anti-Zionism and the anti-Israel stance of the left. In 1982, following false reports of Israeli responsibility for the Lebanese Christian massacre of the Palestinians in Sabra and Shatilla, there was a spate of violent anti-Semitic incidents across the continent. On the other hand, the story of the disproportionate number of Jewish victims among those of the Argentinian military regime's crackdown against urban guerillas is well know. Thus local Jews are assaulted by anti-Semites of both left and right.

World Jewry has made it clear that they will use the economic means at their disposal, principally tourist boycotts, wherever possible to help curb any official support of anti-Jewish or anti-Israel activities. Still, as a result of this perennial insecurity, many of the wealthier Latin American Jews have refuges elsewhere.

Ashkenazim and Sephardim. By and large, discussions of Latin American Jewry focus on the Ashkenazi majority. They dominate the communities, have the strongest connections with their brethren overseas, and produce whatever is written about community life. In fact, approximately one-fifth of the Jewish population of Latin America is

Sephardi, heavily Syrian in composition but with many also from the Balkans and North Africa. These Sephardi Jews maintain their own communal organizations and, because the old-country tie has been the preeminent basis for Jewish continuity, the gap between Ashkenazim and Sephardim has been consistently greater than perhaps anywhere else in the Jewish world. In some countries the Sephardi communities are part of the overall communal confederation, but that is not always so. In Mexico, for example, for many years Ashkenazim refused to accept Sephardi meat as kosher because Sephardim tradition- ally remove the tendon in the hindquarter and the Askhenazim do not.

The Sephardim, despite their smaller numbers, have just as much of a penchant to fragment among country, city, or region-of-origin groups as did the Ashkenazim, so that their weight in the community is even further diminished. Their adjustment, however, has been better in every respect. First, coming from a Mediterranean environment, they fitted into a Latin culture more easily. The Ladino-speaking ones did not even have a language problem, and in general so much of their culture was like that of the new environment that culture shock was minimal. Nor were they looked on as strangers by the indigenous population for the same reasons.

This also had Jewish dimensions. The Sephardim had already learned how to perpetu- ate Jewish life in an environment like that they discovered in Latin America. Moreover, they had not undergone the wrenching of emancipation and even radicalization, which had been the lot of the Jews from central and eastern Europe. Thus, they maintained the old familial and congregational structures that they brought with them and formed a basis for Jewish life in the new setting. As a result, the Sephardim are more Jewish in a traditional way than their Ashkenazi counterparts, although even their children are beginning to feel the effects of the local environment. Perhaps Sephardi assimilation was slowed by yet another factor. The tendency among many Sephardic families, especially those of Syrian background, is to go into business and not to send their children to university, thus eliminating one of the major vehicles encouraging assimilation.

Today there is a Sephardi revival in Latin America, one of the most hopeful signs in Latin American Jewish life. It is most pronounced in Argentina, Brazil, and Venezuela. For the most part it has taken the form of a new associationalism among the younger Sephardim, a movement into more modern and cosmopolitan forms of organization, as distinct from the traditional and highly localistic synagogue. In essence this revival may be considered part of their modernization and secularization; it is something to watch.

The eastern European Jews who immigrated to Latin America in the twentieth century established replicas of the European *kehillah,* without official status but tacitly recognized by Jews and non-Jews alike as the organized Jewish community. The central institutions of these communities have a distinctly public character but no special recogni- tion in public law.[2] Founded by secularists, these communities were built in the mold of modern diaspora nationalism and emphasize the secular side of Jewish life. Because they function in an environment that provides neither the cultural nor the legal framework for a European-model *kehillah,* they must rely on the voluntary attachment of their members. The Latin American communities were successful in maintaining this corporate pattern until recently, because the great social and cultural gap between the Jews and their neighbors aided in giving the Jews a self-image as a special and distinct group, but it has become increasingly difficult to do so as the gap disappears.

Ashkenazim and Sephardim organized separate communities, some by region or city of origin. Just as the Jewish immigrants did not assimilate into their host societies, so, too, they did not assimilate among themselves. In time, these communities loosely confederated to deal with common problems that emerged in their relations with their external environment, chiefly problems of immigration, anti-Semitism, and Israel. Each region-of-origin community, however, retains substantial if not complete autonomy in internal matters and control over its institutions.

Another major difference between Ashkenazim and Sephardim is that the Ashkenazi *kehillot,* as secular ones, were clearly within the *keter malkhut* and indeed had little place for the other *keterim,* whereas the Sephardi congregational communities, as more traditional ones, were located at the nexus between the *keter kehunah* and the *keter torah,* with emphasis on the former. Thus each was rooted in a different domain and consequently organized on different premises. Because the Ashkenazim came to be the overwhelming majority in most Latin American countries, the *keter malkhut* institutions became dominant, and because neither community had much concern with the institutions of the *keter torah,* it remained the weakest domain of all, contributing to the endemic weakness in Jewish life, especially among the young.

In Argentina, Brazil, and Colombia the indigenous federal or quasi-federal structures of the countries themselves influenced the Jews to create countrywide confederations based on territorial divisions, officially uniting state or provincial communities that are, in fact, local communities concentrated in the state or provincial capitals. In the others, the local community containing most of the Jewish population became the countrywide unit, usually by designating its federation as the "council of communities." The community councils of the six Central American countries (Jewish population approximately 7,250) have organized the Federation of Central American Jewish Communities to pool resources and provide services, but it is little more than a paper organization.

One of the extraordinary aspects of the Latin American Jewish communities is their commitment to real elections based on contests between the Zionist and other parties. Not only is this unusual in the Jewish world, but considering the lack of stable electoral politics in most of Latin America it is doubly unique. This is part of the *kehillah* heritage that the Ashkenazim brought with them from eastern Europe as modified by the Zionist commitment of most Latin American Jews.

Although participation in elections has been declining for the past generation, in part because the parties that compete for office are irrelevant to the younger generation, the very fact that the system remains is testimony to the democratic republicanism rooted in the Jewish political tradition and how it survives even under adverse circumstances. Nevertheless, the external world influences the governance of the *kehillot.* Despite the elections the same leadership retains office for decades and if there is a change in leadership it is often accompanied by a period of disorganization bordering on anarchy until a new leadership can reestablish control.

Also imported from eastern Europe was the struggle between the Zionists and the Communists. It is fair to say that every major Latin American community was the scene of a bitter conflict between the two groups. In every one the Zionists triumphed so that the *kehillot* today are all Zionist in their orientation, so much so that the Magbit (Keren Hayesod) provides the major arena for active cooperation on the part of all elements of the community.

Because the Jews are effectively excluded from national politics in most countries except for marginal cases, the *kehillot* become outlets for the political energy of Jews who do not leave the community to integrate with the left. At the same time, the *kehillot* protect the neutrality of the Jewish communities vis-à-vis the external politics of their respective countries. Their aim is to maintain good relations with any government in power and to no small extent they are prepared to stifle dissent within the Jewish community if necessary to do that. That is part of the price of survival in Latin America.

This course of action has both positive and negative consequences. It has enabled Latin American Jewry to survive in a very volatile region, but as with any cautious and defense politics, it alienates the young people who are searching for a more aggressive orientation, particularly in the realm of social reform, a crying need in Latin America. Thus the youth tend to be turned off by the communal institutions and many seek their own political outlets with the radical movements. They find their models in the successive generations of left-wing Jewish intellectuals, who have made important contributions to the larger society.

Even Zionist youth movements such as Hashomer Hatzair have contributed a disproportionate share of Jews who have assumed positions in government, especially the revolutionary governments in Chile and Cuba. Those figures have, as one would expect, dropped their associations with the Jewish people in the process. In something of a continuation of the old Communist-Zionist struggle, the Jewish leftists consider the *kehillot* reactionary outposts of American and Israeli imperialism and therefore to be shunned, while the leaders of the *kehillot* look upon the leftists as dangerous radicals who imperil the Jewish community and therefore to be shunned.

None of these tacitly recognized communal structures have been in existence more than three generations, and the communities themselves originated no more than four generations ago. Most of the smaller ones are just now entering their third generation since they were created by the refugees of the 1930s and 1940s. Consequently, many if not most are still developing an appropriate and accepted communal character.

Not surprisingly, then, the elements of a constitutional crisis of the first magnitude are already present in the Latin American communities. To the extent that a communal structure, based on local territorial divisions rather than on the *landsman* principle, is emerging in these communities, with its accompanying substructure of associational activities whose participants are drawn in because of common interest rather than common descent, this constitutional crisis is being overcome through the rise of new institutions.

The emergence of the Jewish sports or community centers as factors in the local Jewish communities is the major manifestation of this change. As part of their secular ethnic identity, Latin American Jews early on developed sports clubs where they could spend their leisure time associating with one another. Until the 1960s those clubs were essentially private bodies with no Jewish content other than the fact that they were ethnically Jewish. Since then there has been a gradual strengthening of their Jewish and communal character. Their leaders represent the core of the younger generation of Jewish leadership in community after community.

In demographic terms, Latin American Jewry has apparently reached its peak and begun to decline at an even more rapid rate than other diaspora Jewries. Schmelz and Della Pergola estimate that there is a shrinkage of one percent annually through low birthrate, assimilation, and emigration.[3] Not only do the highly urbanized Jews of that region share the general trend in the diaspora of low birthrates, but the region has witnessed an accelerating emigration of Jews, at least since the 1970s. It is estimated that one-fifth of those Jews native to Latin America have settled in Israel and another fifth in the United States, with smaller percentages settling in Europe. Many Jews fleeing Allende's Chile, for example, settled in West Germany, while many Jewish radicals from Argentina went to Spain.

The marked increase in out-marriage indicates that some resolve the dilemmas of being Jewish in Latin America by abandoning the Jewish fold. The Jewish response to intermarriage in Latin America almost assures that those who marry out will stay out. Even the secularists accept the most rigid strictures of Orthodoxy regarding conversions, perhaps because as outsiders they are uncomfortable admitting born non-Jews into their ranks. This "hard line" position is justified as setting an example to young people to avoid intermarriage. Still the intermarriage rate is accelerating as university education becomes the norm for young Jews and, as elsewhere, the university brings them in contact with non-Jews on an equal basis.

Jewish immigration to Latin America has virtually ceased. The last significant influx of Jews took place in 1967 when several thousand Jewish refugees from Egypt settled in Brazil and Venezuela. Even if the restrictive immigration laws that exist in all Latin American countries were not sufficiently discouraging, the Jews themselves would not seek to go to the region. To the contrary, since 1960 there have been substantial out-migrations of Jews from Argentina, Chile, Colombia, Cuba, El Salvador, Mexico, and Nicaragua.

The very modest in-migration of Jews to Ecuador and Venezuela during the same years as a result of the oil boom pales into insignificance in comparison with the out-migration. The only country where the Jewish population seems stable, if not comfortable, and at least plans on remaining for the near future is Brazil. That country, which occupies half the continent, has had a period of economic expansion and capitalist development punctuated, it is true, by economic difficulties but generally upward in a trend of the kind that attracts or holds Jews. As always, the proportion of the "best and the brightest" among the emigrants is high, thereby further weakening the communities that remain behind.

The wave of democratization in Latin America in the 1980s opened the doors for greater participation by Jews in public life, as electoral officials and senior policy-makers, in the universities, and in the mass media. For the first time, many of these prominent people retained serious ties with the Jewish community. At the same time, there are the beginnings of a religious revival in many Latin American communities, through the growing Conservative movement, new and vigorous concentrations of ultra-Orthodox Jews, and in the Sephardic congregations.

The two major Jewish communities in Latin America are Argentina and Brazil, the former with somewhere between 235,000 and 330,000 Jews and the latter with between 100,000 and 150,000. (The wildly divergent estimates of Jewish population are themselves part of the Latin American syndrome.) Whatever future there lies in Latin American Jewry as more than a holding operation lies in these two communities. Argentinian Jewry has been declining as a result of emigration even more than assimilation, while Brazilian Jewry, despite its long-standing assimilatory tendencies, has been growing.

In both cases these Jewries reflect the countries in which they are located. Argentina, which has been de-developing since the beginning of the twentieth century, is presently enjoying a "window" of democracy, but has not overcome its seemingly perpetual socioeconomic crisis. Brazil, on the other hand, despite the fluctuations in its own economic and political situation, has been generally on an upward path in this century and is widely recognized as the awakening giant of Latin America. As always, the Jews are responding accordingly.

The Argentinian Jewish Community

How many Jews are in Argentina is in dispute. The local community for many years estimated its population at half a million. Recent demographic studies have suggested that it is closer to 235,000. Although the first is clearly an overestimate, the second seems to be an underestimate, with the actual figure somewhere between 265,000 and 330,000.

The organization of Argentinian Jewry follows a pattern common to most Latin American Jewries. As groups of Jews reached the shores of Argentina, they established different face-to-face associations—such as synagogues, cemetery associations, *landsmanschaften,* and benevolent societies—based on old-country ties. These localistic organizations provided a collective framework that helped them settle in their new home. However, because they also reinforced the differences among different groups of Jews, the establishment of more comprehensive structures was made difficult.[4]

Within a short time, the strong corporate dimension in Jewish life asserted itself and at least some Jews sought to create more comprehensive frameworks. The need to combat anti-Semitism became a catalyst for the first efforts to build a common structure for Argentinian Jewry. As always, federalism provided the way to recognize yet overcome localism. Argentina, like every other Jewish community, developed federal arrangements of a kind suited to its circumstances: loose confederations of *landsman* organizations dominated by the largest constituent, and tacitly recognized as the Jewish "address" by the authorities. Exactly what has emerged is a matter of dispute among students of Argentinian Jewry. This, in itself, reflects the peculiar ephemerality of that Jewry as an organized entity.[5]

In a sharp reflection of their general marginality and alienation, those who tried to build Jewish life took the *kehillah* patterns they knew from Europe and tried to transpose them to the Argentinian setting. Consequently, the "new" institutions reflected the commitments and quarrels of another time and place, helping to preserve them almost as museum pieces long after they disappeared elsewhere. Originally hailed by Zionists and Jewish nationalists outside Latin America as exemplary structures, in contrast with the institutions of United States Jewry, in the end the *kehillot* have proved to have inherent structural weaknesses directly derived from their lack of relevance to local conditions.[6]

The evolution of Jewish communal and organizational structures in Argentina has both reflected and shaped the growth of the Jewish community. Because more than 80 percent of the Jews live in the Buenos Aires metropolitan area (which may, indeed, contain more than half of the Jews living south of the Rio Grande), a discussion of Jewish communal and organizational structures in Argentina must focus primarily on the federal capital, and only secondarily on the provinces. The congruences of "Jewish organizations of Argentina" and "Jewish organizations of Buenos Aires" is even greater than the population figures alone might indicate, because the principal activities of every "countrywide" organization are in Buenos Aires.

The communal-welfare sphere. The first effort to establish a comprehensive structure for Argentinian Jewry was in 1909, when the short-lived Federación Israelita Argentina was established. It included the Hevra Kadisha (burial society), Talmud Torah (school), Ezra (a welfare society and hospital), and representatives of Zionist and labor groups. Although it failed, it set the direction for more such efforts. In 1916, a more broadly based group made a second effort, convening a "Congress of Argentinian Jews." This time, the old-line Jewish Congregation of Buenos Aires and three Sephardi communities were also willing to join, and the towns in the interior were also represented. Still, the result was more symbolic than real and remained so through the 1920s.

Today, six communal bodies constitute the building blocks of the Argentinian Jewish community: the four distinct Sephardi communities of Buenos Aires; the Asociación Mutua Israelita Argentina (AMIA), which is essentially the Ashkenazi community of Buenos Aires; and the Federación de Comunidades Israelitas (in Hebrew, the Va'ad Ha-Kehillot), which serves as the umbrella organization for the Jewish communities in the provinces. The oldest of the four Sephardi communities is the Congregación Israelita Latina (Jewish Latin Congregation), founded in 1891 by the first immigrants from Morocco and other parts of North Africa. This community has been seriously weakened by intermarriage and assimilation, and by 1968 had only three hundred registered members.

The Asociación Israelita Sefardi Argentina (AISA) was founded in the early years of the twentieth century by Jews from Aleppo. They were later joined by emigrants from the Caucasus and in the 1920s and 1930s from what was then Palestine. "From its inception, this community was distinguished by its extremely religious character and by the close attachment of the majority of its members to their communal institutions."[7] In 1968, the membership of the AISA was about twenty-five hundred.

The third Sephardi community was founded in 1913 by Jews from Damascus, who, in Argentina, as elsewhere, preferred to maintain a distinct distance from the Aleppans. Founded as a burial society and a means of arbitrating disputes among its members, it has come to provide extensive religious and educational services. It was estimated to have thirty-five hundred members in 1968.

The fourth Sephardi communal organization is the Asociación Comunidad Israelita Sefardi de Buenos Aires (ACIS), which grew out of the union of the Ladino-speaking congregations that had established neighborhood synagogues as early as 1914. In 1942 they united to form a single organization for emigrants from Turkey, Rhodes, and the Balkans. The separate character of each congregation continued to be maintained, even to the point where one important synagogue in the community became Conservative while the others have remained Orthodox. The Ladino-speaking community was third in size among the Sephardi communities of Buenos Aires in 1968, with 2,365 member families representing about 7,600 people.[8]

The Sephardim have never developed an effective organization embracing all of these communities. The Argentinian branch of the World Sephardi Federation has been trying to provide a common meeting ground for Sephardim, but most of that stimulus has come from outside the country, with all the limitation that implies. Nevertheless, today the Delegación d'Entidades Sefarditas coordinates Sephardi activities for Israel, and the Entidad Coordinación Sefardita (ECSA) coordinates and integrates activities of the Sephardi communities in Argentina.

The Jewish Congregation of Buenos Aires is the oldest organization in the Ashkenazi community, dating from the 1860s. As the eastern Europeans came, more congregations were founded, the Ashkenazi community became larger and more factionalized, and the demand for a central organizational framework grew. The first organization of financial importance was the Hevrah Kadisha Ashkenazi. This body maintained its monopoly of a service every Jew needed: burial in a Jewish cemetery. Even in a secularized community such as that of the Ashkenazi Jews of Buenos Aires, burial in a Jewish cemetery was considered essential. The Hevrah Kadisha acquired funds from membership fees and payment for burial services. Eventually, there was an increasingly large annual surplus, which was used to meet the financial, social, and cultural needs of its members. "The 'Hevrah Kaddisha' acquired an increasingly central position and in practice an increasingly communal character long before it constituted itself, in 1949, the 'Ashkenazi Community of Buenos Aires.' "[9]

By that time the AMIA had come to include German and central European Jews besides the eastern European Jews who had founded it. As its membership and budget grew, its activities became increasingly diverse. By 1970, for example, it provided 40 percent of the budget of every school associated with its education committee and a tuition subsidy for every pupil in any Jewish school, and not only to pupils in its own schools.

Membership in the AMIA peaked in 1968, with 46,304 member families. Since the beginning of the 1970s, however, membership has declined, despite a minimum annual dues requirement. By 1978, about 20 percent of its membership had dropped out. Nevertheless, the AMIA remains the largest single Jewish organization in Argentina.

The concern of the AMIA has broadened from the Ashkenazi community alone to the future of Argentinian Jewry. The AMIA maintains teachers' seminaries in Buenos Aires and Moisesville, the first of the agricultural colonies, in the province of Santa Fe. It sponsors a network of clubs, cultural activities, and educational projects for the Jewish community, besides subsidizing the budgets of other educational institutions already engaged in such programs. It maintains a *bet din* and a department of religious and rabbinical matters, which constitutes the Orthodox "establishment" in Buenos Aires. It also engages in extensive welfare programs and Zionist activities.

The Federación de Comunidades Israelites has constituent communities in Rosario, Córdoba, Mendoza, Tucumán, and Bahia Blanca. It provides a field-worker who visits the communities to consult with them on educational and communal matters, but the local organizations are generally weak and suffer from the apathy of the local Jews.

The welfare and economic organizations of Argentinian Jewry had their origins in the years when masses of poor Jewish emigrants were arriving from eastern Europe. Earlier emigrants who had already begun to establish themselves set up philanthropic agencies based on different models, resulting in community- or congregation-sponsored clinics, hospitals, and old-age homes.

There were also mutual aid societies organized by settlers from the same village, town, or region. There were trade cooperatives established by the "Jewish" professions: tailors, painters, furriers, knitting manufacturers, furniture and iron goods makers, and so on. There were Jewish banks and credit cooperatives, the most well known being the Banco Israelita del Rio de la Plata, which financed many Jewish enterprises during the forty years of its existence. Its collapse in 1962 precipitated the breakdown of the old Jewish communal order in Argentina.[15] The subsequent collapse of the credit cooperatives in 1970 because of mismanagement completed the job.[16]

The major positive development in the communal-welfare sphere has been the emergence of the great community centers where Argentinian Jews gather to be with one another, as forces in communal life, offering a basis for a pattern of communal organization that will reflect the new Argentinian Jewish reality. The community centers date to the early 1900s when they were organized as sports clubs, but their real expansion came in the postwar generation. Founded as private associations, their role in Jewish life was minimal until recently, when a new generation of leaders came to realize that they must translate these gathering places into vehicles for promoting Jewish identity and survival.

As in every other aspect of communal life, Sephardim and Ashkenazim remain separate in their recreational activities. The Sephardim maintain their Club Atlético Sefardi Argentina (CASA) founded in the early 1900s, which is now ten thousand members strong. Unlike other clubs, CASA maintains a kosher dining room and closes on the Sabbath and Jewish holidays. It expanded its physical plant in the late 1970s.

The oldest Ashkenazi club is the Sociedad Hebraica Argentina, known as the SHA, or the Hebraica, which celebrated its sixtieth anniversary in 1986. It is also the largest, with about twenty-two thousand members. Besides its comprehensive sports program, the SHA offers many social and cultural activities, like those offered by a North American Jewish community center. It cooperates with the Jewish Agency to provide Israel programming and a leadership-training school. It also maintains the largest Jewish library in the country.

Club Nautico Hacoah, more than forty years old, maintains an eleven-story building in Buenos Aires besides its water sports facility twenty miles outside the city in the Tigre resort region. It has eleven thousand members. Maccabi maintains a sports and a cultural program, organizing study groups and university seminars. Its membership is more than nine thousand. It has a building in Buenos Aires and a camping area in the suburbs.

In line with the trend toward greater Jewish involvement, in 1977 the major centers established the Argentina Federation of Maccabi Community Centers (FACCMA) to link them all in their efforts to strengthen Jewish identity. Thirty institutions, Ashkenazi and Sephardi, with a combined membership of twenty-five thousand families, were included in the new federation. The Hebraica, the largest affiliated center, provided FACCMA with office space. The new organization absorbed the older Argentine Maccabi Federation (FAM), which was concerned only with competitive sports. Although the sports program has been continued, FACCMA is specifically committed to strengthening Jewish identity and the revitalization of the Zionist idea.[17] The new body immediately affiliated with the World Confederation of Jewish Community Centers.

The success of these transformed sports clubs reflects the need secular Jews have to find Jewish associations in keeping with their affluent status and the country's general commitment to leisure activities. The cultural activities of the sports clubs are much less popular than their recreational activities. Still, they are beginning to provide a base for the development of a new organizational structure that may overcome the apathy that overwhelms the older, more traditional Jewish organizations.

The external relations–defense sphere. The external relations–defense sphere became the locus for the limited comprehensive communal organization that has emerged. The deep fissures in Argentinian Jewry have kept matters that way. The Delegación de la Asociaciones Israelitas Argentinas (DAIA) is the only group that unites the organizations of the eastern European Ashkenazic, Sephardic, and central European Jews, the Zionist parties, B'nai B'rith, *landsmanschaften,* the major religious congregations, and the major sports organizations. Even fund-raising groups such as the Society of Friends of the Hebrew University are members of the DAIA. (The name of this and other Jewish organizations follows the Spanish usage of *Israelita* rather than *Judia,* which has negative connotations going back to the days of the Inquisition.)

The rise of anti-Semitism in Argentina led to the need to guard the religious rights of the Jewish community. But despite efforts in 1909 and 1916, no roof organization was established.[10] The demand for such a body was further stimulated by an event central to the collective memory of Argentinian Jewry, the Semana Tragica (the tragic week) of 1919: an old-fashioned European-style pogrom. In response, a central committee was

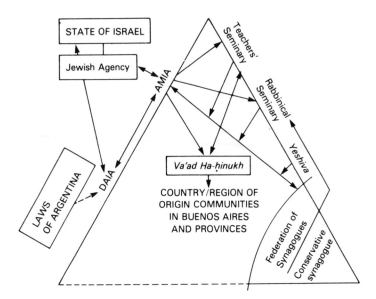

Figure 12.1. The Jewish community in Argentina.

organized, but it disbanded as soon as the crisis had passed. This pattern of temporary alliances formed to deal with specific problems continued during the 1920s.

Ultimately, the emergence of German "scientific anti-Semitism" and its widely popular reception in the Argentine sparked the creation of the first permanent body: the Committee against the Persecution of the Jews in Germany, founded in 1933. It became the Committee against Racialism and Anti-Semitism in 1934, and the DAIA in 1935.

Twenty-eight organizations, all from Buenos Aires, joined the DAIA. These included communal, political, welfare, economic and mutual credit, and cultural and educational organizations. Every major Jewish group operating within the communal consensus was included, with only the Communist and Anarchist organizations remaining outside.[11] The DAIA was constituted on a confederal model; each member organization had equal representation in its general assembly regardless of its size or importance. The larger member organizations frequently complained that tiny, insignificant organizations had the same two votes they did and often sought to change this structure.

Throughout the history of the DAIA, the organization has tried to avoid identification with any party or movement on the Argentinian political scene, to protect itself and the Jewish community in a highly political environment. The Jews are frequently accused of being outsiders, of maintaining dual loyalties, and of not being "true Argentinians." These charges make the community even more reluctant to take sides in political disputes, for "if the side they chose should lose, they would be blamed for the loss by their non-Jewish colleagues, and they would be the first to be punished by the victors."[12]

During its first decade, the DAIA developed a program of information, counterpropaganda, and defense against the verbal and physical attacks of the anti-Semitic and overtly Nazi groups in Argentina. Its second decade coincided with the Perón regime. As the official representative of the Jews of Argentina, the DAIA was put under tremendous pressure to publicly support and identify with Perón. Adhering to its guiding principle of nonidentification, the DAIA refused, and the Perónist Organización Israelita Argentina was established as its rival. This organization also affirmed that it represented all Argentin-ian Jewry and enjoyed Perón's support. Although it failed to bring about the demise of the DAIA, it succeeded in severely damaging those of its activities that involved the state authorities. Partially because of external support from the World Jewish Congress, the State of Israel, and the World Zionist Organization, the DAIA continued its leadership role in the Argentinian Jewish community. By the end of its second decade its member-ship had risen to ninety Jewish organizations in Buenos Aires and sixty-five more in the interior.[13]

The DAIA assisted in founding the Latin American section of the World Jewish Congress and has been its mainstay in Latin America. (Buenos Aires is, in many ways, the world center for Spanish-speaking Jewry.) In return, of course, the World Jewish Con-gress has helped to legitimate the DAIA, has partially financed it, and has given it favored status in the allocations of the Memorial Foundation for Jewish Culture.

The DAIA's relationship with Israel has also been one of mutual support. Besides engaging in public information work for Israel, the DAIA has been an intermediary between the governments of Argentina and Israel during times of strain, such as the Eichmann episode. Because the government and people of Argentina look on the Jewish people as one entity wherever they are located and at Israel as the original homeland of all Jews, the close ties between the DAIA and Israel are expected by non-Jewish Argentinians.[14]

The end of the second decade of the DAIA also marked the end of the Perón regime. The DAIA emerged again as the single undisputed voice of Argentinian Jewry vis-à-vis the government and the outside world. Since then, its agenda has been essen-tially the same: combating anti-Semitism in different forms and guises, protecting the Jewish community from unfavorable laws, propaganda, economic developments, and the like. As the DAIA grew in prestige and sophistication, however, it began to be concerned more and more with the Jewish world outside Argentina. It has done substantial work in cultivating financial and diplomatic support for the State of Israel and for other Jewish communities, notably the Jews of the Soviet Union.

In the 1970s, Argentina passed through a period of civil war, for all intents and purposes. A leftist urban guerrilla movement turned to terrorism, leading to a military counterterrorist response that led to the disappearance of thousands, particularly young people, without a trace, secretly murdered by the counterterrorists. Although not di-rected against Jews per se, it seems that the Jewish community suffered disproportion-ately, if for no other reasons than young Jews represented a disproportionate share of the Argentinian left. We will never know how many of those young Jews had been part of the urban terrorist network and how many were simply removed for their political views or by mistake.

Except in a few individual cases where they had an opportunity to intervene, the Jewish community leadership could do nothing about this at the time and indeed tried to keep a very low profile in the matter even when they took action. This further eroded Jewish confidence in their established institutions. It also stimulated Aliya to Israel as parents either took or sent their teenagers and college-age children to the Jewish state to get them out of harm's way. For Argentinians, Israel "paid off" as a place of refuge for Jews. As many, if not more, Argentinian Jews immigrated to the United States, other Latin American countries, or Europe for the same reasons, substantially reducing the size of the community. It is likely that today, two-fifths of the Jews of Argentinian background—more than 200,000 people—are living outside Argentina.

The Israel-edah sphere. Formal Zionist activity began in Argentina in 1897 with the establishment of a Hovevei Zion group. It grew even in the years that some segments of world Jewry were looking to Argentina as an alternate Jewish national home. Organized Zionism was basically an Ashkenazi activity because Yiddish was spoken at Zionist meetings.

So, too, the Ashkenazim introduced the same party politics that the Jewish pioneers brought to Eretz Israel in the early years of the twentieth century. Therefore, nearly every political party in Israel has its counterpart in the Jewish community of Argentina.

In Argentina, like elsewhere, the Zionists tried to "capture the community," to gain control over the general institutions of Argentinian Jewry. They succeeded in 1956 when the AMIA was authorized by the government to change its internal structure and adopt a new one explicitly based on the Israeli political model. Since then, elections have been by proportional representation in which all Zionist and non-Zionist parties compete. Consequently, the organization has been governed by coalitions that follow the patterns of Israeli politics.[18] At one time, the Zionist parties dominated Jewish affairs, but they have lost their relevance for the younger generation. This is reflected in the steady decline in the number of people voting in the community elections since 1957.[19]

The party system has become increasingly obsolete, a reflection of the commitments of the immigrant generation, and is now being replaced by new forces in the community. As a confederation of independent Zionist bodies, OSA itself has few functions and is more of a forum for interparty jockeying. Nor do the individual parties have much in the way of substantive programs. Zionist educational activity and the promotion of Aliya (immigration to Israel) are undertaken by local representatives of the Jewish Agency or the World Zionist Organization.

The Israeli presence in Argentina is manifested through its embassy and the Jewish Agency; both play active, even catalytic roles in the community, although less so with the newly powerful community centers. Multicountry Jewish organizations such as the World Jewish Congress and B'nai B'rith also maintain regional offices in Buenos Aires. The World Jewish Congress is particularly active in Latin America, which constitutes its main power base outside Europe. In the immediate postwar generation, the WJC reflected the orientations and aspirations of the same pre-World War II European Jewish sources as the Argentinian Jewish leadership, hence there was a natural affinity between the two. Since the WJC entered a new era under Edgar Bronfman's presidency, it has sought a new constituency among the community's new leadership.

United States Jewry established a strong relationship and even presence in Argentina, especially after the fall of Juan Perón in 1953. The Joint Distribution Committee maintains a Latin American office in Buenos Aires and is supportive of local community organization efforts. Until 1978 the American Jewish Committee also maintained an office there. Once very active in Argentina—even publishing a Spanish version of *Commentary* known as *Comentario*—the committee closed its office because of threats to its personnel by government-backed right-wing terrorist groups. Most recently, the North American Jewish community center movement, working through its coordinating body, the National Jewish Welfare Board, has provided technical assistance to the Argentinian sports clubs to increase their Jewish programming and to bring them together in a countrywide confederation.[20]

The religious-congregational sphere. The impact of United States Jewry has been greatest in the religious-congregational sphere, particularly in the work of the Conservative movement. Although the Jewish immigrants organized religious services from the first, among the Ashkenazi Jews religious observance has always fought a losing battle. It is significant that the first "rabbi" of the Jewish Congregation of Buenos Aires was married to a Christian.

Argentinian Jewry can be characterized as somewhere between nonreligious and antireligious. Buenos Aires has fifty-five synagogues, but it is estimated that no more than twenty-five thousand Jews attend High Holy Day services, usually the benchmark of minimal religious behavior among contemporary Jews. Many of the fifty-five synagogues can barely muster *minyanim* (prayer quorums) on the second day of Rosh Hashanah.

Many factors account for religious observance disappearing quickly among the Ashkenazi settlers in Argentina. Among them are (1) the generally nonreligious atmosphere that has always prevailed in Argentina, especially in Buenos Aires, despite the well-nigh universal presence of the Roman Catholic Church and the nominal affiliation of most Argentinians with it; (2) the involvement of the Jewish immigrants in the rebellion against tradition taking place in eastern Europe at the time of their departure; and (3) many eastern European Jews immersed in the cosmopolitan big-city life of Buenos Aires had never lived outside small, mostly Jewish villages and were overwhelmed by the problems of religious observance in a large, cosmopolitan city.

The cogency of the third factor is shown in the history of the Jewish agricultural colonies in Argentina, settled by exactly the same sorts of people as those who settled in Buenos Aires, where religion and the religious way of life flourished. The first attempt to establish a *yeshiva* in Argentina was in one of the settlements in Entre Rios. The first Jewish Congregation of Buenos Aires, founded in 1862, did not have a properly ordained rabbi until 1905 when the Jewish Colonization Association (ICA) sent them one, whom it continued to maintain. Eventually, the prevalent secularism of Argentinian life permeated even the agricultural colonies, so that the second and especially the third generations of colonists were much less observant than the first.

Following the by now classic alliance in the Zionist movement, of the secularist parties with the Orthodox establishment, the AMIA houses the central institutions of Orthodoxy in Argentina, including the chief rabbinate. By and large, the rabbis come from Israel for temporary sojourns of greater or lesser length. The chief rabbinate handles *kashrut,* family affairs, and public relations for the official Jewish community. In addition, the Chabad (Lubavitcher Hassidic) movement has developed some activities in Latin America independently of the establishment.

One of the few bright spots on the Argentinian religious scene is the emergence of the Conservative movement locally in the first postwar generation. Although different forms of non-Orthodoxy existed in Argentina throughout the history of its Jewish community, not until 1958 did an Argentinian congregation become affiliated with the North American variety of Conservative Judaism. In 1963 Marshall Meyer, a young North American graduate of the Jewish Theological Seminary, came to the country, founded Congregación Bet El, and became the driving force in promoting Conservative Judaism locally. Since that year, the Conservative movement in Argentina has succeeded in developing a strong congregational base, establishing a summer Camp Ramah, founding a seminary for the training of Conservative rabbis, the Seminario Rabinico Latino Americano, and in exporting Conservative Judaism to other Latin American countries.

In 1970 twenty-eight hundred families were members of the four Conservative synagogues in Argentina, all of them in Buenos Aires. By 1976 Congregación Bet El with its two synagogues had four thousand members, and seventeen congregations were affiliated with the seminary.[21] Haim Avni states that since 1958 the Conservative movement in Argentina has attracted "large numbers of people who were formerly apathetic to Judaism or even assimilationists, the youth among them being especially prominent."[22]

The North American Reform movement arrived in Argentina in 1965 and established the Emanuel Congregation, which has remained small. There were two other Reform synagogues in Argentina founded by German Jews in the 1930s. The rabbi of Emanuel Congregation also serves as Latin American director of the World Union for Progressive Judaism.[23]

The educational-cultural sphere. Language differences have, until recently, played a major role in shaping Argentine Jewish life. For the Ashkenazim "Jewish" was Yiddish, and vice versa. The sum total of one's identity as a Jew was the sum total of Yiddish newspapers, magazines, books, and theaters, which flourished in Argentina as they did in no other Jewish community in the New World. As the generations pass, however, fewer and fewer Argentinian Jews speak Yiddish as their mother tongue. One tragedy of Argentinian Jewry is that nothing was given to the second and third generations to replace the importance of Yiddish for the first.

Yiddish has always been divisive in the life of Argentinian Jewry, separating Ashkenazim and Sephardim, and has evoked much bitterness among the latter, who have been excluded from many activities that should have been community wide (the OSA, for example) because of the use of Yiddish as the medium of communication. Its use has also alienated much of the younger generation; they do not understand it and equate it with political, moral, and social backwardness. And it has divided the Zionists among themselves, thus greatly restricting the spread of Hebrew language and culture.

For the Sephardim, the traditional Jewish way of life, conducted in Arabic or Ladino, provided the desired cultural framework for many years. More recently, an effort has been made to develop cultural programs for Sephardim of the third and fourth generations who no longer fully share the old ways. The major vehicle for such programs is the Centro de Investigación y Difusion de la Cultura Sefardi (Center for the Investigation and Diffusion of Sephardi Culture).

Since the Holocaust, Spanish has increasingly replaced Yiddish as the language of Jewish cultural expression, but without the culturally minded following that Yiddish had. By and large, the use of Spanish is necessary for those interested in promoting Jewish culture in their efforts to reach out to an indifferent Jewish population—not the cultural tool of a Jewishly aware cultural community. Nevertheless, Jewish organizations continue to publish materials, mostly pamphlets on Jewish topics and contemporary issues related to Jews.

In Argentina, as in other Latin American Jewish communities, Jewish schools are more national-cultural than religious in their orientation. Most people who send their children to Jewish schools are interested in fostering Jewish identity in a cultural sense.[24]

The history of Jewish education in Argentina is reflected in the two organizations that have attempted to provide countrywide support for Jewish schools. The first was the Main Council for Jewish Education in Argentina established by the ICA in 1917 and supported by it through 1939. Even before 1917, the ICA had established and sustained a network of "integral" schools—schools offering general and Jewish studies—in all the agricultural settlements, providing the children of the settlers an elementary education far superior to that offered in the governmental schools.[25] Schools directly or indirectly

supported by the ICA faced some special problems, however, because the ICA emphasized religious studies, Hebrew and Jewish history in the western manner, and rejected
Yiddish culture, which the parents wanted to preserve.

Many teachers in the ICA schools and the members of the community at large
objected to these emphases. In 1934 the Hevrah Kadisha established another organization to provide support for Jewish education, known simply as the Va'ad Ha'Jinuj
(Education Committee). The two organizations continued to exist separately until 1957,
dividing their energies between the schools of the interior served by the Main Council
and the schools of Buenos Aires served by the Education Committee. On December 20,
1956, they finally merged to form the Va'ad Ha'Jinuj Hamerkazi Be-Argentina (Central
Education Council in Argentina).

In 1984 the Va'ad Ha'Jinuj had forty primary schools in greater Buenos Aires and
twenty-two in the rest of the country under its jurisdiction. There were forty-five and
eighteen Jewish kindergartens, respectively. The country also had twenty-eight integral
and supplementary high schools, six *yeshivot,* and six tertiary institutes. Approximately
four-fifths of the students are in greater Buenos Aires.

In 1967 some eighty-nine hundred Jewish children were receiving some kind of
Jewish education. Of that number, 2,450 were enrolled in comprehensive schools and
the rest in very limited supplementary schools. In 1984 the total was 20,339 Jewish
children; 5,621 in preschool, 10,892 in primary, and 3,826 in secondary school. The
1984 figure would seem to represent an astounding increase, but probably simply reflects
more accurate census-taking. What is disturbing about the higher figures is the dropout
rate. Jewish school enrollment per age group peaks in kindergarten and declines significantly from then on.

In 1976, faced with a serious financial crisis that left the school system with a deficit
of approximately one-fourth of the total Jewish education budget, the Va'ad Ha'Jinuj
was reorganized to establish a central education department that would serve the entire
school system. Much of the deficit is being covered by funds from abroad, partly from
Israel channeled through the World Zionist Organization; but Israel has been reluctant
to lend support beyond a certain limit, feeling that the local community should finance its
own education program.

Some schools never came under the aegis of either umbrella organization and
remain independent. Examples are the Sephardi schools in Buenos Aires and the network
of Communist schools. Also standing outside the formal Jewish educational structure are
the ORT (Organization for Rehabilitation through Training) schools, which include
Jewish studies courses for those who want them. But almost all Jewish children who
receive a Jewish education in Argentina do so under the auspices of the Central Education Council.

Several bodies systematically offer post-high school adult education courses. The
Sephardi Centro already has been mentioned. Others include the Escuela de Instructores
y Técnicos en Trabajo Instituciónal (EDITTI) (School for Institutional Leadership Training), sponsored in cooperation with the Jewish Agency and Ha-Midrasha Ha-Ivrit with
more than two hundred students, including secondary school students taking in-service
training. In 1976 the Centro de Estudios Judaicos (Center of Judaic Studies) opened
with the support of the World Zionist Organization and Tel Aviv University to provide
courses that would also help recruit local Jewish leadership.

The Conservative Seminario Rabinico Latino Americano offers the most extensive program. There are three hundred high school and college students in its Hebrew program, adult courses through its Instituto Franz Rosenzweig, a teachers' training program, and thirty rabbinical students. It also has a substantial program for translating and publishing Jewish materials into Spanish. In 1978 the AMIA opened the Instituto de Estudios Judios Superiores.

By and large, Argentinian universities do not include Jewish studies programs. One exception is the School of Oriental Studies of El Salvador Roman Catholic University in Buenos Aires, which offers courses initiated and sponsored by the South American office of the American Jewish Committee and by the Argentinian branch of YIVO, the Yiddish-oriented Jewish research institute.

An important aspect of Jewish education in Argentina is the informal education provided by Zionist youth organizations. During the past twenty-five years, many youth group leaders have been trained as informal educators by the Institute for Youth Leaders from Abroad in Jerusalem. In 1958 the AMIA established a Youth Department and in 1962 a Youth Counselor Corps. There is a Confederation of Argentine Jewish Youth, which, in principle, links all non-Communist Jewish youth groups, but it is basically a "paper" organization.[26]

It is difficult to overestimate the degree to which young people have become alienated from Jewish communal and organizational life. This alienation, as mentioned earlier, can be seen in every facet of organized Jewish life in Argentina and would seem to mark the decline of the community. Israeli researchers find cause for optimism in the increasing numbers of young emigrants from Argentina who have come to Israel since the late 1960s, but from the Argentinian perspective, this can be seen as merely one more sign of the younger generation's alienation from local Jewish life.[27]

The secular nature of the Ashkenazi majority in Argentina has more or less assured that authority and power in the community is located in the *keter malkhut,* whether in the DAIA and AMIA, or more recently in the sports clubs. Representatives of the *keter torah* are not prominent among either Ashkenazim or Sephardim. The weak Ashkenazi rabbinate is subordinate to the *kehillah* and the Sephardi congregations are basically places for prayer, social life, and minimal learning. The one dynamic element outside the *keter malkhut* is the Conservative movement, which has built itself on the elements of *keter kehunah* and *keter torah* as in North America. Significantly, the only way to reach the youth seems to be through the *keter torah,* either in its Conservative, Zionist, or Hassidic versions, which emphasize one or another forms of Jewish learning that give expression to the ideological longings of the young.

By the late 1980s, the contradictory trends built into Argentinian Jewish life have intensified and some unexpected new trends have emerged. While assimilation continued to increase, the inner circles of the community, comprising at least one third of the Jewish population, continue to maintain a vibrant, active, comprehensive kehillah, more integrated in its structure than in the past, emphasizing Hebrew education, strongly intertwined with Israel. The Sephardic community has been reinvigorated, in part because the Sephardic bank, Banco de Mayo, survived the banking crisis that hit the community in the late 1960s and today is able to provide a funding base for Sephardic institutions. The impact of the Conservative movement and its Seminars Rabinico is growing. More unexpected is the emergence of a vigorous, aggressive ultra-Orthodox community with yeshivot and kollelim springing up all over Buenos Aires. All told there is a new interest in Jewish religion among many young people who are searching for a Jewish identity.

Even the communities in the interior are being strengthened with laws migrating south-ward into the country's development areas and organizing command institutions to meet their needs.

Jews are more active and prominent in Argentinian politics and society than ever before, and more of those who are retain their ties with the Jewish community and are even considered to be active in it. The Alfonsin government, in particular, has appointed Jews to prominent positions. For the first time, Jews occupy high positions in the universities. In addition there is now serious Jewish social research being undertaken by local scholars.

The Brazilian Jewish Community[28]

The first Portuguese landing in what is now Brazil took place in 1500. There was at least one Jew on the ship, Gaspar da Gama, a Jewish adventurer from Poland who had been kidnapped and forcibly baptized by the Portuguese in India in 1497. He is reputed to be one of the first two Portuguese to set foot on Brazilian soil.[29]

The Portuguese New Christians, who had been forcibly baptized only three years previously, saw great opportunities in Brazil and in 1502 obtained a concession from the throne to colonize and exploit the land. In later years they took full advantage of this opportunity, and are reputed to be the ones who introduced sugar culture into Brazil. As a result, the country became a haven for Marranos, who were generally left alone, because no local Inquisition was established in Brazil, although after the 1580 unification of Spain and Portugal, Inquisitorial commissions were sent from the Holy Office in Portugal from time to time. Those commissions arrested a number of suspects and sent them to Lisbon for trial, but Brazil continued to be a place of Marrano concentration throughout the sixteenth century, and New Christians contributed heavily to the foundations of Brazilian culture.

The Dutch conquest of Pernambuco in 1630 led many of the Marranos to remove themselves to Dutch territory and return openly to Judaism. They founded congregations in Recife and Paraíba, enrolled in the militia where they had their own Jewish company, and became an active part of the Jewish world. Rabbis, Hebrew teachers, and *hazanim* came to them from New Amsterdam. The Recife community was responsible for many Jewish "firsts" in the New World. As a community it was organized along traditional lines, following the Amsterdam model. The Jewish population peaked at fifteen hundred in 1645 when it comprised approximately 50 percent of the European civilian population in Dutch Brazil.

After a nine-years' war, the Portuguese reconquered the colony in 1654. Because of their prominent role in the colony and its defense, the Dutch secured the Jews' lives and liberty in the capitulation agreement, but all Jews had to evacuate the colony in three months. Most moved to Amsterdam, others sailed to Curaçao, also under Dutch rule, and other Caribbean islands, and twenty-three ended in New Amsterdam to found the first organized Jewish community in what was to become the United States.

This ended organized Jewish life in Brazil until Brazilian independence. Apparently, there continued to be many Marranos in the country. There were periodic investigations, arrests, and punishments throughout the rest of the seventeenth and eighteenth centuries until the Portuguese royal decree of 1773, which ended discrimination against New Christians. Ultimately, the Marranos assimilated into colonial Brazilian society.

Brazil declared independence from Portugal in 1822. Its first constitution, adopted in 1825, retained Roman Catholicism as the state religion but provided for tolerance of other religions. This opened the door for Jewish settlement in the country. Jews, particularly Sephardim from Morocco, had continued to drift into Brazil from time to time. They founded the country's first congregation in Belém, in 1824, even before the formal constitutional change. Belém has been a Sephardi community ever since. Later, other Sephardim gravitated to Brazil, settling in Manaus, in the state of Amazonas (the heart of the Amazon basin), during the economic boom at the end of the nineteenth century. Few Jews settled in the southern part of the country in those years. Organized Jewish life there did not emerge until the last generation of the nineteenth century.

Between 1901 and 1965 there were several attempts at agricultural colonization in Brazil, none of which succeeded. What remains of those efforts are a few descendants who still own land in the colonized areas. The remnants of the last of these colonies were liquidated by 1975. None of this had any influence on the shape of the Brazilian Jewish community except that it brought several thousand Jews into the country.[30]

By World War I, there were between 5,000 and 7,000 Jews in Brazil. Nearly 30,000 additional Jews entered between the end of the war and the introduction of a restrictive immigration policy in 1930. Jewish immigration continued at a diminished rate: some 17,500 refugees entered between 1933 and 1939. After the Sinai Campaign of 1956, 2,500 Jews from Egypt arrived along with another 1,000 from North Africa.

Many of the Jews who arrived in the country did not declare themselves Jews. Hence the official figures for the Jewish population of Brazil have always been underestimates, much as the Jewish estimates have always been excessive. Today it is estimated that there are 110,000 Jews in the country, most concentrated in the two large communities of Rio de Janeiro and São Paulo, which are about equal in size, each with almost 50,000 Jews. Other significant communities are Pôrto Alegre, Belo Horizante, Recife, Coreteba, Belém, and Bahia. Brasília, the capital, has fewer than one hundred Jewish families, and Manaus maintains a community estimated at two hundred. See figure 12.2.[31]

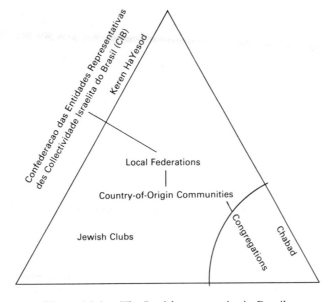

Figure 12.2.   The Jewish community in Brazil.

In contrast with Argentina, Brazilian Jewry has scattered over the entire country and has developed no single center. São Paulo and Rio de Janeiro are co-equal communities with almost the same Jewish populations, though each with its own style of Jewish life. This follows the general Brazilian pattern of spatial and cultural development (table 12.1). Whatever its other benefits, this has not only hindered the development of strong countrywide Jewish institutions, but even of strong local ones to some degree.

Until just before World War I, the only organized Jewish life was in the Sephardi communities in the north. Otherwise, there were only informal *minyanim* and small charitable organizations in Rio de Janeiro and São Paulo. The first officially organized community in the south was in Pôrto Alegre, the capital of the state of Rio Grande do Sul, where the Jews who settled in the abortive agricultural colonies concentrated after their colonies failed. The first organization of the São Paulo Jewish community dates to 1892 and the community itself was founded in 1915 by uniting several philanthropic and cultural associations. Construction of the first proper synagogue in the south was not begun until the end of 1916 in São Paulo. Meanwhile, Jewish organizations were being formed in smaller towns in São Paulo state. A committee was organized in Rio de Janeiro in 1916 to aid war victims in Europe. It united all the existing Jewish societies in the city, most of which had been organized after 1910.

Jewish communal organization took a giant step forward during the 1920s as a result of the "mass" immigration of the time. Zionist parties were organized, a Jewish Communist organization emerged, and a full range of social, religious, and philanthropic institutions was established. However, efforts to organize unified communities on the *kehillah* model did not succeed in Brazil.

Pressure on the Jews and other ethnic minorities to assimilate into Brazilian culture grew in the 1920s and was one reason behind the immigration restrictions imposed. Under the Vargas regime this pressure intensified. In 1938 a government decree prohibited political activities by foreigners and contact with foreign organizations, which led to the forced disbanding of the Zionist organization. In 1941 another decree prohibited foreign language newspapers, which led to the closing of the two Yiddish dailies. By and large these efforts were aimed at the secular activities of the community; and because the communities in the south were overwhelmingly Ashkenazi and emphasized the secular side as other Latin American countries, they were particularly hard hit. Jewish life retreated to the religious-congregational sphere.[32]

Brazil's entry into the war on the side of Allies in 1944 ameliorated some of these pressures. In 1945 the government promulgated a new constitution and in preparation for that event moderated its xenophobic policies. Zionist and other secular Jewish organizations reemerged.

In 1946 and 1947 local federations of Jewish institutions and organizations were formed in the larger communities. This began the constitution of a truly Brazilian Jewish communal structure, which culminated in 1951 with the establishment of the Confederacao das Entidades Representativas des Collectividade Israelita do Brasil (CIB). These organizations began as instruments of the external relations–defense sphere but gradually broadened to include also the communal-welfare and religious-congregational spheres. The Israel-*edah* sphere remained in the hands of the Zionist organizations but in recent years has also become increasingly connected to the framing institutions (figure 12.2).[33]

The principal localistic institutions in the communal-welfare sphere are the Jewish clubs. Each of the two major cities has four such clubs: in Rio the Hebraica, Montesinai, CIB, and ARI; in São Paulo the Hebraica, Maccabi, Circo Israelita, and CID. They are

Table 12.1

Jewish Population of Brazil, by Regions and Selected States, 1940–1980, Absolute Numbers and Percentages[a]

Regions and States	1940		1950		1960[b]		1980[b]	
	Number	%	Number	%	Number	%	Number	%
Total	55,666	100.0	69,957	100.0	86,038	100.0	89,969	100.0
North	1,562	2.8	1,791	2.6	1,390	1.6	1,248	1.4
Thereof:								
Para[c]	995	1.8	1,126	1.6	918	1.1	827	0.9
Nordeste	1,603	2.9	1,913	2.7	1,712	2.0	1,476	1.6
Thereof:								
Pernambuco[d]	1,115	2.0	1,531	2.2	1,292	1.5	1,237	1.4
East	24,274	43.6	30,117	43.1	34,060	39.6	31,549	35.1
Thereof:								
Bahia[e]	955	1.7	1,076	1.5	799	9.3	736	0.8
Minas Gerais[f]	1,431	2.6	1,528	2.2	1,948	2.3	1,525	1.7
Rio de Janeiro[g]	21,666	38.9	27,431	39.2	31,196	36.3	29,139	32.4
South	28,147	50.6	35,988	51.4	48,344	56.2	54,858	61.0
Thereof:								
São Paulo[h]	20,379	36.6	26,443	37.8	37,003	43.0	44,378	49.3
Parana[i]	1,038	1.9	1,340	1.9	2,162	2.5	1,993	2.2
Rio Grande do Sul[j]	6,619	11.9	8,048	11.5	8,720	10.1	8,210	9.1
Center-West	80	0.1	148	0.2	532	0.6	838	0.9
Thereof:								
Distrito Federal[k]	—	—	—	—	114	0.1	625	0.7

[a]Source: Brazil, Instituto Brasileiro de Geografia e Estatistica, various censuses.
[b] Urban population only.
[c]Main city: Belém. [d]Main city: Recife. [e]Main city: Salvador.
[f]Main city: Belo Horizonte.
[g]Until 1960: Combined total of the states of Guanabara (main city: Rio de Janeiro) and Rio de Janeiro (main city: Niteroi). As of 1980, these two states are merged.
[h]Main city: São Paulo. [i]Main city: Curitiba. [j]Main city: Pôrto Alegre.
[k]Main city: Brasilia.

becoming increasingly important in communal affairs as they are in the rest of Latin America.

Jewish schooling in Brazil formally began in 1907 in one of the agricultural colonies. A school was founded in Pôrto Alegre in 1910 and a Talmud Torah in São Paulo in 1916. By 1929 there were twenty-seven schools in the country but only eight hundred pupils all told. Forty years later, there were thirty-three schools with an enrollment of more than ten thousand from kindergarten through senior high school. The state universities of Rio de Janeiro and São Paulo offer courses in Hebrew, and courses are conducted periodically to train teachers for the Jewish schools. The Chabad movement maintains a *yeshiva* in Petrópolis, Rio's mountain retreat. In the early 1980s, there were twenty day schools and two supplementary schools in Brazil with a total enrollment of approximately 10,400 students. Most of the enrollment was in the elementary schools with about a 50 percent attrition rate for high school. Approximately half of all Jewish children are enrolled in Jewish schools. In the small communities the percentage is much higher, at times embracing almost the entire Jewish school-age population. But, conversely, in the major centers it is even lower. Most of the schools have a national-cultural orientation in the Latin American pattern, with only a few being religious in character.

The religious-congregational sphere is even more localistic if possible. Not only is there no countrywide rabbinate, but Rio and São Paulo each have three chief rabbis, one for each of the communities in the city: Ashkenazi eastern European, Sephardi, and German. The *landsmanschaften* have their synagogues and rabbis. There are eighteen synagogues in Rio de Janeiro, most of which claim to be Orthodox. Even so, it is estimated that only one-fifth of the city's Jews are affiliated with the synagogues.

Each congregation represents a specific country-of-origin group and several run their own schools and either run or are closely identified with particular social clubs. Thus they are congregational communities. They can be divided into four groups: Ashkenazic, traditional Sephardic, Ashkenazic Orthodox, and Reform. The latter, the Associacao Religiosa Israelita with a membership of 950 families, is the largest congregation in Rio. It was founded in 1942 by German Jewish refugees. Its present rabbis were trained at the Hebrew Union College in Cincinnati and it is a member of the world Union for Progressive Judaism, but it maintains separate seating and other Orthodox practices.

São Paulo has congregations affiliated with the Conservative movement. There, too, congregations have specific sports clubs. There is a growing ultra-Orthodox community, principally Chabad, but also with an Agudath Yisrael component.

Specifically, Brazilian Jewry is dominated by the institutions of the *keter malkhut*. The reality is that more power is lodged in the sports clubs than in the cosmopolitan institutions of the *keter*. At the same time, the congregations located at the nexus between the *keter torah* and *keter kehunah*, with the emphasis on the latter, play a vital social role because of the nature of the community. Most Brazilian Jewish activity is so private that no set of public institutions can be said to be highly significant on a day-to-day basis.

All told, the Brazilian Jewish community is among the most low-key Jewish communities in the world. In that respect, it is thoroughly assimilated into Brazilian culture. The stereotypical frenzy, often associated with the communities in the Hispanic world, is absent from Brazilian Jewry. Similarly, just as public life in Brazil in general is weak, the public aspect of Jewish life is weak. The Jews do what they must to keep their institutions going, but there is little sign of any drive to improve or strengthen those institutions. Nevertheless, in Rio at least a new, second generation leadership has emerged, which has infused a certain spirit into the community.

It is said that it is easy for different groups to assimilate in Brazil, although no easier than in many countries in the world. Brazilian Jews are no more eager to assimilate than Jews in many other countries, perhaps because they are still a new group on the Brazilian scene, but they do not get passionately involved in fighting assimilation either. Whatever infusions of energy are given to the community come from Israel through the World Zionist Organization–Jewish Agency complex. In that respect, Brazil is like Argentina—big enough to draw on its own resources but still slowly sinking into protectorate status in the *edah*.

Notes

1. For an overview of Latin American Jewry, see Judith Laiken Elkin, "Latin American Jewry Today," *American Jewish Yearbook 1985,* vol. 85, pp. 3–50; U. O. Schmelz and Sergio Della Pergola, "The Demography

of Latin American Jewry," *American Jewish Yearbook 1985*, vol. 85, pp. 51–102; Judith Laikin Elkin, "A Demographic Profile of Latin American Jewry," *American Jewish Archives*, November 1982, pp. 231–48; and Nathan Lerner, "Jewish Organization in Latin America," David Horowitz Institute for Research on Developing Countries, Tel Aviv University, 1974, pp. 4–5. Among English-language works published in the last decade are Judith Laikin Elkin, "The Jewish Communities in 1982," in Jack Hopkins, ed., *Latin America and Caribbean Contemporary Record* (New York, 1984); Judith Laikin Elkin, *Jews of the Latin American Republics* (Chapel Hill, 1976); Judith Laikin Elkin, ed., *Latin American Jewish Studies* (Cincinnati, 1980); Judith Laikin Elkin, ed., *Resources for Latin American Jewish Studies* (Ann Arbor, 1984); Irving Louis Horowitz, "Jewish Ethnicity and Latin American Nationalism," in Abdul Said and Luis Simmons, eds., *Ethnicity in an International Context* (New Brunswick, 1976); Ronald C. Newton, "Indifferent Sanctuary: German-Speaking Refugees and Exiles in Argentina, 1933–45," *Journal of Inter-American Studies* (November 1982), pp. 395–420; Martin H. Sable, *Latin American Jewry: A Research Guide* (Cincinnati, 1978); David Schers, "Anti-Semitism in Latin America," in Salo W. Baron and George S. Wise, eds., *Violence and Defense: The Jewish Experience* (Philadelphia, 1977), pp. 239–53; David Schers and Hadassah Singer, "The Jewish Communities of Latin America: External and Internal Factors in Their Development," *Jewish Social Studies* (summer 1977), pp. 241–58; and Eugene Sofer, *From Pale to Pampa: The Jewish Immigrant Experience in Buenos Aires* (New York, 1982).

2. See Lerner, "Jewish Organization in Latin America."

3. On the demography of Latin American Jewry, see Schmelz and Della Pergola, "The Demography of Latin American Jewry." Because Latin American Jewish communities resist any efforts at census taking out of a not unjustified fear that the hard data would somehow be used to their detriment, given the environment in which they live, our information is based on not necessarily accurate government censuses and estimates by demographers.

4. For a full treatment of the Argentinian Jewish community, see Daniel J. Elazar with Peter Medding, *Jewish Communities in Frontier Societies* (New York: Holmes and Meier, 1983); Haim Avni, "Argentine Jewry: Its Socio-Political Status and Organizational Patterns," *Dispersion and Unity*, vol. 12 (1971), pp. 128–62; vol. 13/14 (1971–72), pp. 161–208; vol. 15/16 (1972), pp. 158–215; Seymour B. Liebman, *Argentine Jewry: Its History, Ethnicity, and Problems*, unpublished report prepared for the Center of Jewish Community Studies, 1975; Robert Weisbrot, *The Jews of Argentina from the Inquisition to Péron* (Philadelphia: Jewish Publication Society of America, 1979); Irving Louis Horowitz, "The Jewish Community of Buenos Aires," *Jewish Social Studies*, vol. 24 (October 1962), pp. 195–222; Victor A. Mirelman, "The Jews in Argentina (1890–1930): Assimilation and Particularism," Ph.D. dissertation (Columbia University, 1973).

5. Thus Haim Avni and Robert Weisbrot argue that the community has a comprehensive organized framework, while Judith Laiken Elkin and Seymour B. Liebman argue that no such framework exists, that references to it fall into the category of Latin American-style projection of popular expectations as assumed reality. See Avni, "Argentine Jewry"; Weisbrot, *The Jews of Argentina*; Elkin, *Jews of the Latin American Republics*.

6. Liebman, *Argentine Jewry*.

7. Avni, "Argentine Jewry," vol. 13/14, pp. 170–71.

8. Ibid., p. 175.

9. Ibid.

10. Avni, "Argentine Jewry," vol. 12, pp. 128–62.

11. Ibid., vol. 13/14, pp. 163–64.

12. Ibid., p. 165.

13. Ibid.

14. Moshe Davis, "Centres of Jewry in the Western Hemisphere: A Comparative Approach," *Jewish Journal of Sociology*, vol. 5, no. 1 (June 1963), pp. 4–26.

15. Avni, "Argentine Jewry," vol. 13/14, p. 205.

16. Liebman, *Argentine Jewry*, pp. 31–32.

17. Naomi Meyer, "Argentina," *American Jewish Year Book 1978*, vol. 78, p. 300.

18. Weisbrot, *The Jews of Argentina*, pp. 87–88, 91–106.

19. In the *American Jewish Year Book 1972*, vol. 73, Nissim Elnecavé reported that the membership of the Organización Sionista Argentina (OSA) was 19,600. Of these, 7,474 went to the polls to elect 21 delegates to the Twenty-Eighth World Zionist Congress in Jerusalem. The estimated membership of OSA in 1978 was 23,000, after a 1976 membership drive, which was deemed successful. The parallel women's group, the Organización Femeniana Argentina (OSFA), on the other hand, exceeded 30,000.

20. Personal interviews with Esther Leah Ritz, president, National Jewish Welfare Board, May 1981.

21. For a survey of the activities of the Conservative movement in Argentina, see Naomi F. Meyer's article "Argentina" in the *American Jewish Year Book,* vols. 78, 79, 80, (1978, 1979, 1980).

22. Avni, "Argentine Jewry," vol. 13/14, pp. 164–65.

23. Ibid., p. 164.

24. On Jewish education in Argentina, see ibid., pp. 182–83; Yaakov Rubel, "The Jewish Educational System in Argentina (1975–1984)," paper presented at the Ninth World Congress of Jewish Studies (1985).

25. Weisbrot, *The Jews of Argentina,* pp. 282–83 and Avni, "Argentine Jewry," vol. 13/14, pp. 197–201.

26. From the Six-Day War through 1974, more than 12,000 Jews moved to Israel from Argentina, according to Israeli figures, 20 percent of whom later returned to Argentina. More than half had received a Jewish education in Argentina, and nearly two-thirds were members of Zionist organizations.

27. For the current state of Argentinian Jewry, see Elkin, "Latin American Jewry Today," pp. 3–50.

28. Data for this section were collected by staff researchers of the Center for Jewish Community Studies/Jerusalem Center for Public Affairs, working in Brazil and Israel between 1968 and 1980. See also Miriam Mundstock, *The Jewish Community of Brazil,* unpublished manuscript prepared for the Center for Jewish Community Studies (1970); Elkin, *Jews of the Latin American Republics;* Elihu Lipiner, "Yidn in Brazil," *Algemeine Entsiclopedia* 5 (1957), pp. 385–404; and Henrique Lemle, "Jews in Northern Brazil," *Reconstructionist,* no. 3 (March 1967).

29. Arnold Wiznitzer, *Jews in Colonial Brazil* (New York: Columbia University Press, 1960) and *The Records of the Earliest Jewish Community in the New World* (1954); Salomão Serebrenick, *Quatro séculos de vida judaica no Brasil 1500–1900,* part 1 of *Breve historia dos judeos no Brasil* (Rio de Janeiro: Ediçoes Biblos Ltda., 1962).

30. Kurt Lowenstamm, *Vultos Judaicos no Brasil,* vol. 2, *Imperio, 1822–1889* (1956); Serebrenick, *Quatro séculos;* Harro O. Sandberg, "The Jews of Latin America," *American Jewish Year Book 1917–18,* vol. 19, pp. 35–105; Elkin, *Jews of the Latin American Republics.*

31. See Schmelz and Della Pergola, "The Demography of Latin American Jewry," pp. 51–105; Geoffrey Paul, "Al HaYehudim be-Brazil," (The Jews of Brazil), *Tefutsot Yisrael,* vol. 19, no. 1 (spring 1981), pp. 101–5 (Hebrew); Henrique Rattner, "Occupational Structure of Jews in Brazil: Trends and Perspectives," paper prepared for the Sixth World Congress of Jewish Studies, Jerusalem, August 1973; *Tradiçao e Mudança: a communidade judaica em São Paulo* (São Paulo: Attica, 1970); *Yishuvim Yehudim be-Brazil* (Jewish Settlements in Brazil), from the archives of the Jerusalem Center for Public Affairs, ca. 1970 (Hebrew).

32. Fritz Pinkus, "Um ensaio acerca da imigraçao judaica no Brasil apos o cataclismo de 1933 e da segunda guerra mundail," in *Revista de Historia* (São Paulo: Universidades de São Paula, Faculdada de Filosofia, Cieneias e Letras, 50 (2), 100, 1974); Moises Senderey, "Brazil under Vargas," in Sander M. Kaplan and Alexander J. Dubelman, eds., *Havaner Lebn: Un curato de siglo Vida Habanera 1931–1957* (Havana, 1958); Robert M. Levine, "Brazil's Jews during the Vargas Era and After," *Luso-Brazilian Review* 5 (summer 1968), pp. 45–58; Alfred Hirshberg, "The Economic Adjustment of Jewish Refugees in São Paulo," *Jewish Social Studies,* no. 7 (January 1945), pp. 31–40.

33. Eliahu Lipner, "A nova imigraçao judaica no Brasil," part 2 of *Breve Historia los Judeos no Brasil* (Rio de Janeiro: Ediçoes Biblos Ltda., 1962); Roman Luftig, "La comunidad israelita de São Paulo," *Comunidades judías de latinoamerica* (1970), pp. 211–14; Eva Nicolaiewsky, *Israelitas no Rio Grande do Sul* (Pôrto Alegre: Editora Garatuja, 1975); Mundstock, *The Jewish Community of Brazil;* Judy Siegel, "Signs of the Jews in São Paulo," *Jerusalem Post* (April 24, 1978); Elkin, *Jews of the Latin American Republics.*

13

Latin American Jewries: The Other Hispanic Communities

There are four other Latin American countries with more than ten thousand Jews—in descending order, Mexico, Uruguay, Venezuela, and Chile. Together they contain about one hundred thousand Jews, or about one-fifth of the Latin American total. The remaining 10 percent of Latin American Jewry are scattered among all the other countries of the region, almost every one of which has a small Jewish community.

Mexican Jewry: Some Persistent Themes

The nearly fifty thousand Jews in Mexico place that community in the intermediate size category in the contemporary diaspora, the fifteenth largest in the world. Long a prosperous community, it has been among the freest of the larger Latin American communities to pursue Jewish life. The present community has just crossed the threshold of its fourth generation of existence—this despite a recorded history of Jews in Mexico that goes back more than 450 years.[1]

Although the story of the contemporary community belongs to the twentieth century, the epic Jewish experience in Mexico is that of the Marranos in the sixteenth and seventeenth centuries. Their story has become increasingly better known in recent years as researchers, drawn to its epic and exotic character, have probed as many aspects as can be documented (in sharp contrast with the scholarly neglect of contemporary Mexican Jewry). Fortunately, the men of the Inquisition were no less committed to documenting every step of their activities than were more recent persecutors of Jews, so the records are rather complete. With all its romantic dimensions, however, it, too, is a story of marginality.[2]

The first of the Marranos came with Cortés and participated in the Spanish conquest of the Aztec empire. Hernando Alonso, of Cortés's band, was the first Jewish martyr on Mexican soil. The complexities of his case are almost paradigmatic for the history of Jewish life in the New World in that period; political as much as religious reasons played a role in his arrest and execution. Whatever the risks, other Marranos followed Alonso and his compatriots to Mexico, where they scattered from Yucatán to the Rio Grande. Seymour Liebman, the leading authority on the subject, has estimated that the Marrano population of Mexico reached at least ten thousand at one point, and was perhaps even greater.

As the Marrano communities flourished, they created a network of underground institutions. They were even able to forge contact with the Jewish community of Eretz Israel, which sent emissaries to Mexican Jewry on several occasions in the four or five generations (nearly 150 years) of its history as an organized body. In the end, however, the combination of inquisitional pressure and assimilation eliminated the community, although consciousness of Marrano origins persisted well into the nineteenth century and, according to Liebman, even into the twentieth. It was only with the arrival of Jews from eastern Europe, who were strangers to Mexican ways, that the last of the descendants of the Marranos abandoned their identity to avoid being identified with the newcomers, or so they say, thus making the break between the two eras of Mexican Jewish history as sharp and deliberate as possible. Despite repeated "discoveries" of people—many of them Indians—who claim Marrano descent, the existence of and the sharp separation between the two communities is part and parcel of the heritage of Mexican Jewry.

The present Jewish community dates its origins to the mid-nineteenth century, which is still something of an exaggeration. Even though a Jewish congregation was founded in the time of Juarez, the Jews who originally came to Mexico were adventurers seeking their fortunes, mostly from the German-speaking countries. They assimilated even more rapidly than the Marranos because they came in a time of emancipation to a country that did not oppress them as Jews. To compound the marginal origins of Mexican Jewry, the first organized expressions of Jewish life in the nineteenth century were religious services conducted by Jews who accompanied the French and their ill-fated puppet Emperor Maximilian during the brief French occupation of the country (1862–67). This community also disappeared.[3]

The first substantial immigration of Jews consisted of Sephardim from the Ottoman Empire and North Africa who came between 1870 and 1890. These included Syrians, Jews who had earlier fled to Morocco because of persecutions in Syria who came as laborers, and Jews from the Balkans, particularly Turkey, who came as part of the general emigration from that area. The Balkans Jews increased in number after the Young Turk Revolution in 1908 and its attendant upheaval. They settled principally in Mexico City and Guadalajara. Many of their offspring became wealthy and even prominent. In the 1880s, two Jews even became generals in the Mexican army. Still, most of them moved to the United States during the Mexican Revolution (1910–20). The first Ashkenazim from eastern Europe entered Mexico by way of Harbin, China, or were adventurers who came from the United States. The Ashkenazim did not become the majority of the Jewish immigrants until World War I and the community's Ashkenazic majority was not really formed until the 1920s.

The Jews who came before the Mexican Revolution opened small businesses or worked as laborers around the country, so that communities were established in at least six cities in the hinterland, aside from the two major ones. Until the 1920s these Jewish settlers were principally Sephardim. None of these communities developed, however; in most cases, the Jews who settled in them or their children left for the larger Jewish communities. By the 1950s only Mexico City, Monterrey, Guadalajara, and Tijuana had a hundred or more Jews. Because most of the small-town Jews were Sephardim, it was easier for those who did not leave to intermarry and assimilate into the local population.

Of the approximately 50,000 Jews in Mexico today, between 40,000 and 45,000 are in Mexico City. Guadalajara has about 3,000 in the city and environs, and Monterrey about 1,500. Many Jews are scattered around Mexico and do not reveal their identity, but contribute secretly to Jewish organizations. Hence, only about 35,000 Jews are recognized by the official institutions of the Mexican Jewish community as linked to the community. Sixty-five percent are Ashkenazim and 35 percent are Sephardim. Curiously, the official Mexican government census, which asks people to state their religious affiliation, registered over 100,000 Israelites (Jews) in 1960. Many of these are Protestants, whose fear of the Catholics makes them try to pass for Jews. Most are members of sects founded by Protestant missionaries, who have become Sabbatarian and self-proclaimed Jews, and are not recognized by the Jewish community. These include the so-called Indian Jews, who attract much attention outside Mexico.

In Mexico, like the rest of Latin America, the Jews' desire to keep their business to themselves led them to develop economic institutions such as banks, mutual savings societies, and even a few producers' cooperatives. The Banco Mercantil was the first Jewish-owned bank, founded by the Jewish lending societies. Today there are several commercial and mortgage banks and about a dozen lending societies that are wholly owned by Jews.

In a relatively short time, Mexican Jews prospered. According to Liebman's estimates, 20 percent of the contemporary Jewish community is wealthy enough to be considered upper class in income, although not necessarily in status. Another 10 percent are in the upper middle class, 50 percent are in the middle class, 15 percent in the lower middle, and 5 percent are poor. Many Jews started as manual laborers; today there are essentially none. Most are retail tradesmen or manufacturers who dominate the textile and clothing industries. A few are in light industry of other kinds. Increasingly, the Jews have entered the professions and there are those in finance. Most of the professionals are doctors because Jews are not encouraged to become lawyers in the Mexican context.

Because the Jews are defined as a religious group, they are subject to the government's restrictions on religion, which in Mexico are substantial because of the long struggle there between liberals and Catholics. Mexican anticlericalism peaked during the 1910 Revolution and it has since been relaxed. Still, no religious group can own land or buildings, but must lease them from the government. Because leases are for ninety-nine years at the equivalent of a dollar per year, the Jewish community has de facto possession of its facilities and is responsible for them, but the threat of government intervention is always there. Government anticlericalism, however, assures religious liberty and restrains the pressure against Jewish life that exists in many Catholic countries.

Today's Jewish community is mainly descended from immigrants who came in the 1920s after the Mexican Revolution had spent its momentum. Thus the Jews have no connection whatsoever with the great events of Mexican history, the century of heroic struggles from the Grito de Hidalgo (the first revolt against Spain) in 1811 to the end of the Revolution. These new immigrants did not knowingly encounter any of the older Mexican Jewish families either. Those families avoided the newcomers and did not want to be identified with them, leaving the newcomers to believe that they were the first Jews to arrive in Mexico. This only added to the discontinuity in Mexican Jewish history.

Like most other Latin American countries, Mexico was a destination of second choice. Almost all the Jews who ended there tried to enter the United States and were unable to for one reason or another. Often they were helped to get to Mexico by American Jewish organizations, particularly HIAS and Bnai Brith. Thus their commitment to Mexico from the first was minimal. It was simply a refuge for them, without any expectations on their part. From the first, they resisted assimilation into Mexican society and culture.

For Jews, Mexico was a land of mystery. The United States already had assumed mythic proportions in the eyes of the world; Jews who immigrated to the United States had a notion of what they were getting into—however obscure and fuzzy their expectations, they still retained some grains of truth. Because Jews did not plan to go to Mexico or most other Latin American countries and Latin America was unknown and uninteresting to Europe, Jews did not know what to expect. The well-recorded history of the Spanish and Portuguese expulsions and inquisitions was hardly a strong recommendation.

Perhaps this is the reason why the first Polish Jews who came to Mexico referred to themselves as Polish rather than Jewish, thinking that it was better to sound like complete foreigners than to evoke ancient symbols of religious hatred. In the end this gave them the label of foreigners when the Jewish label probably would have served them better in the context of Mexican xenophobia and anti-Catholicism. But the only Mexicans the Jewish immigrants encountered were the illiterate and barefoot peasants and lower classes, who lacked even the minimum refinements, as customers or maids. Hence the immigrants acquired a distorted view of Mexican society and culture as extremely primitive and not one that they wished to acquire for themselves or their children.

Organizational choices and their consequences. Not surprisingly, then, the Jews simply transplanted the patterns they knew in the old world. As in Argentina, in the end the model they chose had inherent structural weaknesses derived from its lack of relevance to the local scene.

Mexican Jewry is compounded of four city-communities. All four are confederated in a countrywide umbrella organization founded in 1973, which exists primarily on paper. The local communities originally were organized through federations of *landsmenschaften,* linked through the Comité Central Israelita, in a loose confederation dominated by the largest of its constituents, that also speaks for Mexican Jewry as a whole and is tacitly recognized as the Jewish "address" by the authorities. The original confederation of Jewish communities in Mexico comprised six units: three Sephardi and three Ashkenazi, of which the eastern European Ashkenazi community, Nidje Israel, was—and is—the largest, most powerful, and dominant group. More recently, the confederation has been expanded to also include what elsewhere are called functional agencies, a reflection of the shift now taking place in the Mexican Jewish community as the old country ties fade (figure 13.1). At the same time, the German and Hungarian communities have been absorbed by Nidje Israel. The only institutions not affiliated with *kehillot* are the B'nai B'rith lodges.

The community is governed by volunteer leaders and there are few paid professionals. There is no significant civil service.[4] Its governing body of twenty-two is divided between Nidje Israel with six representatives, three for each of the Sephardic congregations, three for the Consejo de Mujeres, and one each for the two Conservative congregations and the sports club and the joint German-Hungarian Tivka Emunah group. It is funded by assessments in the same proportions.

Mexico suffers from the division between Ashkenazim and Sephardim that prevails in all Latin America. Many Ashkenazim do not even recognize the Sephardim as observant Jews, even though the latter are likely to be more observant than the former. Until recently there was almost no social intercourse between the two groups, even among those who engaged in joint business ventures.

Although the institutions of Mexican Jewry developed out of religious congregations located at the nexus between the *keter torah* and the *keter kehunah,* those congregations over time came to exercise the *keter kehunah* functions as most important. *Keter torah* functions are located in the *batei din* and the schools. The orientation of the community is much more toward institutions associated with the *keter malkhut,* although the lines are more blurred in Mexico than in most other Jewish communities. They are most clearly defined in the Ashkenazi *kehillah,* where the development of a more articu-

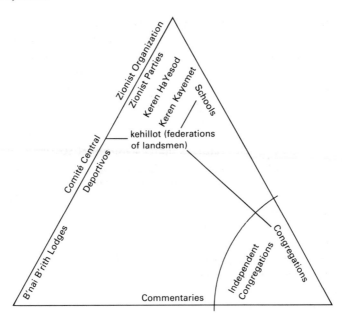

Figure 13.1.   The organizational structure of Mexican Jewry.

lated structure has separated the instrumentalities of the *keter malkhut* from the others and in a short time brought them to dominance.

In the Mexico City community there are four separate *kehillot,* all of which grew out of congregational roots. They still combine the religious-congregational, educational, and communal-welfare spheres. Three of the *kehillot* are Sephardic: the Alianza de Monte Sinai, consisting of Arabic-speaking Jews from Damascus, founded in 1912; the Sociedad Benefiencia del Alicencia Israelita Sedaka y Marpe, consisting of Jews from Aleppo, founded in 1938; and the Unión Sefardi, consisting of Jews from the Balkans, founded in 1923. The Ashkenazim maintain separate *landsmanschaften* and congregations by region of origin, but are united in the Kehillat Nidje Israel, founded in 1922. Their *kehillah* council is structured to provide representation for those constituent bodies. The individual *kehillot* are confederated in the Comité Central of Mexican City Jewry, the organization that undertakes whatever joint functions are necessary. Each *kehillah* raises its own funds for local needs.

The Alianza de Monte Sinai is the oldest community in the country. Its founder, Jacob Granott, was active in the Mexican Revolution, supporting its first leader, Francisco Madero, and maintaining close contact with Pancho Villa and other revolutionary leaders in the north. It is the only Jewish body that has any real identification with that crucial event in Mexican history. Its synagogue was completed in 1913. Although Arabic was originally the common language of the group, later generations have shifted to Spanish. The community maintains a day school from kindergarten through *preparatorio,* the equivalent of the first year of college in the United States. The community now maintains three synagogues in different locations. It offers a full range of religious services and supervises *kashrut* for all the Sephardim. Most of the private life of the community is conducted in the family circle, structured around extended families common to the Arab world. The best estimate places the membership of this community at just under four thousand.

Sedaka y Marpe broke away from the Alianza de Monte Sinai as soon as there were enough Alleppan Jews to develop their own institutions, as they invariably do throughout the Jewish world. The community today has an estimated six thousand members. It maintains two synagogues, a day school from kindergarten through elementary school, followed by a *yeshiva* that meets part time. Although it relies on the *kashrut* supervision of the Alianza de Monte Sinai, it maintains its own burial society.

The Unión Sefardi confines itself to religious services that have incorporated many elements of Reform Judaism. Consequently, it reportedly attracts Ashkenazim who object to the continued use of Yiddish in Nidje Israel. Modest social welfare services are provided by its women's committee. It does not maintain a school, nor does it release membership figures—apparently because the true number would result in higher dues for the Comité Central.

Kehillat Nidje Israel is the largest of the communities. It, too, was founded as a synagogue when the Ashkenazim of Monte Sinai broke away from the Sephardim after an incident in 1922. There were other Ashkenazi worship services operating in the city then and ultimately they all joined the common *kehillah,* but that did not happen until 1954. In the interim, over ten separate congregation-communities developed within the Ashkenazi population, linked only by their use of the same kosher meat services, cemetery, and *mohel,* under the jurisdiction of Nidje Israel. There are separate synagogues for Litvaks and Galitzianers. The Jews from Germany, Austria, and Czechoslovakia who came as refugees from Nazism organized a social and cultural group called Menorah in 1939 and later a Zionist group called Hatikvah. The two were merged in 1948. For many years they maintained Friday night and High Holy Day services, but their children have joined the other Ashkenazi synagogues. Hungarian Jews, who came at the same time, founded their club, Emunah, in 1942, strictly for social purposes.

The unification of the Ashkenazi community was completed between 1954 and 1957. It began with a citywide fund-raising campaign for all Ashkenazi causes and concluded with the formal constitution of a common *kehillah.* Nidje Israel is governed by a council of forty-five, in which are represented the Zionist parties, the Yiddishists, the congregation-communities and *landsmanschaften,* Colegio Israelita (the principal Ashkenazi day school), the Nuevo Colegio Israelita, the youth department, plus different notables selected individually. The Nidje Israel is headquartered in a seven-story Beth Am (House of the People) in Mexico City, which houses the administrative offices, principal synagogue, and facilities for social and communal activities. It still conducts its business in Yiddish and its elections along Zionist lines.

Nidje Israel founded the first Jewish day school in the country, the Colegio Israelita. Instruction was originally conducted in Yiddish. When Hebrew was incorporated into the curriculum, the Yiddishists broke away to form the Nuevo Colegio Israelita, also known as the I. L. Peretz School. The community also established a religious *yeshiva,* Yavne, and it maintains the Tarbut School, which teaches only in Hebrew. In 1963 the Yeshiva of Mexico was established and later was given *kehillah* support. For many years about two-thirds of the Jewish children in Mexico have attended Jewish day schools. There is no common board of education to link the schools and repeated efforts to establish such a body have failed.

The Seminario Idish-Hebreo de Maestros trains teachers for Mexican Jewish schools so successfully that two-thirds of the approximately 150 teachers in those schools are its graduates. However, because knowledge of Yiddish is a prerequisite, Sephardic students are excluded. Because the Sephardic schools also need teachers, they hire Ashkenazi Seminario graduates.

Aside from the synagogues connected with each of the *kehillot,* Bnei Akiva also maintains a *minyan.* There are two Conservative congregations. Beth El, founded by native-born Jews in the 1950s, represents a modernizing trend among Ashkenazim in particular, with its emphasis on the Spanish language and on American-style synagogue services and facilities. It may be the most vital congregation in Mexico. Beth Israel Community Center, founded in 1953 by English-speaking Jews, conducts services and maintains an afternoon school. Although English-speaking, it has developed a mixed membership because it reaches out to Mexican Judaizers and brings them in as converts.

All told, the intimate connections between the religious-congregational and other spheres reflected in the organizational structure have weakened only slightly in recent years. Formal Orthodoxy remains dominant even though most Mexican Jews are far from being observant. Each of the *kehillot* has a *bet din* and only their conversions are recognized in the community. The Conservative congregation sends its converts to the *bet din* of Nidje Israel for the final conversion steps.

Because access to burial in the Jewish cemetery comes through membership in a *kehillah,* even agnostics, atheists, and freethinkers retain their membership in one of the communities and pay their annual dues to be assured of a Jewish burial. The system is strictly enforced, in part because burial fees are still the principal source of communal revenue, generating up to 90 percent of the total. Burials have been delayed until settlements have been reached with families in arrears in their dues and assessments. Thus, between 75 and 80 percent of all known Jews are affiliated with the Jewish communities.

Outside Mexico City, the communities are too small to maintain more than a single organization. The Comunidad Israelita of Guadalajara was founded in 1924. It has fewer than a thousand members (officially, 140 families). The Sephardim and Ashkenazim maintained separate congregations until 1955. The establishment of a common day school helped eliminate the differences. The community also supports the Club Deportivo Maccabi, originally founded by Sephardim and now the center of Jewish life, and a WIZO group. The day school provides classes from kindergarten through *preparatorio.* There is a B'nai B'rith lodge but no local kosher meat. There is also a Conservative congregation for American retirees.

The Monterrey Jewish community has a single Centro Israelita de Monterrey. It maintains a synagogue, the Hativka school from kindergarten through *preparatorio,* in which all but two of the local Jewish children are purportedly enrolled, and a social club, Hativka, the seat of all Jewish activities. The synagogue follows the Ashkenazic rite although it includes the few Sephardic families in town.

The Tijuana Jewish community is concentrated in the Centro Social Israelita de Baja California. Founded in 1965, it provides all the services available in the community— religious, social, and education. Tijuana has no day school, only a part-time religious school, which provides more in the way of community center type activities than Jewish instruction. It is the one community that is growing as Tijuana itself booms. Jewish community centers also exist in Puebla and Torreón.

Mexican Jewry, like other Jewries of Latin America, has gravitated toward its *deportivos* (sports centers), which is the new center of Jewish life. The Centro Deportivo in Mexico City caters to the ordinary Jews; the wealthy have their own club, Belle Vista. The smaller communities also have *deportivos.* In Mexico City, the *deportivo* is the one organization that brings together Jews from all backgrounds and is well funded. It has two kitchens, one kosher and one nonkosher. Though it has a library and offers some cultural activities, it is mainly used for social and recreational purposes.

Almost every Jewish organization in Mexico publishes a periodical, and there are five Jewish newspapers that appear weekly or even more frequently.

External relations–defense sphere. The Mexican attitude toward strangers and Jews in particular is ambivalent. Although Mexico is a xenophobic country, for many years Mexicans also saw their land as a refuge for the homeless. Thus, though they distrusted people from other countries, those who were stateless were welcomed as dispossessed. So, too, Mexico is not a country that is permeated with anti-Semitism, but it has all the anti-Judaism of traditional Catholicism, which, because of the problem of the so-called New Christians, had racial overtones for some five hundred years. By and large, Jews are not considered to be Mexicans but Jews, whose primary ties are to their own country, Israel.

The Jews have responded to this situation on several levels. For most of their relations with the government, influential Jews act as *shtadlanim,* developing close ties with people in high places, which they can then use to secure Jewish interests. On another level, B'nai B'rith lodges, which are in every Jewish community, take community relations as their responsibility. In fact, the Mexican office of the American Jewish Committee is more likely to play a role when organizational activity aside from *shtadlanut* is involved. This may be changing as the Comité Central passes into the hands of the younger generation.

Israel-edah sphere. The Mexican Zionist organizations are responsible for maintaining contact with Israel and conducting activities on its behalf. There are separate countrywide campaigns for the Magbit (Keren Hayesod) and the Keren Kayemet (Jewish National Fund), which are further divided into separate campaigns for Ashkenazim and Sephardim. Each Zionist party conducts a fund-raising campaign for its own needs, and Israeli institutions, particularly the universities, also conduct separate campaigns. Nidje Israel is affiliated with the Latin American office of the World Jewish Congress.

The influence of the United States. Mexican Jewry is constantly if subtly influenced by Mexico's proximity to the United States. Most of the Jews who originally settled in Mexico came because they could not get into the United States, or tried to use Mexico as a springboard for doing so. The children of the community frequently receive their higher education and professional training north of the Rio Grande. There is a constant flow of North American Jewish tourists into Mexico City, some of whom come into contact with the local Jewry.

There are even relatively strong institutional influences. American B'nai B'rith provided direct assistance to the immigrants in the early years. Community relations activities in Mexico were for many years dominated by the American Jewish Committee and the Anti-Defamation League. Mexico was the first Latin American country to have a Conservative congregation, one which usually imports its rabbis from the United States.

Just as Mexico attracts other Americans, it has attracted American Jews as temporary or permanent residents. In general, three groups of American Jews have come to the country. There is a small but growing group of businessmen or people sent by their companies for work assignments in Mexico. These have no intention of becoming permanent residents but sometimes make themselves known to the Jewish community. A second and much larger group consists of retirees who have chosen to live in Mexico because of the good climate and the low cost of living. Most of them gather near

Guadalajara, where they form a formidable share of the small Jewish population, although most of them maintain relatively little, if any, connection with the indigenous Jewish community.

The third group, a fluctuating one, consists of young people who come to Mexico for the experience. Some come as students, others as dropouts either from school or after graduation. They concentrate wherever such populations concentrate, and part of their detachment from American civilization is also a detachment from things Jewish. For more than a few of them, a Mexican sojourn is a step down the road to assimilation in the United States.

With the breakdown of the old order, assimilation has increased in Mexico. Intermarriage has been increasing for the past two decades and Liebman estimates it to be possibly as high as 30 percent. He estimates that half the non-Jewish spouses convert. But in a community where religious observance is minimal, conversion is primarily to preserve the integrity of families. Those who do not convert are also accepted into the family circles, if they are not practicing Christians.

Mexican Jewry has both the conditions and the resources for at least self-maintenance as a community with some amount of outside assistance. (For example, the training of most Jewish professional leadership probably cannot be done locally in a community of that size under any foreseeable circumstances.) Objective and subjective factors also have prevented Mexican Jewry from living up to its potential, factors serious in and of themselves. For the immediate future, Mexican Jewry is faced with the problem of developing its own Jewish personality while not arousing the animosity of xenophobic non-Jews. It also must develop new patterns of Jewish association without abandoning some of the advantages of cohesiveness provided by the older ones.

The Jewish Community of Uruguay

Uruguay affirms that it has a population of forty thousand Jews; if so, this would make it the third or fourth largest Jewish community in Latin America after Argentina, Brazil, and possibly Mexico. Jews did not begin to arrive in Uruguay until late, even by Latin American standards. There is no trustworthy record of Marranos in the region, and the first known Jews in the country date to 1898 when a few drifted in from Argentina. Until the constitution of 1918 separated church and state and protected the rights of aliens, the situation was not encouraging. Still, Jews continued to arrive and in that year there were an estimated seventeen hundred, 75 percent of whom were Sephardim and most of the rest eastern Europeans.

Most of the Jewish community of Uruguay arrived between 1925 and 1928, although there was another spurt of emigration from Central Europe between 1933 and 1940. Almost all live in Montevideo, the capital. Today the percentages are reversed over what they were in 1918: 75 percent of eastern European origin, 13 percent central European, and 12 percent Sephardim. The proximity of Uruguay to Argentina keeps it in the orbit of the larger community.[5]

The first communal organization in Uruguay was Ezra founded by the Sephardim in 1909. The continued immigration brought about a breakdown of the coherence of the small community as *landsmanschaften* and immigrant aid societies proliferated for every possible group. In 1916 the Hevra Kadisha Ashkenazi was founded and in the same year the Sephardim established their Hevra Kadisha, Hesed shel Emet. The German Jews who came after 1933 founded the Nuevo Congregación Israelita, which provided communal, religious, and educational activities for their community.

Zionist activity in Uruguay began in 1911 as an extension of the work of the Argentinian Zionist Federation. After World War I the full range of Zionist parties emerged. Not until 1945 did they federate to form the Consejo Central Sionista, which was reorganized in 1960 as the Federación Sionista Territorial Unificada. The new body, whose formation was stimulated by the World Zionist Organization, was made the official representative of the Jewish Agency in Uruguay.

By and large, the Uruguayan Jewish community is nationalist/secularist in orientation. It is built around four *kehillot:* the Ashkenazi (eastern European) Comunidad Israelita de Montevideo, founded in 1932, with approximately four thousand members; the Comunidad Israelita Sefardita, also founded in 1932, which has fifteen hundred members; the German Nueva Congregación Israelita, founded in 1936, also with fifteen hundred members; and the Societa Hungara de Montevideo, founded in 1942, with two hundred members. Uruguay's four *kehillot* dominate the communal-welfare sphere, their major focus; the religious-congregational sphere, which, except for the Sephardim, is of minor importance in Uruguayan Jewish society; and the Israel-*edah* sphere through the Federación Sionista Territorial Unificada.

All four *kehillot* are united under the Comité Central Israelita (CCI), established in 1940 to represent the Uruguayan Jewish community vis-à-vis the government. The CCI dominates the external relations–defense sphere. It is affiliated with the World Jewish Congress. Its major task is fighting anti-Semitism, which became strong in Uruguay as in the rest of Latin America during the Nazi years and has continued with periodic neo-Nazi outbreaks.

The communities and the CCI are dominated politically by the Zionist parties. In the Ashkenazi *kehillah,* religious matters were separated from other communal-welfare functions in 1942, and are supervised by the Va'ad HaIr LeInyanei HaDat. There is a fifth community, formed by Kehillat HaDat Yireim, ultra-Orthodox Jews who emigrated from Hungary and Transylvania in the 1950s, which stands outside the communal structure.[6]

Non-Zionism is confined to the small group of Jewish radicals including anarcho-sindicalists, Trotskyites, Socialists, and Bundists, who maintain their own organizations. Strongest of these groups are the Communists, known as Progressists in Uruguay. The radicals founded a cultural center as early as 1917, which later became a Progressist stronghold. In the 1930s the Communists could still struggle for control of the community, but the Zionists so overwhelmed them that they have remained only a splinter group. In 1935 the Communists established the Asociación Cultural Jaim Zhitlowsky, which had a youth group and mutual insurance society, the Mutualista Israelita de Uruguay, founded in 1940, and even went so far as to maintain a separate section in the cemetery.

The Ashkenazi and Sephardi communities included educational activities in their programs from their founding. The predecessor of the present Ashkenazi community, the Hevra Kadisha, established a network of schools in 1929 in cooperation with the Jewish Colonization Association (ICA), which brought together some existing institutions and established new ones. The Zionist-oriented Herzl School was founded in 1928. The Sephardi Hevra Kadisha founded the Talmud Torah Eliezer Ben-Yehuda in the same year. Left Poale Zion founded the Shalom Aleichem School in 1941, and the Mizrachi founded its school and the Yeshivat HaRav Kook in 1945, adding a secondary school,

Maaleh, in 1956. The ultra-Orthodox community founded a Talmud Torah and *heder,* Yire'im, in 1948.

Twenty-two hundred students are reported enrolled in the three functioning schools today. Five hundred more are enrolled in the ORT school. All told, they represent less than one quarter of the Jewish school-age population. The largest is the Escuela Integrado, founded in 1962 by uniting several existing institutions. The others are Ariel and Yavne. To serve these schools, a teachers' seminary was founded in 1954 by the Va'ad HaJinukj of the Ashkenazi community, but it is a periodic affair. Coordination of educational activities in the Ashkenazi community is through the Va'ad HaJinukj. Every party and movement has its youth group coordinated by the Federación Juvenil Sionista, founded in 1941, which is represented in the two major countrywide organizations of Uruguayan Jewry.

Cultural activities are now carried on primarily in Spanish, although the older generation still includes a group of Yiddishists and the few Hebraists have their Moadon Ivri. There is some emphasis on translating Jewish writers into Spanish for the small local Jewish intelligentsia. A branch of YIVO maintains an archive and a library, and the Jewish writers and journalists have an association. Uruguay has had an active Jewish press, including daily newspapers in Yiddish, but these are disappearing as the immigrant generation passes.

Almost all these activities are well within the sphere of the *keter malkhut.* Religious activities are principally within the sphere of the *keter kehunah,* with the *keter torah* weak, except in elementary and secondary education, and the modest leadership role which some of the Jewish intelligentsia may play in shaping community attitudes. The traditional *keter torah* role is almost entirely absent in Uruguay, with those Uruguayan Jews concerned about such matters relying on the Argentinian or Israeli rabbinates.

The Jewish Community of Chile

A substantial Marrano population lived in Chile in the sixteenth and seventeenth centuries and gave rise to several famous Inquisition cases. By the eighteenth century they had left or assimilated, founding many of the prominent Chilean families of later centuries. The Chilean Jewish community dates from just before World War I, earlier Jewish arrivals having also assimilated or left. At that time, groups of Ashkenazim from eastern Europe and Sephardim from the Balkans settled in the country. The Sociedad Unión Israelita de Chile, the first Jewish organization, was founded in 1909, and Zionist activity began a year later. But the overwhelming Roman Catholicism of the country led many Jews to hide their identity, and organized life was carried on through societies with neutral names that did not reveal their Jewishness.

In September 1919 the first congress of Chilean Jewry was convened in response to the anti-Semitic events in Argentina that culminated in the semana trágica. The congress was attended by Ashkenazim and Sephardim, representatives of thirteen organizations from six cities, and Indian Judaizers as well. The congress established the Federación Sionista de Chile, which became the framing organization of Chilean Jewry, functioning as a representative body and as a Zionist organization. Thus the annual meeting of Chilean Jewry takes the form of a Zionist congress. In 1920 the Ashkenazi community organizations in Santiago united to form the Circulo Israelita, which links the religious-congregational and educational-cultural spheres. Chile was unusual in that the external affairs–defense and Israel-*edah* spheres were linked from the first, and the institutions normally found in the communal-welfare sphere were in the hands of the religious congregations.

The Zionist monopoly lasted until 1932 when a crisis in the community led to the slow emergence of other institutions that, in time, took over some of the functions of the Zionist federation. The increase in anti-Semitism in the 1930s, the result of a spread of Nazism to Latin America, led to the establishment of a separate representative organization, the Comité Representativo in 1940. In 1943 the Zionist Federation and the Comité Representativo reached a formal agreement dividing responsibilities for their spheres; since then the Comité Representativo has handled the external relations of Chilean Jewry. It is a member of the World Jewish Congress, and the Zionist Federation is a member of the World Zionist Organization. Chilean Jews feel at home in Chile in a way not common to other Latin American communities, yet anti-Semitism is a recurring issue. Nazi organizations are legal and are supported by a large, influential Arab population. The Israel-overseas sphere is the province of the Zionist Federation, the Zionist youth movements, WIZO, and Pioneer Women, and the Centro Universitario, which serves Jewish university students.[7]

The Jews of Chile also felt the need to develop separate health, welfare, and educational institutions. These include the usual welfare societies such as the Bikur Holim and also the Policlínica Israelita to provide medical services. A Jewish legal aid service was established early on. In 1944 the Banco Israelita was organized to serve the Jewish business community.

By and large, grass roots Jewish organization in Chile, like other Latin American countries, is based on country of origin with eastern European Ashkenazim, German Jews, and Sephardim having separate congregations, social groups, and welfare associations. The principal bodies are the Ashkenazi *kehillah,* which grew out of the Hevra Kedisha, which dates to the World War I period; and the Comunidad Israelita Sefardi Magven David founded in 1935. Originally there were two main Ashkenazi groups, Circulo Israelita and Kehilla Ashkenazi whose membership overlapped. They merged in 1982. Relatively more German Jews came to Chile than to many other Latin American countries, in part because Chile already had a long tradition of German settlement, in part because they could get in. They maintain their own Sociedad Cultural Israelita Bnei Yisroel, founded in 1933. There is also B'nei Yisroel founded in 1933. At one time *landsmanschaften,* particularly those of the Polish Jews founded in 1932 and Masje of the Hungarian Jews founded in 1937, were significant.[8] The latter survives as a small body.

Chilean Jewry suffered a severe blow at the time of the election of Salvador de Allende to the presidency, the rise of the Left to power, and the subsequent counterrevolution by the military. Two-thirds of the thirty-five thousand Jews left the country in the wake of those upheavals—the capitalists when Allende assumed power and the leftists when the military took over—although a number subsequently returned. The Jewish community declined to about fifteen thousand today. Some 90 percent of the Jews of Chile live in Santiago, but there are communities in Valparaíso–Viña del Mar, Concepción, Temuco, Valdivia, Coquimbo, Ovalle, Copiapó, Las Arenas, and Arica.[9]

This much reduced Jewish community is carrying on as active a Jewish life as possible, but it has had to consolidate a number of its institutions for sheer lack of numbers. The Comité Representativo had ceased to function during the upheavals, but was reconstituted in 1984. It holds an annual gathering, primarily designed to strengthen Jewish life in the outlying communities. In fact, only Santiago and Valparaíso–Viña del

Mar maintain viable Jewish communities. In the others there are essentially a few Jewish families struggling to preserve their identity.

The communal-welfare sphere includes B'nai B'rith lodges in Santiago, Valparaíso, and Concepción. Bikur Holim continues to be the principal welfare organization. There is also a home for needy children, a home for the aged, and a community center, the Estadio Israelita, founded in 1952, which increasingly has become the focal point of community life.

There are four synagogues in Santiago. The two largest, Askhenazic and Sephardic, are now identified with the Conservative movement. Both have Conservative rabbis of Ashkenazic origin, trained at the Conservative seminary in Buenos Aires. The German Jews maintain a synagogue of their own, and there is a small Ashkenazic Orthodox congregation with a Hassidic orientation founded by Jews from Argentina and Israel. Its rabbi is from Israel. The one synagogue not based on community of origin is the one at the Estadio Israelita, which functions only on the High Holy days and for special occasions.

At one time there were two sports clubs, the older being the Club Atlética Israelita Maccabi, founded in 1948, which was merged with the Estadio Israelita. As elsewhere in Latin America, the sports club is the center of Jewish life.

The educational-cultural sphere comprises a large comprehensive day school in Santiago, the Instituto Hebreo, with fourteen hundred students from kindergarten through high school, and a department of Jewish studies in the University of Chile. ORT maintains a vocational school as part of the comprehensive school complex. The school is under the supervision of a community-wide education committee. The community still maintains two weekly newspapers. *La Palabra Israelita* is controlled by the Ashkenazi *kehilla*.

The key cosmopolitan leaders of the community are the men who head the Committé Representativo, the Zionist Federation, and the local Magbit. Together they form the governing triumvirate of the community. For thirty years, from 1953 to 1983, the key figure in Chilean Jewry was Gil Sinai. He headed the Kehilla Ashkenazi and the Committee Representativo and was the principal contact between Chilean and world Jewry.

The Venezuelan Jewish Community

Venezuela was one of the first newly independent Latin American states to establish religious freedom; it did so in its constitutions of 1819 and 1821. As a result, the first Jewish families settled in Coro about 1820. A Jewish cemetery was established there several years later, which still serves the few Jewish families remaining in that city. By the 1840s, Jewish cemeteries had been established in Caracas, Barcelona, and Puerto Cabello.

Most of these Jews were emigrants from Curaçao, and retained close ties with the Jewish community there. They were Sephardim, descendants of Portuguese Marranos. As the century wore on, the children of these first Jews assimilated or left. Their family names today are found principally among the leading non-Jewish families of the country. While Jews gathered in informal *minyanim* for prayer, no permanent place of Jewish worship was established in Venezuela during the nineteenth century.

The contemporary Jewish community began with the arrival of other Sephardim from North Africa before World War I. Still, the Jewish population remained small. Two hundred forty-seven Jews were recorded in 1891 and only 475 in 1917. That number was almost doubled in the national census of 1926, which, estimating the Jews who did not openly declare their religious affiliation, probably meant that there were about one thousand Jews in the country.

Eastern European Jews began to settle in Venezuela in the interwar generation and were joined after 1934 by refugees from Central Europe, about six hundred of whom arrived during the decade. At the beginning of the postwar generation there were between five and six thousand Jews in Venezuela. Now the Jewish population is estimated at twenty thousand, but there is some serious question as to how this increase came about because the only "mass" immigration in the postwar generation was in 1958 when one thousand Jews from Egypt, Hungary, and Israel were admitted into the country.[10]

More than half of the Jewish community lives in Caracas. The other concentrations are in Maracaibo, Valencia, and Maraque. The organized Jewish community in Maracaibo includes a synagogue, a B'nai B'rith lodge, and a Jewish school.

The Asociación Israelita de Venezuela is the oldest Jewish organization in Caracas. It was founded in the 1920s by the Sephardim. Today it has about eight hundred family members and focuses on a synagogue. The eastern European Ashkenazi community is organized around three congregations: the Unión Israelita, which has about thirteen hundred family members and is somewhere between Reform and Conservative in its practice, the Orthodox Shomrei Shabbat congregation, and the ultra-Orthodox Rabinato de Venezuela. The institution that unites the Jewish community in Caracas is the Hebraica sports and community center, which has become the center of Jewish activity for the younger generation.

The Israel-*edah* sphere is dominated by the Zionist Federation, which dates from 1953. Earlier attempts in the 1920s and 1930s to develop a Zionist federation failed. The federation comprises the Zionist parties, Keren Hayesod, WIZO, Maccabi, and Zionist youth groups.

The framing institution of Venezuelan Jewry is the Federación de Asociaciónes Israelitas de Venezuela, which dominates the external relations–defense sphere and is affiliated with the World Jewish Congress. Its membership includes the communities, the Zionist Federation, and B'nai B'rith, whose two lodges were founded in 1954 and 1956. The *federación* was established in 1965 in response to a surge of anti-Semitism in the country.[11]

In Venezuela almost all Jewish children attend Jewish schools, principally because of their high academic standards. The educational-cultural sphere is dominated by the Colegio Moral Lucas–Herzl Bialik Integrated School, founded in 1947 at the instigation of the Ashkenazi Unión Israelita de Caracas. Children from all the communities attend it. Non-Jewish students, attracted by its high academic standards, represent between 7 and 10 percent of the student body. The school has become known worldwide for its success in Jewish education. Jewish cultural life beyond schooling, however, is very weak.[12]

The Smaller Jewish Communities of Latin America

Bolivia. There were Marranos in Bolivia in the sixteenth century and at least a few Jews passed through the country in the eighteenth and nineteenth centuries. The first permanent settlement of Jews was in 1905. They came from Russia and were followed by another group from Argentina and then by a group of Sephardi families from the eastern Mediterranean. Until the rise of Nazism, there were no more than thirty Jewish families. Seven thousand German Jewish immigrants arrived between 1933 and 1942; most left as soon as they could gain entry to some other country. Now there are no more than a thousand Jews in Bolivia. Most of the Jews are located in La Paz, the capital, but there is a small community in Cochabamba, with a single congregation and a kindergarten.[13]

Jewish communal life in the country began with the founding of the Circulo Israelita in 1935 by eastern European Jews. German Jews then founded the Comunidad Israelita de Bolivia. In the late 1930s, a B'nai B'rith lodge and a Zionist federation were organized. A framing organization was established at the Comité Central Judeo de Bolivia. These groups have together provided the range of communal services, including a cemetary, Hevra Kadisha, Bikur Holim, a home for the aged, WIZO, and a Maccabi sports program. There is a Jewish day school for kindergarten through secondary grades, which attracts many non-Jewish students because of its high standards. Today there are so few young Jews that the school has declined considerably.

Colombia. Marranos reached Colombia with the Spanish conquistadores in the sixteenth century, and a substantial community developed until it was destroyed by the Inquisition in the mid-seventeenth century. Although Roman Catholicism was the only religion permitted until 1853, individual Jews began to settle in what is now Colombia by the end of the eighteenth century, coming in from the Caribbean islands. By the middle of the nineteenth century Jews had settled in all Colombia's port cities and had established a cemetery in Santa Marta. Cemeteries were established in other communities over the next several decades, but not until 1874 was a congregation organized. Most of these early Jews were Sephardim and most assimilated during the nineteenth century.

The Colombian Jewish community was revived just after World War I by Sephardi Jewish emigrants from the Balkans, North Africa, and Syria. They were joined by eastern European Jews and both groups were later augmented by German Jews fleeing Nazism in 1938. The Jewish population of Colombia peaked at eleven thousand at the time of World War II and is now about seven thousand, most of whom are in Bogotá.

Until the 1940s, Jewish life was fragmented among local congregations and welfare institutions, because the Colombian government did not allow any larger organizations. Ultimately, however, the Jewish community was able to establish the Federación General des Comunidades, a representative body affiliated with the World Jewish Congress. It unites all three groups, each with its communal institutions: the Centro Israelita de Bogotá, founded in 1928; the Comunidad Hebrea Sefardi, founded earlier but reorganized in 1943; and the Asociación Israelita de Montefiore, respectively.

There are four synagogues in Bogotá: two Ashkenazi, one Sephardi, and one German; the Colombo Hebrew School from kindergarten through the secondary grades; B'nai B'rith, and a Zionist organization, founded in 1927. The Jews of Cali and the surrounding area are united in the Unión Federal Hebrea, which provides religious and social services. Its constituents include Ashkenazi and Sephardi synagogues and the Jorge Isnaes school that enrolls 92 percent of the Jewish children. Barranquilla is the third organized community in the country.

By and large, the Colombian authorities have not been hospitable to the Jews, desiring them to assimilate but creating an environment not conducive to assimilation. There is considerable Nazi and other anti-Jewish activity. Hence it is not surprising that the younger generation tend to leave the country when they can.[14]

Costa Rica. The first Jews to settle in Costa Rica also came from the Caribbean islands in the nineteenth century but they quickly assimilated. The present Jewish community was founded by Turkish and eastern European Jewish immigrants who came after World War I and German Jewish refugees who came after 1933. Organized Jewish life revolves around the Centro Israelita Sionista. There are organized WIZO and B'nai B'rith groups, other Zionist and youth groups, and La Sociedad de Damas Israelitas de Beneficia. There is a comprehensive school, Instituto Jaim Weizman, attended by 90 percent of the Jewish children. Costa Rican society is not hospitable to unassimilated foreigners, and the Jews are considered in that category. But after an initial period of hostility the government has been friendly. Today there are about twenty-five hundred Jews in Costa Rica.[15]

Cuba. The one thousand Jews remaining in Cuba comprise the remnants of a Jewish community whose population had reached a high of twelve thousand in the 1950s but declined precipitously after the Castro revolution in 1959. It has been declining further ever since.

As a community, Cuba has been a special blend of the Hispanic and North American worlds. It has a Marrano past dating to the landing of Luis de Torres with the first European settlers in 1492. From the mid-seventeenth to the eighteenth centuries a secret community of Jewish merchants carried on an extensive European and North American trade, but they either left or disappeared.

The present community dates to the period immediately after Cuba became independent from Spain in 1898, thereby opening the country for legal Jewish settlement. The first settlers were Jews from Florida who had been supporters of Cuban independence or veterans of the Spanish-American War. They settled in Cuba to take advantage of business opportunities. The community was formally founded in 1904 with the establishment of the Union Hebrew Congregation, affiliated with the American Reform Movement.[16]

About a decade later Sephardi Jews arrived from the Balkans. In 1914 they established the Unión Hebrea Shevet Ajim, an entirely separate entity, although they did receive some aid from the Ashkenazim on an individual basis.

A third wave of emigration from eastern Europe began in 1920. Most continued on to the United States until the immigration laws of 1924 prevented that, leading to a concentration of such Jews in Cuba. They were assisted by American Jewish organizations such as HIAS, the Joint Distribution Committee, and the National Council of Jewish Women. The eastern European Jews established the Centro Israelita as their own communal organization, which benefited from the aid given by American Jews. The Ashkenazi community expanded beyond limited congregational functions to include a welfare program, a medical clinic, a library, a Spanish language evening school, a student center, and a drama club.

The Centro Israelita was strongly identified with Zionism. As a result, the Kulterverein was founded in 1926 under Communist auspices. From then until the late 1930s it competed for control of the Ashkenazi community with the Centro Israelita. Another breakaway group consisted of Orthodox Jews who established Adas Isroel in 1925, which split again in 1929 but was reunited as the Kehillah Ashkenazi Ahdut Israel.

The Asociación Sionista, later the Unión Sionista de Cuba, was founded in 1929 and in the 1930s was divided into the range of Zionist parties. A vocational school was established by ORT in 1935, and a B'nai B'rith lodge was established in 1943. Between 1933 and 1944 from ten to twelve thousand Jewish refugees from Nazism passed through the country, few of them staying.

Problems of representation to the Cuban authorities led to the establishment of the Federación Israelita de Cuba in 1932 in the external relations–defense field. It was replaced by the Comité Intersocial, which functioned between 1932 and 1935 and then the Jewish Committee of Cuba in 1935–36. But cultural distances between the three communities were difficult to bridge. In 1936–39 the Jewish Chamber of Commerce assumed responsibility for defending the Jews against anti-Semitism and representing the community. The Comité Central was reorganized in 1939 and brought together all segments of the community. It was then recognized by the Cuban government, but the basic divisions remained.

After World War II there was another attempt at organizing a common framework, initiated by the Ashkenazi community, which in 1949 founded the Patronada de la Comunidada Hebrea, which built a large community center for the entire community. Except for the Comité Central, the Talmud Torah Theodor Herzl, and the community center, the three communities remained separate.

The Jewish population peaked in 1952 when it was estimated at twelve thousand—75 percent in Havana and the rest scattered throughout the island. Ashkenazim outnumbered Sephardim approximately two to one, while the American community never numbered more than a few hundred. Each of the three communities straddled the communal-welfare, religious-congregational, and educational-cultural spheres, leaving external affairs and defense to the Comité Centrale and Israel-*edah* affairs to the Magbit. In the end, however, the smallness of the Cuban Jewish community also led to a modest measure of integration in the educational-cultural sphere. The Talmud Torah Theodor Herzl, founded in 1924, served children from the three communities from the first and from 1927 on was subsidized by whatever central Jewish community organization existed in the country. In 1939 it became the Colegio Autonomo de Central Israelita. Otherwise the groups established their own schools. There were Sephardi, Zionist, religious, secularist, leftist, and American-style English language schools in the 1950s.[17]

At first, the Castro revolution was viewed sympathetically by many Cuban Jews, and at no point has the revolution been anti-Jewish per se. But its effort to impose communism and destroy the bourgeoisie led thousands of Jews to emigrate, principally to the United States. There they established three Cuban Jewish communities in Miami.

The Jewish community was impoverished by the regime's socializing measures, and by 1963 only 30 percent of the remaining three thousand Jews were employed. The community's schools were consolidated into one, the Albert Einstein School, in the 1960s. The Zionist movement continued until the Six-Day War. Five synagogues continued to cover the range of the communal divisions established fifty years earlier. But although the community's decline has stabilized at one thousand Jews, who have found a way to live with the regime, it is a remnant community.[18]

Dominican Republic. A few individuals made their way to the Dominican Republic while it was under Spanish rule and then in the early years of Dominican independence in the nineteenth century, but all assimilated or left. Only after World War I did eastern European, German, and Hungarian Jews settle on the island; most of them came as refugees after the rise of Nazism. In 1939 there were only forty Jews in the country and by 1943 there were one thousand.

Because the Dominican Republic was the one country that agreed to accept large-scale Jewish immigration before World War II, the Joint Distribution Committee (JDC) tried to establish a colony at Sosua. The effort failed despite the extensive backing given it by the JDC. At its peak, the settlement had five hundred inhabitants. There were less than one hundred left at the end of the first postwar generation.

Organized Jewish life on the island consists of two synagogues: one in Santo Domingo and the other in Sosua, linked in the Comité Central de los Judios de la Republica Dominicana. In 1983 there were an estimated two hundred Jews in the country.[19]

Ecuador. Although there may well have been Jews in Ecuador in colonial times, Jewish settlement in the country hardly antedates the 1930s. About twenty-seven hundred Jews reached Ecuador between 1933 and 1943. In 1950 the Jewish population peaked at four thousand. Today it is estimated to be one thousand.

Freedom of worship was guaranteed by the liberal constitution of 1936, which came at the right time to allow the Jews to organize. Because the Jewish population of the country consists primarily of German Jewish refugees, it is homogeneous; hence it was able to found a single organization in 1938, the Asociación de Beneficencia Israelita, to handle its religious and cultural affairs. That body established a court of arbitration and a Hevra Kadisha. Since then a Zionist federation and B'nai B'rith lodge have been established. There is also a cooperative bank as is typical of many Latin American communities' where Jews do not trust their money to the non-Jewish institutions. Since World War II the Jewish community in Quito has acquired a building, established a home for the aged, and erected a synagogue.

Ecuadoran Jews are even more separated from the local population than in the other Latin American countries because of their internal homogeneity and the particularly sharp division of Ecuadorans into upper and peasant classes. The Jews fall in the the middle where they form a distinctive class as well as a separate ethnoreligious community.[20]

El Salvador. Jewish settlement in El Salvador dates to the first half of the nineteenth century when French Sephardi Jews settled in Chialchuapa, but only a few Jews dribbled into the country over the next century and no communal institutions were established until World War II. The Comunidad Israelita de El Salvador was organized in 1944. It established a cemetery in 1945 and a synagogue in 1950. The Zionist Organization of El Salvador was founded in 1945. With only 350 Jews in the country, there is no Jewish school and little beyond the life of the congregation.[21]

Guatemala. A few Marranos drifted to Guatemala from Mexico and then disappeared. In the mid-nineteenth century, Jews from Germany came and also assimilated. The present community is descended from Jewish immigrants who arrived just before World War I from Germany and the Middle East, who were followed in the 1920s by eastern European Jews. That Jewish community was ruined in 1932 when the Guatemalan government prohibited peddling and many Jews perforce left the country. Few German Jews found refuge in Guatemala because of restrictive legislation.

The eleven hundred Jews in the country are divided into German, Sephardi, and eastern European groups, each with its own institutions. The German Sociedad Israelita de Guatemala and Bet El is affiliated with the Reform movement. The Sephardim have the Magen David and Ashkenazim the Centro Hebreo. There is a Comité Central which confederates the three communities, plus Bnai Brith, WIZO, and the youth groups. All the Zionist groups are linked in the Organización Sionista de Guatemala. There is a small Jewish school.[22]

Honduras. Although there are Inquisition records attesting to the presence of Jews in Honduras in colonial times and a few reached the country in the nineteenth century, no community was established until the arrival of German Jewish refugees in the 1930s.

So few of them arrived that there were never more than two hundred Jews in the country. The families that came in dribs and drabs either left or intermarried. There is a Comunidad Hebreo de Tegucigalpa, which is affiliated with the Federation of Jewish Communities in Central America and Panama, and the ever-present WIZO group, but there is not even a synagogue in Honduras.[23]

Nicaragua. Eastern European Jews who arrived after 1929 established the Congregación Israelita de Nicaragua. A WIZO group was organized in 1941. Most of the 126 Jews who lived in the country in 1968 fled after the Sandanista takeover in 1979 so that today the community is for all intents and purposes extinct.[24]

Panama. Because Panama was part of Colombia from 1821 to 1903, the first Jews who settled in that country were Sephardim from Jamaica who drifted up from the Colombian port cities. A few more arrived at the time of the California gold rush to take advantage of the business opportunities brought by the completion of the railroad across the Isthmus of Panama in 1855. Kahal Shearith Israel, the first Jewish community, was founded in 1876 in the city of Panama, with a synagogue, cemetery, and mutual assistance organization. A Jewish organization was established in Colón at about the same time. The Jewish community grew slightly at the time of the construction of the Panama Canal. In time Kahal Shearith Israel affiliated with the Reform movement, and many of the descendants of its first families have intermarried and assimilated.

An estimated thirty-five hundred Jews lived in Panama in 1982. Most are Sephardim, who maintain the largest community, Shevet Ajim. The third largest congregation is Beth-El, which consists of Ashkenazim who arrived in the 1930s. The three congregations are confederated under a central council, which handles affairs of the community and raises money for Israel. It is affiliated with the Federation of Jewish Communities of Central America and Panama. There are two Jewish day schools, La Academia Hebrea and Instituto Alberto Einstein, which have acquired excellent reputations and between them enroll all local Jewish children and many of the children of the non-Jewish elite, a community center, a B'nai B'rith lodge, the inevitable WIZO, and a students' club.[25]

Paraguay. The Jewish community of Paraguay was founded by Sephardim who emigrated from Eretz Israel and settled there at the time of World War I. They founded the Alianza Israelita as a Hevra Kadisha and a synagogue in 1917 when they were joined by other Sephardim from the Balkans. The first eastern European Jews came in the 1920s and founded an Ashkenazi community, the Unión Hebraica. Paraguay enabled between fifteen and twenty thousand German and central European Jews to find refuge between 1933 and 1939; almost all left as soon as they could. The few who remained established the Unión de Israelitas Pro Socorro Mutual. The Ashkenazim later built a common synagogue.

The two communities have established a common Consejo Representativo Israelita de Paraguay to represent them before the authorities. They have a common school, a sports club, a B'nai B'rith lodge, a WIZO chapter, and one or two youth groups. Although Paraguay became a haven for Nazi war criminals after World War II and has a large Arab population, the Jews have not been disturbed, apparently because the country's lifetime president, Alfredo Stroessner, protects them. About seven hundred Jews remain in the country.[26]

Peru. Peru was one of the two great concentrations of Marranos in the sixteenth and seventeenth centuries. An inquisitional tribunal was established in Lima for all Hispanic South America, and there were regular crackdowns on Judaizers, leading to frequent autos-da-fé. The greatest was in 1634 when so many people were arrested that the economy of Peru collapsed in the wake of the Inquisition's activities. That crackdown led to the greatest auto-da-fé in the New World in 1639. The work of the Inquisition was so effective that by the latter part of the seventeenth century Judaism was wiped out in Peru.

The present Jewish community dates to the mid-nineteenth century when central European merchants and engineers began to settle in the country. They formed a community, La Sociedad de Beneficencia Israelita, in 1870 but later assimilated, so that, although the society continues to exist, not one descendant of the original members is still Jewish. They were succeeded by other central European Jews who continued their traditions, however.

Sephardim began to arrive about 1880, principally from North Africa, and established a community in Quito parallel to the community in Lima. Most later left, leaving behind a group of descendants who still call themselves Hijos des Hebreos (Sons of the Hebrews). After World War I there was a more substantial immigration of Balkan Sephardim to Lima.

In the 1930s there was an influx of German Jewish refugees who strengthened the old German Jewish community. Today there are the usual three Jewish communities in Peru: eastern European Ashkenazi, German, which has inherited the institutions of the 1870 community, and Sephardi. The Ashkenazim are organized in the Unión Israelita and the Sephardim in the Sociedad Beneficencia Israelita Sefardi, each with a synagogue, rabbi, and Hevra Kadisha, but they maintain a common cemetery. The three are confederated as the Asociación des Sociedades Israelitas. There are two homes for the aged, one for the eastern European and one for the central European Jews. There is a Jewish school, the Colegio Leon Pinelo, established in 1946, which enrolls 95 percent of Lima's Jewish children. The Hebraica Sports and Social Club was founded in 1956 as a second generation phenomenon. There is a B'nai B'rith lodge, WIZO, youth organizations, and a monthly Jewish community newspaper, *Nosotros,* published since 1930. Today some five thousand Jews live in Peru.[27]

Notes

1. Seymour B. Liebman, *The Jewish Community of Mexico* (Jerusalem: Center for Jewish Community Studies, 1978); *HaYehudim be-Mexico ve be'Artzot America HaTikhona* (The Jewish Communities in Mexico and Central America) issue of *Tefutsot Yisrael,* vol. 16, no. 1 (January–March 1978) (Hebrew); Isaiah Austri-Dan, "The Jewish Community of Mexico," *Dispersion and Unity,* no. 2 (1963), pp. 51–73.

2. Martin A. Cohen, ed., *The Jewish Experience in Latin America* (New York: Ktav Publishing House, 1971); Corinne Azen Krause, "The Jews in Mexico: A History with Special Emphasis on the Period from 1857 to 1930," Ph.D. dissertation (University of Pittsburgh, 1970) and "Mexico—Another Promised Land? A Review of Prospects for Jewish Colonization in Mexico: 1881–1925," *American Jewish Historical Quarterly,* no. 61 (June 1972), pp. 325–41; Seymour B. Liebman, ed., *Jews and the Inquisition in Mexico: The Great Auto da Fé of 1869* (Lawrence, Kans.: Coronado Press, 1974).

3. Krause, "The Jews in Mexico" and "Mexico—Another Promised Land?"; Harriet Lesser, "A History of the Jewish Community of Mexico City, 1912," Ph.D. dissertation (New York University, 1972); Marlin Zielonda, "The Jews of Mexico," *Year Book of the Central Conference of American Rabbis,* vol. 33 (1923), pp. 425–43.

4. Liebman, *The Jewish Community of Mexico;* Jacob Glantz, *Notes sobres la formación de la comunidad judía de Mexico, Israel y la diaspora en al año 5721 (1960–61),* ed. Enrique Chemilsky (Mexico City, 1962); Jacob Levitz, "The Acculturation of East European Jews in Mexico City, 1920–1946," master's thesis (Wayne University, 1946) and "The Jewish Community in Mexico: Its Life and Education," Ph.D. dissertation

(Dropsie College, 1954); American Jewish Committee, "Summary Report of Mexico City Survey of Jewish Attitudes," report prepared by Manheim S. Shapiro, September 1963; *HaYehudim be-Mexico be'Artzot America HaTikhona,* issue of *Tefutsot Yisrael;* Efraim Zadoff, "Ideological Trends in Secular Jewish Education in Mexico and Argentina, 1935–1955," master's thesis (Hebrew University of Jerusalem, 1980) (Hebrew): Judith L. Elkin, "Latin American Jewry Today," *American Jewish Year Book 1986,* pp. 3–50.

    5. Asher Sapolinsky, "The Jewry of Uruguay," *Dispersion and Unity,* no. 2 (1963), pp. 74–88; World Jewish Congress, *Judíos en el Uruguay* (Montevideo, 1968).

    6. Paula Reicher, "Hapoalim HeYehudim be-Uruguay," (Jewish Workers in Uruguay) (Ramat Aviv: Tel Aviv University, Institute for Zionist Research, 1971) (Hebrew); R. Spiegelman, ed., *Aspectos relaciónados con la formación y desarrollo de la comunidad judía en el Uruguay* (Montevideo: Centro de Estudios Judaicos, 1978); and "Jews of Uruguay," from Archives of the Jerusalem Center for Public Affairs, ca. 1970.

    7. Gunther Bohm, "Judíos en Chile durant el siglo XIX," *Comunidades judías de latinoamerica* (1971–72), pp. 340–66; "Jews in Chile," from the Archives of the Jerusalem Center for Public Affairs, ca. 1970; Moises Senderey, *Historia de la colectividad israelita de Chile* (Santiago: Editorial "Dos Ydische Wort," 1956); Moshe Nes-El, "La imigración judía a Chile durante 1929–1939," *Coloquio,* 7 (1982), pp. 73–88.

    8. Benny Bachrach, "HaYishuv HaYehudi ba-Valparaiso, Chile," *Dispersion and Unity,* no. 2 (June 1960), pp. 40–47; Gunther Bohm, "Juden in Chile," in Rolf Italaander, ed., *Juden in Lateinamerika* (Tel Aviv, 1971); "Jews in Chile"; Mauricio Pitchon, "The Sephardic Jewish Community of Chile," unpublished manuscript, Archives of the Jerusalem Center for Public Affairs; Gunther Bohm, "Chile," *Encyclopedia Judaica,* vol. 5, pp. 462–67.

    9. Judith L. Elkin, *Jews of the Latin American Republics* (Chapel Hill: University of North Carolina Press, 1980).

    10. Elkin, *Jews of the Latin American Republics;* "Venezuela," in *Encyclopedia Judaica,* vol. 16, pp. 90–93; Jacob Beller, *Jews in Latin America* (New York: Jonathan David Publishers, 1969), pp. 68–80.

    11. Beller, *Jews in Latin America;* A. Monk and J. Isaacson, eds., *Comunidades Judíos de Latinoamerica* (1970); "Venezuela," in *Encyclopedia Judaica.*

    12. "Venezuela," in *Encyclopedia Judaica;* and Scharfstein, "Jewish Education in Latin America."

    13. "Bolivia," in *Encyclopedia Judaica,* vol. 4, pp. 1187–88; Monk and Isaacson, eds., *Comunidades Judíos de Latinoamerica,* pp. 36–40; Elkin, *Jews of the Latin American Republics.*

    14. *Skira Klalit al Yahadut Colombia* (General Survey on Colombian Jewry) (Bogotá: Federación Sionista de Colombia, 1974); Tom Price, "The Jewish Community of Colombia," unpublished manuscript prepared for the Center for Jewish Community Studies (1976).

    15. On Costa Rican Jewry, see Tom Price, "The Jewish Community of Costa Rica," unpublished manuscript prepared for the Center for Jewish Community Studies (1976); Scott R. Benarde, "A Contented Corner in Latin America," *Hadassah Magazine* (March 1978), pp. 12–14; Walter Ruby, "Peddlers' Paradise," *The Jerusalem Post Magazine* (October 22, 1982), p. 9; Frank Rasky, "Jews in Costa Rica Proud of Tiny Country," *Canadian Jewish News* (September 26, 1984), p. 42.

    16. Larry M. Becker, "The Jewish Community of Cuba," *Congress Bulletin* (May–June 1971); Abraham J. Dubleman, "Cuba," *American Jewish Year Book 1962,* vol. 63, pp. 481–85; Sandra M. Kaplan and Alexander J. Dubelman, eds., *Un cuarto de siglo vida habañera, 1932–1957* (Havana: Havaner Lebn Almanac, 1958); Ran Leizer, ed., *Continuidad hebrea en tierra Cubana,* Almanaque comemorativo del 25 aniversario del Centro israelita de Cuba 1925–50 (Cuba, 1951); Boris Sapir, *The Jewish Community of Cuba,* trans. Simon Wolin (New York: Jewish Teachers' Seminary Press, 1948) and "Jews in Cuba," *Jewish Review,* no. 5 (July–September 1946), pp. 109–44.

    17. On the organization of the Cuban Jewish community, see Boris Sapir, "Jewish Organizations in Cuba," *Jewish Review,* no. 4 (January–March 1947), pp. 263–81; Everett Gendler, "Holy Days in Havana," *Conservative Judaism,* no. 23 (winter 1969), pp. 15–24; *Havaner Lebn Almanac* (Havana, various dates); Seymour B. Liebman, "Cuba," *American Jewish Year Book 1969,* vol. 70, pp. 238–46; Ann Crittenden, "Jews in Cuba, Once Prosperous, See Community Shrink to 1,500," *The New York Times* (December 12, 1977).

    18. "Cuba," in *Encyclopedia Judaica,* vol. 5, pp. 1146–51; Liebman, "Cuba,"; Elkin, *Jews of the Latin American Republics;* Dubelman, "Cuba."

    19. On the Jews in the Dominican Republic, see Brookings Institution, *Refugee Settlement in the Dominican Republic* (Washington, D.C.: Brookings Institution, 1942); Dominican Republic Settlement Association (DORSA), *Sosua: Haven for Refugees in the Dominican Pepublic,* pamphlet no. 4 (New York, 1941); Hyman Kisch, "The Jewish Settlement from Central Europe in the Dominican Republic," Ph.D. dissertation (Jewish Theological Seminary, 1970); Netam Lam, "From Sosua to Azua," *Hadassah Magazine,* no. 53 (November 1971), pp. 16–17, 38–39; Ben Barber, "Endgame in Sosua," *The Jerusalem Post Magazine,* pp. 7–8.

20. On the Jews in Ecuador, see "Ecuador," in *Encyclopedia Judaica*, vol. 6, pp. 359–60; Abraham Monk and J. Isaacson, eds., *Comunidades Judíos de Latinoamerica* (1968), pp. 82–83; Benno Weiser, "Ecuador: Eight Years on Ararat," *Commentary*, no. 3 (June 1947), pp. 531–36.

21. On the Jews of El Salvador, see "El Salvador," in *Encyclopedia Judaica*, vol. 6, p. 687 and Beller, *Jews in Latin America*, pp. 42–45.

22. On the Jews of Guatemala, see "Guatemala," in *Encyclopedia Judaica*, vol. 7, pp. 956–57; Beller, *Jews in Latin America;* F. Tennenbaum, ed., *La comunidad Judía de Guatemala* (1963); Monk and Isaacson, eds., *Comunidades Judías de Latinoamerica.* pp. 86–88.

23. On the Jews of Honduras, see "Honduras," in *Encyclopedia Judaica*, vol. 8, p. 962; Monk and Isaacson, eds., *Comunidades Judíos de Latinoamerica*, pp. 89–90.

24. On the Jews of Nicaragua, see Walter Ruby, "Speaking to the Sandinistas," *Jerusalem Post* (August 21, 1984); Morton M. Rosenthal, "Nicaragua's Jews: A Second Opinion," *Reform Judaism* (fall 1984), p. 6 and "Nicaragua: Without Jews," *ADL Bulletin* (September 1983), pp. 13–15; "Nicaragua," in *Encyclopedia Judaica*, vol. 12, p. 1135; Beller, *Jews in Latin America*, pp. 145–48.

25. On the Jews of Panama, see Geoffrey Wigoder, "Jews of Panama," *Jerusalem Post* (March 2, 1978); Tom Price, "The Jewish Community of Panama," unpublished manuscript prepared for the Center for Jewish Community Studies (1976); "Panama," in *Encyclopedia Judaica*, vol. 13, pp. 53–54; Monk and Isaacson, eds., *Comunidades Judíos de Latinoamerica*, pp. 102–6, 227–28, 279; Beller, *Jews in Latin America*, pp. 52–57; Dennis C. Sasso, "One Century of Jewish Life in Panama," *The Reconstructionist* (September 1976).

26. On the Jews of Paraguay, see "Paraguay," in *Encyclopedia Judaica*, vol. 13, pp. 85–87; Beller, *Jews in Latin America*, pp. 204–9.

27. On the Jews of Peru, see Judy Siegel, "A Rabbi for Lima," *The Jerusalem Post Magazine* (May 15, 1975), p. 13; "Peru," in *Encyclopedia Judaica*, vol. 13, pp. 322–25; Monk and Isaacson, eds., *Comunidades Judíos de Latinoamerica*, pp. 109–12; J. Toribio Medina, *Historia de la Inquisición de Lima*, 2 vols. (1956); Elkin, *Jews of the Latin American Republics.*

14

The Reshaped Communities of Western Europe

A generation after the Holocaust, there remain, according to the best available figures, some 3.3 million Jews on the European continent, including the Soviet Union. Of this number, 1.3 million are outside the USSR; 80 percent in western Europe. They are concentrated in twenty-eight cities or conurbations with 5,000 Jews or more; 40 percent of 1.3 million are located in Paris and London combined, the two largest communities and the only ones with more than 100,000 Jews. There are six other local communities with 20,000 Jews or more, which means that not only is the total population of European Jewry substantial and even the population outside the Soviet Union considerable, but there are at least eight local communities with Jewish populations large enough to play a role on the world Jewish scene. European Jewry, though not what it once was, still has potential for considerable importance in the Jewish world. But European Jewry often demonstrates more unity in its demographic trends than in any other dimensions, and those trends are not positive.[1]

The European Jewish Scene: An Overview

Taken together, the Jewish communities of Europe constitute the third largest concentration of Jews in the world. Yet what is characteristic of all of them is that, though they have formally recovered to a degree from World War II and the Holocaust, none, with the possible exception of France, will regain its prewar role in the Jewish world or in its host country in the foreseeable future. Almost all suffer from high rates of assimilation and intermarriage, low birthrates, and intense problems of sheer survival. All are to a greater or lesser extent still demoralized and hence unable to take a role in Jewish affairs.[2]

Many of these communities have succeeded in sustaining themselves because they retain some form of official recognition by their host governments. In several, Jews are automatically enrolled as community members by the state unless they deliberately opt out. In a few, the communities have taxing powers or, more common now, a steady income based on a rebate of a small percentage of the state taxes paid by their members. Without these advantages, they would almost certainly be in great financial straits and greater membership difficulties as well.

Leadership in these communities is divided between those who play a major role in the Zionist world and fund-raising for Israel and those whose principal role is in local community affairs. Few of these communities have progressed along the road taken by North American Jewry to integrate the two spheres, even though they are, of necessity,

309

linked. Even in France, where there is a joint campaign, the leadership link is much less pronounced than in the United States. For both groups, leadership remains in the hands of a few notables with a much narrower base than in North America or in Israel. Many of these people play the role they do in community affairs because of a sense of noblesse oblige, or because nobody else is interested, but almost never do they rise out of a cadre of Jewish communal activists who want to move forward in leadership circles. As a result, they are further behind in leadership development programs that will build a new generation of leadership and require assistance from outside Europe to do even the minimum in that regard.

Having despaired of more than a holding action to maintain Jewish life in Europe, European Jewry emphasizes the centrality of Israel much more than do the English-speaking Jewries. The Zionist organizations are still relatively strong, because Zionism still means something even if it is more a matter of lip service than action when it comes to Zionist fulfillment (aliya). Moreover, although Europeans have played down anti-Semitism in the postwar period, the close identification of European culture with Christian religion and the links between church and state that exist in most countries still leave the Jew somewhat on the outside. The rise of anti-Zionism and anti-Israel feeling, especially on the Left, sharpens the Jews' sense of being apart.

The European Jewish response is paradoxical. Jewish education throughout the continent is weak, assimilation is rampant, and secularization is the norm. Sadly, the struggle to cope with these conditions is carried on with half a heart because of the basic demoralization of European Jewry.

The best possibility for an active future for European Jewry lies with the fostering of multicountry links that can bring together the small Jewish communities with the larger ones. This will create a critical mass of Jews who can work together in those areas in which only one or two communities can go it alone. The European section of the World Jewish Congress tries to do this for matters of defense and community relations but has only limited scope. The European Council for Jewish Community Service (ECJCS) tries to do this in the spheres of social services, education, and culture, with limited success because of Europe's diversity. The ECJCS, for example, includes nineteen member countries speaking fifteen languages. In both cases, however, a new generation of leadership is slowly coming to the fore, which may change things to some extent.[3]

During the first postwar generation, European Jewry was a bystander in the growing relationship between Israel and American Jewry. It is understandable why that was so then. Two young, vigorous communities, which had just burst forth to great strength and were actively constructing their futures, found much to say to each other and had the energy to say it. European Jewry, on the other hand, was engaged in painful reconstruction that could not possibly regenerate more than a distant shadow of what had once been. Sapped and weak in the wake of the Holocaust, it had to take a back seat. In the first postwar generation, Europe was, in many respects, a joint protectorate of American Jewry and Israel. It had to rely on the Joint Distribution Committee to make possible much of that reconstruction and on the Jewish Agency to give tone to the communities in an historic demonstration of *edah*-wide partnership.

Now, in the second postwar generation, European Jewry has moved from being a bystander to at least becoming a way station, a stop between Israel and the United States, with a few Israelis and American Jewish leaders coming regularly to Europe to learn about the communities there and to participate in common activities. Consequently, there are now possibilities for European Jewry to move beyond its present situation to become a more active partner in the *edah*. To do so, it must build greater internal unity by strengthening its common instruments, particularly the European Council of Jewish Community Services, as major vehicles for collective action. European Jewry must take its contribution in funds, in professional and voluntary leadership, to the total effort of world Jewry, first by properly serving its local needs and also by assuming an appropriate share of common Jewish responsibilities.

One source of new energy for European Jewry is the new Sephardi presence locally. In the 1930s the Sephardim probably constituted no more than 4 percent of the total European Jewish population. Most were concentrated in the Balkans outside the mainstream of European Jewish life. As a result of World War II and the decolonization that followed it, Sephardic Jewry today comprises approximately one-third of the Jews in Europe outside the Soviet Union. Hence, they constitute a major new factor, particularly in France, the largest Jewish community in free Europe and the fourth largest in the world. The weight of this new Sephardi presence is already being felt in that country. It is characteristic of this new generation that those changes are taking place in Jewish institutions and in the streets, adding new vigor to European life.[4]

In their reconstruction, the Jewish communities of free Europe have had to develop new forms of communal association even while retaining the formal structures of governance of the previous epoch. Most obviously is this so in the countrywide communities organized in the modern epoch as *Kultusgemeinden* (comprehensive state-recognized communal structures) or *consistoires* (state-recognized or semiofficial religious structures).

The Transformation of the Consistorial Communities

Despite their location on or adjacent to a continent in which Jewish life had flourished for at least two thousand years, the present Jewish communities of western Europe are all relatively new. Like the communities of the New World, they are products of the modern epoch, mostly the latter half of that epoch. The countries that had hosted Jewish communities in the distant past had expelled their Jews in the Middle Ages, and Jewish life had been nonexistent within their boundaries for hundreds of years. They welcomed or allowed Jews to return only on the threshold of the modern epoch, granted them citizenship and equal rights during and following the revolutionary upheavals of the eighteenth century, and opened their doors to significant numbers of Jews only in the late nineteenth century. Thus their structures were designed from the first to accommodate the modern temper, emphasizing Judaism as a religion and denying Jewish national existence.[5]

In those countries there was no question of Jewish autonomy in the traditional sense, only the degree to which Jews were free to shape their religious institutions according to their desires. Even that was problematic because western Europe was the home of the modern nation-state, with its strong orientation toward homogeneity and uniformity. Every effort was made by the state to limit Jewish institutions to the religious sphere and then to require those institutions to follow whatever uniform patterns it established for all the religious communities within its boundaries. The result was the establishment of state-recognized or semiofficial community structures at the time of Jewish emancipation in each. The *consistoire* pattern, invented in France, became dominant in western Europe. It was distinguished by its emphasis on the religious dimension of Judaism to the point of emphasizing the *keter kehunah* over the *keter torah* as might be expected in a Roman Catholic country, and on the centralized structure of its institutions, as might be expected in a Jacobin state.[6]

The opening of the postmodern epoch brought a substantial redesign of those institutions in light of the epochal changes wrought by World War II and the establishment of the State of Israel. In every one of the communities with state-recognized religious structures at their base, there has been a serious institutional redesign to give recognition to the renewed acceptance of Jewish peoplehood as a reality. This became more acceptable with the revival of pluralism in the wake of decolonization and the "discovery" of the Third World.

As a consequence, despite its importance during the nineteenth century, only the outlines of the *consistoire* pattern still exist in France. Somewhat more faithful models are found in those countries within the orbit of French culture in Europe and Africa. In some, the *consistoire* still has legal status as a religious body and receives support from government funds, but affiliation with it is entirely voluntary.

In part, the *consistoire* is a casualty of the growing pluralism in the Jewish community. The refugees from eastern Europe and, later, North Africa, who became major, if not the dominant, forces in many of the *consistoire* communities after World War II rejected its exclusively sacerdotal emphasis, and the growth of secularism made Jewish identification through a state-recognized religious structure increasingly incongruous. The new ultra-Orthodox congregations established by some of the refugees rejected the laxity of the official "orthodoxy" of the *consistoire,* and the tasks of communal reconstruction in the aftermath of the war proved too much for the consistorial bodies to handle alone. Above all, the rise of Israel generated demands for mobilization of diaspora political, financial, and organizational resources that went beyond the capabilities of the consistorial structure, requiring more appropriate organizational arrangements. In a larger sense, the times themselves conspired against the old system, as committed Jews the world over rediscovered the national-political aspects of Jewish existence.

New entirely voluntary organizations began to emerge in the framework of the *keter malkhut,* to reach the elements that were otherwise not part of the official community. In the process, they began to assume the functions of "roof" institutions to the extent that the situation in each country encouraged such organizations and in the context of an emerging pluralism in Jewish communal life. Consistorial bodies survived but without the centrality they once had in Jewish life.

Today, four free-world countries maintain state-recognized religious structures: Belgium, France, Luxembourg, and the Netherlands. They contain an estimated 600,000 Jews. In addition, Romania maintains a similar structure for its Jewish community so that some 630,000 Jews live in this framework. If France had not received the large immigration from North Africa, that number would have been at least 50 percent smaller.

The French Jewish Community

For much of world Jewry, revolutionary France was the home of liberty, equality, fraternity, and Jewish emancipation. In the postmodern epoch, France is the largest and most important Jewish community in free Europe. Moreover, its Sephardic majority makes it the only contemporary diaspora community to produce a culture shaped by Sephardic attitudes and mores.

The foundations of the contemporary community. Almost all the Jewish population of France consists of people who settled there since World War I or their descendants. The first two influxes were of east European Jewish refugees after the first and second world wars. The next two influxes were of Sephardic Jews, most particularly from Egypt and western Asia after Israel's Sinai campaign of 1956 and from Algeria and the rest of North Africa after the French evacuation of Algeria in 1960.

The antecedents of the present community structure go back to Napoléon and his restructuring of French civil society at the end of the eighteenth century. Napoléon could remake the Jewish community with relative ease not only because of his own power and appeal or because the French Revolution offered the Jews emancipation and civil rights, but also because French Jewry had no historic organizational base before the Revolution. In the four hundred years after the expulsion of the Jews from France in 1394 there had been no organized Jewish life there. The only Jews in France at the time of the Revolution were barely tolerated handfuls in Bordeaux and Paris, plus the Jews of Alsace, acquired when that territory was conquered and annexed. Only the Alsatian Jews had historic rights of autonomy. The other communities had emerged semi-legally through the slow accretion of crypto-Jewish settlers, who, in the eighteenth century, had formed communal organizations when Jews technically were not allowed to live in France. Even so, Napoléon felt the need to go through the motions of convening a *sanhedrin* and forcing the Jews under French rule to renounce all claims of nationhood and separateness as a prelude to being fully integrated with French culture and society. Moreover, the Jews balked at some of his demands, although they adjusted to them as best they could.[7]

In religious organization as in civil government, the Napoleonic changes outlasted the man. The consistorial system was maintained in the French state throughout the nineteenth century. There were periodic restructurings of the organs of governance and formal changes in the allocation of powers between Paris and the regional consistories, but the *consistoire* was the officially recognized, state-supported framework for French Jewry until the separation of church and state in 1905 at the height of the Third Republic.[8]

The *consistoire* was the first statewide authority ever established for the Jews in France. It consisted of a central *consistoire* headed by the grand rabbi and a council of representatives of each of the regional *consistoires*. The latter consisted of a regional grand rabbi and a council of five laymen. The model was highly centralized in its structure and administration. The French Jewish community is the anomaly among Jewish communities in that there has probably never been another Jewish community as centralized as that of postrevolutionary France.

Paris is the heart of French Jewry, embracing half of the population of the French Jewish community and the seat of its major institutions and leaders. Throughout the nineteenth century Paris benefited from the increasing centralization of French Jewry, and the Paris consistory was synonymous with the central consistory of France. The rabbinical seminary of Metz was transferred to Paris in 1859.

In general, the French authorities sought centralized control, and the Jews constantly tried to loosen the reins. This was manifested in the struggle over the mode of election of the consistorial leadership, which continued throughout the nineteenth century. The non-Jewish authorities favored election by an electoral college; the Jews wanted democratic suffrage.

French Jews also possessed equal rights as individuals and were not legally required to affiliate with the Jewish community. For the authorities, the Jewish community was considered to be a "church," whose principal responsibility was to provide for religious worship and observance. The community was empowered to undertake ancillary activities only insofar as they could be justified from that perspective. Not surprisingly then, the organizational functions of the *consistoire* veered heavily toward the *keter kehunah*. The grand rabbis were the principal leaders and their role was defined as primarily pastoral, although they retained the powers of *halakhic* decision making associated with the *keter torah*. Nevertheless, the Jews succeeded in maintaining some cultural and welfare institutions in this framework, administered by combined lay and rabbinic boards.

Under this regime, the *keter malkhut* was invariably stunted. It emerged in its strongest form in the Alliance Israélite Universelle, French Jewry's contribution to the revival of a structured *edah*. The Alliance was established in 1860 by the lay leadership and because it was secular in its orientation, it was never dominated by the rabbis. It resisted rabbinical involvement except on a nominal basis. Although its activities in France were limited, from the first it attracted the best of the voluntary leadership in the community. Part of its success was due to the support of the French government, which used it as an instrumentality to spread the French language and culture in the Levant. The Alliance succeeded in giving French Jewry a preeminent role in the *edah* for the first time since the emergence of Ashkenazic Jewry in the eleventh and twelfth centuries, by pioneering in the organization of Jewish activity on a worldwide basis. It succeeded because of the image that France had in the minds of nineteenth-century Jews as the fountainhead of emancipation, and hence, for many, the model of what modern Jewish life should be.

After 1905, the *consistoire* lost its official monopoly of Jewish organizational life in France. Slowly, other organizations emerged. Still, no real change took place until after World War I, which brought an influx of Jewish refugees from eastern Europe who were thoroughly unfamiliar with the consistorial pattern and not sympathetic to it. They established their own organizations, in the face of intense opposition by the consistorial "establishment."

In one way, however, these Jews acquired the characteristics of the earlier arrivals. They rapidly came to understand how French culture is antipluralistic and not open to the development of separate identities by French citizens. Hence they either assimilated or otherwise masked their Jewish attachments. This continues to be a major aspect of French Jewish existence. Even though in the second postwar generation, Jews and Judaism have become of major interest in France, most French Jews still have the uneasy feeling that this kind of visibility is not acceptable behavior in the French context and that the Jews who so expose themselves are, in effect, rejecting Frenchification and will ultimately be rejected by France. The principle enunciated during the French Revolution—to the Jews as individuals everything and to the Jews as a people nothing—is the key to the French attitude toward the Jewish population and one which is an omnipresent influence on the shape of the French Jewish community.

During the interwar period there was some organizational ferment in France, whose concrete manifestations were still generally confined to the religious sphere. Liberal and seriously Orthodox congregations and supracongregational organizations developed alongside the *consistoire,* in some competition with it. But not until after World War II did the consistorial system finally give way and the *consistoire* become merely one instrument in the community.

For French Jewry the Holocaust was the second trauma of postrevolutionary modernity (the first was the Dreyfus affair). Once again they were exposed to vicious anti-

Semitism with minimum assistance from their non-Jewish neighbors, who, in the French way, did not want to get involved, and to the active enmity of a large segment of the French population whose anti-Semitism ran deep and who collaborated with the Nazis in the implementation of the "final solution." The Vichy government was, in principle, anti-Jewish but even presumably neutral local officials in France all too often were willing collaborators with the Nazis. Some 83,000 French Jews perished in the Holocaust out of a total prewar Jewish population of 300,000. Jewish institutions, however, continued to function during the war because of the peculiar character of the German occupation of France and the quasi-independent status of the Vichy regime until 1943. Jews were also active in the resistance, which would positively affect their standing in postwar France.

French Jewry in the war's aftermath. The French Jewish community not only needed reconstruction after World War II, but also needed help in absorbing refugees, which was forthcoming principally from the Joint Distribution Committee. The JDC was interested in improving the organizational structure of the community as part of its reconstruction efforts; it played a major role in stimulating the establishment of the Fonds Social Juif Unifié (FSJU), which, in the postwar generation, replaced the *consistoire* as the dominant organization in the community. For the Jews who settled in the country after the war, like those who came in the interwar generation, the consistorial model represented a diminution of Jewish life and its artificial confinement to the religious sphere. Even if they were not interested in being active in the community, they had a set of expectations different from the natives.

In fact, the change was initiated by the old French Jewish establishment when it was still in full control. At the height of the war, French Jewry felt that it needed some instrument to try to confront the Nazis and their Vichy collaborators. In 1944 the leaders of the established community organized the Conseil Représentatif des Juifs de France (CRIF). The CRIF was a late-emerging manifestation of the kind of representative board that had appeared in nonconsistorial communities in the eighteenth and nineteenth centuries. Had it been established earlier, it might have taken dominance from the *consistoire* and held onto it despite the postwar changes. As it turned out, changing realities gave it only a brief moment of centrality until the FSJU emerged and ultimately brought the CRIF under its wing. The present situation can be summarized as follows (see figure 14.1).

The *keter malkhut* in France today is based on three institutions: the FSJU, the CRIF, and the Jewish Agency in France. The FSJU was founded in 1949 at the instigation of the JDC to serve as the internal fund-raising and community-planning arm of French Jewry. The catalytic role of the JDC meant that the American approach of emphasizing the fund-raising body as the framing institution of the community was a factor in the rise of the FSJU to preeminence. From its founding, it dominated the communal-welfare sphere. In many respects it can even be considered the architect of that sphere as separate in France. By mid-generation it had risen to a dominant position in the community. In its original organization, its leadership was restricted to a narrow elite headed by one of the Rothschilds, who in the postwar period as before dominated the main institutions of French Jewry.[9]

After the student revolts of 1968, a drive was begun to democratize the Fonds Social. In the early 1970s, serious steps were taken in that direction, going so far as to introduce public elections for the board. This democratization has had some effect, although turnout is low and the old elites remain clearly dominant.[10] More significant was the expansion of FSJU-supported activities, especially in the educational-cultural

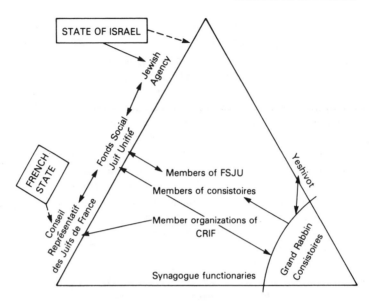

STATE OF ISRAEL

Jewish Agency

FRENCH STATE

Fonds Social Juif Unifié

Members of FSJU

Members of consistoires

Member organizations of CRIF

Conseil Représentatif des Juifs de France

Yeshivot

Grand Rabbin Consistoires

Synagogue functionaries

Figure 14.1.   The structure of French Jewry.

sphere, which reached out beyond the old elites. Moreover, the professionalization of the FSJU's executive leadership had a democratizing effect, especially after the appointment of someone of North African background as executive director at the beginning of the 1980s.

The FSJU manages the Appel Unifié Juif de France, which unites local fund-raising and fund-raising for Israel. The establishment of the Appel as a joint effort involved the FSJU in a conflict with the Keren Hayesod, the fund-raising arm of the World Zionist Organization, which has traditionally been opposed to joint fund-raising appeals, feeling that they dilute support for Israel. The victory of the FSJU in that struggle in all probability marked the turning point in its status in the community, giving it the impetus to assume the dominant position it now holds. With the control over most of the communal funds that the Appel gives it, the FSJU also has been able to move into communal planning, although that is a more recent development.

The CRIF dominates the external relations–defense sphere. It is a classic representative body, embracing religious, Zionist, secularist, and political organizations covering the entire range of French Jewry and is considered the external-relations arm of the community.

The Jewish Agency is an arm of the *edah* that works directly in France to organize and serve French Jewry in matters pertaining to Israel and some educational activities financed with Israeli support. As such, it shares preeminence in the Israel-*edah* sphere with the FSJU. It is something of an anomaly on the world Jewish scene today; in the aftermath of World War II, when French Jewry still could not take care of its own needs, the Jewish Agency came in along with the JDC to provide the Zionist-Israel share of the reconstruction effort and, most particularly, to mobilize French Jewry in support of the Zionist struggle and the new State of Israel. The Agency became deeply rooted in the community in the late 1940s and early 1950s and has continued to maintain a role in community life.

The *keter kehunah* in France continues to be represented by the Consistoire Central

Israélite de France, which is the official representative of French Judaism and dominates the religious-congregational sphere. Moderate Orthodox in orientation, it is responsible for the training and appointment of rabbis, religious educators, *kashrut* supervision, and the application of religious law in personal status matters. The chief rabbi of France, who is the chief representative of the *keter torah,* also stands at the head of the Consistoire Central, whose strength is mainly in Paris and the larger provincial cities.

As a consequence of the struggle between France and Germany for control of Alsace-Lorraine, the Jewish communities in those regions have a separate organizational structure, based on three regional *consistoires,* which are semi-independent of the Consistoire Central. Under the arrangement between France and Germany when Germany ceded Alsace-Lorraine, the French must continue the existing church-state relationship, including government support of religious institutions.

The traditional Orthodox in France were unhappy with the leniency of the *consistoire* and not only organized their own congregations, but in 1952 founded the Conseil Représentatif de Judaisme Traditionaliste de France (CRJTF). The CRJTF, as a more traditional Jewish organization, is less influenced by the French pattern of centralization and is more reflective of the federal dimensions of the Jewish political tradition. Its congregations are independent formally and informally and the CRJTF is just that—a council that unites them for limited purposes where common effort is required.

Liberal Judaism in France, which broke away from the *Consistoire* in the late nineteenth century, is organized in the Union Liberale Israélite, which is affiliated with the World Union for Progressive Judaism. It is a small body, because liberal Judaism has few congregations in France. They are organized in the classic French manner.

The *keter torah* is not strong in France. It is dominated by the chief rabbi of the *Consistoire,* known as the chief rabbi of France, whose tasks straddle the *keter kehunah.* His role as principal bearer of the *keter torah* finds its greatest expression in his formal educational activities rather than through his activities as a *posek.* Other representatives of that *keter* include the regional chief rabbis, who are especially strong in Alsace and Lorraine, and the rabbinical *posekim* of the bodies affiliated with the CRJTF, whose congregations do not recognize the chief rabbinate. Although *yeshivot* have been established in France in recent decades, they are not strong and have little influence beyond their immediate constituencies.

Since modernization, the prominent Jewish intellectuals who define Judaism for French Jews, who are basically not religious, should also be considered in the *keter torah.* In general, intellectuals in France are considered vital in shaping people's self-definition. Thus Jewish intellectuals are important in a way that is much more reminiscent of *keter torah*-style activities than their colleagues anywhere else.

The French Jewish community may be the only one in the world in which the cultural aspect is dominant in the educational-cultural sphere, because of the special emphasis in France on high culture and intellectual activity. As a consequence of that emphasis, Jews in France engage in or support Jewish cultural and intellectual activity as part of being French. Jewish education, however, is weak. For 150 years, French Jews, like those in the United States, rejected separate Jewish education and fought for equal admission to the state schools. Today there is a partial reversal of this trend in the sense that a day school movement has developed in France supported by the highly committed Jews. The French Jewish schools developed about the same time as those in the United States as a result of the postwar influxes. The ultra-Orthodox wanted their own schools from the first, as did many North African Jews.

Most Jewish education in France, however, is still provided through supplementary schools, which were never as strong as in the United States. The strong assimilationist trends in French Jewry until after World War II and the French emphasis on national homogenization did not provide an environment for the development of even supplementary education. Still, no more than 20 percent of Jewish school-age children get a Jewish education of any sort, one of the lowest figures in the Jewish world. Nor is there any proper central organization for Jewish education. Most of the schools are independent, and such technical and professional services as are provided are more often provided by the Jewish Agency than any indigenous body. France relies on Israeli teachers to an extraordinary extent for a community of its size.

France is not a magnet for other Jewish communities in the realm of Jewish education, except, perhaps, for one or two *yeshivot ketanot* (elementary and high school grades only). Instead, French students who want a Jewish education often go elsewhere, particularly to Israel. The Alliance Israélite Universelle has made some effort to remedy this by opening modest educational services for the North African Jewish population in France, including a teachers seminary to train teachers for Jewish schools.

France does not have a well-developed Jewish community center movement. The few community centers that do exist make more of an effort at adult education than in the social and recreational sphere, in keeping with the French spirit.

During the first postwar generation, all three *ketarim* were dominated directly or indirectly by the Rothschild family. There was a Rothschild at the head of every major institution, the FSJU, the CRIF, and the Consistoire Central, and no decision could be made in the community without the assent of the Rothschilds. This both helped and hindered community development. It gave the community great prestige but it also prevented the widening of participation in community affairs and also limited the amount of money that could be raised for the community. As contributors, the Rothschilds were the pacesetters and their contributions did not grow in response to local needs to the same degree that those of their counterparts did in other countries.

In the second postwar generation the role of the Rothschilds is likely to diminish. Here, again, the external environment has played its role. The nationalization of the French banks under the Socialist presidency of François Mitterand actually drove Baron Guy de Rothschild out of the country for a while and the family's political influence declined. At the same time, the Rothschilds themselves were trying to widen participation in the community, perhaps in response to a revolt by elements, principally among the North Africans, that were more militant about communal affairs. At present the French Jewish establishment remains in control but it is not clear what will happen during this generation.[11]

A new Jewish politics emerged because of the Sephardic influx, pitting those Jews who wanted to maintain their Jewish identity against those whom they perceived as either assimilationists or accommodationists. These Jews developed a Zionist-based ideology, which negated the possibilities of a rich Jewish life in the diaspora and focused on Israel as the only hope of the Jewish people yet that only marginally promoted Aliya. These diaspora-based Zionist ideologues challenged the community's ruling establishment along several fronts and were aided and abetted by Israeli emissaries in the country, to the intense discomfiture of the established leadership.

Another matter that brought discomfiture to the Jewish establishment was the emergence of a conscious Jewish effort to exercise political influence on behalf of Israel and Jewish interests. Unlike the pluralistic United States, where Jewish involvement in general politics is accepted as part of normal interest group expression, in France similar activities were always frowned on as assaulting French national unity. The willingness of some Jews to stick their necks out and make it clear to the powers-that-be that their vote was influenced by Jewish issues marked a radical departure from earlier Jewish patterns and can be taken as another sign that the Jewish people is in a postemancipation epoch.

The influx of North African Jews brought about a major transformation in the geography of the French Jewish community. By and large, French Jewry had been concentrated in the country's major cities, overwhelmingly in Paris. The only part of France to have a regional network of Jewish settlements in smaller and larger places was Alsace where the German pattern predominated. However, the North African Jews settled throughout the country. In those years, the Jewish population of France almost doubled. Although the ratio between Paris and the rest of the country remained the same, about half and half, this meant that 100,000 more Jews settled in smaller communities, generating the necessary mass for organized Jewish life in many of these locations. This had immediate organizational consequences, generating organized Jewish life in all parts of the country.

French Jewry may lead the *edah* in its rate of assimilation and intermarriage. Although the influx of Sephardic Jews created a Jewish majority rooted in traditional Jewish culture, the influence of the French environment is such that the Sephardic Jews began to assimilate at least as rapidly as the Ashkenazim, if not more so. In one generation, many of the new immigrants already stopped worrying about the Jewish education of their children, and by the second generation the intermarriage rate was soaring.

In the meantime, the Jewish community of Paris also has undergone a transformation. Paris remains the center of Jewish life in every respect. Even Jewish academics who teach at the provincial universities live in Paris and commute. Other Jews, however, have been rapidly suburbanizing during the entire postwar generation, leading to the development of community institutions throughout the Paris metropolitan region. This has led to a decrease in affiliation in France as elsewhere. Today perhaps a third of the Jews of Paris maintain connections with communal institutions.

All told, the story of postwar French Jewry is one of the development of a more articulated organizational structure for the first time in its history; now at least four of the five spheres are represented by some significant framing institution, and the institutions in each sphere have been strengthened in every arena. Even so, the transformation in the formal organizational structure, though a positive step, was accompanied by substantial internal organizational weakness. The spheres remained dominated by an older communal elite, that, however committed, was unwilling to extend itself beyond certain limits in the development, maintenance, and operation of the institutions of the community. It was easy for the older elite to continue this conservative approach because of the apathy and indifference of a substantial majority of French Jews toward the organized community and to world Jewry in general.

The influx of Eastern European Orthodox Jews created an active Orthodox community outside of and parallel to the mainstream communal institutions; being separatist and inward-looking, however, its impact was confined to its members. The influx of North African Jewry has been the transforming factor as much as there is one; the younger generation of committed North African Jews has launched an assault on the old elite, which increasingly has brought them into positions of power and influence. But the appalling rate of assimilation among North African Jews in France has deprived that new leadership of the backing it might have expected, and the dominance of the Rothschilds acts like a cap on the rise of new leadership that is only now beginning to be jarred loose.

The rise in influence of North African Jews is being felt throughout the community in the second postwar generation. The new chief rabbi of France, elected to replace the Ashkenazi chief rabbi who dominated the first postwar generation, is a Sephardi from North Africa; the new executive director of the FSJU is also. So, too, are most of the younger Jewish intellectuals who have burst forth on the French and French Jewish scenes as the principal delineators of what constitutes Judaism for both religious and nonreligious French Jews.

The Belgian Jewish Community

Although Jews moved in and out of the southern Netherlands (now Belgium) from the thirteenth century onward, the Belgian Jewish community is essentially a product of the modern epoch.[12] Small Jewish communities existed in a few locations in what is now Belgium in the fourteenth century, but they were even more confined to the peripheries and interstices of the society than in the German states or France whence many of them came. In the sixteenth century there was a more visible episode of Jewish presence, this time in Antwerp, which was under Spanish rule. Marranos seeking to escape from the Iberian Peninsula used Antwerp as a transit point on the way to haven in the Ottoman territories. The Marranos developed business interests in Antwerp, which enabled them to travel there from Spain and Portugal, whence they could move eastward. As a result, some stayed on.

Once the eleven provinces of the northern Netherlands successfully revolted against Spain in the late sixteenth century and opened Amsterdam as a haven where Jews could live openly as Jews, Antwerp lost its importance in this respect, and the Jews transferred to the Dutch city. Still, a small community remained in Antwerp, returning openly to Judaism after 1713 when the city came under Austrian rule. Even so there were repeated threats of expulsion until the French conquest of the city in 1794.

Free Jewish settlement in Belgium only came after 1794 when the French revolutionary armies occupied its territory. The French also gave Belgian Jewry its first formal organization beyond the congregational arena, with the establishment of the Consistoire of Krefeld, with approximately eight hundred members. That framework disappeared with the end of the French occupation.

When Belgium gained independence in 1831, the new government officially recognized the Jewish religion and guaranteed the Jews religious freedom. Brussels, the new capital, became the seat of the chief rabbinate established by the government in 1832. The Consistoire Central Israélite de Belgique was organized under government patronage but was not fully recognized until 1870. It followed the French pattern and was centralized in structure.

By that time the Jewish population of Belgium, until the French Revolution predominantly Sephardi, had become overwhelmingly Ashkenazi, as Jews drifted into the country from central and eastern Europe. Only at the end of the nineteenth century, however, was there an influx of Jews from the East who did not assimilate into Francophone culture. This led to a bifurcation of the community, which has persisted to this day. Brussels remained the center of French influence, and a Jewish community developed in Antwerp that was essentially Eastern European. This bifurcation was additionally strengthened by Brussels being the center of Francophone Belgium, or Wallonia, and Antwerp the capital of Flemish-speaking Belgium. Yiddish as a Germanic language found a place in the Flemish regions that it could not find in the French parts of the country. Moreover, the Flemings, increasingly interested in preserving their culture, were more tolerant of Jewish differences and did not exert pressure on them to adopt what was then the dominant language in the country.

Antwerp became a center of the diamond processing industry after the great diamond discoveries in South Africa in the 1880s, and Jews were in that business from the first. This brought growth and great prosperity to the Antwerp community. Orthodox Jews were attracted to the diamond industry, and the Antwerp Jewish community acquired an ultra-Orthodox character, which has been strengthened by each wave of immigration, particularly after World War II. The Jewish population reached twenty-five thousand in 1913 and fifty-five thousand in 1939, which represented about 20 percent of the population of the city. Only eight hundred survived the war by hiding in the city, but many returned after the war, augmented by ultra-Orthodox refugees from eastern Europe. Brussels, however, though remaining nominally Orthodox, was a secularized community with strong assimilationist leanings.

Considering its size, Belgium was relatively hospitable to Jewish refugees from the 1880s to World War II. At the outbreak of the war it was estimated that there was between 90,000 and 100,000 Jews in Belgium, 20,000 of whom were German Jewish refugees who had fled to the country after 1933. No more than 10,000 were Belgian nationals; the rest were refugees who had come in the intervening years but who could not acquire Belgian citizenship. Perhaps half of the Jews fled the country during the German invasion. Of those who remained or returned, 24,000 survived; 13,000 were hidden and most of the others escaped, many to Switzerland and Spain.

The Jewish community maintained a public organization demanded by the Germans and an underground organization throughout the war. The Zionist organizations worked to rescue Jews and even to maintain a *hakhshara* (agricultural training) camp in 1941–42. Jews entered the resistance and went so far as to attack deportation trains to assist deportees to escape. In all this, the Jews had much cooperation from the Belgians, which is why their efforts were successful, especially in comparison with France and the Netherlands.[13]

Because a nucleus of the prewar Jewish community remained in Belgium at the war's end, where they were augmented by those who returned from exile or were liberated from the camps, it was possible to restore Jewish life with relative ease. Belgium continued to be a transit point for Jewish refugees until the mid-1950s. After the war it became easier for new immigrants to obtain Belgian citizenship and most who stayed did so.

The Jewish population stabilized in the 1960s. Brussels is the largest community with approximately 18,000 Jews; Antwerp has a population of 12,000. Other organized communities include Liège (1,000), Charleleroi (500), Ghent, Ostend, and Arles. The Belgian Jews prospered and became typically middle class in a country that is the embodiment of the bourgeois way.

Belgium is the last bastion of the classic consistorial pattern. Judaism is a legally recognized religion and each Jewish community is also legally recognized. There are twelve such recognized communities: four in Brussels, three in Antwerp, and one in each of the other five cities. Ten are Ashkenazi and two Sephardi. Each community elects its synagogue board and chooses its rabbi and *hazzan,* although appointments to the latter two offices must be ratified by the Consistoire Central.[14]

Each community is proportionally represented in the Consistoire Central, which is also the representative body in dealings with the state. The Consistoire Central is responsible for supervising the administration of synagogue properties and examining synagogue budgets and accounts, but it is not particularly interventionist, hence each community essentially manages its own affairs. The *consistoire* appoints a chief rabbi, who is the supreme authority on Jewish religious affairs. The degree of communal autonomy, however, is shown by some of the older communities being essentially expressions of Reform Judaism, others being essentially manifestations of Conservative Judaism, and a few remaining Orthodox.

The Consistoire Central formally links the Brussels and Antwerp communities, but each community goes its own way because of the strong differences in approach to Jewish life that prevail.

Unlike France, the *consistoire* in Belgium has state support as does the Roman Catholic Church. That, in itself, has little influence on Jewish attachment one way or another, although it makes it easier for Belgian Jewish religious institutions to sustain themselves. The chief rabbi, the officially recognized rabbis, and the *hazzanim* are paid by the state, which also pays for the state-recognized teachers who teach Jewish religion in the public schools. The state also provides subsidies for four Jewish day schools, two in Brussels and two in Antwerp, and to other religious and educational institutions.

In a manner reminiscent of every other Jewish community, Belgian Jewry has many organizations—about 100 at last count—divided among all five spheres. Fund-raising follows the pattern of most Keren Hayesod countries, with separate campaigns for Israel and for local needs in both Brussels and Antwerp. In Brussels, the welfare organizations are loosely linked for fund-raising purposes, while in Antwerp they are united in a federated body. Countrywide, besides the Consistoire Central, there is the Conférence Permanente des Oeuvres Sociales Juive de Belgique and La Fédération de la Jeunesse Juive de Belgique in the communal-welfare sphere, and the Zionist Federation of Belgium in the Israel-overseas sphere.

Antwerp is a significant force in the ultra-Orthodox world, a part of the special economy and polity of ultra-Orthodoxy.[15] Almost 80 percent of the diamond exchange was Jewish at the end of the 1960s. The community is homogeneous with almost all the Jews of Polish origin. There are two congregations, Shomrei Hadass and Makhzike Hadass, plus six small Hassidic communities which comprise approximately 12 percent of the Jewish population. There is a small Sephardi community of a few dozen families, which maintains its own synagogue.

Some 90 percent of the children receive a Jewish education in four day schools and *yeshivot* attached to the several congregations and the Hassidic communities. The two principal schools are the Takhkemoni School, sponsored by the Shomrei Hadass congregation, and Jesode Ha-Torah, sponsored by the Makhzike Hadass congregation. The other Jewish organizations are members of Het Centrale Beheer van Joodse Weldadigheid en Maatschappelijk Hulppetton, which serves the communal welfare sphere. It engages in central fund-raising and provides welfare, medical services, social services, financial assistance to those in need, and sponsors youth programs.

The Jews in Brussels and other French-speaking cities are basically modern in orientation and nominally religious if at all, with more involvement in the Brussels Jewish community center than in the synagogues of the *consistoire.* Brussels Jewry is also more divided than Antwerp Jewry and has more visible community conflicts over religious and political issues. There are four recognized religious communities, three Ashkenazi and one Sephardi, plus the Union Israélite Liberale de Belgique, a Reform community.

Until World War II the Brussels Jewish community was second to Antwerp, reaching a peak of about thirty thousand Jews. Today it is the largest Jewish community in the country. Unlike Antwerp it does not have a functioning federation in the communal-welfare sphere but since 1952 has had a common fund-raising body, the Centrale des Oeuvres Sociales Juive, which links fifteen independent institutions. Brussels has two day schools: the Ecole Israélite, which is religious-traditional, and Ganenu, which is more Zionist oriented. The high school is sponsored by the Ecole Israélite.

Unlike France, Jewish intellectuals do not play much of a role in the Belgian Jewish community, just as intellectuals do not play much of a role in Belgian society. Belgium, however, was one of the first Jewish communities to have a center for Jewish studies based at a public university.

The Luxembourg Jewish Community

Luxembourg, with fewer than one thousand Jews, sits in the shadow of Belgium and France. It acquired its consistorial structure because of the influence of those countries and is a faithfully consistorial community because almost all its Jewish life is confined to its religious institutions.

The Netherlands Jewish Community

The Jewish community in the Netherlands was the first modern Jewish community in Europe. The Dutch admitted Jews on terms of reasonable freedom beginning in the late sixteenth century, at the time of the Dutch revolt against Spain. Consequently the Jews developed their communities while interacting as individuals with the larger population.[16]

The first Jewish settlers in the Netherlands were Portuguese Marranos who sought refuge at the peripheries of Spanish-controlled territory (Portugal then was part of Spain) preparatory to escaping beyond. The Dutch revolt offered them a chance to return openly to Judaism and economic opportunities to boot. Their presence rapidly opened the doors to Ashkenazim and made the Netherlands the first Western European country accessible to East European Jews. If the Sephardim were already a presence by 1590, the Ashkenazim became visible by 1620. The first Sephardi congregation was founded about 1600 and the first Ashkenazi congregation in 1635. By the end of the eighteenth century, the Netherlands contained fifty thousand Ashkenazim and five thousand Sephardim. The generation lag is reminiscent of a similar lag in the other direction—in the settlement of twentieth-century Israel—and led to much the same result: a Sephardi sense of superiority over Ashkenazim.

Appropriately the first modern secular Jew, Baruch Spinoza, was a product of Dutch Jewry. In the middle of the seventeenth century, at the opening of the modern epoch, he was the first Jew to cease being part of the Jewish community without feeling the need to be linked with the Christian community, but to be simply a person—a modern man. In doing so he wrought more than a philosophic revolution.

To say that Jews were accepted on something like modern terms does not mean that they were granted formal rights of citizenship or that they did not suffer from anti-

Jewish feeling. Their status was left unclear, a matter for local determination in a polity that was a confederation of provinces. As a result, some cities encouraged Jewish settlement, others were neutral, and others discouraged or even periodically forbade Jews to settle within their limits. The *parnassim* of the Jewish communities were still responsible for guaranteeing the Jews' good behavior in order for them to settle in most cities in the country. The Jews had greater freedom and equality in the economic sphere, hence they not only prospered but supported a flourishing cultural life that made seventeenth and early eighteenth century Amsterdam a world Jewish center.

By the time of the French Revolution, the Sephardim were conservatives. Almost all the Jews who joined non-Jewish liberals to support the Revolution were nurtured in the Ashkenazi community. The Revolution brought the emancipation of the Jews and formal rights of citizenship in 1796. Because the Sephardim kept control of the *kehillah,* the Ashkenazim also used the Revolution as an opportunity to break away and form their own.

In 1810 the state abolished the old communal structure and replaced it with a consistorial one on a federal basis. An upper consistory was provided countrywide linking the "German" and "Portuguese" communities, as they were known. Each province had its consistory. Along with the upper and provincial consistories, the Ashkenazi and Sephardi communities each had their own organizations. Jewish day schools developed with state support after 1821, but after 1857 Jews were required to attend the public schools. Jewish education was relegated to supplementary schools, and not until the twentieth century were Jews able to open their day schools again.

All told, the nineteenth century was a mixed period for Dutch Jewry.[17] As individuals they were able to enter Dutch civil society but at the price of a determined government campaign to assimilate them culturally. They had full freedom of religion but economically difficult times in the Netherlands led to pauperization of more than 50 percent of the community. Toward the end of the century urbanization and industrialization led to an improved economic situation. The Jews were increasingly concentrated in Amsterdam, which, by 1849, had 43 percent of Dutch Jewry and by 1920, 60 percent.

Jewish cultural and religious life deteriorated drastically. Conversion to Christianity, intermarriage, and a low birthrate led to a decline in the Jewish population in the Netherlands in the early twentieth century. The number of mixed marriages increased from 13 percent in 1901 to 41 percent in 1930. This new assimilation went hand in hand with the spurt in Jewish prosperity as Dutch public life opened to the Jews and social integration without conversion became more acceptable.

The growing secularization of Dutch society under Socialist influence seriously affected the Jewish community, whose religious institutions remained firmly Orthodox even if open, but which did not appeal to the new secularists. The organizations of the *keter malkhut* fell into the hands of the non-Orthodox who were basically assimilationists and therefore did little or nothing for Jewish education, emphasizing the welfare institutions of the Jewish community. The Zionist Federation was small but it brought to the country whatever Jewish revival there was.

Major changes in the Dutch Jewish community came after World War I. The Zionist movement launched a struggle to "conquer the community" as the movement did in other countries. After the rise of Nazism in 1933, the Zionists were successful, although nominally the old *parnassim* remained in charge.

When the Germans occupied the Netherlands in 1940 there were 130,000 Jews permanently resident in the country: 121,400 members of the Ashkenazi community,

4,300 members of the Sephardi community, and 4,300 unaffiliated Jews. Tens of thousands of German Jewish refugees had passed through the country but 20,000 had either remained or were caught there at the time of the German invasion. The Germans succeeded in exterminating all but 27,000 of the Dutch Jews by the end of the war. Two thousand managed to escape to other countries, and 10,000 survived in hiding.

The record of the Dutch in the Holocaust was distinctly mixed. The Dutch authorities did not resist the Germans at any point, which eased the German effort and made it that much more successful. At the same time, individual Dutch hid Jews in heroic ways. The pattern was characteristic of the Dutch ambivalence towards Jews, which had manifested itself consistently since the sixteenth century. As a result, Netherlands Jewry suffered more than that of any other western European Jewish community.[18]

There were about thirty thousand Jews in the Netherlands in 1946, including eight thousand Jewish partners in mixed marriages. Emigration, a low birthrate, and a high death rate brought the population down by about six thousand during the next decade. The restored Jewish community spent years in legal and political struggles to regain Jewish property and Jewish souls, particularly children who had been hidden and baptized as Christians. In the end the property plus German reparations brought prosperity to the community, but only three thousand of the approximately thirty-five hundred children hidden by Christians were restored to the Jewish community.

Jewish communal organization was resumed in the framework of the *kehillot* that existed before the war, the Dutch-Israelite for the Ashkenazim, the Portuguese-Israelite for the Sephardim, and the Liberal for the Reform. The first remained by far the largest, including communities throughout the country. The second existed only in Amsterdam with only a handful of families. There were chief rabbis in Amsterdam, The Hague, and Rotterdam, plus a traveling rabbi for the smaller communities. The Liberal community had been developed before the war by German refugees, with earlier attempts at religious reform having failed to attract the Dutch, who preferred to be nonreligious if they dropped away from traditional religion. After the war, however, religious reform attracted an indigenous population who wanted some Jewish affiliation. A small seriously Orthodox community developed in Amsterdam, which has remained within the Ashkenazi community, sustaining whatever religious activities are in the country in more than a formal way. Almost all Jews live in Amsterdam and its environs.

There is almost no cooperation among the three communities in the domains of the *keter torah* and *keter kehunah* but close cooperation in the domain of the *keter malkhut*. One organization, Jewish Social Work, controls and manages the social welfare institutions; funds for them are raised through a common campaign. Money for Israel is raised by Keren Hayesod in a separate campaign.[19]

Curiously, Netherlands Jewry has no significant Jewish organization responsible for the external relations–defense sphere. The Jewish day school provides most of the Jewish educational opportunities.

The Zionist movement gained even more power immediately after the war, dominating the community until most of its leaders settled in Israel after the establishment of the state. The community passed into the hands of those who had settled in for the long term. The general European revulsion against anti-Semitism, which came in the wake of the Holocaust, eased the way for the Jews to integrate even more fully with Dutch life, especially because Dutch sympathies for Israel were pronounced during the first postwar generation.

All this changed after the 1973 Israel-Arab war and ensuing oil crisis. The general

Dutch population became increasingly less sympathetic toward Israel, and anti-Semitism began to reappear in some quarters in the Netherlands. The effects of this on Jewish life will be felt in due course. In the meantime, most of the Jewish community's activities are confined to the communal-welfare and Israel-overseas spheres, with the religious-congregational and educational-cultural sphere diminishing in importance for the younger generation.

The Jewish Community of Great Britain

The modern Jewish community of Great Britain formally dates to 1656. Marranos had been drifting into England singly and in small groups for about 100 years under the tacit protection of the British crown. In that year, Oliver Cromwell, Protector of the Commonwealth, allowed them to establish a house of worship.[20] Thus, the British Jewish community is younger than its American counterpart by two years. The two communities developed along parallel lines over the next three centuries. Both were established on voluntary principles from the first and had no special status in the laws of their host countries. Both were in countries of immigration that attracted Jews escaping from the European continent and the Mediterranean litoral in search of a better life. Moreover, the environments in which both communities developed were liberal ones.

They were very much different, however, in their internal development, in no small part because of the environments in which each was located. The United States was a new society, open for development and the development of new institutions accessible to all comers. Britain was established in the fullest sense of the word, in many respects the least amenable to social change of any of the Western European countries.

Though Jews coming to the United States could almost immediately think of themselves as Americans, Jews in Britain to this day remain separate as Jews in a country that, however hospitable, comprises several indigenous and homogeneous peoples: principally the English, the Scots, the Welsh, and the Ulster Irish. The United States welcomed innovation, including religious innovation, while Britain was most conservative when it came to maintaining the forms of established religion. Following the Anglican style, Anglo-Jewry developed the equivalent of a public Orthodox establishment, whatever the private laxities of its constituents.

American Jewry scattered throughout the United States from the first, building communities from coast to coast. British Jewry was overwhelmingly concentrated in London from the first and has become further concentrated in the twentieth century, just the reverse of what is occurring in the United States.

American Jewry created framing institutions for itself only in the post-World War II generation and through them established the primacy of the *keter malkhut* by way of the communal-welfare sphere. British Jewry succeeded in establishing a framing institution—the Board of Deputies of British Jews—and establishing the primacy of the *keter malkhut* nearly two centuries earlier through the external relations–defense sphere.

The permanent community that Cromwell recognized developed at the time of the English Civil War. The two events were connected in that the spread of Puritanism with its philo-Judaic orientation opened the door for actual Jews to settle in the British Isles. Their readmission was gained in a typically British way. Rather than trying to force through a formal positive act, Cromwell ruled that, because there was no statutory prohibition on Jewish settlement in England, if Jews came to settle, so be it. This is not to say there was no need for legislation to give full rights to British Jewry. In the eighteenth and nineteenth centuries there were acts extending to British Jews the rights of citizenship and political participation, usually by removing general prohibitions or requirements that the Jews and other non-Protestants could not meet.

During its first generation, the community was merely a small Sephardi congregation. In 1701, it was well established enough to build the Bevis Marks Synagogue, the first building constructed expressly for Jewish worship in modern England. That congregation controlled the Jewish community for nearly a century and its *haham* is the chief rabbi of the Sephardim in Britain to this day.

Ashkenazim began to come shortly after the Sephardim, and in the 1690s a small Ashkenazi community was established in London. It divided into two in 1706 and a third Ashkenazi community was formed in 1761. In the eighteenth century, the Jews spread to the English countryside, establishing congregations in at least twelve other cities.

Violent negative public response to the effort to enact legislation to improve the Jewish condition after 1753 led in 1760 to the establishment of the London Committee of Deputies of British Jews, which ultimately became the Board of Deputies.[21] It brought together the representatives of the Ashkenazi congregations to work with the Sephardi congregation in representational matters. The London Committee replaced the Deputados of the Sephardi community, which until 1760 had acted unilaterally to represent English Jewry before the Crown. Hence the name is an Anglicization of a Spanish term even as the act meant the end of the hegemony of the Sephardi minority in England. Shortly after that, representatives of the congregations in the other cities and in the British colonies were brought into the committee.

Meetings of the committee were intermittent until 1835 when a constitution was adopted and the board's representative status was recognized by the British government. The flowering of the board came after 1838 when Sir Moses Montefiore became president, an office which he held, except for one brief interval, until 1874. Membership in the board was based on synagogues until the twentieth century and not until 1886, a year after Montefiore's death, was the Liberal congregation admitted.

The Sephardim retained their dominance throughout the eighteenth century, but after the end of the Napoleonic wars, major Ashkenazi families, particularly the Goldschmidts and Rothschilds, began to emerge as increasingly important in Jewish life. They led the struggle for full Jewish equality, which, in the end, was achieved piecemeal rather than by any single legislative act.

Meanwhile, the Ashkenazi synagogues moved toward congregational union. Nathan Marcus Adler can be considered the first Ashkenazi chief rabbi of the country, because he was elected by the delegates from the London and major provincial congregations. In 1847 he issued laws and regulations for all the synagogues in the British Empire, establishing his authority in a constitutional manner. He served as rabbi until 1891 and was followed by his son.

Just as British Jewry extended its religious control over the British Empire so, too, did the Board of Deputies extend its influence over the entire Jewish world. Under Sir Moses Montefiore, it intervened vigorously in the defense of Jewish rights whenever they were endangered. After the establishment of the Anglo-Jewish Association, the two bodies formed the Joint Foreign Committee (1878), which continued to function until 1917 when it was discredited for its anti-Zionism and disbanded.

The nineteenth century was the glorious age of British Jewry as it was of the British

Empire. A few examples of British Jewish creativity make the point. The *Jewish Chronicle*, founded in 1841, was the first permanent Anglo-Jewish periodical and is now the oldest Jewish periodical in continuous existence. It rapidly became the premier newspaper in the Western Jewish world. In 1855 Jews' College was founded to train ministers of religion for Anglo-Jewry, making it the oldest seminary in the English-speaking world. In 1859 the Jewish Board of Guardians was founded to deal with poor relief. And in 1870 the confederation of the Ashkenazi synagogues of London, which had functioned primarily for charitable purposes and to elect the chief rabbi, was transformed into a union as the United Synagogue, by Act of Parliament.[22]

Meanwhile the Jewish population continued to grow, expanding rapidly after 1880. The few thousand Jews in the country at the end of the eighteenth century reached 65,000 by 1800 and 300,000 by 1914. Jews spread at least in small numbers throughout the British Isles, although the Jewish communities in the so-called provincial cities and towns developed and declined in a generation or two. Their fate coincided with the economic opportunities that they provided for small numbers of Jews balanced against the Jews' desire to live close to one another for mutual support.[23]

Although Jews appeared in Scotland in the late seventeenth century and may even have had a congregation in Edinburgh in the 1780s, the first permanent community was not established until 1816, also in Edinburgh. During the nineteenth century a modest Jewish population took root. There are some fifteen thousand Jews in Scotland, 85 percent of whom are in Glasgow and most of the rest in Edinburgh.[24]

Organized Jewish life appeared in Wales almost half a century earlier, with Jews there from the early eighteenth century and a Jewish community in Swansea founded in 1768. The Cardiff community, founded in 1840, became most important. Of the forty-three hundred Jews in Wales, thirty-five hundred live in Cardiff.[25]

The Jewish community in Northern Ireland is a product of the mass migration of the 1880s and after. The twelve hundred Jews in Northern Ireland live mostly in Belfast.[26] At its peak, British Jewry never exceeded 450,000 and has now declined by more than 10 percent from that high.

The coming of the mass immigration led, as elsewhere, to a proliferation of organizations that fractured the neat pattern of nineteenth-century Anglo-Jewry. The first major break in the unified community came with the establishment of the Federation of Synagogues in 1887 to accommodate the eastern European congregations that did not find themselves attuned to the style of the United Synagogue. From the 1880s to the present there has been a tug-of-war between efforts to create appropriate umbrella organizations or confederations, generally begun by the more acculturated Jews, and the separatist tendencies of the institutions established by eastern European Jews.[27]

The Zionist movement developed in the wake of the First Zionist Congress, and the Zionist Federation was organized in 1899. Although it drew some support from the established community, most of the Anglo-Jewish establishment opposed Zionism. Between 1897 and the Balfour Declaration in 1917 there was a major struggle between the Zionist Federation on one side and the Anglo-Jewish Association on the other. The Balfour Declaration discredited the extreme anti-Zionism of the Anglo-Jewish Association. Shortly thereafter, a generational shift in the leadership of the community led to the emergence of a new pro-Zionist leadership. It included the Ashkenazi chief rabbi, the Sephardic *haham,* and the second Lord Rothschild, all of whom were active Zionists.[28] Thus the pro-Zionists dominated the community during the interwar period, although not until 1943 did they secure control of the Board of Deputies.

The interwar generation was a period of the Anglicization of the immigrants and their children. It also marked the end of the most creative years of British Jewry. By and large the period was devoted to consolidation of the new Jewish population. The United Synagogue built many new synagogues that began to appeal to the second generation of eastern European Jews, as they moved out of the East End into the London suburban boroughs. However, efforts to expand Jewish education failed because they ran against the tide of assimilation.[29]

There was one more influx of immigrants in the wake of the rise of Nazism. The German Jews brought with them both Liberal Judaism and Frankfurt-style ultra-Orthodoxy, strengthening both. Although the beginnings of ultra-Orthodoxy go back to the establishment of the Gateshead Yeshiva in 1927 and the emergence of a Jewish day school movement in the 1930s, it became particularly visible after World War II when eastern European Jewish refugees arrived to strengthen the ultra-Orthodox community. Hungarian Jews were particularly influential in this regard.[30]

British Jewry escaped the fate of the rest of European Jewry in the Holocaust, but the complete mobilization of Britain for six years, the German air attacks, and the long period of shortages resulting from the wartime effort had their effect on the Jewish community, which emerged from the war as exhausted as their non-Jewish neighbors. In some respects the community, whose members prospered economically in the postwar years, has never recovered its vitality. Its preeminence in world Jewish affairs has almost disappeared and its cultural creativity has been stilled.[31]

In 1943 Professor Selig Brodetzky, a Jewish immigrant from Russia and a Zionist leader, was elected president of the Board of Deputies after a carefully planned campaign. He and his colleagues brought about the election to the board that year of a majority committed to the establishment of a Jewish state in Eretz Israel. One of the first steps taken by the board under its new majority was to dissolve its ties with the Anglo-Jewish Association through the Joint Foreign Committee. From then on the board actively backed the Zionist effort. Even the Anglo-Jewish Association grew increasingly neutral and after 1948 became a non-Zionist sympathizer with the state. The neutralization of that body led to the brief existence of the Jewish Fellowship, which was anti-Zionist like the American Council for Judaism, and was dissolved in 1948 with the creation of the state.

In the immediate postwar period, British Jewry had to confront the terrible problem of the struggle of the Jewish Yishuv in Eretz Israel against the British government with all that it meant in exposing Jews in Britain to anti-Semitic attacks. British Jewry stood the test in one of its finest hours, standing firmly behind Zionism and the Yishuv, and throwing its full support behind the Zionist aspirations for a Jewish state.

The 1943 elections marked the transfer of leadership in the British Jewish community from the old establishment to the immigrants of the post-1880s and their descendants. Even earlier, the board had expanded to include representatives of communal organizations of every kind and not simply congregations, which led to a great expansion in its size. From sixty-five members in 1900 it now has approximately four hundred. (The numbers change slightly each triennial election depending on which organizations are represented and in what proportions.)

The structure of the board follows the previously noted pattern common to Jewish bodies. Most of its work is done through its standing committees, which include Law, Parliamentary, and General Purposes; Foreign Affairs; Defense; Education and Youth; Eretz Israel; *shehitah;* Aliens; and the Central Lecture Committee. Although the board functions primarily in the domain of *keter malkhut,* it has formal links with the other *ketarim.* The *shehitah* committee is concerned with matters in the domain of the *keter kehunah,* and the chief rabbi and the *haham* are the constitutionally recognized authorities for the board in matters pertaining to the *keter torah.* Under the board's constitution, the chief rabbi and the *haham* must be consulted on all religious matters. In that respect, the board is the fulcrum of a comprehensive structure that follows the classic triangular pattern (figure 14.2).

The *keter malkhut* dominates the Israel-overseas, communal-welfare, and external relations–defense fields. The last is the most important from an internal British perspective, but the first is increasingly the source of the most energetic leadership in the community. The Joint Israel Appeal, which for many years was a wholly controlled subsidiary of the British Zionist Federation, is now following the model of the United States: to separate itself almost completely from the Zionist movement, in the necessity to reach out to wealthy Jews who, though highly committed to Israel, are not part of organized Zionism. They, in turn, are attracted by fund-raising for Israel; but those who have become involved in the Jewish Agency because of their giving have also become interested in the governance of the *edah,* which has given them a new political concern in the Jewish community. One consequence of this is that, until a few years ago, the dominant role of the Board of Deputies meant that British Jewish parliamentarians were the foremost leaders of the community. Increasingly, the foremost leaders of the community today are the new British multimillionaires who devote their time to Jewish pursuits and who have risen through the Israel-overseas sphere.

Of the three spheres under the aegis of the *keter malkhut,* the communal-welfare is by far the weakest, still consisting primarily of separate institutions. The Jewish Welfare Board, founded in 1859 as the Jewish Board of Guardians, is a loose confederation of institutions. In recent years there have also been changes in this sphere, with the begin-

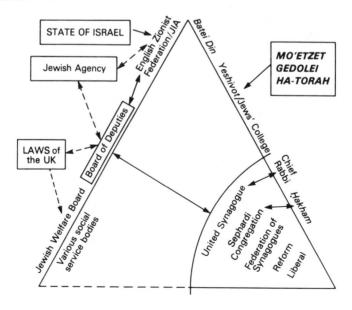

Figure 14.2.   The structure of the British Jewish community.

nings of a common professionalism and some joint fund-raising. This, too, has been stimulated to no little extent by contacts with professional colleagues and their organizations elsewhere in the *edah,* such as the Joint Distribution Committee and the International Conference of Jewish Communal Service.

The United Synagogue, which straddles the *keter kehunah* and the *keter torah,* is the principal but by no means exclusive body in the religious-congregational sphere. The traditionalist nature of British society meant that almost the entire community was willing to accept an Orthodox religious establishment and give it at least nominal allegiance. In the nineteenth century the effort by the United Synagogue to match the English style in religion led to the adoption of the term *minister* to describe the congregational rabbi. The term had value even in Jewish terms because it distinguished between *dayanim* (judges) and *posekim* (*halakhic* decision-makers) as officers of the *keter torah,* who would continue to be called rabbis, and those of the *keter kehunah,* to be called ministers, who served congregations. These ministers adopted Anglican garb, including the priestly collar, and presided over the introduction of Anglican-style decorum in the services.

In the post-World War II period the old-style minister began to disappear. The younger generation often assumed the title rabbi, at least informally, abandoned the clerical collar, and tried to minimize the formality of the service in favor of an increased spontaneity and congregational participation. In many respects the United Synagogue moved to the right religiously after World War II, as the influence of the old families diminished. The new synagogue leadership is more actively traditional, often even Orthodox, while the Bet Din moved the community steadily to the right, responding to the worldwide trend in Orthodoxy and to the immediate competition of the Federation of Synagogues, which grew in strength if not in numbers.

In 1962 Sir Isaac Wolfson, perhaps the single strongest influence in postwar British Jewry, was elected president of the United Synagogue, the first person not from the older families to be so honored. Sir Isaac was sympathetic to the rightward shift in the United Synagogue establishment. At that time studies showed that 61 percent of the Jews of London were members of synagogues, a figure that rose to more than 75 percent in Liverpool and Leeds. The increase followed the common pattern of higher affiliation in smaller communities where Jews feel the need to band together in more structured ways because they lack the population needed to establishing fully Jewish neighborhoods. There were four hundred synagogues registered in 1962. Even then, however, synagogue attendance was low, except for the High Holy Days, with between 15 and 23 percent attending services weekly.

Since then there has been a singular decline in all these measures. The rapid secularization of Great Britain after World War II, which has influenced the Jews perhaps even more than the non-Jews, has generated a falling away from the United Synagogue so much so that the religious life of British Jewry is seriously endangered. At this time less than 50 percent of marriages in which Jews are involved are conducted under the auspices of the rabbinate. Thus we have the paradox of the United Synagogue remaining the dominant religious institution of British Jewry, one that has brooked no serious rivals, but confronting a population increasingly alienated from the synagogue altogether.

The concentrations of strength and dynamism in this sphere are found among the ultra-Orthodox. Their umbrella organization, the Federation of Synagogues, accepts the authority of the Moetzet Gedolei haTorah of Agudath Israel. Although formal authority remains with the chief rabbi and his *bet din,* the *halakhic* pace and standard is increasingly set by the *bet din* of the ultra-Orthodox.

The Sephardi community with its *haham* stands apart from this division in the Ashkenazi world but represents a small minority of the British Jewish population. It is composed of the few descendants of the old families and the influx of Sephardim who came to Britain after World War II from the Islamic countries or former British possessions. Many of these Sephardim have prospered mightily and have risen to high positions in the community.

The Reform and Liberal communities have grown in the postwar period and have opened several new congregations, especially in suburban London. They also founded Leo Baeck College to train their own rabbis. They are associated with the World Union for Progressive Judaism.

A Conservative congregation emerged in the 1960s, headed by the well-known Rabbi Louis Jacobs, who was expelled from the United Synagogue for his modern Orthodox views. His expulsion was a sign of the times and a focal point of a community-wrenching conflict.

In sum, the religious-congregational sphere is divided among five synagogue bodies: (1) the mainstream Orthodox United Synagogue, a centralized union of congregations under the authority of the Ashkenazi chief rabbi; (2) the Sephardi congregations under the authority of the *haham;* (3) the ultra-Orthodox Federation of Synagogues; (4) the Reform and Liberal congregations; and (5) the Conservative congregation. The first three maintain *batei din*. Finally, the *yeshivot* are playing an increasingly important role in the *keter torah*.[32]

The weakest of the spheres in Great Britain is the educational-cultural, which falls foursquare in the *keter torah* in principle but often is under the jurisdiction of the *keter kehunah* in practice.[33] The major ornaments of Jewish education in British Jewry are the Gateshead Yeshiva, Montefiore College, Jews' College, and Leo Baeck College. The Gateshead Yeshiva is the center of a right-wing community that has grown up around it. The other three are more conventional rabbinical seminaries, one for Sephardim, one for Ashkenazim, and one for Reform Jews. They are also considerably weaker, with student populations numbering in the tens. There are seven other, smaller, *yeshivot* in Britain.

World War II stimulated the development of overarching institutions in the educational-cultural sphere. At the outbreak of the war thousands of Jewish children were taken from London to small provincial towns as part of a general evacuation in anticipation of German air raids. The need to provide for their education led to the formation of a temporary Joint Educational Body for the duration of the emergency.

Because of this effort, in 1945 a Central Council for Jewish Education was established, representing the United Synagogue and other Orthodox institutions and with a special executive board for London. Although stimulated by the wartime experience, the new body was also limited by it, because Jewish education during the war had been limited to one hour per week. It took many years to move beyond that after the war. The Central Council chiefly presided over efforts at supplementary education. As day schools emerged they did so on a separate, usually private, basis.

The Orthodox day schools continued after the war as independent institutions and expanded in the 1950s. The Zionist Federation started its day schools in the 1950s. The provincial cities maintained communal day schools and several private Jewish "public schools" were established, foremost being Carmel College, which is renowned in the Jewish world. Jewish boarding schools, or public schools as they are known, combine British and Jewish experiences for primary and secondary education. Other than that, Jewish education is limited and not many young people study in Jewish schools. By and large in Britain as elsewhere the dominance of the religious-congregational sphere in the educational-cultural sphere has worked to the detriment of the latter.

On a more advanced level, a center for Jewish studies of some note has been developed at Oxford University, which relies heavily on visiting scholars, and there are lectures in Jewish studies at other universities. Still, Jewish studies in British universities have not expanded as in the United States, even though there are many programs on paper. Serious Jewish periodical literature is almost nonexistent. The most distinguished of them, the *Journal of Jewish Sociology,* has been kept alive by the efforts of one person working almost alone. The Institute for Jewish Affairs, the policy studies center sponsored by the World Jewish Congress, which has been located in London since the end of World War II, is a major source of Jewish social research in the world and perhaps the principal forum for considering the contemporary Jewish scene in Britain.

Jewish cultural life is even more limited. At one time Britain had a modestly active Jewish cultural scene. Today that cultural scene has diminished substantially. The *Jewish Chronicle,* once the flagship of the Anglo-Jewish press throughout the world, has become little more than a local weekly. The last Yiddish newspaper closed in 1967 and there is no Hebrew newspaper or journal. Adult education is minimal, although the Spiro Institute has emerged as a bright spot on the horizon in recent years.

By and large, the powers-that-be in British Jewry are content with the status quo and do not seek change. At most they bemoan the decline of British Jewry but, like their British peers, do little to try to alter their state.

The Jewish Community of Ireland

Ireland is probably the only European country that never expelled its Jews, partly because it was so peripheral to Europe that few Jews found their way there. On the other hand, the Irish did not encourage Jews to settle among them. The first record of Jews in Ireland suggests that in 1079 a deputation of five Jews tried to gain permission to settle in Munster, then one of the Irish kingdoms, but were sent back. There were other efforts at settlement in the twelfth and thirteenth centuries, mostly by Jews expelled from England, and again at the close of the fifteenth century when a few refugees from the Iberian Peninsula found their way there. But these Jews either left or assimilated.

Organized Jewish life dates to the restoration of the Jews to England and Cromwell's conquest of Ireland. The first community was established in Dublin in 1661. At first, the Sephardim dominated but in the eighteenth century the Ashkenazim came to outnumber them. Nevertheless, the Jewish population so decreased that the synagogue was closed in 1791. Jews were not allowed to become naturalized until 1816, a fact that discouraged Jewish settlement. At that time there were only a few Jewish families in the country.[34]

The community was revived in 1822 when Jews arrived from England, Germany, and Poland. Still, there were no more than 450 Jews in the country in 1881, a number that increased during the great migration. Still, there were never more than 8,000 Jews in Ireland, and in the post–World War II generation their numbers declined to about 4,000. The only functioning community outside Dublin is in Cork, which is diminishing even more rapidly.

The constitution of the Irish Republic, adopted in 1937, recognized Judaism as a minority faith, possessing religious freedom. With Irish independence, the Jews organized their own representative council (1938) and appointed a chief rabbi, detaching themselves from the British Board of Deputies and chief rabbinate. The council is essentially a council of synagogues. Like British Jewry, the community is organized under an Orthodox framework, although there is a small Progressive congregation in Dublin that is outside that framework.

As in Great Britain, the Jewish Representative Council of Ireland is basically an instrument of the *keter malkhut* but it appoints the chief rabbi and *bet din*. Its membership consists of the three main Dublin synagogues, four smaller synagogues, and all other Jewish institutions in the country. There are separate bodies in Dublin for Jewish education, welfare, *shehitah,* youth and student activities, and Zionist affairs. Jewish education in Ireland is more successful than in Britain; 90 percent of Jewish children are in Jewish day schools, both primary and secondary, or afternoon classes, in part because of the strong Roman Catholic influence in the state schools.

The Irish Jewish community is diminishing through emigration, for lack of sufficient economic opportunity to persuade Jews to live in a peripheral place. As a community it has strong roots in Ireland, but they are not enough to overcome pulls to other, more prosperous and central, places.

Notes

1. On the demography of European Jewry, see U. O. Schmelz, *World Jewish Population: Regional Estimates and Projections,* Jewish Population Study Series (Jerusalem: Hebrew University of Jerusalem, 1981) and with Sergio Della Pergola, "World Jewish Population," *American Jewish Year Book 1982,* vol. 82, pp. 285–87; Sergio Della Pergola, "Megamot Demografiot Bekerev Yehudi Ma'arav Europa" (The Jews in Western Europe: The Demographic Aspect), *Tefutsot Yisrael,* vol. 28, no. 4 (winter 1980), pp. 67–94 (Hebrew).

2. Ernest Stock, "The Emerging European Jewish Community Structure," *Jersualem Letter,* no. 46 (March 14, 1982); Daniel J. Elazar, "The New Agenda of European Jewry," *Jerusalem Letter/Viewpoints,* no. 35 (October 17, 1984) and "The Reconstitution of Jewish Communities in the Post-War Period," *Jewish Journal of Sociology,* vol. 11, no. 2 (December 1969), pp. 187–226; Jacob Lestschinsky, "Jewish Education in Europe," *Current Events,* vol. 13 (September 1960), pp. 23–28 and *The Rise and Decline of European Jewry* (New York: Institute of Jewish Affairs, 1951); Nechemiah Robinson, ed., *European Jewry Ten Years after the War* (New York: Institute of Jewish Affairs, 1956); Salo W. Baron, "The Eichmann Trial: European Jewry before and after Hitler," *American Jewish Year Book 1962,* vol. 63, pp. 3–53 and "The Spiritual Reconstruction of European Jewry," *Commentary,* vol. 1, no. 1 (November 1945), pp. 4–5.

3. Elazar, "The New Agenda of European Jewry"; Charles S. Liebman, *On the Study of International Jewish Political Organizations* (Jerusalem: Center for Jewish Community Studies, 1978); Ernest Stock, "The Emerging European Jewish Community Structure" and "Jewish Multicountry Associations," *American Jewish Year Book 1974–75,* vol. 75, pp. 571–97; Josef J. Lador-Lederer, "World Jewish Associations," *Encyclopedia Judaica Yearbook, 1973* (Jerusalem: Keter, 1973).

4. Daniel J. Elazar, *Sephardic Jewry in a New World Role* (New York: Council of Jewish Federations, 1982).

5. Cecil Roth, "The Jews of Western Europe," in Louis Finkelstein, ed., *The Jews: Their History, Culture, and Religion,* 3d ed., vol. 1 (New York: Harper and Row, 1960), pp. 250–86; Raul Hilberg, *The Destruction of the European Jews* (New York: Harper and Row Publishers, Inc., 1961), pp. 363–421; Cecil Roth, "The European Age" and Salo W. Baron, "The Modern Age," in Leo Schwarz, ed., *Great Ages and Ideas of the Jewish People* (New York: Random House, 1956), pp. 267–311 and 315–90; Werner Keller, "Liberation in Western Europe," in *Diaspora* (New York: Harcourt, Brace and World, Inc., 1969), pp. 403–8.

6. Phyllis Cohen Albert, *The Modernization of French Jewry: Consistory and Community in the Nineteenth Century* (Waltham, Mass.: Brandeis University Press, 1977); Paula Hyman, *From Dreyfus to Vichy: The Remaking of French Jewry, 1906–1939* (New York: Columbia University Press, 1979).

7. Diogene Tama, ed., *Transactions of the Parisian Sanhedrin or Acts of the Assembly of Israelitish Deputies of France and Italy* (London: 1807); Raphael Mahler, *A History of Modern Jews, 1780–1815* (London: Vallentine, Mitchell, 1971), pp. 67–72; "French Sanhedrin," *Encyclopedia Judaica,* vol. 14, pp. 840–42; Jacob

Katz, *Out of the Ghetto: The Social Background of Jewish Emancipation, 1770–1870* (Cambridge, Mass.: Harvard University Press, 1973), pp. 139–41.

8. On the history of French Jewry in the nineteenth and early twentieth centuries, see Albert, *The Modernization of French Jewry;* Hyman, *From Dreyfus to Vichy;* B. Blumenkratz, *Histoire des Juifs en France* (Paris: Privat, 1972); Ilan Greilsammer, *The Democratization of a Community: The Case of French Jewry* (Jerusalem: Center for Jewish Community Studies, 1979) and "Jews of France: From Neutrality to Involvement," *Forum,* vol. 28–29 (winter 1978), pp. 130–46; Simon Schwarzfuchs, *Les Juifs de France* (Paris: Albin Michel, 1975); W. Rabi, *Anatomie du Français* (Paris: Editions de Minuit, 1962).

9. See Greilsammer, *The Democratization of a Community* and "Jews of France"; Marc Salzberg, *French Jewry and American Jewry* (Jerusalem: Center for Jewish Community Studies, 1971); Dominique Schnapper, *Jewish Identities in France: An Analysis of Contemporary French Jewry* (Chicago: University of Chicago Press, 1983); Doris Bensimon-Donath, *L'intégration des Juifs Nord-Africains en France* (Paris: Mouton, 1971); O. Klineberg, G. Levitte, and G. Benguigui, *Aspects of French Jewry* (London: Vallentine, Mitchell, 1969); David Landes, "The State of French Jewry," *Moment,* vol. 6, nos. 3–4 (March-April 1981), pp. 12–18; Ilan Greilsammer and Marc Salzberg, "Hakehillah HaYehudit BeTzorfat al Irguniyah" (The Organized Jewish Community of France), issue of *Tefutsot Yisrael,* vol. 16, no. 4 (December 1978) (Hebrew).

10. Greilsammer, *The Democratization of a Community.*

11. Landes, "The State of French Jewry"; Schnapper, *Jewish Identities in France;* Herbert L. Lottman, "The Assimilated Jew, French Style," *Present Tense,* vol. 1, no. 1 (August 1973), pp. 42–44; Albert Memmi, "On Jewishness and the Social Contexts of Jews in France," *The Jewish Journal of Sociology,* no. 1 (January 1970); Arnold Mandel, "France," in *American Jewish Year Book 1984,* vol. 84, pp. 198–204.

12.. Jean-Pierre Francotte, *Les Relations de la Communauté Israélite de Belgique avec le Pouvoir Central (1830–1940)* (Brussels: Centre National des Hautes Etudes Juives, 1972) and "Belgium," in *Encyclopedia Judaica,* vol. 4, pp. 416–18; J. Gutwirth, *Vie Juive Traditionelle* (Paris: Les Editions de Minuit, 1970).

13. Adina Weiss Liberles, *The Jewish Community of Belgium* (Jerusalem: Center for Jewish Community Studies, 1970); W. Bok, *La Population Juive en Belgique au Début de la Guerre et au Cours des Années 1941 et 1942 d'Après Documents* (Brussels: Centre National des Hautes Etudes Juives, 1965); Hilberg, *The Destruction of European Jews,* pp. 382–89; Alex Grobman and Daniel Landes, eds., *Genocide: Critical Issues of the Holocaust* (Los Angeles and New York: The Simon Wiesenthal Center and Rossel Books, 1983).

14. Weiss Liberles, *The Jewish Community of Belgium;* Francotte, *Les Relations de la Communauté Israélite* and *La Vie Juive dans l'Europe Contemporaine* (Paris and Brussels: Centre National des Hautes Etudes Juives and Hebrew University, Institute of Contemporary Jewry, Editions de l'Institut de Sociologie de l'Université de Bruxelles, 1965); W. Bok and B. Goldberg, *Dualité Culturelle et Appartenance* (Brussels: Centre National des Hautes Etudes Juives, 1970); Ernest Stock, ed., *European Jewry: A Handbook* (Paris: European Council of Jewish Community Services, 1982).

15. Jacques Gutwirth, "Antwerp Jewry Today," *Jewish Journal of Sociology,* vol. 10, no. 1 (June 1968), pp. 121–37; Ephraim Schmidt, *Geschiedenis van de Joden in Antwerpen* (History of the Jews in Antwerp) (Antwerp: Druck Excelsior, 1963); D. Wachsstock, "Jewish Antwerp: A Shtetl in Transition," *In the Dispersion* (spring 1966), pp. 68–76.

16. Mozes Heiman Gans, *Memorbook: History of Dutch Jewry from the Renaissance to 1940* (Baarn: Bosch and Keuning n.d., 1971); "The Netherlands," in *Encyclopedia Judaica,* vol. 12, pp. 973–82; Werner Keller, "The Dutch Jerusalem," in *Diaspora* (London: Pitman Publishing, 1971), pp. 317–29; Katz, *Out of the Ghetto.*

17. Gans, *Memorbook;* Ludy Giebels, *De Zionistiche Beweging in Nederland, 1899–1941* (The Zionist Movement in the Netherlands, 1899–1941) (Assen: Van Gorcum, 1975); L. de Jong, *Het Koninkrijk der Nederlanden in de Tweede Wereld Oorlog* (The Kingdom of the Netherlands in the Second World War) (The Hague: Staatsuitgeverij, 1974–76).

18. Joel S. Fishman, "The Jewish Community in Post-War Netherlands, 1944–1975," *Midstream,* vol. 22, no. 1 (January 1976), pp. 42–54; Jong, *Het Koninkrijk der Nederlanden;* Henriette Boas, "The Netherlands," in *American Jewish Year Book 1954,* vol. 55, pp. 205–17; Jacob Presser, *The Destruction of the Dutch Jews* (New York: E. P. Dutton Co., 1969); Veld, *De SS in Nederland: Documenten vit SS-Archieven, 1933–1945* (The SS in the Netherlands: Documents from the SS Archives, 1933–1945) (The Hague: Staatsuitgeverij, 1976); R. Schuursma, "Dutch Fascists' Share in Crime," *Wiener Library Bulletin,* vol. 20, no. 2 (spring 1966), pp. 34–37; Adina Kochba, ed., *Underground of the Zionist Youth in Occupied Holland* (Tel Aviv: HaKibbutz HaMeuhad, 1969) (Hebrew).

19. Fishman, *The Jewish Community;* Maurits Kopuit, "The Netherlands," in *American Jewish Year Book 1973,* vol. 74, pp. 407–21; Han Emanuel, "Experiences Tirées de l'Enquette Demographique sur les Juifs de Hollande," in Francotte, *La Vie Juive,* pp. 65–79.

20. Cecil Roth, *History of the Jews in England* (Oxford: Clarendon Press, 1949); V. D. Lipman, ed., *Three Centuries of Anglo-Jewish History* (London: The Jewish Historical Society of England, 1961) and *Social History of the Jews of England, 1850–1950* (London: Watts and Co., 1954); Raphael Patai, *Tents of Jacob* (Englewood Cliffs, N.J.: Prentice-Hall, 1971), pp. 275–77; A. M. Hyamson, *The Sephardim of England: A History of the Spanish-Portuguese Community, 1492–1951* (London: Methuen, 1951); Todd M. Endelman, *The Jews of Georgian England, 1714–1830* (Philadelphia: Jewish Publication Society of America, 1979).

21. Stuart A. Cohen, "The Conquest of a Community? The Zionists and the Board of Deputies in 1917," *Jewish Journal of Sociology,* vol. 19, no. 2 (December 1977), pp. 157–84; Charles H. L. Emmanuel, *A Century and a Half of Jewish History: Extracts from the Minute Books of the London Committee of Deputies of the British Jews* (London: Board of Deputies of British Jews, 1910); Elsley Zeitlkn, *A Paragraph of Anglo-Jewish History: The Board of Deputies and the B'nai B'rith* (London: Board of Deputies of British Jews, 1936).

22. Stephen Aris, *But There Are No Jews in England* (New York: Stein and Day, 1971); Roth, *History of the Jews in England;* Lipman, *Social History;* C. Russell and H. S. Lewis, *The Jew in London: A Study of Racial Character and Present-Day Conditions* (London: Unwin, 1900); P. Emden, *The Jews of Britain* (London: Sampson Low Marston, 1943); Sir J. Clapham, *An Economic History of Modern Britain, 1850–1886* (Cambridge: Cambridge University Press, 1950–52); N. Barov, *The Jews in Work and Trade* (London: The Trades Advisory Council, 1948); Chaim Bermant, *Troubled Eden: An Anatomy of British Jewry,* (London: Vallentine, Mitchell, 1969) and *The Cousinhood* (New York: Macmillan Co., 1971); W. Bagehot, *Lombard Street* (London: Smith Elder, 1873).

23. On the Jewish communities in England outside London, see M. Goodman, "Liverpool Jewry," *In the Dispersion* (spring 1966), pp. 52–67; Ernest Krausz, *Leeds Jewry: Its Ministry and Social Structure* (Cambridge: Heffer, 1964) and "An Anglo-Jewish Community: Leeds," *Jewish Journal of Sociology* (June 1961), pp. 88–107; R. D'Arcy Hart, *The Samuel Family of Liverpool and London* (London: Routledge and Kegan Paul, 1958); Niggel Grizzard and Paula Raisman, "Inner City Jews in Leeds," *Jewish Journal of Sociology,* vol. 22 (January 1980), pp. 21–34; Meir Persoff and Michael Wallach, "Teshlich Moves Upstream-Maidenhead," *Jewish Chronicle* (September 1982); "Manchester," in *Encyclopedia Judaica,* vol. 11, pp. 858–60; Cecil Roth, *The Rise of Provincial Jewry* (London: The Jewish Monthly, 1950).

24. On the Jews in Scotland, see Chaim Bermant, *Troubled Eden,* pp. 54–59, "Anatomy of Glasgow," *Explorations* (London: 1967), pp. 99–106, and "Scotland," *Encyclopedia Judaica,* vol. 14, pp. 1035–36.

25. On the Jews in Wales, see "Wales," *Encyclopedia Judaica,* vol. 16, pp. 250–51; O. K. Rabinowicz, *Winston Churchill on Jewish Problems* (London: World Jewish Congress, 1956), pp. 167–72; Roth, *The Rise of Provincial Jewry,* pp. 102–4.

26. On the Jews in Ulster, see "Ireland," *Encyclopedia Judaica,* vol. 8, p. 1466; Louis Hyman, *The Jews in Ireland: From the Earliest Times to the Year 1910* (Jerusalem: Israel Universities Press, 1972); Roth, *The Rise of Provincial Jewry.*

27. Bernard Gainer, *The Alien Invasion: The Origins of the Aliens Act of 1905* (London: Heineman, 1972); William Fishman, *East End Radicals, 1875–1914* (London: G. Puckworth and Co., 1975); Barry A. Kosmin, "Immigration without Impact: Some Reflections on the Long-Term Results of the East European Immigration of 1881–1914 on British Jewry," *L'Eylah,* vol. 2, no. 3, pp. 41–44; Lloyd P. Gartner, *The Jewish Immigrant in England, 1870–1914* (London: George Allen and Unwin, Ltd., 1960).

28. See Stuart A. Cohen, *English Zionists and British Jews 1895–1920* (Princeton, N.J.: Princeton University Press, 1982) and "The Conquest of a Community?"

29. Fishman, *East End Jewish Radicals, 1875–1914;* Cecil Roth, *Anglo-Jewish Letters* (London: Soncino Press, 1938) and *Essays and Portraits in Anglo-Jewish History* (Philadelphia: Jewish Publication Society of America, 1962); Maurice Freedman, ed., *A Minority in Britain: Social Studies of the Anglo-Jewish Community* (London: Vallentine Mitchell, 1955); Geoffrey Paul, "A Look at the Community's Past, Present—and Future," *Jewish Chronicle* (November 1978); Stuart A. Cohen and Avihu Zakai, eds., *Hayai haYehudim be-Britania* (Jewish Life in Britain), issue of *Tefutsot Yisrael,* vol. 21, no. 4 (winter 1983) (Hebrew); Bermant, *Troubled Eden.*

30. Norman Cohen, "Trends in Anglo-Jewish Religious Life," in Julius Gould and Shaul Esh, eds., *Jewish Life in Modern Britain* (London: Board of Deputies of British Jews, 1964); Immanuel Jakobovits, "An Analysis of Religious versus Secularist Trends in Anglo-Jewry," in S. L. Lipman and V. D. Lipman, eds., *Jewish Life in Britain* (New York: K. G. Saur, 1983); Chaim Bermant, "The Last Bastion of Tolerant Orthodoxy—Liverpool," *Jewish Chronicle* (November 1981) and "A Religious Revival," *Jewish Chronicle* (November 1978).

31. Cohen and Zakai, eds., *Hayai Yehudim be-Britania;* Gould and Esh, eds., *Jewish Life in Modern Britain;* Freedman, ed., *A Minority in Britain.*

32. Bermant, "A Religious Revival" and "The Last Bastion of Tolerant Orthodoxy—Liverpool"; Nor-

man Cohen, "Trends in Anglo-Jewish Religious Life"; Jakobovits, "An Analysis of Religious versus Secularist Trends in Anglo-Jewry."

33. Jacob Braude, "Jewish Education in Britain Today" and Michael Rosin, "The Jewish Student Today," in S. L. Lipman and V. D. Lipman, eds., *Jewish Life in Britain;* Gerald Cromer and Shelley Schreter, "Jewish Educational Materials in England," *Dispersion and Unity* (winter 1973–74), pp. 192–99; Joseph Hanan, "Jewish Education in Great Britain," *In the Dispersion* (January 1962), pp. 43–53; Ernest Krausz, "Jewish Students in Britain," *In the Dispersion* (winter 1964–65), pp. 85–89.

34. Geoffrey Paul, "Report from Ireland—Jews in the Emerald Island," *Jewish Digest* (July-August 1979); "Ireland," in *Encyclopedia Judaica,* vol. 8, pp. 1463–66; Hyman, *The Jews in Ireland;* Roth, *The Rise of Provincial Jewry;* Yaakov Tsur, ed., *Hatefutsah: Maarav Europe* (The Diaspora: Western Europe) (Jerusalem: Keter Publishing House, 1976), pp. 3–27 (Hebrew); B. Shillman, *Short History of the Jews of Ireland* (Dublin: Cahill and Co., 1945).

15

The Reconstituted Kehillot of Central Europe

The *Kultesgemeinden* of central Europe or their equivalents in areas influenced by central European culture before World War I also have undergone basic constitutional changes in recent years. They have, by and large, lost their power to compel all Jews to be members and must now hold their membership on a voluntary basis. Still, this usually means that all known Jews are automatically listed on the community's rolls but have the right to opt out.

The state-recognized community, once the basis of Jewish life, lost ground in size and importance in the Jewish world when it also lost its compulsory character. Most are declining in population, decimated by war, emigration, and assimilation. Moreover, an increasing (if still small) number of Jews in those communities may be choosing to give up community membership (and the taxes that go with it). Nevertheless, in 1985 about 130,000 Jews lived in such communities.[1]

These communities fall into three groupings: (1) the German-speaking communities of central Europe: Austria, the Federal Republic of Germany, and Switzerland; (2) the Scandinavian communities on Europe's northern periphery; Denmark, Finland, Norway, and Sweden; and (3) the Mediterranean communities of Greece, Italy, and Yugoslavia, which adopted the models of central Europe. Together these form a contiguous bloc of communities covering the European heartland. What distinguishes them are their respective histories.

Structurally, the *kehillah* communities remain neat and all-embracing. All legitimate institutions or organizations function within their overall framework, except where the state has allowed secessionist groups. Countrywide, they are usually organized along conventional federal lines with either "national" and "local" or "national," "provincial," and "local" bodies, each chosen in formal elections and linked constitutionally to one another with a generally clear division of powers. In some, authority is lodged in the local community, perhaps with loose confederal relationships uniting localities. (See figure 15.1.)

The greatest source of strength of the state-recognized communities is in their power to tax or to receive automatically a portion of their members' regular taxes from the authorities. Until World War II, membership in a religious community was compulsory in most of the states in which these communities were found. Hence the communities enjoyed a monopoly of communal governance unless the state also allowed a secessionist community. After the war, that monopoly was broken when state after state eliminated the compulsory features or abolished formal recognition altogether. What remained was their dominance in governance for almost all Jews, who choose to keep their membership.

338

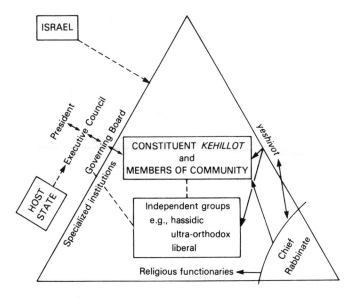

Figure 15.1. Generalized model of the countrywide communities of free Europe.

The Jewish Community in Germany

The long and tragic history of the Jews of Germany is central to Jewish history. Jewish settlement has been more or less continuous, if tenuous, the last two thousand years, punctuated by frequent expulsions and massacres, which constantly disrupted Jewish life and left a residue of deeply ingrained anti-Semitism among the host populations. The Jewish communities have strong traditions of autonomy coupled with the need to cope with waves of persecution culminating in the Holocaust.

Although the first presence of the Jews in German territory goes back to the Roman period, the German states became centers of Jewish life only when Ashkenazi Jewry emerged as a subculture within the Jewish people in the tenth and eleventh centuries. Then it was the locus of the development of the constitutional tradition of the medieval Ashkenazi *kehillah*. The first flowering of Ashkenaz in Germany lasted for a full epoch, from the eleventh to the middle of the fourteenth centuries, when it was destroyed by the massacres and expulsions that came in the wake of the Black Death (1348).[2]

German Jewry hung on for the next epoch, although only in scattered communities and in a constantly diminishing condition. By the beginning of the modern epoch in the middle of the seventeenth century, there were few Jews left in the German states. Hence most of the Jewish community of modern Germany consisted of immigrants who settled in the more liberal German states. The first were Marranos, who settled in Hamburg in the seventeenth century, and Jews living in the areas of Poland and Bohemia that were annexed by Prussia after it emerged as a major European power. The combination of immigration and annexation led to the development of a major Jewish community by the nineteenth century. By the late nineteenth century, Berlin was one of the major centers of Jewish population in the world. German Jewry numbered more than 650,000 when

Hitler took power—this despite the emigration and assimilation that took place regularly throughout the nineteenth and twentieth centuries.[3]

The German Jews were also among the first to lose their autonomy. In the early eighteenth century, at the time of the consolidation of the Prussian state, long before the Jews were emancipated, the rulers of the new German states, wanting to destroy the medieval corporatism that had left Germany divided, struck hard at all separatist institutions in their territories, including the Jewish community. This led the Jews to demand equal rights if they could no longer have autonomy. But it was a slow and painful struggle in Germany because of the negative attitude toward Jews that prevailed throughout the German-speaking world. The issue was complicated by the fact that Napoléon emancipated the Jews when he conquered Germany, thereby linking the Jewish struggle to the enemies of the German people. One of Prussia's first acts after expelling the French was to revoke the emancipation laws.

Not until well into the nineteenth century were German Jews fully emancipated. The constitution of the second German Reich, established in 1870, guaranteed the political and civic equality of all citizens. Jews could vote and be elected to the Reichstag but could not be government ministers. In practice, they were also denied appointment to top university posts. In 1876 Prussia permitted Jews to disaffiliate from the Jewish community without converting to Christianity.

Nevertheless, individual German Jews began obtaining privileges from the beginning of the eighteenth century onward and hence were able to make their contributions to German society. In trying to prove themselves good Germans, they introduced modernization into the Jewish world. The resulting German-Jewish symbiosis led to a flowering on both sides. Germany benefited greatly from the release of Jewish energy, and its redirection served the interests of the new German Empire in almost every field of endeavor. German Jews dominated the modernization of Ashkenazi Jewry. All three major religious movements of modern Jewry—Reform, Conservative, and modern Orthodoxy—originated in Germany. German-speaking Jews laid the foundations of the World Zionist Organization, and modern Jewish thought and literature began in Germany.

After World War I—in which 100,000 Jews served in the German army—all remaining restrictions on the Jews were abolished by the Weimar republic. Jews quickly rose to positions of political power in the liberal and socialist parties and the civil service. The Weimar constitution continued to recognize the right of the Jewish community to collect compulsory dues. At the same time, community organizations were active in every field.

All this ended with the rise of Nazism, which first segregated and persecuted German Jews, then tried to expel them, and finally exterminated those who had not left. The end of World War II found the Jewish community of Germany gone. Most had left between 1933 and 1940 when the gates closed. Although a few thousand Jews survived in the Reich during the war, all of them Jewish spouses in intermarriages who managed to hold on, the last manifestation of the organized community had been abolished by 1942; any Jew who was entitled to membership in it and who had not already fled the country was deported to the death camps.[4]

The end of the war found tens of thousands of Jews on German soil—in concentration camps. Most of them left during the next several years to settle elsewhere, principally in Israel. A small percentage decided to remain in Germany, mostly because of successful business ventures inaugurated while they were in the displaced persons camps. They were joined by a small number of German Jewish refugees who returned after the war to reclaim their property or because they could not adjust elsewhere and longed for the German environment despite all that had happened. About ten thousand of the fifteen thousand German Jewish Holocaust survivors freed in 1945 remained in Germany. They were joined by another nine thousand east European displaced persons, who settled in West Germany between 1945 and 1952. By 1960 some six thousand German Jews had returned.

These two groups were augmented by other refugees who came westward from Poland and later the Soviet Union, plus Israelis who drifted in over the years after the Six-Day War. Slowly a new Jewish community was formed in Germany. On July 17, 1950, the Zentralrat der Juden in Deutschland (Central Council of Jews in Germany) was established with headquarters in Düsseldorf. At first, it was treated as something of a pariah by the rest of the Jewish world because of the natural Jewish revulsion against Germany and even greater revulsion against Jews who would choose to live there after the Holocaust.[5] Until the German government signed the reparations agreement with the State of Israel and the Conference on Jewish Material Claims against Germany in September 1952, German Jewry was outside the world Jewish framework. At that time, however, the Zentralrat also became affiliated with the World Jewish Congress.

The German government, however, did everything it could to encourage Jewish resettlement and the restoration of Jewish community life, as part of its effort to gain legitimization. The federal government and the *länder* immediately restored the official status of the community. The German federal system offered a proper framework for the Jews. The community was reorganized along classic federal lines, with the relationship between each community and the overseeing body delineated in the Germanic way. Like the other religious communities, it has legal standing as the official representative of German Jewry. There is automatic remission to the community of a percentage of the state taxes paid by community members, and the community has custody over prewar Jewish communal property. The Zentralrat receives the 8 percent income tax surcharge paid by every registered member of the community and distributes the money to the communities and their institutions. The only difference is that, in postwar Germany, membership in a religious community ceased to be compulsory as it had been before the war; Jews could opt out or simply not join the community if they did not want to assume the obligations it imposed. The German government provided funds for the reconstruction of synagogues and Jewish institutions, for their maintenance, and for programs that the German Jewish community wanted to foster. The limits were essentially those German Jewry imposed on itself, because the German government was eager to make amends for the Nazi regime. The Zentralrat is also responsible for the external relations-defense sphere, handling representation to the federal government and community relations.

In 1983 there were 28,202 registered Jews in the Federal Republic of Germany. The *American Jewish Yearbook* estimates that there are an additional 25,000 *unregistered* Jews. Although there are seventy-three Jewish communities in the Federal Republic, most German Jews live in the large cities—two-thirds in the six largest. The principal Jewish communities are West Berlin, which consists primarily of native German Jews and their descendants; Frankfurt, 40 percent of whose members are ex-displaced persons and their descendants; Munich, 80 percent of displaced-persons origin; Düsseldorf, Hamburg, and Köln (Cologne). It is an aging community and it also has a high rate of intermarriage.

In 1983 there were 6,548 registered Jews in West Berlin; 4,872 in Frankfurt; 3,920 in Munich; 1,704 in Düsseldorf; 1,391 in Hamburg; and 1,279 in Cologne.

Immigration is insignificant today. Jewish emigration from the Soviet Union and Iran has been reduced to a trickle. The Israeli government has asked the West German government to limit the number of visas it grants Israelis. The West German government even took legal action against three hundred Russian Jews who arrived in Germany by way of Israel, with false papers indicating they had come directly from the Soviet Union. Emigration also is declining; 620 Jews emigrated in 1982.

Still, the community is declining. The ratio of deaths to births is five to one. The intermarriage rate is 78 percent. Until now, the population has been barely maintained through immigration.

The community has established a network of Jewish institutions (see figure 15.2): forty-five synagogues with twelve rabbis who either returned to Germany or came there from other countries, a professional Jewish civil service, and Jewish schools—day schools in Berlin, Frankfurt, and Munich and supplementary schools in other communities. Every community has a social welfare department attached to the Zentralwohlfahrstelle (central welfare office), in Frankfurt. Many communities maintain homes for the aged and summer camps for children. German-language Jewish weeklies are published in Düsseldorf and Munich, and two publishing houses exist in Berlin; one, the Jüdischer Verlag, was reestablished; the other, Ner Tamid, is new.

The Zionist organization and WIZO have branches in most communities. There is regular fund-raising for the Keren Hayesod and Jewish National Fund. The community is a generous contributor and claims to raise the second highest amount per capita in Europe. WIZO, the German section of Magen David Adom, and the German society to further the Israel Cancer Association also raise money.

B'nai B'rith lodges have been established in all the principal cities. It is symbolic of the tenuousness of this new community, however, that rather than referring to themselves as Deutsche Juden (German Jews), they refer to themselves as Juden in Deutschland (Jews in Germany).

Although most of the community is, at best, nominally religious, if that, there are

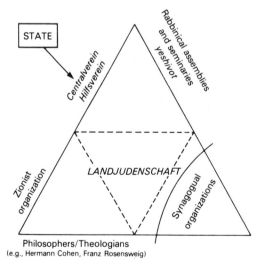

Figure 15.2. The organizational structure of the Jewish community in the Federal Republic of Germany.

an estimated two thousand Orthodox Jews in the country. *Halakhic* decisions are the responsibility of the Conference of Rabbis. An Academy of Jewish Studies has been established at the University of Heidelberg to train synagogue and educational personnel, but it has no permanent faculty.

There are two youth organizations. Bund Jüdische Jugend (the Jewish Youth League) was created in 1979 for youth between the ages of sixteen and thirty-five, to promote Jewish awareness. It has held a number of seminars throughout Germany on Jewish-related topics. The larger Association of Jewish Students in Germany, which claims more than a thousand members, also conducts and participates in seminars in Europe and Israel. It is linked to the European Union of Jewish Students, the Central Council, and the Conference of Rabbis.

In the Israel-*edah* sphere, Israeli leaders, when visiting Germany, usually meet with leaders of the Central Council. Most German Jews have traveled to Israel, and it is has been common to hold bar mitzvah ceremonies there. Israel supplies the community with teachers, principals, and rabbis. The Central Council is affiliated with the World Jewish Congress European Section. The Central Welfare Agency maintains membership in the European Council of Jewish Community Services.

Early in the 1950s the Jewish leadership of the immediate postwar period gave way to a new leadership, in part because the older leaders retired and in part because a series of scandals having to do with the use of restored Jewish property led to several of the older leaders being removed from the scene. Those that took over at this point were still in power in the early 1980s. By the latter years of the decade, they, too, were being replaced, amidst another scandal.

All told, a Jewish community in Germany not only exists but is likely to continue to exist. Whether or not it is likely to play any important role on the world Jewish scene remains to be seen.

The Jewish Community in Austria

The long history of Austrian Jewry is one of point-counterpoint between Jewish efforts to build autonomous communities and to live creative Jewish lives and Austrian persecutions and expulsions.[6] Even when Jews were allowed to live in the country, they were placed under great restrictions, the most galling of which was the limitation of their right to marry. Not until the adoption of the Austro-Hungarian Constitution of December 21, 1867, were Jews fully emancipated, and they were given the right to vote only in 1907. Nevertheless, as early as the eighteenth century, Austrian authorities made deliberate efforts to force the Jews to assimilate, including reorganizing the Jewish communities through a series of laws promulgated in 1789. Those laws were the basis of Jewish communal life throughout the rest of the imperial period.

The Austrian authorities prevented the Jewish communities from fragmenting along Orthodox–non-Orthodox lines by requiring a united community in each town by law. In 1890 legislation was promulgated reaffirming the power of each undivided local community to supervise all religious and charitable institutions in the area and to collect dues. Only Austrian citizens could be elected to the community governing boards.

Parallel to full emancipation and the reorganization of the community was the growth of organized anti-Semitism, which emerged first in Austria as a political force. The Jewish response to anti-Semitism led to the establishment of Jewish political parties in their communities and later, after the franchise was extended to them in 1907, in the general political arena. The assimilationist Jews organized the Öesterreichisch Israelitische Union; the nationalists organized the Jüdisch-Politische Verein, which later became the Jüdisch-National Partei and elected representatives to the Austrian Parliament for a few years before World War I.

The establishment of modern Austria after the defeat of the Austrian Empire in World War I brought little change either in the intensity of Austrian anti-Semitism or in Jewish participation in Austrian political life. In the Jewish communities, the Zionists continued to contest with the assimilationists and in 1934 formed the majority in Vienna and Graz.

The Viennese Jewish community has been the principal one in Austria since the middle of the nineteenth century. In 1846 there were 3,739 Jews in Vienna. That number rose to nearly 200,000 by World War I. In 1936 the 176,034 Jews in Vienna constituted 8 percent of the total population, with fifty-nine synagogues, a Jewish educational network, a rabbinical seminary that was a center of scholarship and rabbinical training, a Hebrew teachers' college, and a full network of welfare, health, education, and sports institutions.

The *Anschluss* led to massive emigration and deportation of Austrian Jews. By the outbreak of the war, almost all the Jewish communities outside Vienna had been dissolved, and the Vienna community was reduced to caring for the aged and infirm who could not leave. It was officially dissolved on November 1, 1942, and replaced with a more limited community council.[7]

Although only a few hundred Austrian Jews survived the war in Austria, many Jews from other countries found themselves there at the war's end because of deportations to forced labor and concentration camps on Austrian territory. Because of Austria's stragetic position as a transit point, the nearly 20,000 Jewish displaced persons in the country in 1945 peaked at 42,500 in late 1946 but declined to less than 1,000 by 1953. During the same period, several thousand Austrian Jews returned to the country from places of imprisonment or refuge and attempted to reestablish organized Jewish life. In 1950, there were 13,396 Jews registered as members of the Jewish community, of whom 12,450 were in Vienna, and the rest in Graz, Linz, Salzburg, and Innsbruck, and scattered in smaller communities. That was the peak permanent Jewish population in the postwar period.[8]

Since then, that number has continued to decrease. Today it is estimated that there are eight thousand Jews in Austria, two-thirds of whom are over fifty years of age. Austria is a transit point for Jews from the eastern bloc seeking refuge in Israel or the West, whether Romanian Jews who have come in a continual stream since the end of the war, Hungarian Jewish refugees who came after the 1956 revolt, or Soviet Jews who come in periodic waves.

Anti-Semitism in Austria has not diminished appreciably even if it had to be expressed more quietly in the first postwar generation. The Austrian government has adamantly refused to provide more than token compensation for its Jewish citizens who were victims of the Nazis, claiming Austria to be a victim itself.

At the end of World War II the four thousand Jews who found themselves in Vienna reconstituted the Jewish community. Its first president was appointed by the occupation authorities but in April 1946 elections were held for the community council. The left-wing unity party won those elections, and the leader of that party was elected president.

Two years later in 1948 the unity party was defeated by a coalition of Zionists and Social Democrats, a sign of the shift away from the Soviet domination of Vienna. A Zionist was elected president. That coalition survived until the elections of December 1949 when the Social Democrats gained a majority of seats on the council. Their man was elected president, remaining in office until 1963 when he was replaced by another Social Democrat. Community elections are generally contested by the Bundwerktätiger Juden (the Jewish Labor Federation), affiliated with the Austrian Social Democratic party; the Zionist Federation, the Orthodox party, and a quasi-Communist list, with the first maintaining a majority on the community board for many years.

The chief rabbinate was renewed in 1948. There are three synagogues in the community: the Central Synagogue, the only one not destroyed in the aftermath of the *Anschluss,* plus two more prayer houses, all under the jurisdiction of the chief rabbi. The community maintains a small day school and two Talmud Torahs for the ultra-Orthodox. Supplementary Jewish education is also provided for students who attend non-Jewish schools.

In the communal-welfare sphere, the community maintains a hospital, old-people's homes, and welfare institutions. Although the community receives a percentage of the taxes paid by its members to the government, its income has not been able to meet its costs and the Joint Distribution Committee has provided assistance, though on a much diminished scale in recent years.

All the communities are united in the Federation of Jewish Communities of Austria, which is dominated by Vienna. The Federation of Jewish Communities dominates the external affairs—defense and communal-welfare spheres. It is a member of the World Jewish Congress European Section and the European Council of Jewish Community Services. All told, however, Austrian Jewry is peripheral even in Europe, not to speak of the larger Jewish world. A declining community, it will be prevented from disappearing only because of the immigration of other Jews in the future.

The Swiss Jewish Community

Of all the state-recognized communities, the Swiss Jewish community has undergone the least change, primarily because of Swiss neutrality during the two world wars, which left its institutions and population intact. Nevertheless, the assimilation and emigration of Swiss-born Jews and the immigration, however limited by the Swiss government policy, of German and East Eurpean Jews because of wartime dislocation, have transformed the content of the community even though its form has changed little.[9] Swiss Jewry is primarily Ashkenazic in origin. Only in the post-World War II period has there been a significant influx of Sephardim from the Arab countries, primarily wealthy, who have organized Sephardi congregations.

The first extensive settlement of Jews in Switzerland came in the thirteenth century when the Swiss republics and cities were beginning to assert themselves as autonomous entities within the Holy Roman Empire. Small Jewish communities maintained themselves in secure circumstances until the Black Death of 1348 when Jews were accused of poisoning the wells and a wave of massacres swept the Swiss cities. By 1349 the Jewish community of Switzerland was almost annihilated. Although groups came back during the next several decades, by the end of the fifteenth century almost all Jews had been expelled. The cohesiveness of Swiss society and the commercial character of the Swiss left no room for Jews to pursue their separate way of life or their traditional occupations without being in severe competition with the indigenous population. Hence they were expelled. The only Jewish population to remain in Switzerland was in the county of Baden, whose Swiss portion, Aargau, retained a Jewish presence until modern times.[10]

The conquest of Switzerland by Napoléon placed the Jewish issue on the Swiss political agenda, but the Swiss refused to grant the Jews citizenship on the grounds that the Jewish people constituted a political rather than a religious body. Jews were permitted to live in Switzerland as resident aliens. Despite the assertion that Jews constituted a separate political entity, the Swiss soon eliminated Jewish communal autonomy. In 1809 the canton of Aargau made Jews subject to all its laws and ordinances, but refused to give them citizenship. Under these arrangements the Jews ceased to be aliens but became dependent on the canton, defined, with usual Swiss precision, as, in effect, a protected polity.

During the first half of the nineteenth century, local Jews, assisted by their brethren in France, Britain, and the United States, struggled to open the rest of Switzerland to Jewish settlement and to gain Swiss citizenship. The Swiss federal constitution was amended in 1866 to grant the Jews freedom of residence throughout Switzerland and guarantee civic and legal equality by eliminating the restriction of civil rights to Christians. But, in the framework of the Swiss federal system, the status of the Jews was dependent on the decision of each canton. The final struggle was stimulated by the actions of the Great Council of Aargau, which had voted to give the Jews full rights in 1862 but had then been turned out by the voters for doing so and retreated to reintroduce a modified version of the 1809 system. Aargau did not change its laws until 1879, after most of the other cantons where Jews lived had done so.

The Swiss people and their government have consistently sent mixed signals to the Jews. For example, kosher slaughtering of four-legged animals was prohibited in Switzerland by popular initiative in 1893. In 1938, however, at the height of the Nazi advance, the Swiss Federal Council enacted a law for protection of democracy, prohibiting public incitement to racial or religious hatred.

Although willing to protect its own Jews, the Swiss government did its utmost to close the doors of Switzerland to refugees from Nazi persecution. This is not the place to tell that shameful story. In the end, only twenty-five thousand Jews were permitted to take refuge in Switzerland and hardly any more were able to pass through on the way to refuge elsewhere. Still, that figure more than doubled the indigenous Jewish population, which needed the assistance of the Joint Distribution Committee to cope with the influx. The Swiss were slightly more generous in 1956 after the Sinai Campaign and the Hungarian uprising, when some Jewish refugees from Egypt and Hungary arrived. But again the emphasis was on taking only those prosperous enough to care for themselves.

Despite these problems, Jews continued to move into Switzerland in the nineteenth century. That population was augmented in the twentieth century as a result of the upheavals of the two world wars. By 1904, thirteen organized local Jewish communities were functioning, to total approximately fifteen hundred family members. In that year, they came together to form the Schweizerischer Israelitischer Gemeindebund (SIG; in French, the Fédération Suisse des Communautés Israélites), a true federation that carefully parallels the Swiss federal structure. By 1970 it had twenty-four member communities with 4,724 family members. The major Jewish communities in Switzerland are Zurich with more than 6,000 Jews, Geneva with more than 3,000, Basel with more than 2,000, Lausanne with more than 1,000, and Berne with about 700.

The governance of the Swiss Jewish community is highly formalistic and low-key in the Swiss way. The SIG is consulted by the Swiss government as the official representative of the Jewish community in anything that the Swiss determine requires the response of the religious communities. Aside from that, its principal functions are to provide services such as care of the aged, youth education (especially summer camps), youth convocations, and trips to Israel. The SIG maintains a Jewish museum in Basel. The SIG is a founding member of the World Jewish Congress and a member of the European Council of Jewish Community Services. It also handles relations between Swiss Jewry and Israel. Unlike many other European communities, the executive director of the SIG is a professional.

The three major Jewish communities have day schools, which attract a substantial portion of the Jewish school-age population. There are two weekly Jewish newspapers, which circulate throughout the country and compete with one another, and local bulletins in each of the major communities.

Agudath Israel has a substantial base in Switzerland, principally in Zurich and Basel. Basel is an ultra-Orthodox stronghold; that group dominates the community but in Zurich it is a separate group within the larger whole. In the twentieth century Zurich Jewry split into three communities: the moderately Orthodox Israelitische Kulturgemeinde (IKG), the Orthodox Israelitische Religionsgesellschaft, and the ultra-Orthodox Agudas Achim. A liberal congregation-community, the Jüdischer Liberale Gemeinde, has been established in Zurich and has acquired a synagogue, community center, and classrooms. It has about two hundred members and is more Conservative than Reform in its orientation. It is not recognized by or allowed to join the SIG and its activities are not listed in the Jewish press. Each community maintains its own institutions and official structure. Sephardi Jews in Switzerland are concentrated in Geneva and Lausanne. They have pursued less of a separatist pattern and instead have become dominant in those two Jewish communities.[11]

Because of its position as a world city, Geneva in the twentieth century became a headquarters city for European Jewry. The Jewish Agency, the World Jewish Congress, the Joint Distribution Committee, and ORT established their European headquarters there. In recent years, however, there has been a shift of these offices to France because of French Jewry's new prominence on the European and world Jewish scene.

The great alpine vacation areas have attracted Jews of all persuasions, including the ultra-Orthodox who together create transient religious communities where there is no permanent Jewish population. Kosher hotels and distinctively garbed people in every major resort offer visible evidence of substantial Jewish populations in each during the appropriate tourist seasons. Such visible Jewish presence as there is in Switzerland is to be found in those resorts, not in the permanently settled communities where the Jews fade into the background as a small minority.

Kehillot of the Scandinavian Periphery

The Scandinavian Jewish communities are relatively new. The oldest one, Denmark, goes back to the beginning of the modern epoch in the seventeenth century; the others were founded in the eighteenth and nineteenth centuries. Most of the Jews living in those communities arrived in the twentieth century, many after World War II. Although the host countries may have practiced discrimination against Jews, officially or unofficially, there is little indigenous anti-Semitism. Nor is there a tradition of Jewish autonomy. Jews could easily assimilate, even before the extention of civil rights to Jewish people, and remaining in the Jewish community was voluntary from the first.

Scandinavia has long been the European periphery, a frontier region in the sense that frontiers are borderlands—in this case the borderlands of a great continent—yet not a frontier in the sense of the cutting edge of civilization. Although long at the edge of Christian civilization in Europe, it has been Christianized for nearly a millennium. For Jews, however, the Scandinavian countries have consistently been at the outer edge or beyond and remain so to this day.[12]

Take the matter of settlement. Most European Jewish communities west of the Rhine were founded after 1650. South of the Baltic Jews returned to countries and regions from which they had been expelled centuries before—whether Hamburg, London, Bordeaux, or others. The Jewish communities founded in Scandinavia in those years were truly new ones and represented first-time Jewish settlement, as much as the Jewish settlement in New Amsterdam founded in 1654 (before any Jewish community in Scandinavia).

Unlike the western European and New World settlements, the Jewish communities of the north never attracted significant numbers of Jews even though they benefited from the modern attitude toward Jews and Judaism as much, if not more, than any of the other communities. Thus the few Jewish communities of Scandinavia were small, scattered outposts of Jewish life, off center stage even for emancipated Jews seeking their fortunes, not to speak of Jews desirous of preserving traditional Jewish lives. The history of Scandinavian Jewry can be summarized as one of successive small waves of settlers coming in when some compelling reason, usually involving persecution and the search for a refuge, turned them northward, followed by periods of establishment and assimilation. As studies of the individual countries indicate, the number of Scandinavian families recognizing their Jewish ancestry far exceeds the number of identified Jews in their respective countries. Only the coming of successive waves of new settlers, small as they might have been, prevented the total assimilation of the existing Jewish communities.

The initial impetus for Jewish settlement in Scandinavia came because of the spread northward of Marranos searching for economic opportunity and peaceful places to rest. For the first century and a half of their existence, roughly from the middle of the seventeenth century until the Napoleonic wars, Jewish communities in Scandinavia were organized like other late medieval communities as semiautonomous *kehillot,* whose authority and status were guaranteed by royal charter. With the coming of emancipation at the beginning of the nineteenth century, the *kehillot* lost their autonomy and were reorganized as more limited religious communities. In return, the Jews gradually gained full citizenship in the respective states of their residence. The first half of the nineteenth century was marked by a struggle for civil rights; the last half was marked by a dual struggle against anti-Semitism and assimilation.

In Scandinavia as elsewhere in Europe, the Holocaust was the culmination of emancipation. The Nazi madness affected Scandinavian Jewry without destroying it. The famous Danish rescue of its Jewish population has become almost legendary. Almost all the Jews of Scandinavia were either residents of neutral Sweden, beneficiaries of the Danish evacuation, or protected by Finland, which, as a German ally, maintained control over its indigenous population (the spectacle of Finnish Jewish soldiers serving side by side with the German army against Russia was one of the more disconcerting phenomena of the war). Only the tiny Norwegian Jewish community felt the brunt of Nazi genocide. A modest number of Jews took refuge in Sweden with the rise of Nazism. Because of the refugees who found their way north, the Scandinavian communities actually were enriched Jewishly by the war.[13]

The Scandinavian countries, particularly Denmark and Sweden, took in a few thousand refugees after World War II and a few thousand more fleeing from the Communist countries because of the troubles of the 1950s and 1960s. These actions, taken together, have made the region more prominent in contemporary Jewish history than it ever was. However, that all of Scandinavia contains fewer than 25,000 Jews out of a population of more than 22 million, or far fewer Jews than the State of Minnesota (34,000 out of 3.5 million), the heartland of Scandinavian settlement in the United States, speaks for itself.

The postwar period brought with it the standard "bundle" of Jewish problems and opportunities. Jewish life again teeters between assimilation and survival; Jewish ties have become primarily associational, replacing traditional systems of belief and patterns of behavior. Israel has become a focal point stimulating Jewish survival yet draining off many of those most committed to Jewish life. Scandinavian Jewry is probably better organized than ever before in its history; at the same time its Jews are increasingly less Jewish in an organic sense.[14]

The Jewish Community of Denmark

Denmark is the oldest Scandinavian Jewish community. Its first Jews arrived in 1622 and in 1657, at the beginning of the modern epoch, a Jewish community was established by Sephardi Jews who took advantage of Denmark's relative liberality. In 1814 the Danish parliament granted religious freedom to all inhabitants, abolished the autonomy of the *kehillah,* and reorganized it under state law. The office of chief rabbi was inaugurated at that time. Jews were granted full citizenship in 1849. Danish Jews had few problems with anti-Semitism, and the story of the rescue of the entire Jewish community by the Danes in World War II is well known. As a result, assimilation has been dominant in the Danish Jewish community; it has been estimated that at least 200,000 Danes have some Jewish ancestry, though there are only 6,000 identified Jews in the country today.[15]

After the first wave of Sephardi Jews there was no serious Jewish immigration to Denmark until Eastern European Jews began to come in the late nineteenth century. A third wave of immigration came because of the Nazi persecutions. The most recent wave consisted of Polish Jewish refugees from Communist regimes, who came in the late 1960s.

Today there are some seventy-five hundred Jews in Denmark. Almost all Danish Jewry lives in Copenhagen. At first, Jews located elsewhere as well, but in the nineteenth century those who did not assimilate moved to the capital. Today only about 1 percent of the Jewish population lives outside that city, mostly in Århus, Denmark's second largest city. Thus the Danish Jewish community is coterminous with the Copenhagen community.

All Danish Jews are automatically enrolled in the Mosaic Community unless they have officially chosen not to belong. All children are registered as community members at birth, thus receiving all the rights and privileges of membership except the right to vote, which they obtain when they reach Danish voting age if they have paid their communal dues.

The community is governed by a twenty-member Board of Delegates (Dele-gaterforsamlingen) elected every two years, which elects a seven-member Board of Representatives (Raprasentaterforsamlingen) as an executive committee. The synagogue has a seven-member board of *gabbaim,* jointly appointed by the Board of Representatives, the Board of Delegates, and the seat-holding male members. There is a five-member education committee appointed by the Board of Representatives, the Ministry of Education, and the Board of Delegates, and a five-member tax committee appointed by the Board of Representatives, the Copenhagen municipality, and the Board of Delegates. The Board of Delegates meets six to twelve times a year to advise the Board of Representatives and to approve the annual budget and all religious appointments.

The Board of Representatives governs the daily affairs of the community. Its members head committees dealing with the old-age home, religious affairs, Jewish education, and cemeteries. It establishes the annual communal tax rate and works out the budget. Taxes are collected by the Danish government and relocated to the community. The Board of Representatives also represents the Danish Jewish community in dealing with the Danish government through the Ministry of Religion, the State of Israel, and other Jewish communities in Scandinavia, Europe, and the *edah.*

The chief rabbi of Copenhagen is the chief rabbi of Denmark. His office is established by the Danish constitution and as such he is responsible to the king as the representative of Danish Jewry. His office keeps the community records and registrations of all births, marriages, divorces, and deaths in the community. He has complete authority under the law in his synagogue and with two other scholars constitutes a Bet Din for conversion and divorce. Because of the tendency of the recent incumbents to lean in the direction of Conservative Judaism, there have been controversies in the community between those who want their rabbis to be more traditional and those who are less concerned about such matters. The rabbinate has been in the Melchior family for several generations.

The community synagogue, erected in 1833, is the central gathering place of Danish Jewry, even though most Danish Jews are unobservant in any traditional sense. The synagogue remains formally Orthodox but is so lax in its Orthodoxy that the truly Orthodox seceded as early as 1910, after a struggle, and established a second congregation called Mahzike Hadas (Upholders of the Religion), which has ties with the ultra-Orthodox world of Agudath Israel and Chabad. All members of Mahzike Hadas belong to the overall community and pay full taxes besides supporting their own institutions and functionaries. About 100 families belong to this subcommunity.

Almost all Jewish boys in Denmark have a bar mitzvah ceremony. At one time Danish law required that all children receive a religious education of some kind as a prerequisite to applying for marriage. This law has been repealed, but the custom is quite entrenched and many girls are also confirmed.

The Karolinskoline, the Danish Jewish day school, provides general and Jewish schooling for the first seven grades. More than half of the Jewish children in Copenhagen attend the school. It is financed by the Ministry of Education (which covers the cost of the general studies program), the Jewish community, and tuition fees. Jewish studies account for between four to six hours per week in the curriculum, about the same as a supplementary Hebrew school in North America. Preschooling for Jews is in the hands of three Jewish kindergartens, one of which is sponsored by the Mahzike Hadas. The members of Mahzike Hadas send their children to public school rather than to the Jewish school and then to their own supplementary educational program. After the age of fifteen, most of their children are sent outside the country to study in *yeshivot* in Belgium or Switzerland. An effort to open a *yeshiva* in Denmark in 1957 failed. Apart from that, Jewish education takes the form of weekend retreats, summer camps, and Israel programs.

The old-age home is the principal social service, because Denmark is an advanced welfare state. Occasionally there is also the need to provide refugee relief.

The present governmental structure of the community dates to 1936 when the Board of Delegates was democratized to allow Jews of eastern European origin to vote and hold office. That change eliminated the oligarchy of the old families. At first, there was a struggle between the two groups, but since the 1930s they have integrated so that this is no longer a point of communal division. Elections are contested by party with differences among the parties based on religious orientation or personalities. Much of the recent struggle has been between those who support the chief rabbi and those who oppose him. Generally speaking, there is a liberal list, traditionally supported by the old Danish families and those who identify with their assimilationist position. The traditional list comprises the active members of the synagogue. Mahzike Hadas frequently presents a third list. When it does not present a list, it will often join with the liberals.

The Jewish Community of Sweden

The Jews who settled in Sweden in the early nineteenth century were primarily from Germany. In the late nineteenth and twentieth centuries, they were primarily from eastern Europe, with the most recent wave coming from Poland after the 1967 Israel-Arab war. Today between fifteen and seventeen thousand Jews live in Sweden, approximately half in Stockholm, another fourteen hundred in Malmö and Göteborg, and the rest scattered in smaller communities throughout the country. Only a third are from families who arrived in the country before 1933, and over half are postwar eastern European arrivals. The intermarriage rate is very high and the birthrate low, so the community, like the others of Europe, is in danger of rapid diminution over the next decades.[16]

Swedish Jewry took a major step toward emancipation in 1838 but it took thirty years before all restrictions against Jews were lifted. Still, in that year the *kehillah* lost its autonomous status to be replaced by local "Mosaic communities" in which membership was compulsory for all Jews. Because Sweden had an established church until 1952, everybody had to belong to some religious body; the only way Jews could leave the community was through conversion. The Mosaic communities did not have juridical autonomy, but they received a share of the state taxes paid by their members. Jews and Catholics received the right to vote in 1870 and to hold political office, but non-Lutherans were not eligible to become ministers of state until 1952. In that year, the Mosaic community was transformed into a voluntary association. Since then some Jews have dropped out of the community but other Jewish resident aliens of Sweden, unable to join the community before, are now eligible to do so and have.

The Central Council of Swedish Jewish Communities comprises thirteen member communities. The council meets periodically to deal with general policy issues, ranging from the problems of kosher slaughtering to the continuity of life in the smaller communities, but in daily affairs the Stockholm Jewish community acts as spokesman for Swedish Jewry. The three major communities serve as focal points for the smaller communities around each. With social services so highly developed in Sweden, the Jewish community has little or nothing to do in that sphere but is active in the educational-cultural, religious-congregational, community relations, and Israel-*edah* spheres. The one welfare role it plays is occasionally providing refugee relief.

Over the years there has been something of a struggle between the Stockholm Mosaiskaverbundet and the Zionist Federation of Sweden, with the first being principally an establishment institution whose control passes from time to time into the hands of younger generation leaders who present themselves as antiestablishment but either are quickly absorbed into the establishment or retire from leadership roles. The Zionist Federation attracts those outside the establishment. It has responsibility for fund-raising through Keren Hayesod and the Jewish National Fund and works with the youth movements, some of whose members are invariably attracted to the leadership of the Zionist Federation when they grow out of the youth movement and do not emigrate to Israel. There are Bnai Brith lodges in Stockholm, Malmö, and Göteborg.

Mainstream Judaism in Sweden is essentially traditional but more in the American Conservative mode than in the Orthodox. The present chief rabbi of the Stockholm Jewish community is a graduate of the Jewish Theological Seminary of America and services in the main synagogue are right-wing Conservative in style. Two small Orthodox synagogues, Yeshurun and Adath Israel are affiliated with the community and have a rabbi from Israel supplied by the Jewish Agency. Göteborg has a liberal rabbi and Malmö a traditional one. By and large, Swedish Jews are not religiously active.

Elections for the local Jewish communities are conducted every three years and follow the electoral system used in Sweden. In the Stockholm Jewish community, partisan elections are conducted with three parties contesting for control: one reflecting the old-time Jewish families with assimilationist tendencies, one a Zionist-oriented party, and the third a young generation-oriented party. The names of these parties change, but this tripartite division generally remains constant.

The Swedish Jewish community places most of its emphasis on education and youth work, fund-raising for Israel, and fostering better Swedish-Israel ties. This does not mean that Jewish education is very deep in Sweden. There is a day school in Stockholm that is always involved in some controversy because it is considered separatist. The day school covers grades one through six only. Supplementary education is dominant in the other communities. When the Swedish Ministry of Education eliminated compulsory instruction in the Christian religion from the schools, the number of Jews who chose to attend classes on Jewish religion diminished.

The Jews of Norway and Finland

The 715 Jews in Norway and the 1,200 in Finland have Jewish communities structured like those in Denmark and Sweden but are much more limited in scope because of their small numbers. Norwegian Jewry is concentrated in Oslo and vicinity or in Trondheim. Because 97 percent of the Norwegian population is affiliated with the state church, the Jews are a tiny minority in an overwhelmingly Lutheran society.[17]

The Finnish Jewish community originated in a way different from those of the other three Scandinavian countries. Because Finland was long part of the Russian empire, the ancestors of most of its twelve hundred Jews arrived there by way of Russia. Almost all Finnish Jews are descended from the Cantonists, Jews kidnapped as children by the Russians to serve in the Czarist army and stationed in Finland; there they organized a Jewish life for themselves. Over half of the Jews in the country are located in Helsinki, the other communities being Turku and Tampere.[18]

Links among the Scandinavian Communities

The Scandinavian countries, except Finland, share a common Nordic linguistic and cultural heritage. Finland, whose population is ethnically different, has been tied to Scandinavia because of its geographic proximity reinforced by a shared political history. While today all four Scandinavian countries (plus Iceland, the Scandinavian frontier) are politically independent, at various times they have been united in different combinations. The rise of modern nationalism led to their successful pursuit of national independence but the subsequent development of the need for international cooperation brought them together through a network of transnational links, principally the Nordic Union. The links gave them something less than confederation but more than a collection of ad hoc sharing arrangements.

This pattern is repeated in Jewish Scandinavia. The four small communities (Iceland has few Jewish families and no organized Jewish life) have created transcommunal institutions and ties. Thus, in the 1950s a pan-Scandinavian Zionist Federation was active; its primary activity was the coordination of charter flights to Israel, the proceeds of which provided money for scholarships to send Scandinavian Jewish youth to study in the Jewish state. When the charter flights were abolished, the federation became inactive except for sponsoring an occasional seminar on a pan-Scandinavian basis.

The Women's International Zionist organization (WIZO) also tries to develop some of its activities on an all-Scandinavia basis to give Jewish women, particularly those in the smaller communities, a sense of belonging to something larger than their local chapters. It, too, seems to have been more active in the past. In 1963 its annual conference voted to admit non-Jewish women to membership if they had close connections to Judaism (apparently meaning that their husbands were Jewish).

The Jewish Agency also conducts many activities on a pan-Scandinavian basis. Its Youth and Hehalutz Department has at times sponsored a one-year program in cooperation with the Paul Baerwald School of Social Work at the Hebrew University to train British and Scandinavian Jewish communal workers (a program discontinued because of lack of British candidates), offered an annual leadership seminar in Scandinavia, and worked with other bodies, including the local Jewish communities, in the development of a Jewish pedagogical and resource center in Malmö to translate educational materials, develop an audiovisual center, and create courses of study for Scandinavian Jews. The World Jewish Congress maintains a regional office in Stockholm, which is designed to serve all Scandinavia. It is a one-man enterprise and is limited accordingly.

The SJUF is the all-Scandinavian youth organization. All Jewish youth and student organizations in Scandinavia are affiliated with it, at least nominally. It holds an annual congress. Its office also rotates between Sweden and Denmark with most of the SJUF executive at any given time composed of members of the host community. It is formally sponsored by the World Jewish Congress, the local communities, and the World Union of Jewish Students, and tries to represent a united voice of youth in the adult community.

Because they live in the one of the most affluent regions in the world, the Jews of Scandinavia are no better candidates for aliya to Israel than those in the other affluent countries. The exceptions are that handful of young Jews who seek fuller Jewish lives and recognize that they cannot live as Jewishly as they wish in the small, assimilated communities of their home countries. They may try Israel and, if religiously Orthodox, are likely to stay. Those who come for what are generally called Zionist motivations are frequently discouraged and return. No figures are available, but there may be a higher number of Scandinavian non-Jews who, in the course of a summer or year-long work experience in the kibbutz, marry Israelis and settle in Israel. Although there is an irony in this situation, it somewhat redresses the negative balance of intermarriage in the Scandinavian countries.

The historical record of the Scandinavian Jewish communities time and again reaffirms their assimilationist tendencies. Although Scandinavia by no means has been free of anti-Semitism, by and large it has still furnished a warm social climate that has encouraged individual Jews to abandon their Jewishness and merge with the peoples among whom they live. In this respect, the Scandinavian countries have been open and have offered, for a few Jews, the possibilities of assimilation that many advocates of Jewish emancipation dreamed about. Only the periodic infusion of new waves of immigrants has revivified the Jewish communities of Scandinavia, either by bringing in Jews of a more traditional bent or by forcing the Jewish communities to activate to receive and care for the immigrants so as not to call attention to the strangers being brought into the midst of highly homogeneous societies.

This tendency to homogeneity directs the course of Jewish life in Scandinavia more than any other external factor. The Scandinavian countries have, in the course of their modernization, become democratic and liberal, but they are not particularly pluralistic because they do not have heterogeneous populations. The Lapps are the only large and distinctive ethnic minority in the region, although each country has pockets of population from one or more of the other ones who often try to preserve their language and customs. Because these pockets usually represent deeply rooted rural settlements, whose origins antedate present state boundaries, they are in a different category entirely. In the urban areas assimilation is the rule. Under such conditions, a small minority like the Jews is vulnerable.

The Jewish response has been characteristic of all modern Jewish communities. In the nineteenth century, when formal religion was the associational bond to hold Jews together, the Jewish community was a religious association, even if its members were not particularly observant. As Jews have shed their traditional habits, customs, and religion, except in its most public formalistic aspects, they have tried to substitute an associational framework as a manifestation of a culturally based ethnicity. Yet, culturally based ethnicity implies some desire to maintain separate customs and minimize deep contacts with people outside one's group. Scandinavian Jews hardly qualify in this sense. Although the Jews who care about their Jewishness are concerned about intermarriage and try to prevent it, they do not, for the most part, try to associate exclusively with one another even outside business hours. That would be too un-Scandinavian. Hence the Jewish communities are not separated, ethnically closed groups.

What, then, remains for Jews seeking to maintain Jewish ties? Paradoxically, they, too, are increasingly bound to the Jewish people through what can only be termed political association. The nature of that political association is not yet fully clear or apparent, especially not to those Jews themselves. The combination of concern for and support of the State of Israel, increasing reliance on the state as a Jewish resource, and a pattern of association in the Jewish community that makes politically oriented institutions vibrant and attractive to younger Jews points strongly toward this conclusion.

Thus, Scandinavian Jewry also reflects a paradox of our times: the strange mixture of full assimilation with Jewish identification primarily political that is coming to characterize so much of postmodern Jewry.

Notes

1. On state-recognized *kehillot* since World War II, see Daniel J. Elazar, *Organization and Status of Contemporary Jewish Communities—5730 (1969–1970)* (Philadelphia: Study of Jewish Community Organization, 1971); Ernest Stock, "The Emerging European Jewish Community Structure," *Jerusalem Letter,* no. 46 (March 14, 1982).

2. For the premodern history of the Jews in Germany, see Irving Agus, *The Heroic Age of Franco-German Jewry* (New York: Yeshiva University Press, 1969); Marvin Lowenthal, *Jews of Germany* (Philadelphia: Jewish Publication Society of America, 1936); Max Margolis and Alexander Marx, *A History of the Jewish People* (Forge Valley, Mass. and Philadelphia: Atheneum and Jewish Publication Society of America, 1969), chaps. 53, 56, 57, 78, 81; Uriel Tal, *Christians and Jews in Germany* (Ithaca, N.Y.: Cornell University Press, 1975); "Germany," in *Encyclopedia Judaica,* vol. 7, pp. 457–504; Michael A. Meyer, *The Origins of the Modern Jew: Jewish Identity and European Culture in Germany, 1749–1824* (Detroit: Wayne State University Press, 1967).

3. On the modern history of German Jewry, see H. G. Adler, *The Jews in Germany* (Notre Dame, Ind.: University of Notre Dame Press, 1969); Alexander Altmann, *Studies in Nineteenth Century Jewish Intellectual History* (Cambridge, Mass.: Harvard University Press, 1964); David Bronson, ed., *Jews and Germans from 1860–1933: The Problematic Symbiosis* (Heidelberg: C. Winter, 1979); Jacob Katz, *Out of the Ghetto: The Social Background of Jewish Emancipation, 1770–1870* (Cambridge, Mass.: Harvard University Press, 1973); W. E. Masse, A. Pauker, R. Ruerup, eds., *Revolution and Evolution: 1848 in German Jewish History* (Tübingen, Germany: Mohr Publishing, 1981); Ismar Schorsch, *Jewish Reactions to German Anti-Semitism 1870–1914* (New York: Columbia University Press, 1972).

4. Lucy Davidowicz, *The War against the Jews, 1933–1945* (New York and Philadelphia: Holt, Rinehart and Winston and the Jewish Publication Society of America, 1975); Nora Levin, *The Holocaust* (New York: Schocken, 1968); John Mendelson, ed., *The Holocaust,* 18 vols. (New York: Garland Publishing, 1982); Herbert Strauss, "Jewish Emigration from Germany: Nazi Politics and Jewish Responses," *Leo Baeck Institute Year Book,* vol. 26 (1981), pp. 343–409; Uriel Tal, *Law and Theology on the Status of German Jewry at the Outset of the Third Reich (1933/4)* (Tel Aviv: Tel Aviv University, faculty of the humanities, 1982); Sarah Gordon, *Hitler, Germans, and the Jewish Question* (Princeton, N.J.: Princeton University Press, 1984).

5. Yehuda Bauer, "The Initial Organization of the Holocaust Survivors in Bavaria," *Yad Vashem Studies,* no. 8 (1970), pp. 127–57; Norbert Muhlen, *The Survivors* (New York: T. Y. Crowell, 1962); Frieda Sachser, "Germany," in *American Jewish Year Book 1983,* vol. 83, pp. 205–9; Henrick Van Dan, "The Jewish Community in Germany," *European Judaism,* no. 1 (1966), pp. 2–10; Jacques Vernant, *The Refugee in the Post-War World* (London: Allen B. Unwin, 1953); Nadine Joseph, "The New Germany," in *Present Tense,* vol. 10, no. 4 (summer 1983), pp. 29–33.

6. J. Fraenkel, *Jews of Austria* (London: Vallentine and Mitchell, 1967); Max Grunwald, *History of the Jews of Vienna* (Philadelphia: Jewish Publication Society of America, 1936); Jacob Toury, "Jewish Townships in the German-Speaking Parts of the Austrian Empire before and after the Revolution of 1848–49," *Leo Baeck Institute Year Book,* vol. 29 (1981), pp. 55–72.

7. Oscar Karbach, "The Liquidation of the Jewish Community in Vienna," *Jewish Social Studies,* no. 2 (July 1940), pp. 255–78; Benjamin Ockstein, *Mauthausen* (Jerusalem: Yad Vashem, 1984) (Hebrew).

8. Marget Feiler, "Austria," in *American Jewish Year Book 1967,* vol. 68, pp. 369–76; Peter Friedlander in *American Jewish Year Book 1976,* vol. 76, pp. 359–71; F. Wilder-Okladek, "The Return Movement of Jews to Austria after the Second World War, with Special Considerations of the Return from Israel," publication of the Research Group for European Migration Problems, no. 16 (The Hague: Martin Nighoff, 1969).

9. Alfred Haessler, *The Lifeboat is Full: Switzerland and the Refugees, 1933–1945* (Zurich: Ex Libris Vertag, 1979) (German); "Rescue to Switzerland: The Musy and Saly Mayer Affairs," in John Mendelsohn, ed., *The Holocaust: Selected Documents in Eighteen Volumes* (New York: Garland Publishers, 1982), vol. 16.

10. "Switzerland," in *Encyclopedia Judaica,* vol. 15, pp. 554–61; Aaron Zwergbaum, "Swiss Jewry," *Tfutsot HaGolah* (winter 1971–72), pp. 153–59 (Hebrew).

11. Henri Elfinbein, "Switzerland," in *American Jewish Year Book 1962,* vol. 63, pp. 316–18; Kurt

Mayer, "The Evolution of the Jewish Population of Switzerland in Light of the 1970 Census," *Papers in Jewish Demography, 1973* (Jerusalem: Institute of Contemporary Jewry of the Hebrew University, 1973), pp. 309–22; Zwergbaum, "Swiss Jewry."

12. For the history of Scandinavian Jewry, see Daniel J. Elazar, Adina Weiss Liberles, and Simha Werner, *The Jewish Communities of Scandinavia* (Lanham, Md. and Jerusalem: University Press of America and Center for Jewish Community Studies of the Jersualem Center for Public Affairs, 1984); K. Wilhelm, "Jewish Communities in Scandinavia," *Leo Baeck Institute Year Book,* vol. 3 (1958), pp. 313–22. See also the following articles in *Encyclopedia Judaica:* "Denmark," vol. 5, pp. 1536–42, "Finland," vol. 6, pp. 1295–99, "Norway," vol. 12, pp. 1222–26, and "Sweden," vol. 15, pp. 545–52; S. Ralph Cohen, "Scandinavia's Jewish Communities," *American Scandinavian Review,* n.d., pp. 126–35; Martin Schiff, "Polish Jews in Scandinavia," *Midstream,* vol. 17, no. 2 (February 1971), pp. 35–42; Julius Margolinsky, "Scandinavia (Including Finland)," in *American Jewish Year Book 1962,* vol. 63, pp. 327–33.

13. H. G. Adler, "Danish Jewry under German Occupation," *The Weiner Library Bulletin,* vol. 9, nos. 1–2 (January–April 1955); Harold Flender, *Rescue in Denmark* (New York: Simon and Schuster, 1963); H. Valentin, "Rescue Activities in Scandinavia," *YIVO Annual of Jewish Social Science,* vol. 8 (1953), pp. 224–51; Leni Yahil, *The Rescue of Danish Jewry* (New York: Columbia University Press, 1970).

14. Elazar et al., *The Jewish Community of Scandinavia.*

15. Adina Weiss Liberles, "The Jewish Community of Denmark," in Elazar et al., *The Jewish Communities of Scandinavia,* part 3; Yitzhak Bezdel, "The Jewish Community of Copenhagen," in *Betfutzot Ha'golah* (spring 1965), pp. 63–65 (Hebrew); "Denmark," in *Encyclopedia Judaica;* Sidney DuBroff, "Polish Jews in Denmark," *Hadassah Magazine,* vol. 52 (September 1970), pp. 36–38; Yehuda Levine, "Jewry of Denmark," *Congress Bi-Weekly,* vol. 33 (January 1965), pp. 7–10; and Ib Nathan Bamberger, *The Viking Jews: A History of the Jews in Denmark* (New York: Sheingold Publishers, 1983).

16. Adina Weiss Liberles, "The Jewish Community of Sweden," in Elazar et al., *The Jewish Communities of Scandinavia,* part 2; Allen Pollack, "Jews in Sweden," *Dispersion and Unity,* 1961, pp. 54–55; "Sweden," in *Encyclopedia Judaica,* vol. 15, pp. 545–52; Yehuda Levine, "The Jews of Sweden and Norway," *Congress Bi-Weekly,* vol. 33 (April 12, 1965), pp. 14–17; Joachini Israel and James Roth, "Self-Image among Jews in Sweden: Theoretical Outline," in *Fourth World Congress of Jewish Studies* (1968), pp. 75–80.

17. See Adina Weiss Liberles and Simha Werner, "The Jewish Community of Norway," in Elazar et al., *The Jewish Communities of Scandinavia,* part 4; Samuel Abrahamsen, "The Sage of Norway's Jews," *Congress Bi-Weekly,* vol. 21 (October 1951), pp. 8–10; "Norway," in *Encyclopedia Judaica,* vol. 12, pp. 1222–26.

18. See Adina Weiss Liberles, "The Jewish Community of Finland," in Elazar et al., *The Jewish Communities of Scandinavia,* part 5; "Finland," in *Encyclopedia Judaica,* vol. 6, pp. 1295–99; Margolinsky, "Scandinavia (Including Finland)."

16

The Mediterranean Communities: A New Focus

The new Sephardi presence in Europe and the reestablishment of the State of Israel suggest the beginning of a turn of world Jewry back toward the Mediterranean basin after five hundred years in which there was a progressive shift away from that great sea, long a heartland of Jewish life. One look at where the Jewish population is and where it is moving, and this turn back becomes evident. As such, it is part of one of the historical cyclical turns that have occurred in Jewish history periodically during the past four thousand years. Hence it is a change with which all Jews must reckon. This, too, offers the new European Jewry a chance to play its role.

The Sunset of Balkan Jewry

This turn back is not immediately true of every part of the Mediterranean world. No region of Europe has a longer history of organized Jewish life than the Balkan Peninsula and the states located in it. The first diaspora communities outside the fertile crescent were probably in that region, and Jewish settlement there has been continuous at least since the days of the Second Temple. During those long centuries, Jewish communal life has had its good periods and bad and has undergone several transformations. It has survived Hellenistic, Roman, Byzantine, and Ottoman rule, and, most recently, has been subjected to the rule of highly nationalistic new states reflecting local ethnic majorities.[1]

The Balkan Jewries include those of Bulgaria, Greece, Romania, Turkey, and Yugoslavia. Turkey is not usually considered a Balkan country but almost all its Jews are part of the Balkan group and live in European Turkey, an extension of the Balkan Peninsula. Romania, usually included as a Balkan country, was originally settled by Balkan Jews, but in the nineteenth century an influx of eastern European Jews brought the community within the Russo-Polish orbit. Bulgaria, which is a Balkan country, does not border on the Mediterranean and is in the Soviet bloc.

The last great tide of Jewish immigration to the Balkans came from the Iberian Peninsula beginning in the fifteenth century as a result of the Spanish expulsion. Capitalizing on a combination of circumstances, the Sephardim brought the Balkans into the mainstream of Jewish life as they had not been for more than a millennium. By their sheer numbers, the Sephardim overwhelmed the indigenous Jewish communities and, in effect, forced them to assimilate into the Judeo-Hispanic cultural and social framework brought from Spain. Ladino became the Jewish language of the Balkans in the way that Yiddish became the Jewish language of eastern Europe. Moreover, exile from their beloved

357

second motherland released great pent-up intellectual energies among the Sephardim, which found their outlet in the Balkan setting.

The result was, at the least, a silver age of Jewish culture bearing a distinctive Sephardi imprint whose impact shaped the Jewish world for two centuries. The cities of the Balkans, with Salonika heading the list, became bastions of Jewish life and culture. Sephardi creativity in *halakhah* and *kabbalah* was nourished in the region and shaped Jewish life and thought from Russia to Latin America. It led, in time, to the last and greatest theopolitical movement of premodern Jewry, the messianic movement of Shabtai Zvi, a product of the Balkan Sephardic world.[2]

Balkan Jewry was first enhanced and then diminished by its location within the Ottoman Empire. The fall of Constantinople to the Ottoman forces in 1453 and the resulting consolidation of Ottoman rule throughout the region, nearly forty years before the Spanish exile, provided Sephardi Jewry with a place of refuge that gave them suffi-cient scope for the exercise of their considerable talents. The Sephardic refugees entered into a virtual alliance with the imperial authorities to cooperate against the common Christian foe. Jewish communities received protected status in the framework of the empire, and the refugees' power in existing communities increased because of their relationship with the imperial authorities.

Balkan Jewry attained its highest development during the century that the Turks stood at the gates of Vienna. With the decline of the empire, the Jewries within its borders also declined. The degree of their decline has been exaggerated because, with the passing of the major centers of Jewish life to other regions, historians of the Jewish people neglected the Balkans. Jewish life continued to thrive and Jewish learning was still cultivated in the great Jewish cities, though with less depth and intensity. Many great works of Balkan Jewish scholarship remain to be rediscovered and no adequate history of its Sephardi age has been written.

In the nineteenth century Balkan Jewry underwent something of a renaissance that was cut short by the emergence of new nation-states out of the ruins of the Ottomans' European empire. The renaissance in its early stages made Ladino prominent as a literary and intellectual medium that paralleled that of Yiddish in the lands to the north. The Balkan *haskalah* (for the renaissance was part of the universal Jewish movement) gave rise to an indigenous modern literature, translations of the major works of European litera-ture into Ladino, more than 250 newspapers and journals, a systematization of Ladino grammar, and the like.[3] It emphasized the modernization of Jewish education and, increasingly, a new political consciousness among Jews—whether identification with local nationalisms or Zionism.

Economically, the condition of the urban communities of the Balkans also im-proved. The improvement was accompanied by substantial population growth through natural increase and migration in the cities. A series of constitutional and administrative reforms within the empire led to the restructuring of Jewish communal organization. Until 1839 the Jews, along with other non-Muslims, were second-class subjects by law. In 1839 Sultan Abdul Medjid published a *firman* (proclamation) bestowing full equality in matters of life and property on all minority groups in all parts of the Ottoman Empire. Some of the consequences of the declaration were official recognition of the Chief Rabbinate and the appointment of Jews to councils and law courts. Jews could become professors and civil servants. Shortly afterward, Jews were admitted to government-supported schools and modern Jewish schools were also established.

In 1855 the community head tax for Jews was replaced by a compulsory army exemption tax, but Jews for the first time could serve in the army rather than paying the tax. During the reign of Abdul Aziz (1861–76), a commission was established at the command of the sultan including the chief rabbi, the president of the Jewish community of Istanbul, and other notables, to define the status of the Chief Rabbinate and unify the Jewish community. Its recommendations were approved by the sultan and put into practice in 1867. The government helped the rabbinate enforce adherence to Jewish religious precepts. At times, government subsidies provided poor Jews with wine and *matzot* for Passover, even though wine is forbidden under Muslim law.

An imperial parliament was inaugurated in 1876 and a constitution was written in which the rights of full equality for minority groups was affirmed. Jews served in this short-lived parliament as representatives of the Jewish community. Nevertheless, the realities of the Jews' position in Ottoman society could not simply be changed by constitutional fiat and they were still considered to be a foreign element by much of the population.

In 1908 the Young Turks overthrew the sultan, Abdul Hamid. Jews participated actively in this uprising. Gedalya Abulafia was a minister in the revolutionary government and the parliament of 1908 included representatives of the Jewish community. After the Revolution, military service became obligatory for Jews (1909), a duty that the chief rabbi willingly supported. Provisions were made for kosher food and Sabbath observance in the army.

The life of the community was drastically changed by the nationalistic revolutions that tore the empire apart in the years before World War I. A Jewish world that had been of one piece for at least four hundred years, whose every link was based on the wholeness of the empire and whose every division cut across the new dividing lines established by the new nation-states was suddenly put in a position of reorganizing its fragments from the ground up. The breakup of the Ottoman Empire had much more effect on Balkan Jewry than did the breakup of the Czarist empire on east European Jewry. Constantinople and Salonika, the empire's principal cities, were also its principal Jewish communities, unlike Moscow and Leningrad, which were peripheral to Jewish life. Their separation from each other and from the other Balkan countries left many smaller communities cut off from their spiritual and cultural centers.

The Jewish communities in the new states had not been linked with one another in any formal way because all had been parts of the same imperial polity. Now they had to forge such links. In doing so, they also modernized their community structures, borrowing from the experiences of the nation-states of Central Europe that had undergone a similar reorganization two to three generations earlier. Thus some versions of the *consistoire* or *Kultusgemeinde* patterns were reproduced in all the new Balkan states, although frequently their external forms masked the continuation of older patterns.

In many respects, the new Jewish communities achieved an organizational coherence they had never before approached. But, as has often been the case, organizational coherence was no indication of communal health. The contrary was true of Balkan Jewry. Successful reorganization came simultaneously with the beginning of extensive modernization, assimilation, and widespread loss of interest in things Jewish. Assimilatory pressures from the host nations began to take their toll. For some, Zionism provided a modern means of resuscitating communal vitality previously based on a common religious faith and culture; for others, organized Zionism was harassed by the host state as inimical to the interests of its new-founded nationalism and could not become an operative force in the community.

World War I only intensified the new states' opposition to anything that smacked of Jewish separatism. The last vestiges of the Ottoman Empire were swept away, and the modern Turkish state rose in its stead to display the same kind of nationalism (in some respects even more xenophobic) that had previously emerged in the Balkan heartland. Like their brethren in Central and Western Europe who had been through a similar experience earlier, the Jews were ambivalent about their status. They welcomed their new rights as individual citizens and began to assimilate into the larger society in most ways but they wished to preserve elements of the Jewish life they had known. During the 1920s and 1930s, they tried to create ways to combine both, often in the face of considerable adversity.[4]

Regardless of local conditions, for most of them World War II mooted the question. The Jewries of Greece and Yugoslavia were destroyed in the Holocaust. Bulgarian Jewry survived only to be engulfed in a Communist takeover, leading them to immigrate en masse to Israel. Although Turkish Jewry was physically least affected by the war, the government's wartime economic measures brought severe hardship to most Jews and stimulated a mass emigration once the Jewish state was established. Thus the once-powerful Jewries of the Balkans, like those of the rest of Europe, were reduced to mere shadows of their former selves. Most of their survivors were reunited in what had once been another corner of the Ottoman Empire and was now the center of the new Jewish renaissance.

The dissolution of Balkan Jewry began before the Holocaust. As with east European Jewry, the upheavals of the late nineteenth century generated a substantial emigration of Jews from the region. Tens of thousands immigrated to the Western Hemisphere, settling in North and South America. Other thousands moved to Eretz Israel before the establishment of the state to take part in its rebuilding. At the turn of the century, the five communities together contained more than half a million Jews—more than the present Jewish population of France. Today fewer than sixty thousand remain—a number approximately equal to the Jewish population of Arizona or Givatayim.

But Jewish communities do not disappear so easily. Thus in the years between 1949 and the present, the Jews who remained in the Balkan lands tried to rebuild their communities on a new and much smaller scale. Under conditions where religious belief and practice have become attenuated and even the most committed Jews have assimilated linguistically and culturally, organizational and associational ties have become more central to Jewish survival than ever before. In this respect the Balkan communities are no different from most of the world's Jewries.[5]

In the end, each of the communities must depend on outside assistance to survive. At least eight multicountry Jewish organizations have made their presence felt in one or more of the five Balkan communities in the twentieth century. The Alliance Israélite Universelle was the first. Its schools played a major role in the modernization of Balkan Jewry at the end of the nineteenth century. Education, however, became a sensitive issue in states experiencing a wave of nationalistic sentiment, and the Alliance was forced to withdraw from the field. Even locally sponsored Jewish schools have had their difficulties, where they have not been forced to close altogether.

The B'nai B'rith was the next outside group to appear in the Balkans, where it became a meeting place for local Jewish elites. As the most prestigious symbol of modern association, B'nai B'rith lodges easily became the places where the decisions shaping local communal life were taken. Although most of the lodges have since disbanded, at least partly because of government opposition to their links with a foreign organization, a few were transformed into independent local clubs and have continued to be important in local Jewish life.

Although Zionism is usually thought to be an "Ashkenazi" movement, the World Zionist Organization became an important presence in all the Balkan states early in its history. Local Zionist societies antedate the first Zionist Congress (1897), and immigration to Israel for rebuilding the land has been a fact of Balkan life for generations if not centuries. The Balkan Jewish community was the first in the world to be dominated by organized Zionism. It is no exaggeration to say that no countrywide Jewish community was ever more thoroughly Zionist in orientation and politics than Bulgaria. Zionism has since become suspect or worse in all the countries under consideration here, for reasons that should be obvious because of their nationalistic stances. As a consequence, organized Zionism was formally eliminated from every one of them.

The World Jewish Congress and its predecessors once had importance in securing and protecting the civil rights of Jews throughout the Balkans. While the WJC's effectiveness—never very great—has probably been diminished further in the aftermath of World War II, it remains a point of contact between world Jewry and the Balkan communities more likely to be tolerated by the current regimes. Even so, formal links are discouraged or forbidden except in Yugoslavia. More acceptable is the European Council for Jewish Community Services, whose communal-welfare, educational-cultural orientation is generally accepted as nonpolitical. The Greek, Romanian, and Yugoslav communities are members of the ECJCS.

The distributive organizations of world Jewry have all played some role in the Balkans. The Joint Distribution Committee, the Claims Conference, and the Memorial Foundation for Jewish Culture were significant in the reconstruction of those communities laid low by World War II. As sources of money and technical expertise, they are substantially responsible for whatever exists today in the way of Jewish services in the Balkans, at least outside Turkey.

In recent years, Israel has assumed a central—if usually unofficial—role in the maintenance of Jewish life in the non-Communist Balkans, with the Jewish Agency as its operative arm. The story of its activities cannot yet be told. Suffice it to say that its effect on Balkan Jewry is a textbook example for those who argue for Israel's centrality in Jewish life. If the Balkan Jewish communities survive as active entities and even participate in contemporary Jewish life, it will be in no small measure because of Israel's active efforts.

The Jewish Community in Turkey

Except for minor incidents of conflict between Jews and Muslims, the Jews in Turkey during the second half of the nineteenth century and the beginning of the twentieth enjoyed good relations, though limited ones, with the majority culture. During World War I, the Jews of Istanbul prospered, encouraging an influx of Jews from other parts of the country. After the Turkish defeat and the collapse of the Ottoman Empire, the Greeks occupied much of Turkey proper (1918–22). Under Greek rule the Jews suffered from repeated outbreaks of anti-Semitism. Finally, the Treaty of Lausanne in 1923 established the present borders of Turkey. After the treaty, large communities, such as Istanbul, Adrianopole (Edirne), and Izmir were returned to Turkish rule.

With international recognition of the new Turkish state, Turkey became a republic under the leadership of Kemal Ataturk, who had led the postwar revolution. Under the Treaty of Lausanne, the Turkish government was forced to recognize the rights of religious and ethnic minorities, who were permitted to have their own institutions, funds, schools, and laws of personal status. The Turkish revolutionary leadership regarded this status as subversive and dangerous, constituting a threat to the country's efforts at political and social integration. Fearing the consequences of hostile feelings, young Jewish intellectuals began intensive propaganda campaigns to influence the community to reject minority status. Moreover, pressure was applied by the government in propaganda campaigns, decrying the Jews as Spanish nationals. Under the combined pressures, the Jewish community, in a document of February 16, 1926, renounced minority status and affirmed the Jews' desire to live as full Turkish citizens. Later, the Greek and Armenian minorities were forced to follow the precedent set by the Jews.

Renunciation of minority status meant the abolition of the Jews' special representation in the Turkish Parliament and their subjection to the full secularizing processes of the revolutionary regime. Turkish Jewry faced many restrictions under the regime of Ataturk, the most important being the gradual ousting of Jews from civil service positions and imposition of discriminatory restrictions on Jews in trade. Until 1945 Jewish soldiers were denied officer status.

Besides specific anti-Jewish acts, the Jewish community of Turkey, like the rest of the population, was made subject to a series of laws designed to make Turkey a secular state. Religious marriages were banned, although Jews were permitted to have a religious ceremony if married first under civil law. The teaching of Hebrew and other religious instruction in Jewish schools were banned. Clergy of all faiths were forbidden to grow beards or wear special garb; synagogues were closed and government support was taken away from Jewish schools.

In July 1934 Muslim masses pillaged Jewish homes and shops in European Turkey and, in a few days, three thousand out of thirteen thousand Jews fled to Istanbul. These were the worst anti-Semitic attacks the Jews of Turkey had experienced in more than a hundred years.

The Turkish government policy was not basically hostile to the Jews as such, but antiforeign and antitraditional. Thus, with the rise of Nazism, permission was granted Jews of non-Turkish nationality living in Turkey to remain and even to bring their families into the country to join them.

To meet the country's financial needs during World War II, the neutral Turkish government approved a capital tax in 1942. The determinants of a taxpayer's assessments were his religion and nationality. The tax for Muslims and foreign citizens was 5 percent of their income or capita, but non-Muslim inhabitants were forced to pay assessments made by special commissions, in accord with the commissions' opinions. As a result, poor artisans and low-wage earners were left destitute, and even the rich were bankrupt because of their inability to liquefy their capital immediately.

In the spring and summer of 1943 the situation of the Jews worsened when the government began deporting non-Muslims, most of whom were Jews. However, by 1944, with the decline of German power, the capital tax was canceled and defaulters were released from prison. Had the Jews not renounced their minority status in 1923, their capital tax assessments would most likely have been set at the same rate as that of the Muslims. As it was, the cruelty and discrimination of the tax had a detrimental psychological effect on the Jewish community and was one of the causes of the mass migration to Israel a few years later. It must be noted, however, that during the war the government took a tolerant and even helpful attitude toward its Jewish citizens and foreign Jews, allowing the Jewish Agency to operate in Turkey, together with the local Jewish community, and to aid in the illegal immigration of European Jewish refugees to Palestine by way of Turkey.

Turkey's regime has been relatively stable since the Ataturk revolution, "guaranteed" by the military. Turkish nationalism, though, remains highly exclusive. Hence the advantages that stability brings, for the greater tolerance of internal differences are undercut by the continuing suspicion of "foreign" elements in Turkish society. Still, because Turkish Jews are a known quantity to their hosts, the Turkish Jewish community can exist on two levels; a recognized outer religious framework protects an informally tolerated communal life of some variety. By and large, Turkish Jews today are concentrated in Istanbul, in greatly diminished numbers after the mass migration to Israel shortly after the state was established. Those who remain tend to be wealthy; they can live comfortably in Turkey and do not want to jeopardize their wealth by leaving.[6]

Jewish efforts to maintain a corporate Jewish life must be undertaken carefully. Turkish law forbids Turkish citizens to have any formal links or even contact with foreign countries or international organizations. The Turkish Jewish community and the agencies in Israel or abroad, whether government, Zionist, or communal, that deal with the community in Turkey are extremely reluctant to have their activities publicized, on the grounds that if neither the Turkish government nor the Turkish people are antagonized, the community will be permitted to continue functioning. The consensus is that the slightest publicity might endanger the status quo. Moreover, because the Turkish regime is basically committed to fostering a secular state, it does not easily encourage more than a modicum of religious activity. Still, in recent decades Islam has secured a more favorable position in the regime, and Judaism has also secured more room to maneuver.

The Democratic party ruled in Turkey between 1950 and 1960. During that period, restrictions on the administration of the Jewish community were eased in return for the Jewish vote. Closed synagogues were reopened and permission was granted for new ones to be built. Hebrew was permitted in the curriculum of the Jewish schools.

Since 1960 a series of military juntas have intervened periodically to take over the reins of government and the military governments actually strengthened freedom of religion by prohibiting distinctions in law based on language, race, religion, or personal convictions. At the same time, in their desire to maintain exclusive control over the country, the military governments at times have intervened in elections for the Jewish Council of Istanbul.

In 1965 the Jewish population was between thirty-five and forty thousand. Estimates in 1980 were as low as twenty-one thousand. Turkish law grants special government recognition to religious communities of more than fifteen thousand members. The heads of such religious communities are granted many of the privileges given to diplomats—a car and chauffeur, a special flag, a special salary, and so forth. The head of the religious community is the official spokesman for the community and represents it to the government. The drop in Jewish population has led to Jewish concern that the formal status of the Jewish community may be endangered.

During the Nazi period, Turkey admitted many European Jews, especially those who had family in Turkey, and German and Austrian professors. Since the end of World War II, except for Turkish Jews who immigrated to Israel and then returned to Turkey, there have been no significant Jewish in-migrations. More than 95 percent of the Turkish Jewish population is Sephardic. About two hundred Karaite families (about one thousand persons) live in the Haskoy section of Istanbul. Their only link to the rabbinite community is the *mohel* who performs their circumcisions.

Jews are known to live in sixteen cities in the country. It is estimated that 84 percent of the entire community lives in Istanbul; in 1927 only 51 percent lived there and in 1904 fewer than 45 percent. Most live in suburban districts. The migration to the suburbs led to the weakening of traditional congregational affiliations, the main means of Jewish identification and affiliation. The government permits the maintenance of existing synagogues but forbids the building of new ones. An exception was made in 1951, when the government granted permission to construct a synagogue on Heybeli Ada, an island near Istanbul. Permission was granted through the good offices of an influential member of the Jewish community, who was also a member of parliament. Another island, Buyukada, also has a new synagogue but it has only a temporary permit.

The economic position of the Jewish community in Turkey is fairly good; better than it was in the 1940s. There are few poor Jews in Turkey, most having immigrated to Israel after the establishment of the state. Those poor remaining are not an undue financial burden on the community. Social service benefits are good, and retired Jews can usually live comfortably on their pensions. Were such people to emigrate, they would lose all these rights.

Anti-Semitism in Turkey can be classified under four separate, if overlapping, headings: (1) government pressure against Jews as part of its pressure against all minority and foreign groups in Turkey, (2) enactments against Jewish religion and culture as part of the government's emphasis on the secularization of Turkish life, (3) overt anti-Semitic attacks because of the higher economic standard of the Jewish community, and (4) anti-Israel acts. There is little or no official anti-Semitism in Turkey. Jews no longer pay special taxes, nor are they treated differently from other citizens in the eyes of the law or with regard to military service. Although the Jews are a small group in a large Muslim majority, they are subjected to no particular harassment. Anti-Semitism in the press is a periodic problem.

The Turkish Foundations Administration, or Vakif, supervises the expenditures and income of all congregations and allows only minimal repairs on religious and communal structures. If requests are presented for more extensive repairs, the community must wait long periods for an answer. In 1972 fourteen people who had been members of Turkey's Central Jewish Communal Council in 1966–67 were arrested for "negligence of duty." The Vakif charged that in 1967 the communal council "misused funds, without approval, on repairs and other work done on Jewish Community properties in downtown Istanbul." The Central Communal Council was asked to explain where the money had come from, as it was a great deal more than appeared on the budget submitted to the Vakif. It was explained that the money had been contributed or loaned by one of the members of the community, who had since emigrated. Although charges were dropped against the defendants, the member who was said to have "contributed" the money has not been allowed to return to Turkey.

In 1973 a group of teachers was arrested for "illegally" teaching Hebrew and Jewish subjects. Under Turkish law, only teachers certified by the state are permitted to teach religion. In Machazike Torah, a religious educational institution chartered by the state, older students and "graduates" teach the younger children, while rabbis teach the older ones. A Muslim teacher at the Jewish day school informed the police that the Jews were teaching illegally. The teachers were arrested and trial procedures begun against them. The charges were quietly dropped later, but these are good examples of restrictions on Jewish life. The restrictions are by-products of Turkish suspicion of Greek and, to a lesser extent, Armenian nationalist activity. They also reflect the government's desire to minimize religious life in Turkey. If Jews were allowed to open new schools where religion was taught, permission would have to be granted to the Muslims and to the other minorities, who are constantly battling the government on this issue.

The Haham Bashi, or chief rabbi, of Turkey is a state official, supported by the state and given the official trappings due the head of a religious community adapted from the Ottoman regime. He presides over a structure that includes a "Conseil Laique," a deliberately French term to describe what is really the *va'ad ha-Kahillah* (communal council), an instrumentality of the *keter malkhut*, except that under Turkish law it must be subordinated to the principal representative of the *keter torah*, whatever the actual practice (fig. 16.1). The actual power of the Turkish Jewish community is located in the Society for the Support of the Poor, formerly the B'nai B'rith lodge, an elite body dating to Ottoman times, which includes the leading members of the community, who share the responsibilities for its governance. Because B'nai B'rith has been banned in Turkey since the Revolution, its former members and those who have followed in their footsteps reorganized in this fashion. The lodge serves as a central source of leadership for the Istanbul Jewish community. The chief rabbi and other rabbis are members, as are almost all the members of the Conseil Laique. The organization determines the lists of candidates for election in most organizations, and its members dominate the active electorate in the community, thus ensuring victory for its lists. The men and women who belong to the lodge are well-to-do, well educated, and are chosen for their leadership potential and interest and their influence in either the Jewish or Turkish communities, or both.

Elections are held for the district councils, and perhaps also for the General Communal Council (Va'ad Hakelali). Elections are also held for the boards of directors of the various communal institutions. Elections usually are pro forma. The chief rabbi reigns more than rules and serves as the formal link to the Turkish authorities.

Until 1949 community roof organizations were tolerated but not recognized. In 1950 new laws required that endowments devoted to religious purpose must be managed independently by a committee chosen by the congregants and that each individual charity must be organized as an independent association. The Conseil Laique was outlawed for a time after 1961 but is now permitted to function without official government recognition.

The only legally recognized countrywide Jewish community structure is the Chief Rabbinate, which maintains liaison with communities throughout the country and represents them in all official business with the government. The current chief rabbi, David Asseo, is Turkish-born. He received his rabbinical ordination in Rhodes and is a university graduate. Although observant himself, he is liberal in his approach to religion, permitting worshipers to ride to synagogue and allowing the use of microphones for the services. There are three rabbis working under him in Istanbul, all of whom studied at *yeshivot* in Israel.

Jewish Istanbul is divided into eight districts, known as Hashgahot, and two subcommunities (Ashkenazi and Italian). Each has a synagogue, administered by a *va'ad ha-Kehillah*. Each council is composed of from four to seven members, depending on the size of the *kehillah*. Each congregation is legally autonomous and is directly responsible to the Vakif, to which it must submit a yearly financial report. Though forbidden by law, the congregations have a unified communal administration. Some forty full-time employees administer the foundations, or Vakifs, of the Chief Rabbinate in Istanbul. The chief

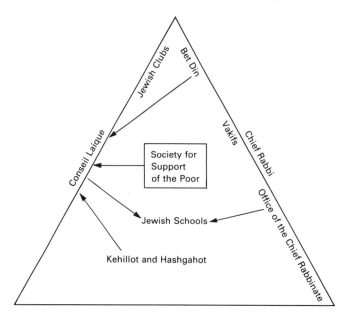

Figure 16.1.   The structure of the Turkish Jewish community.

rabbi appoints a Bet Din, consisting of a Rosh Bet Din (*mara de atra*) and four Hahamim. The Haham Basilik (Chief Rabbinate) and the Bet Din have supervision over marriages, divorces, deaths, births, *kashrut,* and, apparently, education. The Bet Din hears civil arbitration cases but only rarely, because it does not have enough status in the Vakif. The Conseil Laique is the umbrella organization. It has about thirty members. Its fund-raising arm is the "Coordination." The charitable and communal organizations and institutions submit their budget requests to the "Coordination," which provides them with operating funds. The chief rabbi appoints five members to the Conseil Laique, the district councils appoint the others.

Religious life is now at a much lower ebb than in former years. The situation is most critical in the small communities, where there are no religious functionaries of any kind, except a handful of old men who have no formal qualifications but have a great desire to continue the traditions. The Ashkenazi congregation in Istanbul is very small and must pay its members to maintain a *minyan*. The situation is better in the city's Sephardic synagogues, where most Jews attend services on the holidays. In Istanbul ten to fifteen hold services on the Sabbath and holidays. There also are congregations in Adana, Ankara, Bursa, Edirne (Adrianopole), and Izmir.

There is supervised ritual slaughtering in Turkey, but the number of people demanding kosher food is small. The Chief Rabbinate tries to supply *shohetim* to large centers and, in special circumstances, also to outlying communities. However, there is a shortage of qualified *shohetim* willing to live in any communities except Istanbul.

Except for the prohibition on building new synagogues, there have been no recent hindrances of religious observances by the Turkish authorities. However, most of the younger generation are not observant, and many young people are entirely ignorant of Judaism. To counteract this trend, the chief rabbi introduced the bat mitzvah ceremony and gave the bar mitzvah ceremony more communal importance.

The interrelationship between the Bet Din and the Conseil Laique is strong. The Conseil Laique represents the different facets of the community and manages all the community's affairs, as it is unlawful for the rabbinate to deal with finances. It advises the chief rabbi in many fields and is really an all-embracing communal organization. But because it cannot work openly, it is dependent on the Chief Rabbinate to be its spokesman and representative to the government.

Most of the fund-raising for local purposes is carried out by members of the "Coordination," who make systematic annual appeals to each breadwinner, suggesting an appropriate sum according to each contributor's economic situation. This is, in effect, an informal, voluntary communal tax. Another informal tax, called a *kitzbah,* finances the activities of the Chief Rabbinate and community religious services. It is estimated that two-thirds of the community's budget is raised through these and other contributions. The Jewish community also has property granted it in Ottoman times; income from these properties, held by the Haham Basilik Vakif (Foundation of the Chief Rabbinate), constitutes the remaining one-third. Small fees come from weddings, circumcisions, *bar mitzvahs,* funerals, kosher meat, and so forth, and from the sale of seats in most of the synagogues for the High Holy Days.

Contributions to Israel are against the law. It is illegal to take money out of the country, and offenders are severely punished. However, some contributions get to Israel, no doubt with the tacit consent of the authorities.

The first modern Hebrew day school was founded in 1850. In 1868 the Alliance Israélite Universelle began operating. In 1902 one of the large *talmudei torah* merged with one of the Alliance schools in Istanbul; in later years *talmudei torah* in Adrianopole and Izmir did the same. As a consequence of the shift toward a more secular education, the number of students studying in institutions of higher Jewish education (*yeshivot*) diminished so that, though in the nineteenth century Turkey had been renowned for its Jewish scholarship, in the 1960s the one remaining *yeshiva*—the rabbinical seminary—closed for lack of students.

Although the Treaty of Lausanne permitted the minorities to use foreign languages for instruction in their schools, the Jews relinquished this right with other rights when they chose full Turkish citizenship. As a result, by 1928 all Alliance schools, where the language of instruction was French, had either closed or were transferred to the administration of the communities, and Turkish was the only language used. In 1945 the government permitted the introduction of Hebrew and religion into the curriculum on a limited scale (four hours a week); otherwise, the curriculum was the standard one issued by the Ministry of Education. The teachers must be certified by the Ministry of Education, after having taken university or pedagogical courses. Today there is one Istanbul Jewish School, with three sections: a five-year elementary school, a three-year junior high school, and a three-year secondary school, the Lycée B'nai B'rith, founded in 1915. Students pay tuition; the community subsidizes the school to cover the tuition of the needy.

The schools are registered under Turkish law as Turkish Jewish schools, thus excluding children of other nationalities and religions. The elementary school division has an all-Jewish student body. In the junior high and high school divisions more than 90 percent of the children are Jewish; the rest are Muslim. However, in the elementary schools, more than 80 percent of the teachers are Muslim and in the junior high and high school there are only two Jewish teachers; the rest are Muslims, including the principal and assistant principal. The schools provide five hours of Hebrew instruction a week, taught by the community rabbis. There are no formal Judaica classes, but short discussions and explanations about Judaism are given during Hebrew classes. Since the early 1960s, the enrollment in the Jewish school has dropped tremendously. The once high educational level of the schools has dropped considerably in recent years. Children who plan to attend a university or children of wealthier parents usually attend the foreign (mostly English, French, or American) schools or government schools. Part of the decrease in enrollment is caused by the move to the suburbs. Some believe that leaders in the community do not recognize the need to maintain and upgrade Jewish day school education; by sending their children to foreign schools, as most of the wealthy Jews do, they are perpetuating the image of the Jewish schools as second-rate institutions.

The only other Jewish day school operating in Turkey is in Izmir. Founded as a communal high school in 1915, it later became a five-year elementary school. Between 1958 and 1971 there was a secondary school as well.

The other institution that concerns itself with providing a traditional Jewish education is Machazike Torah, affiliated with the rabbinates of Istanbul and Izmir. It provides Talmud Torah classes on Shabbat and Sunday, where prayers and Judaica are taught, and Shabbat and holiday services and social activities. It is estimated that two thousand youth, ranging from six through sixteen years of age, receive religious instruction through Machazike Torah in Istanbul and Izmir. In this way about 50 percent of the Jewish children in Turkey receive some kind of Jewish education.

Machazike Torah also trains *hazzanim, shohetim,* and *mohelim.* Classes in Machazike Torah are led by graduates of the system, including young native rabbis, graduates of Machazike Torah, who, after receiving their rabbinical training in Israel, returned to serve the community. The leaders and supporters of Machazike Torah are not in agreement with the attitudes of the other community leaders and have different priorities for the Jewish community.

There are six Jewish clubs in Turkey, five of them in the Istanbul area and the other in Izmir. There is no organized Jewish social or cultural life in other Jewish communities, except for activities that center in the synagogue, and then only at special times, such as religious holidays or special occasions, such as *bar mitzvahs* and weddings. Most clubhouses contain a discotheque, library, and sports facilities. Often there are classes in Israeli folk dancing, Bible, Jewish history, and Hebrew. Dostluk also has a kosher restaurant. Meeting halls are provided in some cases in the synagogue or community centers. Although formally no different from any other Turkish clubs, these groups quietly sponsor programs dealing with Israel and Judaism. The Organization and Public Relations, Youth and Hehalutz, and Sephardic Communities departments of the World Zionist Organization supply educational materials, lecturers, and entertainers. Events have been held commemorating Yom HaShoah and Yom HaAtzmant.

The Jewish press is represented in Istanbul by two independent Jewish weeklies, *Salom* and *La Vera Luz.* In both papers Ladino is used, written in Turkish orthography. From 750 to 800 families subscribe to *Salom* throughout Turkey and the paper has limited circulation abroad. In general, *Salom* is an antiestablishment publication and frequently attacks the rabbinate and community leaders.

As in most Jewish communities today, Jewish life in Turkey appears to be on the razor's edge. Religious life is diminishing and Jewish education declining, while intermarriage and assimilation are increasing. The Jews who remain in Turkey are content to compromise Jewish identity—if not their own, then that of the coming generations—for economic security and comfort. Even so, they do not feel secure. The Turkish government is not necessarily hostile to the Jews, but its entire orientation makes their position tenuous, especially with regard to organized Jewish life. The attendant compromises, those required by the authorities and those that the Jews make voluntarily to be less conspicuous, combine to weaken the fabric of Jewish life.

The Jewish Community of Greece

At the beginning of the twentieth century there were about 10,000 Jews in Greece. The number grew to 100,000 after the annexation of Thrace, including Salonika, as a result of the Balkan War of 1912–13. Because of Jewish emigration, stimulated by the upheavals in the region, by the outbreak of World War II the Jewish population of Greece had dropped to 77,000. Their political and legal status was good; the Jewish community had been officially registered at the turn of the century as an association and its religious status recognized by royal decree in 1920, in accord with the Greek Constitution. The Jews controlled the markets of paper, textiles, medicines, glassware, ironware, wood, and hides, and were represented in heavy industry, international trade, and banking. Uniquely for the diaspora, much of the Jewish population was employed in manual labor as stevedores, coachmen, and fishermen, and in the crafts. Athens, a minor community during the Ottoman period, grew because of its position as capital, but was a far second behind Salonika.

World War II practically destroyed Greek Jewry. Greece was attacked by Italy on October 18, 1940, and by Germany on April 6, 1941. According to the files of the Salonika Jewish community, 12,896 Jews served in the Greek army as soldiers and officers and thousands of others were in special Jewish sections of the Greek underground. In those parts of Greece held by the Italians, the Jews were not badly treated, but as soon as any area fell into German hands, anti-Jewish measures were immediately put into full effect.

Salonika was occupied by the Germans on April 9, 1941. Between March 1943 and February 1944, 46,091 Jews were deported in nineteen transports to Auschwitz and Bergen-Belsen, 95 percent of whom perished. The same fate befell the Jews of East Thracia and central and eastern Macedonia.

In September 1943, after the Italian surrender, German troops occupied all Greece, including Athens. Eichmann's deputy, Dieter Wisliceny, was immediately directed to Athens. Because of the heroism of the rabbi of Athens, Elija Barzilai, many Jews escaped into the mountains or were hidden by their Greek neighbors and by the Orthodox Church. Still, most of the Athenian Jewish population perished at the hands of the Nazis. A third Axis zone was held by Bulgaria. More than eleven thousand Jews were deported from this area (parts of Thrace and eastern Macedonia). In all, it is estimated that sixty-five thousand Jews were sent to their deaths by the Nazis, about 85 percent of the entire Jewish population.

When World War II ended, ten thousand Jews remained in Greece, almost all of them destitute. Almost all synagogues and centers of Jewish culture had either been destroyed or seriously damaged. Reconstruction of the community was complicated because of the long postwar period of political instability, continual changes in the government, and the extended economic crisis that plagued the country. Half of that number left for Israel or elsewhere in the years immediately after the war.

Immediately after World War II most of the financial help given to the Greek Jewish community came from the American Joint Distribution Committee (JDC) and the Conference for Jewish Material Claims against Germany, which began its work in 1945. These funds were administered by a Center Relief Committee (OPAIE) appointed by the Central Board of Greek Jewish Communities and financed through JDC and through allocations from the administration of Jewish heirless property. Officially, the JDC completed its activities in 1951, but its assistance has lasted much longer. Thus, in Larissa and Volos, apartments were built for Jewish victims of the 1954 and 1958 earthquakes financed by the JDC and the Claims Conference.

The approximately five thousand Jews in Greece today are distributed among fourteen officially organized communities, plus another four that do not have official status but maintain communal organizations. Greek law sets the ground rules. A Jewish community can maintain a recognized community council if it has more than 100 people. If it has between 20 and 100 it may not but it may hold religious services. If it has fewer than 20, it is not entitled to maintain any organized communal activities at all.[7]

The Central Board of Greek Jewish Communities is the overarching body for all Greek Jewry and is legally recognized as such. It functions as the legal guardian of all settlements that do not have communities and is a federal body. The board maintains membership in the World Jewish Congress and the European Council of Jewish Community Services.

The four largest communities are Athens, with slightly more than half the total, Salonika, Larissa, and Volos. The one community that shows any growth is Athens, because of in-migration from the smaller communities. It is the seat of the countrywide institutions of Greek Jewry. The Salonika community is the main contributor to the Central Board of Jewish Communities, and through it to most of the welfare and building projects of the communities. The Salonika community's projects are financed in larger measure by income from its property. There is no community membership tax in Salonika or in the smaller communities, but a monthly membership tax is paid by the community members of Athens. The tax is graduated to each contributor's income.

The Jewish population has more or less stabilized. Greek Jewry suffers from the problems of the rest of European Jewry. However, as long as civil marriage did not exist in Greece, it had a lower rate of intermarriage. Intermarriage meant conversion, either the non-Jewish spouse to Judaism, which is usual, or the Jewish spouse to Greek Orthodoxy, which was once unheard of but is now a growing phenomenon. Still, the marriage of Jewish men to Greek women had become common enough that in 1978 the Central Board of Jewish Communities organized a trial conversion class for women in Athens. However, because of the close ties between the Greek government and the Greek Orthodox Church, this is not something the Jews wish to foster.

By and large, the Jews who have stayed in Greece see themselves as closely connected to their country and loyally involved in its affairs. But the ethnoreligious separation between Jews and Greeks is clear-cut; neither group sees the other as part of some common nationality. Anti-Semitism is a periodic but relatively modest problem.

The Central Board of Jewish Communities was organized in the aftermath of World War II, mainly to channel funds from the JDC and the Claims Conference to the local communities and to represent Greek Jews in their official relations with the government. By and large, it concentrates on its external relations—defense role. In that respect it is more like a board of deputies, leaving the management of the internal activities of Greek Jewry to the local community boards. The one other function the board undertakes is Jewish education, because its auspices are needed to provide Jewish educational opportunities beyond the local schools (figure 16.2).

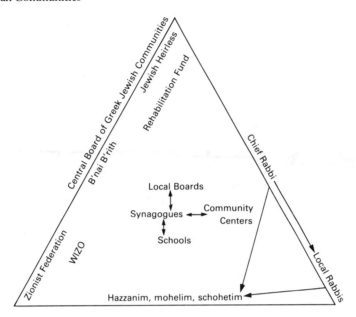

Figure 16.2. The organizational structure of the Greek Jewish community.

Every four years each community sends a number of representatives determined by the size of its local population to a countrywide congress, which selects the general board. Each local community is governed by an elected general assembly. Elections on both local and countrywide planes are of interest to the Jewish community with factional rivalry between Zionists and non-Zionists a reality throughout the electoral process.

The work of the Central Board was disrupted between 1967 and 1974 when Greece was under the rule of the "colonels," but in 1974 the board resumed functioning. The "colonels" were not hostile to the Jewish community, but their generally nationalistic and authoritarian orientation made the Jewish communal leadership cautious. By and large, the Jews are free to express themselves and are allowed to maintain their own routines of life based on the tacit understanding that the Jewish community will preserve substantial autonomy in return for emphasizing its Greek character and not getting involved in Greek politics. The board works closely with Keren Hayesod on fund-raising for Israel, conducted through an independent campaign. Religious functions are the responsibility of the individual community boards.

Other countrywide Jewish organizations include the Zionist Federation, WIZO, and B'nai B'rith. B'nai B'rith in Greece is a particularly respected organization, composed of an active women's section and a men's section, which is more of an ad hoc group called together to discuss special problems confronting the community. Zionists are active members of the organization.

The Zionist Federation of Greece is not only officially chartered as a countrywide body, but because it was defined as a professional group, it continued to hold elections during the military regime. It is nonpartisan in Zionist politics and has become relatively dormant, although periodic attempts have been made to revitalize its leadership. Some of its activities are financed and cosponsored by the Central Board but the ideological differences between the Zionists and the non-Zionists who dominate the board have kept cooperation minimal. The League of Jewish Women, established in 1934 and revived after World War II, is linked to WIZO.

The Jewish Heirless Property and Rehabilitation Fund (OPAIE) also functions countrywide. It was created by government decree in 1949 to handle problems of Jewish heirless property. At the end of the war the total value of heirless property was estimated at between 5 and 10 million dollars. In its first years, the organization was torn between two viewpoints. The Zionists wanted most of the money to be used to resettle immigrants to Israel, while other factions sought to focus on rehabilitation of the Jews remaining in Greece. The quarrel was voiced in the Greek-Jewish press, and finally the World Jewish Congress was called in to mediate the dispute in 1952.

For many years OPAIE was unable to claim the heirless properties it was decreed to receive, for lack of ability to furnish the required proof of death of the concentration camp victims. Such proof required passage of a special law, which neither the Jews nor the government seemed eager to press for. Thus, for several years OPAIE confined its activities to administering heirless properties, the income of which augmented the funds of the Central Board. In the 1960s the board resettled Jews in small dying communities in the hope of protecting Jewish property interests there. Suggestions have been considered several times to disband OPAIE and transfer guardianship rights to the local communities or the Central Board to ensure the continuity of ownership. One major phenomenon of Greek Jewry is that the community has become rich because of the war and would like to find legitimate ways to use the resources that are beyond the needs of the small Jewish community in Greece.

Greek Jews are not particularly religious, although perhaps more likely to maintain a semblance of observance than in the western Jewish communities. Greece has a chief rabbi residing in Athens and other rabbis in Athens and Salonika. There is also a circuit rabbi who serves some of the smaller Jewish communities. There is a fairly full complement of other religious functionaries: *hazanim, shohetim,* and *mohelim,* but keeping them in Greece and training new ones as the existing ones grow older, is a perennial problem. The JDC helps in that regard and the Jewish Agency sends *shlihim* principally for Jewish educational purposes, but also to help in this respect. All religious officials are paid by the community.

Almost the entire Jewish population of Greece is Sephardic, although a few Ashkenazic families in Athens are active in communal affairs. There are no separate organizations for Jews of specific communal backgrounds. On the High Holy Days two separate religious services are held. The main synagogue follows the Sephardic ritual and is frequented by the native Athenian Jews and the Jews who moved to Athens from Salonika; a smaller *minyan* following the older Romaniot (Byzantine Jewish) ritual draws Jews from Ioannina and related communities.

Social custom and family tradition lead almost everyone to attend High Holy Day Services. Many small communities hold services only on the High Holy Days. In the big centers, perhaps half the community attends other festival services, and the number is greatly reduced on the Sabbath. In Athens, services are also held on Mondays and Thursdays when the Torah is read. The synagogue in Athens, built before the war and renovated after, is located in a less fashionable section of the city, which influences poor attendance. In many smaller communities, the synagogues are relics of past communal vibrancy but contemporary dereliction. The synagogue in Rhodes is used as a tourist attraction. In some communities, like Kavalla, the old synagogues have been torn down or sold and smaller ones incorporated into the community center building.

About 70 percent of Jewish children in Greece receive some sort of Jewish education, usually minimal. Teachers are supplied by the Jewish Agency. There are no formal Jewish studies past the sixth grade in Athens and it is even hard to find Jewish children in a day school until then. Nor is the situation in Salonika or Larissa any different. The Salonika community maintains a program of Jewish education in the public schools. In the smaller communities there are supplementary Talmud Torah classes plus summer camps and study programs in Israel. There is a pan-Hellenic Jewish youth movement, which provides some focus for Jewish youth. There is a Maccabi group in Salonika.

The Jewish press in Greece consists of the *Jewish Review,* a fortnightly private publication; *Chronicles,* a monthly publication of the Central Board of Jewish Communities; *Generation,* the monthly of the pan-Hellenic Jewish youth movement; and *Israeli News,* the monthly of the Greek-Israel Association.

In the larger centers, the organizations and institutions described above have their local counterparts. The community board of each community is the ruling body. Because the non-Zionists have always defeated the Zionist list in the elections, subsidiary local groups and institutions are non-Zionist controlled. In general, local communities are too apathetic to have conflicts, and when they do arise the are focused on personality, not ideological issues. People who take office in any organization tend to remain in their positions, locally as well as countrywide, for years.

Most of the communal leaders are prosperous businessmen, and a few are professionals. Women have been playing an ever-increasing role in local affairs in Salonika. Of the twenty members elected to the Thessaloniki General Assembly in 1979, seven were women. Recent elections for the Athens Community Board brought in several young leaders for the first time. A similar trend toward younger leadership was also noted in the elections for the Central Board and the Zionist Federation. Perhaps this marks a turning point in involvement, because earlier very few young people were interested in accepting leadership positions and no organized efforts were made to attract them. More likely, it reflects the generational shift of the mid-1970s.

Because the board of each community is a roof organization, it chooses the boards and committees of the subsidiary institutions, such as community center, school, synagogue, and camp, if they exist. In the small communities, such as Kavalla and Patras, where there are no boards, often one family takes charge of Jewish interests.

There are community centers in Athens, Salonika, Larissa, Volos, Kavalla, Ioannina, Corfu, and Khalkís. The Athens community center complex includes the community offices and the offices of the Jewish Agency, Jewish National Fund, HIAS, the Zionist Center, and the youth club. In Salonika the community has organized a community center with a youth club that serves high school students and young adults. Activities include Hebrew classes for all ages, Judaism classes for children not studying Jewish subjects in school, a club newspaper, various musical activities, and sports. Festival and anniversary programs—including Memorial Day for Salonikan Jewry—are celebrated. In the smaller communities, such as Corfu, Ioannina, and Kavalla, synagogue and community center are often combined. Usually, activities in the smaller communities consist of dances, Ping-Pong, and Hebrew classes. Most of the Jewish youth of those communities attend the activities.

Greek Jewry is more likely to survive because of the organic ties among its members than because of its organizational structure. In this respect, it is typically Mediterranean and as such has a resiliency sometimes belied by the formal picture of the organized community.

The Jewish Community of Yugoslavia

The Balkan Jewish communities must make their place in countries dominated by regimes antagonistic to the notion of pluralism for nonterritorial groups. Yugoslavia is far more liberal in this respect because it is a multinational society. The Yugoslav government has recognized the Jews as a semiautonomous nationality as well as a religious community, though without an indigenous territorial base.[8]

The foundations of modern Jewish life in the south Slav lands came with the major wave of immigration that followed the expulsion of the Jews from Spain in 1492. By the mid-sixteenth century, Sephardic settlers had established communities in Macedonia, Bosnia, and the Dalmatian coast. In the late nineteenth century, many newcomers from Bulgaria and the other Balkan lands joined them.

By contrast, the Ashkenazic communities in the former Hapsburg areas were of fairly recent origin. Until the late eighteenth century, Jews had been banned from residence in Slovenia, Croatia, and the Military Frontier region except in the town of Zemun or Semlin across the Danube from Belgrade. During the nineteenth and early twentieth centuries, many Jews from different parts of the Austro-Hungarian Empire immigrated to the south Slav regions under Hungarian control. Major Jewish communities developed in Croatia-Slavonia and the Vojvodina.

After the occupation of Bosnia-Herzegovina by Austria-Hungary in 1878, some Ashkenazic Jews moved to Bosnia, especially to its capital, Sarajevo. The Ashkenazic community in Belgrade also grew up about the same time. Conversely, a small Sephardic settlement eventually appeared in Zagreb. On the whole, however, the line of demarcation between the Ashkenazim and the Sephardim continued to follow the old border between the Hapsburgs and Ottomans.

After the creation of the Yugoslav state in 1918, the Ashkenazim constituted two-thirds of the Jewish population and the Sephardim the remaining third. The two groups formed separate communities, even when they lived in the same locality. A small Ashkenazi Orthodox group, mainly centered in the Vojvodina, also established its own recognized communities. In 1930 there were 114 organized Jewish communities in Yugoslavia; 38 were Sephardic, 70 Ashkenazic-Neolog, and 6 Ashkenazic-Orthodox. The Sephardic and Ashkenazic-Neolog communities together constituted the Federation of Jewish Religious Communities of Yugoslavia founded in 1919; the Orthodox communities set up their own Union of Orthodox Jewish Religious Communities.

The federation represented the Jewish community to the outside world and administered government subsidies. With the Chief Rabbinate and the Rabbinical Council, it supervised religious and educational affairs and settled religious and other disputes in the Jewish community at large. Nevertheless, organizations such as the Zionist Federation, the Sephardic organization, and B'nai B'rith functioned outside its sphere of influence.

On the eve of World War II, the registered Jewish population in Yugoslavia was 71,342. The Holocaust destroyed over three-quarters of Yugoslav Jewry. The German occupying forces, assisted by local Fascists, systematically exterminated the community.

Some Jews managed to save themselves by joining the partisans or escaping to Italian-held territory.

With the German occupation of Yugoslavia in April 1941 the federation was forced to cease its operations temporarily, but it resumed its activities under its former president in October 1944. In the immediate postwar period it was occupied primarily with the tasks of reconstruction, working with the JDC and, from 1945 to 1952, the Autonomous Committee for Aid, established in conjunction with the JDC. In 1946 there were 12,414 registered Jews in Yugoslavia; about half were Sephardic and half Ashkenazic. Fifty-six Jewish communities were reconstituted under the new Communist regime, the largest of which were Belgrade, Zagreb, and Sarajevo. The distinctions between Sephardim and Ashkenazim, Neolog and Orthodox, were dropped; every local community included all the Jews in its vicinity and all communities belonged to one countrywide federation. The Yugoslav Jewish Federation is recognized as the official representative of the Jewish population. It is structured on federal lines, as befits a country that itself is vigorously federal.

Soon after the creation of the State of Israel, the Yugoslav authorities permitted Jews to emigrate there freely if they so desired. Between 1948 and 1952, 7,578 persons departed for Israel in a series of five *aliyot*. After 1952 the federation reorganized itself and its activities to correspond to the needs of the Jews who remained in Yugoslavia. Its primary focus has shifted from religious to cultural activities. Accordingly, in 1952 the federation formally dropped the word *religious* from its name. Ninety percent of Yugoslavia's declared Jews are registered members.

Of the thirty-six organized Jewish communities remaining in Yugoslavia, the three largest and most important are in Belgrade (with approximately 1,600 Jews), Zagreb (1,300), and Sarajevo (1,100). Some Jewish communal activity is found in eight other cities: Subotica (400), Novi Sad (280), Osijek (220), Rijeka (160), Semun (140), Split (120), Ljubljana (80), and Skopje (50). The remaining twenty-five Jewish communities, with a combined population of approximately 800, exist primarily on paper, because they do not have enough members to support any kind of real communal life. Several of these "communities" have fewer than ten members each. Some 200 Jews are listed as living where there is no formal community whatsoever. All Jewish organizations and institutions are subsidiary to the local community and there are no intermediate territorial bodies. Thus the Federation of Jewish Communities is all-embracing.

The Yugoslav government, as a Communist regime, is cool toward religious identification and expression. Still, it has placed no political obstacles in the way of Jewish religious observance. The Jews are basically nonreligious. Religious institutions, such as they are, function within the framework of the local communities but they play a secondary and limited role in a secular state with a secular society. At one time Yugoslavia had a chief rabbi but the office was abolished at the end of the war. Since 1968 there have been no properly qualified rabbis in the country. Still, some 40 percent of the Jews say they observe some Jewish holidays and customs, and some 30 percent say they attend services at least once a year. Jewish holidays are celebrated by the entire community. Kosher meat, *matzot,* and other religious goods must be imported and are.

Marriage and divorce are entirely under civil control. The Jewish community does not have a Bet Din and does not have the rabbis to establish one. Hence there are no conversions or Jewish weddings. The community is controlled by voluntary leaders and can be seen as having only institutions of the *keter malkhut,* except the synagogues, which are vestigial (figure 16.3).

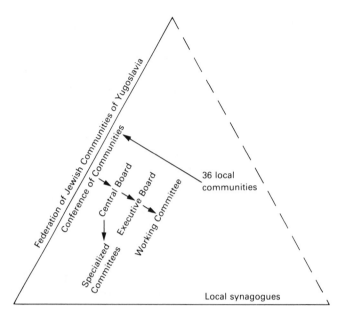

Figure 16.3.   The organizational structure of the Yugoslav
Jewish community.

Membership in the community, compulsory until World War II, is voluntary.
Membership is open to all persons of Jewish descent who do not belong to any other
religious community, and to their spouses and children, even if the spouses are not
Jewish. More than one-third of the community members have only one Jewish parent or
none. Thus the normative definition of who is a Jew in Yugoslavia is a non-*halakhic* one,
developed by the local *keter malkhut*. Most non-Jewish spouses, however, do not join the
community, although a significant minority are active members.

The Federation of Jewish Communities and every local community are required by
Yugoslav law to have written constitutions. Constitutions are revised periodically as is
the practice in Yugoslavia generally. The federation's governing bodies include the Conference of Communities, a Central Board, and an Executive Board, which includes a
working committee and the presidency. There is a supervisory board and subcommittees
for specialized fields such as women, youth, choirs, cultural activities, students, finance
and welfare, interethnic and international relations.

The Jewish community is financed partially by voluntary contributions from its
members and from occasional state subsidies. However, it relies heavily on funds from
outside organizations, such as the Joint Distribution Committee and the Memorial
Foundation for Jewish Culture.

The Conference of Communities comprises representatives of all communities with
at least fifteen registered members and is the ultimate decision-making body of the
federation. Each community elects its delegates, the number determined by the size of
the community. The conference also includes members of the executive board ex officio.
It meets annually. The Executive Board and the other elected bodies are elected every
three years. The Executive Board has twenty-six members. Eleven are from the Belgrade
community; four, including the secretary of the federation and the presidents of the three

major communities—Belgrade, Zagreb, and Sarajevo—serve ex officio; and nine represent the nine largest communities outside Belgrade. One member represents the Directorate of the Home for the Aged in Zagreb. The Executive Board meets at least every two months. Daily business is conducted by the working committee, which consists of the Belgrade members of the Executive Board plus the vice presidents of the federation. The presidency comprises the president and substitute president, both of whom must be from Belgrade, the vice president, and the secretary.

Every local community is governed by a communal council elected annually or biannually with day-to-day administration in the hands of a board composed of the officers plus the heads of the subcommittees and sections. All Jewish institutions and organizations in the locality are members of the local community. Only the largest communities can have such a fully articulated organizational structure; the smaller ones have incomplete organizations that approach this framework insofar as possible.

The principal functions of the Jewish community in Yugoslavia are in the educational-cultural and communal-welfare spheres. The federation also deals with community relations, general fund-raising, and publications. By and large, the community's work is with youth and cultural development because it is limited in trying to secure its survival. It provides some welfare services because Yugoslavia, though a socialistic state, does not have the resources to provide as fine a welfare package as the Jews would like.

The community maintains a major historical museum and archives and also tries to maintain the synagogues and cemeteries that have survived the ravages of war and Holocaust. Because religious activities are minimal, cultural activities—choirs, concerts, libraries and reading rooms, women's activities, and an effort to record local Jewish folklore—are particularly important. The community publishes a bimonthly Jewish review, sent to every registered Jewish household in the country, and an annual Jewish calendar.

Jewish education is primarily a summer activity; an educational camp is conducted each summer for two weeks. Otherwise the only formal Jewish educational institutions are two small kindergartens in Belgrade and Zagreb, where most of the children are non-Jewish. There are informal educational activities built around holiday celebrations. When possible, Jewish youth are sent to Israel for study programs, an arrangement usually tacitly accepted by Yugoslav authorities if it is not made public.

Because it is difficult to find people who will take leadership in the community, elections are for the most part pro forma. They are not contested and there is no party system. There is one submitted electoral list, although the voting is for individuals and therefore there are more candidates than offices.

The principal positions of leadership in the community are found in the Federation, the executive boards of the larger local communities and, to a lesser extent, in the subsidiary bodies, such as the Directorate of the Home for the Aged. Nearly all leadership positions are in the hands of volunteers. The secretary of the federation, the director of the Home for the Aged, the curator of the Jewish Museum, and the youth coordinator may be considered professionals. The voluntary leadership, however, controls the communal institutions, organizations, and decision making. The voluntary leaders are almost all lawyers, doctors, professors, or retired government officials. They are, for the most part, members of the League of Communists. The older ones were partisans in World War II.

The people most active in communal affairs are usually forty-five or older. There are no obvious differences in economic or social status between participants in different institutions or organizations. The main differentiating factors are age and degree of Jewish background. Women are often more active in educational and cultural organizations than men, and men and women share the responsibilities for social and welfare institutions. Those active in synagogues and religious life are usually sixty or older. Otherwise no meaningful distinctions among types of activists can be discerned.

The federation has a long-standing affiliation with the World Jewish Congress as one of its founding members and the European Council on Jewish Communal Services. Since 1953 the president of the federation has held a position on the WJC Executive Board. In 1960 when the European Council on Jewish Communal Services was formed, the then president of the federation helped draft its first statutes. Since 1967 his successor has held the post of first vice president of the council. The federation also has had close ties with the Joint Distribution Committee, the Claims Conference, and the Memorial Foundation for Jewish Culture, it has they have regularly received funds. Close ties are maintained with the Jewish Agency, the World Sephardi Federation, the World Union of Jewish Students, and the International Council of Jewish Women. In short, the community can maintain relations with nearly all world Jewish organizations, except those that specifically include the term *Zionist* in their names. The federation also has developed a network of informal contacts with other eastern European communities and often serves as a bridge between them and world Jewry.

Ties between the Yugoslav Jewish community and Israel have been informal since the Yugoslav government severed diplomatic relations with Israel after the Six-Day War. The two countries still maintain trade connections and the Yugoslav authorities have not interfered directly with the Jewish community's support of Israel. Yugoslav Jews are allowed to travel to Israel freely as tourists. Israelis, too, may visit Yugoslavia with no difficulty. Close personal ties are preserved, especially between Yugoslav Jews and Israeli citizens of Yugoslav origin. Yugoslav Jewish leaders make frequent trips to Israel for official or personal reasons. Every summer, about twenty Jewish students from Yugoslavia attend a special seminar in Israel.

Israel does not officially provide the community with technical assistance, but Israeli "visitors," many of whom were born in Yugoslavia, provide assistance as informal teachers, or *shlihim,* at summer camps. Israelis of Yugoslav descent are an important link between Yugoslav Jewry and Israel. The most important formal contact is probably Hitahdut Olej Yugoslavia, the association of Yugoslav Jews in Israel. (Similarly, the Yugoslav Jewish community maintains close relations with the Association of Yugoslav Jews in the United States, which has its headquarters in New York.) Israel does not provide the community with any financial assistance, but the community occasionally makes contributions to Israel, mainly by way of the Jewish National Fund. Thus contacts have never been broken, but the community of its own volition exercises caution in its relationship with Israel.

The Yugoslav Jewish community is unquestionably the freest Jewish community in any of the Communist countries, no doubt because of the nature of Yugoslav communism. The community is to some extent limited in its activities by the subtle pressure that flows from the general disapproval of religion common to Communist systems and by the official government opposition to Israel. These restrictions, however, have thus far not proved seriously debilitating. Jews are still Jews in the Yugoslav scheme of things—a separate nationality in a federation of nations. That is one of the community's strengths. But it is possible for these Jews, or at least their children if they are intermarried, to assimilate into the ranks of the nation on whose territory they dwell with little difficulty. With a high rate of intermarriage and a great lack of Jewish education, it would seem difficult for the next generation to acquire enough incentive to remain Jewish. From the perspective of the Yugoslav authorities, the Jewish community need not worry about its future; consequently, it may totally assimilate.

What seems clear is that Yugoslav Jewry is a community sustained by its organization. Almost all the content of Jewish life is confined to the organized activities of the community. There is little Jewish life in the home and even less in the synagogues. The Yugoslav Jewish community is a textbook example of an organization sustaining a community. Perhaps the Jewish community of Yugoslavia is doomed to death by natural causes. But it may be that its tight organization combined with the will of those active in it to survive will keep the community alive.

The Jewish Community of Italy

The Jewish community of Italy is the oldest in Europe after that of Greece. The Roman Jewish community sees itself as continuous since the days of the Hasmonaean kings. There was a Jewish presence in Rome during the last days of the Republic, and during the imperial period Jews constituted a significant percentage (estimates are as high as 10 percent) of the Roman population. For as long as the Roman Empire existed the Jews were citizens and as protected as other citizens.

From the fall of the Roman Empire until the "Risorgimento" and the unification of Italy in 1860, Jews could be no more than protected subjects. Because the country was divided into any number of small states, even in bad times Jews could find refuge in one or another. As a result, Jewish life in Italy flourished in a unique way.

There were occasional expulsions but they did not last long. Apart from the years in which the Byzantine Empire brought its highly pro-Christian ideology to bear on public policy, leading to persecutions of the Jews, Italian Jewry had a relatively easy time of it. Italians are not much given to group hatred, and only when the church acted against the Jews settled in its domains did the Jews suffer.[9]

Italy was a crossroads for Jews from east and west, north and south, part of the transmission belt of the traditions of the Jews of Eretz Israel to Ashkenaz a thousand years ago and on the line of migration of the Iberian exiles to the Ottoman Empire five hundred years later. Italian Jewry developed its own customs and a special sense of self-worth that reached its climax during the Renaissance. They participated fully in the cultural revival of the times as Jews, not only contributing their share to Italian culture but also leaving a legacy to Jewish culture that is only now becoming fully known. Hence it is not surprising that in modern times Italian Jews threw themselves wholeheartedly into the Italian effort to attain national unity and greatness. Jews were found across the entire spectrum of political movements once the ghetto walls fell.

While, by and large, Italian Jews left the ghetto under the impact of the French Revolution and the Napoleonic conquest on the Italian Peninsula, they had begun to develop a unique ideology of modernization as early as the eighteenth century, reflecting their previous links with the life of the general community. The Italian Jews did not need to break sharply with their past to modernize, but did so with the rest of Italy. By the mid-nineteenth century they were already active in Italian life and by the end of the century many had begun to assimilate quietly without developing an ideological basis for assimilation, as happened with the Jews north of the Alps. Others tried to develop a Jewish life that enabled them to fit into modern Italian society.

After the unification of Italy, the Jews were granted full citizenship in the new Italian state, and their local Jewish communities were organized along modern lines. It was not until 1911 that the Consortia della Communita Israelita Italiana was established to link these communities. Membership in the Jewish community was made voluntary.

Between World Wars I and II Italian Jewry went from full integration with Italian life to maximum exclusion, beyond what had ever occurred in the past. At first Mussolini's Fascists did not discriminate against Jews. Many Jews even were active in the Fascist movement, some of them quite prominent. Jews were still able to distinguish themselves in the Italian army in the Ethiopian War in 1935–36. After his 1938 alliance with Hitler, Mussolini was gradually compelled to adopt the Nuremberg Laws and first segregate then persecute the approximately fifty thousand Jews of Italy.

World War II brought deportations, though with the reluctant support of the Italians and then only after the German occupation of northern and central Italy in September 1943. By the end of the war, the Italian Jewish community had declined by about 40 percent. Nearly eight thousand were deported and killed in the camps, six thousand converted to other religions, and six thousand left the country. So at the end of the war just under twenty-nine thousand Jews remained in Italy.[10]

In 1943 Italy surrendered to the Allies, Mussolini was deposed, and the new Italian government returned to the traditional ways of Italian tolerance. Hence neither the local Jewish community nor world Jewry viewed Italy as a pariah state with a Nazi past, as was the case with Germany and Austria. Although few of the Jews who fled Italy because of the Nazi-sponsored persecutions returned, there was also no mass postwar exodus. Instead, most of the Jews who remained began to rebuild Jewish life along prewar lines. The indigenous Jewish population was supplemented by several thousand displaced persons who found a haven in Italy. There have been continued, if moderate, increments to the Jewish community as the wealthier Libyan Jews took advantage of their Italian citizenship to follow the Italians when they left Libya. A few hundred Soviet Jews have relocated permanently in Italy and the usual leavening of Israelis has arrived. This has been sufficient to offset the assimilatory tendencies of contemporary Italian Jewry, to keep the Italian Jewish population more or less stable at thirty-two thousand.[11] At the same time, the number of organized local communities declined from seventy to twenty-three between 1930 and 1948. The Holocaust accelerated Jewish concentration in Italy's large cities that grew as centers of Italian life in the aftermath of the unification of the country.

Rome and Milan are the main centers of Italian Jewry. Rome has fifteen thousand Jews and Milan has ninety-five hundred, 44 and 28 percent of the Italian Jewish population, respectively. The Roman Jewish community retains a strong commitment to its ancient traditions. It is the stronghold of the Italian *minhag* (tradition). Milan's community is newer and has a large Lubavitcher Hassidic and other Ashkenazic components. It also has a North African congregation and a congregation of Meshed Jews from Iran. The communities of Turin, Florence, Trieste, and Leghorn have more than a thousand Jews each. They and most of the smaller communities represent the old Sephardic heartland of northern Italy.

At this writing, the shape of the Italian Jewish community may be changing because of the new agreement between it and the government of Italy, which disestablishes the community as part of a general separation of church and state. Until now, the Jewish community has benefited from the arrangement between the Roman Catholic church and the Italian state by having quasi-official status. Mussolini was responsible for establishing the Unione della Communita Israelita Italiana as an obligatory organization for Italian Jewry in 1930, the year after his *concordat* with the Vatican that established the Roman Catholic Church as the state church. Thus the Unione, which is, in fact, a federation of communities, is defined in Italian law as is the status of its individual communities. The country's rabbis are attached to the Unione and through it are authorized to perform marriages. Because of that law, all those considered Jews *halakhically* automatically belong to the community unless they make a formal renunciation of their membership and the Unione receives a portion of the state taxes paid by its members.

Because the law of Italian Jewish communities was promulgated during the Fascist era, it is not surprising that it had antidemocratic features, particularly in its compulsory aspects, which aroused periodic controversy in the Jewish community. Even so, suggestions for reform always caused trepidation among the communal leadership who are fearful of what will happen to the community if the voluntary principle is applied. Membership means obligatory taxes and Italian Jews, like other Italians, may prefer tax avoidance to communal responsibility. The law also fixed in detail the internal financial and organizational structure of each of the local and countrywide communities. In the true Italian manner, there is also a parallel countrywide associational network that provides cultural, fund-raising, welfare, and recreational activities. In this network Italian Jewish vitality is expressed. Still, it is estimated that 90 percent of the Jews living in Italy are members of the community, and the other 10 percent are transients or a few locals who will not register for tax reasons.

The plenary power of the Unione is lodged in a congress composed of members elected by each local community council, which ordinarily convenes once every five years. Elections are usually uncontested. Although this leads to the perpetuation of the same persons in leadership positions, by and large the problem is finding people who will fill a vacuum rather than restraining those who seek dominance.

The congress elects a council and the members of the Consulta Rabbinica, sets policy, and approves the budget for the five-year period. The council has fifteen members plus three rabbis. It elects a president and an executive of three plus a rabbi. The council handles the ordinary governance of the Unione and determines the assessments levied on each community for the activities of the Unione. The budget of the Unione had to be approved by the appropriate ministry of the Italian government (see figure 16.4).

Each local community has a council of between three and fifteen members, depending on the community's size, who are directly elected by all adult taxpaying members of the community who have fulfilled the compulsory education requirements of Italy. Members of the council must be males over the age of twenty-five who have at least graduated from the lower-level schools and "are of religious conduct." Foreigners residing for at least three years in Italy are eligible for council membership provided that they comprise no more than one-third of the council. Each council elects an executive and a president to handle day-to-day governance. Local turnout for council elections is usually low, probably not more than 10 to 15 percent.

Financing of Jewish activities comes from the obligatory taxation of community members, voluntary donations, fees and bequests, income from properties, and some government grants. About 75 percent of Jewish communal expenditures are derived from taxation, about 15 percent from donations, and about 10 percent from properties.

Smaller communities may have functional ties with larger adjacent ones, or even be

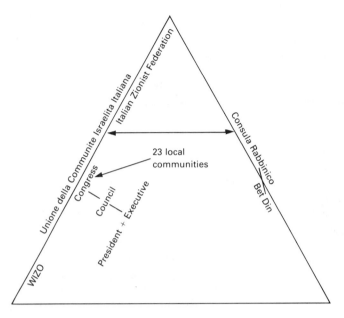

Figure 16.4. The organizational structure of the Italian
Jewish community.

officially incorporated within them. Thus, Siena (100 Jews) is linked with Florence
(1,400 Jews). The ultra-Orthodox communities retain a certain independence but by law
they must also be linked to the Unione. The Italian rabbinical council, the Consulta
Rabbinica, supervises the rabbinate. Each local community is responsible for organizing
all religious, welfare, and cultural services and administers its own property. Most Jewish
life is concentrated in the individual congregations; each maintains its ancient traditions:
Italian, Sephardic, or Ashkenazic.

Local and especially Unione leaders are drawn from the more established elements
in the community, those with the wealth and leisure time to undertake the necessary
activities. A cadre of people is employed by the community, including rabbis; some are
from established rabbinical families but most are from ordinary backgrounds. Community secretaries and administrative staff constitute the Italian Jewish civil service, along
with teachers in the schools. There is a shortage of qualified rabbis. Headmasters and
teachers are trained as required under Italian law, including preparatory courses sponsored by the Jewish community. The Jewish civil service is drawn from among graduates
in law and accounting but have no particular training for Jewish communal work.

External relations–defense. Italian Jewry conducts its external relations–defense activities principally through the Unione, which represents the Jewish community before
the government. It is a reflection of the character of Italian society that, in addition to
quiet diplomacy, the Jewish community has used public action and demonstrations
where necessary to make its point. This is most unusual in Europe where most Jewish
communities maintain a low profile. The principal functions of the Unione are in the
external relations–defense sphere, but it also coordinates activities in other spheres not
conducted in the local communities. Only in the Israel-*edah* sphere does it share control,
nominally at least with the Italian Zionist Federation.

Israel-edah sphere. The Italian Zionist Federation is the principal countrywide organization aside from the Unione, and WIZO is the strongest women's organization, but neither is particularly active. Fund-raising for Israel is conducted by Keren Hayesod in a separate campaign but draws on the same leadership. So, for example, the Italian representative to the Jewish Agency Assembly, in the early 1980s, appointed by the local Keren Hayesod, was not only one of the leaders of the Unione, but was known in Italy as an "assimilationist" in orientation. Italian Jewry plays an active role on the European Jewish scene. The Unione maintains memberships in the World Jewish Congress–European Section and in the European Council of Jewish Community Services.

Religious-congregational sphere. For the religious segment of the Jewish population and some of the nonobservant Jews, the religious institutions are central in Jewish life. The rabbis are the recognized spiritual and religious leaders and the synagogue, besides being a place of worship, becomes a true focus of Jewish life especially during the High Holy Days and periods of crisis, such as the eve of the Six-Day War or the Leningrad trials.

Educational-cultural sphere. A system of Jewish schools recognized by the state combines the syllabus of the state schools with Jewish subjects. Elementary day schools exist in seven communities but there are few Jewish high schools. There is a Collegio Rabbinico Italiano in Rome and the S. H. Margulies Rabbinical School in Turin, which train rabbis, and there are ORT schools for technical courses. The Unione has special sections for cultural activities.

The general openness of Italian society and the absence of serious anti-Semitism have encouraged intermarriage and assimilation, so that although the communities are nominally strong because of their legal status, they are really weak. The social definition of who is a Jew already relates more to personal identification and activity than to *halakhic* canons. The best of the younger generation are likely to emigrate, most to settle in Israel. In sum, the community is in a holding pattern, able to sustain itself primarily through its organizational structure. That structure will have to change as a result of the disestablishment of the Jewish community in 1987. Inevitably, the changes will make affiliation with the community voluntary. The Italian Jewish leadership lives in fear and trembling of what this will mean to organized Jewish life and Jewish survival in Italy.

Congregational Communities of the Iberian Peninsula

There is a third form of Jewish communal organization in Europe, that of the congregational communities. All are located on the Iberian Peninsula, plus Malta. All were organized in the late modern or early postmodern epoch in countries that at first did not formally recognize Jewish religious bodies, hence they never had official status. Once recognized, they remained voluntary, based on local congregational community centers that either embraced the entire community or served as its confederal building blocks.

The Jewish Community of Spain

The rebirth of the Jewish community in Spain is one of the most romantic developments in diaspora Jewish life in the twentieth century. Although the community remains small and in a sense peripheral, even in European Jewish life, it remains the focus of Jewish attention because of the special attachment of Jews for Spain that continues unabated according to all signs. Ironically, nearly five hundred years after the Expulsion, the Spanish Jewish community is one of the few growing Jewish communities in Europe primarily because of the immigration of Jews from Spanish Morocco after the Spanish abandonment of its protectorate there. Today it has an estimated twelve thousand Jews, organized in local congregational community centers in five cities, principally Madrid and Barcelona. The communal leadership is vigorous by European standards and optimistic about the future of Jewish life in Spain.[12]

Although there were always Marranos in Spain, even after the great expulsion of 1492, Jews resumed living there openly as Jews only in the mid-nineteenth century. The present Spanish Jewish community goes back to the Republican edict of religious tolerance of 1868, but it remained quasi-legal until the post-World War II period and has only gained formal status in the postmodern epoch.

The government's relations with the new Jewish communities that sprang up on Spanish soil in the twentieth century were, for a long time, quite ambivalent. Only after the Catholic Church ceased to be the dominant force in Spanish society that it was for centuries did the government give full rights and recognition to the Jewish communities. There have been repeated Spanish government revocations of the 1492 edict of expulsion, mostly at the instigation of Jewish groups interested in making a public relations point. It was finally removed from the statute books in 1968, long after it had become a dead letter. Full freedom of religion was reaffirmed in a 1967 law and at this writing the Spanish Parliament is in the process of enacting legislation giving the Jewish community a legal status commensurate with that of the Catholic Church.

The present Jewish community developed out of a small cadre of Sephardi Jews who returned to Spain from the Balkans before and during World War I. They concentrated in Barcelona and built a community there. A larger contingent of Ashkenazi Jews who sought refuge in Spain during the Hitler period found their way to Spain. Most of them simply passed through the country but three thousand stayed and built a modest Jewish community in Madrid. An even larger contingent of Moroccan Jews who came in the 1950s and early 1960s took over the community and lead it today. They constitute 70 percent of the Jewish population today. These have been joined by Latin American Jews seeking a Spanish-speaking country that would be more secure than their native lands and English Jews looking to retire in the sun not too far from England.

The congregational community centers offer limited Jewish educational and social services. Madrid and Barcelona have had rabbinical leadership since the communities were organized. Elementary Jewish day schools have been maintained in both. Although their formal structure follows the normal congregational pattern, these are communities that are clearly led by a handful of notables.

The community maintains regular contact with the European Council of Jewish Community Services, the World Jewish Congress, and Israel in the usual ways. Because of its attractiveness as a place, in general and Jewishly, Spain has become the venue for a number of international Jewish meetings. For years the community leadership provided an informal bridge between Israel and Spain and then played a significant role in securing Spanish recognition of Israel. The community's leadership is active in the World Sephardi Federation, and through it has begun to appear on the world Jewish scene.

The Jewish Communities of Gibraltar, Portugal, and Malta

Gibraltar is the oldest Jewish community on the Iberian Peninsula. It was established shortly after the British conquest of the rock in 1704. While originally forbidden to settle there under the terms of the 1713 Anglo-Spanish treaty ceding Gibraltar to the British, by 1729 another treaty with the Sultan of Morocco allowed Moroccan Jews to settle there temporarily for business purposes. This led to the development of a permanent community whose legal rights were recognized in 1740. By then, the six hundred Jews settled there constituted one-third of the total civilian population and had two synagogues.

The Jews soon formed the merchant class in Gibraltar, parallel to the British military class, and the Spanish working class. As a result, Sephardic Jews, principally from North Africa, came to Gibraltar by the hundreds to take advantage of the excellent commercial location of the Rock in those days. Subsequently, when the British granted self-government to their colony, the Jews were in the best position to acquire political power since they represented both the educated elite and the middlemen between the Spanish and British. Gibraltar's first chief minister was Sir Joshua A. Hasson, who has held office intermittently since 1964.

At its peak in the mid-nineteenth century, the Jewish population was two thousand. Today, with the commercial importance of Gibraltar almost nil, it has declined to six hundred. In percentage, it has the largest Jewish population in continental Europe, with the Jews constituting some 2 percent of the local population of the island. They are organized into four congregations and several community organizations.[13]

Portugal and Malta are two remnant communities; Malta with only 50 Jews left is a true remnant.[14] Portugal now has about 450 Jews, down from more than 1,000 a generation ago, and is basically focused on one congregation in Lisbon, which was organized at the beginning of the twentieth century and expanded to include wartime refugees, most of whom have left. Its population is declining. There are other congregations in northern Portugal founded by Marranos who returned to Judaism in the 1920s but who remain isolated from the rest of the Jewish world by choice, so as not to antagonize their neighbors.[15]

Notes

1. For the history of Balkan Jewry, see Daniel J. Elazar, Harriet Pass Friedenreich, Baruch Hazzan, and Adina Weiss Liberles, *The Balkan Jewish Communities: Yugoslavia, Bulgaria, Greece, and Turkey* (Lanham, Md. and Jerusalem: University Press of America and the Center for Jewish Community Studies, 1984); L. S. Staurianos, *The Balkans since 1453* (New York: Holt, Rinehart and Winston, 1958); Robert Lee Wolff, *The Balkans in Our Time* (New York: W. W. Norton and Co., 1967); Daniel J. Elazar and Stuart A. Cohen, *The Jewish Polity: Jewish Political Organization from Biblical Times to the Present* (Bloomington, Ind.: Indiana University Press, 1985); Solomon Kalderon and Juda Levi, *Istorija Jevrejskog Naroda, Od Izgona Jevreja sa Pirinejskog Polvostrva do Najnovijeg Vremena* (History of the Jewish People from the Expulsion of the Jews from the Iberian Peninsula to Modern Times), vol. 2 (Belgrade: SJVO, 1935); Vicki Tamir, *Bulgaria and Her Jews* (New York: Yeshiva University Press, 1979); D. Isidoro De Hoyos Y De La Torre (Marqués De Hoyos), *Los Judíos Espanoles en el Imperio Austriaco y en los Balkanes* (Madrid: Impressor de la Real Academia de la Historia, 1904); "Seridai HaKehillot Yayehudiot Beartzot HaBalkan," (The Remnants of Balkan Jewry) *Tefutsot Yisrael*, vol. 12, no. 2 (March-April 1974) (Hebrew).

2. On the Sabbatean movement and its leader, see Gershom Scholem, *Shabbetai Zevi: The Mystical Messiah* (Princeton, N.J.: Princeton University Press, 1973); "Shabbetai Zevi," *Encyclopedia Judaica*, vol. 14, pp. 1219–53; Mortimer J. Cohen, *Jacob Emden: A Man of Controversy* (Philadelphia, Pa.: Dropsie College, 1937); Aron Freimann, *Inyanei Shabbetai Zvi* (The Controversies over Shabbetai Zvi), (Berlin: Mekize Nirdamim, 1912); Stephen Sharot, *Messianism, Mysticism, and Magic: A Sociological Analysis of Jewish Religious Movements* (Chapel Hill, N.C.: University of North Carolina Press, 1982); Itzhak Ben-Zvi, *The Exiled and the Redeemed* (Philadelphia, Pa.: Jewish Publication Society of America, 1961).

3. Isaac S. Emmanuel, *Histoire des Israélites de Salonique* (Paris: Librarie Lipschotz, 1936); Abraham Galanté, *Histoire des Israélites d'Istanbul*, 2 vols. (Istanbul: Hüsnütabiat, 1941–42); Joseph Nehama, *Histoire des Israélites de Salonique*, 5 vols. (Paris and Salonika: Durlacher and Communauté Israélite de Thessalonique, 1935–1978); Elissa Allerhand, "Jews of Salonika Remembered," *Jewish Times* (September 12, 1980); Adolphe Arditty, "Le Vie Juive à Salonique," *Judaisme Sephardi*, no. 64 (September 1938), p. 114; A. Grohmann, "Histoire de Salonique," *Almanach National*, vol. 3 (1911), pp. 78–81.

4. On the late nineteenth century and interwar period, see Harriet Pass Friedenreich, *The Jews of Yugoslavia: A Quest for Community* (Philadelphia, Pa.: The Jewish Publication Society of America, 1979), pp. 55–68; Wayne S. Vicinich, "Interwar Yugoslavia," *Contemporary Yugoslavia: Twenty Years of Socialist Experiment* (Berkeley, Calif.: University of California Press, 1969); Max Laserson, "The Jewish Minorities in the Baltic Countries," *Jewish Social Studies*, no. 3 (July 1941), pp. 273–84; Raul Hilberg, *The Destruction of the European Jews* (Chicago: Quadrangle Books, 1961), pp. 432–73; Robert Seton-Watson, *Eastern Europe between the Wars 1918–1941*, 1st ed. (Cambridge: Cambridge University Press, 1945); Oscar Janowsky, *The Jews and Minority Rights, 1898–1919* (New York: Columbia University Press, 1966); Ezra Mendelsohn, *The Jews of East Central Europe between the World Wars* (Bloomington, Ind.: Indiana University Press, 1983).

5. For a more comprehensive view of the Balkan Jewish community today, see Elazar et al., *The Balkan Jewish Communities*.

6. See Adina Weiss Liberles on Turkey in Elazar et al., *The Balkan Jewish Communities*, pp. 127–70; Shulma Rozanis, *Korot Hayehudai Beturkiyah* (The Activities of Turkish Jews) (Sofia, Tel Aviv, and Jerusalem: Hamishpat Umossad Harav Kook, 1975); David Ahiod, "Judaismo Sobre las Oriclas del Bósforo," *Voz Sepharadi* (July 1966), pp. 7–10; Alan C. Harris, "Report from Turkey," *The Reconstructionist*, vol. 33 (May 3, 1966), pp. 7–15 and (May 17, 1966), pp. 17–24; Avraham Galanté, ed., *Documents Officiels Turcs Concernant les Juifs de Turquie*, 2 vols. (Istanbul: Haim, Rozie and Co., 1931) and *Histoire des Israélites d'Istanbul* and *Histoire des Juifs d'Anatolie*, 2 vols. (Istanbul: M. Babok, 1937–39).

7. See Adina Weiss Liberles on Greece in Elazar et al., *The Balkan Jewish Communities*, pp. 102–26; Jacob Beller, "On Greek Shores," *Jewish Life*, vol. 34, no. 2 (November–December 1966), pp. 43–50; "The 5,000 Jews in Greece," *Israel Horizons*, vol. 21, no. 5 (May–June 1973), pp. 18, 29; Raphael Patai, *Tents of Jacob: The Diaspora Yesterday and Today* (Englewood Cliffs, N.J.: Prentice-Hall, Inc., 1971), pp. 410–13.

8. See Harriet Pass Friedenreich on Yugoslavia in Elazar et al., *The Balkan Jewish Communities*, pp. 12–58; Friedenreich, *The Jews of Yugoslavia;* Savo Lagomdziya, "The Jews of Sarajevo," *World Jewry*, vol. 9 (November-December 1966), p. 25; Yakir Eventov, *Toldot Yehudai Yugoslavia* (The History of Yugoslavian Jews) (Tel Aviv: Hitahdut Olai Yugoslavia, 1971).

9. Ferdinand A. Gregorovius, *The Ghetto and the Jews of Rome* (New York: Schocken Books, 1948); Harry Leon, *The Jews of Ancient Rome* (Philadelphia, Pa.: Jewish Publication Society of America, 1960); Cecil Roth, *The History of the Jews of Italy* (Philadelphia, Pa.: Jewish Publication Society of America, 1946); Hermann Vegelstein, *History of the Jews in Rome* (Philadelphia, Pa.: Jewish Publication Society of America, 1940); Moses A. Shulvass, *The Jews in the World of the Renaissance* (Leiden: E. J. Brill, 1973); "Italy," *Encyclopedia Judaica*, vol. 9, pp. 1115–32.

10. Roth, *The History of the Jews of Italy;* Hilberg, *The Destruction of the European Jews*, pp. 421–32; Mario Giovano, "New Fascists in Italy," *The Wiener Library Bulletin*, vol. 9 (1955), p. 10; Marcel Grilli, "The Role of the Jews in Modern Italy," *Menorah* (autumn 1939), pp. 260–80 and (winter 1940), pp. 60–81 and (summer 1940) pp. 172–97; Massimo Adolfo Vitale, "The Destruction and Resistance of the Jews in Italy," in Yuri Sahl, ed., *They Fought Back: The Story of Jewish Resistance in Nazi Europe* (New York: Crown Publishers, 1967), pp. 298–303; L. Poliakov, "Mussolini and the Extermination of the Jews," *Jewish Social Studies* (July 1949), pp. 249–58; Meir Michaelis, "The Attitude of the Fascist Regime to the Jews in Italy," *Yad Vashem Studies on the European Catastrophe and Resistance*, vol. 4 (1960), pp. 7–41.

11. Chaim Bermant, "Rome Report: 'He No Like to Interfere'," *Present Tense*, vol. 5, no. 2 (winter 1978), pp. 16–18; David Tamar, *Mehkarim Betoldot Hayehudim Be-Eretz Yisrael Uvaltaliyah* (Studies on the History of the Jews in Israel and Italy) (Jerusalem: Reuven Mass, 1973); Luciano Tass, *Yehudei Italiyah* (The Jews of Italy) (Tel Aviv: Ma'ariv and the World Jewish Congress, 1978); Meir Benayahu, *Relations between Greek and Italian Jewry* (Tel Aviv: The Diaspora Research Institute, 1980); Jacob Lestschinsky, "New Conditions of Life among Jews in the Diaspora," *Jewish Journal of Sociology*, vol. 2, no. 2 (1960), pp. 139–48; Eitan Franco Sabatello, "Youth in Italy," *European Jewry*, vol. 5, no. 1 (winter 1970–71), pp. 27–31 and "The Jewish Community in Italy," *Israel and World Jewry* (1971), pp. 72–83.

12. Lavy M. Becker, "Jews in Spain," *The Reconstructionist* (September 1973), pp. 24–28; Jorge Tallet, "Spain: The Jew Within," *National Jewish Monthly*, vol. 14 (July–August 1973), pp. 10–14; Stephen

Klaidman, "Jewish Renaissance—A Spanish Phenomenon," *The New York Post* (January 16, 1973), p. 71; R. D. Barnett, ed., *The Sephardi Heritage* (New York: Ktav Publishing House, 1971).

13. L. A. Sawchuck and D. A. Herring, *The Sephardim of Gibraltar, 1704 to 1939* (Toronto: University of Toronto, 1984) and Sawchuck, "Reproductive Success among the Sephardic Jews of Gibraltar," *Human Biology,* no. 52 (1980), pp. 731–52; R. A. Preston, "Gibraltar: Colony and Fortress," *Canadian History Review,* vol. 27 (1946), pp. 402–23; A. B. M. Serfaty, *The Jews of Gibraltar under British Rule,* 2d ed. (Gibraltar: Garrison Library Printing Press, 1958); W. Stein, "Gibraltar," *The Universal Jewish Encyclopedia* (1939), vol. 4, pp. 605–6; Meir Persoff, "Rock Solid—Gibraltar's Jewish Community," *Jewish Chronicle* (June 1983); "Gibraltar," *Encyclopedia Judaica,* vol. 7, pp. 555–56.

14. "Malta," *Encyclopedia Judaica,* vol. 11, pp. 831–32; Nahum Sloushez, *B'Eretz Hayam* (In the Land of the Sea) pp. 46–66; Cecil Roth, "The Jews of Malta," cited in *The Menorah Journal* (November 1927); S. Assaf, *BeOhalei Ya'akov* (In the Tents of Jacob) (Jerusalem: Mosad HaRav Kook, 5725/1943).

15. Ignacio Steinhardt, "Portugal's Secret Jews," *Jewish Chronicle* (November 29, 1974), p. 15; Jacob Beller, "Jews in Portugal: Past and Present," *Pioneer Woman* (October-November 1973), pp. 10–12; Barnett, *The Sephardi Heritage;* Charles Arnhold, "The Isolated Jews of Portugal," *Jewish Digest* (September 1969), pp. 77–78; Sidney DuBroff, "Jews in Portugal," *Hadassah Magazine* (October 1970), pp. 18–19.

17

Shadow Communities in the Communist World

The long existence of the Jewish people has meant that communities have been established, prospered, declined, and disappeared many times over. This process continues today, perhaps at an intensified pace because of the accelerated pace of life in our times and the combination of great catastrophe and great blessing that brought the modern epoch to a close. We have already noted aspects of this process in describing the individual communities of Europe and the Caribbean. However, there are communities that have been even more devastatingly affected by the changes. These fall into three categories.

The first category consists of old communities where organized Jewish life has almost disappeared because they are in countries subjugated by regimes that prevent Jews from expressing themselves as a community. At most those regimes make limited compromises with the realities of Jewish existence to allow some kind of shadow framework to function. Most of these communities are in the Soviet bloc or in Arab and other Islamic countries. The second category consists of remnant communities where the mass exodus of Jews because of deteriorating local conditions was so complete that organized Jewish life has come to an end or at most has continued on a nominal basis. Most of those communities are in the Islamic world. The third category consists of communities where voluntary emigration in search of greater economic opportunity has slowly reduced them to scattered handfuls of Jews incapable of maintaining a communal life, even though there are no restraints on them doing so. These are mostly communities in the Caribbean and central Africa.

Some attention must also be paid to temporary and transient communities, principally in the Third World. They are of two kinds: (1) those established by Israelis engaged in projects in Third World countries and are there in sufficient numbers to provide the institutional essentials for maintaining an Israeli way of life and (2) those established by American Jews serving in the United States armed forces in countries with no indigenous Jewish communities who must provide for themselves if they wish any shared Jewish life. In some of the second kind, there has been a "fallout," leaving a Jewish residue after the departure of the American armed forces.

All the foregoing may be defined as shadow communities—there, but not really. There are half again as many countries with shadow communities as there are countries with communities more permanently organized. In the Soviet bloc there are somewhere in the vicinity of two million Jews in such communities. Outside the Soviet bloc their Jewish population does not exceed sixty thousand all told.

The communities in the Communist countries of eastern Europe are both remnant and subjugated communities. Most of their earlier residents either died in the Holocaust or emigrated to Israel; the remainder are subject to all the pressures of life in totalitarian states. The communities of Czechoslovakia, Hungary, and Romania have a formal status like that of their sister communities in other continental European countries; within the severe limits imposed on them, they function through state-recognized communal or religious structures. The communities of Bulgaria and Poland are organized under Communist-imposed structures and barely function at all. In the Soviet Union, Jews are forbidden any organization beyond a handful of synagogues and a few "showcase" institutions.

Whatever organized Jewish life there is exists on sufferance of the authorities, and the authorities intervene in Jewish affairs in every way as a matter of ideology and policy. All these communities except the Soviet Union were subjugated after World War II. Russian Jewry, subjugated since World War I, lost the last remnants of its organized communal life in the Stalin purges in the aftermath of World War II.

Perhaps no country in the history of the exile and dispersion of the Jews has been so hostile to Jewish communal organization as Russia.[1] Russia never welcomed Jews as settlers and only acquired a Jewish population by accident, after conquering the territories to the west and south as the muscovites expanded. Not until the latter part of the eighteenth century, when Russia, Austria, and Germany partitioned Poland did Russia acquire a major concentration of Jews who "came with the territory."

The Russian rulers responded negatively to this development. The Russian government forced almost all Jews to remain in Russian Poland, in what was known as the Pale of Settlement, but denied them the right to organize collectively within it. Although the Russians acted to limit and ultimately destroy Jewish autonomy in the manner of the absolutist states to the west, they were not at all open to the suggestion that the Jews be granted even rudimentary civil rights in their regime, much less the political rights.

The Jews had even less of a chance than they had in Poland, where they had originally been attracted by the positive efforts of medieval Polish rulers who saw them as vital contributors to the commerce and prosperity of the country. For the Russians, they were simply an unwanted and distasteful burden. Hence from the first they interfered with Jewish self-government, trying first to limit the *kahal* (the formal name of the framing institutions of the local Jewish communities) and finally, in the mid-nineteenth century, to abolish it altogether as a legal body.[2] Furthermore, unlike in Poland, where even after the Jews were no longer sought after, they were allowed to organize comprehensively in the Va'ad Arba Aratsot (Council of Four Lands), perhaps the most comprehensive countrywide Jewish polity ever to emerge in the European diaspora, the Russians forbade any countrywide Jewish organization.

It would serve little purpose to recount the abysmal history of the Russian government's relations with its Jewish subjects in the past two hundred years. In that respect the Soviet regime has merely continued the Czarist tradition, only more thoroughly and systematically—this despite its initial proclamation of Jewish equality and rights. The Russian policy now as then was summed up by the Czarist Minister Ignatiev who stated that the solution of the Jewish problem in Russia would be that a third would starve to death, a third would convert, and a third would emigrate. The Soviets have mixed their proportions somewhat differently and conversion for them means assimilation to the Communist state but the thrust is the same.

The constant Russian pressure on and harassment of the Jewish community could only produce negative results among the Jews. Beginning in the first generation of the nineteenth century, German-Jewish *maskilim* began to make their presence felt in Russia and within a generation developed a Russian *haskalah*. Its leaders cooperated with the

Russian authorities in the effort to break down traditional Jewish life, in the mistaken belief that modernization would make the Jews acceptable in the non-Jewish world. The Russian authorities exploited this collaboration for their own ends.

Moreover, the authorities corrupted the *kahal* leaders in various ways, not the least of which by requiring them to choose which Jewish children would be sent to the Russian army as cantonists for twenty-five years—in other words, which children would be turned over to the authorities for conversion to Christianity. Under the pressure applied, the *kahal* leaders protected their own and turned over orphans and children of the Jewish poor, which generated class warfare in the community of a kind rarely experienced in Jewish life anywhere and led to the discrediting of the Jewish leadership in the eyes of the general Jewish population.

As a result, by the end of the second generation of the nineteenth century, the organized Jewish community was discredited in the eyes of its members and disestablished by the regime. What took its place was a cacophony of organizations and institutions, which sprang up spontaneously among the Jewish population. These included great *yeshivot* under the guidance of intellectual giants whose influence continues to this day, Hassidic courts under *rebbes* whose dynasties continue to flourish in our time, and local mutual aid and prayer societies uniting tailors or wagon drivers or whomever in a particular city. Whatever the other achievements of these new bodies, they were no surrogate for a comprehensive organized community. Accordingly, Russian Jewry suffered from an inability to defend itself, which was exactly what the Russian authorities wanted.

In the last generation of the nineteenth century powerful popular movements arose to mobilize the Jewish population throughout the Jewish Pale of Settlement. They attempted to fill that gap by mobilizing the Jewish community around one ideology or another and organizing it for what were almost invariably revolutionary purposes, either against the Russian regime or against the Jewish condition in Russia. In the first category was the Jewish Workers Bund, founded in 1897. It sought to give Jewish expression to the revolutionary ferment in Russia at the time through an ideology, "come the revolution," the Jews would be equal citizens of Russia but entitled to preserve their own culture in the new socialist and democratic Russian polity. Part of the Bundists' struggle was directed against Jewish religious tradition, which they viewed as a negative force, retarding the socialist transformation of the Jewish masses.

Taking a very different position was the Zionist movement, which preceded the bund in the form of Hovevei Zion societies founded in the 1880s. It saw the redemption of Russian Jewry as coming only through mass immigration to Eretz Israel. Zionism also acquired full organizational form in the first Zionist Congress. In response to these two movements and other smaller ones, the Orthodox establishment organized Agudath Israel on the eve of World War I in an effort to provide a counterforce.[3]

Thus the Jews of the Russian Empire came to rely on political movements rather than comprehensive communal institutions for coherence. Because they were fragmented in their ideology and aspirations, no single political movement could supply that need. Instead, as the movements grew stronger, the clashes between them grew more intense, with no mediating institutions to moderate them.

Meanwhile, masses of Russian Jews responded to the intolerable situation in another way, by voting with their feet and emigrating westward. More than a third of Russian Jewry left the country in the last generation of the nineteenth century, to transform the Jewish communities of Western Europe and the New World.

The Jews of the Soviet Union

The coming of the Russian Revolution brought with it a promise of change for the better. The liberal democratic regime that took power in March 1917 immediately granted the Jews full civil and political rights. It also authorized them to organize themselves countrywide so that they could participate as a community in the new Russia. But by the time the first all-Russian Jewish Congress could meet in December 1917, the Bolsheviks had already overthrown the Kerensky government and were no more interested in advancing the interests of the Jewish community than were the Czars, despite their strong propaganda to the contrary. They effectively put a stop to all countrywide Jewish organizational efforts aside from those of the Jewish Communists—what became the notorious Yevtsektzia, or Jewish section of the Communist party.

During the years of the civil war, Jews managed to establish democratic local communal structures because the Bolsheviks were not strong enough to stop them. These communities were almost autonomous because in a situation of anarchy they could provide some measure of order and support for their constituents. They were organized democratically around the movements and parties that had emerged in the last generation of the nineteenth century. They competed with one another in democratic elections for seats on the communal governing bodies.

For a brief moment Russian Jewry showed its mettle and acquired communal institutions and political mechanisms and processes worthy of the Jewish political tradition. The spontaneous emergence of those institutions in so short a time and under such difficult conditions is testimony to the Jewish ability for self-government, which is sometimes overlooked in the midst of the surface chaos that often accompanies Jewish politics. However, the Bolsheviks won the civil war and, as soon as they could consolidate their power, they abolished the Jewish communities or, more accurately, forced them to disband. Many of the communal leaders were either imprisoned or murdered. In a few short years the entire effort was a matter of history.[4]

In place of the communities the Bolsheviks established a few cultural institutions with a clearly Communist orientation that were designed to enable the Jews to reach Communism through their own language and culture. This was the Bolshevik pattern throughout Russia. Lenin reluctantly acquiesced to establishing the Soviet Union as a federal state because he had no other way to deal with the nationality problem so as to hold the major portion of the old Russian Empire intact under Soviet rule. The goal of Soviet federalism became one of pouring Communist wine into separate national bottles.

Had the Jews been recognized as another national grouping perhaps they would have found some way to maintain a modicum of Jewish culture as did other nationalities. The Soviets, however, like their Czarist predecessors, remained ambivalent or hostile to Jewish nationality and did not want to grant Jews full recognition in that respect. Only later, for a brief period in the 1930s when Stalin experimented with Birobidjan as a Jewish national home, primarily to compete with Zionism for the hearts and minds of Jews overseas, did anything approaching Soviet recognition of Jewish national rights ever take place. In the 1920s the Jews occupied some kind of indeterminate position between a national grouping and something else. Some were encouraged to establish all-Jewish agricultural colonies in the Crimea in what became semiautonomous counties in that region; others were allowed to flee the country in a last great tide of emigration; and most were simply encouraged to assimilate as individuals by expanding their opportunities in the new, presumably egalitarian Soviet state.[5]

Sad to say, world Jewry cooperated in implementing the Soviet policy, not wanting to recognize Communism for what it was for various reasons. Because most Russian Zionists were Socialists—in many cases radical Socialists with views not dissimilar to those of the Bolsheviks, except that they wanted to build their socialist commonwealth in Eretz Israel—they did not want to believe the truth even when their own members were being persecuted. This was particularly true of those who constituted the Third Aliya to Eretz Israel between 1919 and 1921, which soon became dominant in shaping the Zionist Yishuv. They were so smitten that the more extreme among them actually returned to Russia in 1927–28 to participate in the building of communism in their native land, after being disillusioned with the possibilities of Eretz Israel. Most of these returnees disappeared in the purges of the 1930s, but a few survived to return to Israel in the 1950s and 1960s and to tell their awful tale.[6]

In the West, American Jews who were not necessarily sympathetic to Communism were misled by their basic liberalism to see the Bolsheviks as progressive, if extreme. Hence they used instrumentalities such as the Joint Distribution Committee to provide millions of dollars for the rehabilitation and resettlement of Russian Jewry, most of which ended in the hands of the regime and all of which could have been used to better advantage in Eretz Israel. The JDC reflected the emancipationist ideology of modern Jewry: once Jews were given civil rights in their native lands, they should be encouraged to stay and become productive citizens rather than to seek a solution to their problems in a Jewish national home. The Communists asserted the equality of all races and nationalities and were particularly opposed to anti-Semitism, so the Jews of the West were taken in.[7]

Whatever minor success the Jewish Communists had in building Communist institutions with Jewish cultural content was wiped out between 1936 and 1953, first by the Stalinist purges of the late 1930s, then by the Holocaust, and finally by Stalin's paranoiac assault on the Jews in the five years before his death. The Soviets did allow a few synagogues to continue to exist throughout the country but took every opportunity to close another one so that the number would constantly decrease. There was a chief rabbi of Moscow who presumably spoke for the remnants of religious Jewry in the country but who was clearly a creature of the Communist state. There were one or two vestiges of the Communist experiment in mobilizing the Yiddish language, the Jewish theater, and Jewish writers for the Soviet cause.[8]

This is not the entire picture, however. Although the vast majority of Jews in the Soviet Union were Ashkenazim who lived in the western reaches of the country, the old Pale of Settlement, or in the major cities to which they migrated after the Revolution, perhaps 20 percent of the Jewish population was indigenous to the Muslim territories that came under Russian rule in the nineteenth century and were successfully retained in the civil war. These Jews, part of the Sephardi world in the broader sense of the term, had been less exposed to modernization in the preceding century. They were still strongly rooted in their traditions and were in an environment known for its toughness, much of which they had absorbed.

In the course of the centuries, Jewish communities had developed in Armenia, Georgia, and the Caucasus. Georgian Jewish tradition has it that the first Jewish communities there had their roots in the Assyrian exile of Jews from the northern kingdom of Israel after 721 B.C.E. Those communities came under Muslim rule in the eighth century. All suffered the usual persecutions and attrition. Then, for approximately six hundred years, from the thirteenth to the nineteenth centuries, they were cut off from the major centers of Jewish life. The Russian conquest brought with it restored contact and new persecution.

In their earlier days, these Jewries came within the jurisdiction of the Babylonian Jewish Exilarch and *yeshivot*. After they were isolated, they had to shift for themselves. With the Russian conquest, they came under Russian Ashkenazic influence. At first forbidden to settle there, after 1860 Ashkenazic entrepreneurs, soldiers, and craftsmen arrived and regular contact even led a few of the local Jews to go to Lithuania to study in the *yeshivot* there so as to serve their communities as rabbis. Zionism easily took root among those Jewries and hundreds settled in Eretz Israel, especially in Jerusalem, beginning in 1863.

The Bolshevik Revolution enabled Georgia, Armenia, and other areas to declare their independence, but they were reconquered by the Soviet army within a few years. The local Jews strongly resisted Communist efforts to de-Judaize them. In general, the Soviets had difficulty imposing their will on the non-Russian mountain peoples, and the Jews benefited from Soviet prudence. By and large, they were able to maintain much of their traditional way of life for two generations after the Revolution.

Moreover, only the Jews in the Crimea and the western Caucasus came under German rule and were deported or massacred in the Holocaust. This meant that most of their institutions survived World War II. During the first postwar generation pressure on them increased and the new generation, already educated in state schools, began to drift away from tradition. Soviet pressure grew as more fissures opened in the traditional societies of the regions. Still, a Jewish institutional network survived.[9] The 1959 Soviet census registered 125,000 Jews in the Caucasus, which included the republics of Armenia, Azerbaijan, and Georgia, and the autonomous provinces of Chechan-Ingush, Dagestan, Kabardino-Balkar, and North Ossetia, approximately half of whom were Ashkenazim. In the 1970s the Jews took advantage of the brief period of the more liberalized Soviet emigration policy to leave for Israel. Nevertheless, organized Jewish communities remain throughout the area.

Further to the east are the Jews of Bukhara, once an independent khanate and now a territory in the Uzbek SSR. They are closely related to the Jews of Persia and Afghanistan, with whom they have maintained connections over the years. The Muslims under whose rule they lived were a particularly fanatic lot and persecutions were relentless, at least from the thirteenth century onward, intensifying in the mid-eighteenth century. Hence, when the Russians began their conquest of Bukhara in the mid-nineteenth century, the situation of the Jews actually improved.

Bukharan Jews had a long cultural and literary tradition, writing in both the Tajiki-Jewish dialect and in Judeo-Persian. Halakhically and culturally, they were brought within the Sephardic orbit after 1793, when the Jewish community of Safed sent Joseph ha-Ma'aravi as an emissary to Bukhara. He established their links with the Sephardim of the Mediterranean world. The Bukharan Jews abandoned the Persian Jewish liturgy and adopted that of the Spaniolim. Thus when they began to settle in Jerusalem, they were easily assimilated among the Sephardim there. Hebrew was introduced as a spoken language by the Russian Ashkenazic Zionists at the end of the nineteenth century and soon became the language of instruction in the more forward-looking Jewish schools. The language was still studied legally as late as 1924.

The first Bukharans settled in modern Eretz Israel in 1868. Beginning with the 1882 mission to Bukhara of Rabbi Jacob Meir, who was sent by the Council of the Sephardic community in Jerusalem, Bukharan Jews were stimulated to settle in Eretz

Israel in significant numbers, especially in Jerusalem, where in 1892 they built the Bukharan Quarter. By 1936, there were twenty-five hundred in the country.

At the time of the Russian Revolution, Bukhara sought independence but was finally conquered by the Red Army in 1920 and was forcibly incorporated into the Soviet Union. Because of its non-Russian character, the Soviets showed the same kind of prudence in enforcing Communist ways as in the Caucasus; hence the local Jews were able to preserve more of their way of life than was possible in Russia proper. Jewish cooperatives even had Hebrew names until they were disbanded in the late 1930s, and a Communist newspaper was published in the local Jewish language. In 1939 there were just under 51,000 Jews in Bukhara, a figure which nearly doubled to 94,000 by 1959 as a result of the wartime in-migration of Ashkenazic Jews from other parts of the USSR. Despite Soviet efforts, Jewish life persists apparently unabated. Synagogues remain open and full on Sabbaths and holy days. Kosher meat continues to be available. Bukharan Jews were not included in the emigration of the 1970s. Hence the community remains more or less undiluted.

In 1939 and 1940 the Soviet Union took advantage of its nonaggression pact with Nazi Germany to annex eastern Poland and the three Baltic republics of Estonia, Latvia, and Lithuania. It also forced Romania to surrender Bessarabia. Because all of these territories had high concentrations of Jewish population, the number of Jews in the Soviet Union increased dramatically. These were Jews who had lived under regimes that, no matter how anti-Semitic, had allowed them to preserve their Jewishness and their Jewish institutions. Thus the Soviets inherited a new generation of committed Jews, many of whom had studied in comprehensive Jewish schools in which Hebrew or Yiddish was the language of instruction and most of whom were strongly committed to Zionism.

The Soviets immediately cracked down on these Jewish institutions and closed them in a matter of months, arresting thousands of Jewish teachers, communal leaders, and activists as part of the removal of the indigenous leadership of those formerly independent states. Less than two years later, the Nazi attack on the Soviet Union brought all of those areas under German control and their Jewish populations were well-nigh exterminated. Nevertheless, a generation later, the Jewish revival in the Soviet Union rested heavily on those who survived and retained the Jewish background that they had acquired in the prewar years when those territories were not under Soviet rule.[10]

The nadir of Jewish life in the Soviet Union came in the first half of the postwar generation, between 1948 and the early 1960s.[11] When the State of Israel was established with Soviet support, many Jews thought that it was safe to display their strong support for the reestablishment of Jewish political independence. This expression reached its climax when the late Golda Meir was welcomed as the first Israeli ambassador to the Soviet Union in 1949, with a public outpouring in the streets of Moscow. This so alarmed the Soviet leadership that there was an immediate crackdown on all Jewish self-expression. Most of the remaining synagogues were closed. The few ornamental Jewish institutions that had survived were liquidated as were most of the Jews involved with them, however much they saw themselves as loyal Communists. For the first time in the history of the Soviet Union the regime began to sponsor anti-Semitic propaganda in the mass media.

During this period, the only organized Jewish life of any meaning was that in the Muslim republics and the underground network of Chabad *hassidim,* which tenaciously held on in the other parts of the Soviet Union. Jewish emigration was strictly forbidden along with all other emigration from the Soviet Union. In the late 1950s and the early 1960s a few Russian Jews managed to get out on the grounds that they or their spouses had been Polish citizens before 1939 and hence were entitled to repatriation to Poland. From there most of them moved on to Israel.

The situation changed dramatically after Israel's victory in the 1967 Six-Day War. The rise in Jewish consciousness and pride, which swept the entire Jewish world, also swept Soviet Jewry. Suddenly there were thousands of Jews who wanted to leave the Soviet Union for Israel and were willing to make their demands known. This in turn produced a strong movement for Soviet Jewry in the diaspora, which ultimately secured Israel's backing and intervention on behalf of those Jews who came to be known as "refusedniks."

In truth, the Israeli government was at first ambivalent about taking an activist role because of the problem of its interest as a state in maintaining relations with the Soviet Union. But the pressure of world Jewry led the Israeli authorities to make the hard choice for involvement. Thus began a campaign to "Let My People Go," which led to the emigration of several hundred thousand Jews during the next fifteen years before the gates were closed again.[12]

Equally important, the campaign led to the revival of an underground Jewish life in the Soviet Union: Hebrew language and Jewish cultural study groups, underground publications, theater groups, and *minyanim* for religious services were established, plus whatever else could be done in small groups meeting in private apartments. These myriad activities were connected by a loose but effective communications network and were supplied with materials and encouragement by world Jewry working through a variety of channels.

All this was in addition to the handful of recognized synagogues in the Soviet Union, which, though under government domination, became focal points for public Jewish gatherings as the only places where public Jewish expression was possible. Thus the Moscow synagogue became a point of contact between local Jews and those from outside the Soviet Union, and the street in front of it became a traditional gathering place for Jews seeking to express their identity in public. Simhat Torah gatherings there became world famous, so much so that the Soviet regime tried its best to crack down on them.

In responding to the Jews' struggle to leave the Soviet Union, the Soviet government has increased discrimination against all Jews and has initiated a quasi-official anti-Semitic campaign. Even Jews who do not seek to leave find their careers blocked because they are Jewish.

The 1979 census showed approximately 1,810,000 registered Jews in the Soviet Union, a precipitous drop over the previous census of 2.3 million, even when the Jewish emigration is taken into consideration. The Soviet census records every Soviet resident's nationality, and Jews are legally required to list Yivrei (Hebrew) as theirs. But, in recent years, the Soviet authorities have been encouraging Jews to pass into one of the Slavic nationalities, partly to reduce the number of Jews reported and partly to strengthen the total Slavic versus the Asiatic population in the Soviet Union. Moreover, many Jews have tried to pass to protect themselves in a society that is increasingly anti-Jewish. Hence the Soviet census figures are inaccurate. The 1985 *American Jewish Year Book,* following the Hebrew University demographers, estimates 1,630,000 Jews, for reasons that are not clear. In a more comprehensive discussion of the subject by Leon Shapiro in the 1982 *American Jewish Year Book,* the conclusion is that a more accurate estimate would be 2,619,000.[13]

In a survey conducted by a group of Soviet Jewish scientists in 1976, it was revealed that even a substantial number of those Russian Jews who did not seek to leave the Soviet Union—in all likelihood most of them—wanted to maintain their Jewish identity in some significant way.[14] The feeling of attachment to the Jewish people among those surveyed was expressed in a number of ways. Fifty-nine percent of the interviewees asserted strong social ties with other Jews. Most of the respondents' friends were Jewish. The desire for Jewish social life is best reflected in the finding that 87 percent of the respondents would patronize Jewish meeting places such as coffeehouses or restaurants were they to exist. Almost two-thirds of the respondents stated that they felt an attachment to Jews in other countries. Very few (7 percent) condemned emigration to Israel while 58 percent perceived emigration to Israel as a means of strengthening bonds with the Jewish people and 35 percent expressed a more instrumental approach, seeing emigration as a means of avoiding discrimination and improving living standards.

More than one-third of the interviewees claimed to know Yiddish, and 10 percent more, Hebrew. Fifteen percent claimed serious knowledge of Jewish history and two-thirds more said they knew Jewish history superficially. The respondents demonstrated a high degree of readiness to increase their Jewish knowledge. Ninety-five percent said that they would purchase a book on Jewish history and 87 percent expressed interest in publication of a Russian language periodical devoted to Jewish subjects. Fifty-four percent said that they wanted to learn Hebrew. Eighty-six percent of the sample would prefer that their children study in Jewish educational institutions were such to exist, with 12 percent expressing a preference for schools in which the language of instruction would be Hebrew. Twenty-six percent of the respondents stated a preference for Yiddish-language schools. Almost all (85 percent) said that they would like their children (or grandchildren) to know one of the "Jewish" languages.

Only 7 percent of those interviewed regarded themselves as religious believers. Fifty-three percent stated that, although they did not believe in the Jewish religion, they nevertheless respected it. Seventeen percent expressed a clear atheistic outlook. As a rule, the older respondents, those with less education and lower incomes, and Jews from central Asia were more likely to be religious. Atheism is more frequent among those from mixed families and among students, but not among Jewish scientists and academicians. Most of the interviewees said that they marked the Jewish festivals in some way. Twenty-one percent said that they would attend synagogue regularly were there no hindrances to their doing so, and an additional 50 percent said that they would go occasionally.

At the same time, 60 percent would have liked to see the item concerning nationality deleted from the internal "passport"—the ubiquitous national identity card in the Soviet Union. Fewer than half of the respondents would have preferred the right to choose their nationality on the "passport." Nevertheless, 56 percent of those surveyed would choose explicitly Jewish names for their sons (or grandsons), although most of those would use Jewish names that are generally acceptable in Soviet society. One-third of the interviewees responded that they would object to intermarriage by someone in their family, 22 percent of the respondents took a neutral position on endogamy, and the rest only preferred Jewish spouses.

Some fifty synagogues continue to function, organized as local congregations, and a small number of Soviet students are being trained for the rabbinate at the Jewish

Theological Seminary in Budapest. There are a number of community *sederim* each year and *matzot* are still baked in Moscow.

Other official "Jewish" activities sponsored by the regime include the Soviet Anti-Zionist Committee, established in April 1985. *Sovietishe Heimland,* the Yiddish language magazine published by the Soviet Union of Writers, while hueing the Communist party line, does offer a limited outlet for publishing research on Jewish issues, consideration of Jewish "national questions," and reviewing Hebrew literature. Between 1948 and 1983, ninety-six books in Yiddish were made available in the Soviet Union and *Sovietishe Heimland* publishes twelve booklets annually. There are five Yiddish theater groups including folk theaters in Vilno and Kovno, the Birobidzhan Yiddish Musical Chamber Theater, and theater ensembles in Birobidzhan and Moscow. The *Birobidzhaner Stern* continued to appear as the only Yiddish paper in the Soviet Union and the region has a Yiddish radio station to serve the ten thousand Jews still living in Birobidzhan.

Far more important are the quasi-legal activities of "free" Jews. It is not surprising that a flourishing informal Jewish life has developed within the Soviet Union on a semi-legal basis. It provides a fertile base for Jewish life in the Soviet Union, but there is no sign that the Soviet authorities are likely to permit the open expression of Jewishness in a serious way. At most they tolerate clandestine activities with periodic crackdowns and foster a minimal remnant of organized Jewish life subservient to the regime, asserting that the Jews do not seek any more.

The Jews of Poland

Officially, only 5,000 Jews remain in Poland today. Unofficial estimates suggest that the number is at least double and may be as high as 12,000. Even if that is so, this pitiful remnant of the community of 3,350,000 in September 1939 is perhaps the starkest reflection of the magnitude of the Holocaust.

During the years of ascendancy of eastern European Jewry, Poland was the linchpin of the Ashkenazi world. The first traces of Polish Jewry were to be found between the middle of the eleventh and the middle of the fourteenth centuries. It was in this period the legal status of medieval Polish Jewry was shaped. The first of the general charters dates to 1264. Although the kings protected the Jews, the church actively opposed them, laying the foundations for what was to become the virulent anti-Semitism for which Poles became notorious.[15]

The first major Jewish migration to Poland took place after the expulsions from western Europe in the wake of the Black Death in the middle of the fourteenth century; the Polish-Jewish community as a full-blown entity really dates from that time. In the following 150 years, more than sixty Jewish communities were founded. It was in the latter half of that period that Polish Jewry developed its greatest contribution to Jewish political life, the Va'ad Arba Aratsot.[16] This great political effort was related to the spread of Jewish settlement into the Ukraine in partnership with the Polish nobility, a minor frontier experience in its own right. The effort provoked a response by the Cossacks, who had roamed the Ukraine freely before the arrival of the Poles and were in effect dispossessed by them. They revolted and, in what came to be known as the Chmielnicki massacres of 1648–49, brought an end to the golden age of Polish Jewry.

The Chmielmnicki revolt was followed by Tartar invasions and wars with Russia and Sweden lasting a generation, during which the Jews were everybody's victims. When peace was restored, the communities reconstituted themselves quickly but never recovered the dynamism of the earlier period. They were constantly burdened by expenses for defense, whether outright bribery or taxation, which was simply legalized bribery. Power passed into the hands of ever-narrowing oligarchies with the lower strata of the population being disenfranchised.

The Council of the Four Lands was abolished in 1764 on the eve of the partition of Poland. At that time there were three-quarters of a million Jews in Poland and Lithuania, perhaps 80 percent living in communities of fewer than five hundred Jews, increasingly located in the eastern regions of the kingdom. Between 1772 and 1795 Poland was partitioned between Austria, Prussia, and Russia. Most of the Jews lived in the sections annexed by Russia and during the nineteenth century suffered from the Russian approach to the Jewish problem. The second largest group became part of the Austro-Hungarian Empire and went through emancipation as it took place in Hungary. The smallest group was absorbed into Prussia and later the German Empire and gradually became Westernized in the German Jewish manner.

Throughout what had been Poland the Jewish population grew tremendously during the nineteenth century. Jews were the first to move to the cities in substantial numbers and became dominant in almost every major aspect of urban life. By 1843 approximately 43 percent of the urban population of Russian Poland was Jewish, and in cities with no restrictions on Jewish settlement the average was more than 57 percent. Jews came to dominate trade, banking, and industry.[17]

The status of Polish Jewry deteriorated under the Russian regime so that by the end of the nineteenth century, even though a small Jewish elite was economically prosperous, most Jews were either impoverished or well on their way to impoverishment. This led to the mass emigration of Polish Jews as part of the great flow of eastern European Jews westward. Unlike the situation in Russia, a substantial segment of Polish Jewry identified with Polish national aspirations, fighting on the side of the Poles in the rebellions against foreign rule that took place in the nineteenth century and participating in the literary and intellectual activities that helped shape modern Polish nationalism.

Organizationally the Polish Jewish community was absorbed into the Russian pattern. The local *kahals*, which had long since become oligarchic, became increasingly so under pressure from the Russians. Moreover, Polish Jews were not particularly public-minded in this period, pursuing their individual agendas. Most of the political organization of Polish Jewry, whether traditional or modern, came from the influx of Lithuanian Jews into the territory of the kingdom. The Litvaks were the pioneers of both Jewish nationalism and Jewish socialism. They founded the Hovevei Zion in Poland and the Jewish Bund. By World War I both were well established in Poland, the bund particularly in the urban areas where there was a Jewish proletariat.

During World War I, Polish Jewry was caught in the middle and suffered from the hostility of all the parties with the possible exception of the Germans. After the war, Poland was reconstituted as a politically independent state in the wake of the dismemberment of the German, Austro-Hungarian, and Russian empires. The final boundaries of Poland were fixed in 1921 after a series of wars between the Poles and Lithuanians, Ukrainians, and Russian Bolsheviks. The Treaty of Versailles guaranteed the Jews and other minorities national rights. The provisions of the treaty were incorporated into the Polish Constitution, which had to provide for the third of the new Polish state that was non-Polish because of the way in which the boundaries were drawn at the Poles' request. The Jews were recognized as a separate nationality, but the Polish government, backed by the Polish two-thirds of the population, never really accepted the separate national identity of the minorities.[18]

The Jews did establish a *kehillah* and their own school systems, but the *kehillah* was subject to state regulation in many ways and only the assimilationist Jewish schools received any state support. Nor were the diplomas issued by Jewish high schools recognized by the Polish Ministry of Education. Elections to the *kehillah* were democratic and representation was proportional, but the government often intervened to support the candidates it favored, particularly Agudath Israel, and tightly controlled the budgets of the individual *kehillot*.[19]

The Polish government made every effort to increase the role of the ethnic Poles in their new state, which meant that they discriminated heavily against Jews, who always were disproportionately represented in all those areas of endeavor that the government wanted to make Polish. Thus Jewish ability to get into secondary schools and universities was limited by a *numerus clausus,* efforts were made to deprive the Litvaks of Polish citizenship, and, in general, the government pursued an economic policy designed to bankrupt the Jewish community. The Poles' electoral system was rigged against minorities so that they could not protect themselves politically.

The government pursued a deliberate policy of encouraging Poles to settle in the cities to reduce Jewish dominance. In 1921 the Jewish population of every major city in Poland was at least a third of the total. Warsaw, the lowest, was 33.1 percent, and in Pinsk three-quarters of the inhabitants were Jewish. Even though these percentages declined during the next twenty years they still remained formidable. Moreover, the Jewish population was consistently underestimated in the official statistics, so that the Jews could be further restricted.

All this led to the further impoverishment of Polish Jewry to the point of desperation. Had the gates of the Western countries not been closed in the 1920s, no doubt many Polish Jews would have emigrated. That proved to be an impossibility and, in a catastrophic error, Polish Jewry did not migrate en masse to Eretz Israel while it was still possible to do so. Although the Fourth Aliya was known in Zionist history as the Polish Aliya and made a tremendous difference in the Jewish population of the Yishuv, it was but a drop in the bucket when looked at from the Polish side.

Jewish politics in the postwar period was dominated by the Zionists, particularly the General Zionists who emerged as the strongest force as early as 1919. Their closest allies were the Mizrahi, who followed the policy established early on by the religious Zionist movement to join in coalition with the dominant Zionist party to protect the special interests of religious Zionism. The Socialist-Zionist movements—Hehalutz, Hehalutz Hatzair, Hashomer Hatzair, and others—directed their attention toward Aliya and not toward capturing control of the *kehillah*. They attacked the General Zionists as being for *sejm sionismus* (election to the Sejm—the Polish parliament) instead of Aliya. Hence they did not figure prominently in local politics.

On the other hand, Agudath Israel figured very prominently. It represented a strong minority which gained control over many if not most the local *kehillot* and was supported by the government because its traditional position opposed the effort to stimulate Jewish nationalism in Poland. On the Left, the bund became the dominant Jewish party. The Socialist Zionist parties had less influence, in part because they divided and redivided many times, presumably because of ideological differences. The bund remained openly anti-Zionist and fought the Zionist parties with no little success.

The economic catastrophe of Polish Jewry strengthened the Left in the 1930s. A number of young Jews became Communists and even more joined the bund, which captured control of a number of the major *kehillot*. Unfortunately no party could do anything to improve the Jewish condition given the policies of the government.

In Zionist circles the General Zionists lost ground to the Zionist Socialists and to the Revisionists, as Polish Jews sought more radical solutions to their problems. In particular, Poland became the stronghold of Revisionist Zionism. By the late 1930s, it was the heartland of Betar, the Revisionist youth movement that was to give birth to Etzel (the Irgun Zvai Leumi) and Lehi (the Stern Group). Each party was a movement that provided its own schools, youth groups, and social welfare institutions. Thus joining a party was more than political identification; it was an affiliation with a subcommunity in which one lived much of one's life and received many vital services normally provided by the state. In activities of this kind the parties were successful, particularly in the educational sphere.[20]

This system was transplanted to Eretz Israel during the interwar generation to lay the foundations for the Jewish state that was to emerge later. In many respects this was a new phenomenon in Jewish life—a transference of governance functions and public activities from common institutions to sectarian ones. But it could be seen as a continuation in new form of the division between *hassidim* and *misnagdim,* which emerged in the late eighteenth century, and even of the division between Sadducees, Pharisees, and Essenes of the last epoch of the Second Commonwealth. In each case, when Jews developed sharply different messianic visions, the end result was the development of separate political camps in the largest sense of the term: as subpolities within the *edah,* each of which sought to be comprehensive in scope so that it would embrace every aspect of the lives of its members or adherents. In a few cases these camps acquired territorial expressions but, in most, because of how the Jewish population divided, with people in the same place choosing different visions, they occupied the same territory and hence had to develop strong aterritorial expressions.

The result was something much akin to what Lijphart and others have defined as consociationalism: federations of nonterritorial camps, each based on its own ideology, separated but united by a common sense of national community.[21] The State of Israel was to embody this consociational arrangement, which developed first in Poland and some of the other Eastern European states in the interwar period.

This is not the place to go into the history of the destruction of Polish Jewry during the Holocaust.[22] The Jews began to suffer from the first moment of the invasion: at first through random killings, sadistic abuse, starvation, and forced removal, then through ghettoization and deportation. The 2 million Jews who came under Nazi rule in 1939 were subject to these pressures immediately; the 1.3 million who came under Soviet rule had nearly two years of relative grace before the Nazi terror caught up with them. The systematic murder of the Jews began in the fall of 1940 with the sick and the old. A year later experiments in mass murder were begun. Full scale deportation to the death camps began shortly thereafter and by the fall of 1943 the ghettos had ceased to exist.

The Jews resisted in different ways, from the moral resistance reflected in their efforts to maintain a civilized Jewish life to the very end, to active military struggle in a few of the ghettos and in the forests as partisans. But the hostile Polish environment increased the normal difficulties of resisting a powerful, determined, systematic force that would stop at nothing to achieve its ends.

As soon as possible, the Germans abolished the established Jewish community organizations and substituted the Judenrate, puppet bodies forced to collaborate with the conquerors. The Jewish community simply went underground, maintaining most of its cultural and political organizations to provide a rich fabric of Jewish life in the ghettos. Furthermore, the prewar Jewish relief organizations, including the local ones and the JDC, continued to function until the deportations. The Nazis were amazed at the Jews' ability to adapt to the terrible conditions of ghettoization, to find ways to share their sustenance so that as few as possible died because of deprivation, at least in the early stages when supplies were available, and even to maintain an active political and cultural existence.[23]

It is true that the different parties and organizations remained contentious until awareness of the final solution was upon them, at which point they banded together in a final effort to resist. But with all their contentiousness, they also formed an organized Jewish life in another manifestation of the curious paradox of the Jewish political tradition—in this case under the most extreme circumstances: the strong cultural penchant for organization and self-government along with the equally strong cultural penchant for division into multiple parties and groups, willing to compete furiously with one another.

All told, 89 percent of Polish Jewry was exterminated. Only 300,000 were known to have escaped, of whom 250,000 fled to the Soviet Union and the rest abroad. No more than 2,000 Jews had saved themselves by posing as Aryans. At the end of the war, some 69,000 Jews returned to Poland; 13,000 were Jewish soldiers in the Polish Communist army.

As Poland was liberated, the Jews began to reorganize. In the summer of 1944 a Jewish committee was formed under the auspices of the Polish Committee of National Liberation to provide assistance to Jewish survivors who reached the liberated territories. In October this body was renamed the Central Committee of the Jews of Poland. It consisted of representatives of the different Jewish parties and was dominated by the Zionists. In a short span of time it turned from simply providing material assistance to social and cultural activities too.[24]

By 1945 the Jewish Committee was organized into ten districts, two subdistricts, and about two hundred local communities. Several dozen Jewish cooperatives were founded and thirty-four Jewish farms were established. A Jewish press reemerged with weeklies and biweeklies reflecting the range of political views in the community. The Halutz movements reestablished *hakhshara* farms for training young Jews to pioneer in Eretz Israel. Schools and youth groups were organized. By July, the JDC returned. ORT returned in 1946 and established a network of vocational schools.

By early 1946 some 80,000 Jews were living in Poland. Another 154,000 arrived that summer from the Soviet Union, bringing the total Jewish population to nearly a quarter of a million. The new Communist regime encouraged the reestablishment of Jewish life and also allowed Jews to emigrate freely if they chose. The Zionist movement had the favor of the regime and was particularly active. Societies for art and culture were founded around the country. The Yiddish theater was reestablished. The Jewish Historical Institute began to collect and publish records of the Holocaust. Jewish religious life was resumed, and by 1947 there were thirty-four Jewish schools in the country. The revived congregations joined together as the Union of Religious Communities, which formally joined the Central Committee of Jews in Poland in 1948. The Central Committee was even able to join the World Jewish Congress in 1948.

By that time, however, the true future of Jewish life in Poland had become clear. A year after the war's end there were again pogroms in Poland. In the year between the first pogrom in Kracow on August 11, 1945, and the last in Kielce on July 4, 1946, several hundred Jews were killed. Most of the remaining Jews concluded that they could no longer live in Poland because, despite the Holocaust, nothing had changed. So, in 1946 a mass exodus of the remaining Jews from Poland began. For six months this exodus was semilegal in character, well organized by the Zionist movement. Most of the Jews who left did so by the end of 1946 but even after that, Jews continued to emigrate. By the end of 1947 only 100,000 Jews remained in Poland.

In November 1949 the Zionist parties and the bund were disbanded by order of the Communist government. The Zionists were permitted to leave for Israel, so some thirty thousand additional Jews did so. For six years then, from the beginning of liberation in 1944 until the doors were effectively closed in 1950, Jews kept streaming out of Poland. It is true that the Polish government tried to restore the Jews' confidence that it would protect their security. But the emergence of Stalinist anti-Semitism in the Soviet Union had its effect on Poland, which was then at the height of its Stalinization. This meant that Jewish cultural institutions were closed and the efforts of the Jews to maintain their religious and national existence were treated as antiregime. The Jews realized that the handwriting was on the wall and most of them responded accordingly by voting with their feet.

JDC and ORT were expelled from Poland in 1950. The Union of Jewish Cooperative Societies was forced to merge with the Polish Union of Cooperatives, and the Central Committee of the Jews in Poland was pressured to leave the World Jewish Congress. The final step was the merging of the Central Committee with the Jewish Society of Art and Culture as the Cultural-Social Association of the Jews in Poland—a more acceptable formulation of Jewish identity in a Communist regime. All the Jewish schools were nationalized after they had been forced to eliminate Yiddish as a language of instruction and all teaching of Hebrew. The Jewish Agency was permitted to continue its work for a short while longer, but contact with it was made very difficult.

By 1950, only thirty organized Jewish communities remained in the country. Still, for the next seven years a modestly flourishing Jewish life continued within the limits of "cultural affairs" and with a Communist orientation. In 1957 there was a turn for the better after the revelation of Stalin's crimes by Khrushchev the year before. The Gomulka government allowed the JDC and ORT to return to Poland to help the twenty-five thousand Jews then being repatriated from the Soviet Union. By and large their assistance was to help those Jews pass through Poland to points west, principally Israel. This in turn stimulated the emigration of many of the Jews who had remained in Poland.

In a sense the history of ten years earlier repeated itself. Despite the willingness of the Polish authorities to be more forthcoming on Jewish issues, popular Polish anti-Semitism flared up again and a number of incidents took place that reawakened old fears. As a result, some fifty thousand Jews left Poland in 1958–59, leaving only about thirty thousand in the country, three thousand of whom were supported outright by the JDC, which also financed most of the Jewish communal activities. One benefit of the 1957 liberalization was the revival of a separate Jewish cooperative movement assisted by the government and the JDC in its first stages. It soon prospered and was able to transfer 20 percent of its yearly profits to the Jewish Cultural-Social Association to support the association's activities.[25]

The Six-Day War in 1967 brought another change for the worse in the situation of Polish Jewry. The Polish government, following the Soviet lead, turned actively anti-Israel, and stimulated popular anti-Semitism to divert the public's attention from antiregime demonstrations started by their own students. Jews were persecuted by the government as "rootless cosmopolitans" and driven out of public office. Because most of those who had remained in the country were the ones who had successfully adjusted to the Communist regime, this destroyed the basis of their existence in Poland. This led to a fourth mass emigration in 1968 and 1969, which brought about the virtual end of organized Jewish life. Some fifteen thousand Jews left Poland, most of whom went to Sweden, Denmark, and other western European countries rather than to Israel, because they were dyed-in-the-wool Communists who had long been anti-Zionists.

During 1968 all remaining Jewish youth camps, schools, and clubs were disbanded and the Cultural-Social Association ceased to be active. Yiddish was declared a foreign language, which meant that there could be no Yiddish publications in Poland. This ended even the Communist-dominated Yiddish publishing house and literary journal. The JDC and ORT were expelled again and the Jewish cooperatives were merged into the general cooperative union. Even the Jewish home for the aged was turned into a general institution.[26] What remained in Poland were a few synagogues barely able to muster a *minyan* of congregants. Officially, no more than seven thousand Jews remained in the country. In the next decade Polish Jewry dwindled to a group of aging pensioners unable to emigrate for one reason or another and merely awaiting their final call.

Then in the early 1980s limited contact with the outside Jewish world was resumed. It turned out that the number of Jews in the country was probably double the official figures, and some of those Jews began to identify themselves at least privately to their fellow Jews from the West.[27] Limited Jewish activity resumed beyond the synagogues. The government began to try to restore Jewish monuments to make a better impression on the West and renewed its contracts with Israel. Nevertheless, with the rise of the Solidarity movement, the regime did not hesitate to revive official anti-Semitism and tried to put the blame for Poland's troubles on the pitiful remnant of Jews left in the country.

The Jewish Community in Czechoslovakia

Although Czechoslovakia as a state dates only to 1918, it includes Bohemia and Moravia, which were great centers of Jewish life in the late Middle Ages. The Jewish *va'adim* (community councils) of Bohemia and Moravia flourished at the time of the Polish Va'ad Arba Aratsot (Council of the Four Lands) and Lithuanian Va'ad Lita to form a bloc of comprehensively organized Jewish communal federations stretching diagonally across central and eastern Europe during the sixteenth and seventeenth centuries.[28]

During almost the entire modern epoch, those territories were within the Austro-Hungarian Empire, and the Jewish community structures adapted to the rule of Austria or Hungary. With the establishment of the Czechoslovak republic, the Jews had to reformulate their community organization accordingly. During the interwar period, there were slightly more than 350,000 Jews in Czechoslovakia, nearly 40 percent in Slovakia. Although most of Czech Jewry followed the patterns of central and western European Jewry, in Carpatho-Russia, also part of Czechoslovakia, 65 percent of the Jews were still living in villages in 1930 and represented the most rural Jewish community left in Europe at the time.[29]

From the first, the Zionists were the initiators of Jewish communal organization in the republic. They saw a ready-made opportunity to "conquer the community" because they faced a tabula rasa and did not have to compete with previous established institutions. Moreover, because under the terms of the peace treaty the Jews could claim a substantial measure of autonomy, the Zionists saw a properly organized community as the basis for Jewish national and cultural expression.

The Jewish National Council was established in October 1918, five days before the proclamation of the republic. Within a month the Jewish community federations of Moravia and Silesia accepted the council's authority. In January 1919 Jewish nationalists held a conference in Prague to discuss ways and means to effectuate their program in the communities, out of which emerged the Zidovska Strana, or Jewish party. The Jewish National Council worked to secure Jewish autonomy and to modernize the Jewish population. As a result, many of the communities reorganized themselves on modern democratic lines, expanding the right to vote to include women and Jews who had settled among them from eastern Europe. Secular Jewish schools were established.

This led to the emergence of a Czech assimilationist movement as a counterforce on the one hand, and an ultra-Orthodox party on the other. Both challenged the Jewish National Council's standing as the sole representative of Czech Jewry. In the ensuing struggle, the council won its basic points and the 1920 constitution of the new Czech state explicitly recognized Jewish nationality and minority rights. Every resident of Czechoslovakia was allowed to choose his or her nationality. In 1921, 54 percent of the Jews by religion also identified as Jews by nationality, a figure that rose to 57 percent in 1930. Some 22 percent identified themselves as of Czechoslovak nationality in 1921, rising to 25 percent in 1930. The rest identified themselves as Germans or Hungarians.

The problem of internal religious differences was settled in the individual provinces of the republic. Thus five regional community federations existed in Bohemia and Moravia when Czechoslovakia gained its independence. In 1926 they organized a common Supreme Council of Jewish Religious Communities. In Slovakia and Carpatho-Russia, the Hungarian pattern of Orthodox, Neolog, and Status Quo communities was perpetuated, with the Orthodox maintaining a common organization embracing both regions. After 1923 the Neolog and Status Quo communities merged, establishing the Yeshurun Federation in 1928. As a result there was no chief rabbinate in those regions.

The Jews organized their own political parties to compete in local and state elections. From the first, the Jewish party managed to gain representation on municipal councils but was not able to elect anyone to parliament until 1929. There was a well-articulated party system, which contested the elections within the Jewish community, covering the full spectrum of political viewpoints in central Europe in the interwar period.

The Czechoslovak republic inherited its share of middle European anti-Semitism, which increased as time passed until it became rampant among certain groups after the rise of Nazism. The German takeover of Czechoslovakia in 1938–39 led to a mass emigration of Jews and several tens of thousands escaped. Still more than 100,000 of the 136,000 Jews of Slovakia were killed by the Nazis. Of the 25,000 who survived the Holocaust, most of them left Slovakia after the war and settled in Israel. Of the 122,000 Jews who found themselves in the protectorate of Bohemia-Moravia after the German takeover, about 27,000 escaped, nearly 76,000 died, 10,000 returned after deportation in 1945, and just under 3,000—mostly partners of mixed marriages—escaped deportation and survived the war. Many of them left shortly after.[30]

In early 1948 when the Communists came to power, 44,000 Jews were known to be living in Czechoslovakia. The combination of the Communist seizure of power in February 1948 and the establishment of the State of Israel in May led to the emigration of some 19,000 Jews to Israel between 1948 and 1950 while another 7,000 emigrated elsewhere. The Communist regime closed the doors in 1950, leaving some 18,000 Jews registered with the Jewish community. Two to three thousand succeeded in leaving after 1965, and 3,400 fled after the Soviet crackdown on the Czech effort on liberalization in August 1968.[31]

The estimated Jewish population at the end of 1968 was twelve thousand, mostly elderly. The 1985 estimate was nine thousand and declining. In 1968 the average age of the Jews affiliated with the Council of Jewish Communities in Bohemia and Moravia was sixty, and no more than one twelfth of the Jewish population was between the ages of fifteen and twenty. The situation has become worse from a demographic point of view and the community is more or less waiting to die out.

The old organizational structure was reestablished after World War II. The Council of Jewish Communities in Bohemia and Moravia held its first conference in 1945 with delegates from forty-three communities participating. The Central Union of the Jewish Communities of Slovakia was established by the end of that year. The two bodies established a joint coordinating committee in 1947. The great emigration after the Communist takeover led to the end of organized Jewish life in many communities so that only sixteen were represented in the 1963 conference of the Council, a number that dropped to seven by 1968. At that time there were ten active communities in Slovakia. The largest communities were Prague, with thirty-five hundred members; Bratislava with two thousand; and Kosice with eighteen hundred. The community organizations were all in the *keter malkhut*.

Given the nature of the regime it is not surprising that there was little religious activity and less than a handful of rabbis. In 1984 there were two *minyanim* functioning in Prague on the Sabbath and holidays. Jewish education was even less a reality because there were almost no children except in a few communities in Bohemia and Moravia. The basic functions of the community were to provide or channel welfare or social services for the aged and infirm. All organizational costs were borne by the state. The JDC provided relief funds in the first years after the war, until stopped by the Communists in 1948. The four Jewish old-age homes were the most visible institutions of the community.

For a few years after the war an effort was made to revive the political life of Czech Jewry, primarily under Zionist auspices; both the Central Union and the Council affiliated with the World Jewish Congress. All this ended by 1950 when the Communist takeover was completed. The first half-generation of Communist rule was the period of greatest crackdown on Czechoslovakian Jewry. Early in the 1950s there were the purges of Jewish leaders in the Communist Party and the trial of Mapam kibbutznik Mordechai Oren on charges of spying for the West. Hard-line Communists took over the institutions of the community and forced them to toe the party line.

Some liberalization came from 1966 onward when a more moderate group took over. The community leadership increased its activities and, in cooperation with the state, developed different public expressions of Czech Jewish history as part of the liberalization taking place at the time. Although the liberalization drive ended with the invasion of Soviet troops in August 1968, the Jewish community maintained its improved situation and continued to sponsor lectures and seminars for the few young people who remained. In the 1960s the Jewish community was allowed to resume its ties with the World Jewish Congress and the European Council of Jewish Community Services, even strengthening them in the 1970s. Still, the community has no future under present circumstances.

Jews of the German Democratic Republic

The perhaps one thousand Jews in East Germany are truly a remnant. Formally, they are free to maintain a religious life and there are Jewish congregations as well as a central committee. But, like every other Communist regime, the authorities want to repress Jewish identity as much as possible. Moreover, the advanced age of most of the population makes the matter academic. Nevertheless, more than forty years after the end of World War II, the small community somehow hangs on.[32]

There are eight organized Jewish communities in the German Democratic Republic with a total of fewer than 600 registered Jews: 200 in East Berlin, approximately 70 in Dresden, 50 in Leipzig, and even fewer in Halle, Karlmarxstadt, Magdeburg, Mecklenburg/Schwerin, and Erfurt. The state provides the Jewish community with financial aid including funds for the maintenance of more than 100 Jewish cemeteries and for the restoration of synagogues or the construction of three new ones. The eight communities are organized into the Verband der Judischen Gemeinden DDR (Federation of the Jewish Communities in the German Democratic Republic). Contact with the Jewish world is maintained through informal visits and occasional East German Jewish representation in European Jewish forums.

Notes

1. For the history of Russian Jewry, see S. M. Dubnow, *A History of the Jews in Russia and Poland from the Earliest Times until the Present Day*, 3 vols., trans. from the Russian by I. Friedlaender (Philadelphia: Jewish Publication Society of America, 1916, 1918, and 1920); Louis Greenberg, *The Jews in Russia*, 2 vols. (New Haven: Yale University Press, 1951); Max L. Margolis and Alexander Marx, *A History of the Jewish People* (New York: Atheneum, 1977), chaps. 70, 74, 82, 90; Israel Friedlaender, *The Jews of Russia and Poland: A Bird's Eye View of Their History and Culture* (New York and London: G. P. Putnam's Sons, 1915).

2. For a history of Russian Jewry in the nineteenth century, see I. Levitats, *The Jewish Community in Russia, 1772–1844* (New York: Octagon Press, 1970); J. Frumkin et al., eds., *Russian Jewry 1860–1917*, trans. Mirra Ginsburg (New York: Thomas Yoseloff, 1966); Salo W. Baron, *The Russian Jews under the Tzars and Soviets* (New York: Macmillan Company, 1964); Dubnow, *History of the Jews in Russia and Poland*; Michael Stanislawski, *Tsar Nicolas I and the Jews: The Transformation of Jewish Society in Russia, 1825–1855* (Philadelphia: Jewish Publication Society of America, 1983).

3. On Jewish popular movements in Russia, see Ezra Mendelson, *Class Struggle in the Pale: The Formative Years of the Jewish Workers Movement in Tsarist Russia* (Cambridge, England: University Press, 1970); Henry J. Tobias, *The Jewish Bund in Russia from Its Origins to 1905* (Stanford, Calif.: Stanford University Press, 1972).

4. Gregor Aronson, Jacob Frumkin, Alexis Goldenweiser, and Joseph Lewitan, *Russian Jewry, 1917–1967*, trans. Joel Carmichael (New York: Thomas Yoseloff, 1969); Lionel Kochan, *The Jews in Soviet Russia since 1917* (London: Oxford University Press, 1972).

5. Solomon Schwarz, *The Jews in the Soviet Union* (Syracuse, N.Y.: Syracuse University Press, 1951); "Russia," in *Encyclopedia Judaica*, vol. 14, pp. 459–72; B. West, ed., *Struggles of a Generation: The Jews under Soviet Rule* (Tel Aviv: Massada Publishing Co., 1959); Aronson et al., *Russian Jewry, 1917–1967*; Kochan, *The Jews in Soviet Russia since 1917.*

6. Baron, *The Russian Jews;* Lester Samuel Eckman, *Soviet Policy towards Jews and Israel 1917–1974* (New York: Shengold Publishers, Inc., 1974); Aronson et al., *Russian Jewry, 1917–1967,* chap. 20; David Prital, ed., *In Search of Self: The Soviet Jewish Intelligentsia and the Exodus* (Jerusalem: Mount Scopus Publications, 1982).

7. Yehuda Bauer, *My Brother's Keeper* (Philadelphia: Jewish Publication Society of America, 1974); Jack Diamond, "Jewish Overseas Relief Organizations: Report of a Survey," *Jewish Frontier,* vol. 12 (July 1945), pp. 14–21; Arieh Tartakower and Kurt R. Grossman, *The Jewish Refugee* (New York: Institute of Jewish Affairs of the American Jewish Congress and World Jewish Congress, 1944); Herbert Agar, *The Saving Remnant: An Account of Jewish Survival* (New York: Viking Press, 1960).

8. Yehoshua Gilboa, *The Black Years of Soviet Jewry 1939–1953,* trans. from the Hebrew by Yosef Shachter and Dov Ben-Abba (Boston: Little, Brown and Company, 1971); Joel Cang, *The Silent Millions—A History of the Jews in the Soviet Union* (New York: Taplinger Publishing Company, 1971); Schwarz, *The Jews in the Soviet Union.*

9. *The Jewish Communities of the USSR,* an unpublished report prepared as part of the Study of Jewish Community Organization under the auspices of the Center for Jewish Community Studies (1973); Yitzhak Ben Zvi, *The Exiled and the Redeemed,* trans. I. A. Abbady (Jerusalem: Yad Yitzhak Ben Zvi, 1976).

10. Benjamin Fain and Mervin F. Verbit, *Jewishness in the Soviet Union* (Jerusalem: Jerusalem Center for Public Affairs and Association for Jewish Self-Education/Tarbuth Foundation, 1984); Paul Panish, *Exit Visa: The Emigration of the Soviet Jews* (New York: Coward, McCann and Geoghegan, 1981).

11. Elie Weisel, *The Jews of Silence,* trans. from the Hebrew by Neal Kozodoy (New York: Holt, Rinehart and Winston, 1966); Joseph B. Schechtman, *Star in Eclipse: Russian Jewry Revised* (New York: Thomas Yoseloff, 1961); Boris Smolar, *Soviet Jewry Today and Tomorrow* (New York: Macmillan Company, 1971); William Korey, *The Soviet Cage: Anti-Semitism in Russia* (New York: The Viking Press, 1973).

12. Martin Gilbert, *The Jews of Hope* (New York: Viking/Penguin, 1984); Richard Cohen, *Let My People Go* (New York: Popular Library, 1971); Louis Rosenblum, ed., *The White Book of Exodus* (January–June 1972) (Cleveland: Union of Councils for Soviet Jews, 1973); Robert O. Freedman, ed., *Soviet Jewry in the Decisive Decade, 1971–80* (Durham, N.C.: Duke University Press, 1984); "HaNosherim-HaYehudim Me Brit-HaMoatzot HaPonim Oref le-Yisrael," (The "Noshrim"—Jewish Emigrés from the USSR Avoiding Israel), issue of *Tefutsot Yisrael,* vol. 16, no 2 (April-June 1978).

13. *The Jewish Communities of the USSR,* unpublished report prepared as part of the Study of Jewish Community Organization under the auspices of the Center for Jewish Community Studies (1974); U. O. Schmelz, *World Jewish Population: Regional Estimates and Projections,* Jewish Population Studies Series (Jerusalem: Hebrew University of Jerusalem, 1981); Lukasz Hirszowitz, *The Soviet Census (1979): New Data on the Jewish Minority, Research Report,* no. 5 (London: Institute of Jewish Affairs in association with the World Jewish Congress, April 1980); Leon Shapiro, "Soviet Union," *American Jewish Year Book,* vol. 82 (1982), p. 233.

14. See Fain and Verbit, *Jewishness in the Soviet Union* and Benjamin Fain, Dan Caspi, and Mervin F. Verbit, "Jewishness in the Soviet Union: A Preliminary Report of the First Independent Empirical Study," *Jerusalem Letter,* no. 37 (January 5, 1981).

15. For the history of Polish Jewry, see Bernard D. Weinryb, *The Jews of Poland: A Social and Economic History of the Jewish Community in Poland from 1100 to 1800* (Philadelphia: Jewish Publication Society of America, 1972); Dubnow, *A History of the Jews in Russia and Poland;* Raphael Mahler, *Toledot haYehudim be-Polin* (History of the Jews of Poland) (Tel Aviv: Merhavia Publishers, 1946) (Hebrew).

16. On the Va'ad Arba Aratsot, see "Council of Four Lands," in *Encyclopedia Judaica,* vol. 5, p. 993; "Council of the Lands," *Encyclopedia Judaica,* vol. 5, pp. 994–1003; S. Dubnow, *Pinkas ha-Medinah* (The State Official Minute Book) (Jerusalem: Sifriat Kehillot Yisrael, 1925) (Hebrew).

17. On Jewish life in Poland in the nineteenth century, see "Poland," in *Encyclopedia Judaica,* vol. 13, pp. 732–38; Dubnow, *History of the Jews in Russia and Poland;* I. Halpern, ed., *Beit Yisrael be-Polin* (The House of Israel in Poland) (Jerusalem: Youth Affairs Department of the World Zionist Organization, 1948) (Hebrew).

18. On the minority rights system, see "Minority Rights," in *Encyclopedia Judaica,* vol. 12, p. 47; Oscar Janowsky, *Jews and Minority Rights (1898–1919)* (New York: Columbia University Press, 1933); Jacob Robinson et al., *Were the Minority Treaties a Failure?* (New York: Institute of Jewish Affairs, 1943).

19. On Polish Jewry in the interwar period, see William Glicksman, *Kehillah in Poland during the Inter-War Years: Studies in Jewish Community Organization,* trans. Max Rosenfeld (Philadelphia: M. E. Kalish Folkshul, 1970); Raphael Mahler, *Yehudei Polin bein Shtei Milhamot Olam* (Polish Jewry between Two World Wars) (Tel Aviv: Dvir, 1968) (Hebrew); Jacob Lestchinsky, "Economic Aspects of Jewish Community Organization in Independent Poland," *Jewish Social Studies,* vol. 9 (October 1947), pp. 319–38; Joseph Marcus, *Social and Political History of the Jews in Poland, 1919–1939* (Berlin: Mouton Publishers, 1983); Harry M. Rabinowicz, *The Legacy of Polish Jewry: A History of Polish Jews in the Interwar Period 1919–1939* (New York: Thomas Yoseloff, 1965).

20. Marcus, *Social and Political History,* chap. 16; Rabinowicz, *The Legacy of Polish Jewry;* Myer S. Lew, *The Jews of Poland* (London: E. Goldston, 1944); Ezra Mendelsohn, "The Dilemma of Jewish Politics in

Poland: Four Responses," in B. Vargo and G. L. Masse, eds., *Jews and Non-Jews in Eastern Europe 1918–1945* (New York: Halsted Press, 1974).

21. On consociationalism, see Arend Lijphart, *The Politics of Accommodation: Pluralism and Democracy in the Netherlands,* 2d ed. (Berkeley and Los Angeles: University of California Press, 1975), and Gerhard Lehmbruch, "A Non-Competitive Pattern of Conflict Management in Liberal Democracies: The Case of Switzerland, Austria, and Lebanon," paper presented at the Seventh World Congress, International Political Science Association, Brussels, September 1967.

22. For the history of the Holocaust in Poland, see G. Rietlinger, *The Final Solution: The Attempt to Exterminate the Jews of Europe, 1939–1945,* 2d ed., rev. (London: Valentine, Mitchell, 1968); R. Hilberg, *The Destruction of European Jews* (Chicago: Quadrangle Books, 1961); Louis Falstein, ed., *The Martyrdom of Jewish Physicians in Poland* (New York: Medical Alliance–Association of Jewish Physicians from Poland, 1963); Jacob Apenszlak, ed., *Black Book of Polish Jewry: An Account of the Martyrdom of Polish under the Nazi Occupation* (New York: American Federation for Polish Jews, 1943); and "Poland," in *Encyclopedia Judaica,* vol. 13, pp. 752–76.

23. On Jewish self-government under the Nazis, see Lucjan Dobroszycki, ed., *The Chronicle of the Lodz Ghetto 1941–1944,* trans. Richard Lourie et al. (New Haven, Conn.: Yale University Press, 1984); Yisrael Gutman, *The Jews of Warsaw 1939–1943,* trans. from the Hebrew by Ina Friedman (Bloomington, Ind.: Indiana University Press, 1982); J. Tenenbaum, *Underground: The Story of a People* (New York: Philosophical Library, 1952); Isaiah Trunk, *Judenrat: The Jewish Councils in Eastern Europe under Nazi Occupation* (New York: Macmillan, 1972).

24. On Jewish recovery immediately after the war, see "Poland," in *Encyclopedia Judaica,* vol. 13, pp. 777–83; Yisrael Gutman, *HaYehudim be-Polin Akharei Milhemet Olam Ha-Shniyah* (The Jews in Poland after the Second World War) (Jerusalem: Zalman Shazar Center, 1985) (Hebrew).

25. On postwar Polish Jewish life, see Paul Lendvai, *Anti-Semitism without Jews: Communist Eastern Europe* (Garden City, N.Y.: Doubleday, 1971), pp. 89–240; Josef Banas, *The Scapegoats: The Exodus of the Remnants of Polish Jewry,* trans. Tadeusz Szafar and ed. Lionel Kochan (London: Weidenfeld and Nicolson, 1979); Gershon David Hundert and Gershon Chaim Bacon, *The Jews in Poland and Russia* (Bloomington, Ind.: Indiana University Press, 1984); Peter Meyer et al., *The Jews in the Soviet Satellites* (Westport, Conn.: Greenwood Press, 1971), pp. 207–369.

26. Lendvai, *Anti-Semitism without Jews;* "Poland," in *Encyclopedia Judaica,* vol. 13, pp. 787–83.

27. Field interviews by the author with Jewish travelers who had visited Poland.

28. For the history of the Jews in Bohemia and Moravia, see "Bohemia," in *Encyclopedia Judaica,* vol. 4, pp. 1173–81; Guido Kisch, "Jewish Historiography in Bohemia, Moravia, Silesia," in *The Jews of Czechoslovakia, vol. 1* (Philadelphia and New York: Jewish Publication Society of America and Society for the History of Czechoslovak Jews, 1968); "Moravia," in *Encyclopedia Judaica,* vol. 12, pp. 295–305; Moses Moskowitz, "The Jewish Situation in the Protectorate of Bohemia-Moravia," *Jewish Social Studies,* vol. 4, no. 1 (January 1942), pp. 17–44.

29. On Czechoslovakian Jewry during the interwar years, see *The Jews of Czechoslovakia,* vols. 1–3 (Philadelphia and New York: Jewish Publication Society of America and Society for the History of Czechoslovak Jews, 1968, 1971, and 1984).

30. On the Holocaust in Czechoslovakia, see "Czechoslovakia," in *Encyclopedia Judaica,* vol. 5, pp. 1193–99; F. Steiner, *The Tragedy of Slovak Jews* (1949); Livia Roth Kirchen, *Hurban Yahadut Slovakia* (The Destruction of Slovakian Jewry) (Jerusalem: Yad Vashem, 1961) (Hebrew); "Vatican Policy and the 'Jewish Problem' in 'Independent' Slovakia (1939–1945)," in *Yad Vashem Studies,* no. 6 (1967), pp. 17–53; "Czech Attitudes towards the Jews during the Nazi Regime," *Yad Vashem Studies,* no. 13 (1979), pp. 287–320; *The Jews of Czechoslovakia,* vol. 3, secs. 1 and 2.

31. On the postwar situation, see *The Jews of Czechoslovakia,* vol. 3, sec. 3; Institute of Jewish Affairs, *European Jewry Ten Years after the War,* pp. 82–108; "Czechoslovakia," in *Encyclopedia Judaica,* vol. 5, pp. 1199–1204; Pearl Miller, "Prague's Pride and Prejudice," *The Jerusalem Post Magazine* (June 3, 1983); Erich Kulka, "The Second Murder of Czech Jewry," *The Jerusalem Post Magazine* (May 3, 1974); Meyer et al., *The Jews in the Soviet Satellites;* Heda Kovaly and Erazim Kohak, *The Victors and the Vanquished* (New York: Horizon, 1973).

32. Mark Wood, "Fight for Survival," *Jerusalem Post* (November 14, 1980); Friedo Sachser, "German Democratic Republic," in *American Jewish Year Book 1984,* vol. 84, pp. 210–11, and *American Jewish Year Book 1985,* vol. 85, pp. 240–41.

18

Surviving Communities in the Communist World

The Jewish Community in Hungary

The situation in Hungary stands in stark contrast to the Soviet Union. The seventy thousand Jews remaining after the Holocaust have managed to maintain an active organized Jewish life and in recent years have gained some favorable attention from the regime. The Hungarian Jewish community maintains a full range of synagogues, both Orthodox and Neolog (the Hungarian version of Conservative Judaism); social welfare institutions, mostly for the aged, financed in great part by the Joint Distribution Committee; and a rabbinical seminary, which serves the entire Communist bloc, training rabbis and *hazanim* for those remnant communities.[1]

The first known records of a Jewish community in Hungary go back to the latter part of the eleventh century, at the beginning of the epoch in Jewish history that witnessed the flowering of the medieval Jewish community in Ashkenaz.[2] Apparently the Jews integrated very well because we have records of regular enactments and decrees prohibiting the Jews from mixing in the non-Jewish society or occupying high positions in it. This period of Jewish history ended with the 1349 expulsion in the wake of the Black Death, at the end of the epoch.

Within half a generation, however, the Jews were back in Hungary, but during this epoch in Jewish history, their situation in the areas under Christian rule was very difficult, improving only at the end of the epoch when the Reformation had its effect on segments of Hungarian Christianity. In the meantime a good part of the country was occupied by the Ottomans in the sixteenth century. There the situation of the Jews was considerably eased. As the Turks retreated, many of the Jews left with them.

The Hungarian Jewry of the modern epoch was essentially a new Jewry rather than a continuation of the medieval community, as was true in much of Central Europe. It was the product of a steady migration of Jews from Eastern Europe beginning in the eighteenth century. The Jewish population rose from 11,600 in 1735 to 910,000 in 1910. At first these new Jewish settlers operated under great restrictions as to place of residence and right to marry. They were completely prohibited from acquiring real property. First discussions of the emancipation of the Jews did not begin until the 1830s. Most of the worst restrictions were abolished in 1859 and 1860 and the bill on Jewish emancipation was passed by the Hungarian Parliament in 1867.

With the elimination of all formal restrictions on Jewish participation in Hungarian society, the Jews took a great leap forward in almost every sphere. They gravitated in particular toward the center of the communications network, as Jews do: to the liberal professions, journalism, and the cultural life of the country; marketing of agricultural

409

produce, banking, and the financing of heavy industry. By World War I between 55 and 60 percent of the merchants in Hungary were Jews as were 13 percent of the owners of large and medium-size estates. Twenty-six percent of those who earned their living from literature and the arts were Jews, as were an astounding 42 percent of the journalists, 45 percent of the lawyers, and 49 percent of the doctors. Only in government service was the number of Jews minimal.[3]

In 1895 Judaism was officially recognized by the state and accorded equal rights with Catholicism and Protestantism. Parallel to this leap forward was the emergence of the new anti-Semitism during the last generation of the nineteenth century. Its advocates entered the political arena and even formed a faction of seventeen members in the Hungarian Parliament in 1884. This movement continued into the twentieth century.

Modern Hungarian Jewry was built around three subcultural divisions: those in the northwestern part of the country who were part of the German-speaking world; those in the northeast, who were Galicians; and those in the center, part of the Hungarian cultural heartland. Most Jews identified themselves as members of the Hungarian nation and identified with the Magyars in their struggle against the national minorities, especially because Jewish nationality was not officially recognized.

In religion, the Jews divided into Orthodox, Neolog, and assimilated groups. The modern ultra-Orthodox camp, which has now spread worldwide, emerged in Hungary under the leadership of Moses Sofer, the famous Hatam Sofer of Pressburg who set down the canons of contemporary Orthodoxy at the beginning of the nineteenth century. Two wings of Hungarian Orthodoxy were formed in that century that continue to influence Jewish life throughout the world. The Hatam Sofer and his heirs dominated one wing, and in northeastern Hungary a strong and unique Hassidic movement of the most extreme character developed. Later in that same generation the Neolog movement emerged under the influence of the Haskalah and Reform.

With emancipation, the government convened a general Jewish congress in 1868 whose task it was to establish the basis for an autonomous Jewish community organization under the new conditions. The 220 delegates to the congress included 126 Neologs and 94 Orthodox. The congress broke apart when the Orthodox walked out in response to the majority's refusal to accept the Shulhan Arukh as the basis for the communal constitution. The congress continued in session with the remaining delegates and developed a federated communal structure that shifted the locus of power from the *keter torah* to the *keter malkhut*. The new body consisted of local communities federated into regional unions, which were further federated into a countrywide body whose principal responsibility was to manage relations with the Hungarian government.

This proposed structure required the establishment of a single Jewish community in each locality. But when the Hungarian Parliament accepted the plan in 1870, it made membership in the community optional and provided for those who wished to form separate communities. That decision enabled the Orthodox to go their own way and also allowed some communities to maintain their status as it had been before the new plan was inaugurated. These became known as the status quo communities. By and large they were those that did not want to choose between Neolog and Orthodox trends.

The impact of Hungarian Orthodoxy became worldwide in the twentieth century. Both the Neturei Karta, which developed out of the Kolel Ungarn (Hungarian community) in Jerusalem, who were disciples of the Hatam Sofer, and the Satmar Hassidim had their origins in Hungary. Hence it is no exaggeration to say that the principal opposition to the State of Israel in contemporary Jewry consists of Hungarian Jews or their descendants. In a sense this is ironic because the Hatam Sofer was one of the pioneers in the reestablishment of an active Jewish community in Eretz Israel, encouraging his disciples to settle there, where they became leaders of the Ashkenazi old Yishuv. Although their descendants rejected Zionism, they continued to be concerned with Eretz Israel in the traditional way.[4]

The brief golden age of Hungarian Jewry ended in the wake of World War I. The Communist regime, which took power in Hungary in 1919 after the defeat of the Austro-Hungarian Empire, included a number of Jews, and the counterrevolution that destroyed it was distinctly anti-Semitic. The right wing regime that came to power as a result of the counterrevolution made anti-Semitism government policy, introducing the famous *numerus clausus* in 1920, limiting the number of Jews in postsecondary schools to 5 percent.[5]

Although the *numerus clausus* was relaxed at the end of the 1920s, the effort to separate the Jews from other Hungarians continued. Even such positive actions as granting the Jews the same right of representation in the upper house of the Hungarian Parliament as the other religious communities was part of that process. The Zionist movement was also suspended, although it was allowed to resume its work in 1927.

For about a decade after that, the situation of the Jews improved. Then Hungary began to accept Nazi racial doctrines as its regime was drawn more closely into alliance with the Nazis. Beginning in 1938, "Jewish laws" were passed increasingly restricting Jewish access to the larger society and segregating them as Jews. The communal structure, which had continued after World War I, responded by developing new social service programs to aid those impoverished because of the legislation. Although some Jews at first tried to escape the decree by leaving Judaism (there were as many as five thousand conversions to Christianity after the enactment of the first Jewish law in 1938), there was also a cultural and political revival among Jews, which strengthened the Zionist movement and Jewish religious and cultural life.

The dismemberment of Hungary after World War I and its reduction to the Magyar counties alone halved the number of Jews in the country (473,000 according to the 1920 census). This number further declined in the interwar generation as a result of a very low birthrate, some emigration, and conversions. More than half of the Jews lived in greater Budapest. Sixty-five percent of the Jewish population were affiliated with the Neolog communities, 29 percent with the Orthodox communities, and 5 percent remained in status quo communities. Most of the great Orthodox centers, which had given Hungarian Orthodoxy its power, passed into the hands of Romania, Poland, and Czechoslovakia.

At the beginning of World War II, Hungary reacquired some of this territory as a result of being part of the Axis alliance, so that its Jewish population increased to nearly three-quarters of a million. There were also nearly sixty thousand Christian descendants of Jews identified as racially Jewish under the Nuremberg Laws. As with other countries allied with the Axis, the alliance delayed the destruction of the Jewish communities, but in Hungary the delay was not sufficient to prevent the final solution from being implemented in the end.[6]

The persecutions and massacres began in the territories annexed by Hungary in the summer of 1941. But not until the German occupation of Hungary in March 1944 was Hungarian Jewry exposed to the full fury of the Nazi onslaught. As of that moment only 8 percent of the 850,000 Nuremberg Law Jews had succumbed to Nazi persecution. The changes were felt immediately. On March 20, the day after the German takeover, and even before a new pro-Nazi government was formed, the Jewish community organizations were abolished and a new Jewish Council was set up as the Germans' puppet organization.

This is not the place to go through the history of the Holocaust in Hungary. The destruction of the Jewish community took place within eight months. Mass deportations started in mid-May 1944. By mid-January 1945 the Soviet armies had liberated Budapest, and all Hungary in its post-World War I borders was freed of Nazi rule by early April. By that time, 565,000 Jews had perished. Of the 260,000 who survived, a high proportion were really Christians who had been labeled Jews under the Nuremberg Laws.

In the immediate aftermath of the war, many of the survivors went back to their original places of residence and 266 of the 473 prewar communities were reestablished, only to be abandoned in the following years as the Jews left the provincial areas for Israel, other countries, or Budapest. This emigration was in no small measure because of pogroms that took place in the spring and summer of 1946. The new government repealed all discriminatory legislation, although it did not make any attempt to compensate the Jews for their lost property.

The countrywide institutions of the Jewish community were reestablished, and in December 1948 an agreement was negotiated between the government and the Jewish community that restored official recognition like that given other religious groups. This not only assured the community freedom of religious practice but also gave them state financial support. This agreement was kept in force by the Communist regime, which consolidated its hold on Hungary in 1949, and was renewed in 1968.[7]

One change introduced by the Communists in 1950 was the unification of the Neolog, Orthodox, and status quo communities into a single community organization. Even under the Communist regime the Orthodox community strenuously resisted the unification and as a result was given substantial autonomy within the community. The new organization reflected the division among the three *ketarim* by establishing the National Representation of Hungarian Israelites as the representative of the *keter malkhut* and separate Neolog and Orthodox rabbinical committees to handle the religious affairs of the *keter torah* and *keter kehunah*. The chairman of each committee was recognized as the chief rabbi of his community (figure 18.1).

Immediately after the war the Zionists became dominant in the community, replacing the old Jewish aristocracy, which had been destroyed. The Zionist movement made a great effort to strengthen Jewish education by establishing a network of schools in which Hebrew was the language of instruction, youth groups, camps, and the like. Zionist activities were forbidden under the Communist regime and the Zionist organization was abolished in 1949, its leaders arrested and sentenced to prison.

Although the Communist regime was prepared to recognize Jewish religious rights, it was actively involved in repressing Jewish national identity and the movements that fostered it. Along with the Zionist movement, the Jewish educational institutions were among the first casualties, being absorbed by the state school system as quickly as possible. In addition, Jewish contacts with the rest of the Jewish world were strongly curtailed. The JDC, which had provided $50 million in aid to the Hungarian Jewish community from 1946 to 1952, was expelled in 1953. In addition, Jews suffered from the general economic downturn, a shift to nationalization of the means of production, and Communist oppression in the same way as the general population. Perhaps twenty thousand Jews took advantage of the 1956 uprising to escape the country. This left a

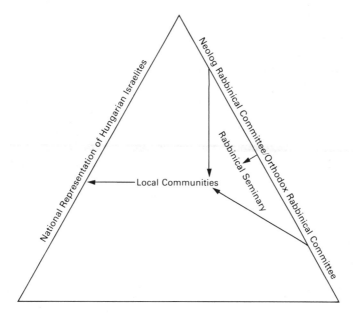

Figure 18.1. The organizational structure of the Hungarian Jewish community.

Jewish community of perhaps eighty thousand, a figure that has declined slightly in the intervening three decades.

At the end of the 1950s, the Hungarian Communist regime inaugurated a period of liberalization from which the Jews benefited like all Hungarians. Although the regime still tried to wean young Jews from their Jewishness, by the 1960s the representatives of the Hungarian Jewish community could again take part in meetings of the World Jewish Congress and the European Council of Jewish Community Services, and could host Jews from other countries. The Memorial Foundation for Jewish Culture was allowed to provide support for the rabbinical seminary and other Jewish cultural and academic institutions in the country.[8]

On the other hand, the survival of organizational forums masks severe assimilation among Hungary's Jews. Besides the pressures of contemporary life affecting Jews everywhere, there are also the problems of living under a Communist regime, whereby career advancement depends on greater conformity to the Communist model, and opportunities for Jewish education and self-expression are limited. Few Jewish boys are circumcised for fear of arousing the antagonism of the authorities. Intermarriage is rife and conversion almost nonexistent for the same reason. Very little remains in the way of Jewish observance among most Hungarian Jews, and it is becoming harder to tell who is a Jew and who is not, from a *halachic* point of view, although, as in every other community, certain sociological norms have been developed to do so. A small kernel of observing Jews remains, but they hardly constitute a handful of Hungarian Jewry.[9]

At this time, some three-quarters of Hungarian Jewry live in Budapest, which has twenty synagogues, including at least one that is properly Orthodox, a network of educational and social services including the rabbinical seminary, and a Jewish high school. There is a Jewish museum and research center devoted to publishing material on Jewish life in Hungary. The rabbinical seminary is the centerpiece of the community, highly touted by the authorities as the sign of the liberalism of the regime.

The Jewish communities of Hungary and Romania remain the freest and most fully articulated in the Communist bloc. As the Jews of Romania emigrate, the more stable Hungarian Jewish community has become the center of Jewish life for eastern Europe, a role that has expanded since the beginning of the 1980s. For example, the rabbinical seminary trains rabbis for other Communist bloc countries, including the Soviet Union. Hungary, then, is the one community in the bloc that is not a remnant community and may have some kind of future.

The Romanian Jewish Community

A strongly Communist regime, Romania has been tolerant in its attitude towards its Jewish community, allowing it substantially free expression as a religious group within the limits of a Communist society dedicated to fostering atheism. Because, like Bulgaria, it sees itself as a homogeneous state, it has discouraged Jewish national expression but has allowed its Jews to emigrate (frequently for a price) to Israel to remove a potentially unassimilable group from its midst. Hence in forty years the number of Jews has declined from nearly 400,000 to fewer than 18,000. Still, organized Jewish communities have continued to function in cities and towns throughout Romania, officially recognized as such, and the community has been able to maintain connections with the rest of world Jewry. All told, however, it is clear that Romanian Jewry is about to become another remnant community.[10]

Although there are traces of Jewish life in Romania from Roman times through the Middle Ages, permanent Jewish settlement there began in the sixteenth century with the arrival of Sephardi merchants from the Ottoman Empire. They first settled in the territories that had come under Ottoman rule and then moved beyond the empire to settle in Walachia and Moldavia, the two Romanian principalities of the time. At least four permanent Jewish communities were established in Moldavia. The Sephardi Jewish community was augmented by Ashkenazim fleeing from Poland and the Ukraine in the wake of the Chmielnicki massacres in 1648–49. Moldavian authorities made an effort to attract Jews in the eighteenth century by offering them special charters, including tax exemptions and plots of land for Jewish institutions. Jews were even given the right to be represented on local councils in Moldavia.[11]

Though the authorities encouraged Jewish settlement, anti-Semitism developed. The principal exponents of anti-Jewish feeling were Greek and Bulgarian merchants and the dominant Orthodox church. In the nineteenth century, with the decline of the Ottoman Empire and the growing influence of Russia and Greece in the Balkans, Romania became increasingly anti-Jewish as it became increasingly independent. From the beginning of the nineteenth century (1819–56), Russia occupied or otherwise dominated the newly independent Romania and introduced extensive anti-Jewish legislation. All earlier privileges were revoked. Between 1856 and 1878 the Romanian provinces were semi-independent under nominal Ottoman suzerainty, at which time their anti-Semitic policies intensified.

At the Congress of Berlin, which led to the granting of independence to Romania in 1878, Jewish civil rights were made a condition of independence by the Western Great

Powers, one which the Romanian government managed not to fulfill. Influenced by Russia and the church, Jews were subjected to the most debasing harassment, so much so that the Great Powers withheld recognition of Romanian independence until effectively bribed by the Romanian government through the redemption of railway shares at six times their quoted value to look the other way. As a result the Romanian Jews were the first to begin the mass emigration from eastern Europe westward, in 1878, in an effort to escape from an intolerable situation.

Until the beginning of the eighteenth century, Jewish communal organization remained local. Then in 1719 the Ottoman authorities appointed a Haham Bashi (chief rabbi), making the position hereditary with a fixed income based on the right of taxation. The Ashkenazim, who by that time began to outnumber the Sephardim, did not recognize the Haham Bashi any more than they had to, and turned instead to their rabbinical authorities. This division became sharper after the rise of Hassidism in the mid-eighteenth century, when many Ashkenazim joined the Hassidic movement and followed their respective *tzaddikim*. In 1819 they succeeded in being exempted from the Haham Bashi's authority, which was confined to "native" Jews: those who were Ottoman subjects, meaning principally the Sephardim. Fifteen years later the institution was abolished.

Along with the office of the Haham Bashi, a Jewish millet (an autonomous ethnoreligious community) was constituted, one of thirty-two based on nationality. It was empowered to collect taxes and its leaders constituted the organized Jewish community. The seat of the millet was in Iasi, and the Sephardic influence was clear in that the head of the guild was known in Hebrew as Rosh Medinah (head of state), in Spanish as Señor, and in Romanian as Starostay. From the Jewish perspective, the Rosh Medinah was the principal officer of the *keter malkhut,* and the Hahum Bashi the principal officer of the *keter torah.* From the Ottoman perspective, the Haham Bashi was at the top of the pyramid and the Starostay was his representative.

The abolition of the office of Haham Bashi in 1834 was accompanied by the abolition of the Jewish millet. The government took over the imposition and collection of the collective tax and communal functions were devolved to the local communities. Not until 1872 was a countrywide Jewish representative body again formed. At that time Benjamin Franklin Peixotto, the American consul in Romania, sent there at the insistence of the American Jewish community to try to improve the conditions of Romanian Jewry, stimulated the organization of the Brotherhood of Zion, which later became the B'nai B'rith, part of the international movement. This lodge, under Peixotto's influence, became the source of a new leadership cadre for Romanian Jewry. This followed the pattern in the Ottoman Empire of using the B'nai B'rith as a club for notables through which they created a vehicle for governance and decision making in a situation in which no formal institutions of Jewish governance would be tolerated by the ruling authorities.[12]

Despite his efforts, Peixotto was convinced that the only solution for Romanian Jewry was mass emigration. Although he convened a conference of world Jewish organizations to deal with the question of Romanian Jewry in Brussels in 1872, he was unable to convince them, with their strong assimilationist tendencies, to advocate such a course of action. Instead they resolved to work for Jewish rights in Romania, a pattern that was to persist until World War II. Shortly after that the Romanian Jews decided otherwise and began to leave the country, especially as their population grew. From 30,000 Jewish taxpayers in 1803 the number had reached 130,000 by midcentury and some 267,000 in 1899. Some 70,000 Jews left Romania in the late nineteenth century, before World War I.[13]

Jews were expelled from the public schools in 1893 and had to create their own modern school system. Jewish community organization emerged around the schools and the welfare activities required by constant expulsions and confiscations, which impoverished most of the Jewish population. These communities were not recognized by law. In an effort to achieve legal recognition, countrywide congresses of communities were held in 1896, 1902, and 1905. They could not work out a mutually acceptable countrywide structure because they were divided between those who wanted to organize principally along religious lines and those who wanted to organize principally as a vehicle for social welfare and education. Jewish assimilationists, who had organized as the General Association of Native Israelites in 1890, and anti-Semites opposed any kind of legal status for the Jewish communities on the grounds that it would prevent Jewish assimilation into Romanian society. Only later when the Zionists gained control of the community was there a concerted effort to achieve Jewish national autonomy.

Romania benefited greatly from World War I, shedding the last remaining traces of Ottoman influence and annexing territories Romanians considered historically theirs in Bukovina, Bessarabia, and Transylvania. Principally as a result of the intervention of the Jewish delegation, the Versailles Peace Conference renewed Western pressure on Romania to grant citizenship to its Jews. The Romanians resisted for four years before formally succumbing in 1923; even then they kept many Jews from acquiring political rights and limited the political rights of those who were granted citizenship. In practice, if not by law, Jews could not enter the civil service or the judiciary, acquire university appointments, or become officers in the army. In short, Romanian Jews were never fully emancipated during the modern epoch. The Romanian Jewish community was given representation in parliament as a minority group under the provisions of the Versailles Treaty providing for minority rights in eastern Europe.

Widespread virulent anti-Semitism continued in the interwar generation, often leading to violence against the Jews. The rise of an indigenous Romanian Fascist movement only added fuel to the fire. More important, from the late nineteenth century onward even the major Romanian parties were anti-Semitic. Where Jews had been able to advance they were expelled and by the end of the 1930s were almost entirely segregated from Romanian life.[14]

It is not surprising then that most of the Jewish population sought national autonomy within Romania, rejecting assimilationism. The Zionists took the lead and the Union of Romanian Jews joined them in this effort after 1919. They submitted Jewish candidates to parliament in 1920. Not until 1926, however, were the Jews first able to elect national Jewish deputies and senators, all from Bessarabia, Bukovina, and Transylvania. Until 1933 the Jewish party was able to send four or five deputies; after 1933 only the chief rabbi, officially a senator, was allowed.

Meanwhile, the Romanian government refused legal recognition of the Jewish community, which left the door open for competing interests to claim leadership of the community and to set up rival communal institutions throughout the country. Finally in 1921 a congress of Jews from the Old Kingdom, Bukovina, Bessarabia, and Transylvania elected a chief rabbi whom they at least recognized. A year later they requested that separate Ashkenazi and Sephardi communities be recognized by the state. The 1923 Romanian Constitution provided for recognition but it took five years (1928) before the parliament enacted the Law of Religions, which recognized Judaism as one of the country's eight historical religions and the Jewish community as a juridical personality in public law. The regulations promulgated by the Minister of Religions in January 1929 to enforce the new law created a period of confusion. Local Romanian officials thought they were empowered to dissolve existing communal boards and appoint new ones. Not until 1932 were matters resolved, and the local communities acquired the juridical status due them. The compromise that emerged recognized Ashkenazi, Sephardi, and, where applicable, separate Orthodox communities.

Meanwhile, in 1925 the Jewish schools finally gained recognition and their students did not have to pass separate state examinations to be granted recognized diplomas. The Jewish community maintained all Jewish schools with only a token subvention from the state.

By this time there were more than three-quarters of a million Jews in Romania, reaching nearly 800,000 in 1924 and dropping slowly after that. Because Romania comprised several provinces, each with its own history and traditions, it is not surprising that the Jewish community adopted a federal structure based on these provincial differences in the framework of the Federation of Jewish Communities of Romania. Bessarabia, which was a center of Jewish culture, became the leading cultural force in the federation, which also included organizations from the provinces of Transylvania, Bukovina, and the Old Kingdom. It should be clearly noted that Romania itself was a highly centralized unitary state, striving for ever greater hierarchical control, especially as the Fascists moved into power.

Romania was seduced into the German camp through sophisticated bribery of its already corrupt political leaders and in September 1940 came under Fascist rule. Under German pressure, it transferred Bessarabia and the northern 60 percent of Bukovina to the Soviet Union and the better part of Transylvania to Hungary and southern Dobruja to Bulgaria. This meant that more than half the Jewish population was severed from the Romanian state. The remaining Jews lost their Romanian citizenship. The Iron Guard, the Romanian equivalent of the Nazi party, tried to stage a coup and failed. In the process, many Jews were killed.

The Romanians joined the Germans in the attack on the Soviet Union in June 1941 and during the next two months assisted in the murder of half of the 320,000 Jews living in Bessarabia, Bukovina, and the border areas of Moldavia. By and large, Romania confined its murderous activities to Jews outside the limits of the Old Kingdom and refused to deport "its" Jews to the camps. After December 1942 the Romanian government was even willing to allow its Jews to emigrate to Palestine. Had the British been willing, tens if not hundreds of thousands of Romanian Jews could have reached Eretz Israel in those years. As it is, the government connived with the Jewish Agency to send some thirteen thousand "illegal" immigrants by ship between 1939 and 1944.[15]

The Union of Jewish Communities of Romania continued to function during the war under one framework or another and consistently intervened to try to save Jewish lives and ameliorate the Jewish condition. It prevented many deportations and even obtained the release of rabbis, communal leaders, and Jewish teachers who had been interned after June 1941 in Romanian concentration camps. Economic pressure and social segregation continued unabated.

At the end of 1941, the union was officially dissolved by the government and replaced by the Central Board of the Jews with new, puppet leadership. The Jewish community responded by forming a Jewish Council whose president was the chief rabbi, Alexander Safran. This body continued to represent the Jews before the government, which did not trust its own instrument. This led within six months to the reintroduction of the real communal leaders into the Central Board, which was thus neutralized, although most of the communal foreign relations work continued to be conducted by the Jewish Council. The council actually succeeded in convincing the Romanian government to repatriate some of the Jews who had been deported to adjacent countries during 1942–43.

The Germans forced the Romanians to formally dissolve the Zionist organization in the summer of 1942 to prevent further emigration of Jews, but this made little difference. The Zionist organization continued to function in a clandestine way. The Joint Distribution Committee continued to work in Romania, at first secretly and then as an autonomous committee of assistance, receiving financing from the Jewish Agency and other world Jewish bodies. In short, Romanian Jewish activity continued in the domains of all three *ketarim* and in all five spheres of communal activity throughout the war.

By early 1944, when it was apparent that the Germans were losing and that the Red Army would shortly overrun Romania, the government's policy became even more conciliatory. By the end of August most of Romania had been conquered by the Soviets. Because of the government's policy, 57 percent of the Jewish population of interwar Romania survived the Holocaust; of those who did not survive, almost all were slaughtered during the first period of the war, during the conquest of Bessarabia and Bukovina. Thus there were more than 340,000 Jews left in Romania at the war's end.

The postwar period, which began in Romania on August 23, 1944, with the fall and arrest of the wartime government, went through four stages. The first lasted until the abolition of the monarchy on December 30, 1947. It was followed by a transition stage as the Communists gradually consolidated their position. From then until 1965 Romania essentially followed the lead of the Soviet Union, although never as extremely with regard to Jewish corporate existence. From 1965 to the present, Romania has pursued an increasingly independent line. Through all this time the organized Jewish community of Romania continued to function in a way that far surpassed that of any other community behind the Iron Curtain.[16]

In 1947 a World Jewish Congress–sponsored registration counted 428,312 Jews in the country. The next year, the Jewish community of Romania began its true decline through emigration. Since then nearly 300,000 Romanian Jews have settled in Israel and about 100,000 have settled in other countries. This emigration was conducted in an orderly manner through the institutions of the community that fostered and facilitated it.

In the transition period immediately after the war, Jewish organizational life functioned openly. The Zionist movement, for example, had 100,000 members in 1948. It participated in the World Zionist Congress in Basel in 1946 and in subsequent world meetings through 1948. After that it was forced to suspend its ties with the outside world and was completely liquidated in March 1949. Romanian Jewry's formal connections with the outside world were severed at that time with the expulsion of the World Jewish Congress and the JDC, although both came back almost immediately through the back door.

In 1945 the Communist party had set up a rival body, the Jewish Democratic Committee, which the party tried to develop into an instrumentality for control of the Jewish community, an effort that failed. It was shelved in the spring of 1949 and officially disbanded in March 1953 when Romania closed down the organizations of all national minorities. From that time on, the Jewish community was left to function through its religious institutions as an officially tolerated religion rather than a nationality.

In 1948 regulations were issued governing the activities of Judaism as a recognized religion and in 1949 the Jews gained equality before the law by being included in the legislation on nationalities. The Jewish communities organized as the Federation of Communities of the Mosaic Religion, whose constitution was approved by the Romanian government on June 1, 1949, under the terms of those regulations. Perhaps ironically, the Romanian penchant for fostering national homogeneity made it easier for the Jews to maintain their separateness because they were no longer bothered by a competing Jewish Communist organization but were able to maintain their *kehillot* as religious communities. Formally, the federation's activities were limited to the religious-congregational sphere and the *keter kehunah* (figure 18.2). The chairman of the federation was the chief rabbi who was also a member of the Romanian National Assembly, ex officio.

Informally, the educational-cultural sphere was allowed to maintain some activities, although Jewish education suffered greatly under the Communist regime. In the years immediately after the war Jewish schools were reestablished; a complete network existed from *hederim* to *yeshivot,* including vocational and academic institutions. In 1948 the Communist regime nationalized all the schools. The government allowed a few schools to continue, with Yiddish as their language of instruction, until 1960. After 1948 such Jewish education as existed was in the hands of private Jewish teachers; their activities were generally tolerated by the authorities. As the Jewish population emigrated and the remaining population consisted increasingly of aging Jews, the number of Jewish schools continued to decrease.

The Romanian government was somewhat more forthcoming with regard to some forms of Jewish cultural expression. Although it closed the extensive network of cultural and literary institutions developed immediately after the war, particularly under Zionist auspices, it did allow a biweekly newspaper in Romania, Yiddish, and Hebrew from 1956 onward, choirs, and a Jewish state theater.

The Federation of Communities of the Mosaic Religion also maintained an active

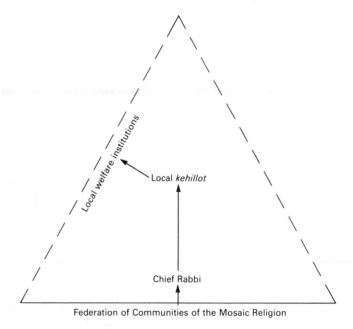

Figure 18.2. The organizational structure of the Romanian Jewish community.

communal-welfare sphere, mostly social welfare programs and institutions, supported by the JDC. The external relations–defense sphere, though having no formally separate organizational structure, was the special domain of the chief rabbi, Moses Rosen, who acquired a worldwide reputation for his ability to advance Jewish interests in his country vis-à-vis the Romanian government. He also personally dominated the Israel-overseas sphere, maintaining connections between the Jewish community and the Jewish state. He negotiated all arrangements with the world Jewish organizations functioning in Romania, or with which Romanian Jewry was allowed to affiliate, including, after the liberalization of the late 1960s, the World Jewish Congress and the European Council of Jewish Community Services.

All told, Romanian Jewry kept itself intact to conduct an orderly self-liquidation. Its future demise as a fully articulated community is well-nigh certain as its population continues to decrease. But as long as there are Jews in Romania, organized Jewish life is likely to continue.

The Jewish Community in Bulgaria

Bulgaria is a textbook example of a Communist regime. Totalitarian to the core, its drive for internal homogeneity is reinforced by a clearly dominant national majority. No strong non-Bulgar minority exists, and Jewish community life is further hampered by the intensely antireligious aspects of Bulgarian communism. On the other hand, the Bulgarians have proved to be relatively tolerant toward "their" Jews. Significantly, the community survives as an organized entity because the authorities feel the need to use an ostensibly Jewish voice to denigrate Israel in the eyes of the surviving Jews.[17]

As in other lands of eastern Europe, Jewish settlement in what is today Bulgaria antedated that of the people who were to become dominant, in this case, the Bulgars. There are records of a Jewish settlement in the first century of the common era and apparently Jews have lived continuously in what is now Bulgaria since then. The Bulgars did not reach the area until the fifth century. As a people, the Bulgars were influenced by Judaism several times during their history. There may even have been a struggle between Jews and Christians over the conversion of what was then a pagan tribe to one of the monotheistic religions; Judaizing practices were part of early Bulgar Christianity. Jewish influence recurred periodically at least until the twelfth century.

After the Bulgars established their state in the sixth century, the country became something of a haven for Jews persecuted elsewhere. In the eighth and ninth centuries Jews fled to Bulgaria from the Byzantine Empire. In the thirteenth century Bulgaria had a small influx of Jews from central Europe fleeing the Crusaders. Hungarian Jews came in the fourteenth century after the expulsion of 1376, and in the fifteenth century Jews came from France and Moldavia after expulsions in those countries.

The biggest influx was that of the Sephardim from the Iberian Peninsula after 1492. They became dominant in the community in the sixteenth century and gained full control over it in 1640 when the Romaniot and Ashkenazic communities, which had maintained themselves as separate legal entities, merged into a single entity dominated by the Sephardim. Thus at the threshold of the modern epoch, Bulgaria became a center of Sephardic Jewish life and culture. This period coincided with Ottoman imperial domination of the country, and the Jews benefited from being part of the empire. In the course of the epoch the Romaniot Jews assimilated entirely among the Sephardim. A small Ashkenazic subcommunity retained its separate identity.[18]

The struggle between the Turks and the Bulgars resulted in a Turkish victory in 1636. Bulgaria became part of the growing Ottoman Empire. This opened the door to even greater opportunity for the Jews. The upshot was that the Jews were much more involved in the life of the general society in Bulgaria than was usual north of the Mediterranean littoral, and Bulgaria was a link between the Sephardic Jews of the Ottoman Empire and their Ashkenazic brethren of Eastern Europe.

Bulgaria gained autonomy and then independence in the nineteenth century. The Turks withdrew from the capital, Sofia, in 1878. Although the Jews in some towns were expelled as supporters of the Turks, by and large they joined with the Bulgarians in welcoming independence. The chief rabbi of Sofia, Gabriel Almosnino, participated in the Bulgarian Constituent Assembly of 1879, ex officio as chief rabbi and representative of the Jews and was one of the signers of the constitution that emerged. In 1880 the Jewish communities were reorganized under Bulgarian law. Although Jews continued to participate in Bulgarian society, anti-Semitism became a staple ingredient of Bulgarian politics, probably as an extreme expression of the revival of Bulgarian national consciousness. Jews were excluded from the key institutions of the new state. This was so despite pressure by the Western powers to guarantee minority rights. The Bulgarians adopted the principles but found ways to make them inoperative in practice.

The office of chief rabbinate was established in 1878. In 1900 a conference of Jewish communities met and adopted a new constitution, which followed the consistorial pattern. There were elected school and synagogue committees in each community, which chose a central council of Bulgarian Jewry independent of the chief rabbi. The chief rabbi was head of the central *bet din,* and there were also rabbinical courts in the three major cities.

The Bulgarian Jewish community was the first to be captured by the Zionist movement. The first Zionist groups appeared in the 1880s as a Sephardic extension of the Hovevei Zion and three Bulgarian delegates participated in the First Zionist Congress in 1897. In 1895, even before the congress, Bulgarian Jews attempted to establish a settlement, Hartuv, in Eretz Israel. The Bulgarian Jewish community was the first to hail Herzl, and the Zionists became the principal power in the community in the early days of the movement.

The Treaty of Neuilly after World War I reaffirmed the principle of equal rights, but the national uprising in 1923 nullified any possibility of implementing its clauses. Instead, anti-Semitism intensified. In the interwar period the Jewish population grew absolutely, reaching 48,565 in the 1934 census but declined relative to the country's total population. By the mid-1930s more than half of Bulgaria's Jews lived in Sofia. Still, many Jews emigrated elsewhere, including Eretz Israel.

The Bulgarian regime became Fascist in the 1930s and allied itself with Nazi Germany in World War II. Consequently, the Bulgarian government introduced comprehensive anti-Jewish legislation in 1941, which began to be implemented in a threatening manner the following year. A program of deportation was begun in the summer of 1942 to remove the Jews from the territories seized by Bulgaria from neighboring countries as a result of its alliance with the Germans.

Early in 1943 the Bulgarian government agreed to turn over the Jews of Bulgaria proper for deportation. But however anti-Semitic the Bulgarian people were, this was too much. Combining humanitarian and political considerations (the Germans had already suffered their debacle at Stalingrad), a protest movement developed, led by the vice president of the Bulgarian Parliament. The movement was joined by other politicians and leaders of the Bulgarian Orthodox Church. They succeeded in stopping the deportations outside the border areas.

Still, the anti-Jewish legislation was rigidly enforced and young Jews were rounded up for work battalions. Preparations were made by the government to resume the deportations, but internal upheavals prevented any policy decisions from being made from the summer of 1943 until the late spring of 1944. At that point the Allies were clearly winning the war, and a new Bulgarian government wanted to extricate Bulgaria from its alliance with the Germans. At the end of the summer of 1944 all anti-Jewish legislation was abolished. Shortly thereafter the Soviet Union invaded Bulgaria, easily overran it, and installed a Communist regime. Organized Jewish life had been officially abolished with the anti-Jewish measures, although it continued in a quasi-legal fashion. After the Soviet occupation, the central Jewish consistory was reestablished as were Jewish communities in thirty-four localities. In 1945 there were 49,172 Jews in Bulgaria according to consistory figures. Thus, the Bulgarian Jewish community survived the Holocaust almost intact, protected by the Bulgarian government, which used its position as one of the Axis states to prevent the Nazis from deporting Bulgarian Jews to the death camps.[19]

Although the Communists emphasized the equal rights of the Jews in a way that was unprecedented in modern Bulgaria, it also tried from the first to control organized Jewish life and ultimately to abolish it as part of the totalitarian takeover of Bulgarian society. Thus the Jews, still reeling from the war, were confronted with a new danger. The organizations of the Jewish community were taken over by Communists and their sympathizers in the Jewish community. Already in January 1945 the Jewish leadership severed Bulgarian Jewry's connections with all world Jewish institutions. The Zionist organization came under pressure and its members were continually harassed. In May 1946 the governance of the central consistory passed into the hands of a coalition of Communists and Zionists, but really under control of the pro-Communist forces.[20]

Consequently, when the State of Israel was declared in 1948, Bulgarian Jewry became the only European Jewish community to emigrate there en masse. Although the Jewish Communists fought the Zionists in Bulgaria, they actively supported those in Eretz Israel in the struggle for the establishment of the state. They were following the Soviet policy of the time, which conveniently coincided with their own Jewish concerns. Thus between September 1944 and October 1948, seven thousand Bulgarian Jews were assisted in getting to Eretz Israel, legally or illegally, although illegal emigration was defined as a crime by Bulgarian authorities until the state was declared. The Zionist emigration suited the purposes of the Bulgarian regime, eager to get rid of all its minorities, hence it was assisted by the government.

About five thousand Jews, or 10 percent of the prewar Jewish community, remained in Bulgaria. For a few years those five thousand maintained a comprehensive organizational framework, even under the Communist regime. The authorities, however, progressively whittled down the scope of the community's activities and finally abolished it as an entity, substituting the "Educational and Cultural Public Organization of Jews of the People's Republic of Bulgaria," which was designed to spread Communist ideology among the Jews. These changes were introduced through the convening of a national conference of the "people's Jewish communities" to make formal decisions to cut back Jewish life. The Sixth National Conference of the Bulgarian Jewish Communities in 1957, after the Sinai campaign, completed the transformation of the old consistory and

Its Rights during the Second World War," in Shaul Esh, ed., *Yad Vashem Studies,* no. 4 (Jerusalem: Yad Vashem, 1960), pp. 261–315; Ira A. Hirschmann, *Caution to the Winds* (New York: McCay, 1962); Josif Toma Popescu, "La Roumanie sauvée de l'Holocauste," *Monde Juif,* no. 105 (1982), pp. 1–11.

16. On postwar Romanian Jewry, see Vago, "Post-War Rumanian Jewry"; World Jewish Congress, *Yahadut Romanyah ba-Tekufah she-le-Ahar ha-Milhamah* and "Rumania" in *Encyclopedia Judaica,* vol. 14, pp. 410–16; and Esther Oren, *Rumanian Jewry 1945–1970,* unpublished report prepared as part of the Study of Jewish Community Organization under the auspices of the Center for Jewish Community Studies (1974).

17. See Baruch Hazzan, *The Jewish Community of Bulgaria* (Jerusalem: Center for Jewish Community Studies, 1974).

18. Vicki Tamir, *Bulgaria and Her Jews: The History of a Dubious Symbiosis* (New York: Sepher-Hermon Press, Inc. for Yeshiva University Press, 1979); "Bulgaria," in *Encyclopedia Judaica,* vol. 4, pp. 1480–94.

19. Tamir, *Bulgaria and Her Jews,* chap. 4; Meyer et al., *The Jews in the Soviet Satellites,* pp. 550–621; B. Arditi, *Yehudei Bulgaria beShnot haMistar haNazi* (Bulgarian Jewry during the Years of the Nazi Regime) (Hulon: Israel Press, 1962) (Hebrew).

20. Baruch Hazzan, "The Jewish Community of Bulgaria," in Daniel J. Elazar, Harriet Pass Friedenreich, Baruch Hazzan, and Adina Weiss Liberles, *The Balkan Jewish Communities: Yugoslavia, Bulgaria, Greece, and Turkey* (Lanham, Md. and Jerusalem: University Press of America and the Center for Jewish Community Studies, 1984), pp. 59–101.

21. Field interviews by the author.

22. "Albania," in *Encyclopedia Judaica,* vol. 2, pp. 522–23 and interviews by the author in 1986.

19

Remnant Communities in the Arab World

The communities in the Arab countries are the remnants of what were, until the rise of Israel, flourishing *kehillot*. Their present state of subjugation or dissolution dates from their host countries' attainment of independence or from the establishment of Israel and therefore reflects another kind of postwar reconstitution. Their subjugation varies from almost complete suppression of all communal and private Jewish activities (Iraq) to government appointment of pliable leadership to manage the community's limited affairs (Tunisia). Only Morocco has allowed its Jewish community to continue to function with a minimum of disturbance, though under close government supervision.

In every one, the situation has deteriorated after each Israeli victory, and the number of Jews remaining in the communities has decreased. Because emigration from the larger ones is possible, it is clear that they, too, are fated to disappear or to become no more than small remnant communities in the near future. In the meantime, communal life proceeds up to the limits of the possible in each of them. This usually means some form of religious life, increasingly limited opportunities to provide children with a Jewish education, and a few limited social services.[1]

The Jewish Remnant in Algeria

Algeria was the site of an ancient Jewish community. Before the Arab conquest the principal Berber tribes were led by rulers who had converted to Judaism even where their tribes were not entirely Judaized. The Jarawa, the leading Judeo-Berber tribe, led the resistance to the Arab conquest. When their leader, known to history as the *kaheena* (priestess) was killed in 693, Berber resistance collapsed and only then was the area conquered. Many of the Berbers converted to Islam, others fled, and the Jewish community was rebuilt principally by Jews coming in from the East.[2]

The Algerian Jewish communities became part of the Mediterranean Jewish world, contributing great scholars and traders to the life of that world in the Middle Ages except when they were overwhelmed by persecution. The community was substantially increased by Spanish Jewish refugees from the persecutions of 1391, most of whom came from Catalonia and the Balearic islands. They became known as the *megurashim* (exiles) and developed separate communities alongside the *toshavim*, or native Jews. The community organization established in the wake of their arrival lasted from the fourteenth century until 1830.

At the time of the French conquest there were thirty thousand Jews in Algeria, whose lives were transformed after coming under French rule.[3] The French rapidly

426

introduced measures to modernize the country including the Jewish community, abolishing the traditional communal organization and replacing it with a formal consistorial structure modeled on that of France and headed by chief rabbis imported from the occupying power. The task of the latter was clearly designed to transform Algerian Jewry into North African versions of Frenchmen of the Mosaic faith. The result was substantial assimilation for many Jews unable to confront the new world, including the abandonment of Judaism altogether. The minority tried to maintain traditional ways unchanged, and a few influential families attempted to synthesize modern French and traditional Jewish culture. In 1870 all Algerian Jews were declared French citizens.

In the 1880s and 1890s a wave of anti-Semitism engulfed Algeria, leading to periodic pogroms throughout much of the country. This anti-Semitism was imported from Europe by the *colons,* the French and Italian Christian colonists of the country. Hence it intensified after the Dreyfus affair. An anti-Semitic party was organized and came to power, but the Muslims did not support it and after 1902 it ceased to exist.

Anti-Semitism persisted, however, and when the Vichy government came to power after the defeat of France by Germany in 1940, the Jews of Algeria, by then 117,646 in number, were deprived of French citizenship. The Algerian administration, now overrun with anti-Semites, applied the Vichy laws as severely as they could—expelling Jewish children from the schools and cooperating with the Nazis toward what was to be an inevitable deportation. The Jews became not only the leaders of the Algerian resistance movement, but almost its total membership, leading an insurrection in Algiers to coincide with the Allied invasion of North Africa on November 8, 1942. Yet after "liberation" by the Allied forces, the Jews suffered further indignities, including the confinement of many in detention camps. It required the personal intervention of President Roosevelt to restore the Jews' French citizenship nearly a year after the invasion, and only in 1957 were they again given full equality.

Algerian Jewry seems to have been consistently governed by a multiple element oligarchy; during the generations only the elements changed. Between 1830 and World War I, the French initiated a shift toward emphasizing the community as a religious body, hence strengthening the power of the modern rabbis, mostly brought in from France, who were more representative of the *keter kehunah* than the *keter torah*. After World War I there emerged a group of modern, non-rabbinical leaders who organized the Comité Juif Algérienne des Etudes Sociales to gain control of the *keter malkhut* and to strengthen it vis-à-vis the other two *ketarim*. The balance they forged persisted until the community's virtual demise.

Algerian Jewry began the postwar period with a reconstitution, culminating in the establishment of the Fédération des Communautés Israélites d'Algérie. An Ecole Rabbinique d'Algérie was established the same year. The Comité Juif Algérienne des Etudes Sociales, which had become the informal power center in the community, resumed its activities in 1948. Though continuing in the framework of the French consistorial system, in practice Algerian local Jewish communities were *kehillot,* each of which functioned autonomously. The sixty *kehillot* were united in a federation which functioned fully until Algerian independence and the exodus of 1961.

When the Algerian civil war began in 1954, the Jewish community was caught in the middle. Once it became clear that France would abandon the territory, the Jews wanted to be recognized as Europeans because they had become so thoroughly Gallicized that they felt no identity with their Muslim compatriots. They succeeded in this and were given asylum in France. By the end of July 1962, seventy thousand Jews had left Algeria for France and another five thousand for Israel. All told some 80 percent of Algerian Jews settled in France. Almost all the Jews who remained in Algeria after it attained its independence retained their French citizenship.

At first the new government maintained a correct relationship with the Jews. In February 1964 the Federation of Jewish Communities of Algeria held a general assembly in Oran to reorganize the remainder of the community. A year later the Boumedienne regime took power in Algeria and the situation began to deteriorate. New and heavy taxes were imposed on the Jews and they were discriminated against in many ways. The government stopped paying rabbis' salaries on the grounds that they were French citizens. The Chief Court of Justice declared that they were no longer under the protection of the law, and an economic boycott was begun against them. The president of the community was brought to trial on grounds that he had connections with Zionism, and one Jew was executed by the regime. Matters peaked at the time of the Six-Day War. The government took over all but one of the synagogues and converted them to mosques. By 1969 only a thousand Jews remained in Algeria, principally those old and infirm who were simply unable to move. By 1980 this number had fallen to three hundred.[4]

The Jewish Community in Egypt

There was no more illustrious Jewish community in the history of the diaspora than Egypt. It is one of the oldest diasporas, dating at least to the destruction of the First Temple when the prophet Jeremiah was carried along by Judeans fleeing their destroyed country to the land of the Nile. A flourishing Jewish community developed, well rooted in the land, even to the point of building the only temple ever in the diaspora.[5] After the Hellenization of Egypt, the Jews were organized as a *politeuma,* a subsidiary polity within the *politea.* Often the Jews were citizens of both. The Egyptian Jews were the first to translate the Bible into a foreign language (the Septuagint), and Jewish philosophy emerged in Alexandria.

This golden age of Egyptian Jewry ended in the diaspora revolt against the Romans in the years 115–17 C.E. The community recovered slowly but ultimately flourished again. It was particularly notable from the conquest of the country by the Fatamids in 969 until the Mamluks took power in the middle of the thirteenth century. Those centuries, well documented in the Cairo Geniza, included the age of Maimonides, who headed the Jewish community in the late 1100s.

Jewish life was difficult under the Mamluks but improved once again after the Ottomans conquered the country in 1517. Although the Ottoman rulers were mostly tolerant toward the Jews, they also were capricious. They relied on Jewish financial agents but also closed synagogues. At the same time, a sprinkling of Spanish Jewish exiles reached Egypt and revived the cultural and religious life of the community. As a result, the community was divided into three subcommunities: the Musta'arbin (the indigenous Arabic-speaking Jews), the Sephardim (the exiles from Spain), and the Mograbim (settlers from North Africa). This followed an old pattern in Egypt whose community had earlier been divided among those who followed the Babylonian *yeshivot* and those who followed the *yeshivot* of Eretz Israel in halakahic practices.

As Egypt declined with the rest of the Ottoman Empire, the life of the Jewish community also declined. Egypt was rediscovered by Europe in the eighteenth century as a result of the Napoleonic wars. Even earlier, in 1768, Ali Bey, the governor of Cairo, took advantage of the Russo-Turkish War to declare himself independent. Though he had to acknowledge nominal Ottoman suzerainty, he and his descendants made Egyptian independence stick.

Muhammad Ali (1805–48) initiated reforms and conquests of other parts of the Fertile Crescent. The prosperity that he brought to Egypt led to a growth in Jewish population. Many Jews came to settle from European countries, particularly the Balkans, and modern schools were established in the community. The vital center of the Jewish community shifted from Cairo to Alexandria, the country's commercial entrepôt. Each European Jewish group founded its own community, although under the authority of the rabbis of the existing ones. Even the Ashkenazim had a community in Alexandria. The rabbinate in Alexandria was particularly modern and emphasized Western as well as traditional education. Hence they played a major role in developing a *halakhic* response to the new technology of modernity, a response subsequently neglected but now being recovered.[6]

The upheavals of the Balkan wars and World War I brought more Jews to Egypt, particularly from Salonika and other Turkish towns. The census of 1917 showed 59,581 Jews and that of 1937, 63,550. Jews entered public life, including two members of the Egyptian parliament and one minister. While some Jews entered the Egyptian nationalist movement, Zionist organizations were also established. Zionism was strengthened during World War I when many Jews from Eretz Israel who were expelled by the Turks found temporary sojourn in Egypt. A Jewish press developed in Arabic, Ladino, and French.

In 1947, 65,600 Jews lived in Egypt, 64 percent in Cairo, 34 percent in Alexandria, and the rest in the provincial cities of Tanta, Port Said, Mansûra, and Ismailia, making Egypt the most urbanized Jewish community in the Afro-Asian world. The community was generally well educated with Jews studying in government and foreign schools. But even before the establishment of Israel and the problems it generated for Egyptian Jewry, the handwriting was on the wall. Egyptian nationalists organized riots against Jewish institutions in Cairo as early as 1945. In 1947 the Egyptian parliament enacted a Companies Law, which required that no fewer than 75 percent of employees of companies in Egypt must be Egyptian citizens. Because only 20 percent of the Jews were Egyptian citizens, most having retained the passports of the European countries whence they came or were stateless, this struck a hard blow at the Jewish community.

The day the State of Israel was declared, Jews were prohibited from leaving Egypt without a special permit. Jewish leaders were arrested. There were bombs and riots in Jewish neighborhoods. The Jews began to lose whatever privileges they had. Between 1950 and 1954 the situation improved under more liberal regimes, and many Jews took advantage of the opportunity to move to Israel, but when Gamal Abdel Nasser seized power in 1954, matters changed for the worse.

The final period in the history of Egyptian Jewry began with the Sinai Campaign in October 1956. Hundreds of Jews were arrested and some 3,000 were interned in detention camps. Thousands were ordered to leave the country within a few days, abandoning all their property, which they were forced to sign over to the government. Approximately 8,000 stateless Jews left the country under the auspices of the American Red Cross. The Egyptian Jewish émigrés scattered throughout the world. Thirty-five thousand went to Israel, some 2,000 to Brazil, 10,000 to France, 9,000 to the United States, several thousand to Argentina, and 4,000 to Great Britain. The 1957 census counted only 8,561 Jews. A decade later the number had been reduced to 3,000.

With the outbreak of the Six-Day War, the last Jewish public officials were dismissed and hundreds of Jews were arrested. Because of the intervention of the Western countries, particularly Spain, most were allowed to leave. By 1970 only a remnant of the community remained.

Jewish community organization continued in Egypt after 1948 as long as there was a community. There was even a well-organized Zionist underground, able to distribute shekels establishing membership in the Zionist movement before the Zionist Congress of 1951. The last Jewish newspaper was closed in 1953. Synagogues, social welfare organizations, and schools were closed in the 1950s, though the Cairo and Alexandrian communities at least formally maintained governing committees. The last chief rabbi of Cairo, who was also recognized as the chief rabbi of Egypt, was deported in 1968.[7]

Fewer than six hundred Jews remain in Egypt today, but since the conclusion of the Egypt-Israel peace treaty, this tiny remnant has been thrust into the limelight in a manner unrelated to its numbers. The opening of the borders has led to a poignant encounter between its members and the Israelis who are either stationed in Egypt on official missions or visiting the country as tourists. It has permitted the community to resume contact with world Jewish organizations, and it has inspired the few hard-pressed but dedicated leaders to carry on with the task of preserving the concrete monuments to a more resplendent past that are in their custody. At best, this handful of men is carrying on a valiant holding operation.

Cairo's Jewish population in 1980 was given as 150 and Alexandria's as 133. There are also another two to three hundred members of the Karaite sect. In the provincial cities that formerly had organized Jewish communities, no Jews remain. Almost all are older people, many of them chronically ill. Women far outumber men, and the number of nuclear families can be counted on the fingers of one hand. There are no children to fill the classrooms of the Jewish school buildings where Muslim children are now being taught.

Though they are vestigial, both communities have managed to preserve a working organization. A strong sense of personal responsibility for somehow keeping the community alive animates the men in charge in both cities. The community still owns fifteen synagogue buildings and four schools. Some years ago, when a financial crisis forced its hand, the committee requested and obtained permission from Chief Rabbi Jacob Kaplan of France to sell one synagogue but is reluctant to sell any of the others. The government has the school buildings under long-term lease for a nominal sum.

Services are held in Cairo's imposing Shaarei Shamayim Synagogue whenever enough people (not necessarily a *minyan*) are available. The emptiness of the synagogue is all the more striking as it has only recently been renovated after years of decay. The historic Ibn Ezra Synagogue, famous as the site of the Cairo Geniza, also has been restored to its former state. No services are held there. The renovation of both was paid for by overseas donors. The situation is similar in Alexandria, except that the grand Eliyahu HaNavi Synagogue was in no need of restoration. Since the last rabbi left Egypt in 1971, the community has been without spiritual leadership. Now the chief rabbinate in Jerusalem sends an Israeli rabbi twice a year.

A major part of the community's annual budget of £E50,000 (about $60,000) goes for aid to needy individuals and families. The rest is spent on salaries and maintenance of the synagogue buildings and offices. Formerly, the members paid a tax to the community; the JDC now covers about half the budget. The JDC connection provides one important link with the Jewish world at large, but emphasizes the community's dependency. By contrast, affiliation with the World Jewish Congress (sanctioned by the Egyptian government) has the symbolic significance of providing equal entrée to world Jewish gatherings. Moreover, the Israeli presence in Egypt since the peace treaty infuses the Jewish remnant with a certain pride and self-confidence.[8]

The Jewish Handful in Iraq

Iraq, ancient Babylonia, was the first great Jewish diaspora community, founded twenty-five hundred years ago. For nearly a thousand years it was the greatest of all diaspora centers, maintaining hegemony over the entire *edah* from the middle of the fifth to the middle of the eleventh centuries C.E. The decline of Babylonian Jewry began even before the Mongol and Tartar invasions but was hastened by the destruction wrought by those central Asian hordes in the thirteenth and fourteenth centuries. The community never completely recovered.[9]

After a series of changes in regime, the Ottoman Turks conquered the country in 1638 and held it until 1917, almost the entire modern epoch. The Jews did relatively well under Ottoman rule, but the general decline of the empire and the bewildering succession of regional rulers kept the community from prospering or progressing. Still, during the nineteenth century the economic situation of the Jews was good. They more or less controlled the country's commerce and exerted substantial influence in government circles. Iraqi-Jewish merchants traded throughout the world and, in partnership with the British, opened up the Far East where they established Jewish communities from Karachi to Kobe. Iraqi Jews were prominent enough in politics to be elected to the Turkish Parliament as delegates from their country after the Young Turk Revolution of 1908. They were among the founders of modern Iraqi literature and did much to advance education in the country.[10]

In 1917 the British conquered Mesopotamia as part of their war against the Turks and ruled first as occupiers and then under a League of Nations mandate until 1932. They installed Faisal, the son of Sharif Hussein of Mecca as King Faisal I. He was a liberal and sympathetic to Jewish interests. Jews were given freedom of religion, education, and employment, and representation in the Iraqi parliament: at first three, one from Baghdad, one from Iraq, and one from Mosul; then after 1946, six, divided three, two, and one, respectively, plus one senator. Jews rapidly advanced in all the institutions of the Iraqi government and continued to be prominent in banking and commerce. They had a particularly advantageous position because so many of them had been educated in Alliance schools, founded in the nineteenth century. Although Baghdad, Basra, and Mosul were the three great concentrations, the Jews were scattered throughout the country. There were probably 100,000 Jews in Iraq at the end of World War I and 150,000 in 1947, two-thirds of whom lived in the province of Baghdad.

The Jews were free enough to organize a Zionist movement and to maintain it from 1918 to 1945. At least four Hebrew language societies were organized in the 1920s and early 1930s as well as a Maccabi sports group. Keren Hayesod organized in the country in 1923 and teachers came from Eretz Israel to teach Hebrew and Jewish history in the Iraqi Jewish schools. After the 1929 Arab riots in Palestine, the government began to attack Zionism and after 1935 the movement had to go underground.

Much of this was a false dawn. Jewish prosperity depended on British government protection. Once Iraq gained its independence in 1932 the government turned against the Jews in an effort to Arabize the civil service and the economic sector. Jews were consistently discriminated against and emigration was made difficult. The culmination of all this was the Shavuot pogrom in 1941. The British intervened, not to save the Jews, but because the pogrom was connected with a pro-Nazi uprising against the Iraqi government and under British auspices peace was restored. As early as 1932, a Zionist underground movement had been organized to prepare for the evacuation of Iraq. It intensified its activities after 1941, when it was better accepted by the community.

As the Jewish-Arab conflict over Palestine intensified, the attitude of the Iraqi government toward the Jews became even more negative. In July 1948 Zionism became a crime, punishable by imprisonment or even death. Hundreds of Jews were arrested and several hanged between May 1948 and December 1949. This led tens of thousands of Jews to flee illegally to Iran. In March 1950 the Iraqi authorities changed their policy and permitted Jews to leave with the proviso that they relinquish Iraqi nationality. In May the legal exodus to Israel began and continued to August 1951. Under the auspices of the Jewish Agency and with the help of the underground Zionist organization, 110,000 Jews left for Israel. Another 13,500 Iraqi Jews arrived in Israel by way of Iran or illegally before May 1950. The Jews had to abandon their property, which was seized by the state.

The remaining Jews were still served by the underground Zionist organization for the next several months, protected by a Jewish self-defense force of some six hundred men, organized by the Hagana. Both were broken up in December 1951 and two of their principals hanged several months later. In January 1952 the six thousand Jews remaining in Iraq were issued new identity cards and forbidden to leave the country. In that year the lone Jewish senator in the Iraqi parliament and the six Jewish members in the lower house were forced to resign, ending Jewish representation in the parliament.

The government reorganized the Jewish community by law in December 1954, further restricting the Jews' rights. Except for short periods, not until 1958 were Jews again allowed to leave the country. For the five years after, under the Qasim regime, conditions improved but when he was overthrown the gates were again closed. By that time the number of Jews had declined to three thousand. The gates continued to open and close with a few Jews leaving each time; the remaining ones maintained basic religious and educational institutions. The Six-Day War led to another round of persecutions and hangings. The climax came between September 1972 and April 1973 when at least twenty-three Jews were murdered by the authorities. The rest fled the country, aided by public protests, so that by the time of the Yom Kippur War only four hundred Jews remained. A few more trickled out during the rest of the decade, leaving approximately that number in the country in the mid-1980s.[11]

A second concentration of Jews was to be found in Kurdistan, a country divided politically between Iraq, Iran, and Turkey. Most of the Jews of Kurdistan were concentrated in the Iraqi section where 146 of 189 Kurdish Jewish communities were located. The Jews were concentrated in the Iraqi cities of Mosul, Kirkuk, Arbil, Amadiya, Zakhu, and Barashi. Because the Jews of Kurdistan spoke their own variant of Aramaic, closely related to that of the Babylonian Talmud, they did not even share a common language with the Iraqi Jews of the Valley of the Two Rivers.

A traditional community down to the very end, trickles of Kurdish Jewish *olim* settled in Eretz Israel from the sixteenth century onward, especially in the eighteenth and nineteenth centuries. Virtually all of Kurdish Jewry migrated to Israel during the mass migration of 1950. Since then, there has been no organized Jewish life in Iraqi

Kurdistan. All that remains of Kurdish Jewry outside Israel are a few surviving villages in Iranian and Turkish Kurdistan.

The Jewish Community of Lebanon

There are sporadic records of a Jewish presence in what is now Lebanon since ancient times, living in the cities and villages of the Lebanon mountains and the adjacent coast. However, not until the late nineteenth century did a serious concentration of Jews develop. Sephardim from Syria, Greece, and Turkey settled in Beirut as that city grew to become the entrepôt of southern Syria and the port of Damascus. The last traditional rural Jewish community in Hasbayya, on the slopes of Mt. Hermon, transferred almost en bloc to Rosh Pina in Eretz Israel in 1888.

By 1929 there were approximately five thousand Jews in Beirut. The estimated number in the country in 1948 was fifty-two hundred, a figure that rose to about nine thousand with the arrival of Jewish refugees from Syria and Iraq after the State of Israel was established. The Lebanese government did not punish its Jews for the "sins" of the Zionists and even granted citizenship to some of the newcomers.

From the first, the Lebanese Jewish community maintained a modified traditional community organization built around local congregations in the cities and villages where Jews lived. Community leadership was in the hands of the heads of the notable families, and communal activities revolved principally around the synagogues, the schools, and basic relief programs. The community leadership represented Lebanese Jewry before the government, often on an informal basis.

Not until 1958 did Jews begin to leave Lebanon, because of the first outbreak of internal unrest that was to fester until it became outright civil war in 1975. Only a few hundred of the Jewish emigrants went to Israel. Most settled in Europe and the United States. Over the next decade the Jewish population decreased to five thousand. The Six-Day War convinced many of these remaining Jews that there was really no Jewish future in the Arab world and another two thousand left within the following year. Still, the Safra and Zilka banks, the two great Syrian Jewish family banks, continued to operate in Beirut until the 1970s.

Throughout this period the Beirut Jewish community maintained its synagogue and communal institutions. There was a community with a synagogue in Sidon and synagogues in the summer resorts in the mountains behind Beirut. The Beirut and Sidon communities maintained Jewish schools for the elementary and early high school grades.

In 1970 the community had further decreased to fifteen hundred. The arrival of the Palestine Liberation Organization after that year and the outbreak of the civil war in 1975 accelerated the community's decline. By 1985 there were fewer than one hundred Jews left in Beirut, the one remaining community. Since 1971, leaders of the community have been kidnapped periodically by Syrian and terrorist organizations, culminating in the kidnapping and murder of the remaining communal leaders in 1985.[12]

The Jewish Community of Morocco

The one Jewish community in the Arab world that has any prospect of surviving is that of Morocco. Though it, too, has drastically declined in size through emigration, particularly to Israel and secondarily to France, Spain, and North America, its members are under no external pressure to leave. Instead, their perceptions of better opportunities or greater security elsewhere have led so many of them to emigrate. As a consequence, most of the community's institutions continue to function, though in more limited form than when the Moroccan Jewish population was at its peak in 1948. Like Iran it combines traditional and modern forms.

Moroccan Jewry, like other old, established Jewish communities, has traditions that local Jewish settlement goes back to the most ancient times. Archaeological evidence proves that there was a Jewish presence in Morocco in the second century of the common era. Apparently, many of the Jews who came to Morocco engaged in highly successful missionary activities, converting some of the major Berber tribes to Judaism in the centuries before the Arab conquest. With the coming of the Muslim armies, many of these Berbers converted to Islam. Others, however, were absorbed into the Jewish community in time. The last of the Jewish Berber tribes did not lose its territorial base until the twelfth century.[13]

As early as the latter part of the sixth century there were close connections between the Jewish communities of Morocco and Spain, with the Jews of Spain fleeing to Morocco at that time to escape the Visigothic persecutions. This pattern was to be repeated at the end of the fifteenth century at the time of the great expulsion. Jews were also involved in the Arab conquest of Spain, which was launched from Morocco with their assistance in 711 C.E.

The history of the Jews in Morocco proper during the Medieval epochs had the usual ups and downs, except that the Jews were subjected to more persecution than was usual in Muslim lands because of the different fanatical Islamic groups that gained control of western North Africa and sometimes Spain itself. This led to many Moroccan Jews moving northward into Christian Spain to escape the periodic persecutions. The situation of the Jews improved toward the beginning of the fourteenth century, but Morocco, like the rest of the Arab world, entered into a period of decline after the middle of that century.

The influx of Spanish exiles after 1492 led to a sharp division in the community between the previous Jewish inhabitants known as *toshavim* (residents) and the new arrivals known as *megurashim* (the exiled). In southern Morocco, the *megurashim* soon dominated integrated communities; in the north the two groups remained separate, with the exiles increasingly dominant. The *megurashim* established their center in Fez and totally absorbed the *toshavim* in Tangier and Tétouan. Elsewhere the two groups did not really merge until the nineteenth century.

During the sixteenth century many Marranos fled from Spain and Portugal to Morocco where they returned to Judaism. Ironically, at that time the Spanish Jewish exiles helped the Spanish and Portuguese establish footholds in Morocco in return for guarantees of rights and benefits. In part, this was because the indigenous Arab government of Morocco was growing weaker, power was being transferred to the countryside, and the Jews had to make the best deals they could. In many of the Berber-controlled areas they made good deals with the Muslims and acquired considerable local power. In others, they were impoverished and subjugated.

Throughout this period there were flowerings of Jewish cultural expression in Morocco and Moroccan Jewry was very much part of the Jewish world, involved in the international commerce that took Jews from the Netherlands to India and affected by the Sabbatean craze that swept the Jewish world in the middle of the seventeenth century. There was considerable cross-Mediterranean emigration in all four directions: Jews from

Livorno and the Netherlands settled in Morocco; Moroccan Jews settled in the new Jewish communities bordering the North Sea, Italy, and the Ottoman Empire. There was also a steady stream of Moroccan Jews to Eretz Israel.

At the beginning of the modern epoch in the latter half of the seventeenth century, Morocco underwent a major political change. It was then that the Alawid Dynasty rose to power, which it has retained to this time. In their rise, the Alawids were assisted by the Jews. The two forged a mutually beneficial alliance, which has also persisted, as reflected in the positive role King Hassan has played in protecting the contemporary Moroccan Jewish community.[14]

Although Morocco had an uneven history in the following generations, Jews were leading figures in the court of the Alawid kings. They were useful as ambassadors, finance ministers, and confidential advisers of the sultans. In the late seventeenth and early eighteenth centuries much of Morocco's foreign relations, particularly with the Christian states, was in the hands of the Jews, who used their overseas connections to protect Moroccan interests. For example, the United States–Moroccan Treaty of 1787, one of the first foreign agreements made by the fledgling republic, was the result of the work of Isaac Cardoza Nunes, a member of the sultan's court, and Isaac Pinto, a Moroccan Jew who had established himself in the United States.

Civil war, an upsurge of Muslim religious fundamentalism, and a series of plagues all coming at the end of the eighteenth century weakened Morocco and opened the door to European influence in the nineteenth century. The European powers also wanted to use the Jews to expand their influence in the country, extending their protection to many Jews and using them as their consular representatives, a sphere in which the Jews had almost a complete monopoly until the last generation of the century.

During the beginning of the last generation of the eighteenth century, many Jewish families emigrated from Morocco in search of opportunity, whether in Europe, the New World, or Eretz Israel. As would be expected, the wealthier families left; they established themselves as part of the larger Sephardi community wherever they settled. The poverty of the lower strata of Jewish society increased during the nineteenth century, becoming grinding by the time the Europeans occupied the country. There are no Jewish population statistics for the period, and estimates of the Jewish population range from 200,000 to 400,000.

All Morocco came under foreign rule when the French established their protectorate in 1912. By then, the country was divided between a Spanish protectorate in the north and the French protectorate in the south, a situation that persisted until 1956 when Morocco gained independence and both foreign powers evacuated Moroccan territory. The Spanish retained only the two coastal cities of Ceuta and Melilla, which had been under their rule from late medieval times.

In 1918 the French authorities affirmed the government's formal recognition of the organized Jewish community of Morocco as established before the protectorate. During the nineteenth century and probably before that, Moroccan Jewry was governed through a system that might be defined as oligarchic republicanism. Countrywide, the Jewish notables in the sultan's court dominated the affairs of the community because of their wealth and access to the foreign suzerain. Locally, councils of notables were elected in each community by the local Jewish population. They were responsible for managing community affairs in the domain of the *keter malkhut*. The leading figures in the community elected a *gizbar* (treasurer), who was responsible for financial matters and could protect their interests. He was an ex officio member of the council and together the council and *gizbar* nominated *dayanim* (rabbinical judges), the leading representatives of the *keter torah*.

These communities were autonomous because the Moroccan authorities had no interest in interfering in Jewish internal affairs. The French limited this autonomy after 1912 and in their decrees of 1918 and 1931. The governance functions of the council and the judicial functions of the *dayanim* were assumed by the protecting power, leaving to the Jewish community the management of educational, religious, and eleemosynary institutions. In typical French centralizing fashion, the Jews lost the right to elect the local committees, which became appointed bodies officially chosen by the grand vizier but really by the protectorate authorities. The local communities were supervised by a Jewish official of the government chosen by the French for his devotion to French interests. As much as they could, the Jewish communities manipulated the choice of committee members to reflect local interests, but they were no longer free to follow their own political tradition as they could before the protectorate.

Before the arrival of the French, communal revenues had come primarily from the tax on kosher meat and from *hekdeshim* (charitable trusts) established by wealthy community members. These arrangements continued after 1912, supplemented by a minimum amount of aid from the Jewish communities overseas plus the generosity of the wealthier Jews of the community. No funds were forthcoming from the state, despite the extension of state control.

Governance of the communities was affected by the social changes wrought by the extension of French influence and later by French rule. The wealthier Jews of the community, who formed the upper class, increasingly turned toward French culture and tried to divorce themselves from the larger Jewish population. French Jews established modern schools in the nineteenth century through the Alliance Israélite Universelle. These rapidly became the focal points for the Jewish assimilationists, where their children could learn French ways and abandon the traditional society out of which they had emerged. As a result, except in Tangier and one or two other communities, this upper class became detached from communal affairs. The only limits imposed on its assimilation into the new French elite were the limits imposed by the French, who were basically anti-Semitic.

Efforts to organize a Zionist movement began in Morocco when the movement emerged in Europe in the late nineteenth century. Organized Zionism, however, had a difficult time gaining a foothold, in part because the French actively discouraged national movements of any kind and in part because the Jews who might have been open to modern Zionism were busy finding their way into the local Frenchified version of Western culture. In the Moroccan context, however, Zionism did not need a separate organizational framework to make its influence felt. Zionist ideas penetrated fully into the community in the interwar generation, particularly into the youth movements and also into other organizations to become the common ideology of the elements of the community who had become modernized but not assimilated.

Although they escaped the full effect of the Holocaust, while the Vichy government controlled the protectorate Moroccan Jews were separated from the larger society by law. In the process relations with their Muslim neighbors also deteriorated. The Vichy government established its version of the Nuremberg Laws despite the opposition of the reigning sultan, Muhammad V, who lived up to the tradition of his family in trying to protect the Jews. Once the Allies had landed in North Africa and Morocco was liberated, Jewish rights, such as they were, were restored, though only in June 1943 when the Gaullists came to power.

When Israel was established in 1948 there were some 265,000 Jews in Morocco. There was almost immediate response by Moroccan Jewry to the reestablishment of the Jewish state. Tens of thousands followed the Zionist emissaries sent to their country and immigrated to Israel. Some 43,000 left in the first three years and 60,000 more left—most but not all to Israel—during the 1950s. Since the 1960s most of the Jews leaving Morocco have chosen destinations other than Israel. The Moroccan Jewish population continued to decline rapidly in that decade, dropping from just under 160,000 according to the 1960 census to an estimated 22,000 in 1968, and perhaps 16,000 to 18,000 in 1982.[15]

As late as 1951, more than a third of Moroccan Jews lived in small towns and villages. By 1961 this figure had dropped to a quarter and by the early 1970s most of the Jews were concentrated in a few major cities, reversing the historic pattern of dispersal throughout the country, which had been characteristic of Moroccan Jewry since earliest times.

Until 1956 no serious obstacles were placed in the way of Jewish emigration to Israel; however, Muhammad V, who otherwise improved the situation of the Jews in Morocco when he brought it to independence in 1956, also imposed an order forbidding them to do so. For five years immigration to Israel was illegal but still substantial: some 47,000 Jews made the trek during that period. When Hassan II ascended the throne on the death of Muhammad V in 1961, the restrictions were lifted. Since then, any Jew has been free to move wherever he wants, although he is still considered by the king to be a Moroccan subject wherever he happens to settle.

Jewish life in Morocco underwent its greatest transformation in the postwar generation, in part because of the sheer demographic changes. Thus, for example, in 1948 the Alliance Israélite Universelle operated fifty-two schools in the country with nearly twenty-two thousand pupils. Until 1956 it was still a growing enterprise, establishing thirty more schools and enrolling nearly twenty-nine thousand students. By 1965, however, the number of students in Alliance schools had dropped to nine thousand, one thousand of whom were non-Jewish. Not only did the Alliance close schools that were no longer needed, but in 1960 the Moroccan government nationalized about a quarter of its schools and opened them to the entire population.

Otzar HaTorah, Chabad, and a group called Em HaBanim established Jewish schools in Morocco in the postwar period and underwent a similar, if less extensive, process. Chabad, in particular, established a presence in Morocco rather incongruously teaching Moroccan Jewish youth Yiddish to spread their message.

Independence improved the condition of the Jews as individuals but brought further restrictions on what remained of Jewish communal autonomy, as the rulers of the newly independent state tried to consolidate Moroccan nationhood. All Zionist activity was forbidden in stages between 1956 and 1959, and many other Jewish organizations were forced to disband. The World Jewish Congress, however, maintained links with Moroccan Jewry throughout this period.

Although a few Jews were influential in Moroccan politics at the outset of Moroccan independence, most were soon replaced. Not until Hassan II ascended the throne did individual Jews again become influential members of the royal court. A select group remains influential today.

Simultaneously, however, there was a rise in anti-Semitism, which had both verbal and physical manifestations. The publication of anti-Semitic literature and, worse, the kidnapping of young Jewish girls, who were then forced to become Muslims, accelerated emigration from the country. As a result, in the 1960s the old Jewish community in Morocco was really dissolved. After the Six-Day War even many wealthy Jews began to leave because of their fears for the future.

This took its toll of Jewish institutions. The All-Moroccan Jewish Council, established by royal decree in May 1945, was torn apart through internal rivalries and dissolved in 1962. In the following decade a new body was established, which biennially convenes a Moroccan Jewish congress, an event that has acquired symbolic importance as a sign of the well-being of Moroccan Jewry under Hassan II. Since 1984 the congress has served as the vehicle for promoting Moroccan-Israeli relations, through the invitation of a substantial Israeli delegation to participate in the event along with Jews from other countries.

After 1967 many local Jewish institutions were closed. The lack of Jewish leadership, particularly rabbis, *dayanim,* and *hazzanim,* was soon felt. Still, a basic community structure remains, with schools, charitable institutions, community councils, synagogues, and the like. Most of the institutions of Moroccan Jewry enjoy extensive aid from world Jewish sources, particularly the JDC, which supports all the school systems and some welfare institutions.

The Jews had preserved their rabbinical courts throughout the period of the protectorate, even though their jurisdiction was severely limited under French rule. In 1956, however, newly independent Morocco transformed them into state courts of law, allowing only the Supreme Rabbinical Tribune to remain independent for another decade (the government abolished it in 1965). Rabbinical judges were appointed judges in the state courts so that their jurisdiction over the Jewish community in personal status matters would come under direct state control. Morocco maintains a chief rabbi, whose functions are limited.

Moroccan Jewry in the 1980s is much like Iranian Jewry in the 1970s, sitting on the edge of a volcano and protected by the grace of the ruling monarch. Even the most devoted supporters of the present government would probably be unwilling to bet on the future of the Jewish community should something happen to Hassan II or if his successor did not share his positive attitude toward the Jews.

The Imprisoned Jews in Syria

Syria, ancient Aram, is Israel's oldest enemy and also the home of one of the oldest Jewish communities in the diaspora, dating to biblical times. Jewish communal life has existed in Syria since the first settlement in the diaspora, with the usual ups and downs. There were large communities in the Roman period, difficult times under the Byzantine rulers, improvements under the Arabs between the seventh and the twelfth centuries, and severe destruction as a result of the Mongol invasions in the thirteenth and fourteenth.[16]

The arrival of Spanish exiles in the early sixteenth century brought about a revival of the Syrian Jewish communities and their transformation as the influence of the more cosmopolitan and sophisticated Sephardim was felt. The arrival of the Sephardim coincided with the conquest of Syria by the Ottoman Turks, which increased trade opportunities and also increased the strength of the Sephardim, who had particularly good connections with the regime. As a result, trade from the western Mediterranean to the Indian subcontinent expanded. Communities prospered in Damascus and Aleppo and in smaller centers throughout the country. The cultural and religious life of Syrian Jewry was strongly influenced by the Jewish community in Eretz Israel, particularly the Kabbalists in Safad.

Aleppo, the center of a region known in Jewish tradition as *aram tzova,* prospered as the crossroads of east-west trade and then declined in the second half of the eighteenth century as its economic base eroded. Conversely, the Jewish community of Damascus rose in importance at that time. Its leaders became increasingly important as ministers and advisers to the local rulers, playing particularly important roles in public finance. Throughout the nineteenth century Jewish families were engaged in local political intrigues. In the nineteenth century new interethnic tensions also developed, bringing blood libels against the Jews on several occasions, including the famous Damascus blood libel of 1840, which was one of the catalytic events in the reawakening of the *edah.*

Muslims, unhappy with the Ottoman rulers' relaxation of discriminatory measures against non-Muslims, rioted against the Christians on several occasions, starting the internecine wars in Lebanon that have continued until now. The Jews were frequently caught in the middle of all this. Moreover, the opening of the Suez Canal almost ended Syria's share of the international trade between Europe and Persia. Syrian Jews started to emigrate in substantial numbers, particularly to the Americas. The Jews of Damascus also began a process of modernization and assimilation, particularly to French culture.

Modernization was much less a factor in Aleppo, which retained traditional patterns. Although many Halabim (Jews from Aleppo) also emigrated to the New World, they have been notably tenacious in retaining their traditional ways generations after leaving their city of origin. Aleppine Jews also emigrated to Eretz Israel as part of the Sephardic proto-Zionist renaissance; fewer Damascene Jews did so.[17]

At the end of World War I the Jews of Syria and Lebanon were concentrated in three large communities: Damascus and Aleppo with about six thousand Jews each and Beirut with some four thousand. Another two thousand were scattered in the smaller communities. During the period of the French mandate there was little Jewish public activity; most Jewish life was confined to traditional and family frameworks. After Lebanon was separated and given its independence in 1943, about fifteen thousand Jews remained in Syria. Ten thousand of them left after the establishment of the State of Israel, stimulated by the 1947 pogroms in Aleppo, in response to the United Nations partition decision.

Since 1948 the condition of Syrian Jewry has become progressively worse. Anti-Jewish laws were promulgated in that year and later, mostly to impoverish the community by preventing the sale of Jewish property and freezing Jewish bank accounts. Much Jewish property was confiscated by the authorities and turned over to Palestinian refugees. Emigration was forbidden. Some Jews who succeeded in getting to Lebanon were returned to Syria by the Lebanese authorities. Others were caught and severely punished, tortured, and even executed, and families of those who did escape were punished. Only twice, in 1954 and 1958, were the frontiers opened to Jews for brief moments.

Today there are an estimated four thousand Jews in Syria, most of whom live in Damascus and Aleppo. There is also a community in Hams and a few Jews in Quamishli. No countrywide Jewish organization is allowed, but each community continues to maintain it own governing committee under the watchful eye of the authorities. The Alliance Israélite Universelle maintains schools in Damascus and Aleppo under strict government supervision, if not control.[18]

The Jewish Community in Tunisia

The Tunisia area is also a site of Jewish settlement since ancient times, perhaps even since the time of Carthage. From time to time the region was the locus of major Jewish centers and many non-Jews converted to Judaism until the Christianization of the Roman Empire put a stop to Jewish proselytization. Still, Judaism spread among the Berber tribes until the Arab conquest of the region and the forced conversion of most of them to Islam.

The Arab conquerors founded Kairouan in 670 C.E. and it soon became a major center of Jewish scholarship. The Jewish community along the Tunisian coast flourished even after the decline of Kairouan, maintaining close contacts with the Jewish communities in other parts of the Mediterranean world, particularly Italy and Spain. As in those countries, individual Jews rose to important positions in the courts of the rulers and used those positions to protect their brethren. The Jewish community was autonomous and led by notables from the rich and well-born families.[19]

Throughout the sixteenth century, the area was the victim of Spanish and Ottoman invasions and counterinvasions, which did not cease until the Ottoman victory in 1574. Communal life was substantially disrupted as a result. The following century, the settlement of Spanish, Italian, and former North African Jews who had removed to Leghorn in Italy in the interests of commerce and then transferred to the coastal communities of northern Africa led to the development of a separate community. These *Grana* (from Leghorn) lived alongside the *Touansa* (natives of Tunisia) in somewhat uneasy coexistence. In 1710 the Grana seceded from the main community and founded their own. The virtual civil war between the Touansa and the Grana was a major feature of Tunisian Jewish life in the modern epoch. The two groups united only in the face of outside danger. In 1899 the authorities forced them to merge formally under a chief rabbi, a common *bet din,* and a single kosher slaughterhouse in each local community, and one delegation to the countrywide council.

Beginning with the period of the French revolution, French influence in Tunisia began to grow. The Jews were strong supporters of the Revolution and its promise of Jewish emancipation. Ultimately, in 1857 they were to be given equality when the Bey of Tunis was forced to do so by Napoléon III and the French navy. Although the resulting Pacte Fondamental was abolished seven years later in the wake of a Muslim revolt against the granting of equality to infidels, continued European intervention served to more or less protect Jewish rights. The French finally made Tunisia a protectorate in 1881. In the meantime, the Alliance Israélite Universelle opened its first school in the country in 1878. From 1910 onward, individual Jews could apply for French citizenship. Except for periodic riots against the Jews, the period of the protectorate was one of relative peace for the Jewish community. Many Tunisian Jews even fought in the French army during World War I.[20]

The Jewish community was reorganized along modern lines in 1888 by government decree, establishing the Caisse de Secours et des Bienfaisance Israélite de Tunis (The Tunis Jewish Welfare Fund). In later years similar funds were organized in the other cities and towns of Tunisia. The fund was supervised by a committee, which also handled the maintenance of synagogues and compensation of rabbis.

A countrywide community council was established in 1921 in which both the Touansa and Grana were represented proportionately. This arrangement continued until 1944 when another government decree forcibly combined the two communities. The council had two divisions, one dealing with religious matters and the other with social welfare. It was financed by taxes on kosher meat and *matzot,* synagogue income, burial services, and government subsidies. The chief rabbi was not a member of the council but could attend meetings as a consultant. In the external relations–defense sphere, the council was responsible for appointing a Jewish representative to the Grand Conseil of Tunisia. It also supported Hebrew cultural activities.

During World War II Tunisia was ruled by Vichy France from June 1940 to November 1942 when it was occupied by the German army until May 7, 1943. During the first period the Jews were subject to racial discrimination under the Nuremberg Laws and during the second to confiscation of property, heavy taxation, service in labor camps, and even deportation to death camps. All this ended when the German army surrendered.[21]

The Jews revived their public life after their liberation. For a brief period they even made progress integrating into Tunisian life. The Destour Independence party even cultivated their support. The last elections for the Jewish community council were held in 1955, just before Tunisia gained independence in 1956.

With independence, the new government embarked on a program of Tunisification, which meant Arabization. Although on the international scene Habib Bourguiba, the leader of the Tunisian independence movement and later life president of the state, appeared moderate, willing to accept Israel's existence for a price, and relatively liberal compared with his Algerian and Libyan neighbors, internally, he was ruthlessly active in suppressing any kind of autonomous Jewish life. The rabbinical court was abolished in 1957 and a year later the Jewish Community Council was dissolved and replaced with a "Provisional Commission for the Propagation of the Jewish Religion," whose members were government appointees. Their task was to prepare elections for a new body that would be a "cultural association" strictly limited to the cultural sphere. No such elections were ever held and the Provisional Commission remained in existence to handle Jewish affairs outside the synagogues. The old Jewish quarter in Tunis was destroyed, ostensibly as part of a slum clearance project. Even the synagogue, the oldest in the city, was leveled and the old Jewish cemetery in Tunis was turned into a public garden. The government stopped subsidizing the Jewish community and when the only Jewish member of the Tunisian cabinet retired, no successor was appointed.

Jewish education in Tunisia had been in the hands of the Alliance Israélite Universelle since the late nineteenth century, but at the time of Tunisian independence only 20 percent of the fifteen thousand Jewish students in the country attended Alliance schools. Almost all the others attended government schools, except on the island of Djerba, where traditional Jewish education was maintained.

The Tunisian Jewish community always had a rich cultural life, unless outside factors were too disruptive to maintain it. This continued to be true in the modern epoch. Jewish works were written and published in Hebrew, Judeo-Arabic, and French well into the 1960s, when government crackdowns eliminated the possibility for doing so. Until independence there was a lively and active Jewish press.

All that could be said in Bourguiba's favor is that he did not encourage persecution of the Jews. Hence, although most of Tunisian Jewry left during the first generation of the postmodern epoch, proportionately more remained and maintained some kind of Jewish life than in any North African country other than Morocco. Jews started to emigrate en masse after 1948 and particularly after 1957. Between 1948 and 1970 more than forty thousand Jews from Tunisia settled in Israel, and nearly the same number settled in France.

The decade of the 1960s was a period of deterioration for the Jewish community. Jews were accused of being unpatriotic and were discriminated against economically. At the time of the Six-Day War there were Muslim riots against the Jews and the Great Synagogue in Tunis was burned. This led to a new wave of emigration. Seven to eight thousand Jews remained in the country in 1968, a figure that dropped to thirty-seven hundred in 1982. Most of the remaining Jews are located in Tunis and on the island of Djerba. The latter group maintains as much as possible of its traditional community. It is subject to periodic outbursts of Muslim anger, usually triggered by some Israel-related event. So, for example, after Israel bombed the PLO base near Tunis in 1985, the Muslims on Djerba rioted and two Jews were killed.[22]

The Jews in Yemen

Although the rediscovery of Yemenite Jewry at the beginning of the Zionist revolution led them to be treated as a lost tribe by the Ashkenazim who were unaware of their existence before the 1880s, the community, though isolated, was in fact always part of the communications network of the Sephardic world. The community apparently goes back at least to the time of the Second Temple, although its traditions date its beginnings even earlier. Its period of greatest prominence was in the sixth century when the Yemeni ruling family embraced Judaism and governed what was effectively a Jewish state for a brief period.[23]

The Jews of Yemen remained within the jurisdiction of the Babylonian *yeshivot* until the latter weakened in the eleventh century, when the community turned to the Egyptian Jewish leadership for guidance. In that period Aden, Yemen's principal port, was an important transit point for Jewish merchants traveling to and from India, which strengthened the Jewish community. Throughout this period the Jews maintained autonomous communal institutions and survived periodic waves of persecution.

The Ottomans conquered Yemen in the mid-sixteenth century and, unlike other parts of their empire where their arrival brought peace, for the Jews their arrival brought great difficulty. The Jews were caught in the cross fire between the Turkish conquerors and the local tribes or were subject to persecution by Muslim zealots, culminating in the destruction of all the synagogues in the capital, San'a, and the expulsion of the Jews in 1676. The local Imams succeeded in driving out the Turks, thereby worsening the Jews' position. Ottoman control was not again extended over the country until 1849 and even then remained nominal.

During the eighteenth and nineteenth centuries the Jews' economic position deteriorated further, although even nominal Ottoman rule brought them greater physical security. The Imam Yahkya revolted against the Ottomans in 1904 and captured San'a a year later. He was to rule until 1948 and, like his predecessors, persecuted the Jews, who remained at the bottom of the Yemeni social order, defined as serfs without rights, severely restricted in their public behavior and private lives, and required to perform degrading tasks.[24]

Jewish life in Yemen continued in the traditional pattern until the end of the nineteenth century. The first "modern" Jewish school was founded in San'a in 1910, leading to a struggle in the community between traditionalists and those advocating change. Because the latter did not find favor in the eyes of the Imam, few changes were introduced before the community's mass emigration. The local communities continued to be governed by councils and *batei din* with the chief rabbi of the San'a community being the Haham Bashi for all of Yemenite Jewry. The last incumbent of that office died in 1932 and no successor was appointed.

From the eleventh through eighteenth centuries, the only hope for Yemenite Jews was the periodic appearance of false messiahs, climaxing in the Sabbatean episode. Pseudomessianism flowered for the final time in the nineteenth century. Three pseudo-messiahs appeared, the last in 1893. In the last generation of the modern epoch, however, this unproductive messianism was replaced by a turning toward Eretz Israel. The first aliya of Yemenites took place in the eighteenth century and led to the foundation of Beth-El, which for nearly two hundred years was the major center of Kabbalists in Jerusalem. In the late nineteenth century, organized aliyot of Yemenite Jews began. Between 1919 and 1948 nearly a third of the Jewish population of Yemen, about sixteen thousand Jews, emigrated to Eretz Israel. Between June 1949 and June 1950 another forty-three thousand were brought by "Operation Magic Carpet." A trickle comprising some thirteen hundred Jews arrived between 1951 and 1954. Thus the community was effectively evacuated.

At that point it was generally believed that the Jewish community in Yemen had ceased to exist. True, one hundred Jews were said to remain, but it was assumed that they were the old and feeble who could not maintain a community life. Subsequently the Kingdom of Yemen underwent a revolution and became North Yemen, suffering a major civil war in the process, which brought about brutal Egyptian intervention. In the process of covering that war, to the extent that it was possible, foreign correspondents began to discover surviving Jewish communities in outlying villages living in groups of extended families and quietly maintaining their own ways.

By 1955 the number of Jews remaining in Yemen was estimated at eight hundred. Since then, there has been a rediscovery of concentrations of Jews who did not leave after 1948, so that today it is estimated that there are at least one thousand Jews in Yemen, now renamed North Yemen, and perhaps as many as six thousand, settled in a number of cities and towns around the country. Within the limits imposed by a hostile government, they maintain their communal and religious existence to the point of continuing to learn Hebrew. The community remains traditionally religious and organized in the traditional way. Schools exist in the larger communities, and in the smaller ones volunteer teachers undertake the responsibility of educating the young semiprivately. There is a full range of religious services.

Economically, the remaining Jews in Yemen are in much the same circumstances as their Muslim neighbors, certainly no worse. In some places they are even allowed to carry weapons for self-defense, although not the *jambiah,* the traditional dagger carried by male Muslims, which is a sign of status. Recently, there have been reports of renewed persecution of those Jews and demands that they be assisted to leave.

The principal contact between the remaining Jews of Yemen and the outside world is through the Satmar Hassidim who cultivate the connection as part of their anti-Zionism. Satmar Hassidim have visited communities in Yemen, accompanied by Yemeni government officials and members of the PLO, since the PLO acts as the intermediary to facilitate the contact for propaganda purposes.[25]

What was once Hadramuth and Aden is now known as South Yemen. The Jewries in those areas were part and parcel of the Yemenite culture area. Although Jews had been in the Hadramuth region since ancient times, Aden did not become a significant settlement until it was conquered by the British in 1839 and turned into a way station on the

British path to South Asia and the Far East. After that, the Jewish population of the city grew and later even became a jumping-off point for the Sephardic migration eastward in the company of the British. In 1839 Jews constituted five hundred of the fifteen hundred residents of Aden. As the city grew so did the Jewish population, although it declined as a percentage of the total. At its peak at the end of World War II there were eight thousand Jews in Aden out of a total population of 100,000.

Under the British the Jews began as builders and ended in the middle management and administrative positions within the British government and as merchants within the community. Because they were fully literate, they became essential middlemen in the British protectorate. The Adeni community became the key in a network that stretched from the heartlands of Yemen to Hong Kong.

Some 70 percent of the Jews of Aden settled in Israel between 1947 and 1949. With the British evacuation in 1968, all the remaining Jews left. Most went to Britain where they settled in London. Others followed the earlier path of Adeni Jews to India, Singapore, Hong Kong, and Australia, while only a few of the poorest settled in Israel.[26]

Notes

1. Norman A. Stillman, *The Jews of Arab Lands* (Philadelphia: Jewish Publication Society of America, 1979); Maurice M. Roumani, *The Case of the Jews from Arab Countries: A Neglected Issue* (Tel Aviv: World Organization of Jews from Arab Countries, 1983); Natan A. Shouraki, *Korot HaYehudim Be-Tzfafon-Africa* (The Saga of the Jews in North Africa) (Tel Aviv: Am Oved Publishers Ltd., 1975) (Hebrew); Mark Robert Cohen, "The Jews under Islam: From the Rise of Islam to Sabbetai Zevi," *The Study of Judaism: Bibliographic Essays* (New York: Anti-Defamation League of B'nai B'rith, 1972), 2 vols.; S. D. Goitein, "Jewish Society and Institutions under Islam," in H. H. Ben Sasson and S. Ettinger, eds., *Jewish Society through the Ages* (New York: Schocken Books, 1971) and *Jews and Arabs: Their Contacts through the Ages,* 3d ed. (New York: Schocken Books, 1974); Shimon Shamir, "Muslim-Arab Attitudes toward Jews: The Ottoman and Modern Periods," in Salo W. Baron and George S. Wise, eds., *Violence and Defense in the Jewish Experience* (Philadelphia: Jewish Publication Society of America, 1977); Government of Israel, "Jews in Arab Lands," *Information Briefing* (Jerusalem: Ministry of Foreign Affairs, 1973); Devora Hacohen and Menachem Hacohen, *One People: The Story of Eastern Jews* (New York: Funk and Wagnalls, 1969); Albert Memmi, *Juifs et Arabes* (Paris: Gallimard, 1974); Y. Schatz and Y. Baiber, eds., *Metzukatam shel HaYehudim Be-Artzot Arav* (Distress of the Jews in Arab Lands) (Jerusalem: Ministry of Education and Culture, 1971) (Hebrew).

2. André Shouraqui, *Marche vers l'Occident: Les Juifs d'Afrique du Nord* (Paris: Presses Universitaires de France, 1958) and *Korot HaYehudim Be-Tzafon-Africa;* E. F. Gauthier, *Le Passé de l'Afrique du Nord: Les Siècles Obscurs* (Paris: Payot, ed. 1942); Michael Ansky, *Yehudei Algeria* (Algerian Jewry) (Jerusalem: Kiryat Sefer, 1963) (Hebrew); H. Z. Hirschberg, *Toldot HaYehudim B'Afrika HaTzafonit* (The History of the Jews in North Africa) (Jerusalem: Mossad Bialik, 1965), pp. 77–88 (Hebrew).

3. Ansky, *Yehudei Algeria;* Attal Robert, "Le Consistoire de France et les Juifs d'Algérie," *Michael,* vol. 5 (1978), pp. 9–16; Shimon Schwartzfuchs, "Shtai Teudot al Yehudei Algeria Le-Akhar HaKivush HaTzarfati" (Two Documents on Algerian Jews after the French Takeover) *Michael,* vol. 5 (1978); Shouraqui, *Korot HaYehudim Be-Tzafon-Africa,* pp. 143–304; Hacohen and Hacohen, *One People.*

4. Shouraqui, *Korot HaYehudim Be-Tzafon-Africa,* pp. 239–304; Ansky, *Yehudei Algeria;* H. Z. Hirschberg, ed., *Mimizrakh U'mima'arav* (From East and West) (Ramat Gan: Bar Ilan University, 1974) (Hebrew); Schatz and Baiber, eds., *Metzukatam shel HaYehudim.*

5. Stanley Lane-Poole, *A History of Egypt in the Middle Ages* (London: Methuen, 1936); William Popper, *Egypt and Syria under the Circassian Sultans, 1382–1486 A.D.: Systematic Notes to Ibn Taghri Birdi's Chronicles of Egypt,* 2 vols. (Berkeley and Los Angeles: University of California Publications in Semitic Philology, 1955–57); Salomon A. Rosanes, *Histoire des Israélites de Turquie et de l'Orient,* 6 vols. (1930–45); Stillman, *The Jews of Arab Lands,* pp. 46–53; Jacob Mann, *The Jews in Egypt and Palestine under the Fatimid Caliphs* (London: Oxford University Press, 1920); Roumani, *The Case of the Jews,* pp. 12–40; Jacob M. Landau, *Jews in Nineteenth-Century Egypt* (New York: New York University Press, 1969).

6. S. Landshut, *Jewish Communities in the Muslim Countries in the Middle East* (London: The Jewish

Chronicle, 1950); Yahudiya Masriya, *Les Juifs en Egypte* (Geneva: Editions de l'Avenir, 1971) and *The Treatment of Jews in Egypt and Iraq* (New York: World Jewish Congress, 1948); Nehemiah Robinson, *The Arab Countries of the Near East and Their Jewish Communities* (New York: Institute of Jewish Affairs, 1951); Yuri Miloslavsky, *Se'irim La'azazel: Zikhronot Asir B'Keleh Mitzrayim* (Scapegoats: Memoirs of a Prisoner in an Egyptian Prison) (Jerusalem: Israel Universities Press, 1970) (Hebrew); Hayim J. Cohen, *HaYehudim B'Artzot Hamizrakh Hatikhon B'yameinu* (The Jews in the Middle East in Our Times) (Jerusalem: Institute of Contemporary Jewry, Hebrew University, 1973) (Hebrew).

7. Masriya, *Les Juifs en Egypt* and *The Treatment of Jews;* Hayim J. Cohen, *HaYehudim B'Artzot Hamizrah Hatikhon B'yameinu;* Gudrun Kramer, *Minderheit, Millet, Nation? Die Juden in Agypten: 1914–1952* (1982), p. 26.

8. Ernest Stock, "Jews in Egypt—1983," *Jerusalem Letter,* no. 60 (June 15, 1983).

9. Jacob Neusner, *A History of the Jews in Babylonia,* 5 vols. (Leiden: E. J. Brill, 1965–70); David Solomon Sassoon, *History of the Jews in Baghdad* (Letchworth: Solomon D. Sassoon, 1949); Roumani, *The Case of the Jews,* pp. 13–22; Stillman, *The Jews of Arab Lands.*

10. Roumani, *The Case of the Jews,* pp. 23–36; Yitzhak Bar-Moshe, *Al-Khuruj min al-Iraq, 1945–1950* (The Exodus from Iraq) (Jerusalem: Sephardic Community Council, 1975) (Hebrew); Avraham Ben-Yaakov, *Yehudei Bavel* (The Jews of Babylonia) (Jerusalem: Ben Zvi Institute, Hebrew University, Kiryat Sefer, 1965) (Hebrew).

11. Hayim J. Cohen, *HaYehudim B'Artzot Hamizrah Hatikhon B'yameinu;* Ezra Haddad, *Yahadut Bavel-Iraq* (Babylonian-Iraqi Jewry) (Jerusalem: Ministry of Education, 1970) (Hebrew); Landshut, *Jewish Communities in the Muslim Countries;* Robinson, *The Arab Countries;* Max Sawdayee, *All Waiting to Be Hanged; Iraq Post-Six Day War Diary* (Tel Aviv: Levanda Press, 1974); Masriya, *The Treatment of Jews.*

12. "Lebanese Jews Shrink to 200," *Jerusalem Post* (October 29, 1980); Menachem Persoff, ed., "A Review of the Current Situation of Jews in Other Arab Lands," in *The Jews in Syria* (Jerusalem: Ahva Press, 1975), pp. 41–43. Stillman, *The Jews of Arab Lands,* p. 204; Landshut, *Jewish Communities in the Muslim Countries,* pp. 54–56; "Lebanon," *Encyclopedia Judaica,* vol. 10, pp. 1542–44.

13. David Corcos, *Studies in the History of the Jews of Morocco* (Jerusalem: Rubin Mass, 1976); Yosef Harari, *Toldot Yehudei MaMaghreb* (History of the Maghreb Jews) (Holon: Yosef Harari, 1975) (Hebrew); Hirschberg, *Toldot HaYehudim;* Avraham Shtal, *Toldot Yehudei Maroko* (A History of the Jews of Morocco) (Jerusalem: Ministry of Education, 1974) (Hebrew).

14. Besides previously cited works on North African Jewry, see *The Jews of French Morocco and Tunisia* (New York: Institute of Jewish Affairs, World Jewish Congress, 1952); Eliahov Eilon, *Les Juifs en Afrique du Nord: Une Chronologie* (Jerusalem: Département de la Jeunesse et du Héhalouts, Division de l'Information, 1975); Devora Hacohen and Menachem Hacohen, *One People.*

15. Joseph B. Schechtman, *On Wings of Eagles: The Plight, Exodus, and Homecoming of Oriental Jewry* (New York: Thomas Yoseloff, 1961); Schatz and Babier, eds., *Metzukatam shel HaYehudim;* Government of Israel, *The Jewish Exodus from Arab Countries and the Arab Refugees* (Jerusalem: Ministry of Foreign Affairs, 1973); Devora Hacohen and Menachem Hacohen, *One People;* Rachel Cohen and David Corcos, "Morocco," *Encyclopedia Judaica,* vol. 12, pp. 341–47; Mark A. Tessler and Linda L. Hawkins, "The Political Culture of Jews in Tunisia and Morocco," *International Journal of Middle East Studies,* vol. 11, no. 1 (1980), pp. 59–86; Mark A. Tessler, "The Identity of Religious Minorities in Non-Secular States: Jews in Tunisia and Morocco and Arabs in Israel," *Comparative Studies in Society and History,* vol. 20, no. 3 (1978), pp. 359–73; Doris Bensimon, "Les Débuts du Movement Sioniste au Maroc: Quelques Documents des Archives Sionistes de Jérusalem," *Michael 5* (1978), pp. 17–80; Norman A. Stillman, "Muslims and Jews in Morocco," *The Jerusalem Quarterly,* vol. 5 (1977), pp. 76–83.

16. Eliahu Strauss-Ashtor, *Toledot HaYehudim BeMizrayim u'veSuria Tahat Shilton haMemelukim* (History of the Jews of Mameluk Egypt and Syria) (Jerusalem: Mosad HaRav Kook, 1970); Stillman, *The Jews of Arab Lands,* pp. 393–405; Persoff, ed., *The Jews in Syria,* pp. 5–22; Albert M. Hyamson, "The Damascus Affair—1840," *Transactions of the Jewish Historical Society of England,* vol. 16 (1952); Moshe Maoz, *Ottoman Reform in Syria and Palestine, 1840–1861: The Impact of the Tanzimat on Politics and Society* (Oxford: Oxford University Press, 1968); Popper, *Egypt and Syria;* "Syria," *Encyclopedia Judaica,* vol. 15, pp. 636–45.

17. Persoff, ed., *The Jews in Syria,* pp. 23–27; Devora Hacohen and Menachem Hacohen, *One People;* Hirschberg, ed., *Mimizrakh U'mima'arav;* Richard F. Nyrop, ed., *Syria: A Country Study* (Washington, D.C.: The American University, 1979), pp. 60–81, 88–89; "Syria," *Encyclopedia Judaica,* vol. 15, pp. 646–49; J. Fried, ed., *Jews in the Modern World,* vol. 1 (1962), pp. 50–90.

18. Persoff, ed., *The Jews in Syria,* pp. 28–39; Fried, ed., *Jews in the Modern World;* Roumani, *The Case of the Jews;* Schechtman, *On Wings of Eagles.*

19. Besides previously cited works on North African Jewry, see S. D. Goitein, "La Tunisie de 11° siècle à la Lumière des Documents de la Geniza du Caire," *Etudes d'Orientalisme Dediées à la Mémoire de Lévi-Provençal,* vol. 2 (1962), pp. 559–79; Felix Allouche, "La Tunisie: Carrefour du Judaisme Antique et Moderne," *Evidences,* no. 5 (November 1949), pp. 5–8; Rodolphe Arditti, "Sur Quelques Epitaphes Importantes de l'Ancien Cimetière Israélite de Tunis," *Revue Tunisienne* (1920), pp. 94–98, 261–66 (1931); pp. 105–19, 404–10 (1932); David Cazès, *Essai sur l'Histoire des Israélites de Tunisie* (Paris, 1888); Shouraqui, *Marche vers l'Occident;* Maurice Eisenbeth, "Les Juifs en Algérie et en Tunisie à l'Epoque Turque (1516–1830)," *Revue Africaine,* vol. 96 (1952), pp. 114–87, 343–84.

20. Allouche, "La Tunisie"; Shouraqui, *Marche vers l'Occident* and *Cent Ans d'Histoire: L'Alliance Israélite Universelle et la Renaissance Juive Contemporaine (1860–1960)* (1965) and *La Saga des Juifs en Afrique du Nord* (1972); Jacques Sabille, *Les Juifs de Tunisie sous Vichy et l'Occupation* (Paris: Centre de documentation juive contemporaine, 1954); R. Attal and C. Sitbon, *Regards sur les Juifs de Tunisie* (Paris: Albin Michel, 1979).

21. Attal and Sitbon, *Regards sur les Juifs de Tunisie,* pp. 182–93; R. Attal, "Les Juifs de Tunisie sous l'Occupation Nazie d'après des Temoignages Oraux," *Le Monde Juif,* no. 44 (October–December 1966), pp. 34–37; Shouraqui, *Marche vers l'Occident;* Sabille, *Les Juifs de Tunisie.*

22. Attal and Sitbon, *Regards sur les Juifs de Tunisie;* Shouraqui, *Marche vers l'Occident* and *Cent Ans d'Histoire;* Shlomo Barad, *Le Mouvement Sioniste en Tunisie* (Tel Aviv: Institut pour la Recherche sur le Mouvement Sioniste et Haloutsique en Pays d'Orient, 1980); "Tunisia," *Encyclopedia Judaica,* vol. 15, pp. 1147–52; Abraham L. Udovitch and Lucette Valensi, *The Last Arab Jews—The Communities of Jerba, Tunisia* (London and New York: Harwood Academic Publ., 1984).

23. "Yemen," *Encyclopedia Judaica,* vol. 16, pp. 739–51; H. Z. Hirschberg, *Yisrael B'Arav* (Israel in Arabia) (Tel Aviv: Mossad Bialik and Massada Press, 1946), pp. 75–111 (Hebrew); S. D. Goitein, *The Land of Sheba and Tales of the Jews of Yemen* (New York: Schocken Books, 1947); Yosef Kapah, *Halikhot Teiman* (Customs of Yemen) (Jerusalem: Ben Zvi Institute, Hebrew University, Kiryat Sefer, 1968) (Hebrew); Mahallal Ha'adeni, *Benin Aden l'Teiman* (Between Aden and Yemen) (Tel Aviv: Am Oved, 1947) (Hebrew); Robinson, *The Arab Countries.*

24. "Yemen," *Encyclopedia Judaica,* vol. 16, pp. 751–59; Manfred Wenner, *Modern Yemen, 1918–1966* (Baltimore: Johns Hopkins Press, 1967); Yehuda Nini, *Yahasan shel Hivat Tziyon VeHatenuah HaTzionit La'Aliyah Mi'Teiman* (The Relationship of Hibbat Tziyon and the Zionist Movement to Yemenite Immigration to Israel) (Jerusalem: Institute of Contemporary Jewry, Hebrew University, 1977) (Hebrew).

25. Roumani, *The Case of the Jews;* Schechtman, *On Wings of Eagles;* Wenner, *Modern Yemen 1918–1966;* Hirschberg, ed., *Mimizrakh U'mima'arav;* Devora Hacohen and Menachem Hacohen, *One People;* Nitza Druyan, *Lo Al Marvad Kesamim* (No Magic Carpet) (Jerusalem: Yad Ben Zvi, 1984) (Hebrew).

26. Ha'adeni, *Bein Aden l'Teiman;* Hirschberg, *Yisrael B'arav;* Hayim J. Cohen, *HaYehudim B'Artzot Hamizrah Hatikhon B'yameinu;* "Aden," *Encyclopedia Judaica,* vol. 2, pp. 262–63; "Habban," *Encyclopedia Judaica,* vol. 7, pp. 1018–20.

20

Declining Communities in Muslim West Asia

Besides the Arab states, the Muslim world includes the rest of western Asia, with its ancient Jewish communities of Iran and Afghanistan, which have been part of the long stream of Jewish history as frontier regions of Babylonian Jewry since biblical times, and Pakistan, that dates to the nineteenth century. They were once closely linked with their brethren in Central Asia, now under Soviet rule, to form a common subcultural area in the Jewish world.[1]

The Jewish Community in Afghanistan

According to Afghani tradition, the leading Afghani tribes—the Durani, Kussatzai, and Afridis—are descended from Jews. More specifically, they claim descent from some combination of the ten lost tribes and King Saul through one of his wives. This tradition is even presented as fact in the tourist guidebooks. It is shared by the Pathans in Pakistan and India. Jewish tradition also regarded Afghanistan, known in medieval times as Khorasan, as the location of the ten tribes.[2]

Jews as such have lived in Afghanistan for several thousand years. During the days of the Babylonian Exilarchate, rejected candidates for the office of Resh Galuta were often exiled to Afghanistan because of its remoteness from the Babylonian center. In medieval times the largest Jewish communities apparently were in Balkh and Ghazni. From the time of the Mongol invasion onward the Jews in Afghanistan were in difficult straits, but perhaps no more so than the rest of the population, because the area was in a constant state of intertribal warfare.

Afghanistan reappears in Jewish history in the nineteenth century when many of the *anusim* (Marranos) of Mashhad in Iran fled there after their forced conversion to Islam in 1839. They revived Jewish life and quickly came to dominate the community, even to the point of making the dominant Jewish language a Judeo-Persian dialect rather than Pashto, which is spoken locally. Jewish scholarship flourished in a modest way and toward the end of the century Afghani Jews began to emigrate to Eretz Israel where they organized a separate subcommunity in Jerusalem.[3]

Jewish community organization consisted of a *hevrah* in each of the three principal cities, composed of all the heads of families, which provided social and burial services. The *hevrah,* something like a town meeting, had some power to punish violators of its ordinances. The head of the community was known as the *kalantor*. He represented it in dealings with the authorities. The *hevrah* and *kalantor* were also responsible for collecting taxes due the government.

447

In 1948 approximately five thousand Jews were living in Afghanistan, principally in Kabul, Balkh, and Herat, the largest community. After the 1933 assassination of King Nadir Shah, the Jews had been banished from the other towns and forbidden to leave their towns of residence without a permit. They voluntarily retreated into their own walled quarters for self-protection. A few managed to flee to Iran or India and from there worked their way to Israel, but until 1950 the government did not allow the others to depart. As soon as permission was granted, almost all of them did, leaving en masse in 1951. Thus, within two years, the Afghani Jewish community almost ceased to exist. Almost all emigrated to Israel. During the next two decades a small number emigrated to the United States.

All told, there were some two hundred Jews in Afghanistan in 1976. There were fifteen Jewish families in Kabul, most native Afghanis and the rest Bukharans who had fled after the Russian Revolution. They maintained a synagogue, a *shohet,* and a rudimentary communal life. They felt secure enough in general but still saw the population as potentially hostile. For example, they did not feel that they could get justice in civil cases in Afghani courts because the Muslim majority believed that any money given to Jews would end up in Israel. Sixteen Jewish families remained in Herat. They maintained four synagogues, at least nominally. By 1985, six years after the Soviet invasion of Afghanistan, the number of Jews in the country had dropped to thirty, all in Kabul. No Jews remained in Herat.

Near Balkh there is a semi-Marrano community whose forefathers were forcibly converted to Islam a century ago. Many of them maintain some Jewish customs, such as lighting candles on Friday night, that reflect their Jewish origins and set them apart from their neighbors.[4] Similar, if less pronounced, phenomena can be found among the Afghani tribes, leading some Jews from outside Afghanistan to be interested in bringing them back to Judaism. Since the Soviet invasion of Afghanistan, there has been no further contact with the Jews there.

The Jewish Community in Iran

The Jewish community in Iran was protected under the Pahlavis. Still, it was no less transformed by the establishment of the State of Israel.[5] Iranian Jews trace their beginnings to the foundation of Persia at the time of Cyrus the Great, some twenty-five hundred years ago. It is possible that Jews lived in what is now Iran even before that, having reached there through the exiles and population exchanges that began with the Assyrian conquest of the northern kingdom of Israel in 721 B.C.E. Yet the antiquity of the community is of little relevance to the present situation. Apart from a common knowledge of the community's former status, there is no organic link between past and present.[6] That is characteristic of Iran in general. Iran is a country whose hidden character stretches back to antiquity yet whose visible institutional structure is without indigenous roots.

The Jews were among the first to follow the path of urbanization and to benefit accordingly. Of the estimated thirty thousand Jews in present-day Iran, some twenty-five thousand live in Tehran, the capital, which has been a city for hardly more than two centuries and became a large city only in the twentieth century. Most of its Jews settled there since 1920. At the end of World War I, Tehran's Jewish population did not reach ten thousand. The great Jewish emigration from the villages began in the 1930s and continued until 1979. The Jewish population of the city at one time exceeded fifty thousand.[7]

There is a small "Iraqi" community in Tehran that numbered some three thousand in 1970. Its members are descended from immigrants to Iran from the areas in the Middle East that recognized the authority of the chief rabbi of Babylonia, as distinct from the Jews of Iran who have had their own religious authorities for the last several centuries. Most came to Iran in the nineteenth century as part of the great Iraqi diaspora that moved eastward in search of economic opportunity and developed outposts throughout Asia from Tehran to Hong Kong. There are few ties between the native Iranian community and the Iraqi Jews, even though most of the Iraqis were born in Tehran to families resident there for several generations.

Only the few thousand Jews remaining in the older cities and towns can possibly have maintained any ancestral connections with long-time places of residence. About half live in the three cities where Jewish communities were traditionally strong: Shiraz, Isfahan, and Hamadan. The rest are scattered among seven smaller communities, including Kerman, Abadan, Kesaye, and Sannandaj, and several thousand are still in villages. All of these are declining communities except Abadan where the oil industry has attracted additional Jewish families to make it the fourth largest Jewish community in the country. Hence, despite premodern elements in its legal status and organizational structure, the contemporary community is no less a product of modern migrations than any contemporary Jewry.

The most tenaciously Jewish community is to be found in Mashhad, whose Jews were forced to convert to Islam in 1831 but subsequently remained faithful to Jewish tradition as Marranos. Because of the problem they faced in preserving their Jewishness, Mashhad Jews came to be much more traditional and loyal to Jewish observance than other Iranian Jews. Many Mashhadis emigrated to Israel in the early 1950s. Some two thousand relocated in Tehran, where they maintain their own synagogues and communal institutions and an active Jewish life. Others became openly Jewish in Mashhad, although they are still counted as Muslims. Mashhad Jews have established communities in Israel (particularly Jerusalem), London, New York, Hamburg, and Milan.

Culturally, Iranian Jewry remains very much the product of its past, and its modern organizational forms are infused with traditional behavior patterns. Descended from families resident in the country for generations and isolated from the rest of world Jewry for centuries, the Jews have assimilated into Iranian culture. Many of their problems as a community are directly related to this assimilation.

Since the establishment of the State of Israel and most pronouncedly since the Khomeini revolution, the Iranian Jewish community has had the characteristics of a community in dissolution. Two-thirds to three-quarters of its members—including many of its potential leaders—have moved to Israel or the West since 1948, principally in two mass migrations, the first to the new state in the early 1950s and the second to western Europe and North America in the 1980s. It was well understood before 1975 that the community would find itself in dire straits overnight should they lose the protection of the Shah. That, indeed, turned out to be the case.

Many of the patterns of association among Iranian Jews still rest on premodern bases. Yet these are survivals from a disappearing past rather than living, developing institutions. Thus synagogues are not formal associations of worshipers in the Western sense, but are places where men come to pray because of special family or communal ties. As the Jews of Iran became less religious, the synagogues were less able to hold them to

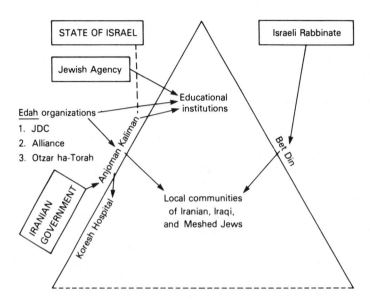

Figure 20.1. The organizational structure of the Iranian
Jewish community before the Khomeini revolution.

the Jewish community—a trend reversed under the Khomeini regime. For most Iranian
Jews, family and interpersonal ties are still perceived to be so important that there is no
felt need for formal organization. Yet the young people going to the university are
mixing with the wider population and breaking away from their family circles so that
these ties are considerably less binding than formerly. Many assimilated Jews are kept in
the Jewish fold because of the country's personal status laws, which require everyone to
belong to some religious community for marriage and inheritance purposes. Iranian Jews
are strikingly committed to pursuing their private interests, first and foremost. Public
business is either neglected or subsumed under private concerns and public-spiritedness
is generally lacking even in the leaders.

Despite the importance of the ancient Persian empires in Jewish history, with two
exceptions the Jews of Persia have played a small role on the world Jewish scene. The
history of Persian Jewry is divided between periods of isolation and of dependence on the
Babylonian Jewish center. Persian Jewry was expected to provide funds for the maintenance of the Babylonian centers, who maintained their authority to appoint *dayanim* and
rabbis for the Persian communities. Nevertheless, the Persian diaspora was at one time a
large one, far larger than the present Iranian Jewish community, with a flourishing
culture including its own language, Judeo-Persian.

The conquest of independent Persia by the Arab Muslims in 642 and the replacement of Zoroastrianism with Islam as the state religion transformed the status of the Jews
and other minority groups into that of second-class subjects. It also ushered in a period
during which Persian Jewry was the source of sectarian divisions, including the Karaite
movement, which, although initiated in the Babylonian centers, was led substantially by
Jews of Persian birth and background. Persia became a major Karaite center and Karaite
communities continued to exist there well into the sixteenth century. It may well be that
the absence of some Jewish practices common to normative (or rabbinic) Judaism, even
among traditional Iranian Jews, stems from the influence of Karaism.

The invasions of the Khans from the Far East in the thirteenth through fifteenth centuries brought an elevation in the status of the Jews, allowed them to participate more fully even in the political life of the times, and made possible a golden age of Judeo-Persian literature. This happy period was followed by the restoration of Muslim rule under the Safavid dynasty beginning in 1502, whose intolerant Shiism reduced Jewish life to conditions of suffering and persecution. Thus, as the world moved into the modern epoch, Persian Jews shared the fate of most of their brethren: falling into the worst and most backward of situations from which they did not emerge until the late nineteenth century. The Jewish population declined, its economic conditions worsened significantly, and it suffered almost total cultural collapse.

Formal links between the Persian Jewish communities and Babylonia were severed by the Safavids, who appointed a local chief rabbi but prevented the development of any other comprehensive Jewish organization or leadership. The Jews of Isfahan, the Safavid capital, became ipso facto the representatives and spokesmen for Persian Jewry under a Nasi (magistrate) and Dayan (judge), but their authority did not officially extend to the rest of the country. Persian Jewry's major contact with the rest of the Jewish world from then on was conducted through emissaries from Eretz Israel, who came regularly to collect funds for Jewish institutions. Many Persian Jews tried to escape their lot by emigrating northward and eastward, where they renewed the Jewish communities of central and south Asia.

The mid-eighteenth century was a period of renewal in Iran under Nadir Shah and several of the largest Jewish communities, including Tehran and Mashhad, date from that period. The opening of the country to European influences in the nineteenth century enabled the great European Jewish *shtadlanim* of the time to intervene on behalf of their brethren. Beginning in the 1860s, Adolph Cremieux and Moses Montefiore took the lead in these efforts, which were then assumed by the Alliance Israelite Universelle and the Anglo-Jewish Association until World War II. Since then, this task has been assumed by American Jewry through its great organizations for overseas relief and, until Khomeini, by Israel. These Jews had influence because of the Iranian government's need for European capital and the Jews' role in the great European capital markets. Moreover, their personal political influence led the local representatives of those governments, particularly the British consuls, to intervene frequently on behalf of the local Jews.

From the 1870s onward, European Jewish leaders negotiated with the shahs to obtain better conditions. Shah Nasr-al-Din was persuaded to issue a *firman* granting Jews protection as a minority. After considerable delay, the Alliance was authorized to open schools, the first of which was founded in Tehran in 1898. Within the next decade similar schools were opened in Hamadan (1900), Isfahan (1901), Sena (1903), Shiraz (1903), and Kermanshah (1904).

American Jewish involvement in Iran began in a limited way during World War I. In 1918, the Joint Distribution Committee (JDC) transferred $15,000 to support needy Jews there through the American Embassy in Tehran. Between 1921 and 1925 the American minister was an American Reform rabbi, Joseph Saul Kornfeld, who frequently intervened on behalf of the local Jewish population.

Liberalization of the Iranian polity in the twentieth century did even more to change the status of the Jews. Although the country's first constitution (1906) made no provision for minority rights or direct Jewish representation in the Majlis (the Iranian parliament), it did open the door to liberal ideas. Jews were active in the constitutional movement and were rewarded by the abolition of the discriminatory provisions in Persian law. Unfortunately, Shah Mazai Har-ed-Din, who had accepted the new liberalization, died within months of the convening of the Majlis and his successor, Muhammad Ali, returned to many of the old ways. Nevertheless, the days of the old regime were numbered. The revolution finally came in 1925, bringing Reza Shah Pahlavi to power.

Reza Shah, who modeled his regime on that of Kemal Atatürk of Turkey, wished to establish a republic but was persuaded that conditions in Iran were not ripe for such a step. So he took the crown for himself. He curbed the power of the Muslim religious authorities, introduced civil government separated from the Muslim religion, and generally tried to modernize Iran by re-creating its pre-Muslim past as the basic national myth.

These steps benefited the Jews indirectly. Jews were also granted the same legal rights as the Muslim majority. Politically, Jewish rights were limited to the election of one member of the Majlis and Jews could not hold important political offices. Aside from the Department of Health, where Jewish doctors were considered desirable, Jews were rarely admitted to the civil service, and no Jews were ever allowed into the ministries of foreign affairs, war, or police. A Jew could theoretically rise to the rank of colonel in the army, but there is no record of Jews having advanced in the regular establishment beyond the lower grades. Thus the Jews remained a national minority in Iranian society, with some protected rights.

In 1941, the English and Russians jointly occupied Iran. Reza Shah's neutralism or perhaps pro-Nazi sympathies led to his deposition by the Allies during World War II. This marked a turning point in the history of Iranian Jewry, for shortly thereafter the United States entered the war and began to replace the British as the premier Western power. After the war, the Americans confronted the Russians, who wanted to continue their occupation of the northern half of the country and, in 1946, forced them to withdraw. Thus Iran came into the American sphere of influence where it remained until the 1979 revolution. As a consequence, Iranian Jewry also passed into the American Jewish sphere of influence.

The twentieth century also brought a slight renaissance in the life of the Jewish community of Iran, which was tied closely to the emergence of Zionism and the revival of the Hebrew language. As a renaissance, it was not of great magnitude nor did it reach a large segment of the population. Among its earliest recorded beginnings were the founding in 1917, in Tehran, of a society for the Hebrew language, which published a textbook for the teaching of modern Hebrew. A history of the Zionist movement written in Persian was published in 1920. The most important contribution of that period was the foundation of the Koresh School, which had Zionist leanings from the beginning. Several Zionist newspapers, particularly *Ha-Geulah* and *Ha-Haim,* were founded in that period but they never could strike roots because of opposition by the regime.

Zionist emissaries reached Tehran in 1929 and 1943 but could do little in the face of the regime's opposition to the spread of Zionism. A small office of the Jewish Agency was opened and continued to function sporadically, primarily to deal with the refugees transferred from Poland and Russia to Palestine by way of Tehran during World War II. Once the state was established, the Jewish Agency expanded its offices in Iran to encourage immigration and was successful for several years in moving masses of Iranian Jews to Israel and in giving assistance to local Jewish educational and cultural efforts. The office continued to function until 1979, when it was hastily evacuated.

The JDC arrived permanently after World War II. The JDC leaders who visited Iran immediately after the war perceived that the local community was in desperate need yet not in a position to undertake any serious action on its own so they decided to make an exception to normal JDC policy and come in to directly operate programs. They have been doing so ever since, continuing on a limited basis under the present regime.

At about the same time, Rabbi Jacob Meir Levy came from Israel to organize the Otzar HaTorah school system, also under American sponsorship. He was a member of Agudath Israel and opposed Zionism. Only after he recognized the local sentiment in the matter did his schools begin to cooperate with the Jewish Agency. For that matter, the agency and the JDC did not see eye to eye at first. The agency viewed the JDC as anti-Zionist because of its efforts in the interwar period to keep the Jews of eastern Europe in their countries of birth rather than encourage them to migrate to Palestine. Echoes of this old conflict appeared in the relationship between the two in Iran. Nevertheless, by the mid-1950s conditions in Iran and the character of the work of the three bodies brought them closer together.

The Soviet-American struggle for control of Iran, which led to the temporary establishment of Azerbaijan as a Communist state in the northern part of the country, also had its effect on the Jewish situation. Some Jews responded to the Soviet effort to win them over by strictly forbidding anti-Semitic activities in the territory under their control. In late 1950 and early 1951, after the Soviets evacuated the area, the local population launched a series of pogroms, which were major factors in encouraging the Jews in northern Iran to leave for Israel. Some twenty-eight thousand of the fifty-five thousand Jews who emigrated to Israel between 1948 and 1968 did so between 1950 and 1952.

Mohammad Mossadeqh rose to power in 1952 and turned Iran leftward. The army deposed him in 1953 and restored the exiled Shah. Mossadeqh's relations with the Jews were ambiguous. He attacked the outside Jewish organizations functioning in Iran as imperialist agents, yet his party appealed to local Jews to join, with some success. His pro-Arab, anti-Israel foreign policy was at least partly inspired by his alliance with the Shi'ite religious leadership and redounded to the disadvantage of the local Jewish population. Perhaps because he wanted the Jews to leave the country, he nevertheless allowed the reestablishment of the Jewish Agency offices in Iran, which had been forced to close in 1948, and even negotiated an agreement between the Bank Meli Iran (Iran's central bank) and Bank Leumi (then Israel's central bank).

With the restoration of the Shah, official government policy changed significantly with regard to Israel. The Shah persisted in defending Jewish interests until his exile. No doubt the support given him by the leading wealthy Jews in his struggle against Mossadeqh played a role in shaping his attitude.

The rise of the Khomeini regime led to retrogression in the status of the Jews and limitations on their community institutions. At first there was direct persecution, including executions of communal leaders because of their connections with the Shah. Later, the situation eased and, for whatever reasons, the Jews who have not fled the country remain in fairly stable condition.

According to Israeli records, 63,143 Jews emigrated from Iran to Israel from the establishment of the state on May 15, 1948, through early 1974, in four waves: from 1950 through 1952, after the Sinai Campaign from 1957 through 1959, from 1962 through 1965, and in the wake of the Six-Day War. A fifth wave came after 1979. Most of the immigration to Israel before 1979 came from the provincial communities. The post-Khomeini emigration, however, was principally from Tehran. Many of the emigrants were wealthy and could reestablish themselves in appropriate style in Beverly Hills, Manhattan, or London.

When they originally came to Tehran, the Jews settled in the Mehalleh, the city's ghetto, one of the truly dreadful slums of the Middle East. Almost all the Jews still lived there through World War II. By 1970 only four thousand Jews remained, the rest having migrated to better neighborhoods as they became more prosperous. The almost universal poverty of Iranian Jewry ended as a result of World War II when some Jewish families attained great riches through wartime market activities. Wartime prosperity gave Iran a lift, which continued and blossomed even more in the 1960s, especially in Tehran. The Jews benefited because of their occupational structure and because most who migrated to Israel were from the poorest segments of the community.

By the 1960s the general economic condition of the Jewish community in Tehran was so good that it was suffering from all the social and moral distortions that new money brings. According to the best estimates, there were at least a dozen Jewish millionaires in Iran in the 1970s, involved in manufacturing plastics and textiles and in foreign trade, automobile agencies, tourism, hotels, and other investments. Some 20 percent of the Jews were prosperous businessmen, owners of stores, sellers of antiquities, carpet manufacturers and sellers, foreign traders, doctors, dentists, and pharmacists. Some 30 percent were lower-middle-class clerks, taxi drivers, and artisans. About 50 percent were still defined as poor by the JDC, including most of the people in the provincial cities. The JDC supported about 30 percent of them.

Iranian society is structured along ethnoreligious lines, hence Jews are Jews to all concerned, although the possibilities for fuller assimilation had increased before the 1979 revolution. There is some conversion to Islam but, as in Mashhad, it is difficult for Jews to deny their Jewishness, even after formal conversion. Under the Shah, intermarriage was a minor but growing problem in the community, as numbers of Jewish young people began attending the university and mixing with non-Jews. This, too, has changed since 1979.

The Jews' flirtation with Baha'ism, a mid-nineteenth century Iranian invention, reflects the universal problem of modern Jewish assimilationism. Apparently many Jews were attracted to Baha'ism. The exact numbers are in dispute, even among the experts, with some suggesting that tens of thousands turned to the new religion, which seemed to offer Jews a way to break out of the confines of the ghetto by embracing a kind of universalism without denying basic Jewish beliefs, only practices. Unfortunately for them, as Islamic heretics Baha'is have been consistently persecuted in Iran, even under the Pahlavis, and are now being exterminated by the Khomeini regime, hence the converts actually lost ground. It is unclear whether they persisted as Baha'is or whether they returned to Judaism. Traditional anti-Semitism in Iran is chiefly anti-Judaism. It always has been strongest where traditional Muslims maintained power. Even under the Shah, where the Shi'ite priesthood was strong, Jews were frequently unable to exercise their civil rights. Now this anti-Jewishness is state policy.

External relations and communal-welfare spheres. The Anjoman Kaliman (Jewish community council), located in Tehran, is the nominal framing institution of Iranian Jewry, recognized by the government as the representative of the Jewish population. In theory, its jurisdiction extends countrywide; in fact, it barely functions even in Tehran. The Iraqis and Mashhadis maintain separate community organizations, based on their synagogues. Shiraz and Isfahan have their own organizations, which are also nominal. Each handles its charitable and educational needs in its own framework.

There is no Iranian Chief Rabbinate to exercise judicial or religious authority over the country. In 1957 an all-Iranian Jewish congress was held to create a countrywide

community were educated in its schools, but after World War II, the heightened importance of English as the second language for Iranians and the evacuation of the provincial cities and villages reduced its potential school population. By the 1960s the Alliance schools were supported by the JDC and the American Friends of the Alliance. Their Hebrew teachers were provided by Otzar HaTorah.

In the 1970s Otzar HaTorah had elementary and secondary schools in Tehran, Shiraz, Kerman, Abadan, and Risaye. It provided Hebrew teachers for the Alliance, ORT, and the locally sponsored Jewish schools. Where the communities supported their own day schools, Otzar HaTorah provided supplementary programs. Thus it had a virtual monopoly of Jewish education in Iran. The growth of the Otzar HaTorah schools was greatly stimulated by the shift from French to English. Moreover, in Tehran, the Alliance schools were located in the Mehalleh, and as the Jews moved away led to a steady deterioration of the quality of the already low-level Jewish education in the country.

Tehran and several of the other larger communities sponsor their own schools. In Tehran the Koresh schools (founded in 1931) are the most significant. The Iraqi Itrifak School in Tehran, founded in 1946, is considered the best Jewish school in Iran. It had eleven hundred students from kindergarten through twelfth grade. A vocational school in Tehran, founded in 1950, is maintained by ORT.

Communal finance. Before local sources provided about 10 percent of the money expended for communal purposes. All the rest came from the outside. The Koresh hospital, ORT, the Alliance, the social welfare committee of the community council, the Koresh school, and the women's committee of the community council all conduct their own fund-raising drives for local needs. When there is a need for money, the communal leaders sell parcels of land that the community has inherited and uses the proceeds to cover expenses. Because land prices have escalated greatly in the growing metropolitan area, this has served to cover such budgetary needs as are recognized locally. Tuition is a source of money for the local schools, ranging from insignificant for the Alliance schools to substantial for the community-run schools. In the provincial cities, the women's committees raise money for local projects, particularly for kindergartens, which are popular activities initiated and supported by the JDC. Other fund-raising is confined to raising small amounts on Pesah and Yom Kippur, primarily for the cemetery and the individual synagogues, though some of the money is set aside for the poor.

Under the Shah, fund-raising for Israel was tacitly permitted and met with somewhat greater success. Officially, the Magbit did not exist in Iran because taking foreign exchange outside the country was illegal. Moreover, raising money for Israel in a Muslim country was fraught with additional problems for the government. Nevertheless, through a series of complicated arrangements, a drive was conducted annually.

The Khomeini regime has actually given the Jewish community something of a new lease on life. The constitution of the Islamic Republic recognizes the Jews as one of the three protected religious minorities, guaranteed "complete freedom in the practice of religious duties and functions, such as in matters of marriage, divorce, inheritance, wills and testaments." Hence the Jewish rabbinical courts have reacquired powers in part taken away under the Shah's secularization efforts.

Not only has the regime allowed the old institutions to continue under new leadership, but its religious tone has led to a religious revival among the Jews, if only in self-defense. In 1981 the Jewish community was given a new religious leader in the form of a new chief rabbi for Tehran, a position often vacant in the past. The same year, the Jewish community elected a new representative to the Majlis, the Iranian parliament, to assume the seat held under the Shah by the executed Habib Elghanian. Synagogue attendance has increased, with the encouragement of the communal leadership, as part of the Jewish effort to increase the legitimacy of Jewish religious observance. Public meetings at which government officials appear are held at the synagogues periodically to strengthen that tie with the regime.

While the Jewish schools have been nationalized and have come under even closer government supervision than in the days of the Shah, the Ministry of Religion provides financing for Jewish religious education, which is compulsory for Jews. Those children not enrolled in Jewish day schools must acquire a Jewish religious education through supplementary schools. As a result, afternoon Hebrew schools have been established. Not only have teachers been trained and hired, but *siddurim* and textbooks have been published with the education ministry's backing. All of this ended what had been a continuing if slow decline in Jewish religious education, paralleling the diminution of Jewish religious commitment.

The Anjoman Kaliman has a new head. Even the Jewish hospital and the welfare institutions continue to operate, though under somewhat additional pressure to provide services for non-Jews, something that was true under the Shah as well.

The major changes have taken place on the survival issues. Most Jews in government posts and at the universities were dismissed after the revolution, and today an estimated 60 percent of the working Jewish population is self-employed, principally in retail businesses and small trades, and another 10 to 15 percent are professionals. Thus Jewish dependence on the outside world for economic sustenance has been reduced to a minimum, involving exchange rather than employment dependency.

Despite official protection, Jews are still subject to harassment on the part of revolutionary guards and the local workers' committees, and there are occasional executions. On the other hand, Jews continue to serve in the Iranian army and several dozen are known to have been killed in the war with Iraq. As the price of all of this, the Jewish leaders are forced to regularly denounce Israel and Zionism.

The Jews in Pakistan

Jews settled in Karachi, now Pakistan's largest city, in the latter part of the nineteenth century. Most were of Bene Israel origin, apparently from the Bombay area. In 1893 the community built the Magen Shalom Synagogue. At the beginning of the twentieth century about twenty-five hundred Jews lived in the city. A second community developed in Peshawar in the northwest frontier province. The Karachi community was organized in the modern Indian manner with the principal organizations outside the synagogue being the Young Men's Jewish Association founded in 1903, the Karachi Bene Israel Relief Fund, and the Karachi Jewish Syndicate to provide housing for poor Jews.

The establishment of Pakistan as an Islamic state caused most of the Jews to move to India, many of whom continued on to Israel or Great Britain. The Peshawar community ceased to exist and by 1968 only 250 Jews remained in Karachi, a number that has dropped slightly. They maintain a synagogue, a welfare organization, and a social club.[9]

Notes

1. Yona Sabar, *The Folk Literature of the Kurdistani Jews* (New Haven and London: Yale University Press, 1982); Reuben Kashani, *Yehudei Afghanistan* (The Jews of Afghanistan) (Jerusalem: Reuben Kashani, 1975) (Hebrew); Itzhak Ben-Zvi, *The Exiled and the Redeemed* (Philadelphia: Jewish Publication Society of America, 1957), pp. 255–70; Raphael Patai, *Tents of Jacob: The Diaspora Yesterday and Today* (Englewood Cliffs, N.J.: Prentice-Hall, Inc., 1971), pp. 247–58; Joseph B. Schechtman, *On Wings of Eagles: The Plight, Exodus, and Homecoming of Oriental Jewry* (New York: Thomas Yoseloff, 1961), pp. 236–37, 243–47.

2. Aryeh Tarkower, *Shivetei Yisrael* (Tribes of Israel) (Tel Aviv: Yavneh, 1966), pp. 249–50 (Hebrew); Raphael Patai, *Golden River to Golden Road: Society, Culture, and Change in the Middle East*, 3d ed. (Philadelphia: Jewish Publication Society of America, 1969); Erich Brauer, "The Jews of Afghanistan," *Jewish Social Studies* (April 1942), pp. 121–38; Ben-Zion Yehoshua, *The Father's Will: Thirteen Folktales from Afghanistan* (Haifa: IFA Publication Series, no. 24, 1969); George Percy Badger, *The Nestorians and Their Rituals*, 2 vols. (London: J. Masters, 1852); Asahel Grant, *The Nestorians or the Lost Tribes* (London: J. Murray, 1841); Patai, *Tents of Jacob*, pp. 253–54.

3. Patai, *Tents of Jacob*, pp. 253–55; Kashani, *Yehudei Afghanistan*; Ben-Zvi, *The Exiled and the Redeemed*; Brauer, "The Jews of Afghanistan"; "Afghanistan," *Encyclopedia Judaica*, vol. 2, pp. 326–28; Nimat Allah al Harawi, *History of the Afghans* (London: S. Gupta, 1965); Louis Finkelstein, ed., *The Jews: Their History, Culture, and Religion*, vol. 2 (Westport, Conn.: Greenwood Press, 1960), pp. 1149–90.

4. Daniel J. Elazar, field notes, Kabul, February 1976. Reuven Kashani, "Afghanistan's Dwindling Community," *Israel Scene*, vol. 6, no. 15 (December 1985), p. 12.

5. This section is primarily drawn from the author's study of the Iranian Jewish community conducted in Tehran in August 1970 and published as Daniel J. Elazar, *The Jewish Community of Iran* (Jerusalem and Philadelphia: Center for Jewish Community Studies, 1975). There is a virtual absence of published materials of quality on contemporary Iranian Jewry. The exceptions to this are Ezra Spicehandler's fine essay, *Yahadut Iran: Kiyyumah u'Ve'ayoteha* (Iranian Jewry), published by the Study Circle on Diaspora Jewry under the auspices of the president of Israel, and Joseph Glanz's comprehensive study of Jewish education, *HaHinukh HaYehudi b'Iran* (Jewish Education in Iran), prepared for the Jewish Agency. These essays can be found in "Yehudei Pras Bezman Hazeh" (The Jews of Iran Today), issue of *Tefutsot Yisrael*, vol. 19, no. 1 (January–March 1975) (Hebrew). Otherwise, the secondary sources proved to be inadequate. Furthermore, documentary material on contemporary Jewish life in Iran, outside the closed files of the Joint Distribution Committee and the Israel Foreign Ministry, consists primarily of reports from Israeli emissaries who have visited the country and a few studies of Jewish education commissioned by the Jewish Agency and COJO.

6. For the history of Iranian Jewry, see Yitzhak Ben-Zvi, *The Exiled and the Redeemed*, pp. 112–19 (on the crypto-Jews of Mashhad) and pp. 255–70, and *Mehkarim u'Mekorot* (Research and Sources) (Jerusalem: Yad yiTzhak Ben-Zvi, 1966); Walter J. Fischel, "Israel in Iran," in Finkelstein, ed., *The Jews*, vol. 2, pp. 1149–90; "Secret Jews of Persia: A Century-Old Marrano Community in Asia," *Commentary*, vol. 7, no. 1 (January 1949), pp. 28–33; "The Jews under the Persian Kajar Dynasty (1795–1925)," *Jewish Social Studies* (1950); "Isfahan: The Story of a Jewish Community in Persia," *Joshua Starr Memorial Volume* (1953), pp. 11–128; "Persia," in *Encyclopedia Judaica*, vol. 13, pp. 302–19; H. Levy, *Tarikh Yahud Iran* (History of the Jews in Iran), 3 vols. (1956–60) (Hebrew); H. Mizrahi, *Yehudei Paras* (The Jews of Persia) (Tel Aviv: Dvir Publishing, 1956) (Hebrew); Ezra Spicehandler, "Iran," *Encyclopedia Judaica*, vol. 7, pp. 1439–44.

7. The material in this section is based on Spicehandler, *Yahadut Iran* and "Iran," *Encyclopedia Judaica*; and the author's field interviews, 1970.

8. The material in this section is drawn from Glanz, *HaHinukh HaYehudi b'Iran*; Mordechai Mevorah, *Report to the World Sephardi Federation* (1974); *Iran* (1973); and the author's field interviews, 1970.

9. "Pakistan," *Encyclopedia Judaica*, vol. 13, pp. 14–15; *Jewish Communities of the World* (London: World Jewish Congress, Institute of Jewish Affairs, 1971), p. 72; Finkelstein, ed., "Pakistan," in *The Jews*.

21

Far-flung Diasporas in the Third World

Because Jews notably gravitate to the most active centers of the world's communications network, few moved south of the Mediterranean littoral or east of western Asia. Neither Africa south of the Sahara nor the rest of Asia offered much opportunity for Jews to pursue the kind of economic activities that have characterized them over the millennia. The two exceptions are Ethiopia and India, both immediately adjacent to ancient west Asian Jewish concentrations. These two countries were settled early in the history of the long Jewish diaspora by adventurous Jewish pioneers from those adjacent lands. In time, they became more or less cut off from their Jewish brethren but managed to survive as indigenous, isolated Jewish communities. Their rediscovery and reconnection with the Jewish people is part of the saga of modern Jewry.

Otherwise, except for isolated occurrences such as the periodic settlement of handfuls of Jews in central Asia and in China between the fifth and the fifteenth centuries (many of the dates are uncertain) and the spread of Marranos, particularly of Portuguese origin, in the Indies and the western Pacific in the sixteenth and seventeenth centuries, no Jewish communities were established in black Africa and Asia east of the Hindu Kush until the modern epoch. In both, when Jewish settlement finally came, it was primarily a by-product of the extension of the Sephardi diaspora southward and, most particularly, eastward.

One of the largely untold stories of modern Jewish history is how Sephardi Jews from Mesopotamia and the Persian Gulf moved eastward in the nineteenth century to found new communities across Asia and on into the Pacific. While most of world Jewry was opening new worlds to the West, these Arabic and Persian-speaking Jews, mostly merchants, followed the tide of empire—particularly the British Empire—as middlemen in the new imperial society and economy. As such, they helped bridge the gap between the colonial rulers and the indigenous populations. These pioneers founded communities in India, Burma, Singapore, Indonesia, Hong Kong, Japan, and the Philippines, bringing organized Jewish life into a world of ancient civilizations, which, except for two small coastal regions of India, had little or no previous contact with Jews.

Small groups of Sephardi merchants and adventurers also followed the Western colonial powers into Africa south of the Sahara. They established small communities in the Belgian Congo, the Rhodesias, and British East Africa. Only at the end of the epoch did Ashkenazi Jewry become significantly involved in this migration, particularly in southern Africa.

In time these communities became more diversified in their Jewish populations and sufficiently established to acquire a "permanent" presence, although they all remained small and most have declined since decolonization. The fortunes of the Jews were tied

460

closely with those of the colonial powers and most did not care to try to make the transition to life within the newly independent African and Asian states. Nevertheless, a few of those communities remain.[1]

The other Jewish presence in these Third World countries is that of Israeli and, to a lesser extent, American Jewish transients. Israelis are sent, often in the thousands, by Israeli companies to undertake projects commissioned by Third World governments and may spend several years in some African or Asian country. Because these projects are of even longer duration and are frequently followed by others, the Israelis establish enclaves wherever there are enough of them, with as full a range of Israeli-style institutions as needed.

The American Jewish presence was particularly prominent from the end of World War II until the American withdrawal from Vietnam in the mid-1970s, that is, for the first postwar generation. It was concentrated in east and Southeast Asia where the American presence was such that the military had permanent bases, which inevitably included Jewish personnel and attracted other Jews because of the business opportunities they provided. With the reduction of the American presence in that part of the world, most of those Jews were transferred or left of their own accord.

In one sense, none of these communities are really significant on the Jewish scene. In another, they represent whatever Jewish bridgeheads there are to the teeming masses of the Third World, whose role in world affairs is likely to grow, however limited some of those regions seem to be in their capacity to modernize. The Asian communities, in particular, have emerged on the world scene as new centers of economic growth. Hence in the twenty-first century we might see a whole different picture of Jewish life in those regions.

The Jewish Community in Ethiopia

Ethiopian Jewish tradition attributes their origins to the offspring of Solomon and the Queen of Sheba. It is more likely that Judaism was spread among them a thousand years later during the Second Commonwealth because of contact with Jews from southern Arabia or Egypt, some of whom may have settled permanently in Ethiopia. Judaism was widespread in Ethiopia until the conversion of the ruling family to Christianity in the fourth century. The mass conversion to Christianity that followed left a minority faithful to Judaism. They were named Falashas (strangers) and were persecuted by the Christian majority, causing them to flee into the interior. In the mountains north of Lake Tana they established an independent kingdom, which lasted until the beginning of the fifteenth century. Later, the Falashas were persecuted, forcibly baptized, and oppressed. Still, they held on to a tenuous autonomy until the middle of the seventeenth century when they finally lost their independence to the Ethiopian rulers.

From the middle of the seventeenth century to the middle of the twentieth, the Jews were essentially impoverished serfs lost to the larger Jewish world. They were rediscovered by European Jews in the last generation of the nineteenth century, but it was not until the beginning of the postmodern epoch that systematic efforts were made to reach out to them. In the late 1970s, at the beginning of the second generation of the new epoch, their continued persecution, now by a Marxist regime, became a major issue on the Jewish agenda and their systematic evacuation to Israel began.

The Ethiopian Jews have retained their traditional tribal-familial organization, which parallels the organization of the other peoples of Ethiopia and harks back to the most ancient forms of Jewish polity. Because they were cut off from *halakhic* Judaism, their religion remained biblical. This meant that as long as they were independent their strongest domains were the *keter malkut*—they literally had kings—and the *keter kehunah*, with the *keter torah* either weak or nonexistent as a separate entity.

Once they lost their independence the strength of the *keter malkhut* diminished, remaining in the hands of elders, and that of the *keter kehunah* grew because their principal leaders were *kaheens* (priests). Thus they may have been the only community in the diaspora to have maintained the *keter kehunah* as a major domain of governance. What is notable about it is that the priests function as a separate caste whose responsibilities are those specified in the Bible, minus the sacrificial system. We know little about the ancient and medieval Falasha kingdom or about the relationship between the present Beta Israel (as the Falashas call themselves) and those antecedent Jews of Ethiopia; hence we cannot compare their present-day organization with that of the past when they were not so poverty-stricken and dispossessed, with all of the concomitant elements of cultural decline associated with massive degradation.

The restored contact between Ethiopian Jews and the rest of world Jewry in the twentieth century was modest and sporadic. There are some disputes as to whether improvement of conditions in the twentieth century was not accompanied by greater persecutions as Ethiopian nationalism became a force against internal differences. In any case, the number of Jews apparently continued to diminish. A few found their way to Eretz Israel in the interwar period and a few others after the state was established. But it was only after the Likud government came to power in 1977 that Prime Minister Menachem Begin set out to rescue them, a process that came at a difficult time: Ethiopia was plunged into civil war after the overthrow of the traditional empire and its replacement by a Marxist regime, and the region was suffering from a series of droughts and famines. What was apparently a majority of surviving Ethiopian Jews managed to trek out of Ethiopia into adjacent Sudan, where they were airlifted to Israel in the latter half of 1984 and early 1985.

There are no reliable population statistics about Ethiopian Jewry though it was generally accepted that there were twenty-five to thirty thousand in Ethiopia before the mass exodus, plus several thousand in Israel who are expected in due course to assimilate in the Israeli population. The evacuation of so many of the community to Israel was thought to have put an end to its indigenous existence, but no more than a year later, new estimates of ten thousand more Jews who remained behind were announced. Their situation is unclear.[2]

The Jewish Community in Kenya

The first Jewish families arrived in Nairobi in the early 1900s as merchants seeking to profit from the construction of the Uganda railways. Nairobi was then no more than a labor camp on the railway. The first synagogue was built in 1913 when there were twenty Jewish families in the city. The number did not grow in the interwar period, but World War II brought about a small influx of Jewish refugees. By 1945 the Jewish community in Kenya consisted of about 150 families, most in Nairobi. They completed a new synagogue in 1955 and reached a peak membership of 165 families in 1967.

The community had a permanent, full-time rabbi until 1965. Since then, there have been temporary rabbis from Israel who have served for set periods. The community is organized on the British pattern, with a Board of Deputies. Besides the board and the synagogue, there is a Zionist organization, which dates to 1909, an aid society, and a Hevra Kadisha. Jewish education is provided through the synagogue. Because Kenya and Israel have maintained ties, formally or informally, throughout the postwar period, many Israelis go to Kenya, some of whom stay there temporarily for economic reasons and add some modest infusions of strength to the community.[3]

The Jewish Community in Zaire

Zaire was known as the Belgian Congo before 1960. The first Jews settled there in 1907 from South Africa. In 1911 Sephardim arrived, principally from the island of Rhodes and other Greek communities. They became dominant in the community, particularly after many of the Ashkenazim left during the Great Depression. After each world war, a few Ashkenazi refugees came too.

By 1911 the resident Jews had organized the Communauté de Congo Belge et du Ruanda-Urundi, which was given legal status by the colonial government. No synagogue was built until 1930, when one was completed in Elisabethville (now Lubumbashi). It housed a community center and such other Jewish institutions as there were in the community. From 1937 onward, there was a resident rabbi. An Association Sioniste de Congo Belge also functioned in this period. Besides the Elisabethville community, there were seventy families in Léopoldville (now Kinshasa) and smaller concentrations of Jews in other Congo towns. Jewish children received instruction in the Hebrew language and Judaism in the government schools; the teachers were paid by the colonial authorities. By 1960 there were twenty-five hundred Jews in the Belgian Congo, half in Elisabethville.

In the civil war that followed the sudden granting of independence to the Congo, many Jews left and the Jewish population was reduced to less than a thousand, mostly in Lubumbashi and Kinshasa. In the intervening twenty-five years the Jewish population continued to decline, so that in the mid-1980s there were no more than two hundred known Jews permanently living in Zaire.

Zaire and Israel established diplomatic relations in 1960 and Israeli technical and military aid missions were prominent in the country until it broke off relations after the 1973 war. Zaire later became the first country to restore relations with Israel, and Israeli technical and military assistance resumed. Hence, besides the permanent Jewish community there are invariably a number of Israelis temporarily living in the country.[4]

The Jewish Community in Zambia

Jews came to Zambia, then Northern Rhodesia, at the turn of the century following British colonial expansion northward. The first two Jewish settlements were at Livingstone and Broken Hill (now Kabwe). When the railroad reached Victoria Falls in 1905, there were enough Jews there to establish a congregation, which by 1910 had thirty-eight members. Jews were pioneers in Northern Rhodesia, opening the country to Europeans. They were involved in ranching, the cattle trade, transportation, and copper mining.

In 1921 forty-eight Jews lived in Livingstone, eleven in Broken Hill, and twenty-five in Lusaka. German Jewish refugees arrived in the late 1930s to increase the size of the community, and the Jewish population reached a peak of close to twelve hundred in the mid-1950s, principally in Lusaka and in five copper belt centers, each of which had small congregations. After the breakup of the Central African Federation and the granting of independence to Zambia, many Jews left. The community was enabled to survive in part because of Israelis temporarily living in the country under the auspices of Solel Boneh, which had construction contracts with the Zambian government. Three hundred Jews lived in Zambia in the early 1980s.

The community is basically congregational. Until the late 1960s it was part of the Central African Jewish Board of Deputies headquartered in Southern Rhodesia and also was part of the Central African Zionist Organization. But after independence in 1964 the government frowned on those ties and the community severed them.[5]

The Indian Jewish Community

India has an indigenous Jewish population rooted in the land for centuries and perhaps millennia. It is the third largest Asian Jewish community after Israel and Iran, and one that promises to remain in existence.[6] Almost all of India's estimated seven thousand Jews are in Bombay and its surrounding areas, including a synagogue in Poona and a declining number of Bene Israel in villages between Bombay and Poona. There are miniscule Jewish communities in New Delhi, Calcutta, and Cochin. Only the Delhi community is holding its own, because it is reinforced by Jews who are in the Indian civil service or the Indian army, and by a constant stream of Jews from other countries stationed in the Indian capital for one reason or another. The Calcutta and Cochin communities are both declining, with fewer than 150 Jews in each. The smaller communities are organized around synagogues, and only Delhi even maintains the notion of Jewish organization beyond the synagogue. As is to be expected, Bombay is the principal center of organized Jewish life.

India is almost unique among countries of the world in that there is no known anti-Semitism nor are Jews looked on as in any significant way different from the many Indian minority religions. Indian culture—its acceptance of diversity and its inherent communalism—has given the Jews a kind of sanctuary that has never been known in the Western world. (For example, Jews appear as a caste in the Indian census.) In the process, Indian Jewry has, perforce, acquired the general characteristics of the Indian population. Their social patterns, psychological characteristics, and culture all bear the marks of the civilization in which they have been located for hundreds if not thousands of years. At its high point in 1948, India may have had as many as thirty thousand Jews.

The Jews of India are divided into three principal groups. The largest is the Bene Israel who are located principally in the state of Maharashtra, in Bombay and environs. They number between five and seven thousand. The second group consists of the Jews of Cochin, now reduced to 75 in Cochin itself, divided into two groups: the so-called white Jews and the so-called black Jews. Both groups have been indigenous to India for centuries—according to their traditions since the time of the First or Second Temples and certainly at least fifteen hundred years. The third group is from the Persian Gulf region. Because most are originally from Iraq, they are known as Baghdadis. Since their arrival early in the nineteenth century, they have remained separate from the indigenous Jews whose Jewishness they regard with great suspicion, to the point of developing their own community institutions. Most left the country for Europe, particularly London, and America, particularly Los Angeles, when the British granted India its independence in 1947.[7]

Most of the indigenous Jews also left India in the late 1940s and early 1950s—for Israel. There was absolutely no pressure from India behind the exodus. Those who left did so mainly to realize the Zionist vision, to seek greater economic opportunity, or to find more pleasant surroundings. Immigration to Israel has almost stopped, though a trickle continues. There is no mass movement, however, and no one is talking about the community disappearing. The number of Jews has been stable for several years now, since the burst of *aliya* after the Six-Day War ceased. It does not diminish because the birthrate replenishes the losses caused by emigration.

Organized Jewish life in Bombay continues despite the *aliya* of most of Indian Jewry. Formally, no organizations have gone out of existence but all are limited in scope and intensity. There are more and, in some respects, better organizations than before. In relation to the organization of the Jewish community, most of its institutions except the synagogue were introduced into the community by immigrants from the West during the past century and a half, many more recently. They have survived in a nonwestern society only because of a handful of leaders. As a result, the communities can barely support the institutions that exist and, in all likelihood, will be even less able to do so in the future.

Communal-welfare sphere. Nominally, the Central Jewish Board is the roof organization that gives the community an address. It was founded during World War II by Victor Sassoon and others for that purpose. Although it claims jurisdiction over all the Jews of India, its work is confined to Bombay and environs because that is where the Jews are. The other communities are too far away, although they occasionally send someone to a meeting.

Most organizations are weak, but there is always one that functions as a catalyst of communal life at any given time. In 1976 it was the Jewish Youth Association of Bombay, an organization of young adults, eighteen to thirty years of age. They did such fund-raising and welfare work as was undertaken in the community, including the Maot Hittim for established residents, the United Israel Appeal, and aid for immigrants to Bombay from the surrounding villages. They organized themselves after the Six-Day War, as a result of its impact. Its members are the activists in the community, as much as there are any. They are strong supporters of Jewish education and serve on the boards of the local Jewish schools.

There is a Bombay Zionist Association, founded in 1920, which has been active in fits and starts. It reached its peak membership of three hundred in the 1970s, but most of its members were only nominally affiliated. There have been two Zionist youth movements in Bombay. B'nei Akiva still exists. Habonim existed at least until 1965 but is no more.

Religious-congregational sphere. The synagogues are the most important continuing institutions. All three world synagogue movements are represented in India, because of the efforts of visitors from the United States who have capitalized on Indian Jewish poverty to enlist synagogues into their respective movements for the most nominal subsidies. The affiliated congregations are all Orthodox in practice. The United Synagogue of India originally consisted of some village synagogues to whom the Conservative movement in the United States sent from five hundred to one thousand dollars annually in a lump sum. Under village conditions, this was enough money to lead to conflicts over its distribution, thus increasing disunity rather than unity. Now it has

Bombay affiliates as well. The Union of Orthodox Jewish Congregations was organized in response to the United Synagogue, but it does not mean much either.

The Gate of Mercy Synagogue is the oldest congregation, founded in the 1790s. It is a corporation with its own governing committee. It owns properties that provide it with an income, so that membership fees are nominal. Hebrew classes are held on its premises, taught by local teachers trained in Israel. It also has a Gemilut Hassadim society and is legally the trustee of the local Jewish orphanage. The synagogue calls itself Conservative but is really no different from an Orthodox congregation in its ritual. Its leadership includes many of the city's most prominent Jews, including in the past at least one mayor of Bombay.

The Jewish Religious Union was founded by Claude Montefiore as a Reform synagogue after World War I. It is the country's only Reform congregation and orthodoxly maintains Reform practices. Its members include the notables of the community, most of whom are in the professions. There are two synagogues supported by the Sassoon family trust funds. They have no membership or governing committees. Jews just come to pray. As such, these synagogues cannot be members of the Central Jewish Board.

India has no rabbis and no *bet din*. Nor has it ever had, except for Rabbi Ezekiel Musleah, a Calcutta native, educated at the Jewish Theological Seminary in New York who served in his native city for a few years in the 1950s, and an occasional "stray" who wandered in for a while. The community has tried to get a rabbi from time to time but cannot pay much and India is India, so they have been unsuccessful.

For a generation, from shortly after India regained its independence until his death in 1981, the Bombay Jewish community was dominated by an extraordinary personality, Hersh Cynowitz, whose official positions were president of the Central Board of Indian Jews and honorary president of the Zionist Organization. Mr. Cynowitz was unique in Bombay. He was born near Bialystok, then in Poland, was trained as a lawyer, worked in the Vilna court system, and was an active Zionist. He came to India in 1943 as a refugee and remained there. Because he was known to the Jewish Agency, he was appointed its representative in India and handled the allocation of immigration certificates to what was then Palestine. He also averred to have organized the first Indian delegation to the World Zionist Congress, in 1946. Of course, he led the delegation. He was a true example of a between-the-wars Polish-Jewish politician. As such, he was automatically part of the "establishment" that dominated Israeli and world Jewish politics until very recently. He really enjoyed the politics of Jewish communal life and its public affairs aspects. For Indian Jewry, he was a "find"—someone who could connect them with the larger Jewish world. Mr. Cynowitz became the contact between Indian Jewry and the rest of world Jewry. More than that, he created the contacts and then channeled them through himself.

Mr. Cynowitz gained his position in India because he filled a vacuum created in the late 1940s. Until then, the community was led by the Iraqi "first families"—the Sassoons, Moses, Khadouries, and so forth. Most of them, however, were cool or cold toward Indian independence and, as the independence movement began to succeed, they moved away. Moses, who was an Indian, brought Cynowitz into the picture. Unlike almost all the Europeans in India at the time, Cynowitz became an Indian citizen, one of the first Europeans to do so. This made him especially meritorious in the eyes of the new government and he never lost the strength it gave him. He also cultivated the Bene Israel and became their leader.

In a way, Cynowitz was a Jewish political "boss." He did favors for people (as he put it, "I am never too busy and when I say I will do something, I deliver"). He made it a point to know everyone. He circulated among people, building up contacts with the authorities and with his "constituents." He maintained his contacts throughout the Jewish world and even did "case work" in Israel for Indian *olim* during his two visits every year. As long as Hersh Cynowitz was alive, Indian Jewry had a strong leader and representation in world Jewish affairs. Since his death, no one has taken his place.

Calcutta was founded and developed by the British and its Jews came, principally from the Arabian Sea littoral, to participate in the commerce of the British Empire. At one time there were six thousand Jews living there. Those who are left are mostly minor clerks or unemployed. There are five synagogues. Magen David is the largest. Attached to it is Neveh Israel (the original congregation on the site). There are two others nearby and a fifth in Chinatown. Three maintain daily *minyanim* by paying all the participants, a substantial benefit in India's economy. A few extra people come on Shabbat, but even on Yom Kippur only about three *minyanim* appear at Magen David. Funds for maintaining the synagogues and *minyanim* come from rentals of the stores located on synagogue-owned properties.

There is no overarching organization in Calcutta. Each synagogue is independent. There are, in addition, some common organizations. These include the Jewish burial board with a paid secretarial position, whose incumbent earns his livelihood as the Jewish functionary in the city. There are also schools for Jewish boys and for girls. In 1976 the boys' school had five students; the girls' school, six. In both, the teachers were Bengalis and no Jewish subjects were taught. The students knew no Hebrew but learned some prayers by rote. The Jewish hospital has been taken over by the government but with the proviso that four beds are reserved for Jews (two male, two female). The hospital is now run down due to what the Jews suggest is mismanagement.

Until the early 1960s, there was a Zionist organization led by a Polish Jewish dentist who lectured at the university. When he moved to Geneva, the organization collapsed. Apparently the community tries to take care of its poor, principally through the dedicated funds of the synagogues. Their major outside Jewish contact was the Jewish Agency *shaliah* in Bombay as long as there was one. He visited them every so often. The Israeli consulate in Bombay handles *aliya* matters.

The Cochin Jewish community is the oldest of all in India. At one time the Jews of Cochin and environs constituted an independent Jewish principality among the many ministates on the Indian subcontinent. Even today the street of the Jews, dominated by its magnificent synagogue, stands in mute testimony to what was once a vibrant Jewish community. Most of the Cochin Jews left for Israel as part of the mass *aliya* from India and all but seventy-five of the remainder have emigrated in driblets since. Some have remained in India, settling primarily in Bombay. Others have moved to Europe and North America, and there has been a constant trickle to Israel. The remaining members of the community play more of a custodial role these days, maintaining what they can of its institutions, customs, and traditions, knowing that in all likelihood they are the last generation of Jews in Cochin.

All that is left of Jewish life in Madras (Tamil Nadu) is the remembered site of an old Jewish centery in the original town site and one Bene Israel girl from Bombay married to a local Hindu. Twice there have been Jewish communities in that southern Indian city. The first time was in the seventeenth and eighteenth centures when Portuguese Marranos and their descendants, and later Ashkenazim from London, joined the British East India Company in its commercial ventures along the Madras coast. These

"Hebrew merchants" were particularly active in the diamond trade and were officially represented in the Madras city government by Jewish aldermen. After World War I, some Jewish refugees from Europe found their way to Madras. They even maintained a Jewish life of sorts, meeting for services at the home of an Austrian Jew named Wolf who functioned as the convenor of the "community." When he died (apparently in the 1950s), the community disappeared as an entity. As late as 1968 there were twenty Jews living in Madras but they have since emigrated.

Because of India's coolness toward Israel, the Israeli government and the Jewish Agency have been able to do little in the country. India does not maintain diplomatic relations with Israel but has allowed an Israeli consulate to be maintained in Bombay. Formally, Israel is entitled to maintain a consul-general, but India used a pretext to expel the last one in 1983 and the consulate is now maintained by junior Israeli foreign service personnel. For about thirty years, from the mid-1940s to the mid-1970s, there was either a Jewish Agency local representative or a *shaliah* from Israel, usually from the Torah Education Department of the agency and later the WZO. He functioned not only as a youth leader and Jewish educator but as a link between Indian Jewry and the Israeli rabbinate for *halakhic* matters.

More recently, the Sephardic Educational Center in Jerusalem has made some efforts to bring Jewish education to Indian Jewish youth, bringing groups to their center in Israel and establishing a winter camp in the Bombay area. At present they are the only Jewish body outside India paying serious attention to Indian Jewry.

The Jews in Hong Kong

When the Chinese ceded Hong Kong to Great Britain in 1842, members of the Sassoon family of Baghdad were among the first outsiders to arrive on the scene. They already had offices in Canton, which they transferred to Britain's new island possession, and were instrumental in developing its port. The Khadouris soon joined the Sassoons, and both families built companies that employed only Jewish managers and clerks, leading to an increase in the Jewish population and the establishment of the Jewish community in 1857. The present synagogue building of the Ohel Leah Synagogue was completed in 1900 and was financed by Sir Jacob Sassoon. The community was almost entirely Sephardic until World War II.

These Sephardic families became the first families of Hong Kong, responsible for much of the colony's development in real estate and public utilities, as well as in commerce. They maintained the few institutions of the community in grand style and also contributed to Jewish causes outside of Hong Kong.

The Japanese occupied Hong Kong immediately upon the outbreak of World War II, and interned the Jews living there. Community life resumed after the war when the Sephardim were joined by a number of Ashkenazim, either refugees or from the United States and Australia with business interests in the crown colony. By 1984 there were 252 Jews in Hong Kong, half Sephardim and half Ashkenazim. Since then the number has declined slightly but has stabilized at about 200. Because Hong Kong is the site of many Jewish business interests, Jews from the rest of the world are frequently to be found traveling to and from this city. There are provisions for kosher food made by a community that otherwise would not necessarily be concerned with such matters. Now that the

British have agreed to relinquish control over Hong Kong to the People's Republic of China by the end of the century, the Jewish community's future is open to question.[8]

The Jewish Community in Japan

If there were any Jews in Japan before the nineteenth century, record of them has been lost. But since Europeans had only sporadic contacts with the island empire until the United States navy opened it in 1853, that is no surprise. Even so, three Jews settled in Yokohama in 1861. By the end of that decade there were about fifty Jewish families from Poland, England, and the United States living in that city. They established a cemetery and burial society and probably a synagogue and school.

Jews from Russia settled in Nagasaki later in the nineteenth century and at least established a cemetery, but as Nagasaki's sea trade moved to Kobe, the Jews also moved there. Jews fleeing from Russia continued to settle in Japan during the time of the Bolshevik revolution. Most transferred elsewhere but a few remained in Tokyo, Yokohama, and Kobe. Thus, in the years immediately after World War I there were several thousand Jews in Japan. Japanese soldiers who fought on the side of the White Russians against the Bolsheviks brought back anti-Semitic literature and ideas in the 1920s, but until the Japanese alliance with Hitler, they made little headway. When the Japanese conquered Manchuria in 1931, tens of thousands of Jews came under their rule with no ill effects, and Japan even opened its doors to a modest number of Jewish refugees from Nazism in the early years of World War II, including the refugees of the Mir Yeshiva who passed through Japan in 1941. Under Nazi pressure the Japanese introduced restrictions on the Jews but basically did not make life any more difficult for them than for other Europeans during the war.

Although many American Jews were involved in the American occupation of Japan between 1945 and 1952, only a few stayed in the country and many of the other Jews left after the war. The Jewish population in Japan declined to about a thousand in 1970, with communities in Tokyo, Yokohama, and Kobe. During the postwar period a few Japanese converted to Judaism as a result of the crisis of belief that engulfed that country after its defeat. They became active publicists of Judaism and Israel. At the same time, a few Jewish soldiers and occupation officials married Japanese girls and settled in Japan.

In the early 1980s there were a reported eight hundred Jews in Japan. Most of the communal activities revolve around the Jewish community center of Tokyo, which includes the Tokyo synagogue. It serves as the center for indigenous Jews, foreign Jewish businessmen temporarily living in Japan, and Israelis. It maintains a rabbi, normally imported from the United States, and a kosher restaurant. There is no countrywide organization and each community center is independent.[9]

The Jewish Community in the Philippines

Because the Philippine Islands came under Spanish rule in the sixteenth century, Marranos found their way to them and were followed by the Spanish Inquisition. At first Judaizers were sent to Mexico for trial and punishment, but beginning in 1580 an auto-da-fé was held in Manila. At least eight Marranos from the Philippines are known to have been tried by the Inquisition in the fifteenth and sixteenth centuries. In any case, the

Marranos who reached the islands were not known to have established organized Jewish life.

Not until the 1870s did Jews begin to settle openly in the Philippines, then still under Spanish rule. The first Jews were from Alsace, but they were the exceptions; most of the Jews who reached the country were Turkish, Syrian, Lebanese, and Egyptian. Later, a small number of Jews from Russia and central Europe found their way to the islands, most by way of the Jewish communities of Harbin and Shanghai.

After the Spanish-American War and the American occupation of the islands, American Jews came to settle. By the early 1930s there were approximately five hundred Jews living in the Philippines. The Jews had conducted services even earlier, but a formal congregation was not organized until 1922 in Manila. A synagogue building was opened in 1924. Although the Philippines were occupied by the Japanese, enough Jewish refugees from World War II reached the islands to quintuple the size of the community by the end of the war. Among the refugees were the community's first rabbi and cantor. By and large, the Japanese did not bother the Jews but did use the synagogue and its social hall to store ammunition. The buildings were destroyed in the fighting as the Americans reconquered the island of Luzon. Not only that, but some 10 percent of the Jews were victims of Japanese atrocities as they retreated.

After the war, most of the refugees moved on. The community was reorganized and the synagogue rebuilt. By the 1960s only 250 Jews remained, approximately half Sephardic and half Ashkenazic. By and large, the wealthy, permanent residents are Sephardim. They are the notables upon whom the community depends but they also have a limited penchant for organizational development, which seems to be a general trait among Middle Eastern Sephardim. They do dominate the life of the one congregation that encompasses all Jews who care to join. The service generally follows the Sephardi *minhag* but the prayers are sung in American Ashkenazi melodies. The Torah reading is according to the Sephardi style. All this is a reflection of the fact that those who lead the service and train the children for bar and bat mitzvah are Sephardim from Syria, Iraq, India, and Hong Kong, while most of the active congregants are Ashkenazim from the United States. Most of the Jews were temporary residents—American Jews stationed there by the United States government or United States business interests. As those diminished, the number of Jews continued to decline, reaching about 150 in the early 1980s. Israel and the Philippines have maintained good relations so that small numbers of Israeli experts have been sent to the country from time to time, many through the United Nations, but not enough to establish any institutions of their own.[10]

The Jewish Community in Singapore

Baghdadi Jews accompanying the Sassoon family established Jewish life in Singapore in 1840, when the British began their development of the island. Although the Magen Avot Synagogue was not opened in its own building until 1878, services were begun almost immediately in a street still known as Synagogue Street. A second synagogue, Chased-El, was built in 1904. Sir Manasseh Mayer who endowed it, also endowed a *talmud torah*. At first, the community was overwhelmingly Sephardi and has remained so, but Ashkenazim from England and the Netherlands and later China, Russia, and Germany also came to Singapore. The community became extraordinarily prosperous. In 1931 the census recorded 832 Jews on the island, a number that increased to 1,500 by the outbreak of World War II.

The Japanese interned many of Singapore's Jews, along with other Europeans, during the war. After the war many left. When Singapore became independent in 1955, an active Jew, David P. Marshall became its first chief minister.

The community maintains a framing institution, the Jewish Welfare Board, which publishes a monthly bulletin. It embraces the two synagogues and the Menorah Club. The community has maintained a single rabbi for both. The Jewish population continued to decline in the 1960s but seems to have stabilized at about four hundred. Because Israel and Singapore have good relations, there are always many Israelis in Singapore, who add an additional complement to the community.[11]

The Jewish Community in Thailand

Thailand is the one Southeast Asian country that never fell under colonial rule. As a result, it also did not attract permanent Jewish residents. Nevertheless, from the beginning of the modern epoch onward, individual Jewish merchants passed through the country to do business there. The first known example is Abraham Navarro from London, sent by the East India Company in 1683. Not until the 1920s did a few Russian Jewish refugees arrive by way of Harbin and settle in Bangkok. They were reinforced after 1933 by some 120 refugees from Nazi persecution. Because most of those Jews left after World War II, no formal community was established until 1964, when the Jewish Association was incorporated. Two years later the community established a community center with a synagogue. Periodic services had been held earlier, and the community received Torah scrolls from the Singapore Jewish Welfare Board in 1960.

The stimulus for organizing the community came from two sources: the Israeli embassy, opened in 1958 and, most important, a United States army chaplain stationed there in the 1960s when Thailand was a base of operations for the United States Air Force during the Vietnam War. At that time only about six Jewish families were permanent residents of Thailand, and the community was actually maintained by the 250 or so temporary Jewish residents in Thailand at any given time. The American withdrawal from Vietnam in 1975 had a serious effect on the Thai Jewish community as its Jewish support system, provided by the military, was drastically reduced. Nevertheless, the community continues to maintain its institutions for the Israeli technical missions, American Jewish businessmen, and others who pass through.[12]

Quasi Communities in the Third World

Quasi communities are Jewries with some attributes of an organized community but with no permanent institutions or settled Jewish population. Most of these quasi communities are outposts established by Israeli and American Jews on missions given them throughout the postwar world. Four, all but one in the Far East, are communities established or given organizational form by Jews serving in the American armed forces. Three of the Far Eastern quasi communities have been in that region since an American "presence" was established there after World War II. Except in China, they were built around religious facilities provided through the military chaplaincy. American Jewish chaplains and soldiers with religious and communal interests managed to mobilize the indigenous Jewish civilian populations wherever there were any. At one time, there were at least three more. French Indochina (the present-day Laos, Cambodia, and the Vietnams) had fifteen hundred Jewish residents before the French evacuation, many of whom left; the others made no effort to perpetuate communal life. New forms of organized life were brought in by the Americans. Thailand was transformed into a permanent one and the others disappeared when the Americans left. The survival of these quasi communities appears to depend on the continued presence of American Jews.[13]

Six of the ten quasi communities, one in south Asia and four in Africa, have been established by Israelis serving in the host countries on diplomatic, technical, or military assistance missions. They are generally built around the provision of educational facilities for the Israelis' children. Because they are in countries with almost no other Jews, they are even more dependent on transients than are the American outposts. There are no population figures for most of these communities because their numbers are constantly fluctuating, but the total may exceed five thousand.

Quasi Communities

U.S. Outposts	Israeli Outposts
Canal Zone	Ivory Coast
China	Liberia
South Korea	Malagasy Republic
Taiwan	Malawi
	Nepal
	Nigeria

Twenty-three countries have permanent Jewish residents (a few with several hundred) but no organized Jewish community life. In eight, there were once Jews in significant numbers; when the majority departed, organized Jewish life ended. The other fifteen simply have too few Jews or have attracted people born Jews who do not care about maintaining their Jewish ties. Perhaps fifteen hundred Jews are scattered throughout these countries.

No organized community life

Aden (2)
Albania (300)
Angola
Botswana
Belize
Burma (50)   The small Jewish community was abandoned after the Japanese invasion (1942) and never restored. The synagogue building is maintained by one of the remaining families.

Burundi
Cambodia
China   China's original Jewish communities disappeared—the last in the mid-nineteenth century. Today there are a hundred families, numbering an estimated five hundred people, in Kaifeng, who recall their Jewish ancestry, at least one of whom has returned to Judaism in the 1980s. Having been rediscovered by world Jewry, oth-

ers are claiming some measure of Jewish identity, primarily for the benefits it seems to offer.

In the mid-nineteenth century, Sephardic merchants and adventurers arrived with the British and organized communities along the Chinese coast. Most shifted to Hong Kong when it became a British colony. There were several waves of eastern and central European Jewish refugees in the nineteenth and twentieth centuries who founded communities in Manchuria and China proper. Shanghai, whose community was founded by Sephardim, benefited from an influx of Ashkenazic, principally Russian, Jewish refugees in the late nineteenth and twentieth centuries, to become a major Jewish community for two generations, from the turn of the century to the Communist victory in 1949. All but the tiniest handful abandoned China in the wake of the Chinese civil war, with most emigrating to the United States, Israel, or Australia. The JDC, which had provided support for the refugee communities when they were in their flower, continued to support the fewer than 100 who remained after 1949. Their numbers have now dwindled to fewer than half a dozen. In addition, there are a few people born Jews scattered around China, Communists who moved from Western lands to participate in the Chinese revolution. Although few hide their Jewish origins, they do not try to maintain any form of Jewish life. Such Jewish life as does exist in China today is organized by American Jews in the United States Embassy in Beijing or in other Chinese cities and consists of services on Yom Kippur and a communal Seder on Pesach, plus a social network, all involving transients.

Cyprus (30)
Fiji
Guyana
Haiti (150)
Indonesia (100)   A small community developed under the Dutch. It was destroyed by World War II and Indonesian revolution. There is no known organized Jewish life.

Libya (20)   Libya once had a flourishing Jewish community, of which an estimated twenty Jews remain. Immigration to Israel accelerated after each Arab-Israel crisis because of local pressure, and the community finally ceased to exist after the 1967 war.

Malaysia
Martinique
Mozambique
Senegal
Sudan
Swaziland
Tanzania
Uganda

Notes

1. Raphael Patai, *Tents of Jacob: The Diaspora Yesterday and Today* (Englewood Cliffs, N.J.: Prentice-Hall, Inc., 1971); David Sitton, *Sephardi and Eastern Jewish Communities of the World Today* (Jerusalem: Central Sephardi Community of Jerusalem, 1974).

2. Itzhak Ben-Zvi, *The Exiled and the Redeemed* (Philadelphia: Jewish Publication Society of America, 1957); Louis Rapoport, *The Lost Jews: Last of the Ethiopian Falashas* (New York: Stein and Day, 1980); A. Z. Aescoly, *Recueil de Textes Falachas* (Paris: Institut d'Ethnologie, 1951); Wolf Leslau, *Falasha Anthology* (New Haven: Yale University Press, 1951).

3. Julius Carlebach, *The Jews of Nairobi 1903–1962* (Nairobi: Nairobi Hebrew Congregation, 1962); "Kenya," in *Encyclopedia Judaica*, vol. 10, pp. 910–11.

4. "Congo, Democratic Republic of," in *Encyclopedia Judaica*, vol. 5, p. 893.

5. "Zambia," in *Encyclopedia Judaica*, vol. 16, pp. 922–23.

6. This section is based on the author's fieldwork in India in 1970, 1976, and 1984.

7. For a history of the Jews in India, see Flower Elias and Judith Elias Cooper, *The Jews of Calcutta* (Calcutta: The Jewish Association of Calcutta, 1974); Daniel J. Elazar, *The Jewish Community of India*, unpublished report prepared for the Study of Jewish Community Organization under the auspices of the Center for Jewish Community Studies (1976); *India Jewish Year Book 1969* (Bombay: Abi-Emu Publishers, 1969); Benjamin J. Israel, *Religious Evolution among Bene Israel of India since 1750* (Bombay: B. J. Israel, 1963); M. D. Japheth, *The Jews of India: A Brief Survey* (Bombay: M. D. Japheth, 1969); Schifra Strizower, *The Bene Israel of Bombay* (New York: Schocken Books, 1971); Ezekiel N. Musleah, *On the Banks of the Ganga: The Sojourn of Jews in Calcutta* (North Quincy, Mass.: Christopher Publishing House, 1975); Eliya Ben Eliahu, *Indian Jewry '84* (Haifa: Ben Eliahu, 1984).

8. "Hong Kong," in *Encyclopedia Judaica*, vol. 8, pp. 963–64; I. Cohen, *Journal of a Jewish Traveller* (London: J. Lane, 1925), pp. 115–21; Dennis A. Leventhal, "The Call of History," *Bulletin* (Association of Former Residents of China), no. 279 (May 1985), p. 9.

9. Abraham Kotsuji, *From Tokyo to Jerusalem* (New York: Bernard Geis Associates, 1964); "Japan," in *Encyclopedia Judaica*, vol. 9, pp. 1280–84; Cohen, *Journal of a Jewish Traveller*; H. Dicker, *Wanderers and Settlers in the Far East: A Century of Jewish Life in China and Japan* (New York: Twayne Publishers, 1962); "Japan: The Jewish Community," in *Bulletin* (Association of Former Residents of China), no. 276 (December 1984), p. 9; Elazar, field notes, 1977.

10. "Philippines," in *Encyclopedia Judaica*, vol. 13, pp. 395–96; G. A. Kohut, in *American Jewish Historical Society Publications*, no. 12, pp. 145–56 (1904); Elazar, field notes, 1985.

11. "Singapore," in *Encyclopedia Judaica*, vol. 14, pp. 1608–9; Cohen, *Journal of a Jewish Traveller*; Elazar, field notes, 1985.

12. "Thailand," in *Encyclopedia Judaica*, vol. 15, pp. 1043–44; Cohen, *Journal of a Jewish Traveller*; Elazar, field notes, 1977.

13. Little systematic information is available about these quasi communities. Journalists' reports, personal accounts written by chaplains, and the like, make up most of the published materials.

22

Building Citizenship in the Renewed Polity

Coping with Millennial Change

The Jewish people today are in the process of millennial change, the kind of change that has not taken place since the triumph of Pharisaic Judaism eighteen hundred years ago or the emergence of the diaspora nine hundred years before that. The Jewish polity must simultaneously encompass, respond to, and give expression to those changes, because the changes are epochal and are taking place on every front. Socially, Jews are increasingly living in a context in which every Jew chooses whether to remain Jewish and, if so, how and to what degree. Jews have not only been absorbed into the emerging world culture that grew out of modern Western civilization, but are among its foremost architects. They have become completely immersed in those strata of the educated for whom these social and cultural realities are most compelling. On the economic front, modern Jews were attracted to commerce and the professions. Postmodern Jews continue in those spheres and have also become managers and technicians, especially in communications. Most are in white collar or service jobs intimately tied up with the postmodern economy. Modernity weakened religious observance for most Jews, but postmodernity has increased the sentimental attachment of those selfsame Jews to a religion that they no longer observe in traditional ways. It also has generated a new Jewish fundamentalism of considerable energy and power.

As always, Jews gravitate to the centers of the communications networks. The migrations of modern and postmodern times reflect this, as have all Jewish migrations since Abraham left Haran for Canaan. This makes Jews more visible, more influential, and far more important than their number warrants. It also makes them more vulnerable in every respect.

With the restoration of an independent commonwealth, Jews have fully returned to the political arena. This requires great structural and constitutional changes in the Jewish polity, which are now in process. There has been a major reordering of authority within the polity; the *keter malkhut* has emerged the strongest of the three *ketarim*, replacing the previously regnant *keter torah*. Significantly, only within the domain of the *keter malkhut* can the different camps and parties in the polity work together. This reordering is a direct result of the breakdown of the unity of the *keter torah* under the pressure of modernity, so that it could no longer maintain Jewish unity. On the other hand, the repolitization of the Jewish people opened new opportunities for the *keter malkhut*.

The *keter malkhut* has developed a new civil religion embracing elements of traditional religion but linking them with modern and postmodern conceits, which is rapidly becoming the dominant mode of Judaism among identifying Jews. The power of the

475

keter malkhut is such that it is beginning to determine citizenship in the Jewish people and its polity. Under contemporary conditions, the answer to the question "Who is a Jew?" is increasingly dependent on the personal identification of eligible or semi-eligible individuals and the level of Jewish activity that they choose for themselves rather than on previously unchallenged *halakhic* canons. Here, too, it is the *keter malkhut* that determines matters—whether through Israel's Law of Return or the setting of standards for membership in diaspora community organizations. What the *keter malkhut* has not done is to develop a systematic way of setting the terms of citizenship. Indeed it may not be possible to do so at this stage in the epochal transformation.

A principal characteristic of this transformation is that Jews are now scattered the world over. A little geography lesson will show the change. The Jewish people emerged at the intersection of longitude 35 east and latitude 32 north. For the first twelve hundred years of their history all the Jews in the world lived within two degrees in any direction of that intersection. Then the range of settlement expanded to encompass an area from latitude 25 to latitude 40 north and longitude 25 to longitude 55 or 60 east. About twenty-three hundred years ago there was another major expansion. Jews spread outward almost from the equator to 50 degrees north and from longitude 5 degrees west to 75 degrees east, but almost all of them still lived in the earlier square. This situation changed little for the next twenty-two hundred years. Almost all Jews lived from latitude 30 to 45 north and longitude 10 west to 70 east. Sephardic Jewry occupied the area from 35 to 45 degrees and Ashkenazic Jewry from 45 to 60 degrees.

Beginning with the age of exploration at the end of the fifteenth century (in which Jews took an active part), individual Jews began to be found throughout the world. By the eighteenth century there were even occasional Jewish communities scattered in the far corners. However, not until the nineteenth century did the Jewish people become worldwide, and only in the twentieth did most of the world's Jews live outside the area between the Straits of Gibraltar and the Persian Desert. The organizational problems that this represents are of a new order, but, fortunately, the technology available to deal with them is of even a newer order. The Jews, geographically more scattered than ever before, are in more instantaneous communication with one another than ever before.

What is important about this transformation is that it is universal. Even those who see themselves as ultra-Orthodox and ultra-Conservative in holding on to tradition have been irrevocably altered by modernity, even if they are unaware of it. Even more striking is the degree to which the modern epoch was an epoch of change for Jews throughout the world, even in those countries that did not undergo what has been termed modernization during its three hundred years.

Every case study in this volume points to the seventeenth century as one of transformation. Anyone even slightly conversant with Jewish history knows that the seventeenth century began an epoch of change for the Jews of western Europe. Returning to that region after centuries, Jews established themselves in the Netherlands, England, northwest Germany, and the Scandinavian countries, to name but a few of the new sites of settlement, under conditions very different from those of the Middle Ages. Experts in Jewish history will recognize the degree to which the Chmielniski massacres in eastern Europe and the Sabbatean episode, which affected the entire Jewish world, both in mid-century, transformed Jewish life in eastern Europe and the Mediterranean littoral. A few aficionados will recall that permanent Jewish settlement in the New World began at the same time. Fewer still know that Jewish communities from Iraq to Morocco also underwent substantial restructuring and greatly changed conditions in that century, which established patterns that persisted until the communities ended three hundred years later.

Thus, even if modernization was not universal, the epoch was universally an epoch of transformation. Moreover, the transformations, particular as they touched each Jewish concentration, moved toward elimination or drastic reduction of Jewish autonomy, seeking to transform the Jews into a religious community rather than a fully articulated civilization. Again, the Emancipation in western and central Europe and its effects are widely known. The emergence of "Frenchmen and Germans of the Mosaic faith" is part of the common knowledge of modern Jewish history. So, too, the absence of traditional autonomous institutions in the New World settlements is widely appreciated. But often overlooked is how the Ottoman period reforms of the 1800s elevated the Haham Bashi (chief rabbi) to preeminence in what was to be a religious hierarchy for the Jewish community with the same intent and, to the extent that they were successful, the same effect. It is not surprising that this was so, because the Sublime Porte borrowed the model, with adaptations, from the French. Consequently, Jewish communities from Bosnia to the Persian Gulf had to respond to modernization after 1840 in their way as much as did European Jewry after 1789.

The institutional response to all this was not easily forthcoming. Throughout the modern epoch most Jewish communities tried to find ways to preserve traditional institutions within the new frameworks dictated by the external powers, in some cases even taking those institutions with them in their migrations to the New World. Latin America is a prime example. Only in the twentieth century, most particularly after World War II with the beginning of the postmodern epoch, have serious new institutional adaptations come to the fore. Those institutions are in some respects unique; in other respects they continue the Jewish political tradition in new forms.

What Kind of Republic?

One point of intersection between the old and the new is in the republican and democratic character of those institutions. As always, Jewish institutions have had to be republican. Every Jewish polity is a commonwealth, belonging to the people it serves. Moreover, that republican tradition continues intact and even stronger since the vast majority of Jews now live in host societies that are also committed to republicanism, thus providing external as well as internal reinforcement.

Less clear is the question of democracy. To the extent that all Jewish organization is republican, there are some democratic elements, perhaps most pronounced in ancient times under the original *edah,* or in medieval times in the small face-to-face communities of Sepharad and Ashkenaz, but never entirely absent. There are always theocratic, nomocratic, and aristocratic elements in Jewish republicanism, too. The Jewish polity was theocratic in the sense that God was deemed to take a direct hand in its affairs in some way and therefore those who spoke in His name had special standing, principally through the *keter torah* but at times also through the other *ketarim.* In fact, the most theocratic periods in Jewish history were also the most democratic, because God's direct rule involved the people as a body more than under nomocratic and aristocratic systems.

Nomocracy began to replace classic theocracy from the time of Ezra and Nehemiah. The recovenanting under those two leaders can be understood as having ended the possibilities of theocracy, that is, the direct rule of God, and replaced them with nomocracy, that is, with the Torah as a mediating institution stronger than either God or his people. It took another six hundred years before the nomocratic principle became preeminent in the *edah*. Once it did, it strengthened the position of the *keter torah,* which was no longer simply a vehicle for transmitting God's instructions or desires but in control of a fully articulated legal corpus that governed every facet of Jewish life.

Those six hundred years were years of struggle between nomocracy and aristocracy. Nomocracy won, but the aristocratic elements survived to counterbalance the nomocratic ones. Political leadership gravitated to the rich and wellborn during the centuries of exile and dispersion, because they were likely to have the best access to the foreign rulers to whom the Jews were subject and could use that access to try to protect Jews and their interests.

Still, the democratic element was never forgotten. Jewish institutions were often more democratic in form than in content, but they could be made democratic in content when the need arose. Jewish history confirms what every political scientist knows: institutions have an impact even when there is a gap between political structure and political behavior. Even when they function as oligarchies, democratic institutions offer a standard and a possibility for change that would otherwise be absent.

In the last analysis, Jewish republicanism is given expression through the balance of power among the *ketarim* rather than through general democratic participation, that is, widespread if not universal suffrage and equality of representation. Perhaps the best way to describe the system is a trusteeship through which republican institutions are constituted by the whole people and then governed by trustees on their behalf. At times those trustees have gained their authority charismatically through *halakhah,* because of their *yikhus* (family lineage) or because of their wealth and social standing. Nevertheless, they have been trustees and are empowered and held accountable as such. In the twentieth century the most common trusteeship has been one of givers and doers, with givers more prominent in the diaspora and doers more prominent in Israel, but both existing in both places.

Nevertheless, since the late nineteenth century there have been periodic efforts to democratize Jewish communities. Sometimes these have masked efforts by small groups of "outs" to challenge equally small groups of "ins." Other times they have been serious efforts to broaden the base of communal decision making.

The State of Israel is the one unqualified expression of this trend. There was never doubt that Israel would be founded as a democratic republic. The closest thing to an issue was the question of whether to give suffrage to women when the Yishuv was given internal autonomy under the British Mandate after World War I. At that time, only the ultra-Orthodox opposed women's suffrage; the Zionist parties, including the religious Zionists, plus the Sephardim of the old Yishuv supported universal suffrage. Israel's Declaration of Independence sets forth the democratic principles on which the state is founded, and, despite occasional scare talk in Israel, there has never been any serious threat to democratic republicanism.

The Jewish communities of Europe reorganized as *kehillot* and those founded in Latin America on the *kehillah* model were also based on the principle of fully democratic elections and, like Israel, tried to ensure that they would be democratic by encouraging party competition. They have had less success, principally because voting is voluntary, and only a few members vote. It is rare that as many as 15 percent of the eligible voters do so, not for lack of opportunity but for lack of interest. Formally, there is probably no signficant community today that does not provide membership voting to elect all or most of its officers. Usually, however, there is no contest for office; candidates are slated by those already in power.

Although some see this as the efforts of an oligarchy to perpetuate itself, it is more often a reflection that people must be encouraged or co-opted to become leaders, and recruitment is more a matter of filling vacuums than seeking dominance. Still, since the mid-1960s there have been challenges to the system in places as diverse as the French Fonds Social Juifs Unifié, the Victoria (Melbourne) Australia Board of Deputies, and the Los Angeles Jewish Federation Council. These challenges have led to the introduction of procedures designed to stimulate turnout and competition, whether through party competition and election days with polling places around the community, or a mail-in ballot, or some combination of these and other devices. All this is to the good, because an open election system, even if it usually is pro forma, acts as a restraining device on the trustees and provides opportunities for real contests when needed, as it has in different communities from time to time. Contemporary Jewish political life is punctuated by surprise challenges in apparently cut-and-dried electoral systems, some of which have been successful and every one of which has influenced officeholders at least to co-opt the opposition and give them a share of the action.

Still, these formal institutions and periodic reform efforts designed to make them as democratic in practice as they appear on paper would not be sufficient were it not for the built-in checks and balances that are a feature of the Jewish polity. These begin with the division of authority and power among the *ketarim* and continue through the multiplicity organizations and institutions that serve the community. This also reminds us that democracy is not merely a question of 50 percent plus one voting for something. That kind of simple-minded majoritarianism, best known as Jacobin democracy because the first to popularize it in modern times were the Jacobins of the French Revolution, is far from being the only kind of democracy or the best. Democracy does require decision making by majorities but in a more complex way.

Making Citizenship Work

Democratic republicanism has five aspects: access, representation, decision making, veto, and rights. Access includes citizenship, suffrage, personal involvement, and accessibility. In a democratic republic, citizenship (or membership) should be open to all who qualify, and the qualification aims for universality. Every citizen or member should have at least formally some way to vote for those who will represent the citizenry in the governance of the polity. Whether that franchise is exercised, and whether, if exercised, there is meaningful political competition is another issue, but the formal right of suffrage must be a keystone of any democratic republic. Beyond suffrage, access has to do with the possibility for citizens or members to be personally involved in the life of the polity by expressing their interests and working together for the common weal. There should also be reasonably equal or at least equitable access to office based on talent and ability open to anyone committed to the principles of the polity.

Representation is the obverse of access and the two go together. When the citizens of a polity cannot assemble as a body, they must rely on representation to maintain their democratic republic. Representation makes it possible to extend the territorial scope of the polity, in the Jewish case worldwide.

Representation in the *edah* has already been discussed. As a practical matter, representation can be either direct or virtual. When direct, representatives speak and act in the name of those who elect them and are responsible to their electors. When virtual, as in the trusteeship, there is generalized responsibility to the community but limited technical ways for those represented to control the representatives.

Decision making in a democratic republic must, in the last analysis, reflect the will of the majority. In the ordinary business of the polity 50 percent plus one vote may be a sufficient majority, but any extraordinary issue requires an appropriate extraordinary majority, especially in a polity based on voluntary adherence. The tendency in the *edah* is to seek consensus or something approaching it rather than minimum majorities. Successful democratic polities have discovered that constitutional issues require both extraordinary and dispersed majorities, if not consensus, so that any constitutional change will be widely accepted in the body politic and not alienate any substantial segment of it. Lack of such majorities has plagued many postrevolutionary regimes; in France, for example, even a nominally successful revolution could not conciliate those who rejected it and bring them into the body politic until DeGaulle did so through the Constitution of the Fifth Republic 170 years later.

The Jewish polity emphasizes consensus or extraordinary majorities because of its voluntary or quasi-voluntary character. However, even where the authority of a state is involved, as in Israel, the variety of visions pursued by its citizens and the intensity with which they are pursued has led to conventional and accurate wisdom that important decisions should be made on as broad a base as possible. That is why Israeli governments seek broad coalitions even to the point of conciliating small nuisance parties. It is why in the diaspora the governing councils of the communities consider victories of 50 percent plus one to be defeats and will not carry out decisions until they have far broader support. This approach is particularly appropriate where the governing bodies comprise trustees who must be careful to exercise their trust properly and not abuse it. What is clear is that the governing bodies of the *edah* or its parts cannot resist majorities even if they tried. Significant in the past generation has been the degree to which even oligarchical communal structures have responded with alacrity to every whisper of dissent by trying to make room for the dissenters rather than risk the formation of majorities opposed to their decisions.

Majority decision making is essential in a democratic republic, but minorities also need protection, sometimes to the point of having veto rights when a majority decision would threaten the very existence of the minority. The principal republican device for constitutionalizing veto powers is the concurrent majority. Where there are recognized camps in the body politic, all must agree to particular decisions in issues of constitutional import. If one or more camps reject the proposed decision, it falls. Where concurrent majorities are fully institutionalized, consociationalism is the result. Israel has been described as a consociational system by many students of Israeli politics, and there are substantial elements of consociationalism in the diaspora communities, which are designed to provide minority veto powers where appropriate, hopefully without allowing those powers to prevent action or ultimate majority rule.

Closely associated with consociationalism and the use of concurrent majorities is the question of rights in a democratic republic. Consociationalism provides protection for minority group rights while preserving the ultimate rights of the majority. There are also individual rights to be preserved and protected. The Jewish political tradition has dealt with individual rights principally in relation to covenant obligations. In other words, they fall within the framework of what the Puritans termed "federal liberty," the right to choose freely to observe the terms of the covenant. Beyond that, every individual has a right to life and dignity in the Jewish political tradition and Jewish political institutions are structured with that in mind. This approach to rights has many possibilities that have been developed in the Jewish political tradition but also has some problems.

In the diaspora, where linkage to the community is voluntary and the scope of the polity is limited, issues of individual rights are rarely raised because there are many ways to avoid clashes between the individual and the community. In the State of Israel these are very real issues. Despite the vociferous demands of a minority who insist on an individualistic approach to individual rights in the style of the United States, and of another minority that would deny individual rights in any matters they have defined as *halakhic,* the State of Israel has developed a policy by fits and starts that falls in the framework of federal liberty. That policy recognizes every individual's inalienable rights and guarantees them within a context that also emphasizes the individual's obligations to the polity.

The sum and substance of all this is that democratic republicanism in the Jewish polity is federal in the largest sense; it is based on a network of covenants that link individuals and camps in a common covenanted community and tries to give them a voice in its affairs and protections for theirs. In governance, most Jewish communities are either representative or multiple-element oligarchies or organized polyarchies, both in the framework of democratic republicanism. In the first, though the emphasis is on governance by trusteeship, the institutions of trusteeship embrace every significant element in the community. In the second, the emphasis is more on direct representation of the significant elements of the community in its governing bodies. Representative oligarchy is probably the most common form; it is the only possible form outside Israel, because of the unbounded condition of diaspora polities. It probably also reflects the reality in Israel at this time.

Beyond that, the *edah* is compounded from subsidiary polities in a federal manner as it nearly always has been. Today that compound has taken the form of a network of authorities linking Israel and the diaspora. The network embraces (1) a *medinah* (politically sovereign state) in Eretz Israel, (2) diaspora *aratzot* (countrywide concentrations of Jews with their own organizational structure but without political autonomy), and (3) *kehillot* (organized local Jewish communities) in both Israel and the diaspora.

Rebuilding the Jewish Polity

The fate of humanity is to be suspended between the messianic and the prosaic, between the quest for grand solutions to our problems and the unspectacular day-to-day tasks of making life livable and worthwhile. The two central fields of human concern, religion and politics, are central precisely because they represent efforts to come to grips with and link the messianic and the prosaic in real life. Every civilization must create viable religious and political beliefs and institutions that enable its members to make that link. The rise and fall of civilizations reflect the cycles of success and failure in efforts to that end.

Jewish civilization has survived because whenever it has been faced with the need to create and re-create beliefs and institutions, it has done so without abandoning its original essence. The key to the success of Jewish religious and political ideas in linking the messianic and the prosaic has been the integration of the two with the life of the community. The health of the Jewish people has depended on that integration and the momentum it has generated to propel Jews toward the creation of the holy commonwealth on earth. Although the ideal of the holy commonwealth cannot be realized by human agency alone, the lives of the members of the community are transformed by their common striving. The continuous task of the Jewish polity, then, is to strive for the holy commonwealth through the development of the proper combination of the messianic and the prosaic.

In our time, the Jewish people has been greatly stimulated—or, more accurately, revived—through actions and by events of messianic import. One result of this is that many Jews have believed it sufficient for maintaining their Jewishness to identify with those messianic events while ignoring the more prosaic aspects of Jewish living. Realistically, however, the potentialities made possible by the messianic thrust of recent Jewish history can be realized only through the prosaic activities that shape the everyday lives of Jews. To that end, an alive, properly structured and working Jewish polity is an absolute necessity.

The involvement of Jews in such a polity must be understood as something much more than choosing to participate as one would in a fraternal or service organization or a local philanthropy. Instead, proper involvement must be understood as a matter of *citizenship*. A common task of all Jews is to build that sense of citizenship in the Jewish polity and then use it to build the kind of commonwealth desired. The Jewish polity today suffers because its members and, sometimes, its leaders have a deficient sense of citizenship. That deficiency, in turn, reflects a deficient sense of being part of a Jewish public. To be a res publica—to have republican government—there must be a public. The problem of the public is a serious one today, not only for Jews but for the world. It is a prominent issue in the political theory literature of the West in the seventeenth and eighteenth centuries, which laid the foundation for modern democratic republicanism.[1]

It should be obvious that the existence of a public involves consent. The Jewish people answered that question millennia earlier; but precisely at the time that moderns were forging a new kind of consensus to constitute themselves into a public, Jews were losing the basis for their consensus because of their transition to modernity.

During the modern epoch, the problem for the *edah* was how to maintain some kind of public when individual Jews were becoming full members of the publics of the countries in which they were located. In the twentieth century, particularly after 1948, a shift occurred. Today the problem is no longer how to make Jews willing to be members of two publics simultaneously, but one of being unable to maintain any public at all. This is probably true for most if not all the Western world except Israel and perhaps Switzerland. The sense of public has diminished so substantially that the republican foundations of Western civilization and of Jewish life in the diaspora are threatened. Most problems that Jews have today derive from Jewish expressions of this republican crisis, this crisis of the public.

What constitutes the Jewish public? The classic Jewish texts discuss this question. For example, there is a *midrash* that plays on *tzibbur,* the Hebrew word for public. *Tzibbur* is spelled in Hebrew צִיבּוּר, which can be read as initials for *tzaddikim* (righteous people), *benonim* (ordinary people), and *reshaim* (wicked people). Every *tzibbur* includes righteous, ordinary, and wicked people. The question then becomes, Who sets the tone? Only if the *tzibbur* is written with the *tzade* first, the *bet* second, and *resh* last, is it possible to have one. When that begins to break down, the *tzibbur*—the public—goes.

A clear understanding of what constitutes public life emerges from the Bible. The transformation of the Jewish people from simply being a nation like all others into a people is decisive in Jewish history. The Jewish people was considered a *goy,* a nation, *k'khol hagoyim,* like all the nations, until it covenanted with God and then it became an *am,* a people. A *goy* usually is based on prior kinship but any group of people under any sort of government, or even with an appropriate common identity, can be a *goy.* It does not have to be a republic; it can be under the worst of regimes, but it can still be a nation.

An *am* is a nation with a purpose or vocation. As such, its polity must be based on some form of consent; consequently, it has a public aspect. This is implicit in the biblical text, which makes it clear that when the Jews became an *am,* they also become an *edah;* the two events were simultaneous. Part of becoming an *am* is the acquisition of some kind of common political organization. These two terms suggest the two aspects of Jewish identity, kinship and consent. *Am* emphasizes kinship; *edah* emphasizes consent.

Consent (from Latin *consentire,* to feel together, agree) is best generated by assembling before Sinai or Shechem or on the Moabite plain as was done in ancient Israel, or on the Rutli field in medieval Switzerland, or on the plain in the old Icelandic republic to hearken to the Law Speaker. Consenting is congregating in the courtyard of the Temple and hearkening to Ezra reading the Torah or in a town hall in Massachusetts agreeing to laws and leaders. But that kind of consenting happens only under special circumstances or in small groups. (In Iceland up to twenty thousand people assembled on the plain every year; slightly smaller groups gather annually for the *Landesgemeinden* that still operate in some Swiss cantons.)

That kind of assembly is not the only way consent is given. It is a good way, if it can be done, although it usually becomes a ritual rather than the product of real deliberation. Even so, participation means consenting. Hence the rituals of consent are important.

Jews, recognizing the importance of assembling to consent, have developed ways to ritualize continual consenting. According to Jewish tradition, Jews not only received the Torah at Sinai but must reaffirm their acceptance of it every day. Much of Jewish liturgy is ritualized assembling to renew consent to *Adonai* (God), *am,* and *edah.*[2] That is why Jewish prayer is so different from Christian prayer and why Jews must pray in a community (defined by the *halakhah* as an assembly of at least ten adult males, the minimum needed to accomplish any communal purpose from an individual mourner saying *kaddish* to establishing a fully articulated communal structure). It is why so many modern Jews assemble in the synagogue for so-called social reasons rather than prayer; they understand what assembling is for, though perhaps some cannot articulate this understanding. It is why the principal Hebrew name for synagogue is *bet knesset,* house of assembly (in the political or constitutional sense)—synagogue is the Greek translation of *bet knesset.*

The contemporary trend toward privatization overwhelms the notion of public obligation or responsibility and makes it extraordinarily difficult to build any kind of consensus. If the only consensus is that everybody is free to "do his own thing," it is difficult even to protect the rights of people to do their own things, because for some people the things they want to do will interfere with others. Admittedly, the public posture states that one is free to "do his own thing" so long as it does not hurt anyone else. But who is judge of what hurts someone else? That has become the problem.

Since the beginning of political thought, political theorists have demonstrated, in an intellectually satisfying way, that the results of such privatization can lead only in one direction—to what the Bible terms *hamas,* senseless random violence, the breakdown of civilization. This is the conclusion whatever theory one follows. To a theorist this is an interesting problem; to a human being it is potentially dangerous. The Bible identifies *hamas* as the only reason for which God is willing to destroy the world.[3]

In 1835 Alexis de Tocqueville wrote: "If a people is unable to discern the causes of their own wretchedness, they are likely to fall sacrifice to the ills of which they are ignorant."[4] He was referring to this problem of excessive privatization, which he foresaw as the tendency in modern democracy unless it was very careful about the direction it took. Today his words have special relevance.

As a consequence of the transformations of the contemporary world, the Jewish polity must deal simultaneously with the Jewish public as one and as congeries of specialized publics through which Jews participate in Jewish life. Formerly it was possible to see these groups simply as parts of one public. Take the question of Jewish "giving." At one time, for example, it was likely that all the big givers in a community socialized with one another almost exclusively, shared the same views, identified with the same public and private institutions, and belonged to the same congregation and club; one could see them as a kind of public. The range of interests of Jewish "big money" has grown in the past generation as the number of Jewish wealthy has increased. In the larger communities there no longer are personal connections between people of substance. Even support for Israel is no longer through one common channel. Younger people of wealth, whether or not they give to the magbit through normal channels, also are establishing new funding mechanisms to support alternative institutions in Israel.[5] This is a major shift in the one sphere that had seemed immune to fragmentation.

Elitism is another danger. Nothing will destroy democratic republicanism faster than if a few people become the only public committed to making the republic work. If most people pursue their private pleasures without regard to anything beyond them, or if they express only an occasional nod toward civic responsibility based on habit, or vote in occasional elections but show little interest beyond these gestures, it is easy for that to happen. Those people interested in public affairs—and there will always be people who are—will come to see themselves as the only reference group worth consideration.

What has happened in the last generation to the concentric circles of the model presented in chapter four reveals something about the direction in which the Jewish people is headed. What was visible at the beginning of the generation with regard to the separation between the inner circles of people who are more involved and more committed, and the outer circles that are drifting farther and farther away, is becoming even more true. As the gap between the outer and the inner circles becomes a vacuum, it will begin to erode the middle circles. People who still see themselves as committed Jewishly do not see themselves as part of a Jewish public nor are they concerned about being citizens. On the contrary, they look around and see that most Jews whom they know as Jews are uninterested. They see most institutions as institutions that have been privatized. Thus they maintain their Jewishness on a private basis. This is a dangerous trend for Jews. One can only wonder how long they can perpetuate such attitudes as individuals without succumbing to the forces of assimilation; it is equally dangerous and weakening to the Jewish community.

On the other side of the ledger, as the inner circles have grown closer, there has been greater interaction among the different publics within them. In the United States, for example, in the first postwar generation, the separation between Orthodox and non-Orthodox publics was almost total, with the Orthodox separate from the mainstream of American Jewish life. Today there is much less separation in the matters affecting the *keter malkhut*. As a result, more Jews from each community are now aware of what the others are about and have more contacts with one another than ever before. On one hand, this has led to greater conflict, as propinquity often will. On the other, there is reason to expect that, if present trends continue, there will be a stronger alliance forged between the Jewish community federations and at least some elements of the Orthodox community than between the federations and the Reform and Conservative establishments. A relationship may even develop between the federations and the Orthodox camp like that in Israel between the dominant political parties and the parties of the religious camp, or like that between federations and the Reform congregations during the early years of the federation movement seventy to eighty years ago, because of the symbiosis of interests developing between them.

This is one example of how, as the federations have become the framing institutions of the American Jewish community, they increasingly establish the parameters of the American Jewish organizational mosaic. This brings them to interact with all the other elements in it—with some more intimately and clearly, with others less so. This development has created an opportunity for the federations to build a larger Jewish public as well as their own publics.

In diaspora communities where Orthodoxy remained the public norm, the principal division was between religious and secular Jews. The militant Jewish secularists who emerged from the eastern European milieu in the late nineteenth century refused to have anything to do with Jewish religion. Where the secularists dominated the community as in Argentina, Jewish religious institutions were left to wither on the vine. Where the religious institutions dominated, as in Britain, the secularists were simply left outside the community. In Israel the two groups reached a political modus vivendi because both were forced to function within the framework of a bounded society and neither could simply go its own way. But on the human level, the emphasis was on as complete a separation as possible. Thus separate publics were created that were comprehensive in scope.

The separation of the circles in the diaspora has led to a breakdown of the separation between religious and secular Jews in the inner circles. Secularism as an ideology has almost disappeared as nonobservant Jews have become neo-Sadduceans. The paradoxical situation may be that of Israel, where the successful relationships have encouraged polarization by enabling each public to develop its way of life with a minimum of interaction. Even so, because of the smallness of the Jewish state, there must be a degree of interaction. It is the task of the institutions of the state to foster a common Israeli-Jewish public, but although this was assumed to be almost exclusively a state function in the early days of statehood—such was the thrust of *mamlakhtiut*—it is now clear that "public building" is not a task only for governments; it also requires work on the part of the civic sector. Although Israel has preserved a far greater sense of public than the western diasporas, it is coming to recognize that there must be an alliance of government and civic bodies that will work at strengthening that sense of public if it is to survive the first flush of statehood.

Citizenship and Holy Commonwealth

The biblical vision for the Jewish people requires them to build a holy commonwealth; with equal emphasis on both dimensions. There can be no redemption if either is missing or deficient. What is important is not the polity itself but the purposes it serves, yet those purposes cannot be served without the polity. What the polity tries to be, what Jews strive to become, by working together in a commonwealth spread over space and time, helps define its purpose and justification.

The Jewish polity exists by virtue of what might be called a religious mystique, an orientation toward a better future, based on a sense of the Divine presence. It is directed toward nothing less than the redemption of humanity. That is the kind of polity for which Jews must be concerned, always remembering that redemption, far more than charity, begins at home.

The Jewish polity is organized on a dual basis rooted in kinship and consent. Jews are Jews by birth; to some extent that is enough to shape their fate. Yet, in the end, being Jewish is a matter of voluntary consent. People born Jews must still choose to be Jewish. Individual Jews have always been able to leave the fold. Even in the worst of times, there were ways out. The Holocaust came close to being the exception, but even while millions were being killed in Europe, we have no idea how many Jews outside Europe disappeared through assimilation.

There is, therefore, a difference between being born a Jew and being a true citizen of the Jewish polity. Born Jews and persons who become Jews have a right to citizenship but must choose to exercise that right. Similarly, there is a difference between being simply a citizen—a person who identifies with the Jewish community, who joins a congregation, contributes to a Jewish fund-raising campaign, or whatever—and a *good* citizen. The kind of civic commitment to the Jewish polity, to the commonwealth that is and to the commonwealth that could be, makes the difference between being a citizen and being a good citizen.

To build good citizenship in a proper commonwealth Jews must reckon with their present situation as honestly as possible. They must build upon its possibilities just as they must struggle against its deficiencies. They must struggle against some hard truths and even some uncomfortable ones.

Little need be said about the revival of the sense of kinship among Jews. The impact of the Six-Day War, the new ethnicity, and the new anti-Semitism have been widely discussed. Something else, however, has happened to Jews in the diaspora to stimulate a new sense of Jewish identity. Many diaspora Jews, particularly the most successful, have discovered that they have reached the limits of integration. Jews have discovered that a Jew can assimilate completely. They have also found that a Jew who does not want to disappear can become an active, full member of the larger society while retaining his Jewish identity. But a Jew who is an active, full member of that society reaches a point where he must limit his involvement or give up his Jewishness. This is not simply true of Sabbath observers who rapidly come to that point. It is equally true of the nonobservant. This is not a condition that Jews impose on themselves; it is a condition that is imposed on them. The choice is not forced by persecution or even negative pressures; it is based on positive factors.

American Jews have been the first to face this choosing precisely because Jews have been so successful in the United States. If we could probe the thoughts of the top leadership of American Jewry, who have been successful in general affairs, we would probably find that many now recognize that they could go further; but to do so they would have to give up their Jewish involvements—not because of any formal anti-Jewish pressure, but because there are certain activities, even aside from religious observance, that mark Jews as being apart. For example, living up to the expectations of the Jewish community in contributions to Jewish causes sets them apart. The American example is the best, because in the United States Jews are least set apart. A Jew may be the biggest contributor to the United Fund in town; but if his contribution to the United Jewish Appeal is as big or—usually—bigger, it will draw attention to him as more than simply an "American." It is hard to define what "simply an American" means, but there is such a

The school is one of the most important political institutions of the Jewish polity. If the Jewish polity were enclosed in a territory, in a box, an army would stand at its borders and defend it. But the Jewish polity does not have borders that an army can defend. Israel has borders, and Jews the world over support Israel so that it can support an army to defend its borders. But the world Jewish commonwealth does not have any borders; its care can be strengthened only through learning and through places where people can learn.

The history of the Jews has been a history of communities built around schools. They are the key institutions because they convey learning. Greek civilization survived for five hundred years after the Roman conquest of the Greek city-states, because the Greeks, like the Jews, had developed academies and they could live around those academies. When the academies failed, Greek civilization disappeared. The Jewish people has never allowed its academies to fail. Its task is to build schools and then to create learning societies around them—learning societies in a Learning Society.

The Demographic Challenge

Regaining a Jewish rhythm and reestablishing Jewish turfs will be helpful only if there are enough Jews. The tragic demographic situation of contemporary Jewry is a major problem in the building of a good Jewish commonwealth. The situation is tragic but is not a tragedy in the classic sense. It is not inevitable but is all the more tragic for being caused by bad or wrong choices made by Jews as individuals that have affected the whole people. The nineteenth century was a period of Jewish population explosion; the number of Jews in the world increased sixfold. But, as each Jewish community became modern, its birthrate began to drop. By the 1930s the birthrate of western European Jewry had dropped below the replenishment level. This became the situation in the United States after the baby boom that followed World War II, a baby boom which was more a product of American societal norms than Jewish concern.

In short, contemporary Jews were the first to accept zero population growth, even after losing six million people, more than one-third the Jews in the world, in the Holocaust. And they have been successful at it. As a result, even if fewer Jews slide out by assimilation, not many people may be left in the diaspora to be Jewish. It is not likely that diaspora Jewry will disappear, but the Jewish population in the diaspora will fall rapidly in the next generation. Between disappearance of people through assimilation and the drop in the Jewish birthrate, the diaspora is likely to lose at least two million Jews during the next fifty years. Many will just fade from the picture as Jews. A "saving remnant" will remain, but the Jewish people will be much weaker internally and externally.

Ironically, Israel may become the world's largest Jewish community by backing into that position. Positive birthrate and ability to retain those born Jews could bring its Jewish population past that of the United States not long after the turn of the century.

Demographic decline means that the Jewish polity will have fewer human and economic resources to draw upon, and Jews' influence in the larger society will diminish.[7] Even with the will and energy that Jews can command, 10 or 12 million people cannot do the work of 14 million. Even with zero population growth the rule in the West, Jews will be a smaller part of the total population in those countries and less able to defend their legitimate interests. In the United States, for example, at their high point,

Jews represented approximately 3.5 percent of the total population. During the "golden age" of the 1950s, they dropped to 3 percent. American Jewry is now down to 2.7 percent and has not yet begun to lose in absolute numbers, which will begin soon.

The unfavorable situation of the Jews vis-à-vis the West pales when we take the whole world into consideration. In the light of the population explosion in the Third World, the Jewish situation is even more critical. With Israel perennially having difficulties with the Afro-Asian bloc willing to do the bidding of the Arabs—in part because of a mistaken assessment of the Jewish state as a colonialist imposition—the Jewish political situation is likely to become even more difficult if the number of Jews grows smaller. All this is reinforced by the contemporary temper, which emphasizes quantity over quality and makes assessments about what is important on the basis of sheer numbers. Thus the importance of the Jewish people is diminished—despite its seminal role in world affairs—even among many who should know better.

Jews must address themselves to this problem of numbers. Jews can do something about the problem of zero population growth, if not individually then at least by twos. They can at least seek to replace the lost six million before following the fashions of their environment.

The Jewish polity can also do something about losses through intermarriage by fostering the right kind of conversion. It must be understood that conversion means acquiring a new "citizenship" and not simply changing one's "church." What Jews are asking people to do when they convert is not simply to adopt a new set of religious beliefs, although that is part of it, but to become part of a people and public. Taking on citizenship is different from merely changing one's time and place of worship, and it must be approached differently. With that concept in mind, the community could begin to develop some standards and insist on them.

Migration and Citizenship

A different aspect of contemporary Jewish life that affects Jewish citizenship is the renewed—or continuous—effect of Jewish migration. More than one hundred years after the beginning of the great emigration of European Jewry to new worlds, the Jewish people confront a mass migration of Jews nearly parallel in size and scope. Millions of Jews are once again on the move, most pulled this time by the positive attraction of new locations—Israel, the United States, the suburbs, the Sunbelt, or what have you—rather than pushed by unbearable conditions in their countries or communities of origin. This new great migration lacks the drama of its earlier parallel, but its implications for Jewish life are no less great.

Migration must be considered one of the central themes of the Jewish experience. No other people, not even the American people, has been so thoroughly shaped by migration, or so fully embraced migration as a means to deal with its problems of survival and even development. Jewish history can be read as a kind of point-counterpoint between the historical realities of Jewish existence and the idealized expectations of finding a final destination—Eretz Israel—that will break the migratory cycle. The dialectic of these two themes is with us today as before, despite the realization of the first plateau of the Zionist dream, the reestablishment of the State of Israel as the place where Jews should be able to come to rest forever.

Jewish history begins with an emigration, that of Abraham from Mesopotamia to

Canaan, which was to become Eretz Israel, in a deliberate effort to break with his past environment to begin building the new society. The Bible says: "Go thou from your land, your kith, and your father's house to a land that I [God] will show you." The establishment of the Jewish people on constitutional foundations was associated with a second emigration, the Exodus from Egypt. The detachment from Egypt as a place and the migration itself were major elements in bringing about the reconstruction of the people, as habits of slavery were purged during a generation of wandering in the desert. Then for six hundred years the Jews had a haven in their land, and migration virtually ceased to be a factor in Jewish life. The emigration that closed that period, the forced exile of important elements of the ten northern tribes (722 B.C.E.), represented an emigration from the Jewish fold.

In the wake of the destruction of the First Temple (586 B.C.E.), the Jews revived their ability to turn migration to useful ends. Through their exile to Babylonia and then the return of part of them to Eretz Israel, they created a new theological perspective and socioreligious base, which enabled the Jewish people to survive and develop. The migrations surrounding the first exile and return are paradigmatic of the effect of migration on the Jewish people in subsequent epochs; Jews migrated out of necessity more than choice but capitalized on that necessity to undertake the periodic institutional and ideational adaptations required to continue as a creative and dynamic people.

From then on, migration became a regular feature of Jewish life. In the epoch immediately following the return, Jews began to migrate voluntarily as well as from need in their search for opportunity, establishing communities throughout the ancient world by using the patterns of communal organization and Jewish observance developed through the Babylonian experience. The mixture of migration by choice and by necessity became a standard feature of the Jewish experience and has remained such to this day.

By and large, migrations occurred because of forces or circumstances external to the Jews involved. Thus during the Middle Ages, when Jews were settled in relatively small political entities whose rulers vacillated between friendly and hostile policies toward their Jewish subjects, the Jews themselves encouraged migration to keep their options open and to protect themselves against these vagaries of mood and behavior. In the modern epoch, Jews adopted a policy of encouraging emigration only when efforts at local emancipation failed to achieve full Jewish rights and equality. There also has been an enduring Jewish policy commitment to encourage migration to Eretz Israel. This remains a sine qua non of Jewish public policy, as it has since the beginning of Jewish history.

The modern epoch was one of almost continuous migrations for the Jewish people, climaxing in the last two generations of the epoch, from the late 1870s until just after the establishment of the state. During that time, the geography of the Jewish world was radically transformed in what can only be described as a paroxysm of intercontinental movement. When the dust settled early in the 1950s, there was a general feeling in the Jewish world that the great era of migration had ended and that migration would decline as a significant factor in Jewish life.

Although there are fewer migrants in any one year, today migration again has become significant for the Jewish polity. In the 1960s mass migrations resumed, first the exodus of North African Jews to France after the French evacuation of Algeria, followed by the success of world Jewry in temporarily opening the doors of the Soviet Union and other east European countries. Other, more modest, sources of migration since then include Jews from countries of the Southern Hemisphere—Argentina, Chile, Zimbabwe,

South Africa—seeking safer homes. A fourth is the small but still significant Aliya to Israel of Jews from the West. There is the migration of Israel *yordim,* which assumed substantial proportions in the late 1970s. In the 1980s the migration of Iranian and Ethiopian Jews occurred because of the Khomeini revolution and the continuous persecution of the Falashas by the Ethiopian government. Except for the Western *olim* and Israeli *yordim,* all of these intercontinental moves have involved migration from felt need.

All told, since 1960 the number of intercontinental migrants can be estimated at no less than one million (table 22.1). Most have moved from one diaspora country to another, not to Israel, despite its availability and its efforts to encourage Aliya.

In addition to the intercontinental migrations, there has been extensive voluntary intracontinental migration. In North America, for example, the movement of Jews from the northeastern United States to the South and West has taken on mass proportions, particularly since the 1960s. Parallel to it is the migration from eastern Canada to the Canadian West or to the United States Sunbelt. Accurate figures are hard to come by, but no less than one and a quarter and perhaps as many as one and a half million Jews have been involved in such migrations since the end of World War II. A similar phenomenon is happening in a more modest way in Europe, with Jews from the cold climates of northern and western Europe retiring to the warmer climates of southern Europe.

No discussion of contemporary migratory trends would be complete without reference to the interurban migration characteristic of the metropolitan frontier. In North America, this is manifested in the movement from the former central cities to the suburbs and from suburb to suburb or from suburb to exurb. In Israel there is a similar extensive migration from city to city in the same metropolitan regions in the Israelis' perennial search for better housing. The same phenomena are manifested in Europe, Latin America, South Africa, and Australia, although perhaps in a slightly slower-paced way. Those migrations account for at least eight million more Jews. In sum, only a small minority has not changed its place of residence in some significant way since the end of the mass migration to Israel in 1952.

The implications of this for those engaged in the governance of the Jewish polity are exceedingly important. How much time is taken up in dealing with the consequences of migration? How many institutions have been established, closed, adapted, or reconstituted because of migration? How much of the social fabric with which Jews are familiar and on which they have counted for the maintenance of Jewish life has been rent? We do not have precise answers to these questions, but in the larger sense we know the answers.

The Jewish response to this phenomenon falls into three categories: (1) institutional response to the migrants—what is done, if anything, to help them migrate and to absorb them in their new homes, (2) social adaptations as a result of migration—changes in the way Jews live because of changing their place of residence, and (3) constitutional and institutional adaptations—how Jews transform their institutions to cope with the changes brought about by migration.

During the past century a network of organizations has developed in the Jewish polity to handle the problems of "recognized" Jewish migrants by helping them secure the right to migrate, helping transfer them, or absorbing them at the end of their journey. Jewish leaders make public careers in these organizations and a civil service has developed to run them. The Jews have become so good at handling such migrants that at least since the flow of refugees from Cuba to the United States in the early 1960s, American Jewish organizations have been called on by the United States government to assist it in refugee

Table 22.1
Estimated Jewish Intercontinental Emigration since 1960

From	Low Estimate	High Estimate
North Africa	320,000	320,000
USSR and eastern Europe	350,000	460,000
Southern Hemisphere	70,000	80,000
Western countries	50,000	70,000
Israel	205,000	300,000
Iran	60,000	70,000
Ethiopia	15,000	15,000
	1,070,000	1,315,000

Source: Author's compilation from organizational records and reports, census, and demographic studies.

absorption. There is no more experienced body of people in the world than the Jewish civil service engaged in this enterprise.

Modern migrations have been a major factor in the transformation of Jewish life in the diaspora from its traditional organic to an associational basis, whereby Jews function as Jews by joining Jewish organizations rather than through living in an organic Jewish setting. For example, migration has had a major role in bringing about the disappearance of the "Jewish street" and its replacement by institutional ties. Postmodern migrations have taken many Jews beyond associationalism to cut them off from any serious institutional ties to the Jewish community because of where they have settled. Associational ties can survive without the Jewish street but to be sufficiently "dense" they require a Jewish neighborhood, which is what replaced the Jewish street for a while. Recent migrations, however, have even destroyed Jewish neighborhoods in many parts of the diaspora. This matter must be of serious concern to the Jewish community.

One task of the Jewish people is to build and maintain an appropriate institutional framework to accommodate this apparently continuous movement and to develop better ways and means to deal with the seemingly "perpetual motion" of Jews. Doing so is all the more necessary now in an age when public institutions have taken responsibility for dealing with human problems far beyond what was customary a century ago. Earlier great migrations took place when laissez-faire was the accepted response of public bodies, when individuals and families had to shift for themselves. Even then Jewish communities responded beyond the demands of laissez-faire to help their brethren; this gave the Jewish people a head start in preparing for what is now the accepted role of public institutions.

Citizenship, Vision, and Politics

All the achievements in reconstituting the Jewish polity make it possible to foster the kind of Jewish unity that only a sense of citizenship can create: a unity based on a positive sense of the Jewish role in the world and a clear vision of Jewish purpose rather than simply on the recognition that, by accident of birth, Jews are in the same boat. The sense of purpose and vision is essential. As a future-oriented people, Jews need a sense of purpose to maintain their collective health. As the prophet said, "Without vision, the people perish." All Jews will not necessarily agree on the essence of that vision or how to achieve it—as a people they seldom have—but it is possible to develop sufficient agreement in certain spheres to maintain the collective health of the Jewish body politic.

Differences of opinion, conflict, and negotiation are implicit in this model. Citizenship can exist only where there is a polity, and a polity, by definition, requires a politics—the continuous effort to balance interests and ideals to pursue common goals and to do so creatively with one's fellows in the community. A true Jewish politics will be a prime indicator of the seriousness of the Jewish enterprise.

Fortunately, Jews are a learning people as well as a doing people. When they really want to do something, they are successful at it. Perhaps this is why they were given the Torah; if not told how to channel their extensive energies, they would energetically pursue self-destructive (and perhaps generally destructive) courses of action. With a sense of purpose and vision, Jews can foster a true Jewish polity that will foster the messianic pursuit of justice in the framework of the prosaic organization of powers and programs.

Notes

1. John Dewey, *The Public and Its Problems* (New York: Holt, Rinehart and Winston, 1927); Robert J. Pranger, *The Eclipse of Citizenship: Power and Participation in Contemporary Politics* (New York: Holt, Rinehart and Winston, 1968); Vincent Ostrom, *The Political Theory of a Compound Republic* (Blacksburg, Va.: Virginia Polytechnic Institute, Center for the Study of Public Choice, 1971).

2. See Gordon Freeman, *Politics of Prayer,* Working Paper No. 5 of the Workshop in the Covenant Idea and the Jewish Political Tradition (Jerusalem and Ramat Gan: Center for Jewish Community Studies and Bar Ilan University Department of Political Studies, 1977).

3. On *hamas* in the Bible, see Gen. 6:11, 6:13, 49:5; Exod. 23:1; and Deut. 19:16.

4. Alexis de Tocqueville, *Democracy in America,* trans. Lawrence Mayer (Garden City, N.Y.: Doubleday, 1969).

5. See Eliezer Jaffe, *Giving Wisely: The New Israel Fund* (Jerusalem: Koren, 1982); Matthew Nesvisky, "Unlimited Partnership," *Moment,* vol. 9, no. 5 (May 1984), pp. 30–39; Danny Siegel, *Danny Siegel's Tzedakah Report,* published annually.

6. See Abraham Joshua Heschel, *The Earth is the Lord's* (New York and Philadelphia: Harper & Row and Jewish Publication Society of America, 1950).

7. On demographics, see the *American Jewish Year Book 1984,* vol. 84 and O. U. Schmelz, *World Jewish Population, Regional Estimates and Projections,* Jewish Population Studies Series (Jerusalem: Hebrew University of Jerusalem, 1981).

Appendix 1

A Note on Sources

There are four sources of data on which this book is based.

1. The books and articles cited in the footnotes and the journals I have read faithfully for at least thirty years and, for a few, the past forty, as well as back issues for an additional twenty to thirty years where they exist.

2. Interviews and conversations with almost every figure in world Jewish affairs who played a prominent role in the postwar generation. These include formal and informal interviews under different circumstances, often in the heat of action; conversations on Israel-diaspora relations with every prime minister of Israel, every chairman of the Jewish Agency Executive since the establishment of the state, and both chairmen of the Board of Governors of the reconstituted Jewish Agency. The only leader whom I never personally interviewed or talked with was Nahum Goldmann. That is an experience I regret to have missed, but he is sufficiently on record about everything dealt with in this work to have made his contribution through bibliographic sources. I also had many occasions to talk with his colleagues who dominated the important positions of the World Jewish Congress during the Goldmann years.

3. The country studies conducted personally or by the staff of the Study of Jewish Community Organization, now part of the Jerusalem Center for Public Affairs. I did not conduct every country study personally, but I did undertake a number of them and directly supervised the rest. Through the SJCO, we did fieldwork in Argentina, Australia, Austria, Belgium, Brazil, Bulgaria, Canada, Chile, Cyprus, Czechoslovakia, Denmark, Egypt, Finland, France, Germany, Greece, Hong Kong, Hungary, India, Iran, Iraq, Ireland, Israel, Italy, Japan, Lebanon, Libya, Mexico, Morocco, the Netherlands, New Zealand, Nicaragua, Nigeria, Norway, Panama, Poland, Portugal, Romania, South Africa, Spain, Sweden, Switzerland, Syria, Thailand, Turkey, the USSR, the United Kingdom, the United States, Venezuela, Yugoslavia, and Zimbabwe. In every case we followed the research guide, *Studying Jewish Communities* (Appendix 2). Each study included the mining of documentary sources, existing secondary literature, and extensive interviews with knowledgeable participants and observers. In many cases, we published country reports or studies, including the following:

BOOKS (All books are publications of the Jerusalem Center for Public Affairs.)

The Balkan Jewish Communities: Yugoslavia, Bulgaria, Greece, and Turkey—Daniel J. Elazar, Harriet Pass Friedenreich, Baruch Hazzan, and Adina Weiss Liberles (1984)

Community and Polity: The Organizational Dynamics of American Jewry—Daniel J. Elazar (1980)

The Governance of the Canadian Jewish Community, ed. Daniel J. Elazar and Harold Waller (forthcoming)

Israel: Building a New Society—Daniel J. Elazar (1986)

Jewish Communities in Frontier Societies: Argentina, Australia, and South Africa—Daniel J. Elazar with Peter Medding (1983)

495

The Jewish Communities of Scandinavia: Sweden, Denmark, Norway, and Finland—Daniel J. Elazar, Adina Weiss Liberles, and Simcha Werner (1984)

Jewishness in the Soviet Union: Report of an Empirical Study—Benjamin Fain and Mervin Verbit (1984)

The Jews of Yugoslavia: A Quest for Community—Harriet Pass Friedenreich (1979)

The Other Laws: The Shephardim Today—Daniel J. Elazar (1988)

REPORTS, WORKING PAPERS, AND OTHER SEPARATELY PUBLISHED ITEMS (All publications listed in this section are available through the Jerusalem Center for Public Affairs.)

The Activity Spheres of the American Jewish Community—Daniel J. Elazar (1972)

American Jewry and the Yom Kippur War: A First Assessment of the Community Response—Daniel J. Elazar (1974)

The Canadian Jewish Community: A National Perspective—Harold M. Waller (1977)

"Civil Judaism" in the United States—Jonathan S. Woocher (1978)

Decision-Makers in Communal Agencies: A Profile—Daniel J. Elazar (1973)

The Decision Makers: Key Divisions in Jewish Communal Life—Daniel J. Elazar (1973)

Decision Making in the American Jewish Community—Daniel J. Elazar (1972)

The Democratization of a Community: The Case of French Jewry—Ilan Greilsammer (1979)

French Jewry and American Jewry—Marc Salzburg (1971)

The Geography of American Jewish Communal Life—Daniel J. Elazar (1973)

The Governance of the Jewish Community of Calgary—Harvey Rich (1974)

The Governance of the Jewish Community of Edmonton—Jennifer K. Bowerman (1975)

The Governance of the Jewish Community of Hamilton—Louis Greenspan (1974)

The Governance of the Jewish Community of London—Alan M. Cohen (1974)

The Governance of the Jewish Community of Montreal—Harold M. Waller and Sheldon Schreter (1974)

The Governance of the Jewish Community of Ottawa—Zachariah Kay (1974)

The Governance of the Jewish Community of Toronto—Yaakov Glickman (1974)

The Governance of the Jewish Community of Vancouver—Edna Oberman (1974)

The Governance of the Jewish Community of Windsor—Stephen Mandel and R. H. Wagenberg (1974)

The Governance of the Jewish Community of Winnipeg—Anna Gordon (1974)

The Jewish Community of Belgium—Adina Weiss (1970)

The Jewish Community of Bulgaria—Baruch Hazzan (1974)

The Jewish Community of Delaware—Adina Weiss and Joseph Aron (1976)

The Jewish Community of Denmark—Adina Weiss (1977)

The Jewish Community of Finland—Adina Weiss (1977)

The Jewish Community of Greece—Adina Weiss (1974)

The Jewish Community of Iran—Daniel J. Elazar (1975)

The Jewish Community of Mexico—Seymour B. Liebman (1978)

The Jewish Community of Norristown, Pennsylvania—Adina Weiss and Joseph Aron (1976)

The Jewish Community of Sweden—Adina Weiss (1977)

The Jewish Community of Turkey—Adina Weiss (1974)

Jewish Survival and American Jewish Leadership—Daniel J. Elazar (1973)

The Jewries of Scandinavia—Daniel J. Elazar (1977)

The Jews of Norway—Simcha Werner and Adina Weiss (1977)

In the Absence of Hierarchy: Notes on the Organization of the American Jewish Community—Ernest Stock (1970)

On the Study of International Jewish Political Organizations—Charles S. Liebman (1978)

The Organization and Status of Contemporary Jewish Communities 5730 (1969–1970)—Daniel J. Elazar (1971)

Preliminary Bibliography for the Comparative Study of Jewish Community Organization—Daniel J. Elazar (1970)

Sephardic Jewry in the United States: A Preliminary Institutional Profile—Daniel J. Elazar et al. (1978)

Studying Jewish Communities: A Research Guide—Daniel J. Elazar (1970)

Today's Sephardim in Perspective—Daniel J. Elazar (1982)

Trend Report on Jewish Social Research in Britain—Ernest Kraus (1971)

ARTICLES

"Building Jewish Citizenship in the Emerging American Jewish Community," Daniel J. Elazar, *Forum*, no. 23 (spring 1975), pp. 5–17.

"The Communal Organization of South African Jewry," Steven Aschheim, *Jewish Journal of Sociology*, vol. 12, no. 1 (June 1970), pp. 201–31.

"Consensus and Community in Israel," Asher Arian, *Jewish Journal of Sociology*, vol. 12, no. 1, (June 1970), pp. 39–53.

"A Contemporary Paradox: Israel and Jewish Peoplehood," Peter Y. Medding, *Forum*, no. 26/1 (1977), pp. 5–16.

"How 'Durban' Reacted to Israel's Crises: A Study of an American Jewish Community," Ernest Stock, *Forum*, no. 23/2 (1975), pp. 38–60.

"In the Absence of Hierarchy: Notes on the Organization of the American Jewish Community," Ernest Stock, *Jewish Journal of Sociology*, vol. 21, no. 2 (December 1970), pp. 195–200.

"Israel, American Jewry, and the Re-Emergence of a World Jewish Polity," Daniel J. Elazar in *Annual of Bar-Ilan Studies in Judaica and the Humanities XVI–XVII* (1979).

"The Institutional Life of American Jewry," Daniel J. Elazar, *Midstream*, vol. 17, no. 6 (June/July 1971), pp. 31–50.

"Jewish Multicountry Associations," Ernest Stock, *American Jewish Year Book 1974–75*, vol. 75, pp. 571–97.

"Jews of France: From Neutrality to Involvement," Ilan Greilsammer, *Forum*, nos. 28–29 (winter 1978), pp. 130–46.

"The Legal Status of American Jewry," Daniel J. Elazar and Stephen R. Goldstein in *American Jewish Year Book 1972*, vol. 73, pp. 3–94.

"The New Sadducees," Daniel J. Elazar, *Midstream*, vol. 24, no. 7 (August/September 1978), pp. 20–25.

"A Note on the Structural Dynamics of the American Jewish Community," Daniel J. Elazar, *Judaism*, vol. 20, no. 3 (summer 1971), pp. 335–40.

"On the Study of the Financing of Jewish Community Activities," A. A. Kessler, *Jewish Journal of Sociology*, vol. 12, no. 1 (June 1970), pp. 89–100.

"Patterns of Jewish Communal Participation," Daniel J. Elazar, *Congress Bi-Weekly*, vol. 39 (March 24, 1972), pp. 7–9.

"The Political Tradition of the American Jew," Daniel J. Elazar in *Traditions of the American Jew*, Stanley M. Wagner, ed. (New York: Center for Judaic Studies of University of Denver, 1977), chap. 5.

"The Reconstitution of Jewish Communities in the Post-War Period," Daniel J. Elazar, *Jewish Journal of Sociology*, vol. 11, no. 2 (December 1969), pp. 187–226.

"The State of World Jewry: A Contemporary Agenda," Daniel J. Elazar, *Forum*, vol. 25, no. 2 (1976), pp. 51–62.

"The Sunset of Balkan Jewry," Daniel J. Elazar, *Forum*, vol. 27, no. 2 (1977), pp. 135–41.

"Toward a Jewish Definition of Statehood for Israel," Daniel J. Elazar, *Judaism*, vol. 27, no. 2 (spring 1978), pp. 233–44.

"Towards a Renewed Zionist Vision," Daniel J. Elazar, *Forum*, vol. 26, no. 1 (1977), pp. 52–69.

JOURNALS AND SERIAL PUBLICATIONS

(1) Issues of *Tefutsot Yisrael* (Hebrew quarterly copublished by the Jerusalem Center for Public Affairs and the American Jewish Committee) devoted to products of the study.

The American Synagogue: Its Uniqueness and Future (summer 1982)

Israel-Diaspora Relations (spring 1984)

The Jewish Communities in Scandinavia: Association and Assimilation (March 1977)

The Jewish Community in Mexico and Central America (March 1978)

The Jewish Community in Montreal: Facing Quebec Nationalism (June 1977)

The Jewish Federation: "Kehillot" American Style (spring 1982)

Jewish Life in Britain (winter 1983)

The Jewish Population in the Diaspora/Demographic Analyses and Forecasts (winter 1980; double issue)

The Jews in Australia (June 1979)

The Jews of France in Troubled Times (winter 1982)

The Organized Jewish Community in France (December 1978)

Pluralism and Equality/The Community Relations Agenda of American Jewry (summer 1981; double issue)

The Remnants of Balkan Jewry (March–April 1974)

(2) *Jerusalem Letter/Viewpoints* (An English language periodical published twice monthly providing up-to-date and often behind-the-scenes information on and analysis of significant developments in Israel, the Jewish world, and the Middle East.)

JL7—"French Jewry and the French Elections—I," Ilan Greilsammer (March 12, 1978)

JL8—"French Jewry and the French Elections—II," Ilan Greilsammer (April 16, 1978)

JL11—"The Jews of Quebec and the Canadian Crisis," Daniel J. Elazar (May 19, 1978)

JL25—"Soviet Jewry: Its Sources of Information and Images of Israel," Dan Caspi (December 4, 1979)

JL27—"The Movement of M'sorati Judaism in Israel," Batya Stein (February 19, 1980)

JL30—"American Jewish Political Activism in the 1980s: Five Dilemmas," Jonathan S. Woocher (July 1, 1980)

JL33—"Jewish Religion and Politics in Israel," Daniel J. Elazar (October 12, 1980)

JL37—"Jewishness in the Soviet Union: A Preliminary Report of the First Independent Empirical Study," Benjamin Fain, Dan Caspi, and Mervin F. Verbit (January 5, 1981)

JL44—"Jews on the Move: The New Wave of Jewish Migration and Its Implication for Organized Jewry," Daniel J. Elazar (January 10, 1982)

JL46—"The Emerging European Jewish Community Structure," Ernest Stock (March 14, 1982)

JL60—"Jews in Egypt—1983," Ernest Stock (June 15, 1983)

JL65—"American Jews and Israel: Pragmatic, Critical, But Still in Love," Steven M. Cohen (September 18, 1983)

JL67—"Federation Allocations for Jewish Education and Other Local Services: A Comparison," Alysa M. Dortort (November 24, 1983)

JL71—"Israeli Emigres and the New York Federation: A Case Study in Ambivalent Policymaking for 'Jewish Communal Deviants'," Steven M. Cohen (June 19, 1984)

VP32—"Zionism as a Strategy for the Diaspora: French Jewry at a Crossroads," Shmuel Trigano (April 5, 1984)

VP35—"The New Agenda of European Jewry," Daniel J. Elazar (October 17, 1984)

UNPUBLISHED REPORTS

Argentine Jewry: Its History, Ethnicity, and Problems—Seymour B. Liebman (Slightly different version published in *Midstream*, vol. 21, no. 1 [January 1975], pp. 59–66.)

Background Information on German Jewry—Jesse Fried (1984)

The Jewish Communities of the USSR (1974)

The Jewish Communities of Brazil—Miriam Mundstock (1970)

The Jewish Community of Colombia—Thomas L. Price (1976)
The Jewish Community of Costa Rica—Thomas L. Price (1976)
The Jewish Community of India—Daniel J. Elazar (1976)
The Jewish Community of Italy—Henryk Zvi Geller (1973)
The Jewish Community of Panama—Thomas L. Price (1976)
The Organized Jewish Community in France—Marc Salzburg (1974) (Ph.D. dissertation)
Rumanian Jewry 1945–1970—Esther Oren (1974)
The United Jewish Federation in Norfolk, Virginia—Ephraim Inbar (1981)

Field notes are also available through the Jerusalem Center for Public Affairs for the following countries not cited above: Ireland, New Zealand, Portugal, Rhodesia (Zimbabwe), Switzerland.

4. My participation in Jewish affairs, first in the United States from involvement in the establishment of a Young Judea chapter in Denver in 1942 to the present; in Israel from my first summer as a student in 1953 to the present; and on the world Jewish scene from 1968 to the present. Although I would not have wanted to base this book only on my experiences as a participant—it is not a memoir—those experiences have proved invaluable in giving me insight into world Jewish affairs and the affairs of most major communities in the *edah*, have helped me understand better what we have studied and its meaning, and have added much to my store of knowledge that could not have been gained through any study from outside alone. No doubt participation also brings with it some limitations, especially those derived from commitment, for I am committed to the Jewish people, their *edah*, civilization, religion, and state, and these undoubtedly color my perceptions of the world Jewish polity. I make no apology for those biases because I believe that political science is enriched by commitment, as long as it is declared, kept under control, and used to advance systematic analysis, not to skew it.

Appendix 2

Studying Jewish Communities

A RESEARCH GUIDE

I. Background Information on the Jewish Community

Note: The information required to answer the questions in this section should be gathered from documentary and secondary sources, census data, and the like, rather than by interview unless no such sources are available.

A. *Jewish Settlement and Population*
    1. What is the countrywide Jewish population?
    2. Which are the major Jewish settlements? List them. Give their Jewish populations.
B. *Immigration and Emigration, Internal Migration*
    1. When did the present Jewish population or their ancestors settle in the country? In the local community? If the present Jewish community was formed by waves of immigration, identify as many of them as possible.
    2. Where (from which countries or regions) did the immigrants originate?
    3. What is the order of migration (i.e. who came when) to the country as a whole? To particular local communities?
    4. Is there any significant in-migration today? If so from where? Significant in which way (number, particular skills, particular attitudes)?
    5. Do immigrants from different countries or regions maintain themselves as distinct groups? Do they organize to do so? If so, how? Are there ties between Jews of different countries of origin? Institutional? Organizational? Social? Are there conflicts?
    6. Is there any significant emigration from the country? If so, who is leaving? To where?
    7. Is there significant migration from locality to locality? From where to where? Are the Jews moving to suburbs in significant numbers?
    8. In general, is the community a growing one? A stable one? A declining one?
C. *Historical Development of the Jewish Community*
    Briefly, trace the development of the Jewish community emphasizing its organized life and the history of its organizations and institutions. Where possible, relate the development of organized community life to the factors delineated in A and B. (Note: This section should be devoted to general historical themes; specific historical background should be provided where relevant for subsequent section in the *Guide*.)
D. *Social and Economic Background*
    This section is designed to provide a summary of information from existing demographic and sociological studies relevant to this study. The questions in this section are designed to aid in the identification and meaningful interpretation of data gathered through standard methods of demographic records, not to obtain statistical data by interview. Answers to them should be obtained whenever possible from existing studies.
    1. Summarize the basic population data, including such items as (a) number and size of

500

households, (b) age and sex distribution of the population, (c) educational background, (d) geographic distribution of Jewish population.

2. What statistical data are available regarding Jewish background, identification, and affiliation of the total Jewish population? Consider such factors as (a) religious identification and affiliation, (b) organizational affiliation, (c) religious participation and observance, (d) Jewish education, (e) use of Jewish communal facilities and services, (f) contributions to Jewish organizations and institutions, and (g) location of the Jewish population and institutions.

3. What data are available regarding attitudes of the Jewish population toward Judaism, Jewishness, and the Jewish Community? Consider such factors as attitudes toward religion, Jewish tradition, Jewish education, residence patterns, communal activity, and intermarriage.

4. What do the Jews do for a living? Or what are the occupations and economic activities? (Provide statistical data where available.)

5. What is the general economic condition of the Jewish population? Countrywide? In particular communities?

6. Is there much intermarriage? (Give statistics where available.) If so, do many of the non-Jewish partners convert? Are they accepted by the Jewish community if they do? Are Jewish partners to mixed marriages accepted by the Jewish community even if their spouses have not converted?

E. *The Jewish Community and the General Environment*

1. Who is considered Jewish by the Jewish community? Who is not who might be?

2. Who is considered to be Jewish by the non-Jewish community? When is a person of Jewish descent not considered Jewish by the Gentiles?

3. To what extent is anti-Semitism present in the general community? Perceived to be present by the Jews? A factor in the Jewish-Gentile relations? A factor directly affecting the organized Jewish community? To what extent did it exist in the community's perceived past? To what extent does anti-Semitism today or consciousness of past anti-Semitism shape the structure and activities of the Jewish community?

4. Is the Jewish community and/or its leadership aligned (formally or informally) with any political segment within the country? If so, with whom and why?

5. To what extent do non-Jews concern themselves with Jewish life and the problems of the Jewish community? Do the general media convey information about Judaism, Jews, or Israel that influences or affects the Jewish community? Are the general media more or less important than the specialized Jewish media in providing Jews with such information and in shaping their self-perceptions? What role do Jews and the Jewish community play in shaping non-Jewish treatment of Jewish issues?

II. The Structure of the Jewish Community

A. *Structure of the Jewish Community Countrywide*

1. How is the Jewish community structured countrywide? Is there a coherent overall structure? If so, describe it.

2. To what extent is the community structured on territorial lines? If so, how? List the significant territorial components (organized local communities; state, provincial, or other kind of intermediate communities).

3. To what extent is the community structured according to the country, region, or language of origin of the Jewish population? If so, how? List the significant institutional and organizational components that reflect this (e.g., congregations, *landsmanschaften,* "communities").

    4. To what extent is the community built around specialized organizations and institutions (e.g. ideological groups, synagogues, community centers, political clubs, schools)? If so, how? List the significant organizational and institutional components.

    5. Is there an all-embracing communal organization? If so, how would you describe its place in the structure? If not, who speaks for the Jewish community on a countrywide basis? Have there been any efforts to create an all-embracing community organization? If so, what happened to them?

    6. Which are the several most important institutions and organizations in the community? List and describe them. Why are they particularly important? What is their strength?

    7. What is the place of religious institutions in the community?

B.   *Membership, Affiliation, and Identification with the Jewish Community*

    1. Who is considered a member of the Jewish community? Under what conditions is a potential member of the community considered to be outside it?

    2. Is there a means of formally affiliating or identifying with the community? If so, how does one do so? Is there compulsory affiliation or automatic enrollment in any form? If so, describe it. Is it possible to opt out? If so, how? Is membership an individual or family matter?

    3. Are there quasi-formal ways of affiliation or identifying (e.g. contributing money)? If so, what are they?

    4. Is membership in particular institutions or organizations (e.g. congregations, community centers, welfare federations) tantamount (or equivalent) to membership in the community? If so, which organizations?

    5. What percentage of the eligible Jewish population affiliates with the community?

    6. Who does not affiliate? Why?

    7. Of those who do not affiliate, are there any who profess to be Jewish? If so, how do they manifest their Jewishness?

    8. Is it possible for a person to successfully deny his Jewishness? How would he go about it?

C.   *Legal Status of the Jewish Community*

    1. Are there special laws that define the existence of the Jewish community? General laws applying to every "religious" or "national" community? Is there a communal body that is informally recognized by the government as the representative of the Jewish population? Recognized in any other way?

    2. How do the various organizations and institutions serving the community acquire legal status? Through the community as an entity? As separate entities? Are any organizations or institutions formally recognized by the government for special purposes?

    3. What jurisdiction do the general courts have over Jewish matters? Do they use Jewish law in deciding Jewish matters?

    4. Are there Jewish courts? Are they formally recognized by the government? Informally recognized? What is their jurisdiction? Who makes use of them?

    5. What jurisdiction do Jewish authorities have over matters of personal status? Marriage and divorce?

    6. Does the state enforce or administer any Jewish laws (e.g. dietary laws)?

    7. Does the community have a written constitution? If so, how and when was it adopted? Who prepared it? How is it changed? What status does it have in the eyes of the non-Jewish authorities?

D.   *Structural Dynamics of the Jewish Community*

    1. Is there any one local community or small group of communities that dominates the countrywide communal structure? That is essentially synonymous with it? If so, which? Why?

    2. Are there Jewish "communities" or organizations that stand outside the formal community structure? If so, which? List them. Why do they remain outside?

E.   *Structure of Intermediate (State, Provincial, Land) Jewish Communities*
     Answer the same questions as those included under II A. through D.
F.   *Structure of Local Jewish Communities*
     Answer the same questions as those included under II A. through C., possibly excepting II
     C. on legal status.

III. The Functions of the Jewish Community

A.   *The Scope of the Community's Activities*
     1. Identify the major activities undertaken by the Jewish community or any of its institu-
         tions and organizations. List and describe them.
     2. Who is served through these activities? What percentage of the Jewish population is
         reached through them? (Use hard data where available; otherwise seek the best available
         estimates.)
     3. Insofar as possible, evaluate the importance of these activities in the lives of the individ-
         ual Jews (or Jewish families) who comprise the community.
     4. Roughly rank the perceived importance of these activities to the community as a whole.
B.   *Specific Functions*
     Describe the character and scope of the following functions. Indicate who is responsible for
     them, the institutional and organizational structure that serves them, their relative impor-
     tance in the community, and the constituencies to which they are most closely related.
     1. Cultural Activities
     2. "Defense" and Political Affairs
     3. Education
     4. Fund-raising
     5. Press
     6. Religious Services
     7. Social Services
     8. Sports and Recreation
     9. Welfare
     10. Youth Activities
     11. Other
C.   *Functions of Intermediate (State, Provincial, Land) Jewish Communities*
     Answer the same questions as those included under III A. and B.
D.   *Functions of Local Jewish Communities*
     Answer the same questions as those included under III A. and B.

IV. Political Dynamics of the Jewish Community

A.   *Governance of the Countrywide Jewish Community*
     1. Who governs the Jewish community and its institutions? How?
     2. How are the governing bodies organized?
     3. How are their members chosen? Are there elections? If so, who has the right to vote?
         Who actually participates in the elections? Are voting results available? (Collect any that
         are.)
     4. Are elections considered an "issue" in the community or are they pro forma?
     5. Who nominates candidates? Is there a party system? Are there continuing factions in the
         community?
     6. Are elections contested? If so, which ones? Under what conditions?
     7. Do officeholders tend to remain in office long? Is there much rotation in offices? Does
         the leadership tend to perpetuate itself? How are leaders moved out of office?

8. Are there connections between the important institutions and organizations in the community? If so, in what ways? If not, why not?
9. If there are connections, are they institutionalized? Informal? Personal?
10. How do the leaders of the various institutions and organizations relate to one another?
11. To what extent is there overlapping organizational activity?

B. *Governance of Intermediate (State, Province, Land) Jewish Communities*
Answer the same questions as those included under IV A.

C. *Governance of Local Jewish Communities*
Answer the same questions as those included under IV A.

D. *Community Finance*
1. How is the Jewish community and its activities financed? Countrywide? Locally?
2. What share of the funds are raised through voluntary contributions? Through government or other non-Jewish communal (e.g., United Fund) grants or subventions? Through taxes? Through fees (for services)? For the community as a whole? For specific institutions, organizations, and functions?
3. How is money raised? What means are used? Who is responsible for mobilizing funds? Managing them? Allocating them?
4. What is the pattern of allocation of communal funds?
5. What correlation exists between the sources of funds and the distribution of power in the community?

E. *Consensus and Conflict in the Community*
1. Is there any common ideology (explicit, implicit, or latent) that binds the community together? If so, what is it and from where does it draw its force?
2. Is there a set of perceived interests that binds the community together? If so, what are they?
3. What decisions must be made on the basis of principle by common agreement?
4. What problems or issues generate community conflicts? Why?
5. How are conflicts expressed?
6. How are they dealt with?
7. To what extent are conflicts in the community based on personal grounds? Ideological grounds or grounds of principle?
8. Are there some problems or issues confronting the community or its members that are just not discussed? If so, what are they? Why are they avoided?
9. What are the outermost limits beyond which conflict within the community is not tolerated?

V. Leadership and Participation in the Jewish Community

A. *The Character of the Community's Leadership and Activists*
1. What are the principal positions of leadership in the community? Which positions are occupied by volunteers? By professionals?
2. What are the respective roles of voluntary and professional leadership? Where and to what extent is voluntary leadership real and where is it nominal? Where and to what extent do professionals control community institutions, organizations, and decision making?
3. What opportunities are there for communal activity?
4. Who becomes active in the community? How do they go about it?
5. Are there visible differences in their economic or social status, in educational level, in occupational patterns, or in personal tastes and interests between participants in different institutions and organizations?
6. Who is active in

    a. Synagogues? Religious organizations?

    b. Jewish educational institutions? Cultural organizations?

    c. Jewish health, welfare, and social service institutions?

    d. Umbrella or roof organizations? General fund-raising organizations?

    e. Zionist organizations? Israel-oriented organizations?

    f. "Defense" organizations?

    g. Other

B. *Participation in Community Affairs*

Note: "Participation" here refers to broad-based participation, not simply leaders.

1. Describe the patterns of participation in community affairs.
2. What forms of participation are available? To whom? Who participates? In which activities? What pressures encourage participation? Discourage it?
3. Is there a division of functions (formal or informal) between men and women? If so, describe it.
4. What roles do youth play in the community?

C. *Voluntary Leaders*

1. What are the occupational patterns of the voluntary leadership?
2. What is their economic status?
3. Where were they born? What is their family background?
4. Do the voluntary leaders achieve their positions by virtue of any special talents, skills, or characteristics (e.g. intellectual, monetary, religious observance, heredity)?
5. How are voluntary leaders recruited? How are potential leaders identified? Is a special effort made to recruit potential leaders? If so, describe how. Are younger people recruited into leadership positions?
6. Does activity or leadership in some institutions serve as a springboard for becoming active or attaining leadership in others?
7. To what extent is voluntary leadership in the community compartmentalized? Circulatory? Overlapping?

D. *Professional Leaders*

1. Which are the main positions occupied by professional leaders in the community? List and describe them.
2. Who are the professional leaders? What are their social and educational backgrounds? Where were they born? What are their family backgrounds?
3. How are professional leaders recruited? To what extent are they specifically trained for their positions or fields?

E. *Leadership and Representation*

1. To what extent is the community's leadership representative of the community? Explain your answer.
2. Is the degree of representativeness (or lack thereof) institutionalized? Is it the result of accidental or pragmatic considerations?
3. Is there any special group considered by the community to be entitled to leadership positions?
4. Is there any group in the community that considers itself responsible for the provision of community leadership? Considers itself entitled to provide such leadership by special right?
5. To what extent does the leadership of the various organizations overlap?
6. To what extent is there sharing or rotation of offices among a small group of key people?

F. *Leadership and Decision Making*

1. What is the relationship between leaders (volunteers and professionals) and the positions they occupy (i.e. do the positions carry significant authority, power, or influence with them)? Review by major position.

2. Are there figures in the community who are particularly powerful or influential regardless of the positions they hold? Or regardless of whether they hold positions at all? If so, who are they? What are the sources of their power or influence?

3. Who makes decisions on the following matters in the community? How are they made?
   a. general policy matters?
   b. matters affecting relations with non-Jews or the host country?
   c. matters affecting Jewish religious observance?
   d. Jewish educational matters?
   e. fund-raising?
   f. other community matters?

VI. Intercommunity Relations

A. *Within the Country*

   1. To what extent are there structured linkages between countrywide and local (and intermediate) communities? Institutions? Organizations? How are these connections manifested? What forms do they take?

   2. To what extent is there structural separation between countrywide and local communities? Institutions? Organizations?

   3. To what extent are the informal connections between countrywide and local (and intermediate) communities? Institutions? Organizations? How are such connections manifested? What forms do they take?

   4. How do the countrywide and local (and intermediate) communities share or divide tasks? Responsibilities?

   5. What kinds of conflicts or disagreements occur between communities, institutions, or organizations? Cite examples, where possible. Are there any persisting conflicts that continue to shape intercommunity, interinstitutional, or interorganizational arrangements?

   6. Are there transfers of funds from one community (or its institutions or organizations) to another? If so, from which to which? For what purposes? Through what vehicles or under whose auspices?

B. *Between Countries*

   1. Is the community as a whole affiliated with any worldwide or regional Jewish organizations? If so, which? What kinds of relationships have developed between them and the community? What is their role in the life of the community?

   2. Are individual institutions or organizations within the community affiliated with any worldwide or regional counterparts? If so, which? Describe the relationship. If not, why not? (If the community has political parties, are they connected with other Zionist or Israeli parties?)

   3. What kinds of informal ties exist between the community and the rest of world Jewry?

   4. Does the community (or its institutions or organizations) contribute funds to support projects or activities in other communities (excluding Israel)? Does it provide professional or technical assistance? Guidance? If so, to whom (or which)? For what purposes? How? Through what vehicles or under whose auspices? Since when? Indicate sums wherever possible.

   5. Does the community (or its institutions or organizations) receive funds from other communities (excluding Israel)? Professional or technical assistance? Guidance? If so, from which? For what purposes? How? Through what vehicles or under whose auspices? Since when? Indicate sums wherever possible.

C. *Between the Community and Israel*

   1. What kinds of ties, formal or informal, exist between the community, its institutions, organizations, and members, and Israel?

2. What role does Israel play in the life of the community? What role do Israel, leaders, and officials play (e.g. Israel: diplomats stationed locally)?

3. Does Israel (including Israel-based institutions) formally provide the community with any professional or technical assistance (e.g. teachers, *shlichim*)? Guidance? If so, what kinds? For whom? Under what circumstances? Through which agencies? What assistance does Israel (or do Israelis) provide the community informally?

4. Does Israel (including Israel-based institutions) formally provide the community with any financial assistance? If so, what kinds? Under what circumstances? Through which agencies? Indicate sums wherever possible.

5. Does the community (or its institutions, organizations, or members) contribute funds to Israel? If so, to whom and how much? For what purposes? Through which agencies? Indicate sums wherever possible.

VII. Sources and Bibliography

A. *Published Sources of Data*
  1. List historical and contemporary studies of the community or any of its organized segments. (Obtain copies whenever possible.)
  2. Have there been any sociological or demographic studies of the Jewish community (countrywide or local communities) since World War II? Published? Unpublished? List them. (Obtain copies whenever possible.)
  3. Are there any other sources of demographic data that you know of (e.g. census data)? (Obtain copies whenever possible.)

B. *Unpublished Sources of Data*
  1. List unpublished manuscripts, theses and dissertations, oral history materials, etc. pertaining to the community or any of its organized segments.
  2. Are there any archives or collections of relevant data in the community or elsewhere?

C. *Interview Data*
  1. List all persons interviewed in the course of the study. Provide background information on each interviewee and his or her role in the community.
  2. Supply interview protocols for each interview with head notes according to the following format.
      a. Name of interviewee
      b. Date of interview
      c. Total and position of interviewee
      d. Place of interview
      e. Personal background of interviewee (in a general sense) including such items as place of birth, occupation, role in the Jewish community, etc.
      f. Time of interview
      g. Name of interviewer

Index

Abdul Hamid, 359
Abulafia, Gedalya, 359
Academy of the Hebrew Language, 74
Adelaide Hebrew Congregation, 250
Afghanistan, Jewish community in, 447–48
African Jewish community, 131; in France, 317,
    318, 319–20; in North Africa, 95, 113,
    128, 154, 156–57, 239
Afrikaner National Party, 83
Afrikaners, 207, 211
Afro-Asian Jewish community, 156, 189
Agency Board of Governors, 140, 141–42
Agudath Israel, 47, 49, 68–69, 71, 97, 105,
    108, 118–20, 163, 183, 186, 190, 191,
    242, 249, 263, 350, 380, 399
Ahad Ha'am, 172
Albania, Jewish community in, 423
Alberta, Canada, 200
Alfonsin government, 280
Algeria, Jewish community in, 426–28; French
    influence on, 426–27; organization of, 427
Ali, Muhammad, 429
Alianza de Monte Sinai, 291–92
Aliya: Fourth, 399; Russian-Jewish, 139, 146;
    Third, 392
Aliyah Department, 139, 146
Aliyot, Zionist, 158
Alliance Israélite Universelle, 72–73, 79, 85, 87,
    118–20, 128, 134, 314, 318, 437, 439,
    440, 441, 451, 455, 456–57
Almogi, Yosef, 145
Almosnino, Gabriel, 421
Alonso, Hernando, 287
Alsace-Lorraine, 67, 317, 319
Am, 483
America Israel Public Affairs Committee, 78
American Academy for Jewish Research, 74
American Jewish Committee, 71, 77, 78, 115–
    16, 135, 217, 222, 275
American Jewish Community Federations, 42.
    See also Federations, American Jewish
    Community

American Jewish Congress, 77, 217, 221, 222
American Jewish Council, 124
American Jewish Joint Distribution Committee
    (JDC), 72, 83, 86., *See also* Joint Distribu-
    tion Committee
American Jewish Year Book, 341, 395–96
American Zionist Federation, 217
Anglo-Boer War, 75, 240, 242
Anglo-Jewish Association, 79, 251, 327, 329
Anglo-Jews, 199, 205, 207, 220, 243
Anschluss, 344
Anshei Knesset HaGedolah, 29, 173
Anti-Defamation League of B'nai B'rith, 77, 78,
    116, 294
Anti-Semitism, 75, 77, 79–80, 84, 115, 136,
    149–50, 176, 206, 210–11, 226, 235,
    239, 254; in Algeria, 427; in Argentina,
    272–73; in Austria, 343–44; in Bulgaria,
    421–22; in Chile, 298; in France, 314–
    15; in Germany, 339; in Greece, 370; in
    Hungary, 410, 411; in India, lack of,
    464; in Iran, 454; in Iraq, 431–32; in
    Italy, 383; in Latin America, 264; in Mo-
    rocco, 437–38; in Netherlands, 326; in
    Poland, 397, 402; in Romania, 414, 416;
    in Turkey, 361–62, 364; in USSR, 392,
    394
Anti-Zionism, 86, 127, 162, 211, 227; in Eu-
    rope, 310; in Great Britain, 327, 329; in
    Latin America, 264
Antwerp, 320–21
Appel Unifié Juif de France, 316
Arab-Israeli Conflict, 225, 325
Arab world, 128, 131; and republicanism, 25
Aratzot, 71, 108
Argentine Jewish community, 72, 75, 78, 84, 87,
    98, 125, 126, 130, 135–36, 137, 197,
    200, 201, 204, 268, 269–80; in United
    States, 274
Argentina Federation of Maccabi Community
    Centers, 272
Argentina Jewish community education, 262–63

509